Welcome to

Research in Education

with Research Navigator™

This text contains some special features designed to aid you in the research process and in writing research papers. As you read this textbook, you will see special Research Navigator™ (RN) icons cueing you to visit the Research Navigator™ Web site to research important concepts of the text.

To gain access to Research Navigator™, go to **www.researchnavigator.com** and login using the passcode you'll find on the inside front cover of your text.

Research Navigator™ includes three databases of dependable source material to get your research process started.

■ **EBSCO's ContentSelect Academic Journal Database**   EBSCO's ContentSelect Academic Journal Database contains scholarly, peer-reviewed journals. These published articles provide you with specialized knowledge and information about your research topic. Academic journal articles adhere to strict scientific guidelines for methodology and theoretical grounding. The information obtained in these individual articles is more scientific than information you would find in a popular magazine, in a newspaper article, or on a Web page.

■ *The New York Times Search by Subject Archive™*   Newspapers are considered periodicals because they are issued in regular installments (i.e., daily, weekly, or monthly) and provide contemporary information. Information in periodicals—journals, magazines, and newspapers—may be useful, or even critical, for finding up-to-date material or information to support specific aspects of your topic. Research Navigator™ gives you access to a one-year, "search by subject" archive of articles from one of the world's leading newspapers—*The New York Times*.

■ **"Best of the Web" Link Library**   Link Library, the third database included on Research Navigator™, is a collection of Web links organized by academic subject and key terms. Searching on your key terms will provide you with a list of five to seven editorially reviewed Web sites that offer educationally relevant and reliable content. The Web links in Link Library are monitored and updated each week, reducing your incidence of finding "dead" links.

In addition, Research Navigator™ includes extensive online content detailing the steps in the research process, including:

■ Starting the research process

■ Finding and evaluating sources

■ Citing sources

■ Internet research

■ Using your library

■ Starting to write

For more information on how to use Research Navigator™
go to **www.researchnavigator.com**

RESEARCH IN EDUCATION

RESEARCH IN EDUCATION

Evidence-Based Inquiry

James H. McMillan
Virginia Commonwealth University

Sally Schumacher
Virginia Commonwealth University

PEARSON

Boston • New York • San Francisco
Mexico City • Montreal • Toronto • London • Madrid • Munich • Paris
Hong Kong • Singapore • Tokyo • Cape Town • Sydney

Senior Editor: *Arnis E. Burvikovs*
Series Editorial Assistant: *Kelly Hopkins*
Marketing Manager: *Tara Kelly*
Editorial-Production Service: *Omegatype Typography, Inc.*
Manufacturing Buyer: *Andrew Turso*
Composition and Prepress Buyer: *Linda Cox*
Cover Administrator: *Linda Knowles*
Electronic Composition: *Omegatype Typography, Inc.*
Interior Design: *Roy Neuhaus*

For related titles and support materials, visit our online catalog at www.ablongman.com.

Between the time website information is gathered and then published, some sites may have closed. Also, the transcription of URLs can result in typographical errors. The publisher would appreciate notification where these errors occur so that they may be corrected in subsequent editions.

Many of the designations used by manufacturers and sellers to distinguish their products are claimed as trademarks. Where those designations appear in this book, and Allyn and Bacon was aware of a trademark claim, the designations have been printed in initial or all caps.

Library of Congress Cataloging-in-Publication Data

McMillan, James H.
   Research in education : evidence-based inquiry / James H. McMillan, Sally
Schumacher.—6th ed.
      p. cm.
   Includes bibliographical references and index.
   ISBN 0-205-45530-1
   1. Education—Research. 2. Education—Research—Evaluation. 3. Educational statistics.
I. Schumacher, Sally. II. Title.

LB1028.M365 2006
370'.7'2—dc22

                                                                        2005043005

Printed in the United States of America

10 9 8 7 6 5 4 3 2 1   10 09 08 07 06 05

Brief Contents

Contents

PART III

QUALITATIVE RESEARCH DESIGNS AND METHODS   313

CHAPTER 12
Designing Qualitative Research   314

CHAPTER 13
Qualitative Strategies   339

Preface

In the last few years, there have been major developments in the field of educational research and evaluation. Most important, empirical research has become essential for making decisions and for forming and changing policies (e.g., data-driven decision making). Educators are now expected to understand and critique studies that can be used as evidence for changing curriculum, instruction, counseling, assessment, and other educational practices. Researchers have more stringent standards for conducting quality research that must be met. At the federal level, legislation related to the 2001 law, No Child Left Behind, and the Education Sciences Reform Act of 2002, has resulted in a new definition of *scientifically based education research*, which is being used pervasively to evaluate and synthesize research and to provide the basis for program evaluation. The sixth edition of *Research in Education: Evidence-Based Inquiry* has been revised to respond to these changes and, at the same time, maintain a balanced emphasis on both quantitative and qualitative methods. Our goal is to provide a comprehensive yet relatively nontechnical introduction to the principles, concepts, and methods currently used in educational research and evaluation.

Students enrolled in their first educational research course typically have two instructional needs. Some plan to do additional work in statistics, research design, qualitative methodologies, and evaluation. In addition to mastering the fundamental principles of research, these students need to develop both an awareness of the breadth of educational research and a broad conceptual base for understanding more technical and advanced aspects of research. Other students, whose immediate career goals lie more in educational practice than in conducting research, need to understand key research terms, gain practice in reading studies critically, know how research designs and procedures may affect empirical findings, and understand applied and evaluation research. *Research in Education* is designed to meet both of these instructional needs.

RATIONALE FOR THE TEXT

Educational research has become more diverse during the past few decades. It is now well established that quantitative, qualitative, and mixed-method inquiry contribute significantly to the field of knowledge in education. Our experience is that by learning about both quantitative and qualitative research and by changing "lenses" when viewing education, students gain a deeper understanding, knowledge, and appreciation for each of these traditions in educational research as well as for mixed-method designs.

NEW AND IMPROVED FEATURES

There are several significant changes in the sixth edition that improve student learning:

- All chapters have undergone substantial revision.
- Four new complete published research articles have been added.
- The number of excerpts from published articles has been increased to 166, from 78 different journals.
- A new chapter has been added on mixed-method designs, secondary data analysis, and action research.
- "Alerts" have been added to emphasize key points.
- "Misconceptions versus Evidence" boxes have been added to show the importance of accurate interpretations of research findings.
- Research Navigator Notes have been added to link to relevant illustrations from articles in the Research Navigator database.
- A new appendix on writing research proposals has been added.
- The book's Companion Website has been expanded.
- The design of the book has been improved, including the use of boxes and color.

ORGANIZATION OF THE SIXTH EDITION

The sixth edition is divided into six parts. Part I (Chapters 1 through 5) defines *research* as scientific, evidence-based inquiry that is designed to produce knowledge and to improve educational practice. We briefly introduce quantitative and qualitative research; delineate the functions of basic, applied, and evaluation research; and then describe the limitations of educational research. We present an overview of research designs, techniques, and formats. Selection, formulation, and statements of both quantitative and qualitative problems are discussed and illustrated. The literature review chapter (Chapter 4) includes updated techniques for computer searches, presented in easy-to-follow steps, as well as guidelines for writing literature reviews in quantitative and qualitative research. The Internet chapter (Chapter 5) introduces essential skills for using the vast resources of the World Wide Web for educational research. Specific Internet websites that focus on educational research are identified and reviewed.

Part II (Chapters 6 through 11) introduces quantitative designs by presenting fundamental principles of sampling, measurement, and experimental validity. Descriptive statistics are presented to provide a foundation for understanding the more detailed coverage of measurement. Nonexperimental designs are covered in Chapter 9, followed by experimental and single-subject designs in Chapter 10. We have retained the nontechnical introduction to inferential statistics. Computations are reserved for Appendix D.

Part III (Chapters 12 through 14) begins with an introduction to designing qualitative research, which emphasizes research questions and significance, design, purposeful sampling, and strategies to enhance validity, usefulness, reflexivity, and field work ethics. Chapter 13 on qualitative strategies covers entry into the field, participant-observation, in-depth interviewing, and supplementary techniques. Chapter 14 on qualitative data analysis presents coding, categorizing, and pattern-seeking strategies along with a current discussion of qualitative data analysis (QDA) programs and software websites. Various narrative structures are described.

Three emerging methodologies are identified in Part IV (Chapter 15): mixed-method designs, secondary data analysis, and action research. These contemporary approaches represent new directions and possibilities.

Part V (Chapter 16) addresses analytical research of past or recent events, including concept analysis and historical research. A new section on oral history has been added. We emphasize the search and criticism of sources.

Part VI (Chapter 17) returns to a more general discussion of educational evaluation research and policy analysis. Three approaches to evaluation are briefly described. Policy analysis presents an overview of research methods and cost analysis.

INSTRUCTIONAL AIDS

In each chapter, we have retained a number of instructional aids to assist students: a concept map at the beginning, a list of key terms, application problems, and criteria for evaluating studies conducted by different methodologies. We believe the instructor, rather than the book, should determine the course objectives and level of student competency. Given that, the book has been organized so that the instructor can emphasize general knowledge, certain methodologies, or specific skills, such as making an annotated bibliography on a topic, writing a critical literature review, developing a preliminary proposal with a problem statement and design, or conducting a small-scale study. We have used numerous approaches to meet different student and programming needs.

The book's Companion Website has been continued in this sixth edition and can be accessed by students at www.ablongman.com/mcmillanschumacher6e. It includes chapter objectives and outlines, application exercises, web links to additional resources, and multiple-choice questions on chapter content. The Instructor's Manual provides course objectives, alternative course organizations, teaching techniques, PowerPoint presentations, and test items for each chapter.

A major instructional aid in this book is the use of excerpts from published studies in all chapters except 1 and 17. Excerpts were chosen to represent different disciplines and to be applicable to the practices in a variety of education areas, such as administration, supervision, instruction, special education, early childhood, counseling, adult education, and programs in noneducational agencies. Most of the excerpts have been updated for this edition. The excerpts are especially helpful in gradually introducing students to the style and format of a published article.

ACKNOWLEDGMENTS

Because this book has resulted from a merging of our specializations as researchers and professors, there is no senior author; each author has contributed equally to the book. Many other people also contributed to this endeavor.

We gratefully acknowledge the support of our colleagues, mentors, and friends, who are too numerous to name. We especially thank our master's degree and doctoral candidates, who challenged us to be more explicit. And we thank those individuals who reviewed this book, whose ideas, criticisms, and suggestions helped shape this new edition. The reviewers for the first edition were H. Parker Blount, Georgia State University; Alice Boberg, University of Calgary; David J. Cowden, Western Michigan University; Jane A. Goldman, University of Connecticut; Harry Hsu, University of Pittsburgh; Sylvia T. Johnson, Howard University; Stephen Olejnick, University of Florida; and Robert J. Yonker, Bowling Green State University. The reviewers for the second edition were Gerald W. Bracey, Cherry Creek Schools, Colorado; Jane A. Goldman, University of Connecticut; Harry Hsu, University of Pittsburgh; and Herman W. Meyers, University of Vermont. The reviewers for the third edition were Jane A. Goldman, University of Connecticut; Laura Goodwin, University of Colorado at Denver; James McNamara, Texas A & M University; Bud Meyers, University of Vermont; Anton Netusil, Iowa State University; Ellen Weissinger, University of Nebraska; and Wen-Ke Wang, National Changhua Normal University in Taiwan. Reviewers for the fourth edition included Laura Goodwin, University of Colorado at Denver; Judith A. Kennison, Ithaca College; Anton Netusil, Iowa State University; and Ellen Weissinger, University of Nebraska. The fifth edition reviewers included David Anderson, Salisbury State University; Shann Ferch, Gonzaga University; Brian Hinrichs, Illinois State University; Daniel Robinson, University of Louisville; David Tan, University of Oklahoma; and James Webb, Kent State University.

We are indebted to our thoughtful reviewers for the sixth edition: Florence A. Hamrick, Iowa State University; James R. Martindale, University of Virginia Health System; Stephen K. Miller, University of Louisville; and Susan Mulvaney, California State University at Long Beach.

Although some of the chapter reorganization of this edition is new, we hope that it facilitates teaching and learning. We would appreciate receiving comments and suggestions from colleagues and students as we gather material for the seventh edition. Feel free to contact us by e-mail (jmcmillan@vcu.edu).

We especially appreciate the continued guidance and support of our Senior Editor, Arnis Burvikovs, and Senior Development Editor, Virginia Blanford. We also appreciate the special assistance that Donna Simons, Kelly Hopkins, Megan Smallidge, and Audry Stein, all from Allyn and Bacon, provided during the revision and production phases. Special recognition is given to Donna Jovanovich for revising and expanding the Companion Website, which was done by Jeff Oescher for earlier editions, and to Rich Mohn for proofreading the website content. Finally, our families—Donald F. X. and Marcia Schumacher and Janice McMillan—have provided continued encouragement for this exciting, if at times difficult, undertaking.

James H. McMillan
Sally Schumacher

Using Research Navigator™

This edition of *Research in Education* is designed to integrate the content of the book with the following resources of Research Navigator™, a collection of research databases, instruction, and contemporary publications available to you online at www.researchnavigator .com

- **EBSCO's ContentSelect Academic Journal Database** organized by subject, with each subject containing leading academic journals for each discipline.
- *The New York Times,* one of the most highly regarded publications of today's news. View the full text of articles from the previous year.
- **Link Library** connects users to thousands of websites for discipline-specific key terms.
- **Research Review and Preparation.** A special section called "Understanding the Research Process" helps you work your way through the research process.

CONNECTING THE BOOK WITH RN

As you read this book, you'll see special Research Navigator™ (RN) icons cueing you to visit the ContentSelect database on the Research Navigator™ website to expand on the concepts of the text and to further explore the work being done in the field of Educational Research. RN learning aids in the book include:

1. **Marginal keyword search terms.** Appearing in the margins of the text, these already tested terms will guide your search on topics relevant to the course content and will yield an abundance of sources from a variety of perspectives that will broaden your exposure to key topics. Begin by searching the ContentSelect database, and then check out the other databases as well.
2. **Applied research activities and projects.** At the end of each chapter, special RN exercises provide more practice using the ContentSelect database in Research Navigator™ and move you beyond the book to library and field research.

It's now time to enter Research Navigator™. Purchase of this book provides you free access to this exclusive pool of information and data. The following walk-through illustrates, step-by-step, the various ways this valuable resource can make your research process more interesting and successful.

Research Navigator.com

8.1 Discriminant Validity
Accession No.: 7409893

REGISTRATION

In order to begin using Research Navigator™, you must first register using the personal access code found on the inside of the front cover of your book. Follow these easy steps:

1. Click "Register" under New Users on the left side of the home page screen.

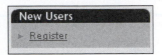

2. Enter the access code exactly as it appears on the inside front cover of your book or on your access card. (Note: Access codes can only be used once to complete one registration. If you purchased a used text, the access code may not work.)

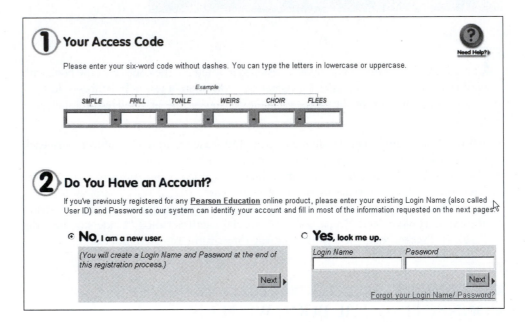

3. Follow the instructions on screen to complete your registration—you may click the Help button at any time if you are unsure how to respond.
4. Once you have successfully completed registration, write down the Login Name and Password you just created and keep it in a safe place. You will need to enter it each time you want to revisit Research Navigator™.
5. Once you register, you have access to all the resources in Research Navigator™ for six months. Each time you enter Research Navigator™, log in by simply going to the "Returning Users" section on the left side of the home page and type in your LoginID and Password.

GETTING STARTED

You're now official! The options available to you on Research Navigator™ are plenty. From Research Navigator™'s home page, you have easy access to all of the site's main features, including a quick route to the three exclusive databases of source content. If you are new to the research process, you may want to start by browsing "Understanding the Research Process."

This section of the site can be helpful even for those with some research experience but who might be interested in some helpful tips. Here you will find extensive help on all aspects of the research process including:

- Introduction to the Research Paper
- Gathering Data
- Searching the Internet
- Evaluating Sources
- Organizing Ideas
- Writing Notes
- Drafting the Paper
- Academic Citation Styles (i.e., MLA, APA, CMS)
- Blending Reference Material into Your Writing
- Practicing Academic Integrity
- Revising
- Proofreading
- Editing the Final Draft

COMPLETING RESEARCH

The first step in completing a research assignment or research paper is to select a topic. Your instructor may assign you a topic, or you may find suggested topics in the margins or at the end of chapters throughout this book. Once you have selected and narrowed your research topic, you are now ready to *gather data*. Research Navigator™ simplifies your research efforts by giving you three distinct types of source material commonly used in research assignments: academic journals (ContentSelect), newspaper articles (*The New York Times*), and World Wide Web sites (Link Library).

1. EBSCO's ContentSelect

The first database you'll find on Research Navigator™ is ContentSelect, which contains the EBSCO Academic Journal and Abstract Database containing scholarly, peer-reviewed journals (such as *Journal of Education Policy* and *Assessment & Evaluation in Higher Education*). The information obtained in these individual articles is more scientific than information you would find in a popular magazine, in a newspaper article, or on a Web page. Searching for articles in ContentSelect is easy!

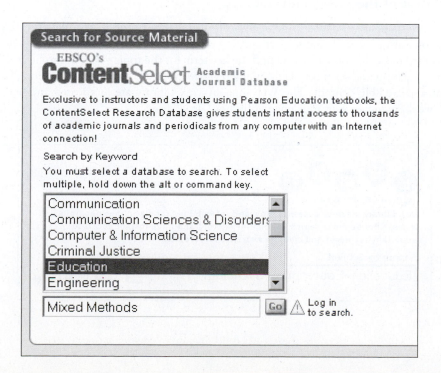

Within the ContentSelect Research Database section, you will see a list of disciplines and a space to type keywords. You can search within a single discipline or multiple disciplines. Choose one or more subject databases, and then enter a keyword you wish to search. Click on "Go."

Now you'll see a list of articles that match your search. From this page you can examine either the full text or the abstract of each of the articles and determine which will best help with your research. Print out the articles or save them in your "Folder" for later reference.

2. The New York Times

Searching *The New York Times* gives you access to articles from one of the world's leading newspapers. The first step in using the search-by-subject archive is to indicate the subject area you wish to search. You have the option of searching one specific subject at a time by highlighting the subject area or searching all subjects by highlighting "All." Click on "Go" now for a complete listing of articles in your chosen subject area that have appeared in *The New York Times* over the last year, sorted by most recent article first. For a more focused search, type a word, or multiple words separated by commas, into the search box and click "Go" for a list of articles. Articles can be printed or saved for later use in your research assignment.

3. "Best of the Web" Link Library

The third database of content included on Research Navigator™ is a collection of Web links, organized by academic subject and key terms. To use this database, simply select a subject from the dropdown list and find the key term for the topic you are searching. Click on the key term and see a list of editorially reviewed websites that offer educationally relevant and credible content. The Web links in Link Library are monitored and updated each week, reducing your incidence of finding "dead" links.

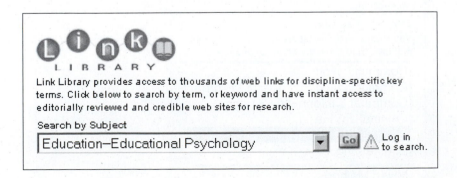

USING YOUR LIBRARY

While Research Navigator™ does contain a vast amount of information to assist you with your research, it does not try to replace the library. After you have selected your topic and gathered source material from the three databases of content, you may need to go to your school library to complete your research. Finding information at the library, however, can seem overwhelming. Research Navigator™ provides some assistance in this area as well. Research Navigator™ includes discipline-specific "library guides" for you to use as a road map. Each guide includes an overview of the discipline's major subject databases, online journals, and key associations and newsgroups. Print them out and take them with you to the library!

CAUTION! Please note that the Research Navigator™ site undergoes frequent changes as new and exciting options are added to assist with research endeavors. For the latest information on the options available to you on Research Navigator™, visit www.researchnavigator. com.

RESEARCH IN EDUCATION

FUNDAMENTAL PRINCIPLES OF EDUCATIONAL RESEARCH

What is scientific, evidence-based inquiry? Are there guiding principles for conducting a research study? Educators who are unfamiliar with scientific methods frequently ask these questions. They may also ask, Why are research results considered more useful in making decisions than the experience and advice of others? How does research influence educational practice? What kinds of studies are done in education? Is there a systematic way to evaluate a research article?

Chapters 1 and 2 answer these questions by providing an introduction to the field of educational research, an overview of research designs, and an explanation of the formats of quantitative and qualitative research journal articles. This introduction will familiarize readers with basic terminology and fundamental concepts of research. *All* research begins with a problem statement and requires a literature review. Chapter 3 explains how to recognize, state, and evaluate a research problem. How should a problem be stated in order to be useful in planning a study? What should a problem statement convey to the reader? How are problem statements evaluated? Chapter 4 shows how related literature is used to enhance a study. Why is a literature review important? What sources are available for conducting a literature review? How does one conduct a computer search of the literature, given that much of it is now contained in online databases? How is a literature review organized and evaluated? Chapter 5 shows how the vast resources of the Internet can be used in many ways to enhance educational research. How is the Internet organized? How are directories and search engines used? What are some useful websites?

Together, these five chapters present basic principles of research that students need to understand to conduct, read, and analyze different types of research and methodologies. Subsequent parts of this text will discuss in greater detail the designs and procedures for specific methodologies.

1 Introduction to Evidence-Based Inquiry

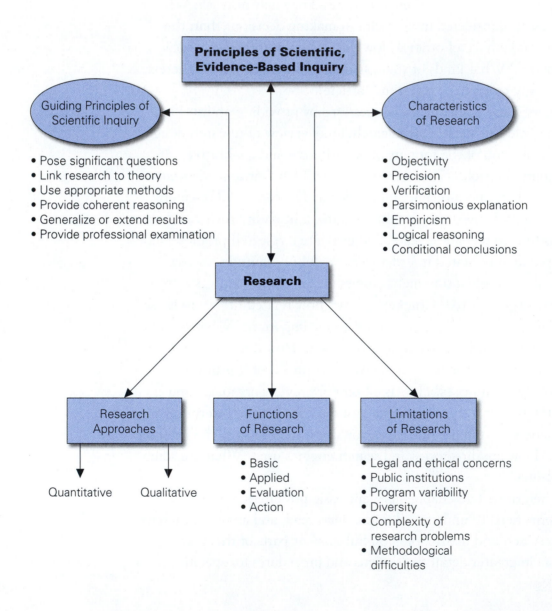

Principles of Scientific, Evidence-Based Inquiry

Guiding Principles of Scientific Inquiry

- Pose significant questions
- Link research to theory
- Use appropriate methods
- Provide coherent reasoning
- Generalize or extend results
- Provide professional examination

Characteristics of Research

- Objectivity
- Precision
- Verification
- Parsimonious explanation
- Empiricism
- Logical reasoning
- Conditional conclusions

Research

Research Approaches

Quantitative   Qualitative

Functions of Research

- Basic
- Applied
- Evaluation
- Action

Limitations of Research

- Legal and ethical concerns
- Public institutions
- Program variability
- Diversity
- Complexity of research problems
- Methodological difficulties

KEY TERMS

replication

evidence-based inquiry

generalization

research

research methods

objectivity

verification

explanation

empirical

data

basic research

theory

applied research

evaluation research

action research

The times we live in are truly amazing in terms of the possibilities for educational research! Powerful tools have been afforded us through the variety of technology and research methods that have been refined throughout the last half century. These tools and methods allow us to address challenging questions and to have greater confidence that our results will be valid and useful. More important, there is a renewed interest at all levels of education for decisions to be data driven and based on hard evidence. This has resulted in a greater need for all educators to understand, conduct, and use research findings.

This chapter introduces educational research by describing the development of knowledge to improve educational practices. Educational research is guided by six principles of scientific, evidence-based inquiry that are applied to both quantitative and qualitative research approaches. Educators and other professionals use basic, applied, evaluation, and action research for different purposes, and some features of education limit scientific studies of educational phenomena.

Most important, Chapter 1 introduces the language and the logic of research used in reading and conducting studies. Research Navigator Notes provide article accession numbers to an online journal database housed at www.MyLabSchool.com. The articles in this database illustrate the chapter content, and these references appear in all chapters. In addition, a brief example of Misconception vs. Evidence appears in most but not all chapters to illuminate how evidence-based knowledge can be misinterpreted or misused.

EDUCATIONAL RESEARCH IN THE TWENTY-FIRST CENTURY

For the foreseeable future, the nature of educational research will be strongly influenced by federal policies. The newly formed Institute of Education Sciences (IES) provides leadership in expanding scientific knowledge and understanding of education from early childhood through postsecondary study. The IES's mission is one of "building evidence-based education" that supports learning and improves academic achievement and access to educational opportunities for all students (see www.ed.gov/about/offices/list/ies/index.html).

Evidence-based studies recently published in professional journals illustrate the variety of topics that interest educators and the public. Consider these examples:

Burko, H., Wolf, S. A., Simmone, S., & Uchiyama, K. P. (2003). Schools in transition: Reform efforts and school capacity in Washington state. *Educational Evaluation and Policy Analysis, 25*(2), 171–201.

Dieker, L. A., McTigue, A., Campbell, G., Rodrequez, J., Savage, M., & Jackson-Tomas, A. (2003). Voices from the field: Teachers from culturally and linguistically diverse backgrounds entering the profession through alternative certification. *Teacher Education and Special Education, 26*(4), 328–340.

Drummond, K. V., & Stipek, D. (2004). Low-income parents' beliefs about their role in children's academic learning. *Elementary School Journal, 104*(3), 197–214.

Farkas, R. D. (2003). Effects of traditional versus learning-styles instructional methods on middle school students. *Journal of Educational Research, 97*(1), 42–51.

Frykholm, J. (2004). Teachers' tolerance for discomfort: Implications for curricular reform in mathematics. *Journal of Curriculum and Supervision, 19*(2), 125–149.

Harrington, T. E., & Pourdavood, R. G. (2002). Exploring the evolving nature of three elementary preservice teachers' beliefs and practices: Three parallel case studies. *Focus on Learning Problems in Mathematics, 24*(1), 45–64.

Honig, M. I. (2003). Building policy from practice: District central office administrator's roles and capacity for implementing collaborative education policy. *Educational Administration Quarterly, 39*(3), 292–338.

Lewis, A. E. (2001). There is not "race" in the school-yard: Color-blind ideology in an (almost) all-white school. *American Educational Research Journal, 38*, 781–811.

Meier, K. J., & Wilkins, V. M. (2002). Gender differences in agency head salaries: The case of public education. *Public Administration Review, 62*(4), 405–412.

Morris, D., Bloodgood, J., & Perney, J. (2003). Kindergarten predictors of first- and second-grade reading achievement. *Elementary School Journal, 104*(2), 93–110.

Preston, J. A. (2003). "He lives as a *Master*"; Seventeenth-century masculinity, gendered teaching, and careers of New England schoolmasters. *History of Education Quarterly, 43*(3), 350–371.

Windschitle, M., & Sahl, K. (2002). Tracing teachers' use of technology in a laptop computer school: The interplay of teacher beliefs, social dynamics, and institutional culture. *American Educational Research Journal, 39*, 165–205.

Why Is Educational Research Important?

Why has educational research become a valuable source of information? We suggest six reasons for the importance of evidence-based inquiry.

First, *educators are constantly trying to understand educational processes and must make professional decisions.* These professional decisions have immediate and long-range effects on others: students, teachers, parents, and, ultimately, our communities and nation. How do educators acquire an understanding to make decisions? Most of us tend to rely on several sources, including personal experience, expert opinion, tradition, intuition, common sense, and beliefs about what is right or wrong. Each of these sources is legitimate in some situations, yet in other situations, each source may be inadequate as the only basis for making decisions.

Second, *noneducational policy groups, such as state and federal legislatures and courts, have increasingly mandated changes in education.* How do policy groups acquire their views of education and obtain their information about schools and instruction? Most policy-makers prefer to have research-based information relevant to the specific policy issue. Many state legislatures mandate state education departments to conduct studies on state educational policies. Both federal and state departments of education also commission funded studies. Researchers are increasingly being asked to work on complex problems in highly politicized environments.

Third, *concerned public, professional, and private groups and foundations have increased their research activities.* Professional educational associations, teacher labor unions, Parent-Teacher Associations, and foundations such as the National Science Foundation have conducted or commissioned studies on topics of special concern to the organization.

Fourth, *reviews of prior research have interpreted accumulated empirical evidence.* For example, studies on retention indicate that retaining a child in a grade serves few educational purposes. Other research reviews have addressed such topics as thinking aloud and reading comprehension; hypermedia and learner comprehension, control, and style; why parents become involved in their children's education; parameters of affirmative action in education; teacher efficacy; the effects of single-sex and co-educational schooling on social, emotional, and academic development; and teacher occupational stress, burnout, and health. Other research reviews identify areas of needed research.

Fifth, *educational research is readily available*. Research about educational practices is found in professional and research journals, funding agencies' published reports, books, library databases, newspapers, television, and the Internet. Although the quality of the research may vary with the specific source, educational research is very accessible.

Sixth, *many educators who are not full-time researchers conduct studies to guide their decisions and to serve as efforts in classroom, school, and system accountability*. Teachers can conduct action research that is relevant for their needs and for the issues about which they feel passionately, such as second-language students, students with disabilities, and teaching approaches in school subjects. Educators often collaborate to conduct research and to form partnerships in projects. Seemingly insignificant findings can add to the current body of evidence in the search for answers to important educational questions. Furthermore, all educators must be able to demonstrate effectiveness in an age of accountability. Educators also need to interpret results accurately and to be responsible in their use of research findings. Evidence-based inquiry provides valid information and knowledge about education that can be used to make informed decisions.

Because research systematically describes or measures phenomena, it is a better source of knowledge than one's own experiences, beliefs, traditions, or intuition alone. Some studies are abstract and provide general information about common educational practices and policies; this type of research influences the way one thinks about education. Other studies provide detailed information about specific practices at particular sites, such as a school, a classroom, or a program; this type of research can be used immediately to improve or justify a specific practice.

Developing Knowledge to Improve Educational Practices

The impact of educational research on schools and policy-makers seeking to improve educational practices may be seen as a process. Figure 1.1 shows the five phases of the process of developing evidence-based knowledge to improve educational practices: (1) identification of research problems, (2) empirical studies, (3) replications, (4) research synthesis and review, and (5) practitioner adoption and evaluation. The [identification of research problems] (Phase 1) begins with determining valued outcomes. Practical fields, like education, are concerned with valued outcomes such as learning. Research questions and problems come from the following sources: common observation, practical wisdom, policy controversies, prior research, and new methods applied in the study of education. Researchers conduct evidenced-based studies (Phase 2), and then they attempt research **replication**[1] (Phase 3) with different subjects and in a variety of settings and circumstances. In research synthesis and review (Phase 4) comparable studies are systematically evaluated and statistically or narratively summarized. Such an analysis helps to organize and make sense of the overall findings of prior research. Thus, the preponderance of evidence from many careful studies, rather than a few exact replications of the original research,

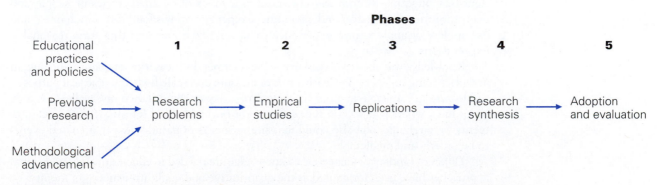

FIGURE 1.1   **Development of Evidence-Based Knowledge to Improve Educational Practice**

builds an evidence-based body of knowledge in education. Practitioners and policy-makers can reasonably accept the implications of research findings that are consistent without harmful side effects. Continuing local evaluation (Phase 5) is the final phase in the process.

To illustrate the potential impact of evidence-based research on educational outcomes, here are some examples of practices that were found to be effective, or "what works" (National Center for Educational Evaluation and Regional Assistance, 2003):

- **One-on-one tutoring by qualified tutors for at-risk readers in grades 1–3** The average tutored student read more proficiently than approximately 75 percent of the untutored students in the control group.
- **Life-skills training for junior high students** Implementing a low-cost, replicable program reduced smoking by 20 percent and serious level of substance abuse by 30 percent by students' senior year compared to the control group.
- **Reducing class size in grades K–3** On average, students in small classes scored higher on the Stanford Achievement Test in reading/math than 60 percent of the students in regular-sized classes.
- **Instruction for early readers in phonemic awareness and phonics** The average student in these interventions read more proficiently than approximately 70 percent of the students in the control group.

Clearly, the federal emphasis is on supporting a new generation of rigorous research.

The National Center for Educational Evaluation and Regional Assistance (NCEE) was established as part of the IES's goal to focus on evidence-based program effectiveness and impact questions. The NCEE recently initiated several program effectiveness studies in the following areas: preschool reading, reading instruction in the primary grades, teacher preparation, professional development, educational technology, remedial reading, after-school programs, English-language learning, and charter schools. All of these nationally funded evaluation studies provide either two or three years to address the bottom-line question of causality: Did Program X raise student achievement? The NCEE supports only those studies that can provide credible scientific evidence. The results of these studies will be widely disseminated in scholarly and professional journals.

RESEARCH AS SCIENTIFIC, EVIDENCE-BASED INQUIRY

Conducting research is a relatively new activity in the history of education, just as the concept of providing a free public education for all children is relatively modern in the history of humanity. In the early centuries, before reading and writing were common, individuals developed knowledge of the world around them primarily by two means. The first was through one's own personal experiences along with observation of others' experiences. Collective wisdom was conveyed as a series of detailed stories of people and events. Stories provided an understanding, a repertoire of wisdom from which one could extrapolate or apply known experience to an unknown area and thus form reasonable expectations.

Knowledge was also developed in another manner: by measuring or quantifying human activities using numbers. The early units of measure and scale had very practical purposes: to measure in a reliable manner the length of a day or the distance one walked. A mile was a mile, whether it was on flat, soft sand or on rocky, hard terrain. If these measurements were reliable, one also could measure segments of natural laws that caused events to be orderly and predictable.

Different kinds of evidence-based knowledge are needed in education. Two traditional approaches have been formalized as the quantitative and qualitative modes of inquiry. To the reader, the most obvious distinction between these two research approaches is the form of data presentation. Quantitative research presents statistical results using numbers; qualitative research presents data as a narration with words. These two research methods, however, are distinguished by far more than this obvious difference, which will be explained later in the chapter.

Guiding Principles of Scientific, Evidence-Based Inquiry

Education is a highly contested field of inquiry for two reasons: Values play a central role, and an educational intervention, when extensively investigated, seldom has only one main effect. Both positive and negative unintended consequences are often important. The accumulation of scientific knowledge over time is circuitous and indirect. Making a judgment on the effectiveness of a treatment is complex and requires a myriad of considerations.

1.1 Education Sciences Act
Accession No.: 10755456

The National Research Council (NRC) recently convened a committee of scholars to address two questions of interest to educators: "What constitutes 'scientifically based' research of educational phenomena?" and "Is scientifically based research the only or the best approach to studies which are meaningful in education?" (Eisenhart & Towne, 2003). Although the NRC's report, *Scientific Research in Education* (2002), focused on the first question, much of the subsequent public and academic debate addressed both questions.

To address the first question, some modifications must be made regarding the profound impact of the academic disciplines' standards for research rigor. What comprises rigorous research principles is somewhat different in each of the disciplines. Moreover, among the disciplines, there are variations in designs and methods, both in the process of conducting a study and in the rigor of the criteria. **Evidence-based inquiry** is the search for knowledge using systematically gathered empirical data. Unlike opinion or ideology, evidence-based inquiry is conducted and reported in such a way that the logical reasoning can be painstakingly examined. The term *evidence-based* does not refer to ritualization and using narrow forms of investigation, nor does it necessarily refer to following formal procedures. A study is evidence based when investigators have anticipated the traditional questions that are pertinent and instituted techniques to avoid bias at each step of data collection and reasoning. If the errors or biases cannot be eliminated, investigators discuss the potential effects of these issues in their conclusions.

Scientific inquiry, including educational research, is guided by six principles (National Research Council, 2002). Each is briefly explained in a following section with certain modifications, some of which were reflected in scholarly reviews of the report (Erickson & Gutierrez, 2002; St. Pierre, 2002). It is important to note that these principles are not absolute; they can serve only as guides when applied to education.

Guiding Principle 1: Pose Significant Questions That Can Be Investigated Empirically
The quality of a posed question often determines whether a study will eventually have an impact on the current state of knowledge. A question may be investigated to fill a gap in prior knowledge, to seek new knowledge, to identify the cause or causes of some phenomenon, or to formally test a hypothesis. A good question may reframe a prior research problem in light of newly available methodological or theoretical tools. The significance of a question can be established by citing prior research, relevant theory, and important claims regarding practice or policy. A question may even be articulated at the end of a study, when the researcher has a better understanding of the phenomenon.

Guiding Principle 2: Link Research to a Relevant Theory or Conceptual Framework
Much of scientific inquiry is linked, either explicitly or implicitly, to some overarching theory or conceptual framework that guides the entire research process. Sometimes, the conceptual framework is not formally stated but is easily recognized by the community of scholars working in the particular discipline. For example, the concept of *culture* provides a framework for anthropologists, just as the notion of *group* or *community* often frames the work of sociologists. Theory enters the research process in two important ways. First, scientific research is usually guided by a conceptual framework or theory that suggests possible questions or answers to questions posed. In a second, more subtle way, a conceptual framework influences the research process in the selection of what and how to observe

TABLE 1.1   Guiding Principles of Scientific, Evidence-Based Inquiry

1. Pose significant questions that can be investigated empirically.
2. Link research to a relevant theory or conceptual framework.
3. Use methods that allow direct investigation of the research question.
4. Provide a coherent and explicit chain of reasoning.
5. Replicate/generalize or extend across studies.
6. Disclose research to encourage professional scrutiny and critique.

Adapted from National Research Council (2002). *Scientific research in education.* Committee on Scientific Principles for Education Research. Shavelson, R. J., and Town, L., Eds. Center for Education, Division of Behavioral and Social Sciences and Education. Washington, D.C.: National Academy Press.

Research Navigator.com

1.2 Evidence-Based Research
Accession No.: 11092781

(i.e., methodological choice). Thus, the conceptual framework or theory drives the research question, the use of methods, and the interpretation of results (see Table 1.1).

Guiding Principle 3: Use Methods That Allow Direct Investigation of the Research Question   A method can only be judged in terms of its appropriateness and effectiveness in undertaking a particular research question. Scientific claims are strengthened when they are tested by multiple methods. Specific research designs and methods are best suited to specific types of questions and can rarely illuminate all the questions and issues in a given line of inquiry. Very different methodological approaches must often be used in different parts of a series of related studies.

Debates about the merits of various methods, especially quantitative versus qualitative, have raged for years. Simply stated, the method used to conduct scientific research must fit the question posed, and the link between question and method must be clearly explained and justified. Fortunately, a wide range of legitimate methods is available.

Guiding Principle 4: Provide a Coherent and Explicit Chain of Reasoning   A logical chain of reasoning, which proceeds from evidence to conclusions, is coherent, shareable, and persuasive to the skeptical reader. The validity of inferences made through this process is strengthened by identifying limitations and biases, estimating uncertainty and error, and systematically ruling out other plausible explanations in a rational, convincing way. Detailed descriptions of procedures and analyses are crucial.

Most rigorous research—quantitative and qualitative—embraces the same underlying logic of inference. Nonetheless, the nature of the chain of reasoning will vary depending on the design, which will, in turn, vary depending on the question being investigated.

Guiding Principle 5: Replicate/Generalize or Extend across Studies   Scientific inquiry emphasizes checking and validating individual findings. However, the role of contextual factors and the lack of control that exists in social settings make replication difficult. In both social sciences and education, many generalizations are limited to particular times and places. And because the social world changes more rapidly than the physical world, social generalizations usually have shorter life spans than generalizations in the physical world.

Some quantitative research aims at replication and generalization. **Generalization,** in research, is the extent to which the results of one study can be used as knowledge about other populations and situations. For instance, the findings of one quantitative study may also describe the current status of another group and its members' opinions, beliefs, and actions. The goal of most qualitative research, however, is to illuminate what is unique and to understand the particulars of a specific situation (i.e., case) in all its complexity. A body of scientific knowledge is built through the *logical extension* of findings, rather than through the *statistical generalization* of such information. The term *extension of findings* (sometimes used synonymously with *analytical synthesis, extrapolation, transferability,* or *assertion)* means that others can use the information to understand similar situations and can apply the information in subsequent research. Knowledge is produced not by replication but by the preponderance of evidence found in separate case studies over time.

Guiding Principle 6: Disclose Research to Encourage Professional Scrutiny and Critique   Scientific research does not contribute to a larger body of knowledge until its findings have been widely disseminated and undergone professional scrutiny by peers. The intellectual debate at professional meetings, in collaborative projects, and in other situations provides a forum by which scientific knowledge is refined and accepted. A collaborative, public critique is a sign of the health of scientific inquiry.

No single study or series of related studies can satisfy all six of the guiding principles. A single study may adhere to each principle in varying degree, and the extent to which it does assists in gauging its scientific quality. The features of education and of educational research, in combination with the guiding principles of science, set the boundaries for the design of a study. The design per se does not make the study scientific. A wide variety of legitimate scientific designs are available for educational research, ranging from experiments to in-depth qualitative case studies (National Research Council, 2002). To be scientific, the design must allow empirical (i.e., evidence-based) investigation of an important question, suggest appropriate methods for exploring the question, account for the context in which the study occurred, utilize a conceptual framework, demonstrate a chain of logical reasoning, and disclose results to encourage professional examination.

Definition of Research

Briefly defined, **research** is the systematic process of collecting and logically analyzing data for some purpose. This definition is general because many methods are available to investigate a problem or question. While educational research is not limited to the approaches used in the physical and natural sciences, the word *research* should not be used indiscriminately to describe what is actually casual observation and speculation. **Research methods** (sometimes called *methodology*) are the ways in which one collects and analyzes data. These methods have been developed for acquiring knowledge by reliable and valid procedures. Data collection may be done with measurement techniques, extensive interviews and observations, or a set of documents.

Research methodology is systematic and purposeful. Procedures are not haphazard; they are planned to yield data on a particular research problem. In a broader context, the term *methodology* refers to a design whereby the researcher selects data collection and analysis procedures to investigate a specific research problem.

The Characteristics of Educational Research

The following characteristics are common to many types of evidence-based research conducted in education: objective, precise, verifiable, explanatory, empirical, logical, and conditional. Taken together, these characteristics describe the nature of research (see Table 1.2):

1. **Objectivity** Objectivity is both a procedure and a characteristic. To the lay person, objectivity means unbiased, open-minded, not subjective. As a procedure, **objectivity** refers to data collection and analysis procedures from which a reasonable interpretation can be made. Objectivity refers to the quality of the data produced by procedures that either control for bias or take into account subjectivity.

2. **Precision** Technical language is used in research to convey exact meanings. Expressions such as *validity* and *reliability* in measurement, *research design, random sample,* and *statistical significance* convey technical procedures. Other phrases, such as *constant*

TABLE 1.2 **Characteristics of Educational Research**

Characteristics	Quantitative	Qualitative
Objectivity	Explicit description of data collection and analysis procedures	Explicit description of data collection and analysis procedures
Precision	Measurement and statistics	Detailed description of phenomenon
Verification	Results replicated by others	Extension of understandings by others
Parsimonious explanation	Least complicated explanation preferred	Summary statements
Empiricism	Numerical data	Narrative
Logical reasoning	Primarily deductive	Primarily inductive
Conditional conclusions	Statements of statistical probability	Tentative summary interpretations

comparison and *reflexivity,* refer to strategies in qualitative inquiry. Precise language describes the study accurately so that the study may be replicated or extended and the results may be used correctly.

3. ***Verification*** To develop knowledge, a single study attempts to be designed and presented in such a manner to allow **verification**—that is, the results can be confirmed or revised in subsequent research. Results are verified in different ways, depending on the purpose of the original study. If the research tests a theory, then further testing with other groups or in other settings could confirm or revise the theory. Most qualitative studies, however, provide descriptive interpretations about the selected situation or case. These interpretations are extended but not replicated in subsequent research of other similar situations for revision. Qualitative research is not verified in the same manner nor to the same degree as quantitative research.

4. ***Parsimonious explanation*** Research attempts to explain relationships among phenomena and to reduce the **explanation** to simple statements. The theory "Frustration leads to aggression" is an explanation that predicts, and it can be tested for verification. The summary generalization "Teacher learning and curriculum change cannot be isolated from the social situations in which the curriculum is implemented" (Tobin & LaMaster, 1995) is an explanation that can be investigated further. The ultimate aim of research is thus to reduce complex realities to simple explanations.[2]

5. ***Empiricism*** Research is characterized by a strong empirical attitude and approach. The word *empirical* has both lay and technical meanings. The lay meaning of *empirical* is that which is guided by practical experience, not by research. According to this pragmatic perspective, if it works, it is right; regardless of the reasons, it must be right because it works. To the researcher, **empirical** means guided by evidence obtained from systematic research methods rather than by opinions or authorities. Generally, an empirical attitude requires a temporary suspension of personal experience and beliefs. Critical elements in research are evidence and logical interpretations based on the evidence.

To a researcher, evidence is **data,** that is, results obtained from research from which interpretations or conclusions are drawn. In a general sense, the terms *data, sources,* and *evidence* are used synonymously, to mean information obtained by research methods. Test scores and computer printouts, field notes and interview records, artifacts and historical documents are all called *data.*

6. **Logical reasoning** All research requires logical reasoning. Reasoning is a thinking process, using prescribed rules of logic, in which one proceeds from a general statement to the specific conclusion (deduction) or, the reverse, from specific statements to a summary generalization (induction). Both kinds of reasoning are employed in the research process, regardless of the type of design or method being used.

7. **Conditional conclusions** One misconception of research is that the results are absolute. This is incorrect. As noted by a leading educational researcher, "Behavioral science and research does not offer certainty. (Neither does natural science!) It does not even offer relative certainty. All it offers is probabilistic knowledge. If A is done, then B will probably occur" (Kerlinger, 1979, p. 28). One way of defining *research* might be to say that it is a method of reducing uncertainty. The social sciences have more uncertainty than the physical sciences.

Drawing conditional conclusions is central to research. All scientific research contains restricted interpretations. Both quantitative and qualitative research statements have implicit or explicit conditional conclusions. Researchers thus often write that their results "tend to indicate" or "are suggestive."

The Research Process

The research process typically involves several phases. These phases are not always sequential nor are they an orderly step-by-step process. Research is more an interactive process between the researcher and the logic of the problem, design, and interpretations. Here is a summary of the process, with variations noted (see Figure 1.2):

1. **Select a general problem.** The problem defines the area of education in which research will be conducted, such as instruction, administration, adult education, or special education.

2. **Review the literature on the problem.** The most important literature is prior research and theory, but other literature may be useful. In some studies, an exhaustive

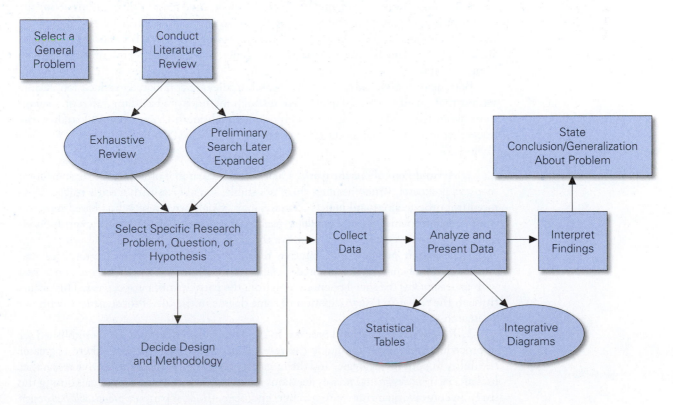

FIGURE 1.2   **The Research Process**

literature review is done before one collects data. In other studies, the literature review is tentative and preliminary before data collection and then expanded as data are collected.

3. ***Decide the specific research problem, question, or hypothesis.*** This requires the investigator to select whether a quantitative or qualitative mode of inquiry is appropriate for the research problem. If a qualitative approach is selected, the research problem or question is a preliminary guide and will become more specific as the research progresses.

4. ***Determine the design and methodology.*** The researcher decides from whom data will be collected, how the subjects will be selected, and how data will be collected.

5. ***Collect data.*** Ethical and legal concerns regarding data collection and analysis must also be resolved.

6. ***Analyze data and present the results.*** Usually, summary visual representations are used, such as statistical tables and integrative diagrams.

7. ***Interpret the findings and state conclusions or a summary regarding the problem.*** Decisions are made about the reporting format appropriate for the purpose of the study and the intended audience or readers. The research process may be relatively short, or it may take several years or longer.

The inquiry process is essentially one of reflection. Each decision made by the researcher is reported explicitly, often with a rationale for the choice. It is an exciting intellectual process, one that uses different skills in the various phases.

QUANTITATIVE AND QUALITATIVE RESEARCH APPROACHES

As noted earlier, the terms *quantitative* and *qualitative* are used frequently to identify different modes of inquiry or approaches to research. The terms can be defined on two levels of discourse. At one level, quantitative and qualitative refer to distinctions about the nature of knowledge: how one understands the world and the ultimate purpose of the research. On another level of discourse, the terms refer to research methods—how data are collected and analyzed—and the types of generalizations and representations derived from the data.

Both quantitative and qualitative research studies are conducted in education. Purists suggest that quantitative and qualitative research methods are based on different assumptions about the world, the research purpose, research methods, prototypical studies, the researcher role, and the importance of context in the study (Denzin & Lincoln, 2000) (see Table 1.3):

1. ***Assumptions about the world*** Quantitative research is usually based on some form of *logical positivism*, which assumes there are stable, social facts with a *single reality*, separated from the feelings and beliefs of individuals. Qualitative research is based more on *constructionism*, which assumes *multiple realities* are socially constructed through individual and collective perceptions or views of the same situation.

2. ***Research purpose*** Quantitative research seeks to establish relationships and explain *causes* of changes in measured social facts. Qualitative research is more concerned with *understanding* the social phenomenon from the participants' perspectives. This occurs through the researcher's participation to some degree in the life of those persons while in a research role.

3. ***Research methods and process*** In quantitative studies, there is an established set of procedures and steps that guide the researcher. In qualitative studies, there is greater flexibility in both the strategies and the research process. Typically, a qualitative researcher uses an *emergent design* and revises decisions about the data collection strategies during the study. In contrast, quantitative researchers choose methods as part of a *pre-established design* before data collection.

TABLE 1.3   Quantitative and Qualitative Research Approaches

Orientation	Quantitative	Qualitative
Assumptions about the world	A single reality, i.e., measured by an instrument	Multiple realities, e.g., interviews of principal, teachers, and students about a social situation
Research purpose	Establish relationships between measured variables	Understanding a social situation from participants' perspectives
Research methods and process	Procedures (sequential steps) are established before study begins	Flexible, changing strategies; design emerges as data are collected
Prototypical study (clearest example)	Experimental design to reduce error and bias	Ethnography using "disciplined subjectivity"
Researcher role	Detached with use of instrument	Prepared person becomes immersed in social situation
Importance of context	Goal of universal context-free generalizations	Goal of detailed context-bound summary statements

4. ***Prototypical studies*** The quantitative researcher employs *experimental* or *correlational* designs to reduce error, bias, and extraneous variables. The prototypical qualitative study of ongoing events is an *ethnography*, which helps readers understand the multiple perspectives of the social scene or system by the persons studied. Whereas quantitative research seeks to control for bias through design, qualitative research seeks to take into account subjectivity in data analysis and interpretation.

5. ***Researcher role*** The ideal quantitative researcher is *detached* from the study to avoid bias. Qualitative researchers become *immersed* in the situation and the phenomenon being studied. For example, qualitative researchers assume interactive social roles in which they record observations and interviews with participants in a range of contexts. Qualitative scholars emphasize the importance of data collected by a skilled, prepared *person* in contrast to an *instrument*. Qualitative research is noted for "disciplined subjectivity" (Erickson, 1973) and "reflexivity" (Mason, 1996), that is, critical self-examination of the researcher's role throughout the entire research process.

6. ***Importance of the context in the study*** Most quantitative research attempts to establish *universal, context-free generalizations*. The qualitative researcher believes that human actions are strongly influenced by the settings in which they occur. The researcher cannot understand human behavior without understanding the framework within which subjects interpret their thoughts, feelings, and actions. This framework or context is noted by the qualitative researcher during data collection and analysis. Qualitative research develops *context-bound* summaries.

Many of these distinctions between quantitative and qualitative research are not absolute when one conducts research or reads a completed study. Experienced researchers can and do combine both quantitative and qualitative research methods in a single study in order to investigate a particular research problem (see Chapter 15). However, combining both approaches in a single study is more difficult than it may appear (Tashakkori & Teddlie, 1998). The distinctions, however, are useful devices in an introduction to research for describing and understanding research methods, a goal of this textbook.

Research
Navigator.c⊛m

1.3 Qualitative Research
Important
Accession No.: 4886856

THE FUNCTIONS OF RESEARCH:
BASIC, APPLIED, EVALUATION, AND ACTION

The purpose of research is based on the anticipated use of its findings. Basic, applied, evaluation, and action research differ essentially in the degree to which they facilitate decision making.[3] They do not differ, however, in terms of being evidence based. Most studies are designed and judged as adequate for one type of research and as less adequate for other types of research.

Basic Research

The exclusive purpose of **basic research** (sometimes called *pure* or *fundamental research*) is to know and explain through testing specific theories that provide broad generalizations. A **theory** predicts and explains a natural phenomenon. Instead of explaining each specific behavior of adults, for example, the scientist seeks general explanations that link different behaviors. Noted scholar Fred N. Kerlinger (1986) defines a *theory* as a set of interrelated constructs and propositions that specify relations among variables to explain and predict phenomena. By explaining which variables relate to which other variables and how, the scientist can make predictions. For instance, if one can predict from variable A (say, test anxiety) to variable B (test performance), then one can deduce the possibility of control through intervention with, say, instruction on test-taking skills.

A theory may or may not have empirical support. When a theory has considerable empirical support, it is called a *scientific law*. A scientific law such as the law of gravity is generalizable—that is, it explains many individual cases.

Basic research is not designed to solve social problems. The scientist is preoccupied with developing knowledge but is not required to spell out the practical implications of his or her work. Both goals usually cannot be achieved by a single study. Basic research, after considerable time, can indirectly influence the ways people think and perceive phenomena. Much valuable social science research, however, is *not* specifically theory oriented. While having modest, limited, and specific aims is good, formulating and verifying theories is better because theories are more general and explanatory.

Applied Research

Applied research is conducted in a field of common practice and is concerned with the application and development of research-based knowledge about that practice. Medicine, engineering, social work, and education are all applied fields. Applied research (as opposed to basic research) produces knowledge relevant to providing solutions to general problems. In other words, applied studies focus on research problems common to a given field.

In the field of education, applied research usually focuses on problems that need to be solved to improve practice. To the extent that general theories are tested, the results may be generalized to many different educational settings. For example, basic theories of human memory, developed through basic research, could be tested in a new curriculum to discern improved retention of science concepts. Other examples of applied research in education are studies that compare different teaching styles, identify characteristics of effective schools, and examine the effects of lengthening the schoolday on student achievement. Educational research thus focuses on knowledge about *educational* theories and practices, rather than on *universal* knowledge.

Because applied research usually investigates problems that are integral to making decisions, its impact may be immediate. Depending on the topic of study, applied research also may have an indirect effect over time by influencing how practitioners think about and perceive common problems.

Evaluation Research

Evaluation research focuses on a particular practice at a given site. The practice may be a program, a product, or a process, but the site is crucial. Evaluation research assesses the *merit* and *worth* of a particular practice in terms of the values operating at the site. Evaluation determines whether the practice works—that is, Does it do what is intended at the site? Evaluation also determines whether the practice is worth the associated costs of development, implementation, and widespread adoption. Those costs may involve materials, space, staff development, teacher morale, and/or community support.

Evaluation focuses first on the concerns and issues related to the practice at a given site. Such studies can add to existing knowledge about a specific practice and stimulate further research and methodological development. For example, a series of evaluative studies on a particular practice at diverse sites, such as Title IV (Head Start) classrooms, or on the change process within a large organization can add to existing knowledge in the applied field.

Action Research

Action research involves the use of research methods by practitioners to study current problems or issues. Teachers conduct these studies or play important roles in the research process. Action research may focus on three levels: individual teacher research, research by teams in a single school or department, and schoolwide research. Because the focus is on a solution to common issues or everyday concerns in classrooms or a school, the results of action research tend to be localized. Rigorous research control is not essential, and both quantitative and qualitative research approaches may be used.

A more recent variation is *collaborative action research* (Oja & Smulyan, 1989; Stinger, 1996; Stringer, 2004), in which practitioners conduct the inquiry with the help of a consultant. For example, teachers may work with university-based researchers in their classrooms doing participatory research. Collaborative action research usually focuses on both the processes and the outcomes of a change strategy, such as a staff development program.

Many aspects of action research are similar to those of the qualitative approach. Often, both numerical data and qualitative data are used. Important elements of action research include (1) making a time commitment, (2) viewing collaboration as valuing each person's contribution and level of engagement, (3) developing trusting relationships, (4) appraising one's actions, especially professional actions, throughout the process, and (5) accepting change as crucial to remaining an effective teacher.

The *purpose* of research and the *quality* of research are two separate dimensions of inquiry. Researchers use the same kinds of designs and methods for these different types of research. The criteria for determining the quality of a study is related to the design and procedures chosen for the question being investigated. As such, there can be poorly designed basic research and excellent applied studies. Similarly, small-scale action research can be well designed, and large-scale evaluation studies may provide questionable information because of procedural difficulties.

LIMITATIONS OF EDUCATIONAL RESEARCH

Education, as an interdisciplinary field of inquiry, has borrowed concepts and theories from psychology, sociology, anthropology, political science, economics, and other disciplines. Theories based on concepts such as *role, status, authority, self-concept,* and the like have been tested in education, and new educational concepts have emerged. Evidence-based educational research uses methodologies developed originally in the social sciences. Psychology, especially measurement, has traditionally dominated educational research. Other methodologies employed in education are the sociological survey, anthropological

Research Navigator.com

1.4 Disciplines in Research
Accession No.: 2816948

participant observation, historical research, and political analysis. While these approaches are often modified for educational research, doing so rarely violates the discipline from which the method was drawn.

The presence of many disciplinary perspectives in education research has at least two implications for evidence-based inquiry. First, since different disciplinary perspectives focus on different parts of the education system, many legitimate research frameworks and methods are available (National Research Council, 2002). But, because most disciplines focus on different parts of the educational system, this also means that contradictory conclusions are possible. Second, advances in educational research often depend on advances in related disciplines and fields.

> **MISCONCEPTION** The recent federal emphasis on scientific inquiry implies that this approach is the *best way* or even the *only way* for educators to make decisions.
>
> **EVIDENCE** Cognitive studies of administrator decision making suggest that logic, experience, ethical concerns, and legal ramifications are more important than scientific inquiry in making many decisions.

The field of education is often compared to that of medicine, where scientific studies play a role in determining health policy and medical practice. Educational scholars, however, contend that the two fields and their research constraints are not analogous. Social science is often contrasted with physical science, but as noted educational researcher David Berliner recently wrote (2002, p. 18), "We do our science under conditions that physical scientists find intolerable." In addition to a number of institutional and methodological constraints, cost is a "major concern in a field [i.e., education] that is widely considered to be underfunded" (Viadero, 1999, p. 34).

The development of a scientific basis for educational knowledge is limited by a set of features specific to education. Most practitioners are well aware of these features, but these aspects also affect research activities. Education is multilayered, constantly shifting, and involves interaction among institutions (e.g., schools, universities, families, communities, and government). It is value laden and embraces a diverse array of people and political forces. Because the U.S. educational system is so heterogeneous and the nature of teaching and learning so complex, research generalizations are limited in scope and thus application.

Furthermore, educational research relies on having relationships with professional practitioners. No study can be conducted without the participation of or cooperation of professionals. Educational research depends on its links with practice, which exist along a continuum: Some types of research involve only a short, distant, one-time interaction, whereas others require long-term, full partnerships or collaborations with schools or other agencies.

Educational research is limited by the following six constraints, which ultimately influence the knowledge gained about education through research (see Figure 1.3):

1. *Legal and ethical considerations* Educational research focuses primarily on human beings. The researcher is ethically responsible for protecting the rights and welfare of the subjects who participate in a study, which involves issues of physical and mental discomfort, harm, and danger. Most studies require that informed consent be obtained from the subjects, their parents, or a relevant institution, and laws are in place to protect the confidentiality of the data and the privacy of the subjects.[4] These principles often impose limitations on the kinds of studies that can be conducted in valid ways in education. For example, the physical and mental discomfort of subjects may affect the length of testing periods, the replication of studies, the types of treatments, and ultimately the research questions investigated.

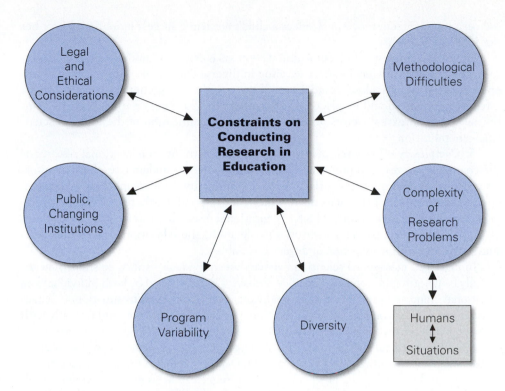

FIGURE 1.3 **Constraints on Educational Research**

2. *Public institutions* Education is a public enterprise that is influenced by the external environment. Since the report of a presidential commission, *A Nation at Risk,* was issued in 1983, the United States seems to be in a constant process of reforming its schools. Legislative mandates and judicial orders have changed the structure of schools and added, deleted, and modified programs. As waves of reform have swept the schools, instability has occurred in curriculum, standards, and accountability. Longitudinal and replication studies that evaluate changing clientele, programs, and institutions are difficult to conduct. In addition, the ultimate effects of these changes on schooling may not be known because such effects often occur years later, outside the educational setting.

The public nature of education also influences the kinds of research questions investigated. In most studies, the subjects and other groups are made aware of the research topic. Some topics may be too controversial for a conservative community or too divisive for a given institution's staff. Some studies are not conducted because the subsequent reactions may be detrimental to maintaining an educational organization.

3. *Program variability* A third constraint on research in education is the wide variety of programs that exist, often with the same core name. Even within reform movements, state and local control of education markedly shapes how instructional programs and other changes are implemented. Evaluations of curriculum changes may be influenced by high-stakes accountability systems and national college entrance exams. Researchers must specify the local and state conditions under which their findings were produced.

4. *Diversity* The U.S. population is becoming increasingly diverse, and this is mirrored in American neighborhoods and schools. The linguistic diversity that characterizes many schools is the most obvious manifestation of this trend. But beyond the common characteristic of lacking English fluency, there are notable differences between students from newly arrived immigrant families and those whose families have lived in this country for generations. Along with linguistic diversity come differences in culture, religion, academic preparation, and ties to the homeland. The parents' education and current

socioeconomic circumstances may affect a child's academic success more than his or her not speaking English.

Examining linguistic and sociocultural contexts is critical to understanding the ways in which cultural differences affect learning in diverse classrooms. Attention to different contexts implies close coordination between the researcher and practitioners. Greater emphasis should be placed on the impact of schooling on diverse populations of students. Contextual factors neccessitate a careful delineation of the limits of scientific generalization.

5. *Complexity of research problems* Another constraint on educational research is the complexity of research problems. The people involved—students, teachers, administrators, parents, and members of the collective community—are complex human beings, and they actively select the elements to which they respond. Furthermore, different individuals process ideas differently. Much of educational research illustrates the complexities of individual differences. Thus, within a single study, the educational researcher deals simultaneously with many, often ambiguous, variables.

In addition, most social scientists believe that individuals cannot be studied meaningfully by ignoring the context of real life. Behavior is determined by both individual and situational characteristics, and to study individuals without regard to situational characteristics would be incomplete. Thus, educational researchers must contend not only with individual differences among people but also with a myriad of situational elements.

6. *Methodological difficulties* The final constraint on educational research is methodological difficulties. Educational research measures complex human characteristics, as well as thinking and problem-solving skills. Moreover, to measure achievement, intelligence, leadership style, group interaction, or readiness skills involves formulating conceptual definitions and deciding issues of validity. Some educational research has become possible only as valid and reliable instruments have been developed. Other difficulties are the inappropriate use of methodology and reporting practices (Daniel, 1999).

Qualitative research also has methodological difficulties, especially those inherent in employing multimethod strategies, addressing the reflexive research role, and making explicit the data analysis techniques used. Qualitative research is sometimes criticized by the conventional viewpoint for its lack of reliable and generalizable findings, but case study designs provide context-bound summaries for understanding education and for future research (Peshkin, 1993).

Despite these difficulties, educational research has made considerable gains in evidence-based knowledge. The features of education and of educational research, in combination with the guiding principles of scientific inquiry, set the boundaries for the design of a study. As noted earlier, however, the actual design of the study does not make it scientific. A wide variety of legitimate scientific designs are available for education research, ranging from experiments to in-depth qualitative case study designs (National Research Council, 2002). To be scientific, the design must allow empirical investigation of an important question, account for the context in which the study occurred, use a conceptual framework, demonstrate a chain of logical reasoning, and disclose results to encourage public examination.

SUMMARY

This chapter has discussed the six guiding principles of scientific, evidence-based inquiry; the development of educational knowledge; the characteristics of educational research; distinctions between quantitative and qualitative research; the functions of research; and the limitations of educational research. The major ideas in this chapter can be summarized as follows:

1. Evidence-based inquiry uses systematically gathered, empirical data that are reported in such a way that the

logical reasoning that underlies them can be painstakingly examined.

2. The process of developing educational knowledge involves identification of research problems, empirical studies, replications, research synthesis, and practitioner adoption and evaluation.

3. The guiding principles of scientific inquiry are to pose significant empirical questions, to link research to theory, to use appropriate methods for investigating the research question, to demonstrate a specific chain of reasoning, to generalize or extend across studies, and to disclose results for professional scrutiny.

4. *Research* is the systematic process of collecting and logically analyzing data for some purpose.

5. Characteristics of research in education are objectivity, precision, verification, parsimonious explanation, empiricism, logical reasoning, and conditional conclusions.

6. Quantitative and qualitative research, differ in terms of their assumptions about the world, research purposes, research methods and processes, prototypical studies, research roles, and the importance of consid-

ering context in the physical, behavioral, and social sciences.

7. Applied research tests the usefulness of scientific theories in an applied field and investigates relationships and analytical generalizations common to that given profession.

8. Evaluation research assesses the merit and worth of a specific practice at a given site or several sites against one or more scales of value.

9. Action research involves teachers using research methods to study classroom problems.

10. The scientific quality of a study depends on the design and methods used, not the type of research (e.g., basic, applied, evaluation, or action research).

11. Education is an interdisciplinary field of inquiry—that is, educational researchers borrow concepts and methodologies from other academic disciplines and apply them in educational research.

12. Educational knowledge is limited by ethical and legal concerns, the public nature of education, program variability, diversity, the complexity of research problems, and methodological difficulties.

RESEARCH NAVIGATOR NOTES

Reading the following articles will help you understand the content of this chapter. Go to the education database (included in the EBSCO database) in Research Navigator; use the Accession Number to find the article.

1.1   *Education Sciences Act*
Sroufe, G. (2003). Legislative reform of federal education research programs: A political annotation of the Education Sciences Reform Act of 2002. *Peabody Journal of Education,* 78(4), 220–230. Accession Number: 10755456.

1.2   *Evidence-Based Research*
Mayer, R. E. (2003). Learning environments: The case for evidence-based practice and issue-driven research. *Educa-*

tional Psychology Review, 15(4), 359–367. Accession Number: 11092781.

1.3   *Qualitative Research Important*
Pugach, M. C. (2001). The stories we choose to tell: Fulfilling the promise of qualitative research for special education. *Exceptional Children,* 67(4), 439–454. Accession Number: 4886856.

1.4   *Disciplines in Research*
Spidler, G., & Hammond, L. (2000). The use of anthropological methods in educational research: Two perspectives. *Harvard Educational Review,* 70(1), 39–49. Accession Number: 2816948.

CHECK YOURSELF

Multiple-choice review items, with answers, are available on the Companion Website for this book.

www.ablongman.com/mcmillanschumacher6e

APPLICATION PROBLEMS

Research results can be used in a number of ways:

A. to influence the way the reader thinks or perceives a problem
B. to generate decision making that leads to action
C. to generate a new research question or problem

The following are examples of research results. In which of the ways just listed might each be used? Provide examples. There is not a single correct answer. For feedback, compare your answers with the sample answers in the back of the book.

1. A teacher reads a research study reporting that children from broken homes are more likely to exhibit deviant behavior in schools than are children from intact homes.
2. A study reports that a test measuring reading comprehension in grades 1 through 4 has been validated on students in grades 1 and 2 but not those in grades 3 and 4.
3. An educational historian notes that a well-known study of the organization of public schools from 1900 to 1950 stops short of the 1954 Supreme Court ruling on "separate but equal."
4. Upon reading the results of a survey of the parents of his school pupils, a principal realizes that the parents do not understand the new report card and grading system.
5. A curriculum developer field tests a pilot module of a strategy to help adult basic education teachers teach a reading strategy. The results of a representative sample of the teachers in the state suggest that the module should be revised to include a rationale for the strategy, a clear specification of the type of student who would benefit from the strategy, and alternative techniques to respond to student difficulties.
6. Previous research indicates that school systems have been tightly structured organizations with hierarchical authority. A professor of school administration recalls that several superintendents and principals have seen many elements of autonomous behavior by principals and teachers at the school level, even though no empirical studies have reported this.

NOTES

1. Boldfaced key terms are defined in the Glossary at the end of the book.
2. Qualitative researchers debate whether the explanations are propositions, assertions, summaries, naturalistic/summary generalizations, or conclusions. See Stake (1995), Lincoln and Guba (1985), and LeCompte and Preissle (1993).
3. The authors recognize that the distinctions among basic, applied, evaluation, and action research are oversimplified and overemphasized in this discussion for illustrative purposes.

4. The laws, passed in 1974, are the Family Education Rights and Privacy Act, the National Research Act, and the Privacy Act. Although there is consensus about the intent of these laws, the interpretation of the regulations varies. A researcher abides by the procedures of the agency for which data are collected.

Research Designs and Reading Research Reports

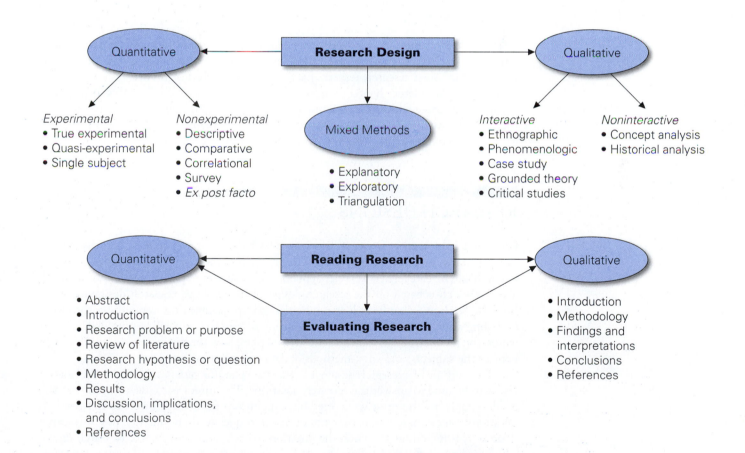

KEY TERMS

research design	interactive
experimental	ethnography
true experimental	phenomenological study
random assignment	case study
quasi-experimental	grounded theory
single-subject	critical studies
nonexperimental	noninteractive
descriptive	analytical research
comparative	concept analysis
correlational	historical analysis
correlation	mixed-method
survey	explanatory
ex post facto	exploratory
secondary data analysis	triangulation
qualitative	

This chapter completes our overview of educational research. Its goals are to introduce terminology related to the way research is designed and to acquaint you with the organization of published research reports. Each of the research designs will be examined in greater detail in a later chapter. Our experience in teaching research is that it is best to become acquainted with these research design terms and concepts as early as possible. As they are reviewed in the context of actual studies and explained in greater detail, you will gain a more complete understanding and have increased retention.

RESEARCH DESIGNS

Chapter 1 examined how research can be viewed as scientific inquiry and disciplined inquiry, that approaches to research can be primarily quantitative or qualitative, and that research can be categorized as basic, applied, evaluation, or action. Another way to think about research is based on the research design of the study. A **research design** describes how the study was conducted. It summarizes the procedures for conducting the study, including when, from whom, and under what conditions the data will be obtained. In other words, the research design indicates the general plan: how the research is set up, what happens to the subjects, and what methods of data collection are used.

The purpose of a research design is to specify a plan for generating empirical evidence that will be used to answer the research questions. The intent is to use a design that will result in drawing the most valid, credible conclusions from the answers to the research questions. Since there are many types of research questions and many types of research designs, it is important to match the question to an appropriate design. Research design is a very important part of an investigation, since certain limitations and cautions in interpreting the results are related to each design and because the research design determines how the data should be analyzed.

To help you identify and classify different research designs, we have classified them as three major categories: quantitative, qualitative, and mixed method. The first two are the most common. Within each major category, there are different types. These types of designs, listed in Table 2.1, are often used to describe the research (e.g., "This is an experimental study," "This is a case study," "Correlational research was used"). The designs will

TABLE 2.1   Research Designs

Quantitative		Qualitative		
Experimental	**Nonexperimental**	**Interactive**	**Noninteractive**	**Mixed-Method**
True experimental	Descriptive	Ethnographic	Concept analysis	Explanatory
Quasi-experimental	Comparative	Phenomenologic	Historical analysis	Exploratory
Single-subject	Correlational	Case study		Triangulation
	Survey*	Grounded theory		
	Ex post facto	Critical studies		
	Secondary data analysis			

*Surveys are classified here as a type of research design. Surveys can also be classified as a type of data collection technique.

be reviewed briefly in this chapter and revisited in detail in later chapters. Once you become familiar with the primary orientation of each design it will help you identify that design when reading studies or when thinking about a study of your own.

ALERT!   The debate as to whether using a quantitative, qualitative, or mixed-method approach is best has been resolved by matching appropriate designs to research questions.

It should be noted that these categories are independent of the classification of research as basic, applied, or evaluation. That is, for example, basic research can be experimental or nonexperimental, applied research can be single-subject or correlational.

QUANTITATIVE RESEARCH DESIGNS

Quantitative research designs were initially developed from research in agriculture and the hard sciences. These fields of study adopted a positivist philosophy of knowing that emphasized objectivity and quantification of phenomena. As a result, the research designs maximize objectivity by using numbers, statistics, structure, and control.

A very important subclassification of quantitative design is experimental/nonexperimental. Once you have determined that the study being reviewed is quantitative, then you should think about whether it is experimental or nonexperimental. This difference has major implications for both the nature of the design and the types of conclusions that can be drawn.

Experimental Designs

In an **experimental** design, the researcher manipulates what the subjects will experience. In other words, the investigator has some control over what will happen to the subjects by systematically imposing or withholding specified interventions. The researcher then makes comparisons either (1) between subjects who have had and others who have not had the interventions or (2) between subjects who have experienced different interventions. An experimental design also has a particular purpose in mind: to investigate cause-and-effect relationships between interventions and measured outcomes.

Here we will describe the three most common experimental designs. Chapter 10 will present these designs and others in greater detail.

True Experimental   The unique characteristic of a **true experimental** design is that there is random assignment of subjects to different groups. With **random assignment,** every subject used in the study has an equal chance of being in each group. This procedure, when carried out with a large enough sample, helps ensure that there are no major differences between subjects in each group before intervention begins. This enables the researcher to conclude that the results are not due to differences in characteristics of the subjects or to most extraneous events.

The physical and biological sciences frequently use true experimental designs because they provide the most powerful approach for determining the effect of one factor on another. In these disciplines, it is also relatively easy to meet the conditions of random assignment and manipulation. For example, if a group of farmers wants to determine which of two fertilizers causes the best growth, they can divide large plots of land into smaller sections and randomly give some sections fertilizer A and the others fertilizer B. As long as the same amount of rain and sun and the same insect problems and other factors affect each section—which would probably be the case—the farmers can determine which fertilizer is best. In the social sciences, however, and especially in education, it is often difficult to meet these conditions. True experiments are especially difficult to employ in applied research, in which researchers minimize changes to naturally occurring conditions.

Quasi-Experimental   A **quasi-experimental** design approximates the true experimental type. The purpose of the method is the same—to determine cause and effect—and there is direct manipulation of conditions. However, there is no random assignment of subjects. A common situation for implementing quasi-experimental research involves several classes or schools that can be used to determine the effect of curricular materials or teaching methods. The classes are intact, or already organized for an instructional purpose. The classes are not assigned randomly and have different teachers. It is possible, however, to give an experimental treatment to some of the classes and treat other classes as controls.

Single-Subject   Research in education has been influenced heavily by a tradition in which groups of subjects, rather than individuals, are studied. In many situations, however, it is impossible or inconvenient to study entire groups of subjects. Furthermore, the researcher may be interested in one or two subjects, not large groups of subjects. **Single-subject** designs offer an alternative by specifying methods that can be used with a single individual or just a few subjects and still allow reasonable cause-and-effect conclusions. Similar to quasi-experimental research, there is direct manipulation but no random assignment in single-subject research.

Nonexperimental Designs

Nonexperimental research designs describe things that have occurred and examine relationships between things without any direct manipulation of conditions that are experienced. There are six types of nonexperimental designs: descriptive, comparative, correlational, survey, *ex post facto,* and secondary data analysis.

Descriptive   Research using a **descriptive** design simply provides a summary of an existing phenomenon by using numbers to characterize individuals or a group. It assesses the nature of existing conditions. The purpose of most descriptive research is limited to characterizing something as it is.[1]

Comparative   In a **comparative** design, the researcher investigates whether there are differences between two or more groups on the phenomena being studied. As with descriptive designs, there is no manipulation or direct control of conditions experienced; even so, the comparative approach takes descriptive studies a step further. For example, rather than simply describe pupil attitudes toward discipline, a comparative study could investigate whether attitudes differed by grade level or gender. Another example would be to compare the grades of athletes and nonathletes. Often, comparative modes of inquiry are used to study relationships between different phenomena, for example, the relationship between participation in athletics and grade-point average.

Correlational   **Correlational** research is concerned with assessing relationships between two or more phenomena. This type of study usually involves a statistical measure of the degree of relationship, called **correlation.** The relationship measured is a statement about the degree of association between the variables of interest. A *positive correlation* means that high values of one variable are associated with high values of a second variable. The relationship between height and weight, between IQ scores and achievement test scores, and between self-concept and grades are examples of positive correlation. A *negative correlation* or relationship means that high values of one variable are associated with low values of a second variable. Examples of negative correlations include those between exercise and heart failure, between successful test performance and feelings of incompetence, and between absence from school and school achievement.

Survey   In a **survey** research design, the investigator selects a sample of subjects and administers a questionnaire or conducts interviews to collect data. Surveys are used frequently in educational research to describe attitudes, beliefs, opinions, and other types of information. Usually, the research is designed so that information about a large number of people (the population) can be inferred from the responses obtained from a smaller group of subjects (the sample).

Ex Post Facto   An *ex post facto* design is used to explore possible causal relationships among variables that cannot be manipulated by the researcher. The investigator designs the study to compare two or more samples that are comparable except for a specified factor. The possible causes are studied after they have occurred. Rather than manipulate what *will* happen to subjects, as in experimental designs, the research focuses on what has happened differently for comparable groups of subjects, then explores whether the subjects in each group are different in some way. For example, an important question concerning day care for children is the relative effect the type of day-care program may have on school readiness. Some day care programs are more academic than others. Since it would be very difficult to manipulate experimentally the type of day care a child attends, an ex post facto mode of inquiry would be appropriate. The investigator would identify two groups of children who have similar backgrounds but who have attended different types of day care. The subjects would be given a school readiness test to see whether those who attended a highly academically oriented day-care facility differ from children who attended a less academically oriented day-care facility.

Secondary Data Analysis   Often, researchers have access to data that others have gathered and conduct analyses using these data. This type of research design is called **secondary data analysis.** Secondary analysis is becoming more popular as large federal and state data sets are released to the public. Good examples include test score data and data relevant to the No Child Left Behind (NCLB) Act, passed in 2001. According to the NCLB, for example, student test score data must be reported for different types of students (e.g., students with disabilities, English-language learners, African American students). Researchers can take these data and conduct studies that compare achievement among the groups or that examine trends.

QUALITATIVE RESEARCH DESIGNS

Qualitative research designs use methods that are distinct from those used in quantitative designs. To be sure, qualitative designs are just as systematic as quantitative designs, but they emphasize gathering data on naturally occurring phenomena. Most of these data are in the form of words rather than numbers, and in general, the researcher must search and explore with a variety of methods until a deep understanding is achieved. Qualitative designs can initially be classified as *interactive* or *noninteractive* and then further delineated within each of these major types.

ALERT!   Researchers use a number of different terms to describe methods that are *qualitative*. Be sure to check the meanings of terms used by individual researchers.

Interactive Methods

Interactive qualitative methods use face-to-face techniques to collect data from people in their natural settings. Five interactive designs (as listed in Table 2.1) are ethnographic, phenomenological, case study, grounded theory, and critical studies. These designs can be organized by (1) a focus on *individual lived experience*, as seen in phenomenology, case study, grounded theory, and some critical studies, and (2) a focus on *society and culture*, as defined by ethnography and some critical studies.

Ethnography   An **ethnography** is a description and interpretation of a cultural or social group or system. Although there is considerable disagreement about the meaning of the term *culture*, the focus is on learned patterns of actions, language, beliefs, rituals, and ways of life. As a process, ethnography involves prolonged field work, typically employing observation and casual interviews with participants of a shared group activity and collecting group artifacts. A documentary style is employed, focusing on the mundane details of everyday life and revealing the observation skills of the inquirer. The collective informants' point of view is painstakingly produced through extensive, closely edited quotations to convey that what is presented is not the fieldworker's view but authentic and representative remarks of the participants. The final product is a comprehensive, holistic narrative description and interpretation that integrates all aspects of group life and illustrates its complexity.

There are several variants of ethnography. Whereas many anthropologists employ participant observation in ethnographic studies of a culture, educational researchers utilize the technique to produce micro-ethnographies (Erickson, 1973; LeCompte & Preissle, 1993; Wolcott, 1995). A *micro-ethnography* is a participant observation study of one aspect of a cultural component (e.g., education) such as participants in an educational activity (an urban classroom or principals in an innovative program).

Phenomenology   A **phenomenological study** describes the meanings of a lived experience. The researcher "brackets," or puts aside, all prejudgments and collects data on how individuals make sense out of a particular experience or situation. The aim of phenomenology is to transform lived experience into a description of "its essence—in such a way that the effect of the text is at once a reflexive reliving and reflective appropriation of something meaningful" (Van Manen, 1990, p. 36). The typical technique is for the researcher to conduct long interviews with the informants directed toward understanding their perspectives on their everyday lived experience with the phenomenon.

Case Study   A **case study** examines a *bounded system*, or a case, over time in detail, employing multiple sources of data found in the setting. The case may be a program, an event, an activity, or a set of individuals bounded in time and place. The researcher defines the case and its boundary. A case can be selected because of its uniqueness or used to illustrate an issue (Stake, 1995). The focus may be one entity (within-site study) or several entities (multisite study).

Grounded Theory   Although the hallmark of qualitative research is detailed description and analysis of phenomena, **grounded theory** goes beyond the description to develop *dense* (detailed) concepts or conditional propositional statements that relate to a particular phenomenon. The term *grounded theory* is often used in a nonspecific way to refer to any approach to forming theoretical ideas that somehow begins with data. But grounded theory methodology is a rigorous set of procedures for producing substantive theory. Using a constant comparative method, the data analysis simultaneously employs techniques of induction, deduction, and verification. The researcher collects primarily interview data, making multiple visits to the field. The initial data collection is done to gain a variety of perspectives on the phenomena; then, the inquirer uses constant comparison to analyze across categories of information. Data are collected until the categories of information are *saturated*. At this point, the researcher selects the central phenomenon, develops a *story line*, and suggests a conditional matrix that specifies the social and historical conditions and consequences influencing the phenomenon.

Critical Studies   Researchers who conduct **critical studies** draw from critical theory, feminist theory, race theory, and postmodern perspectives, which assume that knowledge is subjective. These researchers also view society as essentially structured by class and status, as well as by race, ethnicity, gender, and sexual orientation. Thus, a patriarchal society maintains the oppression of marginalized groups (Lather, 1991). Critical researchers are suspicious of most research designs for ignoring the power relations implicit in the data collection techniques and for excluding other ways of knowing. Whereas feminist and ethnic research focus on gender and race as the problem of a study, postmodernism and critical theory tend to focus more on society and social institutions.

Noninteractive Methods

Noninteractive designs, sometimes termed **analytical research,** investigate concepts and events through an analysis of documents. The researcher identifies, studies, and then synthesizes the data to provide an understanding of the concept or a past event that may or may not have been directly observable. Authenticated documents are the major source of data. The researcher interprets facts to provide explanations of the past and clarifies the collective educational meanings that may be underlying current practices and issues.

Examples of analytical research include concept analysis and historical analysis. **Concept analysis** is the study of educational concepts such as *cooperative learning, ability grouping,* and *leadership* to describe the different meanings and appropriate use of the concept. **Historical analysis** involves a systematic collection and criticism of documents that describe past events. Educational historians study past educational programs, practices, institutions, persons, policies, and movements. These are usually interpreted in the context of historical economic, social, military, technological, and political trends. The analysis examines causes and the subsequent events, often relating the past to current events.

MIXED-METHOD RESEARCH DESIGNS

The use of **mixed-method** research designs, which combine quantitative and qualitative methods, is becoming increasingly popular because many situations are best investigated using a variety of methods. With mixed-method designs, researchers are not limited to using techniques associated with traditional designs, either quantitative or qualitative. For example, a study of how teachers apply the results of high-stakes tests to their instruction might use a written questionnaire to survey a large number of teachers, as well as qualitative interviews to probe the reasons for the use documented in the survey. An important advantage of mixed-method studies is that they can show the result (quantitative) and explain why it was obtained (qualitative).

ALERT! The overall credibility of a mixed-method study depends on the independent quality of the quantitative and qualitative designs used as well as the interplay between them.

Explanatory Designs

How mixed-method designs are used can vary considerably, depending on the weight given to each approach and when each is used. It is common, for instance, to use methods sequentially. In an **explanatory** design, which may be the most common type, quantitative data are collected first and, depending on the results, qualitative data are gathered second to elucidate, elaborate on, or explain the quantitative findings. Typically, the main thrust of the study is quantitative, and the qualitative results are secondary. For example, this kind of design could be used to study classroom assessment and grading. A large sample of teachers could be surveyed to determine the extent to which they use different factors in classroom assessment and grading; this would provide a general overview of the teachers' practices. In a second phase, teachers could be selected who represent extremely high or low scores on the factors in the survey. These teachers could then be interviewed using a qualitative method to determine why they used certain practices. Thus, the qualitative phase would be used to augment the statistical data and thus explain the practices.

Exploratory Designs

In a second type of mixed-method design, the qualitative data are gathered first and a quantitative phase follows. The purpose of this kind of study, which is called an **exploratory design,** is typically to use the initial, qualitative phase with a few individuals to identify themes, ideas, perspectives, and beliefs that can then be used to design the larger-scale, quantitative part of the study. Often, this kind of design is used to develop a survey. By using a qualitative component in the beginning, researchers are able to use the language and emphasis on different topics of the subjects in the wording of items for the survey. Doing so increases the validity of the scores that result because they will be well matched with how the subjects, rather than the researchers, think about, conceptualize, and respond to the phenomenon being studied.

Triangulation Designs

The third kind of mixed-method study is called a **triangulation** design. In this design, both qualitative and quantitative data are collected at about the same time. Triangulation is used when the strengths of one method offset the weaknesses of the other, so that together, they provide a more comprehensive set of data. To the extent that the results from each method converge and indicate the same result, there is triangulation and thus greater credibility in the findings. Theoretically, the triangulation design is used because the strengths of each approach can be applied to provide not only a more complete result but also one that is more valid. An example of a triangulation design would be a study on school culture. A quantitative survey of school culture could be used in conjunction with focus groups of students, teachers, and administrators. The more the survey results match the focus group results, the greater the validity of the conclusion that a certain type of culture exists in the school. The advantage of using the survey is that a large number of students, teachers, and administrators can be represented, and the advantage of using the focus groups is that descriptions are provided in voices specific to each group.

READING AND UNDERSTANDING RESEARCH REPORTS

Research is reported in a variety of ways, most commonly as a published article or as a paper delivered at a conference. The purpose of the report is to indicate clearly what the researcher has done, why it was done, and what it means. To do this effectively, researchers use a more or less standard format. This format is similar to the process of conceptualizing and conducting the research. Since the process of doing research is different for quantitative compared with qualitative methods, there are differences in the reporting formats used for each approach. Mixed-method studies, as might be expected, combine elements of both quantitative and qualitative report formats. While there is typically one review of the literature, there are often separate Methodology sections for the quantitative and qualitative parts of the study. Explanatory studies present quantitative methods first, exploratory studies present qualitative methods first, and triangulation studies present both at the same time.

All research reports, however, share this common, simple sequence:

$$\text{Question} \rightarrow \text{Method} \rightarrow \text{Conclusion}$$

The article or paper will begin with a question, summarize the methods used, and end with one or more conclusions.

At this point, it will be helpful simply to jump in, so to speak, and to begin reading research reports. Two articles have been provided in this chapter to get you started: one quantitative study and one qualitative study. Each contains notes to help you understand what you read, but you are not expected to comprehend everything. That will come with further experience and study. Each type of research is introduced with a description of the major parts, and each article is followed by questions that will help you understand what is being reported.

In reading research it is important to judge the overall credibility of the study. This judgment is based on an evaluation of each of the major sections of the report. *Each part of the report contributes to the overall credibility of the study.*

How to Read Quantitative Research: Anatomy of an Experimental Example

Although there is no universally accepted format for reporting quantitative research, most studies adhere to the sequence of scientific inquiry. There may be variation in the terms used, but the components indicated below are included in most studies:

1. Abstract
2. Introduction
3. Statement of research problem or purpose
4. Review of literature
5. Statement of research hypotheses or questions
6. Methodology
   a. Subjects
   b. Instruments
   c. Procedure
7. Results
8. Discussion, implications, conclusions
9. References

Abstract   The *Abstract* is a short paragraph that summarizes the entire journal article. It follows the authors' names and is usually italicized or printed in type that is smaller than the type in the article itself. Most abstracts contain a statement of the purpose of the study, a brief description of the subjects and what they did during the study, and a summary of important results. The abstract is useful because it provides a quick overview of the research, and after studying it, the reader usually will know whether to read the entire article.

Introduction   The *Introduction* is typically limited to the first paragraph or two of the article. The purpose of the introduction is to put the study in context. This is often accomplished by quoting previous research in the general topic, citing leading researchers in the area, or developing the historical context and/or theoretical rationale of the study. The introduction acts as a lead-in to a statement of the more specific purpose of the study. In Excerpt 2.1, the introduction includes the first nine paragraphs.

Research Problem or Purpose   The first step in planning a quantitative study is to formulate a research problem or purpose: that is, a clear and succinct statement that indicates the purpose of the study. Researchers begin with a general idea of what they intend to study, such as the relationship of self-concept to achievement, and then they refine this general goal to a concise sentence that indicates more specifically what is being investigated—for example, What is the relationship between fourth graders' self-concept of ability in mathematics and their achievement in math as indicated by standardized test scores?

The *Research Problem* or *Statement of Purpose* can be found in one of several locations in articles. It can be the last sentence of the introduction, as in Excerpt 2.1, or it may follow the review of literature and come just before the methods section.

Review of Literature   After researchers formulate a research problem, they conduct a search for studies that are related to the problem. The *Review of Literature* summarizes and analyzes previous research and shows how the present study is related to this literature. Often, the theoretical rationale for the study is included. The length of the review can vary, but it should be selective and concentrate on the way the present study will contribute to existing knowledge. As in the example, it should be long enough to demonstrate to the reader that the researcher has a sound understanding of the relationship between what has been done and what will be done. There is usually no separate heading to identify the review of literature (Excerpt 2.1 does have one, however), but it is always located before the methods section.

Research Hypothesis or Question   Following the literature review, researchers state the hypothesis or question. Based on information from the review, researchers write a *Hypothesis* that indicates what they predict will happen in the study. A hypothesis can be tested empirically, and it provides focus for the research. For some research, it is inappropriate to make a prediction of results, and in some studies, a research question rather than a hypothesis is used. Whether it is a question or a hypothesis, the sentence should contain objectively defined terms and state relationships in a clear, concise manner, as do the hypotheses in our example (i.e., the last two sentences before the *Method* section).

Methodology   In the methods or *Methodology* section, the researcher indicates the research design, subjects, instruments, and procedures used in the study. Ideally, this section contains enough information to enable other researchers to replicate the study. There is usually a subheading for each part of the methods section.

In the *Subjects* subsection (sometimes referred to as the *Participants* or *Data Source*), the researcher describes the characteristics of the individuals from whom information was gathered. There is an indication of the number of subjects and the way they were selected for the study.

The *Instruments* subsection describes the techniques used to gather information. There should be an indication of the validity and reliability of the results for each measuring device to show that the techniques are appropriate for the study. Sometimes examples of items are included to help the reader understand the nature of the instrument.

The *Procedure* or data collection subsection is used to explain how the study was conducted. The authors describe when the information was collected, where, and by whom. They describe what was done to the subjects (i.e., the intervention) and the manner in which the data were collected. It is important to provide a full description of the procedures. There needs to be sufficient information so that the reader would know how to proceed in replicating the study. The procedures may also affect the ways subjects respond. Readers thus need to examine the procedures carefully in interpreting the results.

Results   A summary of the analyses of the data collected is reported in the *Results* or *Findings* section. This section may appear confusing to the beginning researcher because statistical language, symbols, and conventions are used in presenting the results. The results are usually indicated in tables and graphs within the text of the article. The results should be presented objectively without interpretation or discussion, summarizing what was found. (Sometimes, interpretation will follow the results in this section.) Since the Results section contains crucial information in the article, the reader must be able to understand and evaluate the material. This is important in order to avoid uncritical acceptance of the conclusions. At this point readers should not be concerned with understanding all statistics presented in Excerpt 2.1.

Discussion, Implications, and Conclusions   In this section, the researchers indicate how the results are related to the research problem or hypothesis. It is a nontechnical interpretation of whether the results support a hypothesis or answer a research question. If the study is exploratory or contains unexpected findings, the researchers explain why they believe they obtained these results. The explanation should include an analysis of any deficiencies in the methodology utilized and an indication of other research that may explain why certain results were obtained. This section is also used to indicate implications of the study for future research and practical applications and to give overall conclusions. This section is identified by several different labels. The most common are *Discussion*, *Conclusion*, and *Summary*.

References   A list of references and reference notes that are cited in the article follows the discussion. The style of the notation will vary. The journal in which Excerpt 2.1 was published uses the most recent APA (American Psychological Association, 2001) format.

Guidelines for Evaluating Quantitative Research

There is no agreed-upon method for or approach to reading research articles. Some readers begin with the conclusion, and others follow the written sequence of the article. Our experience suggests that a reader should begin with the abstract and then scan the introduction, research problem, and conclusion sections. If after reading these sections, the reader is still interested in the article, then he or she should start at the beginning and read the entire article more carefully. Whenever reading research, one should keep in mind the practical or meaningful significance of the study. Research is significant if there are no serious weaknesses in the design and the differences obtained between groups or individuals or relationships reported are large enough to suggest changes in theory or practice.

Other questions also should be kept in mind in reading research. While readers need to become acquainted with these considerations now, a full understanding and application of the questions is expected only after further study of each topic. The following questions, organized according to each major section of a quantitative research article, constitute a guideline for evaluating quantitative investigations.

Research Problem or Purpose

1. How clearly and succinctly is the problem or purpose stated?
2. Is it sufficiently delimited to be amenable to investigation? At the same time, does it have sufficient practical or theoretical value to warrant study?
3. Does it have a rationale? Has the problem been studied before? If so, should this problem be studied again? Is the study likely to provide additional knowledge?
4. Will the findings give rise to further hypotheses, thereby increasing the probability of adding to existing knowledge?

Review of Literature

1. How adequately has the literature been surveyed?
2. Does the review critically evaluate previous findings and studies, or is it only a summary of what is known?
3. Does the review support the need for studying the problem?
4. Does the review establish a theoretical framework for the problem?
5. Does the review relate previous studies to the research problem?

Hypotheses or Questions

1. Are any assumptions advanced with respect to the hypotheses or questions?
2. Are hypotheses consistent with theory and known facts?
3. Are they testable?
4. Do they provide an expected result?

Methodology

1. Are the procedures, design, and instruments employed to gather the data described with sufficient clarity to permit another researcher to replicate the study?
2. Is the population described fully? Did the researcher use the total population, or was there a sample used? If a sample is used, is it representative of the population from which it was selected?
3. Is evidence presented about the validity and reliability of the scores?
4. Was a pretest used? Was there a pilot study? If so, why? What were the results? Was the problem or question or procedure changed as a result of the pretest or pilot study, and if so, was this modification justifiable or desirable?
5. Are there any obvious weaknesses in the overall design of the study?

Results

1. Were statistical techniques needed to analyze the data? If so, were the most appropriate and meaningful statistical techniques employed?
2. Have the results been adequately and clearly presented?
3. Is there reference to *practical* as well as *statistical* significance?

Discussion, Implications, Conclusions

1. Are the conclusions and generalizations consistent with the findings? What are the implications of the findings? Has the researcher overgeneralized the findings?
2. Does the researcher discuss the limitations of the study?
3. Are there any extraneous factors that might have affected the findings? Have they been considered by the researchers?
4. Are the conclusions presented consistent with theory or known facts?
5. Have the conclusions (both those relevant to the original hypothesis and any serendipitous findings) been presented adequately and discussed?

EXCERPT 2.1   Anatomy of a Quantitative Research Article

The Effects of Computer-Assisted Instruction on First Grade Students' Vocabulary Development

Charlotte Boling, *The University of West Florida*

Sarah H. Martin, *Eastern Kentucky University*

Michael A. Martin, *Eastern Kentucky University*

The purpose of the present study was to determine the effect of computer-assisted instruction on first grade students' vocabulary development. Students participating in this study were randomly divided into experimental and control groups. The students in both groups were involved in DEAR (Drop Everything And Read) as part of their instruction in a balanced literacy program. During their normal DEAR time, the control group used a book and tape to explore stories. The experimental group explored stories using computerized storyboards. The results of the study show a significant difference for both groups on pre and posttests. However, the mean difference demonstrates a much larger gain for students in the experimental group.

Abstract

What can teachers do to insure that the children they teach will develop into successful readers? This is a question that has puzzled the educational community for years. Most educators have their individual opinion as to how the reading process occurs. Morrow and Tracey (1997) state that some educators believe in a behavioristic approach where reading is taught in a skills-based environment through a prescribed curriculum. Others believe in a more constructivist approach where a relationship between the context and child must be developed where students build knowledge and gain skills through immersion in a literature-rich environment (Czubaj, 1997; Daniels & Zemelman, 1999). Whatever one believes, these approaches to reading instruction—behaviorist or constructivist—continue to be the subject of debates in our classrooms and communities.

Introduction—Significance of topic

The core beliefs that teachers possess have a great impact on students learning to read. Teacher's personal beliefs concerning the processes involved in learning to read greatly influence their instructional choices. A teacher's beliefs are based on his or her personal knowledge, experiences with instructional techniques, and the way students respond to the instructional strategies in classroom situations (Dillon, 2000; Howard, McGee, Purcell, and Schwartz, 2000; Kinzer and Leu, 1999). Therefore, while teachers maintain their core beliefs about how children best learn to read, they are continuously striving to find the technique(s) that will have the greatest impact on their students.

Since the early 1920s, educators have used a multi-sensory approach to teaching reading by combining reading, writing, and speaking in a natural context and not through deliberate teaching (Chall, 1992). This has been particularly useful in the teaching of vocabulary. It stands to reason then that the most active vocabulary growth occurs in the early years of life. A child learns to connect an object with the sight, sound, smell, taste, and feel associated with the object. This experience is followed by certain sounds made to represent the object. Thus, communication begins and the concept associated with the object develops into vocabulary. For example, a child understands the physical properties of an apple. He knows how the object looks, tastes, feels, smells, and sounds. A loving parent then builds vocabulary in a natural context by adding the word associated to this object—apple. Then, this label is connected to the experience. "You are eating an apple."

Introduction—Background on importance of vocabulary

As the vocabulary increases, children realize words are used in many contexts. Children must then reach beyond the actual word and activate their schema of the context in which the word is used to understand the meaning. For example, the word "mouse" can have different meanings, such as, a small rodent or a computer device. A child needs

(continued)

excerpt 2.1 (*continued*)

to experience words being used in different contexts to understand the complexity of our language. The more children experience vocabulary in context, the sooner they will begin to realize that it is the concept of the word in question in the given context that provides meaning.

As a child progresses through the various aspects of literacy development (listening, speaking, reading, and writing), their communication skills become more interdependent upon vocabulary development. Vocabulary development involves understanding the 'labeling' that goes with the 'concept' that makes the word meaningful. It is acquired through direct experience, multiple exposure, context, association, and comprehension. As students become comfortable with new vocabulary words, they are more likely to use the words when communicating.

> **Introduction—Background on importance of vocabulary (continued)**

Elements of our 'Technological Age' often influence the instructional decisions that teachers make in the classroom. One such decision is the role that computers will play in the reading development of the children one teaches. Computer-based teaching and learning has produced positive effects in the classroom. Students seem to be motivated by learning through this medium (Forcier, 1999). Therefore, it is essential that today's teachers change as our society changes (Hoffman & Pearson, 2000). Children who enter today's primary classrooms have been processing multi-sensory concepts for most of their young lives. Home computers, interactive games, television, the Internet, and software companies capitalize on this multi-sensory concept.

Software companies have developed many programs for beginning reading that appeal to the senses and interests of the young child who is learning to read. This multimedia concept stimulates the learner with sight, sound, and action while integrating skills necessary for language development. Instructional technology offers virtual multi-sensory perception that should provide meaningful instruction.

> **Introduction—Background on importance of technology**

Teacher-centered instruction is one approach to the use of instructional technology in the classroom (Forcier, 1999). The teacher-centered approach is similar to the direct-instruction approach in that the teacher is directing the children through the learning in order to achieve the goals of the lesson. One category of the teacher-centered approach is computer-assisted instruction. When using computer-assisted instruction the teacher organizes the learning situation. He/she selects the targeted learning goal, situates the learning environment, and then allows exploratory time as students engage in learning. The teacher then monitors the learning activities and modifies the instructional level as needed to meet the various needs of the children involved.

> **Introduction—Importance of teacher-centered instruction**

Classroom teachers have the unique opportunity to infuse a variety of technological components with multi-sensory learning while situating the learning situation. One area where this is especially true is in the teaching of reading to young children. The research study being reported employed a teacher-centered, computer-assisted instructional technique that situated progressive reading material in an attempt to answer the following question:

Will a computerized multi-sensory approach to the teaching of reading increase first-graders' vocabulary development?

> **Research question**

Review of Literature

> **Major heading**

Many software programs offer 'read alongs' and 'edutainment' that assist students as they learn letter sounds, vocabulary concepts, comprehension, and to enjoy literature. Interactive multimedia allows the printed word to take on sight, sound, and action which visually and mentally stimulates the individual.

One such program is DaisyQuest I and II (Mitchell, Chad & Stacy, 1984–2000). An in-depth study investigated the phonological awareness in pre-school children utilizing this software (Brinkman and Torgesen, 1994). Each child in the treatment group interacted with a computerized story concerning "Daisy the friendly dragon". A computer, monitor,

> **Summary of findings from previous study**

e x c e r p t   2 . 1   (c o n t i n u e d)

mouse, and standard headphone were provided to allow the child, as he/she listened to the story, to discover clues revealing where the dragon was hiding. The clues were revealed by correctly answering at least four correct answers in a row. The skills assessed were rhyming words, beginning sounds, ending sounds, middle sounds, and whether a word contained a given number of sounds. This study revealed that children in the treatment group responded at a higher and faster rate of reading readiness than children in the control group. Not only did the children in the treatment group gain knowledge to aid in their ability to read; these pre-schoolers had fun!

Summary of findings from previous study (continued)

In another study, two literacy teachers (one a Reading Recovery teacher, the other a Title 1 Reading Teacher) wrote simple, predictable texts using a multimedia software, HyperStudio (Wagner, 1978–2000). These teachers created 'talking books' for their students with a focus on high-frequency words with graphics and animation to offer sight, sound, and movement. Students enjoyed experiencing the stories as the computer 'read' the story to them as the cursor (pointing finger) touched each word. This process came full circle by the end of the school year, as these students were writing and reading their own stories. Students were then encouraged to use invented spelling, graphics, and sounds, while they created their own stories using the Kid Pix Software program (Hickman, 1984–2000). "The computer serves as a motivational tool in their journey to literacy" (Eisenwine & Hunt, 2000, p. 456).

Summary of findings from previous study

There are many reasons why computer-assisted reading instruction has been effective. The computer provides immediate responses and practice for the child learning a skill. Struggling readers interface with the computer and practice a skill without embarrassing situations in the classroom. Interaction with a multi-sensory format provides motivation and a positive attitude toward reading and learning (Case & Truscott, 1999; Forcier, 1999).

Shows significance of technology

A word of caution accompanies much of the literature warning educators to focus on the targeted instructional goals and not be 'enchanted' by the entertainment that makes software packages so appealing (Case and Truscott, 1999; Sherry, 1996). While this multi-sensory approach is highly motivating for young readers, the instructional purpose is to enable them to become better readers. Educators should choose the types of software and technological resources carefully in order to maximize learning without being entangled in the 'bells and whistles'.

Indicates criteria for selecting software

The benefits of using instructional technology include "an intrinsic need to learn technology . . . motivation increases engagement time . . . students move beyond knowledge and comprehension and into application and analysis . . . and students develop computer literacy by applying various computer skills as part of the learning process" (Dockstader, 1999, p. 73). As Ray and Wepner (2000) suggest, the question as to whether or not technology is the valuable educational resource we think it is may be a moot point since it is such an integral part of our lives. However, the question concerning the most productive methods of using technology in the classroom still needs to be addressed. Therefore, the purpose of this study was to investigate the effects of computer-assisted instruction on first grade students' vocabulary development. Specifically, this study investigated the impact of the WiggleWorks program (CAST & Scholastic, 1994–1996) on first grade students' vocabulary development.

Shows need for study

Purpose

Research problem

Method

Sample

Identifies subjects

A first grade classroom at a mid-Atlantic elementary school was selected for this research project. The subjects were 21 first-grade students. There were 10 boys and 11 girls involved in this study. The ethnic background of this class was as follows: 13 Caucasian students, six African American students, one Hispanic student, and one Pakistani student. Students were from a lower socioeconomic status and had limited exposure to educational experiences

Convenience sample

Description of subjects

(continued)

excerpt 2.1 (continued)

outside the school. The subjects were assigned to either the control or experimental group by using a table of random numbers and applying those numbers to the students. Ten students were assigned to the control group and 11 to the experimental group.

Random assignment (low number of students in each group)

Computer Assisted Program

The WiggleWorks (1994–1996) software program was used in this study. Co-developed by CAST and Scholastic, Inc., this program offers a literacy curriculum based on a combination of speech, sounds, graphics, text, and customizable access features. The software program features 72 trade books, audiocassettes, and a variety of computer-based activities. Students use the trade books and audiocassettes to read independently with or without the support of the audiocassette. Using the software program, students may listen to a story, read along with a story, or read a story silently. As they read, students are encouraged to review the suggested vocabulary words by selecting My Words. Students may listen to a pronunciation of the word by clicking on it or hear the word contextually in the story. Students may add new words to their vocabulary list by clicking on the selected word and the plus sign or remove words by clicking on the subtraction sign. Students may read and reread the story as they wish. Students may also create word families or practice spelling using a magnetic alphabet.

After listening to or reading a story, students have the option of composing their own stories. WiggleWorks provides a story starter, cloze-structured text, or free writing to help young students write their story. After composing a story, students may illustrate personal stories using basic drawing tools, stamps of the story characters, and/or story event backgrounds. Students may share their stories with others by recording their stories or printing the story and creating a book. These functions are available in a Read Aloud, Read, Write, My Book, and Magnet Board menu available to the individual user.

WiggleWorks is a managed instructional system. The management functions allow the teacher the opportunity to customize the computer-assisted instruction for each child. For instance, in Read Aloud, the settings can be adjusted so that the story is read to the student using a word-by-word, line-by-line, or whole-page approach. The management system also keeps a running log of individual and class activities. The Portfolio Management feature provides a reading record for each child (tracks the stories read, date and time individual stories were read, etc.), including reading and writing samples. The WiggleWorks software program provides a multimedia approach to literacy while supporting traditional methods with the accompanying trade books and audiocassettes.

Detailed description of intervention

Variables

The research project tested the independent variable of computer-assisted instruction on reading vocabulary development. Eleven students received the treatment monitored by one of the researchers. The dependent variable was a pre and post vocabulary test. The test was an independent word list administered by the researcher to the experimental and control group at the beginning and end of each session.

Intervention (independent) and outcomes (dependent)

Measurement

How data are collected

The instrument used to determine the effect of computer-assisted instruction on vocabulary was a pre and posttest designed by one of the researchers. Six high-frequency vocabulary words from each of the seven stories were selected by the researcher and placed on an independent list. The independent list of words served as the pre and post vocabulary test for each. All results were compared to determine the effect the treatment had on these subjects.

Locally developed instrument

Procedure

How intervention was implemented

As a part of the regular curriculum, all students received reading vocabulary instruction. The teacher utilized the reading instructional curriculum adopted by the county which consist of reading text books, related materials, and charts provided by the publishing company. Students participated in daily reading instruction. Each student in the class was

e x c e r p t   2 . 1 (c o n t i n u e d)

randomly assigned into two groups: a control group and an experimental group. In an attempt to limit extraneous learning, both groups continued to receive regular reading instruction by the researcher/teacher. The regular reading curriculum had a twenty minute time block where students participated in a DEAR (Drop Everything And Read) program. The researchers used this block of time to implement this research project.

Seven pre-determined stories were used for this research project. The stories were available on book and tape as well as interactive, computerized storyboards. The control group experienced the story in a variety of ways. First, they listened to the assigned story as the teacher/researcher read the story to them. Next, students listened to the story on tape and read along with an accompanying book. Lastly, students were provided with an assortment of literature: library books, classroom literature, or the student's personal books to read at their leisure after the pre-determined book and tape assignment had been completed. During that twenty-minute time span, the 10 students in the experimental group visited the Media computer lab and explored the same story using the computerized storyboard. A computer, monitor, mouse, and headphone were provided for each subject. During the first session, the teacher/researcher explained the working mechanics of the computer laboratory and answered any questions from the students. Then, the lessons began as students listen to enjoy the story. Next, the students revisited and identified words unknown to them by clicking on the word. The computerized storyboards serve as a remediator. These subjects saw the printed word highlighted and heard as the word was produced in sound. Students were required to listen to the story once while reading along. After completing those requirements, students could listen and/or read any story previously read or any story at a lower level. Students were introduced to a new Wiggle-Works story every other day. During this project, students experimented with seven different stories that became progressively more challenging. The ability levels of the stories ranged from Kindergarten to second grade. The project continued for six weeks.

More detail about intervention and procedure

Results

The results were analyzed using a Paired-Samples T-test. An alpha level of .05 was set incorporating a two-tailed significance level. The analyses showed significant positive changes for both groups. The mean scores confirm that students using computerized storyboards demonstrate significant gains in their ability to recall a greater amount of new vocabulary words (See Table 1). The pre and posttest were analyzed using a Paired-Samples T test. The results demonstrate a statistically significant difference ($p > .002$) in the experimental (computer) group. A significant difference ($p > .01$) was also found (See Table 2) in the control group (Book/Tape).

Pretest-posttest analysis

Description of results

The mean scores of the pre and post vocabulary tests indicate a significant gain in the experimental (computer story board) group (MeanPre = 3.7; MeanPost = 16.9). A further analysis involving the reading ability of the individual students demonstrated that students with higher reading ability scored higher in the experimental and control groups than

Introduction of second independent variable

TABLE 1   Means and Standard Deviations

Group	Pretest		Posttest	
	M	SD	M	SD
Computer	3.7	4.37	16.9	13.17
Book/Tape	1.8	2.68	5.45	6.07

Mean scores

Standard deviation

(continued)

excerpt 2.1 (*continued*)

TABLE 2   Paired-Samples T-test

Group	df	t	P
Computer	9	4.18	0.002
Book/Tape	10	3.17	0.010

— Inferential statistical test

average ability or low ability student. Those students who were performing successfully in their reading scored significantly higher than those students who were performing at a lower level.

— Introduction of second independent variable (continued)

Discussion

The stories selected for this project were progressively more challenging so as to meet the needs of as many young readers as possible. Students with greater reading ability scored higher on the pretests and showed greater improvement on the posttests. These students seemed to possess a greater command of reading and technological skills required in maneuvering the storyboards.

— Summary of results

Students with less reading ability did not gain as much from the experience. While they seemed to enjoy the stories, they were greatly challenged by the pre and posttest. These students would have been more successful with stories developmentally appropriate for their reading ability. Overall, the ability level of the students in the classroom seemed to mirror their performance in the computer-based reading instruction. Strong readers worked somewhat independently, average-ability students were at an instructional level with reading and technology skills, while students with less reading ability needed assistance with reading and technology. Students in the experimental group (computer storyboards) were greatly motivated by the use of computers. They enjoyed the interactive, multi-sensory aspect of learning. This was evidenced by the students' request to spend more time listening to stories on the computers. Multi-sensory teaching seemed to make their learning fun.

— Additional results and explanation of results

Implications and Significance

This research project was designed to investigate the effects of computer-assisted instruction on first grade students' vocabulary development. With the integration of sights, colors, sounds, actions, plus the printed word, vocabulary lessons took on a new meaning. Students recognized the word on sight, remembered the word through association and phonemes, and quite a few could use the word as a part of their spoken and written vocabulary. Students were able to recognize the words in isolation and in text.

— Conclusions

Overall, implications of this research project are that a 20-minute DEAR time using computerized storyboards directly results in improved vocabulary development among first grade students. Learning new vocabulary words took place at a faster pace with greater accuracy than with the direct teaching format. "Technology brings to your classroom the capability of connecting dynamic, interactive vocabulary learning with reading, writing, spelling, and content learning." (Fox and Mitchell, 2000, p. 66)

— Findings related to previous research

Computerized classroom instruction does not infer inflated test scores or a magic potion for teaching. It is a motivating medium that enhances good teaching. The infusion of technology and literacy is a lifelong learning gift we create for our students.

— Significance

e x c e r p t   2 . 1 *(c o n t i n u e d)*

Recommendations

Computer-assisted instruction has a positive influence on student's motivation, interest, and learning. This research project validates the effect that computer-assisted instruction has on first graders vocabulary development during a crucial time when they are learning to read. To improve upon this study, a concentrated effort should be made to determine the developmental reading level of each student. Students could then receive more individualized instruction at their appropriate reading level. Additionally, teachers/researchers need to move students from dependent direct instruction to more independent learning. A natural follow-up to this study could be to see if this move to more independent learning is facilitated by differing uses of technology in the classroom.

Restatement of conclusion

Suggestions for future research

References

Brinkman, D. & Torgeson, J. (1994). Computer administered instruction in phonological awareness: evaluation of the DaisyQuest program. *The Journal of Research and Development in Education, 27* (2), 126–137.

Case, C. & Truscott, D. M. (1999). The lure of bells and whistles: choosing the best software to support reading instruction. *Reading and Writing Quarterly, 15,* (4), p. 361.

Chall, J. (1992). The new reading debates: evidence from science, art, and ideology. *Teachers College Record, 94,* (2), 315.

Czubaj, C. (1997). Whole language literature reading instruction. *Education, 117* (4), 538.

Daniels, H. and Zemelman, S. (1999). Whole language works: sixty years of research. *Educational Research, 57,* (2), 32.

Dillon, D. R. (2000). Identifying beliefs and knowledge, uncovering tensions, and solving problems. *Kids insight: reconsidering how to meet the literacy needs of all students* (pp. 72–79). Newark, DE: International Reading Association.

Dockstader, J. (1999). Teachers of the 21st century know the what, why, and how of technology integration. *T.H.E. Journal, 26* (6), 73–74.

Eisznwine, M. J. & Hunt, D. A. (2000). Using a computer in literacy groups with emergent readers. *The Reading Teacher, 53* (6), 456.

Forcier, R. C. (1999). Computer applications in education. *The computer as an educational tool* (pp.60–93). Upper Saddle, NJ: Prentice-Hall. Inc.

Fox, B. J. & Mitchell, M. J. (2000). Using technology to support word recognition. spelling. and vocabulary acquisition. In R. Thurlow, W. J. Valmont, & S. B. Wepner (Eds.). *Linking Literacy and Technology.* Newark, DL: International Reading Association. Inc.

Hickman, C. (1984–2000). Kid Pix. Deluxe Version. [Unpublished computer software], Available: http://www.pixel poppin.comlkid-pix/index.html

Hoffman, J. & Pearson, P. D. (2000). Reading teacher education in the next millennium: what your grandmother's teacher didn't know that your granddaughter's teacher should. *Reading Research Quarterly, 35,* (1), 28–44.

Howard, B. C., McGee, S., Purcell, S., & Schwartz, N. (2000). The experience of constructivism: transforming teacher epistemology. *Journal of Research on Computing in Education, 32,* (4), 455–465.

Kinzer, C. K. & Leu, D. J. (1999). *Effective Literacy Instruction.* Upper Saddle River, NJ: Prentice-Hall, Inc.

Mitchell, C. & S. (1984–2000). DaisyQuest. [Unpublished computer software]. Available: http://www.greatwave.com/html/daisys.html

Morrow, L. M. & Tracey, D. H. (1997). Strategies used for phonics instruction in early childhood classrooms. *The Reading Teacher, 50,* (8), 644.

Ray, L. C. & Wepner, S. B. (2000). Using technology for reading development. In R. Thurlow, W. J. Valmont, & S. B. Wepner (Eds.). *Linking Literacy and Technology.* Newark, DL: International Reading Association, Inc.

Sherry, L. (1996). Issues in distance learning. International *Journal of Educational Telecommunications, 1* (4), 337–365.

Wagner, R. (1978). HyperStudio. [Unpublished computer software]. Available: http://www.hyperstudio.com/

WiggleWorks [Computer Software]. (1994–1996). New York: CAST and Scholastic, Inc.

References in APA format

Title of journal article: initial cap only

Title of journal: cap each word

Year published

Pages

Volume

Title of book: initial cap only

Chapter in a book

Publisher

Journal title and volume number italic

Web reference

Source: From Boling, C., Martin, S. H., & Martin, M. A. (2002). The effects of computer-assisted instruction on first grade students' vocabulary development. *Reading Improvement, 39*(2), 79–88. Provided by Reading Improvement, Phillip Feldman, Ed. Reprinted by permission.

How to Read Qualitative Research: Anatomy of a Qualitative Example

There is greater diversity in the formats used to report qualitative research than in the formats typical of quantitative studies. While there is not a single mode for representing qualitative research, many published reports have four major sections: Introduction, Methodology, Findings, and Conclusions. In contrast to those found in quantitative studies, however, these sections may not be identified clearly or may be identified by descriptive terms related to the topic. Excerpt 2.2 provides an example of a qualitative research article.

Introduction   The *Introduction* provides a general background of the study, indicating the potential importance of the research. It summarizes the general intentions of the investigator, along with a general statement of the research problem or purpose. For a journal article, usually only one of many research foci are reported. The introduction includes a preliminary literature review to present possible conceptual frameworks that will be useful in understanding the data and results. The review justifies the need for a descriptive case study. The introduction may also indicate the structure of the rest of the report.

Methodology   The *Methodology* section describes the design of the study, including the selection and description of the site, the role of the researcher, initial entry for observation, the time and length of the study, the number of participants and how they were selected, and data collection and analysis strategies. This information is needed to evaluate the soundness of the procedures. The amount of detail contained in this section will vary, depending on the type of research report. In relatively short published articles the methodology may be part of the introduction.

Findings and Interpretations   In this section, the researcher presents the data that were gathered, usually in the form of a lengthy narrative, and analyzes the data. This should be done in sufficient detail to allow the reader to judge the accuracy of the analysis. The data are used to illustrate and substantiate the researcher's interpretations. Analysis is often intermixed with the presentation of data. The data are often in the form of quotes by participants. It is important to indicate the purpose of data analysis and to describe what has been learned by synthesizing the information. Because the presentation is in narrative form, there are frequently a number of descriptive subtitles connoting different findings.

Conclusions   The *Conclusion* usually includes a restatement of the initial focus of the study and how the data results and analyses impinge on that focus. Implications of the results can be elaborated, as well as implications for further research.

References   The References section provides full bibliographic information for all previously completed work that is cited in the article. While APA format is common, some journals have a unique style.

Guidelines for Evaluating Qualitative Research

To understand qualitative research, it is necessary to carefully read the entire report. This is how readers are able to identify with the investigators and understand how they have come to their conclusions. The process by which this occurs is important, and to understand this process, it is necessary to read from beginning to end. As with quantitative studies, certain questions should be asked about the report to judge its quality.

Introduction
1. Is the focus, purpose, or topic of the study stated clearly?
2. Are there situations or problems that lead to the focus of the study? Is there a rationale for the study? Is it clear that the study is important?
3. Is there background research and theory to help refine the research questions?

4. Does the introduction contain an overview of the design?
5. Is the literature review pertinent to the focus of the research? Is the literature analyzed as well as described?

Methodology

1. Are the particular sites described to identify their uniqueness or typicality?
2. How was initial entry into the field established?
3. How was the researcher's presence in the field explained to others? What was the role of the researcher?
4. Who was observed? How long were they observed? How much time was spent collecting data?
5. Does the researcher report any limitations to access of pertinent data?
6. Are the data representative of naturally occurring behavior?
7. Are limitations of the design acknowledged?

Findings and Interpretations

1. Are the perspectives of the different participants clearly presented? Are participants' words or comments quoted?
2. Is contextual information for participants' statements provided?
3. Are multiple perspectives presented?
4. Are the results well documented? Are assertions and interpretations illustrated by results?
5. Is it clear what the researchers believe the data indicated? Are personal beliefs kept separate from the data?
6. Are the interpretations reasonable? Were researcher preconceptions and biases acknowledged?

Conclusions

1. Are the conclusions logically consistent with the findings?
2. Are limitations of the research design and focus indicated?
3. Are implications of the findings indicated?

EXCERPT 2.2   Anatomy of a Qualitative Research Article

The Developmental Progression of Children's Oral Story Inventions
Eugene Geist   Jerry Aldridge

This study investigated stories that children created after being told the Grimm version of selected tales. These stories were told as an instruction to the children on story structure and to familiarize children with ideas of plot, character, and conflict in stories. This cross-sectional study considered what differences are evident in the oral fairy tales that children tell at different ages. Stories from children in kindergarten, first grade, second grade, and third grade were collected and analyzed. For the purpose of this study, the following research questions were asked. These questions guided the research and eventually became the major coding categories.

1) Is there a developmental difference in the type of story (i.e., personal narrative, fantasy, realistic fiction) children tell when they are asked to invent a fairy tale?
2) Are there developmental differences in the content of children's stories among age groups?
3) Are there developmental differences in how children organize the content of their invented fairy tales?

— **Abstract (rather long)**

(continued)

e x c e r p t 2 . 2 (c o n t i n u e d)

A qualitative research methodology was used for this study. Children's orally invented stories were tape recorded and transcribed. The data were analyzed using content analysis of the transcripts.

This study Indicates that children's orally told invented fairy tales can be used (a) to promote cognitive development, (b) to assess cognitive development, and (c) to Identify emotional conflicts that children are experiencing. This study also indicates that second grade is a good time to promote creativity and imaginations as this was the age in which children were most confident in their Imaginative abilities.

Abstract (continued)

Few studies have been conducted on children's oral story inventions (Aldridge, Eddowes, Ewing, & Kuby, 1994). Studies on children's interest in folk and fairytales have not touched on children's invented "fairy tales" and how they can reflect developmental issues. There have been many examinations of written retellings of fairy tales (Boydston, 1994; Gambrell, Pfeiffer, & Wilson, 1985; Morrow, 1986). However, few works have examined oral stories invented by children. Invented oral stories can give a valuable insight into a child's cognitive, affective, and creative development (Allan & Bertoia, 1992; Markham, 1983; Sutton-Smith, 1985).

Suggests need for study

This study investigated stories that children created after being told the Grimm version of selected tales. These stories were told as an instruction to the children on story structure and to familiarize children with ideas of plot, character, and conflict in stories. The Grimm (1993) versions were chosen because the literature suggests that they are the closest to the oral tradition (Zipes, 1988). This cross-sectional study considered what differences are evident In the oral fairy tales that children tell at different ages. Stories from children in kindergarten, first grade, second grade, and third grade were collected and analyzed (Geist & Aldridge, 1999).

General research problem

For the purpose of this study, the following research questions were asked. These questions guided the research and eventually became the major coding categories.

1) Is there a developmental difference in the type of story (i.e., personal narrative, fantasy, realistic fiction) children tell when they are asked to invent a fairy tale?
2) Are there developmental differences in the content of children's stories among age groups?
3) Are there developmental differences in how children organize the content of their invented fairy tales?

Research questions

Method

A qualitative research methodology was used for this study. Children's orally invented stories were tape recorded and transcribed. The data were analyzed using content analysis of the transcripts. According to Carney (1972), "content analysis is any technique for making inferences by objectively and systematically identifying specified characteristics of messages" (p. 25).

Overall research design

A semistructured interview format was used to collect data. The children were asked to make up a fairy tale and tell it to the researcher. The researcher prompted the subject if there was a long pause. The researcher also had the child start over if the child was engaging in a retelling of a story that the researcher recognized. The data were then analyzed using a content analysis.

Researcher conducted all interviews

Participants

Not "subjects"

Convenience sampling was the method used to select study participants. The classrooms chosen were believed to facilitate the expansion of a developing theory because the sample was homogeneous. All subjects were African American and from low socioeconomic families. The subjects for this study were students in four classrooms at an elementary

Indicates characteristics of participants

e x c e r p t 2 . 2 *(c o n t i n u e d)*

school in a low socioeconomic area of an urban city in the Southeastern United States. The racial make up of the sample was 100% African American.

Data Collection

Each classroom participated in a 45-minute lesson on fairy tales and story structure each day for 4 days. The lesson consisted of reading and discussing the plots and characters of fairy tales. After the 4 days, the children were asked, individually, to make up a fairy tale and tell it orally. The stories were tape recorded and transcribed. A content analysis of the transcripts was performed as described by Carney (1992).

> **Indicates characteristics of participants (continued)**

> **Data gathered as tape-recorded interviews**

> **Data analysis**

One kindergarten, one first-grade, one second-grade, and one third-grade classroom, each with approximately 15 students, participated in this study. Each classroom was given an identical session on fairy tales and story structure. This session consisted of reading fairy tales to the students and discussing the aspects of the story. The specific description of the 5 days of storytelling and discussion are found in Geist and Aldridge (1999). These procedures were modified from Allan and Bertoia (1992) by Boydston (1994). Allan and Bertoia developed a procedure to initiate the discussion of fairy tales. This outline was used for seventh graders, however, because this study was interested in students in kindergarten, first, second, and third grades, a procedure modified by Boydston (1994), was used for this study. Boydston's outline was developed for second graders but is appropriate for the ages targeted in this study.

> **Shows modification of previously used methods**

Data Analysis

Analysis of the data was generated from the transcripts of the audiotapes. The research questions served as a guide for conducting the analysis. Each question became a major coding category broken down by age. The results of each age were then compared to each other to build a model of children's invented fairy tales. Bogdan and Biklen (1992) stated that preassigned coding systems are developed when researchers explore particular topics or aspects of the study.

> **Coding emerges from the data for many qualitative studies**

Inter-rater reliability was conducted on this study by having an educational professional with extensive knowledge of fairy tales and their form, function, and uses independently categorize the data. Another rater was trained in content analysis and was experienced in the content analysis method. This researcher had performed qualitative studies on fairy tales and children's storytelling in the past. The two raters participated in two practice sessions of reading and analyzing children's oral invented stories.

The recordings were transcribed and copied. The independent rater and the researcher received identical copies of the transcripts. Because the three foreshadowed questions were used as a framework for the categories, the independent rater was given a copy of the foreshadowed questions. Each rater read the transcripts as many times as needed and noted themes related to genre, content, and organization. Each rater then independently compared the common themes from each grade and constructed a model for genre, content, and organization.

> **Use of trained, independent rater improves credibility**

Both raters discussed the method for analysis before beginning. When a theme or thread was identified, it was highlighted by a colored marker that identified it with other items that belonged with that thread. The rater wrote notes in the margin next to this highlighted text. Then all of the text passages with the same color highlight were collected by grade. The rater then reread the passages and came up with a phrase or word that best described the common characteristics of those passages. The descriptive phrases were then compared to the phrases for the other grades to determine if a model could be constructed. Often, there was more than one model that was evident in each of the categories.

These themes and models were then compared. The themes and models that were consistent between the two raters were retained and clarified. The themes and models that were not consistent between the two raters were not included. Each story

(continued)

was then categorized independently by each rater into the rough model that had been developed.

Results

Findings from this study suggest a developmental shift in the genre, content, and organization of children's oral invented stories. The genre of the children's stories moved from the fantastical to stories based on personal experiences. Kindergarten children told mostly fantasy stories, first and second graders told mostly realistic fiction, and third graders told mostly personal narratives. **Results directly related to research question**

The content of the children's stories showed development in two areas. First, there was development in the basis of their stories. Kindergarten children based their stories on previously heard material, first graders based theirs on familiar surroundings, second graders based their inventions on their imagination, and third graders tended to base their stories on personal experiences.

Second, there was development in how parents were depicted in the stories. Kindergartners, first, and second graders depicted parents as heroes and comforters. Third graders depicted parents as authority figures.

The content of the stories of all the grades contained reflections of the children's fears and concerns from everyday life. Fears about being kidnapped or other stresses, such as performance anxiety and social pressures, were reflected in their stories. **Examples from participants**

The organization of the stories moved from disjointed sentences to a coherent whole story. States that could be delineated were (a) disjointed, (b) phrase disjointed, (c) short-utilitarian, (d) sidetracked, and (e) coherent whole.

Genre

Inquiry paradigm

The development of genre moved from the fantastical notions of kindergartners to the realistic personal narratives of third graders. Kindergartners told fantastical stories of talking umbrellas, flying to Mars, magic, and evil witches that turned children into food. First and second graders told realistic fiction stories about hunters, kings, queens, and an occasional witch; however, almost all of the actions of the characters were in the realm of possibility. Third graders tended to tell personal narratives that related directly to their life experiences; they were simply retelling events that happened to them or to someone they knew. **Detail provided to show depth of understanding**

The study suggests the genre was influenced by 3 things. First it was influenced by the classroom context. In the kindergarten classroom, the researcher observed a lot of fantasy literature. Children heard stories daily about talking animals and fantastical actions in the books the teachers read to them. However, as the grades progressed, the researcher observed that the teachers provided more realistic literature and less fantasy. This, In turn, affected the genre of the stories that the children told. Second was the children's developing understanding of the difference between fantasy and reality. As children begin to understand the concept of causality and move into concrete operations, the concept of what is possible and logical versus what is illogical, magical and impossible becomes more delineated. The second and third grade stories reflect this move toward reality based stories. Third, was the base material that children chose. As we have already mentioned, children tended to choose more personal material as they got older until at third grade, they tell personal, true to life personal narratives. Obviously, this shift is going to affect the genre of the story that they tell. This will be discussed further in the examination of the content of the children's stories. **Explanation of overall findings concerning genre**

Content

There were two developmental themes that could be delineated in the content of the children's stories. The first was the basis that the children used to construct their stories. The

e x c e r p t   2 . 2   (c o n t i n u e d)

second was the role of parents in the children's stories. Third, the content of all the grades contained reflections of children's fears and concerns.

Children in kindergarten based their stories on previously heard material. They did not appear confident in their ability to be successful in making up a story on their own, so they used stories that they had heard or read recently to build their story around. First graders were a little more sure of themselves so they did not need specific stories on which to base their inventions. However, they still needed to base the settings and characteristics on things that were familiar to them. This gave them the framework for their stories. By second grade, the children did not need outside structure on which to build their stories. They could rely on their imagination completely as the basis for their stories. In third grade, the surge of imagination noted in second grade appeared to be gone. Either by discouragement or development, children had given up on imagination as the basis of their stories. These children told personal narratives that used personal experiences as the basis for their inventions. These types of stories required little or no imagination.

A second developmental theme evident in the content of the children's orally invented stories was that at around third grade children began to consider peers, rather than parents, as their primary social contacts. This transition was reflected in their stories. In kindergarten and first grade, children were still primarily dependent on their parents for social and emotional interaction. However, around second grade they began to bond with peers, and the peer group became their primary social group with many third graders.

Before third grade, parents in children's stories were heroes and comforters. It was they who rescued the child from the grasp of the monster. A major shift had occurred In the third graders' stories, when parents were depicted as strict authority figures who were present to judge and punish. Third grade children's stories showed a common theme of fear of parental reprisals in this sample.

The stories also show a reflection of children's fears and anxieties. Children are surrounded with stress that is often not released. Stories offer children this release. The stories of all the grades contained personal reflections of fears and stresses. Especially prevalent were fears of kidnap and murder. The children in this particular school had experience with a classmate being kidnapped and murdered so it is not surprising that this fear appeared in their stories.

Right margin annotations:
Researcher opinion

Researcher synthesis of findings from each grade level

Researcher reflection on characteristics of participants

Organization

Three developmental aspects of children's organization of invented stories were determined in this study. These included:

1) There was a clear developmental sequence to the way children organized their stories.
2) Egocentrism decreased through interactions in the social environment.
3) The distinction of the difference between fantasy and reality developed with age.

Even after the children were involved in the 4-day workshop on fairy tales, a developmental pattern still emerged. This suggests that there are aspects to children's understanding of story structure that is developmental and cannot be totally directly taught. The workshop focused on the characters, settings, plot, and organization of fairy tales. The children were instructed that fairy tales have a clear beginning, middle, and end; the beginning contains an introduction of the characters, setting, and problems; the middle of the story discusses how the characters go about solving the problems; and the end of the story contains the resolution. Thus, the children were familiar with the parts of the stories, and still a majority of the children were unable to use the information gen in the workshops to construct a coherent whole story. This suggests that the progression through stages of organization is developmental and not based on training.

Right margin annotations:
Review of salient characteristics of context

Conclusion

Implication of conclusion

(continued)

e x c e r p t   2 . 2   (c o n t i n u e d)

There was a cognitive developmental sequence in the organization of children's oral invented stories. So distinct were the differences, a developmental model can be proposed based on the data. The first stage can be characterized by the children's being unable to form a coherent ordered whole story. They told disjointed stories in which individual thoughts were juxtaposed. This is consistent with the findings of Piaget (1958) that children could not order a story into a coherent whole until about the age of 8.

Synthesis of data to suggest model

In the second stage, the children could string a series of thoughts together into coherent phrases, however, the phrases of about two or three sentences were juxtaposed against other phrases to which they had little relationship. In the third stage, children told short, utilitarian stories that just included the basics of a story with no elaboration. The children were attempting to keep their stories ordered and coherent and, if there was too much information, they got confused.

The fourth stage showed the result of this confusion. Children got sidetracked because they included more elaboration and lost track of the original story line. Eventually, they got back on track, and ended the story on the same theme with which they started. The final stage was characterized by children telling a coherent, elaborate story from beginning to end without getting sidetracked.

Conclusions and Implications

This study showed that literacy is not totally in the domain of social knowledge. The learning of words, letters, and rules of language must be passed down through the culture; these aspects of literacy cannot be invented by children without help. However, there are aspects of literacy that involve what Piaget deemed logico-mathematical knowledge. This study suggests that story structure is, at least partially, logico-mathematical knowledge. The part-whole relationship (Piaget, 1970) plays a part in the structure of children's stories. The children in this study all received direct instruction on story structure, but still a developmental sequence was evident. Children's understanding of story structure Is dependent on more than direct instruction.

Findings related to previous research

Story structure is learned through interaction with text and words rather than through direct instruction. Children will invent story structure by telling and writing stories. The reactions from the audience and from their rereading or listening to other students' stories cause disequilibrium, which according to Piaget (1970), leads to development.

This study indicates that children's orally told invented fairy tales can be used (a) to promote cognitive development, (b) to assess cognitive development, and (c) to identify emotional conflicts that children are experiencing. This study also indicates that second grade is a good time to promote creativity and imaginations as this was the age in which children were most confident in their imaginative abilities.

Overall conclusions

Orally invented stories can be used to promote cognitive development. Each time children tell a story, they must attempt first to order it mentally. This mental activity promotes the construction of knowledge. A developmental sequence to the organization of orally told stories appears evident from the stories children told in this study. To promote the movement through these developmental stages, children must be provided with the opportunity to tell stories to an audience and receive social interaction. Each time the child tells a story, the reaction from the audience causes disequilibrium. If the audience does not understand the story, the child must examine why the audience did not understand it. This type of construction through social interaction was also described by Kamii (2000) in math development. This works just as well for storytelling. The feedback from peers helps the child to overcome the limitations of egocentrism and egocentric thought.

Implications

Points related to previous research

Orally told invented fairy tales can also be used for assessment of children's cognitive abilities. This can give a teacher an idea of the areas in which a child might need work. This study was consistent with Piaget (1952) with regard to developmental sequences through which children must progress. This sequence can be used to assist in screening students who might need assistance.

Implications

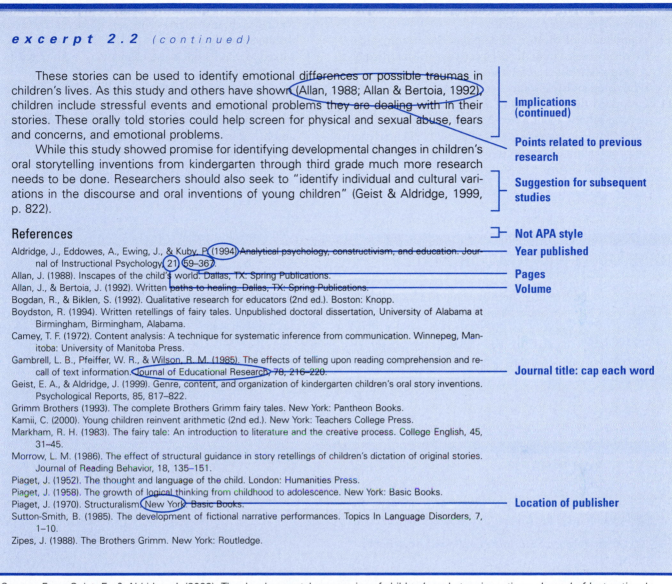

excerpt 2.2 *(continued)*

These stories can be used to identify emotional differences or possible traumas in children's lives. As this study and others have shown (Allan, 1988; Allan & Bertoia, 1992), children include stressful events and emotional problems they are dealing with in their stories. These orally told stories could help screen for physical and sexual abuse, fears and concerns, and emotional problems.

> **Implications (continued)**
>
> **Points related to previous research**

While this study showed promise for identifying developmental changes in children's oral storytelling inventions from kindergarten through third grade much more research needs to be done. Researchers should also seek to "identify individual and cultural variations in the discourse and oral inventions of young children" (Geist & Aldridge, 1999, p. 822).

> **Suggestion for subsequent studies**

References

> **Not APA style**

Aldridge, J., Eddowes, A., Ewing, J., & Kuby, P. (1994). Analytical psychology, constructivism, and education. Journal of Instructional Psychology, 21, 59–367.

> **Year published**

Allan, J. (1988). Inscapes of the child's world. Dallas, TX: Spring Publications.

> **Pages**

Allan, J., & Bertoia, J. (1992). Written paths to healing. Dallas, TX: Spring Publications.

> **Volume**

Bogdan, R., & Biklen, S. (1992). Qualitative research for educators (2nd ed.). Boston: Knopp.

Boydston, R. (1994). Written retellings of fairy tales. Unpublished doctoral dissertation, University of Alabama at Birmingham, Birmingham, Alabama.

Camey, T. F. (1972). Content analysis: A technique for systematic inference from communication. Winnepeg, Manitoba: University of Manitoba Press.

Gambrell, L. B., Pfeiffer, W. R., & Wilson, R. M. (1985). The effects of telling upon reading comprehension and recall of text information. Journal of Educational Research, 78, 216–220.

> **Journal title: cap each word**

Geist, E. A., & Aldridge, J. (1999). Genre, content, and organization of kindergarten children's oral story inventions. Psychological Reports, 85, 817–822.

Grimm Brothers (1993). The complete Brothers Grimm fairy tales. New York: Pantheon Books.

Kamii, C. (2000). Young children reinvent arithmetic (2nd ed.). New York: Teachers College Press.

Markham, R. H. (1983). The fairy tale: An introduction to literature and the creative process. College English, 45, 31–45.

Morrow, L. M. (1986). The effect of structural guidance in story retellings of children's dictation of original stories. Journal of Reading Behavior, 18, 135–151.

Piaget, J. (1952). The thought and language of the child. London: Humanities Press.

Piaget, J. (1958). The growth of logical thinking from childhood to adolescence. New York: Basic Books.

Piaget, J. (1970). Structuralism. New York: Basic Books.

> **Location of publisher**

Sutton-Smith, B. (1985). The development of fictional narrative performances. Topics In Language Disorders, 7, 1–10.

Zipes, J. (1988). The Brothers Grimm. New York: Routledge.

Source: From Geist, E., & Aldridge, J. (2002). The developmental progression of children's oral story inventions. *Journal of Instructional Psychology, 29,* 33–39. Reprinted with permission of the Journal of Instructional Psychology.

SUMMARY

This chapter has provided an overview of common terminology of types of research designs and the standard formats of published articles. The major points in this chapter are as follows:

1. Research design is the general plan of the study, including when, from whom, and how data are collected.
2. In experimental research, the investigator studies cause-and-effect relationships by manipulating a factor and seeing how that factor relates to the outcome of the study.
3. True experimental research is characterized by random assignment of subjects to groups.
4. Quasi-experimental research investigates causation without random assignment.
5. Single-subject research investigates the causal relationship between a factor and the behavior of a single individual.
6. *Nonexperimental* is a generic term that refers to research in which there is no direct control over causation. Nonexperimental designs can be classified as descriptive, comparative, correlational, survey, ex post facto, and secondary data analysis.
7. Interactive qualitative modes of inquiry use face-to-face data collection to construct in-depth understandings of informants' perspectives.

8. An ethnography is a detailed description and interpretation of a culture or system.

9. A phenomenological study describes the meanings of a lived experience from the perspective of the informants.

10. A case study investigates a single bounded system over time using multiple sources of data.

11. Grounded theory is used to develop detailed concepts or propositions about a particular phenomenon.

12. Critical studies emphasize the subjectivity of knowledge and contemporary perspectives of critical, feminist, and postmodern theory.

13. Noninteractive qualitative modes of inquiry, or analytical research, investigates concepts and events through document analysis.

14. Mixed-method studies use elements of both quantitative and qualitative designs.

15. Quantitative studies follow a well-established format and contain similar sections. In qualitative studies, the format will vary but will usually include an introduction and literature review, methodology, findings and interpretation, and conclusions.

RESEARCH NAVIGATOR NOTES

Research Navigator.c⊛m

Reading the following articles will help you understand the content of this chapter. Go to the education database (included in the EBSCO database) in Research Navigator; use the Accession Number provided to find the article.

2.1   *Qualitative Research Methods*
This article reviews the rationale for using qualitative data as evidence for a conclusion. Accession Number: 10614569.

CHECK YOURSELF

Companion Website

Multiple-choice review items, with answers, are available on the Companion Website for this book.

www.ablongman.com/macmillanschumacher6e.

APPLICATION PROBLEMS

1. Classify each study described below as a type of research design: experimental, nonexperimental, quantitative, qualitative, or mixed-method.
   a. A pilot investigation of the validity of the Back Stroke Test to identify problem swimmers
   b. A comparison of the effect of two reading programs on fourth-grade classes in Kalamazoo
   c. An investigation of the structure of attitudes of college students
   d. The effect of extrinsic rewards on the motivation of randomly assigned children to play groups
   e. A survey of principals' general attitudes toward collective bargaining as well as interviews with a small number of principals

   f. A study of the relative effectiveness of different counseling techniques used by counselors over the past five years
   g. An investigation of the difference in attendance between students in two high schools with different leadership styles
   h. A posttest-only study of the effect of humorously written review sentences on comprehension for two groups of children
   i. A study of the meaning of merit pay to teachers

2. Locate one quantitative and one qualitative journal article. For each article, identify the major sections and answer the questions provided in the guidelines for evaluating each type of article. Rate the overall credibility of each article.

3. Write a brief statement that indicates which type of research design—quantitative or qualitative—is used most commonly in your field of study.
4. Ask a professor in your field of study how he or she reads a research article. Ask about what he or she reads first, second, and so forth. Also ask what your professor does about statistical procedures included that he or she does not understand and what features he or she focuses on to judge the overall credibility of the study.

NOTE

1. We restrict the use of descriptive design to situations in which comparisons or correlations are not used only to provide a way to distinguish these designs from others. It would not be uncommon to find researchers using descriptive and nonexperimental designs interchangeably.

3

Research Problems: Statements, Questions, and Hypotheses

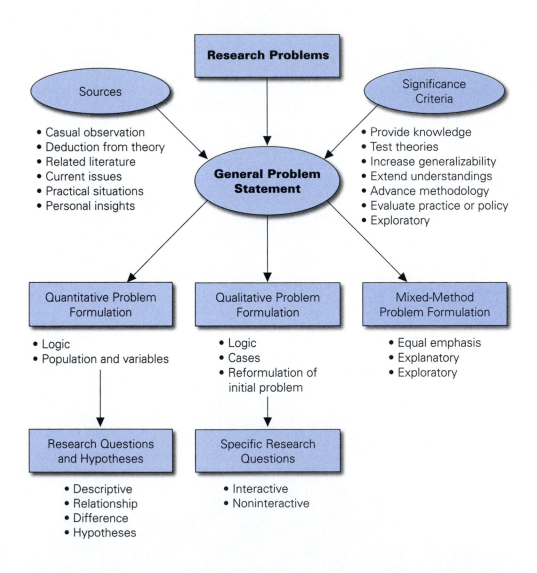

KEY TERMS

research problem
quantitative:
   construct
   variable
   categorical variable
   continuous or measured variable
   independent variable
   manipulated or experimental variable
   dependent variable
   predictor variable

criterion variable
operational definition
research hypothesis
qualitative:
   case
   qualitative field records
   narrative descriptions
   synthesized abstractions
   foreshadowed problems
   significance of the problem

Perhaps the most difficult aspect of research is formulating a clear, concise, and manageable research problem. As explained in this chapter, the statement of the research problem is crucial because it communicates to others the focus and importance of the problem, the educational context and scope, and the framework for reporting the results.

This chapter also discusses common sources used to generate research problems and criteria for evaluating their significance. Quantitative problem formulation uses reasoning to link the constructs, variables, and instruments. Qualitative problems are reformulated as the researcher builds from field records of social situations of a selected case and later relates them to broader phenomena. Criteria for judging the adequacy of the problem statement are addressed in this chapter, as well.

THE NATURE OF RESEARCH PROBLEMS

Asking questions about educational practices constitutes the initial step in research. Some questions, although important, may not connote research problems as stated. A **research problem** implies the possibility of empirical investigation—that is, of data collection and analysis.

Vague propositions and value questions are not research problems per se. Questions such as How can we prevent student dropout? and propositions such as Democratic institutions are a natural manifestation of the American culture are too vague to be researchable. Value questions ask which of two things should or should not be done. As stated, value questions, cannot be investigated empirically. In the process of asking such questions, however, a researchable problem may emerge.

A research problem is formally stated to indicate evidence-based inquiry. Quantitative research problems may be phrased as statements, questions, or hypotheses. Some examples of quantitative research problems are:

- What are the attitudes of the parents toward a school's student retention policy?
- Is there a difference in motivation between age cohorts of male and female graduate students?
- There is a positive relationship between school climate and student achievement.
- The purpose of this research is to study adolescent loneliness.

Each of these statements implies data collection and analysis.

Qualitative research problems are phrased as research purposes or questions but *never* as hypotheses. Qualitative problems usually are phrased more broadly than quantitative problems by using terms such as *How? What?* and *Why?* Stating the situation or context limits the problem. A qualitative study might examine in detail, for instance, one specific situation, person, state, or historical period. Some examples are:

- An interpretative research design was used to examine urban middle school students' meanings attributed to teachers' caring relationships.
- What does being a "single parent" mean to teachers who have young children to rear—how does being a single parent affect their parenting, job, and social roles?
- The purpose of this study is to examine and analyze the development of female academies in Vermont.

Sources of Problems

A problem is identified initially as a *general topic*, and after much preliminary work, the general topic is focused as a *specific research problem*. But where does one begin to find even general topics? The most common sources are casual observations, deductions from theory, reviews of the literature, current social issues, practical situations, and personal experiences and insights:

- **Casual observations** are rich sources of questions and hunches. Decisions frequently are made based on assumptions about the effects of practices on pupils or staff, without empirical data. Evidence-based inquiries often start with observations of certain relationships, routine ways of doing things, and innovations. Each of these inquiries may solve a practical problem, propose a new theory, or identify variables not yet in the literature.
- **Deductions from theory** also can suggest research problems. The applicability of a theory to a specific educational problem is unknown until tested empirically. Such a study could verify the usefulness of a theory for explaining one or more educational occurrences.
- **Related literature** may suggest a need to replicate a study to increase the generalizability and validity of those previous findings. In many instances, it is impossible to randomize the subjects, which limits the generalizability of the findings. When studies have been replicated, researchers can have more confidence in the findings. Citing related literature enables qualitative studies to extend the empirical understandings to other situations.
- **Current social and political issues** in U.S. society often lead to educational research. For example, the women's movement raised questions about sexual equity in general and about gender stereotyping in educational materials and practices. Similarly, recent immigration policies have suggested research questions about multiculturalism in education.
- **Practical situations** may suggest evaluation and policy studies. Questions for such research may focus on educational needs; information for program planning, development, and implementation; and the effectiveness of a given practice.
- **Personal experience and insights** may suggest research problems that can be examined in depth through qualitative methodologies. For example, a teacher who has worked with exceptional children can recognize more readily the meanings in a situation involving such children than an ethnographer who has had no prior contact with exceptional children. Being able to empathize and being able to recognize the subtle meanings in a situation are important skills in most qualitative research.

Formal Problem Statements

Researchers use formal problem statements to guide their research. Such a statement introduces the reader to the importance of the problem, places the problem in an educational context, and provides the framework for reporting the results. The problem statement orients the reader to the significance of the study and the research questions or hypotheses to follow.

The Focus, Educational Context, and Significance of the Problem   In any well-written problem statement, the reader is not kept in suspense but rather told directly and immediately the general focus, educational context, and significance of the problem. For example, in Excerpt 3.1 the reader is told about the expected shortage in the number of

EXCERPT 3.1 Problem Statement: Framework

Who will lead the schools during the 21st century? . . . The problem is exacerbated by . . . teacher reluctance to enter administration coupled with the number of administrator retirements present a significant challenge to boards, superintendents, and communities. . . .

To help find a solution to this problem, a study was conducted of 189 master's students enrolled in a Midwestern university's educational leadership program. Students completed a survey identifying factors that influenced their decision to apply for an administrative position. (p. 75)

Source: From Cooley, V., & Shen, J. (1999). Who will lead? The top 10 factors that influence teachers moving into administration. *NASSP Bulletin, 83*(606), 75–80.

school administrators and about teachers' reluctance to enter administration. The study was conducted to identify factors that influenced teachers' decisions to apply for an administration position.

A Framework for Results and Conclusions   The problem statement also provides the framework for reporting the conclusions (e.g., what information will be presented). Excerpt 3.1 exemplifies the framework for the findings of a study. Ten factors that teachers consider in applying for administrative positions were reported and discussed in that study, with implications for recruiting and retaining a new generation of school leaders.

Qualitative problem statements also provide the framework for reporting the findings and interpretations. For example, in a recent study, the research problem was to report the "findings on the perception of poor single mothers regarding the helpfulness of their support systems in enabling them to work" (Wijnberg & Weinger, 1998). The findings were organized as early dreams, perceived network support and resources, coping styles, and social support when ill.

The introductory paragraphs of a study are difficult to write, as they must convey a lot of information succinctly. Researchers frequently rewrite these paragraphs as they formulate the significance of the study and research questions. They may even write the final version of the introduction after the study has been completed. Regardless, researchers begin with an initial problem statement to guide their activities.

PROBLEM FORMULATION IN QUANTITATIVE RESEARCH

Asking questions about a general topic is the starting point for defining a research problem. Then, the problem is narrowed to specific research questions or hypotheses. For example, the topic of educational policy-making might focus on school board policies, and that broad topic might be narrowed to certain policies, such as fiscal, student, or personnel. The topic can be focused even more: Is the interest in the antecedents to the policies, the process of policy-making, or the consequences of the policies for whom? From one general topic, a number of questions can thus be generated. Suppose the selected topic is instruction. Again, one could ask similar questions: What kind of instruction? Is the focus on the antecedents, the process, or the consequences? Is the interest in students of specific ages or with certain characteristics?

If the problem is too general, then the results will be difficult to interpret. Ultimately, the researcher has to make decisions about the selection of variables, the population, and the *logic for the problem*. This means that the initial problem statement is usually revised many times. The logic of quantitative problems is illustrated in Figure 3.1.

FIGURE 3.1   Quantitative Research: The Logic of Constructs, Variables, and Operational Definitions

The Logic of Constructs, Variables, and Operational Definitions

To formulate a problem, researchers begin with an abstract construct, logically link that construct to a set of variables, and then decide the operational definition for each variable. The reasoning process moves from an abstract construct to less abstract variables to a selected instrument. The arrows in Figure 3.1 indicate that several decisions are made and reviewed *before* data are collected.

Constructs   In research, an abstract concept is called a **construct.** Often derived from theory, a construct expresses the idea behind a set of particulars. Examples of constructs are motivation, intelligence, thinking, anxiety, self-concept, achievement, and aptitude. Another way to define a construct is to say that it is created by combining variables in a meaningful pattern. Such variables as visual perception, sight/sound discrimination, audio acuity, and left-to-right orientation are meaningfully combined to suggest the construct of reading readiness.

Variables   A **variable** is an *attribute* or *level* that expresses a construct and has different values, depending on how it is used in a particular study. There are several kinds of variables. A variable used to separate subjects or entities into two or more attributes is a **categorical variable.** Categorical variables may have only two attributes (e.g., male/female, married/single, and pass/fail) or more than two levels (e.g., income level, educational attainment, religious affiliation). A **continuous** or **measured variable** is one in which the attribute or level of an entity is measured and can assume an infinite number of values within a range (e.g., socioeconomic status, test score, and age). Each variable should be a separate and distinct phenomenon. Educational research investigates many factors as variables: classroom variables (e.g., teaching styles, interaction patterns, cognitive levels of questions); environmental variables (e.g., parental educational level, social class, family structure); and personal variables (e.g., age, gender, intelligence, motivation, self-concept).

Types of Variables   In experimental research, one variable precedes another, either logically or in time. The variable that comes first and influences or predicts is called the **independent, manipulated,** or **experimental variable**—that is, the variable that is manipulated or changed by the researcher to investigate the effect on a dependent variable. The second variable, which is affected or predicted by the independent variable, is the **dependent variable** (see Excerpt 3.2). The independent variable is the *antecedent*; the dependent variable is the *consequence*. The dependent variable is labeled as such because its value depends on and varies with the value of the independent variable. Suppose a researcher wants to see the effect of the timing of a review on social studies achievement. The researcher will manipulate the timing of the review—immediate and delayed—and then measure the effects on social studies achievement.

In nonexperimental research, the independent variable *cannot* be manipulated. For example, a study of the effect of school size (independent variable) on achievement (dependent variable) may use large, medium, and small schools (levels of the independent variable). Obviously, the researcher will not manipulate the sizes of the selected schools but will choose the schools from enrollment records. In some correlational research, the antecedent variable is called the **predictor variable** and the predicted variable is called the **criterion variable.** In a study that examines the relationship of scores on the Scholas-

EXCERPT 3.2   Experimental Research: Independent and Dependent Variables

Research questions to examine the effects of teaching a lesson of emotionally charged issues on achievement, attitude, . . . [using Multisensory Instructional Packages {MIP}]:

1. Will there be significantly higher student achievement test gains when the Holocaust is taught using the MIP as opposed to when it is taught traditionally?

2. Will there be significantly higher student attitude test scores toward instruction methods when the Holocaust is taught with the MIP as opposed to when it is taught traditionally? (p. 43)

Source: From Farkas, R. D. (2003). Effects of traditional versus learning-styles instructional methods on middle school students. *Journal of Educational Research, 97*(1), 42–51.

tic Aptitude Test (SAT) to success in college, the predictor variable is the SAT scores and the criterion variable is college success. In other correlational studies, there is no obvious antecedent variable; such is the case in considering the relationship between self-concept and achievement. The researcher here is not interested in prediction but in determining the strength and direction of the relationship between the variables (see Excerpt 3.3). Some researchers use the terms *independent* and *dependent* with correlational and other non-experimental research when it is clear that one variable precedes the other variable or that categories have been created to allow comparisons.

In most descriptive research and some survey research, there is only one variable of interest. For instance, a study that describes the reading achievement of second-graders or a survey of parental attitudes toward a school policy contains only one variable of interest (see Excerpt 3.4).

EXCERPT 3.3   Correlational Research: Predictor and Criterion Variables

The present study has two main purposes: (1) to develop a comprehensive set of kindergarten prereading tasks that would predict reading achievement at the end of first and second grade, and (2) to determine at what point in the kindergarten year—beginning, middle, or end—the various tasks would exert maximum predictive power. (p. 95)

Source: From Morris, D., Bloodgood, J., & Perney, J. (2003). Kindergarten predictors of first- and second-grade reading achievement. *The Elementary School Journal, 104*(2), 93–110.

EXCERPT 3.4   Survey Research: Variable of Interest

To obtain information about low-income parents' beliefs about their role that could help guide future efforts to increase . . . their participation. . . . (1) How much parents from diverse backgrounds value involvement in their children's schooling; (2) what factors are associated with differences among parents in the belief about involvement; and (3) what parents say, in their own words, they should be doing to help their children succeed in school. (pp. 200–201)

Source: From Drummon, K. V., & Stipek, D. (2004). Low-income parents' beliefs about their role in children's academic learning. *The Elementary School Journal, 104*(3), 197–214.

TABLE 3.1   Examples of Variables and Constitutive versus Operational Definitions

Variable	Constitutive Definition	Operational Definition
Self-concept	Characteristics used to describe oneself	Scores on the Coopersmith *Self-Esteem Inventory*
Intelligence	Ability to think abstractly	Scores on the Stanford-Binet
Teacher with-it-ness	Awareness of student involvement and behavior	Results of the *Robinson Scale Teacher With-It-Ness*

A variable may be independent in one study and dependent in another; a variable also may be a predictor or a criterion variable. How the variable functions (e.g., as independent, dependent, predictor, criterion or as the only variable of interest) in a given study depends on the purpose, logic, and design of the study. The problem statement is phrased to indicate the function of the variable(s) in the proposed study and thus implies the design.

Operational Definitions   Each variable in a quantitative study must be defined operationally and subsequently categorized, measured, or manipulated. A constitutive (i.e., dictionary) definition defines a word by using other terms, such as defining *anxiety* as "apprehension or vague fear." In contrast, the researcher uses an **operational definition,** which assigns meaning to a variable by specifying the activities or operations necessary to measure, categorize, or manipulate that variable. An operational definition tells the researcher and the reader what is necessary to answer the question or test the hypothesis. Variables frequently can be defined operationally in several ways, and some operations may be more valid for certain research problems than others. The operational definition for a variable is often not as valid as the researcher desires. To conduct an evidence-based inquiry, however, one must define each variable operationally.

Table 3.1 provides some examples of variables, each described with a constitutive definition and an operational definition.

Problem Formulation

A useful procedure for transforming a general topic into a manageable problem is to identify the population, the variables, and the logic of the problem. Suppose a supervisor is interested in determining whether organizing programs for gifted elementary students in different ways will affect student creativity. The gifted programs are organized as: (1) special programs, in which students remain together for a comprehensive program; (2) pullout programs, in which students attend regular classes except for two hours' daily instruction by selected teachers; and (3) enrichment programs, in which students complete enrichment activities as an extension of their regular instruction. The research question is, Is there a difference in creativity (the dependent variable) among gifted elementary students (the population) who participate in a special program, a pullout program, or an enrichment program (three levels of one independent variable)? This question is narrowed to the degree that it identifies the population and the two variables. The logic behind the question is clear because the relationship between the independent and dependent variable can be identified.

A question phrased as Does mainstreaming do any good? is too broad and has neither a population nor variables. The researcher must narrow the problem to be more specific:

Is there a difference between high school students' (the population) attitudes toward students with disabilities (the dependent variable) who participated in a six-weeks mainstreamed class and the attitudes of those students who did not participate in the class (two levels of the independent variable)? Now the question is focused. In addition, it implies an experimental design, and the logic behind the problem is explicit.

By identifying the types of variables and the population, the researcher clarifies the focus and logic of the problem. This process is not easy; it requires rewriting and reconceptualizing the problem. Reading literature, brainstorming with others, and talking with experienced researchers all can help in clarifying a problem. Once the idea is clearly in mind, the researcher can write a formal problem statement.

ALERT! It is better to do the preliminary work necessary to write a problem statement that has a specific purpose than to proceed with a broad statement and purpose.

Specific Research Questions and Hypotheses

In a quantitative study, the research problem may be stated as a question or a hypothesis. The question format is often preferred because it is simple and direct. Psychologically, it orients the researcher to the immediate task: to develop a design to answer the question. Research questions may be descriptive questions, relationship questions, or difference questions. Each type of question implies a different design (see Figure 3.2).

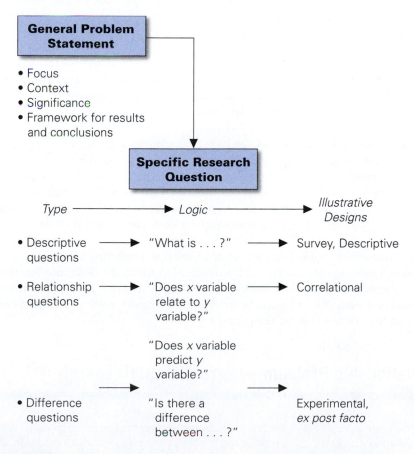

FIGURE 3.2 **Logic of Quantitative Problem Statements and Specific Research Questions**

EXCERPT 3.5   Descriptive Problem—Survey Research

In the present study, we examine the degree to which exemplar teachers reported using cooperative learning versus the degree to which they would prefer to use this method, as well as the relative use of each element of cooperative learning. (p. 234)

Source: From Lopata, C., Miller, K. A., & Miller, R. H. (2003). Survey of actual and preferred use of cooperative learning among exemplar teachers. *Journal of Educational Research, 96*(4), 232–239.

Research Navigator.com

3.1 Relationship Questions
Accession No.: 12103384

Research Navigator.com

3.2 Difference Questions
Accession No.: 12010631

Research Navigator.com

3.3 Difference Questions
Accession No.: 11453638

Descriptive Research Questions   Descriptive research questions typically ask What is? and imply a survey research design. These terms, however, are not always used in the wording of the research question. For example, a research question may be What is the achievement level of our fourth-grade students on the Iowa Test of Basic Skills? Evaluation research often investigates the perceptions of groups concerned with a practice, such as What are the administrators' opinions of a program? Which of the alternative bus routes do our pupils' parents prefer? and What does the staff perceive as our most important instructional needs? (see Excerpt 3.5).

Relationship Questions   A relationship question asks, What is the relationship between two or more variables? and implies a correlational design. For example, Does self-concept relate to achievement? asks a question about the relationship between one variable (self-concept) and another (achievement). Studies that determine the best predictors for a variable, such as predictors of college success, imply relationship questions between the possible predictor variables—such as high school grade-point average and class rank, recommendations, and participation in extracurricular activities—and the dependent variable, college success. Excerpt 3.6 illustrates a problem statement that implies a relationship question between selected long-range predictors and children's social adjustment. The problem statement also suggests the design for the study.

Difference Questions   A difference question typically asks Is there a difference between two groups or two or more treatments? This type of question is used when the study compares two or more observations. Asking Is there a difference? rather than Is there a relationship? between two or more observations clarifies the underlying logic of the study. Questions such as Is there a difference between pretest and posttest scores? are more useful than those phrased Is there a relationship between pretest and posttest scores? (see Excerpt 3.7).

If the researchers firmly believe that in addition to predicting a difference between two or more variables, they can predict the direction in which the difference lies, then the direction should be stated in the research question. The question Is there a difference in pretest and posttest scores? may thus be stated Is there greater mastery of reading comprehension on the posttest than on the pretest?

EXCERPT 3.6   Relationship Problem—Correlational Research

In this study, I examined variables that predict how African American parents and guardians of school-aged children rate their children's elementary and secondary school teachers, and the public school system as a whole. (p. 279)

Source: From Thompson, G. L. (2003). Predicting African American parents' and guardians' satisfaction with teachers and public schools. *Journal of Educational Research, 96*(5), 277–285.

EXCERPT 3.7   Difference Questions—Experimental Research

RQ 1: Are there significant differences in student affective learning between traditional classroom instruction and instruction through a game/simulation?

RQ 2: Are there significant differences in student cognitive learning between traditional classroom instruction and instruction through a game/simulation?

RQ 3: Are there significant differences in student motivation between traditional classroom instruction and instruction through a game/simulation? (p. 38)

Source: From Garard, D. L., Hunt, S. K., Lippert, L., & Raynton, S. T. (1998). Alternative to traditional instruction: Using games and simulation to increase student learning and motivation. *Communication Research Reports, 15*(1), 36–44.

Research questions are *not* statistical questions stated for data analysis. A statistical question may be phrased Is there a statistically significant difference between A and B variables? or Is there a statistically significant relationship between A variable and B variable? Statistical questions are stated in the Methodology section of a study. Research questions are stated in the Introduction and suggest the design.

Research Hypotheses   A **research hypothesis** is a tentative statement of the expected relationship between two or more variables. Problem statements and research hypotheses are similar in substance, except that research hypotheses are declarative statements, more specific than problem statements, clearly testable, and indicative of the expected results. For the research problem, Is there a relationship between review and cognitive retention? the research hypothesis might be There is a positive relationship between review and cognitive retention. Empirical testing is feasible to the extent that each variable can be manipulated, categorized, or measured. Although the word *relationship* is not used in every hypothesis, relation expressions such as *will achieve, produces, is a function of,* and *effects* connect the variables.

A hypothesis implies an if/then logic. Most hypotheses can be put into an if/then form to indicate the relationship between variables—for example, If perceived student differences, then greater differences in teaching behavior; If a remedial course, then higher reading comprehension; and If democratic leadership style, then faculty satisfaction. The logic is similar for a hypothesis with more than two variables.

A hypothesis is a conjectural explanation of phenomena that is accepted or rejected by empirical evidence. In the preceeding examples, a remedial reading course explains higher achievement and a democratic leadership style explains faculty satisfaction.

To be useful in research, a hypothesis should meet several standards:

1. *The hypothesis should state the direction of the relationship.* A statement such as If teacher feedback, then student science achievement implies a relationship but is not a hypothesis. The directional hypothesis might state Teacher feedback will relate positively to student science achievement or There is a positive relationship between teacher feedback and student science achievement. When a treatment is administered to one group of subjects but not another, researchers should hypothesize directional differences—for example, Fifth-grade students who receive microcomputer-assisted instruction will have higher math achievement than comparable students who did not receive microcomputer-assisted instruction.

2. *A hypothesis should be testable.* A testable hypothesis is verifiable; one can draw conclusions from empirical data that indicate whether the hypothesized consequences did or did not occur. To be testable, a hypothesis must include variables that can be measured or categorized by some objective procedure (see Excerpts 3.8 and 3.9). For example, because one can classify first-grade students as having attended preschool or not into two levels, a hypothesis might state Children who attend preschool will have higher scores on a scale of social maturity than children who do not attend preschool.

EXCERPT 3.8   Research Hypothesis

Boys and girls who attend single-sex Catholic secondary schools score higher on tests of academic achievement and self concept than their counterparts who attend coeducational Catholic secondary schools. (p. 493)

Source: From LePore, P. C., & Warren, J. R. (1997). A comparison of single-sex and coeducational catholic secondary schooling: From the national educational longitudinal study of 1988. *American Educational Research Journal, 34*, 485–511.

EXCERPT 3.9   Research Hypothesis

The foregoing literature review suggests that parents who attend school meetings or conferences and interact with school personnel are likely to have children who demonstrate higher levels of achievement at school than children of parents who fail to participate in their child's school program. (p. 92)

Source: From Shaver, A. V., & Walls, R. T. (1998). Effect of Title 1 parent involvement on student reading and mathematics achievement. *Journal of Research and Development in Education, 31*, 90–97.

3. *A hypothesis should offer a tentative explanation based on theory or previous research.* A well-grounded hypothesis indicates that there is sufficient research or theory for considering the hypothesis important enough to test. A research hypothesis usually is stated after a literature review, at which point the researcher has knowledge of the previous work or theory. In many areas of education, however, there is little conclusive evidence, and only some educational research can serve as a basis for the research hypothesis.

> **MISCONCEPTION**   Girls achieve less than boys in mathematics in primary school, and few girls pursue math- and science-related majors in college even though their SAT scores are similar to those of boys.
>
> **EVIDENCE**   After changing the research problem, it was found that fewer girls than boys took advanced high school mathematics courses to prepare for math- and science-related college majors.

4. *A hypothesis should be concise and lucid.* In its simplest form, a hypothesis should have logical coherence and a clear order of arrangement. Brief statements aid both the reader and the researcher in interpreting the results. A general rule is to state only one relationship per hypothesis. Although a researcher may have one general hypothesis, it is better to rephrase it into more specific hypotheses for clarity.

PROBLEM FORMULATION IN QUALITATIVE RESEARCH

Problem formulation in qualitative research begins with selecting a general topic and a mode of inquiry (i.e., interactive or noninteractive). The topic and methodology are *interrelated* and selected almost simultaneously, rather than in separate research steps. For example, an early research decision is whether to examine ongoing or past events. Suppose that a study of current phenomena requires the researcher to have access to a site or to a group of people who shared some social experience, such as working in the same school system or participating in a special project or a class. A study of past events will require that archival collections of primary documents be made available to the researcher. These considerations will begin to shape and influence the selection of a general topic.

Qualitative researchers begin by narrowing a general topic to a more definitive topic. A principal may notice that a growing number of African American women are seeking promotions in a large urban district. The researcher will begin to wonder What experiences have veteran African American women principals had that may provide useful directions to future administrators? As another example, suppose that a researcher notices that deaf children and their hearing peers in a public school often fail to communicate. The researcher might ask How does this failure affect the children's cognitive and social development?

Many qualitative research interests come from personal experience—a long-time concern or interest in a topic developed from opportunities in one's current biography and personal background. Prior experience gives the researcher physical and/or psychological access to present or past social settings. In other words, research problems lie in many personal situations and experiences, as well as in general reading, which need only to be recognized as potential research problems. Thinking further, puzzling, and being aware of qualitative research traditions enable researchers to establish the logic behind the problem.

The Logic of Qualitative Field Records, Descriptions, and Abstractions

Qualitative research, in contrast to quantitative research, employs primarily *inductive reasoning* but deductive reasoning is used at selected times. The problem is most clearly stated after much data collection and preliminary analysis. The researcher obtains comprehensive field records of a present or past situation, which give detailed descriptions of people's perceptions and social realities, and then forms abstractions from these descriptions to explain the phenomenon. Inductive reasoning allows one to explore and discover with an emerging research design, rather than test deductions using theories from a predetermined design. The research problem is typically reformulated during data collection so that the data closely represent the reality of the shared social experiences.

Problem formulation begins with the selection of a particular case for in-depth study. The inductive process is schematically represented in Figure 3.3. Note that the arrows in

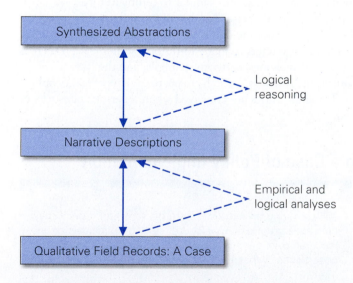

FIGURE 3.3   The Logic of Qualitative Research: Field Records, Descriptions, and Abstractions

the center of the figure go in two directions (i.e., from the bottom upward and from the top downward) to illustrate the use of both inductive and deductive reasoning.

Qualitative Field Records: A Case   Researchers select a specific case for in-depth study. A **case** is a particular social situation chosen by the researcher in which some phenomenon will be described by participants' perceptions. The researcher also decides on a primary qualitative methodology (e.g., participant observations, in-depth interviews, or analysis of documents). In selecting a case, the researcher limits the research problem to a particular context, such as foreign-born teachers in a school district who speak English as a second language, informal mentors working with native Mexican adolescents in an urban setting, or teachers implementing a mathematics curricular reform. Thus, the researcher selects a particular case, rather than variables, to gain an understanding of a broader phenomenon. The broader phenomenon in Excerpt 3.10 is leadership in policy implementation and school change.

Qualitative field records, which are obtained over a lengthy time period, include data such as participant observation field notes, interview tapes, and researcher notes about historical documents. Each field note, transcript, or document note contains the date of occurrence and the context, such as the social scene, situation, and participants. The field data collected initially may lead to collecting data from other people, sites, and archive collections, as the researcher discovers more aspects about the selected case. In other words, the term *case* does not refer to one person or one archival collection or one locale but to the *social situation* examined. Data collection strategies are adjusted to obtain a holistic view of the phenomena and then to study certain aspects in depth.

Narrative Descriptions   Researchers construct from the data **narrative descriptions,** or detailed accounts of the people, incidents, and processes. The entire narrative description is completed after data collection because of the discovery orientation of the research. To inductively generate a descriptive narration, certain kinds of data must be in the field notes, transcripts, or notes of historical documents.

Descriptive narrations, sometimes called "rich" or "thick" description told in "loving detail," contain at least four elements: people, incidents, participants' language, and participants' "meanings":

1. *Participants* are described as individuals who have different personal histories and display different physical, emotional, and intellectual characteristics in various situations.
2. *Incidents* form a narration about the social scenes, similar to telling a story.
3. Descriptions emphasize the *participants' language,* not that of researchers or of social science. For instance, participants' names for incidents, locations, objects, special events, and processes are all noted. Language refers to many forms of communication such as verbal and nonverbal expressions, drawings, cartoons, symbols, and the like.
4. Descriptions emphasize *participant "meanings,"* which are people's views of reality or how they perceive their world. These meanings are conveyed when a person states *why* or *because* an event happened.

EXCERPT 3.10   Understanding a Case of Policy Implementation

The purpose [is] . . . to explicate the concept of transition leadership and its centrality to understanding policy implementation and school change through a case study of one district and its school principals. . . . This study rests with understanding the actions principals define for themselves during an extreme state of transition. Specifically, our research questions explore, How do principals define leadership in transition? Where do they see leadership possibilities? What are their leadership priorities? (pp. 473–474)

Source: From Goldring, E., Crowson, R., Laird, D., & Berk, R. (2003). Transition leadership in a shifting policy environment. *Educational Evaluation and Policy Analysis, 25*(4), 473–488.

Synthesized Abstractions   Researchers generate abstract summaries from the data to produce **synthesized abstractions** or summary generalizations and explanations of the major research findings of a study. Synthesized abstractions may take different formats, such as a list of narrative themes, "lessons learned," the essence of a shared experience, a delineated concept, or an assertion or propositional statement. The researcher constructs a picture that takes shape as he or she collects data and examines the parts. The subtle meanings of the phenomenon can be understood more clearly by the readers.

Problem Reformulation

A qualitative research problem is reformulated several times *after* the researcher has begun data collection. The research problem is stated initially in planning for the study, reformulated during early data collection, and reformulated as necessary throughout data collection. The continuing reformulation of the research problem reflects an emergent design. Reformulation relates to changing data collection strategies to acquire the totality of the phenomena and then to study some aspect in greater depth. The specific research problem evolves and is condensed toward the end of data collection. In most publications, the condensed version of the research problem often is not the same problem that initiated the research (see Excerpt 3.11).

Foreshadowed Problems   Qualitative researchers begin with **foreshadowed problems,** or anticipated research problems that will be reformulated during data collection. The statement of foreshadowed problems depends to some extent on prior knowledge of the events and processes at a site, of the people to be interviewed, and of archival collection documents. Thus, foreshadowed problems are not directly derived from an exhaustive literature review but rather from the researcher's initial experiences in planning the study. A preliminary literature review, however, aids the researcher in phrasing the foreshadowed problems.

Foreshadowed problems are usually phrased as broad, general questions, focusing on the What? How? and Why? of the situation. The What? refers to who, when, where, and which social scenes occur. The How? refers to the processes to be examined and what influenced them (see Excerpt 3.12). The Why? refers to participant "meanings," or people's explanations for the incidents and social scenes observed. Each of these questions is deliberately broad to allow for discovery and development of an emergent design.

Condensed Problem Statements   A condensed problem statement may be written any time during or after data collection. It is usually the selected major research question that will focus the entire report. The title, literature review, and discussion often use abstract terms of qualitative scholars; however, the research problem may or may not be phrased in descriptive terms (see Excerpt 3.13).

E X C E R P T   3 . 1 1   Initial Problem and Reformulation from the Sites

[Initially] show how teachers and their administrators were attempting to come to terms with top-down, . . . [state], and district mandates to make more and better use of computer technologies in teaching and learning. . . .

How are existing power relations in schools reinforced and/or reorganized by the introduction of computer technologies? How do these new technologies change the work of teaching and how do these changes undermine or encourage the teacher's . . . sense of control and ownership? . . . These questions emerged from a series of conversations and experiences we had with individual teachers . . . [who] consistently raised issues of gender inequities both in the context of schooling and in relation to the technology itself. . . . *[We] did not set out to study gender.* (pp. 170, 171)

Source: From Jenson, J., & Rose, C. B. (2003). Women@work: Listening to gendered relations of power in teachers' talk about new technologies. *Gender and Education, 15*(2), 169–181.

EXCERPT 3.12 Ethnographic Problem Statement and Research Questions

Social relationships for people with disabilities have been a central concern . . . for many years. So too have sibling relationships. Specifically, we will report the findings of a case study of the sibling relationships of Raul, a young man with Down syndrome. . . . We focused on the following questions:

1. What are the predominant types of interactions between the siblings and Raul?
2. How does Raul participate in these interactions?
3. How do the observed sibling interactions compare to findings about Raul's interactions with nondisabled peers at school? (pp. 289, 291)

Source: From Harry, B., Day, M., & Quist, F. (1998). "He Can't Really Play": An ethnographic study of sibling acceptance and interaction. *JASH: Journal of the Association for Persons with Severe Handicaps, 23*(4), 289–299.

EXCERPT 3.13 Qualitative Problem Statement

Working as a principal in any large, urban school today can be both a difficult and dangerous assignment. However, a growing number of African American women administrators are seeking promotional opportunities to lead in schools. . . . Listening to and recording veteran African American women principals' experiences may provide useful direction to future administrators who aspire. (p. 339)

Source: From Bloom, C. M., & Erlandson, D. A. (2003). African American women principals in urban schools: Realities, (re)constructions, and resolutions. *Educational Administration Quarterly, 39*(3), 339–369.

Statements of Qualitative Research Purposes and Questions

Qualitative studies contain statements of research purposes and questions that imply the inductive logic for the problem at hand. The statement of research purpose is the final condensed version of the initial problem statement. Specific research questions may be stated or implied. The statement of purpose implies the chosen qualitative mode of inquiry: interactive or noninteractive research.

Qualitative Problem Statements and Questions   The qualitative research traditions of ethnography, phenomenology, case study, grounded theory, and critical study focus on current phenomena for which data can be obtained through interacting with the participants in a selected social situation (see Excerpt 3.14).

Historical Problem Statements and Questions   Historical research problems focus on past events and often require access to documents in historical archives. A historical study

EXCERPT 3.14 Qualitative Problem Statement

The following questions are addressed: . . .

In what ways do foreign-born ESL teachers draw on their experiences as foreign-born residents living in the United States to open or close new social networks for their students?

How can these practices be seen as a way of breaking down the power differentials between minority and majority groups? (p. 128)

Source: From Case, R. E. (2004). Forging ahead into new social networks and looking back to past social identities: A case study of a foreign-born English as a second language teacher in the United States. *Urban Education, 39*(2), 125–148.

EXCERPT 3.15   Historical Problem Statement

By the century's end, vacation schools offering summer recreation and industrial education to the children of the urban, immigrant poor became yet another philanthropic program to enter the public school domain. What hap- pened to vacation schools in New York City as a conse- quence of public administration is the focus of this article. (p. 18)

Source: From Gold, K. M. (2002). From vacation to summer school: The transformation of summer education in New York City, 1894–1915. *History of Education Quarterly, 42*(1), 18–48.

may begin when archival documents are made available to scholars. Such a study may also begin when only a few people remain of those who experienced the event, such as a labor strike over the right of married women teachers to be tenured (see Excerpt 3.15). Because back issues of major newspapers and journals are often stored on data disks and available on the Internet, more historical research can be done today than in the past, when only bound collections of information existed. In addition, many public agencies now keep their permanent records in easily accessible formats.

PROBLEM FORMULATION IN MIXED-METHOD RESEARCH

Like a study that is either completely quantitative or qualitative, a mixed-method investigation begins with identification of a general problem, which provides a context and background. Identifying the general problem is followed by indicating a more specific purpose for the study. At this point, the researcher could indicate that a mixed-method design will be used and write specific quantitative research questions and foreshadowed problems. In addition, some researchers present more specific questions and problems after their review of the literature.

Since a good research problem implies the design, the research questions and foreshadowed problems should be presented in a way that is consistent with how the methods will be used. The *relative importance* of how each method functions in the study should be communicated (e.g., whether a quantitative or qualitative approach is emphasized or both are given equal weight) along with the overall purpose of the research. Knowing the relative importance of each method used in the study helps determine the type of mixed-method design.

Equal Priority to All Questions   When a variety of questions are asked and all are equally important, then both quantitative and qualitative data are collected at about the same time. The research questions and foreshadowed problems are usually presented together. Doing so communicates that both kinds of data have equal priority. Suppose a researcher is interested in studying beginning teachers and has formulated this general problem: What kinds of help are most important in ensuring the success of beginning elementary teachers? The following questions are more specific:

1. To what extent have several kinds of help been received by beginning elementary teachers? (quantitative)
2. How do beginning elementary school teachers rate the helpfulness of the assistance received? (quantitative)
3. How does the elementary school principal rate the helpfulness of assistance provided to beginning teachers? (quantitative)
4. Why have certain kinds of assistance proven most helpful? (qualitative)
5. How does the context of the teaching situation influence the need for different kinds of assistance? (qualitative)

The first three quantitative questions could be addressed with an instrument that lists the types of assistance received (e.g., from a mentor, principal, other teacher) and provides a rating scale for evaluating the extent of helpfulness. The qualitative questions (items 4 and 5) could be answered by conducting interviews with teachers and principals at about the same time that the surveys are being completed. Findings from both kinds of data would be analyzed and interpreted to determine if similar results are obtained. The questions imply a *triangulation design* because using both methods provides a more complete result.

Measured Results Explained by Qualitative Data   Suppose these research questions were being considered: Are there differences in the amounts of helpful assistance that beginning teachers receive? If so, how do beginning teachers explain why some types of assistance are helpful and others are not? Researchers must see the results of the first question to decide if they need further data to explain the findings. A survey could be used to identify individual teachers who have received the greatest amount of effective assistance and those teachers who have received the least amount of assistance. Once those individuals have been identified, qualitative interviews could be conducted with a small sample from each group. The interviews could explore reasons that particular kinds of assistance were helpful or not helpful. The research design could be represented like this:

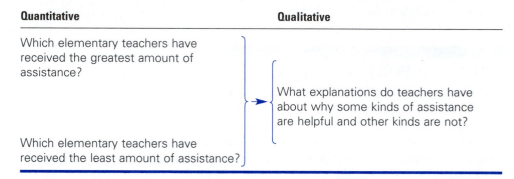

Quantitative	Qualitative
Which elementary teachers have received the greatest amount of assistance?	What explanations do teachers have about why some kinds of assistance are helpful and other kinds are not?
Which elementary teachers have received the least amount of assistance?	

When data are collected sequentially—quantitative first, qualitative second—the quantitative phase provides general results that are then explained with qualitative data. When data are collected sequentially, an *explanatory design* is implied.

Qualitative Questions, Then Quantitative Questions   When there is little prior research on a topic or a practice is new, qualitative methods may be used first to investigate the scope of the phenomenon, followed by quantitative methods. The data identified in the qualitative phase will then be investigated in a more structured way using quantitative approaches. For example, in a study of beginning teacher assistance, it may be necessary to explore the types of assistance received before measuring the relationship among the types. The quantitative results extend what is found in the qualitative phase. The following research design could be used:

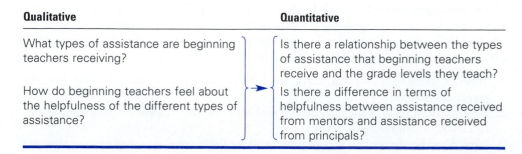

Qualitative	Quantitative
What types of assistance are beginning teachers receiving?	Is there a relationship between the types of assistance that beginning teachers receive and the grade levels they teach?
How do beginning teachers feel about the helpfulness of the different types of assistance?	Is there a difference in terms of helpfulness between assistance received from mentors and assistance received from principals?

When qualitative methods initiate the inquiry and are then followed by quantitative techniques, the problem implies an *exploratory design*. Exploratory designs are often used to develop instruments. A topic will be studied in depth to clarify all important dimensions, and then these dimensions will be used as a framework for developing a questionnaire. For instance, a researcher could spend considerable time in a school observing the nature of school climate and then use that information to develop an objectively scored instrument that captures all aspects of school climate.

THE SIGNIFICANCE
OF PROBLEM SELECTION

The **significance of the problem** is the rationale for a study. It justifies why an evidence-based inquiry is important and indicates the reasons for the researcher's choice of a particular problem. Because research requires knowledge, skills, planning, time, and fiscal resources, the problem to be investigated should be important. In other words, the study should have a potential payoff.

A research problem is significant when it aids in developing theory, knowledge, or practice. That significance increases when several reasons can be provided to justify the inquiry. Justifications may be based on one or more of the following criteria: whether the study provides knowledge about an enduring practice, tests a theory, is generalizable, extends understanding of a broader phenomenon, advances methodology, is related to a current issue, evaluates a specific practice at a given site, or is an exploratory study.

Knowledge of an Enduring Practice   The study may provide knowledge about an enduring educational practice. Perhaps previous research on the practice has been done, but this particular research problem has not been investigated. The practice being studied may be common to many schools but not necessarily found in every school. The study will add knowledge about an enduring common practice (see Excerpt 3.16).

Theory Testing   The study may be significant because it tests an existing theory with a verification design. The focus may be on social science theories of child or adult development, organizational development, conflict, and so on. Educational theories may focus on curricula, instructional models, staff development, learning styles, teaching strategies, or the like. By testing a theory in different situations or on different populations, the researcher may modify or verify it.

Generalizability   The study may be designed so the results will be generalizable to different populations or practices. A study may replicate or include other variables not investigated in previous research, or it may call for using a different population than the original research to enhance generalizability (see Excerpt 3.17).

Extensions of Understanding   Many qualitative studies conducted in the phenomenological tradition extend understanding, rather than generalizability. By describing a selected case of a social situation in detail, such a study provides an understanding of the

EXCERPT 3.16   Significance: Add to Knowledge
of an Enduring Practice

The study adds to parent involvement research by examining parents' beliefs about involvement in different domains. (p. 201)

Source: From Drummon, K. V., & Stipek, D. (2004). Low-income parents' beliefs about their role in children's academic learning. *The Elementary School Journal, 104*(3), 197–214.

EXCERPT 3.17 Justification: Replication and Generalization

Thus, the objective of the present inquiry was to replicate and extend the work of Witcher, et. al. (2001). Specifically our purpose was to investigate what preservice teachers view as important characteristics of effective teachers. (p. 118)

Source: From Minor, L. C., Onwuegbuzie, A., Witcher, A. E., & James, T. L. (2002). Preservice teachers' educational beliefs and their perceptions of characteristics of effective teachers. *Journal of Educational Research, 96*(2), 116–127.

phenomena observed. That understanding provides an image or configuration of reasonable expectations that might be useful in similar situations.

Methodological Advancement The study may be significant because it increases the validity and reliability of an instrument or uses a methodology different from the methodologies used in previous studies. Much of the research on educational measurement investigates questions related to assessment, such as testing procedures, the order of the items on an instrument, the item format or response set, and the information processes of the respondent. Another study may develop a statistical or methodological technique and elaborate on its usefulness for research.

Current Issues The study may focus on a social issue of immediate concern. As mentioned previously, organized political movements such as those for women's rights and civil rights have generated educational research. Public recognition of social problems has frequently led to assessment of their educational effects. The increasing prevalence of single-parent families, for example, has raised questions about the impact of single parenting on student self-concept and achievement. Similarly, studies on the instructional effects of students having laptops and Internet access have originated from social concerns about living in a highly technological society (see Excerpt 3.18).

Evaluation of a Specific Practice or Policy at a Given Site The study may evaluate a specific practice or policy for decision makers at a given site or for external groups. Evaluation research determines worth: Does the practice need improvement? Is it effective? Should its usage be expanded? Similar questions are addressed in policy studies. Such research supplies information for immediate use in site decision making, which may be at the local, state, or national level. While the study is not concerned initially with generalizability or theory development, it may have implications for developing such knowledge (see Excerpt 3.19).

Exploratory Research Exploratory research is usually conducted in new areas of inquiry, and such studies may be quantitative or qualitative. For example, a study might field test

EXCERPT 3.18 Justification: Current Issue

[Being aware of] the No Child Left Behind Act . . . can enable educators to get a head start not only on hearing the concerns of African American parents but also on improving their relations with these parents and seeking effective ways to improve the quality of education that they offer to African American students. (pp. 277, 279)

Source: From Thompson, G. L. (2003). Predicting African American parents' and guardians' satisfaction with teachers and public schools. *Journal of Educational Research, 96*(5), 277–285.

EXCERPT 3.19   Justification: Evaluation of a New Program at a Site

[For] our research project, "The Effects of Standards-Based Assessments on School and Classrooms," [we] selected Washington because of the newness of its reform effort. We decided to study implementation at the local level, per-suaded by the generally accepted belief that large-scale re-forms succeed or fail based on issues of local implementation. (pp. 171–172)

Source: From Borko, H., Wolf, S. A., Simone, G., & Uchiyama, K. P. (2003). Schools in transition: Reform efforts and school capacity in Washington state. *Educational Evaluation and Policy Analysis, 25*(2), 171–201.

EXCERPT 3.20   Significance: To Develop Components of a Concept

The purpose [is] . . . to begin the process of fleshing out the construct of leadership content knowledge, [that is] . . . how and why subject matter knowledge matters in educational leadership; . . . [to] analyze three cases of instruc-tional leadership [principal, associate superintendent, and central office team], . . . and [to] examine each for evidence of leadership content knowledge in use. (p. 424)

Source: From Stein, M. K., & Nelson, B. S. (2003). Leadership content knowledge. *Educational Evaluation and Policy Analysis, 25*(4), 423–448.

EXCERPT 3.21   Justification: Explore to Develop Theory

Several objectives guided this study. Specifically . . . to (1) identify and explore (and ultimately develop a concep-tual framework for) the various domains of discomfort that teachers face; (2) explore dimensions within these various discomfort domains that define whether moments of dis-comfort for students and teachers become debilitating or educative; (3) explore the impact of discomfort on teacher's beliefs and pedagogical practices; and (4) explore the notion of teaching *toward* discomfort. (p. 130)

Source: From Frykholm, J. (2004). Teachers' tolerance for discomfort: Implications for curricular reform in mathematics. *Journal of Curriculum and Supervision, 19*(2), 125–149.

a particular assessment format to determine whether it can be used by sixth-grade students and if it discriminates against any particular student groups. Qualitative exploratory stud-ies often examine phenomena that have not been studied previously. Some exploratory studies develop theory or components of a concept (see Excerpts 3.20 and 3.21).

STANDARDS OF ADEQUACY FOR PROBLEM STATEMENTS

Research problems are critically evaluated on the three elements discussed in this chap-ter: the statement of the general research problem, the significance of the problem, and the specific research purpose, question, or hypothesis. In addition, other criteria may be applied.

General Research Problem The following questions appraise the general statement of the problem:

1. Does the statement of the general research problem imply the possibility of empirical investigation?
2. Does the problem statement restrict the scope of the study?
3. Does the problem statement give the educational context in which the problem lies?

Significance of the Problem Readers assess the significance of the problem in terms of one or more of the following criteria:

- Develops knowledge of an enduring practice
- Develops theory
- Generalizable—that is, expands knowledge or theory
- Provides extension of understandings
- Advances methodology
- Is related to a current social or political issue
- Evaluates a specific practice or policy at a given site
- Is exploratory research

Specific Research Question or Hypothesis Different criteria are applied in the evaluation of quantitative, qualitative, and mixed-methods research questions.

Quantitative

1. Does the specific research purpose, question, or hypothesis state concisely what is to be determined?
2. Does the level of specificity indicate that the question or hypothesis is researchable, or do the variables seem amenable to operational definitions?
3. Is the logic of the research question or hypothesis clear? Are the independent and dependent variables identified?
4. Does the research question or hypothesis indicate the framework for reporting the results?

Qualitative

1. Do the research questions, foreshadowed problems, and condensed problem statement indicate the particular case of some phenomena to be examined?
2. Is the qualitative methodology appropriate for the description of present or past events?
3. Is the logic of the research reasonably explicit?
4. Does the research purpose indicate the framework for reporting the findings?

Mixed-Method

1. Is the relative emphasis of each method made explicit?
2. Is the order in which quantitative and qualitative data are collected clear (e.g., how each type of data will be used in the study)?

Other Criteria for Standards of Adequacy Before conducting a study, the researcher, a possible funding agency, review committees, and other groups also evaluate the problem according to additional criteria. These criteria concern the ability of the researcher to conduct the study and the feasibility and ethics of the research design. Typical questions asked include the following:

1. Is the problem one in which the researcher has a vital interest and a topic in which the researcher has both knowledge and experience?
2. Are the problem and the design feasible in terms of measurement, access to the case, sample, or population, permission to use documents, time frame for completion, financial resources, and the like?
3. Does the researcher have the skills to conduct the proposed research and to analyze and interpret the results?

4. Does the proposed research ensure the protection of human subjects from physical or mental discomfort or harm? Is the right of informed consent of subjects provided? Will ethical research practices be followed?

SUMMARY

This chapter has examined the major aspects of research problem statements, problem formulation in quantitative and qualitative research, the significance of the problem, and standards of adequacy for a problem statement. The primary concepts can be summarized as follows:

1. A research problem implies the possibility of empirical investigation.
2. Sources for research problems are casual observations, theory, literature, current issues, practical situations, and personal insights.
3. A research problem statement specifies the focus, educational context, importance, and framework for reporting the findings.
4. In quantitative research, deductive logic is employed in selecting the construct, variables, and operational definitions.
5. A construct is a complex abstraction and as such is not directly observable. A variable is an event, category, behavior, or attribute that expresses a construct and has different values, depending on how it is used in a study.
6. Variables may be categorical or continuous. Variables may be dependent, independent, manipulated, experimental, predictor, or criterion variables in different designs.
7. An operational definition assigns meaning to a variable by specifying the activities or operations necessary to measure, categorize, or manipulate the variable.
8. To formulate a quantitative problem, the researcher decides the variables, the population, and the logic of the design.
9. Specific quantitative research problems may ask descriptive, relationship, or difference questions or state a hypothesis.
10. In qualitative research, the general topic, the case, and the methodology are interrelated and selected interactively, rather than in separate research steps.
11. A case is a particular situation selected by the researcher in which some phenomenon will be described by participants' "meanings" of events and processes.
12. A qualitative study employs logic to use field records to generate a descriptive narration and to develop abstractions from that narration.
13. Qualitative field records, obtained over a lengthy time, are recorded as participant observation notes, transcripts of in-depth interviews, and researchers' notes of historical documents.
14. Qualitative descriptions are detailed narrations of people, incidents, and processes that emphasize participants' "meanings."
15. Qualitative research problems are reformulated several times during data collection, while quantitative research problems are stated before data collection begins.
16. Mixed-method problem statements indicate the relative importance of quantitative and qualitative data (i.e., how the method will function in the design).
17. A research problem is significant if it provides knowledge about an enduring practice, tests a theory, increases generalizability, extends empirical understanding, advances methodology, focuses on a current issue, evaluates a specific practice, or is an exploratory study.
18. Problem statements are judged by the criteria for statement of a research problem, the problem significance, the specific research questions or hypotheses, and the appropriate logic and feasibility.

RESEARCH NAVIGATOR NOTES

Research Navigator.com

Reading the following articles will help you understand the content of this chapter. Go to the education database (included in the EBSCO database) in Research Navigator; use the Accession Number provided to find the article.

3.1 Relationship Questions
Bodine, A. (2003). School uniforms, academic achievement, and uses of research. *Journal of Educational Research, 97*(2), 67–73. Accession Number: 12103384.

3.2 Difference Questions
Box, J. A., & Little, D. C. (2003). Cooperative small-group instruction combined with advanced organizers and their relationship to self-concept and social studies achievement of elementary school students. *Journal of Instructional Psychology, 30*(4), 284–287. Accession Number: 12010631.

3.3 Difference Questions
Denner, P. R., Richards, J. P., & Albanese, A. J. (2003). The effect of story impressions preview on learning from narrative

text. *Journal of Experimental Education, 71*(4), 313–333. Accession Number: 11453638.

3.4   Reformulation Example
Jenson, J., & Rose, C. B. (2003). Women@Work: Listening to gendered relations of power in teachers' talk about new technologies. *Gender and Education, 15*(2), 169–182. Accession Number: 9756400.

3.5   Qualitative Research
Ukrainetz, T. A., & Fresuez, E. F. (2003). "What isn't language?": A qualitative study of the role of the school speech-language pathologist. *Language, Speech, and Hearing Services in School, 34*(4), 285–299. Accession Number 11021893.

3.6   Condensed Problem Statement
Cho, S., Singer, G. H., & Brenner, M. (2000). Adaptation and accommodation of young children with disabilities: A comparison of Korean and Korean American parents. *Topics in Early Childhood Special Education, 20*(4), 236–250. Accession Number: 3933327.

CHECK YOURSELF

Multiple-choice review items, with answers, are available on the Companion Website for this book.

www.ablongman.com/mcmillanschumacher6e

APPLICATION PROBLEMS

1. The following are examples of research topics. Indicate the decisions necessary in order to conduct the study, and restate each as a useful research question.
   a. Effects of different ways of learning social studies
   b. Effects of cooperative versus competitive instruction on attitudes toward learning
   c. Opinions of parents toward education
   d. Family characteristics and school attendance
   e. Validity of the Wechsler Intelligence Scale for Children (WISC) for school performance
2. Write a directional hypothesis for the following problem statement, and identify the type of variables in the hypothesis: Low-achieving students frequently respond positively to behavior modification programs. Is there any relationship between the type of reward (tangible or intangible) and the amount of learning?
3. State a hypothesis based on each of the following research questions:
   a. What is the effect of individualized and structured social studies on high school students?
   b. Are there any differences in students' engagement in tasks when a teacher uses a positive introduction and when a teacher uses a neutral introduction to tasks?
   c. Does nonpromotion of elementary pupils improve their social adjustment?
   d. Do teachers' perceptions of job stress differ among teachers of mildly retarded, moderately retarded, and nonretarded children?

4. In the following qualitative problem statements, identify the case to be studied:
   a. This study describes and analyzes how women faculty members at an urban university perceive their professional and personal lives and how they integrate their lives.
   b. School board records of a suburban school system were analyzed for the ideologies articulated by various school board members to legitimize systemwide curriculum policies from 1950 to 1980.
   c. The research problem is to describe how Sue Olson, a first-year elementary school teacher, learns a professional role with students, faculty, administrators, and parents and how she develops meaning for teacher professionalism.
   d. The research problem is to describe and analyze a faculty social system in the implementation of an innovative middle school program for grounded theory.

Read the following full-text studies. Go to the education database (included in the EBSCO database) in Research Navigator; use the Accession Number provided to find the article. Answer the following questions.

5. Box, J. A., & Little, D. C. (2003). Cooperative small-group instruction combined with advanced organizers and their relationship to self-concept and social studies achievement of elementary school students. *Journal of*

Instructional Psychology, 30(4), 284–287. Accession Number: 12010631.

   a. What is the operational definition for each dependent variable?

   b. Is each operational definition valid for the study? Why?

   c. Could the operational definitions influence the varied results?

6. Ukrainetz, T. A., & Fresuez, E. F. (2003). "What isn't language?": A qualitative study of the role of the school speech-language pathologist. *Language, Speech, and Hearing Services in School, 34*(4), 285–299. Accession Number: 11021893.

   a. What is the selected case?

   b. How many people and settings constitute the case?

   c. Who are the ancillary participants?

7. Denner, P. R., Richards, J. P., & Albanese, A. J. (2003). The effect of story impressions preview on learning from narrative text. *Journal of Experimental Education, 71*(4), 313–333. Accession Number: 11453638.

   a. What are the independent and dependent variables?

   b. What is the operational definition for each level of the independent variable?

   c. Why was a second experiment done?

8. Cho, S., Singer, G. H., & Brenner, M. (2000). Adaptation and accommodation of young children with disabilities: A comparison of Korean and Korean American parents. *Topics in Early Childhood Special Education, 20*(4), 236–250. Accession Number: 3933327.

   a. How many people and locations constituted the case for this article?

   b. What does the word *comparison* mean in this study?

   c. What is the topic of each specific research question?

   d. Are the findings organized by the specific research questions?

4

Literature Review

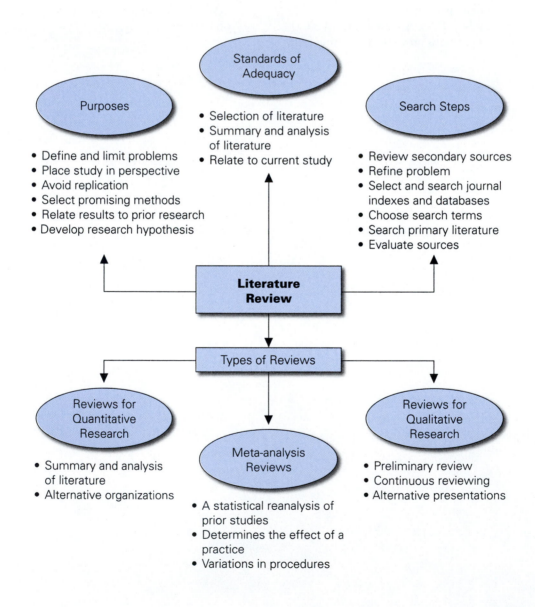

KEY TERMS

literature review

electronic resources

related literature

secondary literature

primary literature

ERIC

ERIC digests

report literature

preliminary search

exhaustive search

thesaurus

refereed

meta-analysis

A literature review, if conducted carefully and presented well, will add much to an understanding of the research problem and help place the results of a study in a historical perspective. Without conducting a review of the literature, it is difficult to build a body of scientific knowledge about educational phenomena.

During the last three decades, the landscape of literature searches has changed dramatically. Once done manually, such searches are now done electronically, whether on the Internet with a computer, or by accessing the many electronic databases available. Because of the accessibility of so much literature, the reviewer must be an *active decision maker* at every step of the process. Otherwise, he or she may be lulled into letting the computer do the selecting of relevant literature, rather than being extremely discerning in making his or her own choices.

This chapter explains the purposes of the literature review and the steps involved in searching for relevant secondary and primary literature. Most literature reviews comprise a narrative, interpretive criticism of the existing research. Literature reviews for quantitative and qualitative research are described. Later in the chapter, the discussion turns to meta-analysis, a literature review that statistically summarizes the results of prior research. Finally, standards are provided for evaluating narrative literature reviews. Because use of the Internet is now essential in reviewing the literature, some Internet resources are examined in this chapter. Chapter 5 reviews additional Internet resources and provides Internet addresses.

FUNCTIONS OF A REVIEW OF RELATED LITERATURE

An interpretive review of the literature is exactly that—a summary and analysis of the relevant literature about a research problem. A **literature review** illuminates the related literature to enable a reader to gain further insights from the study.[1]

Literature includes many types of sources: professional journals, scholarly books and monographs, government documents, dissertations, and electronic resources. **Electronic resources** include various types of literature published on the Internet, a global network of computer databases. Some refereed journals and conference proceedings are published only electronically.

Related literature is that which is directly relevant to the problem, such as previous research investigating the same variables or a similar question, a theory and the testing of the theory, and studies of similar practices. Thoroughly researched topics in education usually have sufficient research pertinent to the problem. New and little-researched topics usually require a review of any literature that is related in some essential way to the problem.

Purposes of a Literature Review

A review of the literature serves several purposes in research. The knowledge gained from the literature aids in stating the significance of the problem, developing the research design, and relating the results of the study to prior knowledge. A review of the literature enables the researcher to do the following:

1. **Define and limit the problem.** Most studies that add to education knowledge investigate only one aspect of a larger topic. By becoming familiar with the major works on that topic and the possible breadth of that topic, the researcher can refine his or her general idea to a specific problem.

2. **Place the study in a historical perspective.** To add to the knowledge in any sub-field, researchers analyze how their study relates to existing literature. A researcher may state that the research of A, B, and C has added a certain amount to the body of current knowledge, that the work of D and E has further added to that knowledge; and that this study extends knowledge by investigating the stated question.

3. **Avoid unintentional and unnecessary replication.** Conducting a thorough search of the literature enables the researcher to avoid unintentional and unneeded replication. The researcher, however, may deliberately replicate a study for verification.

4. **Select promising methods and measures.** As researchers sort out the knowledge on a subject, they assess the research methods that have been used to establish that knowledge. Analysis of instruments, sampling, and methods of prior research may lead to a more sophisticated design, the use of a different instrument, a more appropriate data analysis procedure, or an improved methodology for studying the problem.

5. **Relate the findings to previous knowledge and suggest further research.** The results of a study are contrasted to the findings of previous research in order to determine how the study adds new knowledge. Most researchers suggest directions for further research based on insights gained from conducting their studies.

6. **Develop research hypotheses.** In some quantitative studies, researchers use the literature to justify the formulation of specific research hypotheses. Previous studies may suggest certain results, and the hypotheses should be consistent with those studies. Sometimes, researchers use theories, rather than empirical studies, to justify research hypotheses.

Steps in Writing a Review of the Literature

The review of the literature is usually done in broad, sequential steps. Researchers often return to prior steps, however, as they gain understanding of the topic or restate the problem. The general steps for reviewing the literature include the following:

1. **Analyze the problem statement** to identify concepts and variables that suggest topic areas and key terms to search.

2. **Read secondary literature** to define the problem in more precise terms and to locate primary literature.

3. **Decide the search strategy for primary literature** such as deciding if this is a preliminary search or an exhaustive search.

4. **Transform the problem statement into search language and conduct a search.** The key terms appropriate for searching databases may be used in different combinations.

5. **Evaluate the pertinent primary literature** for inclusion in the review.

6. **Organize and logically group selected literature.** Empirical studies may be classified in several ways: by the variables, by the populations, by historical order, by similar results, or by designs and methods.

7. **Write the review** to provide readers with an understanding of the problem and the need for or importance of the research.

SOURCES FOR A LITERATURE REVIEW

Although a review emphasizes primary literature, secondary literature is also useful. **Secondary literature** reviews prior research and gives a quick overview of empirical studies on the topic. This literature eliminates much of the technical information about the original study but cites extensive references. Research and theoretical reviews may be found in monographs, encyclopedia articles, and journals that contain reviews.

Primary literature is the original research study or writing by a theorist or a researcher. Primary literature contains the full text of a research report or a theory and thus is more detailed and technical. These materials are published in journals, research reports, monographs of single studies, and dissertations and are also placed in databases.

Primary and secondary literature provide different information and are used in different ways in the search process. Secondary literature provides general background information and gives clues for searching primary literature. Primary sources provide detailed information of current research, theories, and methods used to investigate the problem.

ALERT!   Recent primary literature, not secondary literature, is the essence of a review!

Sources for Secondary Literature

Recognized authorities write reviews of original studies when sufficient work has been done to enable a critical assessment of the stature of the knowledge. The topics for reviews are usually selected by a committee of researchers and scholars who are aware of current issues and research. When work on a topic is ongoing, conducting a thorough review may not be warranted for several years. Thus, some reviews may appear dated yet provide useful information.

Research Navigator.com

4.1   Library Use

There are several advantages to starting with secondary literature instead of primary literature. First, secondary literature gives the researcher knowledge of the research on the topic to the date of publication. Second, these sources can help refine a problem to a more specific research question. Third, secondary literature helps identify primary literature through the bibliography. Last, secondary literature can provide a cluster of key terms about the topic to use in a search. The following sections describe the usefulness of some of the secondary sources listed in Table 4.1 (see Excerpt 4.1).

Quarterly and Annual Reviews   General references provide reviews on topics selected from the entire field of education. Quarterly and annually published reviews give detailed syntheses of narrow topics along with exhaustive references. Usually, the author has a conceptual framework, which provides the criteria for selecting the reviewed study.

Professional Books   Professional books, including some textbooks, give detailed analyses of broad fields from particular perspectives. The subject index of *Books in Print,* which cites *all* currently published books, is available online in most libraries.

Encyclopedias   Reading the short, authoritative summary of a topic in an encyclopedia is helpful in the early stages of a review. The *Encyclopedia of Educational Research,* with over 250 articles and extensive bibliographies, represents a comprehensive analysis of 15 or more fields of educational research. There are also more specialized encyclopedias, which

EXCERPT 4.1   Review in a Secondary Source

Results of the analyses showed no significant differences on any of the student participation variables as a result of class size. . . . Observations were made in Grades 4 and 5 rather than in earlier grades and students had only at-tended small classes for 1 year and then changed to larger classes. Patterns of engagement behavior may be relatively stable by this time and difficult to change. (p. 326)

Source: From Finn, J. D., Pannozzo, G. M., & Achilles, C. M. (2003). The "why's" of class size: Student behavior in small classes. *Review of Educational Research, 73*(3), 321–368.

TABLE 4.1 Selected Sources for Reviews of Secondary Literature

General References

Review of Educational Research (1931–present, journal)

Review of Research in Education (1973–present, annual book)

Educational Psychology Review (1989–present, journal)

Yearbook of the National Society for the Study of Education (1902–present, annual)

Encyclopedia of Educational Research, 6th ed. (1992)

Books in Print

Specialized References

Handbook of Educational Psychology (1996)

Handbook of Qualitative Research in Education, Second Edition (2000)

Handbook of Reading Research (2002)

Handbook of Research on Curriculum (1996)

Handbook of Research on Educational Administration (1999)

Handbook of Research on Mathematics Teaching and Learning (1992)

Handbook on Research on Multicultural Education (2001)

Handbook of Research on Music Teaching and Learning (2003)

Handbook of Research on School Supervision (1998)

Handbook of Research on Social Studies Teaching and Learning (1991)

Handbook of Research on Teacher Education (1996)

Handbook of Research on Teaching, 4th ed. (2001)

Handbook of Research on Teaching the English Language Arts (2003)

Handbook of Research on the Education of Young Children (1993)

Handbook of Schooling in Urban America (1993)

Handbook of Research on Science Teaching and Learning (1994)

Handbook of Special and Remedial Education: Research and Practice (1995)

Handbook of Sport Psychology (2001)

Yearbook of Adult and Continuing Education (1976–present)

Yearbook of Special Education (1976–present)

The Second Handbook on Parent Education (1989)

International Handbook of Bilingualism and Bilingual Education (1998)

International Handbook of Early Childhood Education (1992)

International Handbook of Women's Education (1990)

contain articles about certain topics, such as early childhood education, special education, school administration and supervision, teaching and teacher education, and so on.

Specialized Handbooks and Yearbooks   Handbooks and yearbooks that specialize in certain areas of practice and research are similar to encyclopedias, with several exceptions. The authoritative chapters in specialized handbooks and yearbooks are usually more comprehensive and longer than those in encyclopedias but also more narrowly focused. If a handbook or yearbook exists on the topic one wishes to review, that would be a better place to start. One example is the *Annual Review of Research for School Leaders.*

Other Specialized References   Other handbooks and encyclopedias, primarily from social science disciplines, may serve as secondary sources for literature reviews. Specialized references, for example, are available in anthropology, social psychology, aging, child psychology, adolescent children, organization management, political science, and other disciplines.

Databases and Indexes   Another approach is to locate secondary sources from databases and indexes, which are typically used for locating primary sources. For example, in addition to primary materials, the Education Resources Information Center, or **ERIC,** provides citations to books, book chapters, literature reviews, guides, and opinion papers.

One of the most helpful secondary sources included in ERIC is the collection of **ERIC digests,** short reports that synthesize research and ideas about contemporary educational issues. There are more than 2,400 full-text digests in the ERIC database. In general, many of the indexes listed in Table 4.2 also provide online access to some secondary literature. By using various search options, which are often found in the "Advanced Search" section within a database, a search can be limited by type of publication.

Online Library Catalogs   Most libraries have online catalogs of their books, which allow you to conduct different types of searches. Not only can you search by author or title, but you can also search by additional commands that allow you to target a specific topic or field of study. (This is explained in the section on conducting a search.)

Each library will have somewhat different procedures for searching its catalogs and accessing its different databases. And so while the basics will be very similar for all libraries, you will need to become acquainted with the specific searching procedures of the library in which you are working.

Sources for Primary Literature

Primary literature includes empirical studies, research reports, government documents, and scholarly monographs. Indexes identify primary published literature, giving the location of each source and an abstract. Selected sources for a review of primary literature are listed in Table 4.2. Most of these are available on the World Wide Web.

The most thorough indexing and abstracting service for education periodicals is provided by ERIC (Education Resources Information Center). ERIC has established a database of literature since 1966. This database contains 1.1 million bibliographic citations to a broad collection of education-related resources. In 2004 ERIC instituted a new process for obtaining and selecting documents and journals to include in the database. The standards and criteria now used are provided on the ERIC website (www.eric.ed.gov). This means that some journals that were included in ERIC prior to 2004 may not be included after 2004.

Current Index to Journals in Education (CIJE)   *CIJE* abstracts from over 1,000 education journals and periodicals, from 1969–2004. It also indexes educationally relevant articles from such periodicals as the *Personnel Journal* and the *Journal of Family Counseling*.

Resources in Education (RIE)   *RIE* indexes and abstracts from 1969–2004 non-journal documents or what is called **report literature,** documents other than journals, which include speeches and presentations made at professional meetings, monographs, final reports of federally funded research, state education department documents, final reports of school district projects, and the like. *RIE* documents from 1969–2004 are in the ERIC Document Microfiche Collection, which is available in universities, state departments of education, and many public school systems. Beginning in 2004 non-journal documents from 1993 to the present are available online at no cost.

ALERT!   For many educational topics, *CIJE* or *RIE* is the best place to start searching for the most recent relevant sources.

TABLE 4.2   Selected Indexes for Primary Literature

Type of Source	Related Index/Indexes
Educational journals	*Current Index to Journals in Education (CIJE)*
Report literature	*Resources in Education (RIE)*
General and educational periodicals and monographs	*Education Index* (1929–present)
Selected abstracts and indexes in specialized areas	*Psychological Abstracts* (PsycINFO) (1887–present)
	Sociological Abstracts (1953–present)
	Exceptional Child Education Resources (1966–present)
	Physical Education Index (1970–present)
	State Education Journal Index (1963–present)
	Educational Administration Abstracts (1966–present)
	Higher Education Abstracts (1965–present)
	Sociology of Education Abstracts (1965–present)
Government documents	*Monthly Catalog of U.S. Government Publications* (1895–present)
	Digest of Educational Statistics (1962–present)
	American Statistics Index (1973–present)
Dissertations and theses	*Dissertation Abstracts International* (1861–present)
Citation indexes	*Arts and Humanities Citation Index* (1975–present)
	Science Citation Index (SCI) (1945–present)
	Social Science Citation Index (SSCI) (1956–present)

Educational Index   The *Educational Index* primarily references educational periodicals, yearbooks, and monographs. It indexes more than 300 journals but does not provide annotations and abstracts. If an exhaustive search is required, the *Educational Index* is useful because it provides coverage since 1929. Most reviewers use *CIJE* from 1969 to date but use the *Educational Index* for enduring topics.

ALERT!   Because the *Educational Index* is not limited to scholarly journals, key term searches can retrieve information from educational articles in nonrefereed journals, such as *School Shop* and *Library Talk*.

PsycINFO   PsycINFO, sponsored by the American Psychological Association (APA), covers all types of scholarly documents, including journal articles, books, book chapters, technical reports, and dissertations. References are provided to studies in cognitive, social, and moral development; learning processes; and classroom, peer, and teacher effects on learning. The articles have been carefully selected for behavioral relevance from education-related journals. Retrospective coverage of literature, updated monthly, is available as far back as 1887.

Selected Abstracts and Indexes in Subjects Related to Education   The sources discussed thus far have very broad coverage for most problems in educational research. Several other abstracts and indexes, however, have more narrow coverage, focusing on single subjects related to education. If a research problem is limited to a specific topic, a thorough search would include the more specialized reference, including the following:

- *Psychological Abstracts*, published in print format monthly by the APA since 1927, indexes and abstracts more than 950 journals, technical reports, monographs, and other scientific documents in psychology and related disciplines. *Psychological Abstracts* usually provides more thorough coverage than *CIJE* of educational problems related to psychological topics such as human development, counseling, exceptional children, and learning.
- *Sociological Abstracts*, which is similar to *Psychological Abstracts*, has been published five times a year since 1953. Because its subject index uses single terms, the reviewer must check the abstract to determine the article's relevance.
- *Exceptional Child Education Resources (ECER)*, published since 1969, uses a format similar to that of *CIJE*. Many of the 200 or more journals it covers are not listed in *CIJE*.
- The *Physical Education Index*, published quarterly since 1970, provides a subject index on educational topics and specific sports. It also indexes sports medicine.
- The *State Education Journal Index*, published twice a year since 1963, is a subject and bibliographic index on articles from about 100 state education journals. These journals cover a broad range of topics and are useful primarily for such state-level issues as federal aid, collective bargaining, and teacher certification.
- *Educational Administration Abstracts*, published since 1966, abstracts articles from about 100 journals. The references section classifies abstracts into 42 subjects and provides author and journal indexes but not a subject index.

Government Documents Indexes   The *Monthly Catalogue of United States Government Publications* indexes books, pamphlets, maps, and periodicals of all types—over 15,000 per year. All of the publications are organized alphabetically by department and bureau with monthly and annual indexes by author, title, and subject and by series/report numbers. The *Digest of Educational Statistics*, published annually, contains demographic statistics and some longitudinal analyses of enrollment, staffing, student retention rates, and educational achievement at all levels of education. The *American Statistics Index*, published monthly and annually, cites publications of departments and agencies other than the U.S. Department of Education. For example, information on vocational education, emolument, and specialized training programs, welfare recipients with children in school, and drug abuse may be collected by the U.S. Departments of Agriculture, Commerce, Health and Welfare, and Justice.

Dissertation Abstracts International   This resource abstracts dissertations that have been accepted by more than 375 institutions in the United States and Canada. Most dissertations and theses are original and unpublished studies and thus primary research.

Citation Indexes   Citation indexes enable a researcher to determine the impact of a key study or theory on the works of other scholars and researchers. This is particularly important if the first work was controversial, began a subfield, or initiated a series of studies. The *Science Citation Index (SCI)* and the *Social Science Citation Index (SSCI)* provide bibliographic information for all the references that cited the earlier work. Psychology citations are indexed in *SCI*, and education and psychology are indexed in *SSCI*.

STEPS IN CONDUCTING AN ELECTRONIC SEARCH

Before conducting any search of the literature, you should become thoroughly familiar with the library you plan to use. It is best to have someone orient you to the library, showing you where reference materials, microfiche collections, and journal indexes are located.

Most important, you need to understand the computer software that is used. If a reference librarian or an instructional technology specialist is assigned to or knows about educational literature, he or she will be especially helpful, and you should feel free to ask questions. Searching the literature can be quite time consuming, and the librarians are there to help you. Many students are surprised at how long it takes to do a review. It is not unusual to do a number of different searches as you increase your understanding of your research question and its ramifications.

The steps that are summarized in the sections that follow begin with secondary sources. However, because the use of computers and accessing databases via the Internet have made searching for primary sources more efficient, many researchers start with them instead (Step 3). This can be done if the researcher has already done considerable reading in the topic being investigated or if the proposed study is one of many on the same topic. Regardless, when initially investigating the topic, it is still best to start with *secondary* sources. By following a set of sequential steps, you will increase the quality of the search and be able to locate the most appropriate studies more quickly (see Figure 4.1).

Step 1: Use Secondary Sources to Locate Reviews and Related Literature

Libraries have computerized catalogs of their books, which allows you to conduct different types of searches. Not only can you search by author or title, but you can also search by using additional commands that allow you to target a specific topic or field of study. The most commonly used commands are *subject* and *keyword*, and both are used with logical connectors such as *and, or,* and *not.*

Keyword searching with connectors will result in a precise retrieval. Such a search is used when you have incomplete information about an author or title and the subject headings are too broad. If the keywords *cooperative learning* and *achievement* are connected with *and,* the search will be narrowed to records that contain both of these terms. Using *not* as a connector will also narrow the search by including records with one term but not the other. For instance, searching on *cooperative learning not achievement* will exclude any record that contains the term *achievement* even if *cooperative learning* is in the record. If the *or* connector is used, the search will be broadened to records that have either term.

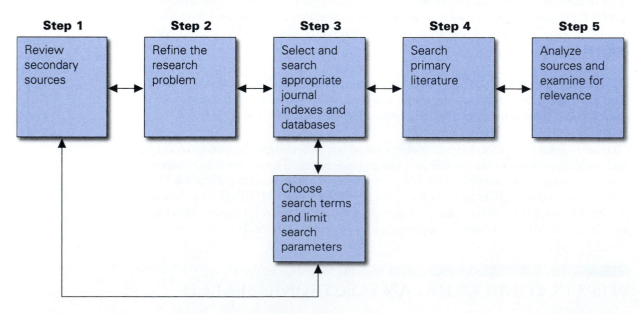

FIGURE 4.1   The Literature Search Process

Another approach to identify secondary sources is to use one of the databases that can be accessed through a search engine on the World Wide Web such as *Ovid* or *First-Search*. FirstSearch allows you to electronically search Education Abstracts Information, a database that contains English-language periodicals and yearbooks. Subjects include administration, teaching methods and curriculum, literacy, government funding, and more.

ALERT!   FirstSearch may be used for an initial search. However, it contains limited sources to educational literature compared to the ERIC system, which retrieves only educational sources.

An additional approach to identify secondary sources is to use indexes and databases that are more typically used for locating primary sources. For example, besides indexing primary sources, ERIC provides citations to books, book chapters, literature reviews, and opinion papers. As noted earlier, the ERIC digests are among the most helpful secondary sources included in ERIC. In general, many of the indexes listed in Table 4.2 also provide online access to some secondary literature. By using various search options which are often found in an "Advanced Search" section, you can usually limit your search by type of publication.

Again, each library will have somewhat different searching procedures for both its catalogs and its online materials. Although the basics are similar for all libraries, you will need to become acquainted with the specific search procedures in the library in which you will be working.

Step 2: Refine the Research Problem for Key Concepts

The initial research problem is often general and somewhat tentative. At this stage, the researcher thinks that the problem may be adequate but that it needs to be more specific and limited. By reviewing secondary literature and related primary literature, he or she will learn how others have defined the problem in more specific ways. The researcher will find ideas and examples to help delimit the problem, and concepts and variables will be clarified as he or she finds operational definitions. Most important at this time is to identify the key concepts that will help you select the appropriate journal indexes and specialized indexes for use in searching for primary literature (see Table 4.3).

The process of refining a research problem can be frustrating. Typically, an initial problem that seems to have merit will be revised as the researcher reviews previous studies. A new problem will be formulated, and often it too will be revised as further literature is reviewed. This pattern of reviewing and revising may be repeated many times.

In addition, the researcher must decide the type of search to be done: a preliminary search to select a research problem; an exhaustive review for a thesis, dissertation, or major study; or an update of a previous literature review. A **preliminary search** to refine a problem usually examines about 10 of the most recent references from one or two databases. The search is limited by the numbers of years and databases. An **exhaustive search** of the literature is done for a narrowly focused problem and examines more than 10 years of materials and perhaps multiple databases. However, doing a keyword search with an Internet search engine for either type of search will not be sufficient; the researcher will eventually have to go to specialized indexes, abstracts, and databases to obtain quality primary sources.

Using the term *recent* to describe the literature obtained in a search is somewhat misleading. It usually takes six months to a year for a manuscript that has been accepted for publication to actually be published. It may take as long as two years for a book or a collection of chapters written by different authors to be published. *Recent* is therefore a relative term in this context.

TABLE 4.3   Selected Indexes, Abstracts, and Databases
ERIC
Exceptional Children Educational Resources
PsycINFO [Psychological Abstracts]
PsycARTICLES
Books in Print
Social SCISEARCH and Backfiles [*Social Science Citation Indexes*]
GPO Monthly Catalogue [*Monthly Catalogue of U.S. Government Documents*]
Public Affairs Information Service [PAIS]
Legal Resources Index [LAWS]
Sociological Abstracts
Family Resources [NCFR]
Ageline [AARP]
National Rehabilitation Information Center [NRIC]
National Institute of Mental Health Database [MCMH]
Resources in Vocational Education
Sport Database
Bilingual Education Database
Dissertation Abstracts On-line
National Newspaper Index

Step 3: Select and Search Appropriate Journal Indexes and Databases

Many indexes can be used to locate research in education. By selecting an index, you are choosing a database and, consequently, the sources to be searched. Each database has its own search procedures and options. Although there is much overlap of sources between some databases, some sources are unique to certain databases. In addition, different indexes provide a range of aids to the reviewer, such as annotations, abstracts, and different searchable fields to refine a search. Figure 4.2 shows an annotated sample ERIC journal entry.

The PsycINFO database, also mentioned earlier, contains bibliographic sources from the literature in psychology and related disciplines (including education), and the citations are available in computerized and print formats. The entire PsycINFO database is online at most libraries (www.psyinfo.com). PsycINFO contains abstracts of articles from more than 1,800 journals, as well as abstracts of books, book chapters, dissertations, reports, and other documents. PsycARTICLES (www.psycinfo.com/psycarticles) contains the full text of 49 APA journals and also covers over 165 education and education-related journals. Sample topics include learning, students, teachers, educational testing and measurement,[2] counseling and guidance, family issues, social processes, and social behavior.

Both the ERIC and the PsycINFO databases can be accessed via the Internet. This allows students and other researchers to conduct their searches of these databases from any location with Internet access.

Once the database has been selected, then the proper search terms and search parameters must be decided. Indexes organize the literature by subject, title, key terms, and author. To select the most appropriate key terms for a topic, you should use a **thesaurus** of terms for that database. For most searches of educational literature, it is best to use the *Thesaurus of ERIC Descriptors*. The *Thesaurus of ERIC Descriptors* is essentially a list of terms, or *controlled vocabulary*, by which ERIC citations are indexed. It organizes the terms alphabetically and defines each one so that the researcher can match his or her definition

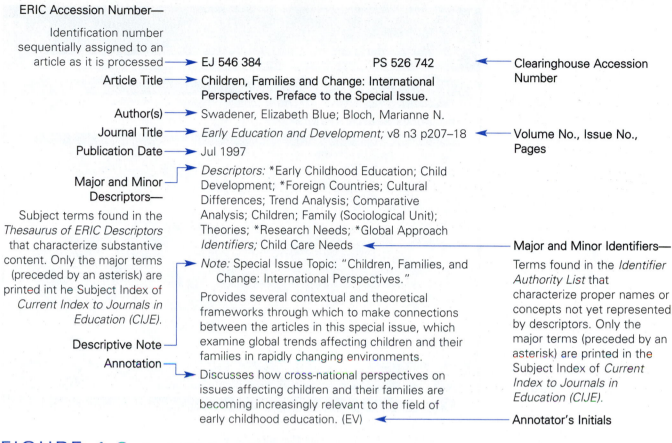

ERIC Accession Number—

Identification number sequentially assigned to an article as it is processed ──► EJ 546 384   PS 526 742   ◄── Clearinghouse Accession Number

Article Title ──► Children, Families and Change: International Perspectives. Preface to the Special Issue.

Author(s) ──► Swadener, Elizabeth Blue; Bloch, Marianne N.

Journal Title ──► *Early Education and Development;* v8 n3 p207–18   ◄── Volume No., Issue No., Pages

Publication Date ──► Jul 1997

Major and Minor Descriptors—

Subject terms found in the *Thesaurus of ERIC Descriptors* that characterize substantive content. Only the major terms (preceded by an asterisk) are printed int he Subject Index of *Current Index to Journals in Education (CIJE).*

Descriptors: *Early Childhood Education; Child Development; *Foreign Countries; Cultural Differences; Trend Analysis; Comparative Analysis; Children; Family (Sociological Unit); Theories; *Research Needs; *Global Approach

Identifiers; Child Care Needs   ◄── Major and Minor Identifiers—

Terms found in the *Identifier Authority List* that characterize proper names or concepts not yet represented by descriptors. Only the major terms (preceded by an asterisk) are printed in the Subject Index of *Current Index to Journals in Education (CIJE).*

Descriptive Note

Note: Special Issue Topic: "Children, Families, and Change: International Perspectives."

Provides several contextual and theoretical frameworks through which to make connections between the articles in this special issue, which examine global trends affecting children and their families in rapidly changing environments.

Annotation

Discusses how cross-national perspectives on issues affecting children and their families are becoming increasingly relevant to the field of early childhood education. (EV)   ◄── Annotator's Initials

FIGURE 4.2   Sample ERIC Journal Article Entry

to the one used in the indexes. Once the researcher has identified the best thesaurus descriptors, he or she uses them to continue the search. The thesaurus also indicates terms that are closely related to the descriptors, both more broad and more narrow terms. For example, suppose you are searching for sources about this research problem: What is the effect of teaching style on student achievement? The key terms are *teaching styles* and *student achievement*. Figure 4.3 shows the entry for *teaching styles* in a recent ERIC *thesaurus*. Note that this term has been used as an ERIC descriptor since 1966. It is wise to look at the definitions of the related terms because one of them may be closer to what you mean by *teaching styles* than the definition in the ERIC system. Related terms are also used in conducting an exhaustive search of the literature. The only way to learn if a descriptor will be useful in identifying literature related to your research problem is to use it to locate articles and reports and then to examine the titles and abstracts. If the materials seem promising, it makes sense to use that descriptor. If you find a research article that matches almost exactly what you mean by *teaching styles*, then you should note the descriptors (sometimes called *key terms* listed by the authors or editors on the first page of the article or the descriptors assigned to it in the index). These key terms may be useful in identifying the most relevant studies.

To research a problem that is psychologically oriented and that involves searching the psychological literature, you should consult the *Thesaurus of Psychological Index Terms* before searching the PsycINFO database. The terms in this index are different from those in ERIC.

The search begins when you go online and access the page of the database website that allows you to enter appropriate terms. The first choice you will make is which terms to use in your search. Before starting to search, you should limit your search parameters to locate

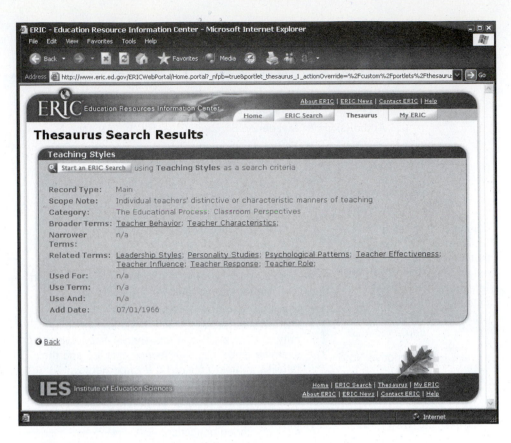

FIGURE 4.3   **Sample Thesaurus Entry**

the literature most relevant to your problem. These parameters are very important and must be attended to *before* submitting your search. Figure 4.4 shows a recent ERIC webpage.

ALERT!   The ERIC website and database are periodically redesigned by a U.S. Department of Education contractor. The current webpage may look different and provide different options depending on the search engine. Check with a reference librarian at your library for the current status of ERIC.

This webpage offers the choice to narrow your search by specifying the type of publication. By using the pull-down menus, you can limit your search exactly. For example, to conduct an initial search, it is usually wise to limit your search to journal articles published over the last 10 years. When the sources are displayed, you can review each in greater detail by clicking on its title to reveal the full abstract and bibliographic information.

Step 4: Search Primary and/or Secondary Literature

Most searches must be tailored even further to identify a reasonable number of sources that appear to be closely related to the research problem at hand. The most common way of delineating the search is with the logical connector *and*. Using *and* will reduce the search because the computer will look only for entries that are categorized by all the descriptors indicated. For example, a search of *teaching styles* **and** *elementary education* would have fewer "hits" than using only *teaching styles*. (*Teaching styles* alone would include elementary, middle, and high schools, as well as colleges and universities.) If a third descriptor,

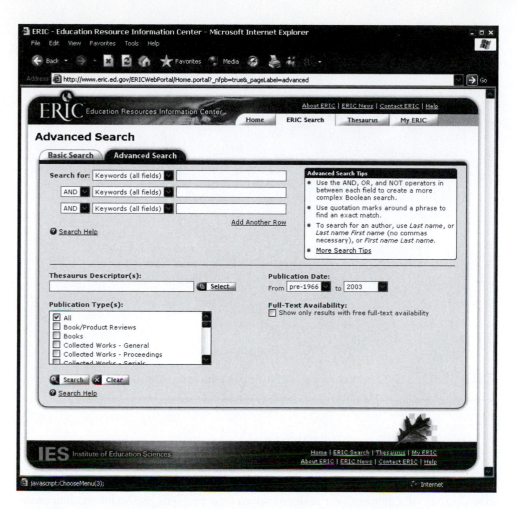

FIGURE 4.4   **Sample Limits for ERIC Searching**

achievement, were added, the search would be even further refined. This process of narrowing the search is illustrated in Figure 4.5. (The numbers of entries were retrieved in March 2003 and are those entered between 1993 and 2003.)

If your search produces very few "hits," then you should try using other major descriptors or related descriptors in your search. Each entry in ERIC can have up to six major descriptors. You can also broaden your search by using the connector *or.* For example, a search of *teaching styles* **or** *teaching behaviors* **and** *elementary education* **and** *achievement* would locate articles that contain either *teaching styles* or *behaviors* and both of the other two descriptors.

Once you have limited your search to a workable number of title entries, then you should examine each source in greater detail to determine if it would be beneficial to obtain the entire article. The more detailed information on the screen will indicate whether the record is in *CIJE* or *RIE* (i.e., *CIJE* entries have *EJ* accession numbers and *RIE* entries have *ED* accession numbers). In addition, it will include complete bibliographic information and an abstract. After reading the abstract on screen, many researchers initially rank each citation by degree of potential usefulness, such as 3 for "most important," 2 for "possible use," and 1 for "irrelevant." Most libraries have the capability to print out information from the screen or to save it to your own diskette.

Primary sources are reported in a wide variety of journals. In fact, there are hundreds of them that differ greatly in quality. Journals that submit all of the manuscripts sent to them to a *blind review process* are considered to have more articles of quality. (In a blind

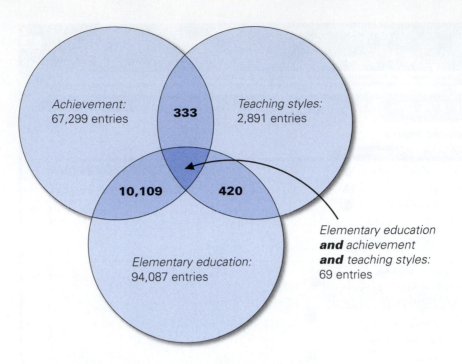

FIGURE 4.5   **Narrowing an ERIC Search with *and***

review, the names of the manuscript's authors are omitted when it is sent to reviewers for the purpose of reducing reviewer bias.) Two or three reviewers, all experts on the topic investigated, will comment on the significance of the problem, methodology, data analysis, contribution of the findings and conclusion, and other aspects of the manuscript. Usually, reviewers are asked to recommend whether the manuscript should be published as submitted, revised and resubmitted, or rejected. Rarely do reviewers recommend to publish something as submitted. Indeed, a journal's rejection rate is often used (and justifiably so) as a barometer of its quality. A journal is said to be **refereed** if this review procedure is followed. Conversely, a journal is nonrefereed if it does not use external reviewers to evaluate manuscripts. Regardless, just because a study is published, that does not mean that it contains good research, so you may want to learn which journals in your area are regarded as high-quality publications.

Step 5: Analyze Sources and Examine for Relevance

To locate a specific source, you must know how your library is organized and especially how it provides access to journals. Journals may be found in a variety of formats, including online, print, and microform.

Sources that are not available locally or by Internet may be obtained through interlibrary loan or by obtaining a photocopy from another library. Some database services, such as *Psychological Abstracts*, provide the author's address. By conducting an Internet search or using a directory of membership for the American Education Research Association or the American Psychological Association, you could locate and write the author for a reprint of an article or paper. The source also might be available for purchase through a service such as Infotrieve (www4.infotrieve.com) or Ingenta (www.ingenta.com) or at the journal publisher's website. No article reproduction service covers all of the ERIC-indexed journal titles, however.

After obtaining copies of the articles that seemed most important based on reading the abstract and considering the journal's reputation, your next task is to read the study to see if it will be useful in one's review. At this stage, you will probably reject some of the articles as not pertinent. Usually, researchers continue searching until they have 15 to 30 articles. You will always locate and read more studies than you will eventually use in a review.

A *mediated online search* is used when the reviewer has found insufficient literature by searching the library-mounted databases and now needs to search distant indexed databases. This type of search is conducted by a search analyst or librarian. The cost is based on how long the analyst or librarian is connected to a database and how many citations are saved. To minimize the cost, it is important to work with the search analyst to select the appropriate descriptors before going online.

EVALUATE, SUMMARIZE, AND ANALYZE PRIMARY SOURCES

The first requirement of conducting a good review is to select good studies to summarize and analyze. Use these three criteria to evaluate your primary studies:

1. *Credibility* Does the study appear objective, are the conclusions reasonable, and was the methodology appropriate for the investigation? (Many of these issues are discussed in later chapters.) Other indicators of credibility center on the author, his or her prior research, if the study was supported by external grants or funds, and if it is one of a line of inquiry by the author.

2. *Journal reputation* Is the journal refereed or not? Journals sponsored by national associations tend to have excellent reputations and use a blind review process.

3. *Relevance* Each study should be clearly related to the research problem or provide background or a historical perspective. Because one cannot include every study in a review, recent, well-done, and representative studies should be selected for review.

As you read each study, it is useful to record your notes electronically or on index cards (e.g., 5" × 8" size), which can be easily organized in different ways. You should begin by reading the abstract of the article, if there is one, and the purpose or research problem. Next, you should read the results and decide if it is worthwhile to read the article more carefully and take notes on it. At this point, you may have to discard some of the articles as not useful.

If you decide to use the article, then you should begin taking notes by writing down the complete bibliographic information, by summarizing the research problem as briefly as possible, and by underlining or circling the independent and dependent variables. Next, you should indicate in outline form the design (i.e., subjects, instruments, procedures) and then summarize the results and conclusions. On the back of the index card, you should record interesting and insightful quotations, weaknesses or limitations in the methodology, analysis of the data and conclusions; and how the study may be related to the research problem. You can use a code to indicate your overall judgment of the article. If you find it closely related to your research problem and highly credible, you might rate the article as an A (see Excerpt 4.2); if somewhat related and credible, a B; and so on.

It is also helpful to develop a code that indicates the major focus of the study by topic. For example, in reviewing studies on student engagement, you may find that some studies examine the effect of engagement on student achievement, that some focus on strategies to improve student engagement, and that others emphasize different approaches to student engagement depending on the type of students. Each of these could be identified using a code or notation on the card, such as "Effect on ach.," "Improv. engage.," and "Approaches."

EXCERPT 4.2   Analysis of a Prior Study

In another study addressing the utility of portfolios, Wolf, Lichtenstein, Bartlett, and Hartman (1996) investigated the first-year results of the . . . school district's teacher evaluation system in which teacher portfolios figured heavily in pay-for-performance decisions. They found that, of 829 teachers eligible to participate in the program, 266 submitted portfolios. Of the 266 teacher portfolio partici-pants, 236 or approximately 90% of these who applied, were awarded an outstanding designation and a $1000 cash bonus. "As measured by the general reaction of teachers, administrators, and the public, the overall pay-for-performance program was a success" (Wolf et al., 1966, pp. 284–285).

Source: From Tucker, P. D., Stronge, J. H., Gareis, C. R., & Beers, C. S. (2003). The efficacy of portfolios for teacher evaluation and professional development: Do they make a difference? *Educational Administration Quarterly, 39*(5), 572–603.

ORGANIZING AND WRITING A LITERATURE REVIEW

The nature of the written review of literature will depend on whether the study is quantitative or qualitative. Quantitative reviews are often detailed and found in the beginning sections of articles. Qualitative reviews tend to be brief in the beginning but more integrated throughout the complete articles.

Quantitative Reviews of Literature

The review of the literature can be organized in several ways, but the most common approach is to group studies that investigate similar topics or subtopics. This can be done more easily if you coded the studies as you read them. Index cards about articles with one code can be put in one pile, those with another code in a second pile, and so forth. The cards or articles then can be put in order, usually with articles related to the problem in a more general way first and those more specifically related to the problem last. Within each article topic, it may be possible to organize the studies by date, with the most recent studies last. This arrangement provides a sense of the development of the research over time. Studies that are only generally related to the research problem should be summarized briefly. If several studies have similar results, they should be grouped and their findings summarized as such—for example, "Several studies found that teachers' expectations are related to student achievement (Jones, 1978; Smith, 1984; Watson, 1982)."

ALERT!   A literature review should *not* be organized by study, with each paragraph in the review dealing with a different study.

The following steps will be useful for reviewing studies that are closely related to the research problem:

1. Provide a brief summary of the article.
2. Analyze the study. The analysis is important because it demonstrates that one is not accepting the study as credible without critically examining the methodology of the research to evaluate the contributions of the results.
3. State explicitly how the reviewed study is related to the research problem. A critical examination shows the relationship of the proposed study or current study to previous literature. This step is essential for ensuring that the results contribute to the current body of knowledge and for generating ideas for future research.

For a few studies, then, specifically those that are closely related to the problem, the review should include three elements: a *summary* of the study, an *analysis* of the study, and a statement of how the study *relates* to the research problem (see Excerpt 4.3). The review should not contain long quotations or use the same wording in discussing different studies.

Quotations, in general, should be used sparingly and only when a special or critical meaning cannot be indicated using your own words. You should use short sentences, as well as transitional sentences, to provide a logical progression of ideas and sections.

Some reviews are organized in alternative ways, depending on the type of study and the topic researched. For instance, reviews may be organized by (a) variables, (b) treatments, (c) research designs and methods, (d) different results from investigations of the same problem, or (e) any combination of these (see Excerpt 4.4). A study that is better designed than the previous research emphasizes methodological criticism (see Excerpt 4.5).

The length of the review depends on the type of study, its purpose (e.g., class paper, thesis or dissertation, manuscript for publication, etc.), and the topic. The literature review

Research Navigator.com

4.3   Avoid Plagiarism

EXCERPT 4.3   Relating Prior Research to Current Study

It would seem, however, that studies on the relationship between families and Black college students are more limited. The present study was designed to examine this gap in the literature on Blacks in higher education. The purpose of this study was to explore the role of family in the life of African American college students. (p. 494)

Source: From Herndon, M. K., & Hirt, J. B. (2004). Black students and their families: What leads to success in college. *Journal of Black Studies, 34*(4), 489–513.

EXCERPT 4.4   Organizing Previous Studies by Similar Conclusions

Despite more than 30 years of extant scholarship, . . . the myth remains that the ideal leader for most schools conforms to a White, masculine stereotype, especially at the secondary level (Brunner & Peyton-Caire, 2000; Murtadha & Larson, 1999; Shakeshaft, 1989). The educational literature offers limited knowledge construction based on data gathered from African American women principals (Alston, 2000; K. W. Collins & Lightsey, 2001; Henry, 2001; Lomotey, 1989). (p. 346)

Source: From Bloom, C. M., & Erlandson, D. A. (2003). African American women principals in urban schools: Realities, (re)constructions, and resolutions. *Educational Administration Quarterly, 39*(3), 339–369.

EXCERPT 4.5   Methodological Criticism

Although results supported the effectiveness of cooperative learning, school favorableness toward cooperative learning might have created a selection bias that threatened the validity of the results. Specifically, schools whose faculty agreed to implement the structured model of cooperative leaning were included in the treatment group. Despite this weakness, Stevens and Slavin (1995) contended that cooperative learning positively affected academic achievement. (p. 233)

Source: From Lopata, C., Miller, K. A., & Miller, R. H. (2003). Survey of actual and preferred use of cooperative learning among exemplar teachers. *Journal of Educational Research, 96*(4), 232–239.

for an exploratory study may not be very long, whereas that in a thesis or dissertation may be 30 or 40 typed pages. A lengthy review requires structuring with major and minor headings and periodic summaries. Excerpt 4.6 is an example of a quantitative research literature review.

Qualitative Reviews of Literature

Similar to a review of quantitative research literature, a review of literature in qualitative research is used to document the importance of the topic. Otherwise, the literature is used

EXCERPT 4.6   Quantitative Research Literature Review

Often, African American and Hispanic parents do not attend school functions. Consequently, there is a widely held belief among educators in poor and urban schools that those parents do not care about their children's education (Delpit, 1995; Flores, Tefft-Cousin, & Diaz, 1991; Poplin & Weeres, 1992; Thompson, 2002). Moreover, in its Schools and Staffing Surveys for 1990–1991 and 1993–1994, *The Digest of Education Statistics* (U.S. Department of Education, 1999) reported that lack of parent involvement was a great concern for many public school teachers.

Summary

Some researchers have found that there is a mismatch between teachers' perceptions of parent and guardian involvement and reality (Flores et al., 1991; Poplin & Weeres, 1992). For example, Thompson (2002) conducted a study of the K–12 schooling experiences of nearly 300 African American students in a southern California region that had many underperforming schools. Although there was a widespread assumption among educators in the region that the parents and guardians of most children of color were apathetic about their children's formal education, Thompson found that when the African American students in her study were asked to rate the level of their parents' involvement, the majority of students rated it as excellent or good. The students' ratings were compared later with data from African American parents in the same region. The overwhelming majority of the parents also rated their involvement in their children's education as excellent or good (Thompson, 2003). Furthermore, in their examination of the National Education Longitudinal Study data, Cook and Ludwig (1998) found that African American parents were as involved in their children's education as were White parents from similar socioeconomic backgrounds. These findings are similar to those of other researchers who found that educators are not always the most reliable judges of parent involvement (Flores et al., 1991; Poplin & Weeres, 1992).

Analysis

Furthermore, some researchers have specifically described the positive correlation between parent involvement and the schooling experiences of African American students. . . . Floyd (1995) examined variables that contributed to the academic success of a group of lower socioeconomic status (SES) African American high school students. She found that good parental relationships or positive relationships with other adults played an important role in the students' academic success. Wilson and Allen (1987) studied African American adults to identify links between educational attainment and family practices. They concluded that parents play a significant role in their children's education. Clark (1983) studied the home environments of high- and low-achieving poor African American high school seniors and found that parents of high achievers used regular routines to assist their children academically. Conversely, the parents of low achievers were so overwhelmed by adversity that they made few positive contributions to their children's formal schooling. . . .

A logical first step is for educators to begin to listen to the voices of parents in order to hear their concerns. In an effort to begin this discussion, I sought to provide educators with feedback from African American parents about their children's schooling experiences. In this study, I examined variables that predict how African American parents and guardians of school-aged children rate their children's elementary and secondary school teachers, and the public school system as a whole. (pp. 278–279)

Related to current study

Source: From Thompson, G. L. (2003). Predicting African American parents' and guardians' satisfaction with teachers and public schools. *Journal of Educational Research, 96*(5), 277–285.

EXCERPT 4.7 Providing a Conceptual Framework and Relating to Current Research

Building on the work of Weedon (1987), Peirce (1995) developed a concept of *social identity* . . . as 'the conscious and unconscious thoughts and emotions of the individual, her sense of herself and her ways of understanding her relation to the world' (p. 32, quoted in Peirce, 1995). In opposition to the Western notion of identity as centered, singular, and unitary, [social identity] takes on three characteristics. . . . This article uses Peirce's (1995) conception of social identity as a means to identify the unique qualities that the foreign-born ESL teacher brings to instruction and curriculum. (pp. 126–128)

Source: From Case, R. E. (2004). Forging ahead into new social networks and looking back to past social identities: A case study of a foreign-born English as a second language teacher in the United States. *Urban Education, 39*(2), 125–148.

differently in qualitative research. Rather than provide a detailed analysis of the literature prior to the methods section, the review is a preliminary one. A qualitative review simply introduces the purpose of the study and the initial broad questions that will be reformulated during data collection. Qualitative researchers usually provide the conceptual framework that they began with, as well (see Excerpt 4.7).

Unlike a quantitative researcher, a qualitative researcher conducts a continuing literature search during data collection and analysis. This approach to reviewing the literature merely reflects the discovery orientation typical of qualitative research. A continuing literature review is done because the exact research focus and questions evolve as the research progresses. Using this approach, the researcher can better understand what he or she is actually observing and hearing. The literature may provide meaningful analogies, a scholarly language to synthesize descriptions, or additional conceptual frameworks to better organize the findings. As with quantitative research, the literature review in qualitative research is integrated with the discussion and conclusion sections of the article or report. At this point, additional new literature may be introduced to better explain and interpret the findings. Thus, by the completion of a study, the researchers have done an extensive literature review (see Excerpt 4.8).

The literature review in a qualitative study is (a) presented as separate discussion and/or (b) integrated within the text. Seldom is an entire section of a journal article or an entire chapter in a report called a "Literature Review." The literature is found in the introduction and the more detailed discussion is located in the concluding interpretations of the study. Given the format required by some journals, a "Literature Review" header may be provided for readers.

META-ANALYSIS LITERATURE REVIEWS

Unlike a narrative criticism of the literature, a **meta-analysis** is a review that uses statistical techniques to summarize the results of prior studies that have been independently conducted. Because this type of review has only recently been published, there are some concerns about its credibility. The ERIC digest *Meta-Analysis in Educational Research* and the spring 2001 issue of the *Review of Educational Research* both discuss the relative merit of different meta-analyses. These sources illustrate the strengths and limitations of meta-analysis and show how researcher judgment is always an important influence in interpreting data. (For a more detailed discussion, see J. E. Hunter [2004] *Methods of meta-analysis: Correcting error and bias in research findings* [2nd ed.].)

Statisticians have long noted that in many applied fields, the treatment effects are small and therefore difficult to detect in a single study. A natural question is whether the

EXCERPT 4.8 Qualitative Research Literature Review

Background

The interrelationships among gender, higher education, and inequality in the workplace have been examined from diverse theoretical perspectives and through a number of different disciplines. Probably the most influential idea to account for women college students' lower career aspirations and their resignation to accepting lower-paying, less prestigious careers has been that institutions of higher education discourage or discriminate against women (Astin 1978; Dweck et al. 1978; Hall and Sandler 1982; Holmstrom and Holmstrom 1974; Sadker and Sadker 1994; Stacey et al. 1974; Sternglanz, and Lyber-Beck 1977). . . . — **Summary**

Holland and Eisenhart's [1990] long-term study of women students on two southern campuses moves away from social reproduction theory to a theory of "cultural production." Their approach allows us to see students as active agents who construct "systems of meaning" through which they relate to and act within their world. The most important construction that Holland and Eisenhart uncover in their study is a "culture of romance" that privileges males and is generated within student peer groups. Some women students fall into the "culture of romance" as they become discouraged in their studies. . . . — **Summary of major study**

The Holland and Eisenhart study provides rich material on women students' ideas about romance and marriage, but, curiously, it does not touch on students' ideas about motherhood or how these ideas might be related to students' decisions about their careers. By contrast, Anne Machung's (1989) study of Berkeley students, conducted at about the same time, indicates that senior women students planned to interrupt their careers for child rearing. Likewise our study reveals that a "culture of motherhood" rather than a "culture of romance" may lie behind women students' lower career aspirations. — **Analysis of second major study**

Granted, this difference between our findings and those of Holland and Eisenhart may be partly because of the different foci and methods of these two studies. The Holland and Eisenhart research focused only on women students, whereas our study compared women and men. This allows us to highlight those views of women students that stood out in strong contrast to those of men, in particular their contrasting views about the compatibility between their careers and their roles as parents. Another difference is that our study looked at students only over one academic year, whereas Holland and Eisenhart followed a group of women students over several years during and after college. This allowed them to document the women's lowering aspirations and their increasing involvement in romantic relationships over time, whereas our methods could not detect major shifts in students' interests and involvements. Yet we were able to uncover something that may have been missed in the Holland and Eisenhart study. Our study shows that a perceived incompatibility between motherhood and full-time careers is a central theme in students', especially women students', discussions of their futures. (pp. 68–70) — **Analysis and relationship to current research**

Source: From Stone, L., & McKee, N. P. (2000). Gendered futures: student visions of career and family on a college campus. *Anthropology and Education Quarterly, 31*(1), 67–89.

aggregate of studies might not have statistical and practical significance even though no single study does. Thus, meta-analysis determines the size of the effect of educational practices investigated in a number of individual studies.

A key concept in any synthesis is *pattern*. The distinction between primary analysis and meta-analysis may be analogous to the distinction between taking observations at ground level and taking observations from the air. As one rises in an airplane, the precision achieved at ground level lessens and is replaced by a greater recognition of patterns. Thus, the pattern of skyscrapers that is indiscernible when driving into a large city becomes more evident from a higher-elevation vantage point. Second, the conclusions based on a meta-analysis can be stronger than those of the component studies because pooling of data generally increases statistical power of the *effect size*.[3]

The Research Process

The steps to conduct integrative research reviews are similar to the tasks of original research. Cooper (1998) characterized rigorous research synthesis as having five phases: problem formulation, data collection, data evaluation, analysis and interpretation, and public presentation. Each phase of the review involves methodological issues and requires subjective decisions that can lead to procedural variations which can profoundly affect the outcome of the review. Obviously, the validity of the conclusions of research or research reviews depends on the decisions made in each phase. Each of these phases is summarized in the following list from the viewpoint of helping readers evaluate a research synthesis:

1. ***Problem formulation*** To formulate a research synthesis problem, the reviewer decides what questions or hypotheses to address and what evidence should be included in the review. Meta-analysis procedures are primarily used to integrate research results and are seldom applied to theoretical or methodological literature.

2. ***Data collection*** This phase involves the specification of procedures to be used in finding relevant reviews. Whereas the primary researcher samples individuals, the reviewer, in a sense, retrieves researchers. In reality, reviewers are not trying to draw representative samples of studies from the literature, but they are attempting to retrieve an *entire population* of studies. This goal is rarely achieved, but it is more feasible in a review than in primary research. The investigator hopes the review will cover all previous research on the problem.

To minimize bias in data collection, a reviewer should use more than one major database, informal communications, and the bibliographies of past researchers or reviews. Reviewers should be explicit about how studies were gathered, providing information on sources, years, and keywords used in the search, and they should present whatever indices of potential retrieval bias are known to them. Characteristics of individuals used in the separate studies should be summarized.

3. ***Data evaluation*** The data evaluation phase involves specifications about decisions concerning evidence that will be included in the review. Both primary researchers and research reviewers examine their data sets for extreme values, errors in recording, and other unreliable measurements. In addition, the research reviewer should discard data because of questionable research design validity. In other words, the reviewer makes either a discrete decision—whether to include or exclude the data in the review—or a continuous decision—whether to weigh studies dependent on their relative degree of trustworthiness. Most social scientists agree that methodological quality should be the primary criterion for inclusion.

4. ***Data analysis and interpretation*** In contrast to primary study reviewers, meta-analysis reviewers interpret data using rules of inference that build on standard statistical techniques. Analysis and interpretation methods are frequently idiosyncratic to the particular reviewer. This leads to criticisms of subjectivity and a concern that a variety of methods have been introduced into the reviewing process. Further, quantitative reviewing is based on certain premises. The basic premise is that a series of studies was selected that address an identical conceptual hypothesis.

Methods for data analysis range from simple vote-counting methods to sophisticated statistical techniques to obtain indices of the effect size. Either the results or the raw data of each component study can be integrated. Reviewers should be careful to distinguish between study- and review-generated evidence.

5. ***Public presentation*** The presentation of a meta-analysis involves decisions about what information should be included in the final report. Two primary threats to validity are the omission of details on how the review was conducted and the omission of evidence about variables and moderators of relations that other inquirers may find (or will be) important to the hypothesis. Slavin (1984) suggests that the effect size for each study should be included and that the coding of studies on various criteria should be presented.

STANDARDS OF ADEQUACY

The adequacy of a narrative literature review is judged by three criteria: the selection of the sources, summary and analysis of the literature, and the relevance of the literature to the current study.

Selection of Literature
1. Is the purpose of the review (preliminary or exhaustive) indicated?
2. Are the parameters of the review reasonable? Why were certain bodies of literature included in the search and others excluded?
3. Is primary literature emphasized in the review and secondary literature, if cited, used selectively?
4. Are most of the sources from reputable, refereed journals?
5. Are recent developments in the literature emphasized in the review?
6. Is the literature relevant to the problem?
7. Are complete bibliographic data provided for each source cited?

Summary and Analysis of Literature
1. Is the review organized by topics or ideas, not by author?
2. Is the review organized logically?
3. Are major studies discussed in detail and the actual findings cited?
4. Are minor studies with similar results or limitations summarized as a group?
5. Is there adequate analysis or critique of the methodologies of important studies so that the reader can determine the quality of previous research?
6. Are studies compared and contrasted and conflicting or inclusive results noted?
7. For some basic and applied studies and qualitative research, is the conceptual framework or theory that guides the study explained?

Relationship to Current Study
1. Does the summary provide an overall interpretation and understanding of prior research?
2. Does the review of major studies relate explicitly to the research problem and methods?
3. Do the methodological analyses provide a rationale for the design to follow?
4. Does the review of the literature help establish the significance of the research?

A literature review is not judged by its length or by the number of references it includes. Rather, it is judged in the context of the proposal or the completed study. The problem, the significance of the study, and the research problem all influence the type of literature review.

SUMMARY

This chapter summarized the reasons for conducting a literature review, the nature of the search process, literature reviews in quantitative and qualitative studies, and meta-analysis. In summary:

1. Literature for review is taken from journals, reports, monographs, government documents, dissertations, and electronic resources.
2. Reviewing the literature enables the researcher to define and limit the problem, to place the study in historical perspective, to avoid unnecessary replication, to elect promising methods, to relate the findings to prior research, and to suggest research hypotheses.
3. Primary literature is essential in a review; secondary literature, however, provides useful information to get started.
4. The process of reviewing the literature is as follows: analyze the problem, read secondary sources, decide on a search strategy, transform the problem into search language, conduct the search, evaluate obtained sources, organize notes, and write the review.
5. Secondary literature is a synthesis of original work and usually consists of articles in general and specialized educational journals, annuals, yearbooks, handbooks, encyclopedias, and books.

6. Primary literature is the original empirical study or writings of a researcher, which is found by using indexes, abstracts, and databases.

7. Steps in conducting a search are to review secondary sources, to refine the research problem, to select and search appropriate indexes and/or databases, to search primary literature, and to analyze sources for relevance.

8. A reviewer reads each source that was obtained, summarizes and analyzes it using notes on index cards, and then organizes the cards according to a classification system of merit or worth.

9. Sources are evaluated by three criteria: credibility, journal reputation (i.e., refereed or nonrefereed journal), and relevance to the current research.

10. The steps in writing a review are to provide a summary and analyze the studies, stating explicitly how the reviewed study is related to the research problem.

11. In quantitative research, the literature review is usually organized by topic: summarizing the minor studies as a group, analyzing the major studies individually, and usually proceeding from the most general topic to the most related topic. There are alternative ways to present the literature in quantitative research.

12. In qualitative research, a preliminary literature review suggests the need for the study and the conceptual framework employed, but the literature search continues during data collection and analysis. Literature is presented in the introductory discussion and integrated within the text.

13. A meta-analysis uses statistical techniques to summarize the results of prior studies that were independently conducted.

RESEARCH NAVIGATOR NOTES

The following Home Page Tabs will help you in understanding the content of this chapter. Go to the Research Navigator home page.

4.1 *Library Use*
Read Home Page, Tab 3 "Using Your Library"

4.2 *Locating Sources*
Read Home Page, Tab 2 "Finding Sources"

4.3 *Avoid Plagiarism*
Read "Understanding & Avoiding Plagiarism" located on the Home Page, Tab 1 "The Research Process"

CHECK YOURSELF

Multiple choice review items with answers are available on the Companion Website for this book.

www.ablongman.com/mcmillanschumacher6e

APPLICATION PROBLEMS

1. Suppose that a supervisor wants to locate mathematics curriculum guidelines and evaluation studies of mathematics programs formulated under Title I of the Elementary and Secondary Education Act and those most recently done through Chapter 1. Which database and type of search would be most efficient?

2. Below is a problem statement and descriptors for each concept. The descriptors are listed in order of importance to a literature search.

How do teacher-questioning techniques affect fourth-grade students' learning in social studies?
A. questioning techniques
B. questioning
C. questioning behavior
D. questions
E. achievement
F. skills
G. recall

H. social studies
I. history
J. upper elementary
K. elementary education
  a. Direct a narrow search to obtain pertinent literature using *and* to join the descriptors from A through K that most closely match the research question.
  b. Direct a more thorough search using *or* to join the different key terms for the same concept and using *and* to connect the descriptors A through K.
3. A reviewer has classified his or her relevant sources in the following manner:
A. evaluations of behavior modification programs: effects on instructional approach, teacher questioning style
B. descriptions of behavior modification programs and management implications
C. evaluations of behavior modification programs and management implications
D. theories of stimulus-response learning

E. studies of operant conditioning on animals
   Organize these in order for a literature review on the problem of "evaluation of instruction, student behavior, and learning in a behavior modification program."
4. Using the Research Navigator Home Page Tab 5: Endnotes and Bibliography, do the following:
A. Name three bibliographic styles.
B. Using Figure 4.2, Sample ERIC Journal Article Entry, write a bibliographic citation in APA style.
C. Write an intext citation in APA style for the article in Figure 4.2, Sample ERIC Journal Article Entry.
D. Write an APA citation using this information for the following online journal article. Retrieved on July 23, 2005, from *Journal of Bibliographic Research*, volume 5, pages 117–123. The authors are G. VandenBos, S. Knapp, and J. Doe. The article was published in 2001. The name of the article was "Role of Reference Elements in the Selection of Resources by Psychology Undergraduates."

NOTES

1. The authors greatly appreciate the assistance of James Ghaphery, Virginia Commonwealth University Reference Specialist, in preparing this chapter.
2. References for measurement are cited in Chapter 6.

3. Effect size (ES) is, in principle, the difference on a criterion measure between an experimental and a control group divided by the control group's standard deviation. The interpretation of ES is discussed in Chapter 11.

Educational Research on the Internet

James Ghaphery

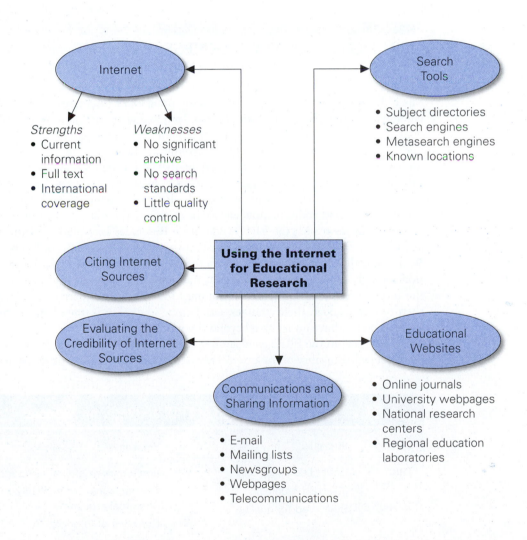

KEY TERMS

Internet
ERIC
controlled vocabulary
subject directories
search engines

metasearch engines
retrieval algorithms
newsgroups
mailing lists
real time

The information in this chapter, like the Internet, is a work in progress. No matter how quickly these words are rushed to press, Web addresses will have changed, new websites will have emerged, and new search engines will have surfaced. It is also safe to say that the technology behind the Internet will continue to change the ways in which information is organized and presented. With that in mind, this chapter will focus on those strategies and concepts for Internet research that should stand the test of time.

STRENGTHS AND WEAKNESSES OF THE INTERNET FOR EDUCATIONAL RESEARCH

Since the **Internet** encompasses a worldwide network of interconnected computers, the amount of information that researchers today have at their fingertips is truly unprecedented. The challenge is to find *quality* information. A careful consideration of the Internet's strengths and weaknesses will help determine when and how to search the Internet for a specific topic. The Internet is particularly good at delivering current and targeted information about a specific topic. On the other hand, the Internet does not serve as an exhaustive source for educational research. It is not organized with the educational researcher in mind and generally has not been reviewed for accuracy or quality.

A comparison with the **ERIC** (Education Resources Information Center) database, as shown in Table 5.1, illustrates both the strengths and limitations of Internet research. With the ERIC database, you can search through the contents of more than 1,000 education journals dating back to 1966, all at the same time. In comparison, when searching the Internet for education journals, you must find out which journals have websites and then browse through their archives, usually one journal at a time. Further, most online journals do not have an archive beyond the past five years.

Every item in the ERIC database has been assigned a series of subject headings. The consistency and quality of these subject headings allows you to retrieve specific informa-

TABLE 5.1 Comparison of ERIC and Internet Sources

Source	Strengths	Weaknesses
ERIC	Controlled vocabulary	Limited international coverage
	30+ year archive	Abstracts instead of full text of journal articles
	Reviewed for quality	Currency of information
Internet	Current information	No significant archive
	Full text on-line journal articles	No search standards
	International coverage	No quality control

tion from the database. The Internet does not have such a system of **controlled vocabulary.** There is no thesaurus to consult to find out what the best search terms are. For example, if you were looking for educational research about teenagers, would the best search term be *teens*, *adolescents*, or *high school and middle school students?*

Everything that you find in ERIC has been through some type of review process. Many journals in ERIC have an editorial staff of experts who judge the quality of all of the submissions. This does not mean that everything in ERIC should be accepted as without fault, but it is certainly better reviewed than the Internet. Anyone (from a teenager to a respected scholar) can publish a webpage. While there is an appealing democratic beauty to the Internet, it is crucial to evaluate the quality of Internet sources.

ALERT!   Most sources on the Internet are not reviewed for quality.

Even though ERIC offers a more comprehensive, better-organized, and peer-reviewed set of information about educational research, the Internet does have its own advantages. If a journal has an online version, you will be able to browse the most recent literature that might take many months to appear in ERIC. Abstracts are the norm for entries in ERIC, whereas online journals will often contain the full text of each article. While ERIC covers educational research and issues in the United States very well, the Internet offers wider access to educational research from other countries. You will also find other useful information on the Internet beyond journal articles and research reports, such as statistics, e-mail links to experts, governmental information, data sets, and discussion forums.

Fortunately, you are not limited in your research to either the Internet or journal indexes like ERIC. In framing your research question, think about the type of information that each might offer. This, in turn, will help with your searches in each source. For example, you would certainly want to know what the research on your topic has been for the past 10 years as well as in the past months. By combining the Internet with the research tools that were presented in Chapter 4, you can capture a well-rounded and diverse portrait of the research literature in the area being investigated.

AN INTERNET RESEARCH STRATEGY

The research strategies discussed in Chapter 4 are also relevant to Internet research. Before you start typing words into the first search engine that comes along, it is very important to have a focused search strategy with a number of key terms and subject headings. Based on that search strategy, you must choose from an assortment of secondary finding tools including *subject directories* and *search engines*. Once you have identified appropriate Internet search tools, pay attention to the various search options that each one offers, and construct your computer search accordingly. Finally, evaluate the sources that you find for their quality and relevance to your research question.

Choosing the Right Internet Search Tool

Each Internet search company (e.g., Yahoo!, and Google) compiles its own database of Internet sites. When you search the Internet, you are really searching these databases. That is, your search does not go out onto the Web and look at every page in existence. In choosing an Internet search tool, it is important to determine the quality, content, organization, and scope of the data behind the scenes. The three primary types of Internet search utilities are *subject directories, search engines,* and *metasearch engines.* (See Table 5.2 for selected examples of each.) Understanding the differences among these will improve your Internet searching considerably.

TABLE 5.2 Internet Search Tools	
Subject Directories	
About	http://about.com
Complete Planet	www.completeplanet.com
Internet Public Library	www.ipl.org
KidsClick!	http://kidsclick.org
Librarians' Index to the Internet	http://lii.org
Link Library	www.researchnavigator.com
WWW Virtual Library	http://vlib.org
Education Subject Directories	
Education Index	www.educationindex.com
Educator's Reference Desk	www.eduref.org
Search Engines	
AlltheWeb	www.alltheweb.com
AltaVista	www.altavista.com
Google	www.google.com
Lycos	www.lycos.com
MSN Search	http://search.msn.com
Yahoo!	www.yahoo.com
Metasearch Engines	
Metacrawler	www.metacrawler.com
Search.com	www.search.com
Vivisimo	http://vivisimo.com

Subject Directories   Internet **subject directories** are the "Yellow Pages" of the Internet, where you are able to browse through lists of Internet resources by topic. Typically, each topic is located within a hierarchy of subjects. For example, in a subject directory there may be a choice for *education*, then numerous choices under that subject such as *universities, K–12, government, history*, and so on. Examples of subject directories include WWW Virtual Library, Librarians' Index to the Internet, and the Link Library of Research Navigator.

The advantage of subject directories is that the content has been reviewed and organized by a human! Subject directories rely on teams of editors who have knowledge of specific disciplines. Thus, under each category, you will find a high degree of relevance and quality. Subject directories are often the quickest way to assemble a manageable list of Internet resources for a topic. Here are some research questions that would be especially good for a subject directory:

- Where can I find a list of educational associations?
- Where can I find the Web addresses to the department of education from each state?
- Where can I find a listing of online education journals?

Although subject directories are especially well organized, they are much smaller than the average search engine. For example, Librarians' Index to the Internet contains only 12,000 Internet resources, compared to more than 4 billion webpages included in Google. On the other hand, each entry in Librarians' Index to the Internet contains a written description that helps evaluate the site. Often, the best search strategy in using a subject directory is to steer clear of the search box and to use the categories instead. The search function of a subject directory is most useful when you are not sure what category to choose for a particular subject. For example, in the Yahoo! directory, it is somewhat difficult to find information about Montessori education, especially if you choose the education category *K–12.* If you search Yahoo! for *Montessori education,* you will find that it is listed in the education category *theory and methods.*

Specialized subject directories can also be useful to the researcher. In the field of education, there are several subject directories, such as the *Educator's Reference Desk,* that select websites with the educator in mind. A final strength of subject directories is that they can point you to areas of the Internet that are hidden from the larger search engines. This area is often referred to as the "invisible Web" or "deep Web." Much of the invisible Web is made up of searchable online databases. Some subject directories, such as Complete Planet, focus exclusively on the invisible Web.

Search Engines   Search engines are large, searchable databases of webpages. Whereas subject directories are assembled and organized by human editors, search engines are compiled in an automated fashion. Each search engine uses a "spider" or "robot" that trolls through the Web from hyperlink to hyperlink, capturing information from each page that it visits. Therefore, the content of each search engine is dependent on the characteristics of its spider:

- How many pages has it visited?
- How often does it visit each page?
- When it visits, how much of the webpage does it record?

A recent study in the journal *Nature* (Lawrence & Giles, 1999) concludes that search engines have plenty of room for improvement. There are an estimated 800 million webpages available to search spiders. Yet less than 20 percent of these pages appear in even the largest search engines. In terms of freshness, the addition of new pages or modifications can take several months. Especially interesting is that there is not a consistent amount of overlap between search engines. *This means that the Internet researcher is wise to try searches in several search engines.* The authors of the *Nature* study also consider the effect of "spidering the Web" to create a search engine database. They suggest that this practice gives greater weight to popular sites (which have many links pointing to them) and dilutes the presence of the scholarly information available on the Web.

Despite the limitations of search engines, they do index billions of Web pages. Search engines offer a quick way to search for specific words that may appear in webpages. Here are some research questions that would be especially appropriate for a search engine:

- Are there any webpages that cover standardized testing in the state of California?
- Are there any webpages that deal with John Dewey's *Democracy in Education?*
- Are there any webpages with a biography of Paulo Freire?

In searching through a large set of data, like a search engine does, there are a number of strategies to keep in mind. The concepts discussed in Chapter 4 about computer searching, such as using logical connectors, apply to Internet searches as well. Note that in all of the examples above, you would want to combine two or more concepts for an effective search. Your Internet searching will be more effective by paying attention to search language, special search features, and the most relevant search results.

Metasearch Engines   A **metasearch engine** submits your search to multiple search engines at the same time. Examples of metasearch engines include Vivisimo and Metacrawler. Metasearch engines can be especially useful since studies have shown that each search engine includes pages that others do not. On the other hand, no single metasearch engine includes all of the major search engines. Also, you cannot take advantage of the specific search language or features that are native to each search engine. For this reason, it is best to use search engines for your complex Internet searching and to rely on metasearch engines for searches that are very simple, say, one or two words (especially if those words are uniquely

Research Navigator.com

5.1 Using Internet Search Engines.
Accession No.: 4098282

spelled). With metasearch engines, it is especially important to pay attention to relevancy, since you have less control over how each search engine interprets your metasearch query. Here are some examples of good questions for a metasearch engine:

- Are there any webpages that mention the Australian Ngarkat Conservation Park?
- Are there any webpages that mention Jonathan Kozol?

Consult these sites for the latest information about Internet search directories, search engines, and metasearch engines:

- Search Engine Showdown   http://searchengineshowdown.com
  From subject directories to metasearch engines: reviews, statistics, and search tips for the Internet researcher.
- Search Engine Watch   www.searchenginewatch.com
  Includes search tips as well as ratings of the major search engines.

Search Language   No standard search language is valid across all search engines. Some search engines understand logical connectors like *and,* whereas others insist that you use a + before each word if you wish to limit your results to combined terms. Despite the lack of standards, several features are common to most search engines. For example, even though some engines use *and* while others look for +, the feature of combining more than one idea into a single search is available in most search engines. One of the best places to find out about each engine's search language is its online "Help" page. It is even advisable for seasoned Internet searchers to revisit the page of their favorite search engine periodically.

Special Search Features and Relevancy   Search engines continue to make advancements in the area of special search features. You will find these on the "Advanced Search" option within most search engines. Special search features help you construct very complex searches through the selection of various options from a menu. Special search features include the ability to limit your search by language, date, location, and media (such as audio or images). For example, by using Yahoo's advanced search menu, it is possible to access images of robots that are located only on pages hosted by the Massachusetts Institute of Technology.

In addition to search options, you should also be familiar with the **retrieval algorithms** of various search engines. *Retrieval algorithms* determine both how many pages each search retrieves as well as how the results of each search are ordered. The retrieval algorithm is a mathematical formula that weighs factors such as page popularity and how many times and where search terms appear in each document. For example, if you were searching for *Max Apple,* the webpages that appear at the top of your search results should be the most relevant. Perhaps these pages had both words *Max Apple* as part of their title, whereas the webpages that appear at the very end of your search results might simply have the word *apple* somewhere in their text. If your results start to look less and less relevant, don't keep looking through the same list; move on to a new search or a new search engine.

Blurring the Lines   The difference between a *search engine* and a *search directory* is often difficult to discern. The advanced search technology that makes it easier to find the information you need often masks the type of tool that you are using. In a search engine, there will often be an associated directory listing. For example, when you search Yahoo!, your search will also be matched against the Yahoo! directory for categories that may be relevant to your search.

Many search engines and subject directories are, in fact, *businesses,* which support much of their operation through advertising. So-called "sponsored links" will appear in your search or directory results when a company pays for its inclusion. Often, but not always, such results will be labeled.

Beyond Webpages: Scholarly Communication

Perhaps the most revolutionary aspect of the Internet is its ability to connect people with shared interests. This is especially powerful in highly technical and specific areas of study, where geographical boundaries might otherwise hinder communication between a limited number of experts. For example, it might be hard to find a group of scholars in any one location who were all interested in the sociology of education. Through the Internet, however, such groups are able to form and discuss various issues specific to their field of study. Through the use of e-mail, mailing lists, newsgroups, and conferencing, educational researchers are able to access the "braintrust" of their peers and need not feel isolated by location.

E-mail   E-mail can be an especially valuable tool in conducting research. The speed and ease of e-mail communication allows you find resources and experts. Through e-mail it is possible to easily contact researchers, librarians, and institutions in order to get guidance on a specific research question. E-mail is also an excellent way to collaborate with colleagues on works in progress by sharing ideas, drafts, and files.

Newsgroups and Mailing Lists   On the Internet, there are literally thousands of **newsgroups** and **mailing lists** covering every conceivable interest. For example, there is a mailing list called *arlist-1* that is dedicated solely to the discussion of action research. Most Internet browsers include a *news reader*, which allows you to locate groups and to read and post messages. A mailing list is similar to a newsgroup, except that the messages are transmitted as e-mail and are therefore available only to individuals who have subscribed to the mailing list. Research Navigator's Library Guide to Education (www.research navigator.com/library/lg_education.html) includes a menu of selected discussion groups. It is also possible to search an archive of past discussion by using a variety of search tools, including Google Groups (http://groups.google.com).

Conferencing and Telecommunications   One of the fastest-growing aspects of conducting business, either in the business world or at universities, is through Internet telecommunications and collaboration. Examples include chatting, video and audio conferencing, online data collection, and networked, shared folders in virtual offices or workspaces on the Web. Free or fairly inexpensive software is available to help academics and researchers communicate in **real time** through these convenient and time-saving resources. (Real time is immediate communication.) New technology is being developed daily as the need arises and the benefits and savings of its use for educational research are still being explored.

Current Awareness Services   To help you navigate this vast field of information, there are some strategies that will help you locate sources that are up to date. Many online journals provide free "alert" features, whereby they e-mail the most recent table of contents. Furthermore, some electronic journals have advanced features that allow you to select an article of interest and to get an alert when a future article references that original article.

Internet search engines and subject directories have also entered the field of current awareness. For example, Google provides a news alert service that sends you an e-mail whenever a news story mentions the words you selected in conducting an earlier search. Likewise, Librarians' Index to the Internet provides a weekly e-mail of new and noteworthy websites. The use of a *weblog* (or *blog*) is another emerging way for individuals and groups to post their news and thoughts online. Blogs are often syndicated on webpages and through *RSS (really simple syndication)*. You can subscribe to any number of RSS feeds and receive a compilation of selected blogs and news right on your desktop. A website sponsored by the Teachers College of Columbia University, www.tcrecord.org, offers a blended approach to scholarly communication within education, providing discussion forums, reviews, a searchable archive, and e-mail alerts.

See Table 5.3 for an overview of available current awareness services.

Known Locations

A final method of Internet research is to go directly to Internet sites that are known for their quality and authority. This is certainly important, given the amount of time that it takes for fresh information to appear in subject directories and search engines. For

TABLE 5.3 Selected Current Awareness Services

Service	Address
All About RSS	www.faganfinder.com/search/rss.shtml
Google News Alert	www.google.com/newsalerts
Librarians' Index to the Internet News	http://lii.org/search/ntw
Listing of Education News and Awareness Sources	www.lib.uchicago.edu/e/su/edu/news.html
Teachers College Record	www.tcrecord.org

example, if you didn't visit the website of your favorite online journal, you would miss out on the articles from the current issue.

A good starting point for Internet research is your library's webpage. Many college and university libraries have developed research guides for various disciplines, including education. If you want to explore research guides from other libraries, a comprehensive international listing of library webpages can be found at Libweb (http://sunsite.berkeley.edu/Libweb).

Educational agencies are often represented within international, federal, state, and local governmental webpages and offer access to a number of resources. Government websites are especially rich in statistical data and reports. Other sources for known locations include national associations and organizations, nonprofit organizations, newspapers, and online journals. In the following pages, we will highlight a number of websites that exemplify the type of quality that you should demand from Internet resources. Perhaps you will even add some of them to your own list of known locations for scholarly research.

EDUCATION WEBSITES

Government Websites

The U.S. Department of Education website (www.ed.gov) is an authoritative and reliable resource that contains research reports, statistics, current news, and current legislation relating to education. In addition to this federal level of information, there are resources for specific states. A listing of all of the state education agencies, along with thousands of other organizations, is available through the Education Resource Organizations Directory (http://wdcrobcolp01.ed.gov/Programs/EROD), which is compiled and run by the U.S. Department of Education.

Institute of Education Sciences

The Education Sciences Reform Act of 2002 initiated a number of important changes to the U.S. Department of Education. Perhaps most significant, it authorized the creation of a new agency, the Institute of Education Sciences (IES) (www.ed.gov/about/offices/list/ies). The IES seeks to advance the field of educational research through a scientifically rigorous and evidence-based approach. It consists of the National Center for Education Research (http://ed.gov/about/offices/list/ies/ncer), the National Center for Education Statistics (http://ed.gov/about/offices/list/ies/nces), and the National Center for Educational Evaluation and Regional Assistance (http://ed.gov/about/offices/list/ies/ncee).

National Center for Education Research (NCER) The NCER supports research that provides "scientifically rigorous" findings pertaining to educational policies, practices, and problems. There has been much debate about what is meant by scientifically rigorous. According to the NCER website, the goal is to "provide scientific evidence of what works, for whom, and under what conditions." While the agency maintains that both quantitative and qualitative research can be scientifically rigorous and contribute to solving educational problems, there is a rather strong preference for quantitative studies, specifically randomized experiments.

Many NCER programs extend beyond the U.S. Department of Education to other agencies, foundations, and universities. These programs are often supported through a network of 12 national research and development centers, which seek research-based answers to a wide range of topics, including early childhood education, student learning and cultural and linguistic diversity, adult education, reading and literacy, and gifted and talented students. Most of the centers are located within universities, and many partner with other agencies.

ALERT!   Find a national center of interest to you at www.ed.gov/about/offices/list/index.html?src=gu.

National Center for Educational Evaluation and Regional Assistance (NCEE)   The NCEE is responsible for evaluating the impact of federal programs on student achievement, for synthesizing and disseminating information from studies, and for providing technical assistance to programs and projects that target student achievement. Both ERIC and the What Works Clearinghouse are contained in the NCEE. See Table 5.4 for examples of the kinds of initiatives that the NCEE supports.

TABLE 5.4   Examples of NCEE Studies: 2003–2004

Study	Description
Early Reading First National Evaluation	This congressionally mandated study will assess improvement in child outcomes and literacy instruction associated with the receipt of Early Reading First program grants.
Development, Implementation, and Impact Evaluation of Academic Instruction for After-School Programs	The new after-school academic enrichment curriculum will be pilot tested with randomized experiments in five after-school centers during the 2004–2005 schoolyear and more fully the following year.
Remedial Reading Programs—Power4Kids/Closing the Gap	A field test evaluation will be conducted of intensive and well-implemented remedial reading programs for third- and fifth-graders whose verbal knowledge scores are between the fifth and thirtieth percentiles.
Impact Evaluation of Teacher Preparation Models	This study will assess the effects of two types of teacher training on students' achievement.
Evaluation of the Effectiveness of Educational Technology Intervention	This study will assess the impact of using educational technologies that are intended to improve student achievement in reading and mathematics.
Optimizing Educational Outcomes for English Language Learners	This evaluation will compare the outcomes of enhanced versions of structured English immersion and transitional bilingual education programs that differ in the amount of Spanish language used for instruction to the outcomes of typical existing programs.
Evaluation of the Impact of Charter School Strategies	The purpose of this initiative is to evaluate achievement gains of middle school students attending charter schools.

Regional Educational Laboratories   This national network of 10 Regional Educational Laboratories (REL) (www.relnetwork.org) is supported by the U.S. Department of Education and specifically the Institute of Education Sciences. The REL Network provides targeted research in specific areas of educational practice and school reform.

One way the laboratories carry out this mission is to provide a strong Web presence. Each laboratory has a regional focus as well as an assigned national leadership area for topics such as assessment of educational achievement, technology, and teaching diverse learners. The REL Network also features a searchable database of all publications from the laboratories. Figure 5.1 presents the search page for the Regional Educational Laboratories Network. Note how you can limit your search to a particular lab or search the databases of all the labs at one time.

Online Journals, Reviews, and Abstracts

While most high-quality educational research is published in peer-reviewed scholarly journals or presented at scholarly conferences, information from journals and conferences is increasingly available on the Web. In many cases, journals that have been strictly published on paper are now available electronically as well, either as a part of a larger database (e.g., Research Navigator) or as single products.

The following three websites maintain extensive listings of electronic journals in education:

- Electronic Journals in the Field of Education   http://aera-cr.asu.edu/links.html
- Education Journals and Newsletters   www.scre.ac.uk/is/webjournals.html
- Education-Line   www.leeds.ac.uk/educol

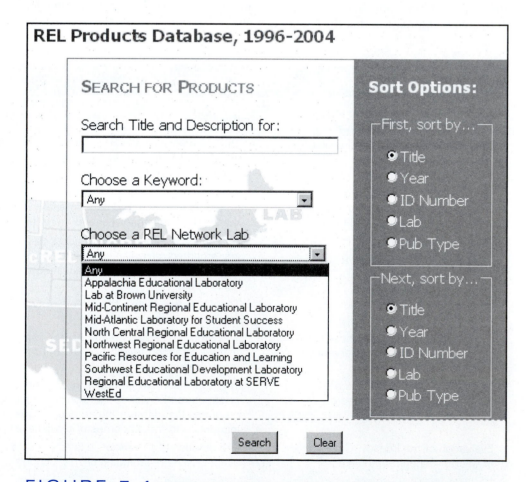

FIGURE 5.1   Regional Educational Laboratories (REL) Network Search Page

Many of these listings indicate whether a title is free, scholarly, peer reviewed, or full text. Most university libraries also maintain institution-specific subscriptions to electronic journals. In addition to journal listings, Education Line hosts an archive of reports, conference papers, working papers, and preprints in the fields of education and training.

Two websites that index conference proceedings and other research reports are the Education Policy Analysis Archives (http://olam.ed.asu.edu/epaa) and the Qualitative Report (www.nova.edu/ssss/QR). Both sites contain full-text access to more than 10 years of articles.

Statistics

Many statistical resources are available to you on the Internet, and you can access them by visiting the websites listed in Table 5.5. Often, these datasets are ideal for conducting replication studies, secondary data analysis, and other investigations without collecting original data. In addition, many of these statistics can be downloaded in multiple formats, allowing you to analyze them through different statistical packages, such as Excel, Statistical Package for the Social Sciences (SPSS), and Statistical Analysis System (SAS).

Professional Associations

Almost all of the larger professional associations have a substantial Web presence. At each group's site, you can find useful information such as lists of members and faculty, publications, resolutions, and links to other websites. By visiting these pages, you can learn about and obtain educational research and also get a feel for the culture and activities of these various organizations. Just type in the name of the association in a search engine, and its homepage will come up.

Two national societies, the American Educational Studies Association (www3.uakron.edu/aesa) and the American Education Research Association (www.aera.net), provide valuable information for educational researchers. Their websites both contain news, conference information, research reports, and other information relating to research in the field of education. Research Navigator's Library Guide to Education www.research navigator.com/library/lg_education.html) includes a listing of other education associations across many specialties.

Clearinghouses

In 1966, the U.S. Department of Education established the first ERIC clearinghouses to help contribute to the ERIC database and to disseminate information about their specific

TABLE 5.5	Internet Datasets	
Site	**Address**	**Description**
National Center for Education Statistics	http://nces.ed.gov	U.S. Department of Education providing multiple sources of educational research collections
Statistical Abstract of the United States	www.census.gov/statab/www	Includes data from private as well as government sources
Fedstats	www.fedstats.gov	Contains data from 14 federal agencies
American National Election Studies	www.umich.edu/~nes	Data about U.S. politics and political candidates and office holders
Eurostat	http://europa.eu.int/comm/eurostat	European statistics
UNESCO	http://unescostat.unesco.org	Wide range of international educational statistics maintained in the UNESCO database

subject areas. With the advent of the Internet, the clearinghouses posted a considerable amount of research on their websites.

The ERIC clearinghouses were closed, however, at the beginning of 2004, as part of the Education Sciences Reform Act of 2002. Many organizations have worked to archive and continue the outreach mission of the clearinghouses. Due to these efforts, much of the information the clearinghouses collected is still available, and it serves as an excellent starting point for educational research in many areas:

- Adult, career, and vocational Education   www.cete.org/acve
- Assessment and evaluation   http://edresearch.org
- Counseling and student services   http://counselingoutfitters.com
- Disabilities and gifted education   www.cec.sped.org
- Educational management   http://cepm.uoregon.edu
- Elementary and early childhood education   http://ecap.crc.uiuc.edu/info
- Information and technology   www.eduref.org
- Languages and linguistics   www.cal.org
- Reading, English, and communication   www.kidscanlearn.com
- Rural education and small schools   www.ael.org/cress
- Science, mathematics, and environmental education   http://stemworks.org
- Social studies/Social science education   www.indiana.edu/~ssdc/ssdc.htm
- Teaching and teacher education   www.aacte.org
- Urban education   http://iume.tc.columbia.edu

EVALUATING AND CITING SOURCES ON THE INTERNET

Evaluating Internet Resources

Many Internet sites contain materials that are not of sufficient quality to be used for educational research. You can evaluate Internet materials by asking the following questions:

- Who is the author or publisher of the information?
- What is the author's reputation and qualifications in the subject covered?
- Is the information objective, or is there a noticeable bias?
- Are the facts or statistics verifiable?
- Is there a bibliography?
- Is the information current?

Checklists like this have only limited usefulness. The final key to evaluating any type of research is to carefully read and analyze the content. It is also helpful to find a variety of sources, so that you can compare and contrast them and arrive at a fully informed view of the subject. If you are interested in learning more about evaluating sources on the Internet, go to Evaluating Websites for Educational Uses: Bibliography and Checklist (www.unc.edu/cit/guides/irg-49.html). See also Excerpt 5.1.

Research Navigator.c☉m

5.2 Evaluating Online Information.
Accession No.: 3206835

EXCERPT 5.1   Evaluating Internet Research

One of my seventh graders was so excited when he got his first computer that he spent much of his time on it. His love of technology led him to the Internet, and he soon built his own Web site. His site is now among the millions of sites on the Internet, and if you search for a site on computer repair and network consultation, you may have to wait for his services—because he needs to be home in time for dinner.

Source: From Caruso, C. (1997). Before you cite a site. *Educational Leadership, 55*(3), p. 24.

Citing Internet Sources

As with all other research, it is important to document your sources so that other researchers can visit the same sites you found. One of the unique things about documenting Internet sites is that the addresses can often change. For this reason, most citation formats encourage you to include the date that you accessed the site.

Most educational research is documented in APA format. You can find the APA's official guideline for citing electronic sources in the APA's *Publication Manual* (APA, 2001) and on the APA's webpage (www.apastyle.org/elecref.html).

Here is an example of an APA citation of an online journal article:

VandenBos, G., Knapp, S., & Doe, J. (2001). Role of reference elements in the selection of resources by psychology undergraduates. *Journal of Bibliographic Research, 5,* 117–123. Retrieved October 13, 2001, from http://jbr.org/articles.html.

More examples of APA and other styles—such as Modern Language Association (MLA), *Chicago Manual of Style* (CMS), and Turabian—can be found through Research Navigator (i.e., Endnotes and Bibliography) (www.researchnavigator.com/bibliography/rncite.html). The Landmark Citation Machine (www.landmark-project.com/citation_machine) is another worthwhile tool that not only offers examples but also includes interactive tools that create the appropriate citation style for you.

PUTTING IT ALL TOGETHER: AN INTERNET SEARCH

Now that you have an understanding of the different types of Internet search tools and strategies, you are ready to work through an example of an Internet search (see Figure 5.2). We ran several searches for the topic *charter schools* in April 2004. Starting with a large search engine, we searched for the words *charter schools* and *research*. The first 10 results led to both relevant and varied sites. By exploring links to advocacy groups, such as the Center for Educational Reform and the Canadian Charter Schools Centre, along with those to more nonpartisan organizations, such as the Education Commission of the States, we identified numerous online research studies.

Also within the results was a link to a 1995 online journal article from *Education Policy Analysis Archives (EPAA)*. While this article is dated by Internet standards, it provides excellent background information and a link to a more recent article from the same journal. This is an especially interesting aspect of online journals: linking articles backward and forward to each other. Likewise, our search results also included a listserv message about charter schools, which alerted us to a charter school electronic mailing list (and its searchable archive). We limited an advanced search in another search engine to just government websites and retrieved 18,000 results, including links to U.S. Department of Education research, state information, and federal legislation.

By repeating our search in a subject directory, we found the Charter School Development Center and Charterschools.org (sponsored by the U.S. Department of Education). The subject directory also provided a description and independent review of each site. Moving on to known locations, we searched both the Department of Education website (www.ed.gov/index.jhtml) and the National Center for Education Statistics (http://nces.ed.gov). These searches led us to even more material, including 500 entries from the Department of Education (e.g., current information on grants) and more than 20,000 hits through the National Center for Educational Statistics. A search of the REL Network produced a wealth of information (800 hits), including regional perspectives and conference proceedings. Finally, we established a Google News Alert for the words *charter schools,* and on the first day alone, we had breaking news from six different states.

In reviewing these results, we noted that each search led to unique material. Furthermore, by following the links, we found other sites that were not included in any of our

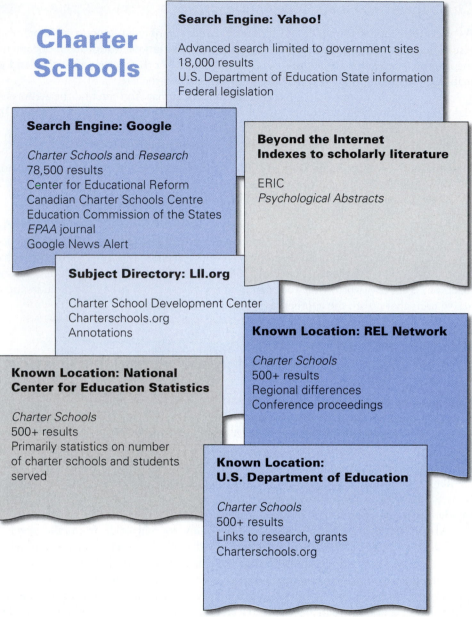

FIGURE 5.2 Sample Search Using Multiple Search Strategies

original results. Clearly, it pays to search across a variety of sources. You will also want to supplement online research with the scholarly literature found through indexes such as ERIC and *Psychological Abstracts*.

ALERT!   For further exploration of research on the Internet, try the following:

- http://lib.berkeley.edu/TeachingLib/Guides/Internet/FindInfo.html
- www.sou.edu/library/searchtools
- http://library.albany.edu/internet

SUMMARY

The following statements summarize the major aspects of conducting educational research on the Internet:

1. The Internet is a series of interconnected computers and contains a wealth of information for the educational researcher.
2. The strengths of using the Internet for educational research include access to full-text documents, the most current research, discussion forums, and information from around the world.
3. The Internet does not contain controlled vocabulary, consistent quality, or a significant archive for educational research.
4. The three primary types of Internet search tools are subject directories, search engines, and metasearch engines.
5. Subject directories contain lists of websites organized by topic.
6. Search engines are large searchable databases of websites.
7. Metasearch engines simultaneously query multiple search engines.
8. Each search tool has its own search features and strengths.

9. Scholars and researchers are able to share information over the Internet through the use of e-mail, mailing lists, newsgroups, and teleconferencing.
10. Accessing known locations on the Internet such as associations, newspapers, online journals, government pages, and statistical sites can lead the researcher to high-quality information.
11. Finding datasets on the Internet is a good way to find existing statistical data and build on past studies.
12. National research centers and regional educational laboratories sponsored by the U.S. Department of Education are excellent resources for combining educational research with practice.
13. Since just about anyone can post a webpage, it is especially important to evaluate the quality of the information you find on the Internet.
14. No single search tool can access everything that is available on the Internet.
15. It is best to try searches across a number of different search tools and known locations.

RESEARCH NAVIGATOR NOTES

Reading the following articles will help you understand the content of this chapter. Go to the education database (included in the EBSCO database) in Research Navigator; use the Accession Number provided to find the article.

5.1 *Using Internet search engines*
This article provides further details and strategies for conducting effective online searches, including "Tips and tricks." Accession No.: an4098282.

5.2 *Evaluating Online Information*
American Psychological Association consumer guide to evaluate the credibility of websites. Accession No.: an3206835.

CHECK YOURSELF

Multiple choice review items, with answers, are available on the Companion Website for this book:

www.ablongman.com/mcmillanschumacher6e.

APPLICATION PROBLEMS

1. A school administrator needs to locate samples of Internet policies and guidelines for the state of Georgia. Which Internet search tools and searches will find the most relevant information? In addition, what are two known locations that might help with this research?

2. Would you trust this website? How would you verify that it is legitimate?

Feline Reactions to Bearded Men

www.improbable.com/airchives/classical/cat/cat.html

Author's credentials: Catherine Maloney, Fairfield University, Fairfield, Connecticut

Abstract: Cats were exposed to photographs of bearded men. The beards were of various sizes, shapes, and styles. The cats' responses were recorded and analyzed.

Research methodology: While each cat was viewing the photographs, it was held by a laboratory assistant. To ensure that the cats were not influenced by stroking or other unconscious cues from the assistant, the assistant was anesthetized prior to each session.

Entry from bibliography: Boone, Patrick, "Cat reactions to clean-shaven men," in *Western Musicology Journal*, March/April 1958, vol. 11, no. 2, pp. 4–21.

3. Visit the U.S. Department of Education's website (www.ed.gov) and locate at least one set of online statistics about education. Write a brief annotation of the data, including the title, the Internet address, a summary, and one statistic.

QUANTITATIVE RESEARCH DESIGNS AND METHODS

*P*art II presents the designs and methods of quantitative research. Chapter 6 presents fundamental principles of sampling, measurement, and research design. Next, Chapter 7 reviews descriptive statistical concepts and procedures that are essential to understanding quantitative studies. Score validity and reliability, sources to use to evaluate instruments, and different ways of collecting quantitative data are presented in Chapter 8. These principles are useful in answering questions such as How can researchers summarize large amounts of data? Why is variability of results important? How can relationships be measured? What are the types of evidence researchers use to make valid inferences from subjects' responses? How do researchers establish reliability? What are the advantages and disadvantages of questionnaires compared with interviews? How are questionnaires designed? How is observational research or survey research conducted?

The next two chapters summarize the essentials of quantitative research designs. Chapter 9 considers descriptive, comparative, correlational, predictive, and *ex post facto* designs, and Chapter 10 covers experimental and single-subject designs. The last chapter in this part, Chapter 11, is a conceptual introduction to inferential statistics. The intent is to provide an understanding of the logic of probability as applied to testing hypotheses and questions. Basic terminology and statistical procedures are presented to enable a reader to interpret the results sections of quantitative research and a researcher to select appropriate statistical procedures, based on the design of the study.

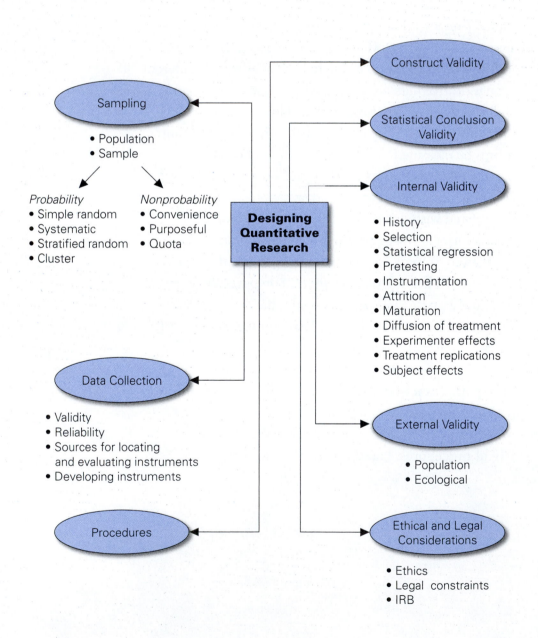

KEY TERMS

research design
credibility
variability
sources of variability
MAXMINCON
subjects
participants
sample
population
probability sampling
random sampling
simple random sampling
systematic sampling
stratified random sampling
proportional sampling
nonproportional sampling
cluster sampling
multistage cluster sampling
nonprobability sampling
convenience sampling
purposeful sampling
quota sampling
instrument validity
instrument reliability
statistical conclusion validity

internal validity
construct validity
external validity
plausible rival hypotheses
history
selection
statistical regression
pretesting
instrumentation
attrition
maturation
diffusion of treatment
experimenter effects
treatment replications
subject effects
demand characteristics
inadequate explication of
   the constructs
mono-operation bias
mono-method bias
population external validity
ecological external validity
Hawthorne effect
informed consent
internal review board (IRB)

Designing quantitative research involves choosing subjects, data collection techniques (e.g., questionnaires, observations, or interviews), procedures for gathering the data, and procedures for implementing treatments. Together, these components constitute the methods part of the study. The essential elements of designing quantitative research will be discussed in this chapter, with an emphasis on important principles for conceptualizing and planning a study. Each of these components will be discussed, with attention to principles in each component that enhance the quality of the research. Important ethical and legal considerations in planning and conducting research will be discussed, as well.

THE PURPOSE OF RESEARCH DESIGN

As introduced in Chapter 2, the term **research design** refers to a plan for selecting subjects, research sites, and data collection procedures to answer the research question(s). The design shows which individuals will be studied and when, where, and under which circumstances they will be studied. The goal of a sound research design is to provide results that are judged to be *credible*. **Credibility** refers to the extent to which the results approximate reality and are judged to be accurate, trustworthy, and reasonable. Credibility is enhanced when the research design takes into account potential sources of error that may undermine the quality of the research and may distort the findings and conclusions. By carefully designing the study, the researcher can eliminate or at least reduce sources of error. Not every potential source of error can be controlled completely in research conducted in field settings, such as schools, but there are principles for planning research to minimize such influences.

In quantitative research, researchers consider different *sources of variability*. **Variability** refers to how much observations of something take on different values. For example, we know that our mood varies day to day, just as we know that a student's academic performance will not be the same each time he or she completes a test.

From the standpoint of design, it is important to recognize and control three **sources of variability:** systematic, error, and extraneous. *Systematic variance* is related to the variables that are being investigated. What you want is a design that will *maximize* this kind of variation. For instance, when studying the relationship between engaged time and achievement, you would want to design the research so that the two variables of interest, engagement and achievement, both have high variability. If, say, all the students received the same or very similar achievement scores, then you would not be able to demonstrate the relationship.

Similarly, in an experiment, you want to maximize the variance of the dependent variable when comparing the groups. This is often accomplished by making sure that the treatments in the study will potentially produce quite different results. For example, systematic variance is likely to be greater in a study comparing individualized instruction with small-group discussion than comparing two kinds of small-group discussion formats.

Error variance is something to be minimized. It includes sampling and measurement error and other kinds of random events that make it difficult to show relationships. *Extraneous variance* needs to be controlled. This kind of variability affects relationships directly, rather than in a random fashion. For instance, in examining the relationship between test scores and class size, the socioeconomic status of the students would be a variable that would need to be controlled. That is, you would get a better estimate of the relationship if the effect socioeconomic status, which is related to achievement, were removed statistically.

It is helpful to use the following acronym to remember the three sources of variability in designing and evaluating research: **MAXMINCON.** Quantitative research needs to MAXimize systematic variance, MINimize error variance, and CONtrol extraneous variance. Methods to achieve these goals are summarized in Table 6.1 and will be discussed in further detail in later chapters.

TABLE 6.1 Principle of MAXMINCON

MAXimize Systematic Variance	MINimize Error Variance	CONtrol Extraneous Variance
1. Use design measures that provide sufficient variability.	1. Standardize measurement procedures.	1. Make potential confounding variables constant.
2. Use a sample to provide sufficient variability.	2. Use measures with high reliability.	2. Use random assignment; matching, if random assignment is not possible.
3. Use design interventions that are very different.	3. Aggregate individual scores into group scores.	3. Build a possible confounding variable into the design as another independent variable.
	4. Use large samples.	4. Use statistical adjustment procedures to help control the effects of confounding variables.
	5. Assure standardization in implementing the intervention in an experiment.	

SUBJECTS: POPULATIONS AND SAMPLES

One of the first steps in designing quantitative research is to choose the subjects. **Subjects** (abbreviated as S) are the individuals who participate in the study, and from whom data are collected. In an experiment, for instance, each person who is given an intervention and whose response is measured is a subject. In a nonexperimental study, individuals whose present or past behavior is used as data are considered subjects. For example, a researcher might use 2004 tenth-grade test scores; each tenth-grader who provided scores would be considered a subject. In some studies, the term **participants** is used rather than subjects.

Collectively, the group of subjects or participants from whom the data are collected is referred to as the **sample.** The sample can be selected from a larger group of persons, identified as the population, or simply refer to the group of subjects from whom data are collected (even though the subjects are not selected from the population). The nature of the sampling procedure used in a particular study is usually described by one or more adjectives, such as *random sampling, convenience sampling,* or *stratified sampling.* This describes the technique used to form the sample.

We will consider two major categories of different sampling techniques: probability and nonprobability. First, though, some further discussion of *population* is needed.

What Is a Population?

A **population** is a group of elements or cases, whether individuals, objects, or events, that conform to specific criteria and to which we intend to generalize the results of the research. This group is also referred to as the *target population* or *universe*. The target population is often different from the list of elements from which the sample is actually selected, which is termed the *survey population* or *sampling frame*. For example, in a study of beginning teachers, the target population may be first-year teachers across the United States in all types of schools. The survey population may be a list of first-year teachers from 24 states. Thus, although the intent of the research is to generalize to all beginning teachers, the sampling frame places some limitations on such generalizations.

It is important for researchers to carefully and completely define both the target population and the sampling frame. This begins with the research problem and review of literature, through which a population is described conceptually or in broad terms. A more specific definition is then needed based on demographic characteristics such as age, gender, location, grade level, position, and time of year. These characteristics are sometimes referred to as *delimiting variables*. For example, in a study of rural first-grade minority students, there are four delimiting variables: rural, students, first-grade, and minority. A complete description is then included in the subjects section of the report.

Probability Sampling

In **probability sampling** subjects are drawn from a larger population in such a way that the probability of selecting each member of the population is known. This type of sampling is conducted to efficiently provide estimates of what is true for a population from a smaller group of subjects (sample). That is, what is described in a sample will also be true, with some degree of error, of the population. When probability sampling is done correctly, a very small percentage of the population can be selected. This saves time and money without sacrificing accuracy. In fact, in most social science and educational research, it is both impractical and unnecessary to measure all elements of the population of interest.

Several methods of probability sampling can be used to draw representative, or *unbiased,* samples from a population. Each method involves some type of **random sampling,** in which each member of the population as a whole, or of subgroups of the population, has the same chance of being selected as other members in the same group. Bias is avoided with random sampling because there is a high probability that all the population characteristics will be represented in the sample. If the correct procedures are not followed, though, what may seem to be random sampling will actually produce a biased sample (biased in the sense that certain population characteristics are over- or under-represented). For example, you may think that you can obtain a random sample of college students by standing by a busy corner and selecting every third or fourth student. However, you may not be able to keep an accurate count, and you may inadvertently select more males or females or more older or younger students. Such a procedure would result in a biased sample.

ALERT!   A very common mistake is for researchers to generalize their results far beyond the characteristics of their sample. Using probability samples enhances the credibility of researchers' generalizations.

The concept of inferring what is probably true for the population from a sample is very important. As illustrated in Figure 6.1, once the sample has been selected, it is used to make inferences about the population. This always involves some degree of error. The degree of error is inversely related to the sample size—that is, the larger the sample size, the less the likelihood of error in making inferences about what is true for the population.

Simple Random Sampling   In **simple random sampling,** subjects are selected from the population so that all members have the same probability of being chosen. This method is often used when the population is small. For example, a common type of simple random sampling is drawing names out of a hat.

With a large population, it is necessary to use a more precise procedure. One such procedure is to use a table of random numbers, which is a set of randomly assorted digits. (A table of random numbers is illustrated in Appendix C.) Suppose, for example, that a researcher has a population of 100 third-graders and wants to select 20 by simple random sampling. First, each third-grader in the population is assigned a number from 001 to 100. (It could be 00 to 99.) Second, the researcher randomly selects a starting point in a table of random numbers. Then he or she reads all three-digit numbers, moving either across rows or down columns. The researcher follows the three-digit rows or columns while selecting 20 three-digit numbers between 000 and 100. Table 6.2 contains an example of simple random sampling. Five of the 20 subjects chosen to be included in the sample are circled, beginning with the top left and moving down each column.

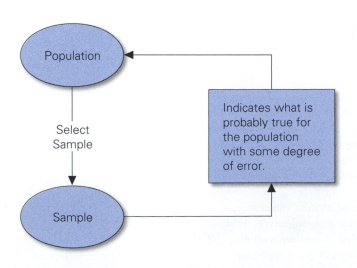

FIGURE 6.1   **Relationship of Sample to Population**

TABLE 6.2	Randomly Assorted Digits	
46614	20002	17918
16249	05217	54102
91530	62481	05374
62800	62660	20186
10089	96488	59058
47361	73443	11859
45690	71058	53634
50423	53342	71710
89292	32114	83942
23410	41943	33278
59844	81871	18710
98795	87894	00510
86085	03164	26333
37390	60137	93842
28420	10704	89412

EXCERPT 6.1   Simple Random Sampling

The sample (*n* = 600) was randomly drawn from the enrolled population of University of Florida (UF) undergraduates (30,866) who were 18 years of age or older and holding a free computing account. . . . Because other population characteristics were not considered relevant to the research questions for this preliminary investigation, we chose not to draw a stratified sample.

Source: From Pealer, L. N., Weiler, R. M., Piggs, Jr., R. M., Miller, D., & Dorman, S. M. (2001). The feasibility of a web-based surveillance system to collect health risk behavior data from college students. *Health Education and Behavior, 28,* 547–559.

A more efficient and increasingly popular way to draw a simple random sample is by using an appropriate computer software program, such as SPSS. This is especially easy and effective if the sampling frame is in an electronic format. Excerpt 6.1 provides an example of simple random sampling.

Systematic Sampling   In **systematic sampling,** every nth element is selected from a list of all elements in the population, beginning with a randomly selected element. Suppose there is a need to draw a 10 percent sample from a population of 100. A number from 1 to 10 is randomly selected as the starting point. If 5 is selected, every tenth name on the list will then be selected: 5, 15, 25, 35, and so on. This approach can be used only when the researcher has a sequential list of all the subjects in the population, but it is easier than simple random sampling because not every member of the population needs to be numbered.

Systematic sampling is illustrated in Figure 6.2. From among 60 students, we need to select 6 to be in our sample (10 percent). We would randomly select a number from 1 to 20 (say, 2), and then select every twelfth student for our sample.

There is a possible weakness in systematic sampling if the list of cases in the population is arranged in a systematic pattern that is related to what is being investigated. For

10 percent sample (every 10th student):

2   12   22   32   42   52

FIGURE 6.2   **Systematic Sampling**
Source: Adapted from Babbie, 1998.

EXCERPT 6.2 Systematic Sampling

Three samples were drawn from this study. They were samples of (a) practicing teachers, (b) college sophomores beginning a teacher education program, and (c) college seniors completing a teacher education program (but prior to student teaching). For the first sample, survey forms were mailed in a rural western state to 700 teachers randomly selected from the State Department of Education list of all licensed educators.

Source: From Green, K. E. (1992). Differing opinions on testing between preservice and inservice teachers. *Journal of Educational Research, 86,* 37–42. Reprinted by permission.

example, suppose we are sampling teachers from many schools and the list obtained from each school is rank ordered in terms of length of service. If this cyclical pattern (referred to as *periodicity*) is related to every nth subject, the sample would systematically exclude teachers with certain ages and not represent the population. Alphabetical lists do not usually create periodicity and are suitable for choosing subjects systematically.

An advantage to systematic sampling is that if the population is rank ordered on a variable that is related to the dependent variable, this ordering has the effect of stratifying and making sure that the sample is represented by each level of that variable. For instance, if the population list is ordered by aptitude test scores (highest scores first, followed by lower scores), when we then select every nth subject we will be assured that all levels of aptitude will be represented in the sample. Systematic sampling is illustrated in Excerpt 6.2. In this study, the first of three samples, practicing teachers, is selected randomly from a list.

Stratified Random Sampling   A common variation of simple random sampling is called **stratified random sampling.** In this procedure, the population is divided into subgroups, or strata, on the basis of a variable chosen by the researcher, such as gender, age, location, or level of education. Once the population has been divided, samples are drawn randomly from each subgroup. The number of subjects drawn is either *proportional* or *nonproportional*. **Proportional sampling** is based on the percentage of subjects in the population that is present in each stratum. Thus, if 40 percent of the subjects in the population are represented in the first stratum, then 40 percent of the final sample should be from that stratum. In **nonproportional** (or disproportionate) **sampling,** the researcher selects the same number of subjects to be in each stratum of the sample.

Whether proportional or nonproportional, stratified random sampling is often more efficient than simple random sampling because a smaller number of subjects needs to be used. As long as the characteristic used to create the strata is related to the dependent variable, then using a stratified sample will result in less sampling error. Dividing the population into subgroups also allows the researcher to compare subgroup results.

Excerpts 6.3, 6.4, and 6.5 illustrate the use of stratified random sampling. In Excerpt 6.5, for example, the researchers have stratified the teacher population on the basis of grade level and scores on the EFT (Embedded Figures Test) and the student population by class-

EXCERPT 6.3 Stratified Random Sampling

The samples of telephone numbers used in telephone interview surveys are based on a random digit stratified probability design. The sampling procedure involves stratifying the continental U.S. into 4 time zones and 3 city-size strata within each time to yield a total of 12 unique strata.

Source: From Saad, L. (2000). Most working women deny gender discrimination in their pay. *Gallup Poll Monthly, 413,* 35–36.

EXCERPT 6.4   Stratified Random Sampling

A stratified random sample of schools was selected across population density (i.e., urban, suburban, and rural), enrollment (i.e, 0–599, 600–999, 1000 and greater), and school levels (i.e., middle school and high school). Percentages of schools across population density and enrollment [and level] were established to maintain a sample consistent with the overall make-up of schools in Maryland.

Source: From Maccini, P., & Gagnon, J. C. (2002). Perceptions and application of NCTM standards by special and general education teachers. *Exceptional Children, 68*(3), 325–344.

room. The sampling is diagrammed in Figure 6.3. To ensure that the final sample has a sufficient number of subjects in each group, nonproportional sampling is used.

Cluster Sampling   Cluster sampling is similar to stratified random sampling in that groups of individuals are identified from the population and subjects are drawn from these groups. In **cluster sampling,** however, the researcher identifies convenient, naturally occurring groups, such as neighborhoods, schools, districts, and regions, not individual subjects, and then randomly selects some of these units for the study. Once the units have been selected, individuals are selected from each one.

Cluster sampling is needed in studies in which the researcher cannot obtain a complete list of all members of the population but can identify groups, or clusters, of subjects. For example, it would be very unusual to have a single list of all of the individuals participating in adult literacy programs in a state. However, all of the literacy centers in the state (which are known) could be sampled and then individuals could be sampled from the lists provided by the selected centers.

Thus, cluster sampling consists of at least two stages. Using more than two stages (e.g., school districts, schools within districts, classrooms within schools, students within classrooms) would be called **multistage cluster sampling.** We could begin by sampling 40 of 150 school districts, then 6 classrooms in each of the 40 districts, and then 10 students in each classroom (or all students in each classroom), using simple random or systematic sampling. Multistage cluster sampling is often used in states using geographic designations or districts as units that are initially selected, with schools selected from the geographic areas or districts. Cluster sampling usually results in a less representative sample of the population than either simple or stratified random sampling. See Figure 6.4, which illustrates different sampling procedures.

EXCERPT 6.5   Stratified Random Sampling Participants

Thirty-six female elementary school teachers were randomly selected from a volunteer pool in a southern school district. The sample consisted of 18 second-grade teachers and 18 fifth-grade teachers and was restricted to female teachers, since there were few male teachers in the school district at the primary level. Based on the EFT* scores, 9 teachers at each grade level were randomly selected from those who were field independent, and 9 others were selected from those who were field dependent. There were 12 students (6 males and 6 females) who were selected randomly from each teacher's classroom for purposes of testing. The second-grade children ranged in age from 7 years to 7 years 11 months, whereas the fifth-grade children ranged in age from 10 years to 10 years 11 months.

*EFT refers to the Embedded Figures Test.

Source: From Saracho, O. N., & Dayton, C. M. (1980). Relationship of teachers' cognitive styles to pupils' academic achievement gains. *Journal of Educational Psychology, 72,* 544–549.

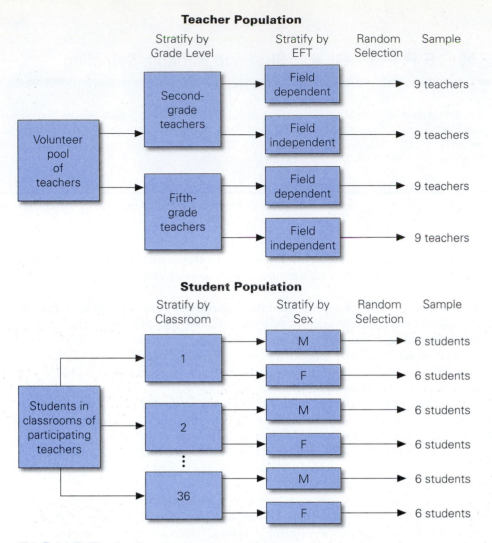

Teacher Population

FIGURE 6.3 **Stratified Random Selection of Subjects for Saracho and Dayton Study**

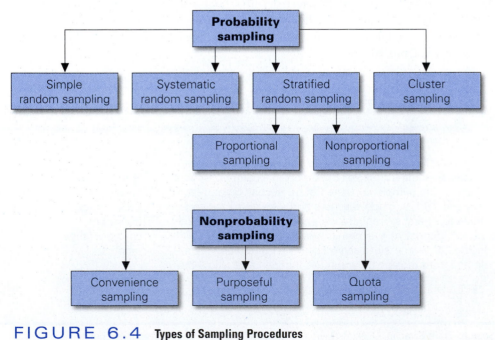

FIGURE 6.4 **Types of Sampling Procedures**

Nonprobability Sampling

In many educational studies, particularly experimental and quasi-experimental investigations, probability samples are not required or appropriate, or it may be impossible or unfeasible to select subjects from a larger group. Rather, **nonprobability sampling** is used. In fact, this form of sampling is the most common type in educational research. Nonprobability sampling does not include any type of random selection from a population. Rather, the researcher uses subjects who happen to be accessible or who may represent certain types of characteristics. For example, this could be a class of students or group gathered for a meeting. Many circumstances bring people together in situations that are efficiently and inexpensively tapped for research.

We will consider three types of nonprobability sampling: convenience sampling, purposeful sampling, and quota sampling. Additional nonprobability sampling techniques are covered in Chapter 12 for qualitative designs.

Convenience Sampling   In **convenience sampling** (also called *available sampling*) a group of subjects is selected on the basis of being accessible or expedient. It is convenient to use the group as subjects. This could be a university class of a professor who is doing research on college student learning styles, classrooms of teachers enrolled in a graduate class, school principals who participate in a workshop or conference, people who decide to go to the mall on Saturday, or people who respond to an advertisement for subjects. While this type of sample makes it easier to conduct the research, there is no precise way of generalizing from the sample to any type of population. This means that the generalizability of the findings will be limited to the characteristics of the subjects. This does not mean that the findings are not useful; it simply means that caution is needed in generalizing. Often, researchers will describe convenient samples carefully to show that although they were not able to employ random selection, the characteristics of the subjects matched those of the population or a substantial portion of the population.

Although we need to be very wary of convenience samples, they often provide the only possibility for research. Also, the primary purpose of the research may not be to generalize but to better understand relationships that may exist. In such a case, it may not be necessary to use probability sampling. Suppose a researcher is studying the relationship between creativity and intelligence, and the only possible sample consists of children in an elementary school in his town. The study is completed, and the results indicate a moderate relationship: Children who are more intelligent tend to be more creative. Because there is no probability sampling, should we ignore the findings or suggest that the results are not credible or useful? That decision seems overly harsh. It is more reasonable to interpret the results as valid for children similar to those studied. If the school serves a low socioeconomic area, the results will not be as useful as they would be if the school represented all socioeconomic areas. The decision is not to dismiss the findings but to limit them to the type of subjects in the sample. As more and more research accumulates with different convenient samples, the overall credibility of the results will be enhanced. Excerpt 6.6 is an example of using a convenient sample.

EXCERPT 6.6   Convenience Sampling

During the fall of 2002, the researcher surveyed the population of interest (specifically inservice teachers) with respect to their assessment literacy. The group of inservice teachers consisted of 197 teachers, representing nearly every district in a three-county area surrounding the researchers' institution. The schools were selected based on convenience due to their geographic location.

Source: From Mertler, C. A. (2003). Patterns of response and nonresponse from teachers to traditional and web surveys. *Practical Assessment, Research, & Evaluation, 8*(22). Retrieved May 10, 2004, from http://PAREonline.net/getvn.asp?v=8&n=22.

EXCERPT 6.7   Purposeful Sampling

Participants were chosen from three pullout resource room programs for students with mild disabilities. Participants met the following criteria:

1. They were identified as having LD under the 1986 Oregon administrative rules;

2. They were participants in special education programs;
3. They had an active Individualized Education Program (IEP) in reading; and
4. They had parent permission and gave their own permission to participate in the study.

Source: From DiCecco, V. M., & Gleason, M. M. (2002). Using graphic organizers to attain relational knowledge from expository text. *Journal of Learning Disabilities, 35*(4), 306–320.

Purposeful Sampling   In **purposeful sampling** (sometimes called *purposive, judgment,* or *judgmental sampling*), the researcher selects particular elements from the population that will be representative or informative about the topic of interest. On the basis of the researcher's knowledge of the population, a judgment is made about which subjects should be selected to provide the best information to address the purpose of the research. For example, in research on effective teaching, it may be most informative to observe expert or master teachers, rather than a sample of all teachers. To study school effectiveness, it may be most informative to interview key personnel, rather than a random sample of the staff.

As we will see in Chapter 12, there are several types of purposeful sampling procedures for qualitative investigations. In quantitative studies, the emphasis is more on relying on the judgment of the researcher to select a sample that is representative of the population or that includes subjects with needed characteristics. That is, the emphasis tends to be on representativeness, while qualitative researchers are more interested in selecting cases that are "information rich." Excerpts 6.7 and 6.8 are examples of using a purposeful sampling procedure in a quantitative study.

Quota Sampling   **Quota sampling** is used when the researcher is unable to take a probability sample but is still able to select subjects on the basis of characteristics of the population. Certain quotas are established so that the sample represents the population according to these characteristics. Different composite profiles of major groups in the population are identified, and then subjects are selected, nonrandomly, to represent each group. For example, it is typical to establish quotas for such characteristics as gender, race/ethnicity, age, grade level, position, and geographic location. The advantage of this type of sampling is that it is more representative of the population than is a purposeful or convenience sample, but there is still great reliance on the judgment of the researcher to select the subjects.

Nonprobability sampling has two major limitations. First, the sample is not representative of a larger population, so generalizing is more restricted. The generalizability of the findings will be limited to the characteristics of the subjects. This does not suggest that the findings are not useful; it simply means that greater caution is necessary in

EXCERPT 6.8   Purposeful Sampling

Data for the study were collected in 16 high schools in California and Michigan. The 16 schools were chosen purposefully to guarantee diversity in secondary-school teaching contexts in terms of state policies, district resources, school organization, and student composition.

Source: From Raudenbush, S. W., Rowan, B., & Cheong, Y. F. (1993). Higher order instructional goals in secondary schools: Class, teacher, and school influences. *American Educational Research Journal, 30,* 523–553.

generalizing the results. Often, researchers will describe the subjects carefully to show that although they were not selected randomly from a larger population, the characteristics of the subjects appear representative of much of the population.

A second limitation is that a nonprobability sample may be biased. This is particularly true for *volunteer samples*, in which subjects volunteer to participate in the research. Studies indicate that volunteers differ from nonvolunteers in important ways. Volunteers tend to be better educated, of higher social class, more intelligent, more sociable, more unconventional, less authoritarian, less conforming, more altruistic, and more extroverted than nonvolunteers. These characteristics could obviously affect the results, leading to conclusions that would be different if a probability sample were used. For example, suppose a researcher wants to survey students on their attitudes toward the college they attended. Letters are sent to the graduated class of 500; 25 agree to come back to campus for interviews. Is it reasonable to conclude that the attitudes of these 25 volunteer students are representative of the class?

MISCONCEPTION   Some would argue that North Dakota and Minnesota have the strongest high schools because students in these states score highest on the SAT. However, this finding is a reflection of sampling.

EVIDENCE   Most students in these states take the ACT; only the best students need to take the SAT and actually do so. As a result, these students' scores are very high. In sum, the SAT scores of students in Minnesota and North Dakota are not truly representative when compared to the scores of students in other states, where almost all students applying to college take the SAT.

In deciding on a sampling procedure, it is helpful to keep in mind the strengths and weaknesses of the different procedures, as summarized in Table 6.3. The final choice of procedure will depend on your purpose, availability of subjects, and financial resources.

Sample Size

The number of subjects in a study is called the *sample size*, represented by the letter n or N. The general rule in determining sample size is to obtain a sufficient number to provide a credible result. This usually means obtaining as many as possible. However, in situations in which a random sample is selected from a large population, a sample size that is only a small percentage of the population can approximate the characteristics of the population satisfactorily. Rowntree (1941) illustrated this point many years ago in a study of the percentage of income that was spent on rent by five categories of working-class families in England. Data were collected for the entire population and compared with the data that would have been reported by different sizes of random samples. As indicated in Table 6.4, there was little difference between a sample size of 2 percent (1 in 50) and 10 percent (1 in 10).

There are essentially two approaches to determining adequate sample size. One uses published tables or sample size calculators (easily found on the Internet), based on established formulas. The tables and calculators use information provided by the researcher to determine what size of sample is needed for a given level of precision. This works well for some studies, but often the information needed is not readily available. A second approach uses various rules of thumb or general guidelines. It turns out that these more informal procedures are used most in educational research. For example, when a population is very large—say, greater than 10,000—the size of the sample needed will usually range from 1,000 to 1,200. A 5 percent sample from a population of 2,000 (i.e., 100) would be insufficient. A 5 percent sample for a population of 40,000 is twice as many as needed.

Research Navigator.c⊕m

6.1 Sampling
Accession No.: 8752465

TABLE 6.3 Strengths and Weaknesses of Sampling Methods

Sampling Method	Strengths	Weaknesses
Probability		
Simple random	Easy to understand Little knowledge of population needed Free of subject classification error Easy to analyze and interpret results	Requires numbering each element in the population Larger sampling error than in stratified sampling for same sample size
Systematic	Simplicity of drawing sample Easy to understand Free of subject classification error Easy to analyze and interpret results Subjects do not need to be numbered	Larger sampling error than in stratified sampling for same sample size Periodicity in list of population elements
Proportional stratified	Allows easy subgroup comparisons Usually more representative than simple random or systematic Fewer subjects needed if strata are related to the dependent variable Results represent population without weighting	Requires subgroup identification of each population element Requires knowledge of the proportion of each subgroup in the population May be costly and difficult to prepare lists of population elements in each subgroup
Nonproportional stratified	Allows easy subgroup comparisons Usually more representative than simple random or systematic Fewer subjects needed if strata are related to the dependent variable Assures adequate numbers of elements in each subgroup	Requires subgroup identification of each population element May be costly and difficult to prepare lists of population elements in each subgroup Requires weighting of subgroups to represent population
Cluster	Low cost Efficient with large populations Permits analysis of individual clusters	Less accurate than simple random, systematic, or stratified May be difficult to collect data from elements in a cluster Requires that each population element be assigned to only one cluster
Nonprobability		
Convenience	Less costly and time consuming Ease of administration Usually assures high participation rate Generalization possible to similar subjects	Difficult to generalize to other subjects Less representative of an identified population Results dependent on unique characteristics of the sample Greater likelihood of error due to experimenter or subject bias
Purposeful	Less costly and time consuming Ease of administration Usually assures high participation rate Generalization possible to similar subjects Assures receipt of needed information	Difficult to generalize to other subjects Less representative of an identified population Results dependent on unique characteristics of the sample Greater likelihood of error due to experimenter or subject bias

TABLE 6.3   *(continued)*

Sampling Method	Strengths	Weaknesses
Quota	Less costly and time consuming Ease of administration Usually assures high participation rate Generalization possible to similar subjects Tends to provide more representative samples than convenience or purposeful	Requires identification information on each subject Difficult to generalize to other subjects Less representative of an identified population Results dependent on unique characteristics of the sample Greater likelihood of error due to experimenter or subject bias More time consuming than convenient or purposeful

Further informal criteria are summarized in the following list:

1. **The type of research** Correlational research should have a minimum of 30 subjects, and in research comparing groups, there should be at least 15 subjects in each group. (Some highly controlled experiments will contain as few as 8 to 10 subjects in each group.) In survey research studies, there should be about 100 subjects for each major subgroup that is analyzed and 20 to 50 subjects in minor subgroups.
2. **Research hypotheses** If the researcher expects to find small differences or relationships, it is desirable to have as large a sample as possible. For example, the effect of coaching courses on standardized test scores will produce relatively small but important practical differences. This effect would be generally undetectable in studies with small numbers of subjects.
3. **Financial constraints** Obviously, the cost of conducting a study will limit the number of subjects included in the sample. It is best to estimate these costs before beginning the study.
4. **Importance of results** In exploratory research, a smaller sample size is acceptable because the researcher is willing to tolerate a larger margin of error in the results. In research that will result in the placement of children in programs or in the

TABLE 6.4   Percentage of Income Spent on Rent

Income Class	Number of Families	Population Data	Sample Size			
			1 in 10	1 in 20	1 in 30	1 in 50
A	1748	26.5	26.6	25.9	28.3	27.1
B	2477	22.7	22.9	23.5	22.3	22.6
C	2514	19.8	18.1	17.2	17.2	18.0
D	1676	15.8	16.0	14.4	17.1	16.9
E	3740	11.3	11.0	10.1	11.2	11.5

Source: From *Poverty and Progress: A Second Social Survey of York,* by B. S. Rowntree, 1941, London: Longman, Green. Reprinted by permission of The Joseph Rowntree Charitable Trust.

expenditure of a large amount of money, however, it is imperative for the researcher to attain a sample large enough to minimize error.

5. ***Number of variables studied*** A larger sample is needed for a study that has many independent or dependent variables or for a study in which many uncontrollable variables are present.

6. ***Methods of data collection*** If methods of collecting information are not highly accurate or consistent, a larger sample will be needed to offset the error inherent in the data collection.

7. ***Accuracy needed*** The accuracy of the results (i.e., the degree of confidence that can be placed in a statement that the sample data are the same as for the population) is greater as the sample size increases. As the study by Rowntree (1941) demonstrates, however, a point of diminishing returns is reached as the sample size increases to a certain percentage of the population.

8. ***Size of the population*** As the size of the population increases, the researcher can take a progressively smaller percentage of subjects from the population.

ALERT!   In small sample studies, finding "no difference" or "no relationship" usually means that the conclusions that follow from the results are not credible.

DATA COLLECTION TECHNIQUES

Research involves gathering information about the variables in the study. The researcher chooses from a wide range of techniques and approaches for collecting data from the subjects. Each method has advantages and disadvantages, and the specific approach adopted should be the best one for answering the research question.

At this point it is important to understand two basic principles of measurement that are common for all methods: validity and reliability. Knowledge of these principles is used both to choose instruments and to evaluate the adequacy of data collection reported in research studies. Both will be examined in greater detail in Chapter 8.

Instrument Validity

Instrument validity is the extent to which inferences and uses made on the basis of scores from an instrument are reasonable and appropriate. Validity is a judgment of the appropriateness of a measure for specific inferences, decisions, consequences, and uses that result from the scores that are generated. In other words, validity is a situation-specific concept; it is dependent on the purpose, population, and situational factors in which measurement takes place. The results of a test, questionnaire, or other measure can therefore be valid in one situation and invalid in another.

This definition has important implications for designing and evaluating research, since findings are directly related to the measure that is used. The investigator who is designing research should first clearly define the inferences, uses, or decisions that will be made from the results. Then an instrument should be selected that provides good evidence that making such inferences or decisions is valid.

Instrument Reliability

Instrument reliability refers to the consistency of measurement, or the extent to which the scores are similar over different forms of the same instrument or occasions of data collection. The goal of developing reliable scores is to minimize the influence on the scores of chance and other variables unrelated to the intent of the measure.

EXCERPT 6.9   Instruments Section

Future Career Preference

Girls rated the probability of entering each of 19 potential job or career categories on a 7-point scale ranging from "very unlikely" to "very likely." Each category was presented with a label, followed by a brief description (e.g., food service, like waiter, waitress, cook, food preparation). The categories that involved science were (a) health paraprofessional, (b) health professional with a bachelor's degree, (c) science- or math-related professional with a bachelor's degree, (d) health professional with an advanced degree, and (e) science professional with an advanced degree. Examples and degree qualifications were given for each category. Ratings for all five categories were averaged to create a single score for a science career (alpha = .78); ratings for categories (b) and (d) were averaged to create a health professional score (alpha = .81); and ratings for categories (c) and (e) were averaged to create a physical science professional score (alpha = .77).

Source: From Jacobs, J. E., Finken, L. L., Griffin, N. L., & Wright, J. D. (1998). The career plans of science—talented rural adolescent girls. *American Educational Research Journal, 35*(4), 681–704.

The specific methods for estimating and reporting reliability are very precise and are explained in detail in Chapter 8. Designers and readers of research should interpret reliability in much the same way as validity, looking for evidence that sufficient reliability of each score is documented. Also, many studies fail to support their hypotheses because of significant errors in measuring the variables. (With more reliable measures, the hypotheses might be supported.)

In reading the instruments section of a study or in designing data collection, there are a few questions to keep in mind:

1. Are the scores reliable for the subjects of the particular research?
2. Are the characteristics of the subjects used to establish validity and reliability similar to the characteristics of the subjects in the study?
3. Are the instruments used the best ones? Would others be more reliable and provide more valid results?
4. Why did the researcher choose these instruments?
5. Are the instruments described well enough or referenced to allow another researcher to replicate the research?

Excerpt 6.9 is from the instruments section of a study. The extent of the description provided is about what is expected in reporting most types of research.

Sources for Locating and Evaluating Existing Instruments

In conducting research, the researcher should choose an instrument that has established the reliability and validity he or she needs and that will provide sufficient variability of scores. Although reliability and validity are the most important considerations in selecting an instrument, there are other considerations, such as purchasing costs, availability, simplicity of administration and scoring, copyright limitations, level of difficulty, and appropriateness of norms.

While it is often difficult to find an instrument that will meet all of the criteria a researcher might have, there are thousands of instruments, and it is probable that one is available that can be used intact or modified to meet a specific purpose. The easiest way to locate existing instruments is to use sources that summarize information on several measures. The sources in the following list are widely used and accessible:

Tests in Print, Volume 6, published periodically by the Buros Institute of Mental Measurement (Murphy, Plake, Impara, & Spies, 2002): Provides a summary of tests reviewed in all preceding mental measurement yearbooks.

Handbook of Research Design and Social Measurement, 6th edition (Miller & Salkind, 2002): Reviews and critiques popular social science measures.

Index to Tests Used in Educational Dissertations (Fabiano, 1989): Describes tests and test populations used in dissertations from 1938 to 1980; keyed by title and selected descriptors.

Commissioned Reviews of 250 Psychological Tests (Maltby, Lewis, & Hill, 2000): Contains brief reviews of tests published in the 1990s. Provides variable measured, description, sample tested, reliability, validity, where test can be found, and evaluative comments.

Directory of Unpublished Experimental Mental Measures, Volume 8 (Goldman & Mitchell, 2002): Describes nearly 1,700 experimental mental measures that are not commercially available. Includes references, source, and purpose on topics ranging from educational adjustment and motivation to personality and perception.

ETS Test Collection and *Testlink Test Collection Database:* The Educational Testing Service (ETS) has developed several sources that describe more than 20,000 tests and instruments. The database covers published and unpublished measures in several areas, including achievement, attitudes and interests, personality, special populations, and vocation/occupation. Each of over 200 separate bibliographies describes instruments and appropriate uses and can be ordered from ETS. *Tests in Microfiche* lists unpublished research instruments, also in a wide variety of areas.

Tests: A Comprehensive Reference for Assessments in Psychology, Education, and Business, 10th ed. (Maddox, 2003): Provides descriptions of over 3,100 published tests, including purpose, cost, scoring, and publisher.

Test Critiques, Volumes 1–10 (Keyser & Sweetland, 1984–1994): Gives in-depth evaluations for widely used, newly published, and recently revised instruments in psychology, education, and business. Contains user-oriented information, including practical applications and uses, as well as technical aspects and a critique by a measurement specialist. The companion, *Test Critiques Compendium*, reviews 60 major tests from *Test Critiques* in one volume.

Mental Measurements Yearbook (MMY; Buros Institute of Mental Measurement): Provides reviews of commercially available tests in several areas, including character and personality, achievement, and intelligence. References for most of the tests facilitate further research. The MMY has been published periodically for 60 years. The Buros Institute website (www.unl.edu/buros) includes *Test Reviews Online*, which allows electronic searches of the Buros database.

Tests and Measurements in Child Development: Handbook I and II (Johnson, 1976): Two volumes describe about 900 unpublished tests and instruments for children through age 18.

Sourcebook of Mental Health Measures (Comrey, Backer, & Glaser, 1973): Describes about 1,100 instruments related to mental health, including juvenile delinquency, personality, and alcoholism.

Handbook of Family Measurement Techniques (Touliatos, Perlmutter, Straus, & Holden, 2000): A three-volume set provides overviews and reviews of hundreds of instruments used to measure family variables.

Socioemotional Measures for Pre-School and Kindergarten Children: A Handbook (Walker, 1973): Describes instruments to measure attitudes, personality, self-concept, and social skills of young children.

Handbook for Measurement and Evaluation in Early Childhood Education (Goodwin & Driscoll, 1980): A comprehensive review of affective, cognitive, and psychomotor measures for young children.

Dictionary of Behavioral Assessment Techniques (Hersen & Bellack, 1988): Provides descriptions of approximately 300 instruments that assess psychological and behavioral traits.

In addition to these sources, online resources are very helpful. An excellent one is by the American Psychological Association (www.apa.org/science/faq-findtests.html). The Buros Institute's *Test Reviews Online* (http://buros.un1/edu/buros/jsp) is also excellent. The ERIC database (www.eric.ed.gov) allows online searches by the name of the instrument.

Developing Instruments

Although many instruments are available, there are occasions when researchers have to develop their own measures. The most common situation that requires a locally developed measure is evaluation research for a specific setting. Unless the research will have an important direct impact on programs or individuals, it is unusual for the researcher to systematically establish reliability and validity (as summarized in Chapter 8) prior to conducting the study. A more common approach is to develop an instrument that seems reasonable and to gather pilot data on it to revise as needed. While it is probably not necessary to establish sophisticated estimates of reliability and validity, it is still possible for the instrument to be of such inferior quality that the results attained will be uninterpretable. Thus, it is important for a researcher to follow a few basic steps when faced with the development of an instrument:

1. Become acquainted with common approaches to measuring the trait or behavior of interest. Many existing sources summarize approaches for measuring such variables as achievement, attitudes, interests, personality, and self-concept.
2. Write out specific objectives for the instrument, with one objective for each trait or behavior of interest.
3. After reading about the area and conducting discussions with others about what approach would best measure the trait, brainstorm several items for each objective.
4. Ask professionals who are knowledgeable in the assessed area to review the items: Are they clear? Unbiased? Concise? Are the meanings the same for all readers?
5. Find a small sample of individuals who are similar to those who will be used in the actual study and administer the instrument to them. This could be referred to as a *pilot test* of the instrument. Check for clarity, ambiguity in sentences, time for completion, directions, and any problems that may have been experienced.
6. Check for an adequate distribution of scores for each item in the instrument. If all the responses to an item are the same, it will be difficult to know whether the question is inadequate or whether the trait actually lacks variability. As long as the responses result in a spread of scores, the chances are good that the item is an adequate measure of the trait.
7. Revise, delete, and add items where necessary, depending on feedback from the sample subjects in the pilot test.

PROCEDURES

In a quantitative study, the researcher plans the procedures that will be used to collect data and, in the case of experimental research, the nature and administration of the experimental intervention. The researcher decides where the data will be collected (e.g., in a school, city, or laboratory setting), when the data will be collected (time of day and year), how the data will be collected (by whom and in what form), and, if necessary, specifics of the experimental treatment. Any procedures used to control bias (e.g., counterbalancing the order of instruments to control subject fatigue or boredom or being sure observers are unaware of which group is receiving the treatment and which is the control) are planned and implemented as part of the procedures. In reporting the study, the researcher should present the procedures in sufficient detail to permit another researcher to replicate the study.

DESIGN VALIDITY

In the context of research design, the term *validity* (sometimes referred to as *experimental validity*), means the degree to which scientific explanations of phenomena match reality. It refers to the truthfulness of findings and conclusions. Explanations about observed phenomena *approximate* what is reality or truth, and the degree to which explanations are accurate comprises the validity of design.

There are four types of design validity in quantitative research:

- **Statistical conclusion validity** refers to the appropriate use of statistical tests to determine whether purported relationships are a reflection of actual relationships.
- **Internal validity** focuses on the viability of causal links between the independent and dependent variables.
- **Construct validity** is a judgment about the extent to which interventions and measured variables actually represent targeted, theoretical, underlying psychological constructs and elements.
- **External validity** refers to the generalizability of the results and conclusions to other people and locations.

These four types of design validity can also be expressed as questions to be addressed in considering the overall quality of the findings and conclusions:

- Is there a relationship among the variables? (Statistical conclusion validity)
- Is there a causal relationship between the intervention and the dependent variable? (Internal Validity)
- What is the nature of the constructs? (Construct validity)
- What is the generalizability of the results? (External validity)

In designing or reading quantitative research with these four types of design validity in mind, it is necessary to consider who will be assessed (subjects), what they will be assessed by (instruments), how they will be assessed (procedures for data collection), and, for experimental designs, how experimental interventions will be administered. Once statistical conclusion validity has been assured, then it is important to ask Is there anything that occurred or was done that could provide an explanation of the results by means of a rival hypothesis? *Rival* is used in the sense that it is in addition to the stated hypothesis or intent of the research. (A rival hypothesis to the study of whether smoking causes lung cancer, for example, is that diet may contribute to the cause of lung cancer.) This question represents the search for extraneous variability in internal validity.

Campbell and Stanley (1963) refer to such explanations as **plausible rival hypotheses.** The search for plausible rival hypotheses is essential to ensure the quality of the research. Consider, for example, the questions below. Each addresses a possible source of error that could lead to a plausible rival hypothesis that might explain results:

1. Does the researcher have an existing bias about the subjects or about the topic researched?
2. Are the subjects aware that they are being studied?
3. Are the subjects responding honestly?
4. Did both groups receive the intervention as described?
5. Does the sex of the interviewer make a difference?
6. Did very many subjects drop out before the end of the study?
7. Did the time of day the research was done affect the results?

If the researcher believes that the conditions of data collection might affect the results, the study can be designed to ensure that all conditions are as similar as possible. For example, in an observational study of the relationship between teacher behavior and student attention to material, the time of day the observer records data and the subject matter of the lesson (e.g., mornings versus afternoons, math versus history) could make a difference in student attention. One way to control this potential source of error is to make sure that all the observations are done at the same time of day during lessons on the same topic. In this example, the researcher could also control these potential influences by making them independent variables. This could be achieved by assigning observers to each subject of interest and having each topic observed in both the morning and the afternoon. Then the researcher could assess the effect of time of day and subject, rather than simply control for it.

In quantitative studies, control of possible extraneous variables is essential, although educational research rarely exhibits the degree of control evident in studies of physical phenomena or psychology. Thus, the researcher must search constantly for factors (extraneous variables) that might influence the results or conclusions of the study. For quantitative research, the concept of internal validity describes the efficacy with which extraneous variables have been controlled. The concern is with the way the procedures, sampling of subjects, and instruments affect the extent to which extraneous variables are present to complicate the interpretation of the findings. A study high or strong in internal validity successfully controls all or most extraneous variables so that the researcher can be confident that, for instance, X caused changes in Y. Studies low or weak in internal validity are difficult to interpret, since it is impossible to tell whether the results were due to the independent variable or to some extraneous variable that was uncontrolled or unaccounted for. It is important for researchers to be aware of common factors that may be extraneous and to conceptualize and read research with these factors in mind. Since complete control of extraneous variables in educational research is difficult, if not impossible, all relevant threats to internal validity that cannot be prevented should be accounted for in interpreting the results.

Statistical Conclusion Validity

In quantitative research, statistics are used to determine whether a relationship exists between two or more variables. The issue is the extent to which the calculated statistics accurately portray the actual relationship. Doing the statistics is the first step in determining results, interpretations, and conclusions. In other words, statistics guide the findings. While we have not yet discussed typical statistical procedures, it is important to realize that certain factors may invalidate the statistical results. That is, there are reasons that researchers may draw inferences about the relationship between variables that are incorrect. While a complete consideration of these factors, or "threats," as they are called, is beyond the scope of this book, being familiar with these ideas is important to readers.

Shadish, Cook, and Campbell (2002) list nine threats to statistical conclusion validity. The first seven are pertinent to our discussion:

1. **Low statistical power**   An incorrect conclusion of no relationship due to lack of power, or the ability to detect relationships.
2. **Violated assumptions of statistical tests**   Violated assumptions may under- or overestimate the size of a relationship.
3. **"Fishing" and error rate problem**   Repeated tests for statistical significance can inflate statistical significance.
4. **Unreliability of measures**   Measurement error weakens relationships.
5. **Restriction of range**   Reduced, small differences among a set of scores weakens relationships.
6. **Unreliability of treatment implementation**   Unstandardized treatments underestimate the effects of an intervention (also referred to as *treatment fidelity*).
7. **Extraneous variance in the experimental setting**   Features of an intervention setting may inflate error, making it more difficult to show a relationship.

You may notice that much of the error caused by these factors makes it more difficult to show relationships. This is a critical feature for research that concludes, based on lack of statistical significance, that there really is no relationship. In this case, threats to statistical conclusion, if present, invalidate no-relationship conclusions. (We will return to this subject in Chapter 11.)

Internal Validity

Internal validity is strongest when the study's design (subjects, instruments, and procedures) effectively controls possible sources of error so that those sources are not reasonably related to the study's results. Several categories or types of threats to internal validity are pertinent to most quantitative studies. Each of these threats is described and illustrated in a following section. These categories are taken from Campbell and Stanley (1963), Cook and Campbell (1979), Shadish, Cook, and Campbell (2002), and McMillan (2004). It is best to keep in mind that the names of these various threats to internal validity should not be interpreted literally. Often, each has a broader meaning than the name may suggest at first. While some of the names are unique to this book, most were originally conceived for experimental research. While many of the threats relate to both experimental and nonexperimental designs, some only make sense in the context of an experiment.

Two conditions must be present to establish whether a threat is plausible: (1) the threat is present for only one level of the independent variable, and (2) the threat is related to the dependent variable. Suppose a researcher is investigating the effect of a special training program for school counselors. If the group receiving the program is more experienced than the comparison group and experience influences the dependent variable, then a clear threat to internal validity will compromise causal inferences.

History   In the context of internal validity, **history** refers to extraneous incidents or events affecting the results that occur during the research. This is a threat to any research that is conducted across time, and it becomes more serious as the time between measures increases. If some event occurs during the study that is plausibly related to the dependent variable, it is difficult to know if the independent variable, the event, or a combination of the two produced the result. In this sense, the event is *confounded* with the independent variable; the two cannot be separated.

History can occur *within* the study when subjects are affected by something that happens during the treatment in an experiment or *outside* the research setting. For example, suppose a class is studying the Far East and researchers are trying to determine what effect this unit has on students' multicultural attitudes. During the unit, a major crisis occurs in China. If the students are affected by the crisis, which in turn influences the way they respond to a multicultural attitude questionnaire, this event will constitute a history threat to the internal validity of the study. History threats can also occur within a research setting. For example, a series of unexpected announcements that distract a class receiving one method of instruction adversely will affect the influence of the lesson. Students in this class might score lower than other classes, but the researcher will not know if this result is caused by the distraction or the method of instruction.

Selection   There are two types of selection threats to consider: those that occur in experiments and *ex post facto* designs and those that are related to sampling. In experiments, groups of subjects are formed in order to study an independent variable of interest. If there is a systematic difference between the groups, however, the results may be due to these existing differences. The threat of **selection** exists whenever groups of subjects cannot be assigned randomly. While there are several approaches that help control this problem in cases where randomization is undesirable or impossible (e.g., matching, testing subjects more than once, adjusting posttest scores on the basis of initially measured group characteristics, and giving each group every treatment), the researcher should always be concerned with this important threat.

Consider, for example, a teacher who wants to investigate whether the mastery or inductive approach is best for teaching adjectives and adverbs. The teacher secures the cooperation of another class in order to conduct a study. The two teachers flip a coin to decide who will use the discovery approach and who will use the mastery approach. The teachers assess achievement by giving each group a pretest and a posttest to determine growth in knowledge. It happens, however, that the average IQ score of the mastery group is 115 while that of the discovery group 95. Here selection is a major problem, since we would expect the higher-IQ group to achieve more than the lower-IQ group under almost any condition. If uncontrolled and unaccounted for in some way, then such a threat to internal validity could render the study useless. The teacher would falsely conclude that the mastery learning method is more effective, when its apparent success is really due to initial differences in ability.

As discussed previously, selection is also related to the manner in which the researcher chooses a sample. As pointed out, a common problem in research is using volunteers for the sample. The volunteer group may be more motivated or motivated for special reasons; hence, they will respond differently to the treatment or questions than a nonvolunteer group will respond.

Statistical Regression   **Statistical regression** (also called *regression artifacts*) refers to the tendency of subjects who score very high or low on a pretest to score closer to the mean (i.e, *regress* to the mean) on the posttest, regardless of the effects of the treatment. All measures have some degree of error, and statistical regression occurs because of changes in error from the pretest to the posttest. Scores on a posttest will be different from the pretest for students on the basis of mathematical probability alone because of this error. For groups of students who score either very high or very low on a pretest, this error works to change the scores on the posttest so that they are closer to the mean of the posttest than they were to the mean of the pretest.

To illustrate this concept, think of Figure 6.5 as representing the same test taken twice by two groups of students in a class in which the average score is 100. The average score for the Superstars on the first test was 150, whereas the score for the Challengers was 40. On the second test, we would expect the average score for the Superstars to be

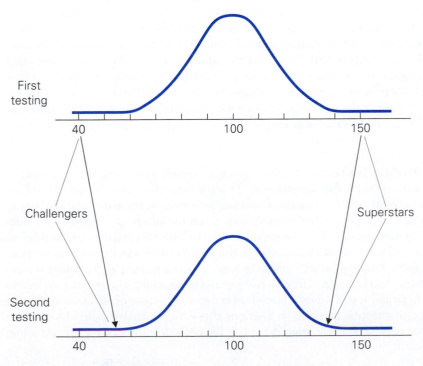

FIGURE   6.5   **Illustration of Statistical Regression**

lower and the Challengers' score to be higher, even if their true ability or knowledge remains the same.

Regression is a problem whenever the researcher purposely chooses groups on the basis of extremely high or low scores. For example, a school district may want to implement a special program to improve the self-concept of children who score low on a self-concept inventory. An assessment of the impact of the program could examine self-concept scores after the program (in a posttest), but the researcher would have to keep in mind that even if there is no program effect whatsoever, the initially low scores (on a pretest) would improve to some degree because of statistical regression. Similarly, it is usually difficult to find positive changes in programs for gifted children. (Because of regression, posttest scores will tend to be slightly lower on average.)

Pretesting   Whenever research utilizes a pretest (i.e., some form of measurement that precedes a treatment or experience), it is possible that the test itself will have an impact on the subjects. Just taking a pretest could provide the subject with motivation or practice on the type of questions asked or familiarize the subject with the material tested. This kind of **pretesting** (or *testing*) effect is found in experiments measuring achievement over a short time and in research on attitudes or values when a single group is given a pretest and a posttest. If an attitude questionnaire is used as a pretest, simply reading the questions might stimulate the subject to think about the topic and even change attitudes. A researcher might, for instance, be interested in evaluating the effect of a series of films on changes in students' attitudes toward children with physical disabilities. The researcher would give a pretest, show the films, and then give a posttest to find out whether changes have occurred. Any observed changes, however, might be caused by the pretest. The items in the questionnaire could have been enough to change the attitudes. Pretesting is not a threat for nonexperimental designs.

Instrumentation   A threat to internal validity that is related to testing is called **instrumentation.** It refers to the way changes in the instruments or persons used to collect data might affect the results. This threat is particularly serious in observational research, when the observers may become fatigued or bored or change in some other way so as to affect the recording of data. A good example of how instrumentation could affect results occurs when scores from the same standardized test are used to track achievement across several years. If there has been a renorming of the test and a new form, it is problematic to compare results from the old test with those from the new one. The 1995 renorming and other planned changes in the Scholastic Assessment Tests (SAT) is a good illustration of how this can lead to errors in interpretation, since the meaning of the same score, for example, 500, is different in the new form. *Testing* is a change in the subject resulting from taking the test, while *instrumentation* is a recorded change in the results from inadequacies of the testing.

Attrition   Attrition (also called *mortality*) occurs in a study when subjects systematically drop out or are lost during the investigation. This is a threat to many longitudinal studies that last over several weeks or months. For example, a study of the effect of a program to assist low-achieving ninth-graders conducted between the ninth and the twelfth grades would have apparent success if the lowest-achieving students dropped out of school before twelfth grade and were not even included in the posttest analyses. For most nonexperimental and short-duration research, attrition is not a threat unless the treatment is especially demanding and systematically causes low-performing subjects to drop out. In studies that have differential loss of subjects from different groups because of selection bias or the nature of the treatments, mortality is a serious threat to internal validity. Mortality is essentially the same problem as selection, but it happens after the study is already set up and under way.

Maturation   Maturation refers to changes in the subjects of a study over time that affect the dependent variable. Subjects develop and change as a part of growing older, and in interpreting research that occurs over an extended time, such changes should be considered. Some changes, such as getting hungry, tired, bored, or discouraged, can occur in a relatively short time and are also considered maturational threats to internal validity. Suppose a researcher is investigating the attitudes of fourth-graders toward reading, mathematics, and science. The researcher has developed an instrument and gives it to all subjects in the same way. It takes the subjects a half hour to finish the reading instrument and another half hour to complete the mathematics questions. How will they respond to the science instrument? They will probably be tired, bored, and inattentive, and maturation would thus be a major problem in using their responses to the science items as an indication of their attitude toward science. Other examples are students who become more knowledgeable because of experience and first-graders who learn to dribble a basketball not because of an effective teacher but because they are maturing physically.

Diffusion of Treatment   In an ideal experimental design, an intervention is given to one group, and the control or alternative condition group never comes in contact with the experimental intervention. For instance, if a psychologist is studying cheating behavior and manipulates the incentive to cheat as the independent variable, one group might receive a high incentive for cheating and the other group a low incentive, but neither group would be aware of the treatment the other group was receiving. If, however, a teacher decided to test this notion with a class of students and told half the students they would receive a high incentive and the other half that they would, at the same time, receive a low incentive, then each group would know the conditions of the other. In such circumstances, the treatments would be diffused throughout all subjects. It is possible that both treatments could affect either group, resulting in **diffusion of treatment.** Diffusion also occurs if the effects of the treatment spread to subjects in a control or comparison group.

Experimenter Effects   **Experimenter effects** refer to both deliberate and unintentional influences that the researcher has on the subjects. This may be reflected in differential treatment of subjects, such as using a different voice tone, being more reassuring to one group than to others, reinforcing different behaviors, displaying different attitudes, selectively observing different subject responses, and any other demeanor that influences either the subjects' behavior or the evaluation of the behavior by the researcher. Experimenter effects also occur if the characteristics of the investigator or person collecting data, such as clothing, age, sex, educational level, and race, affect subjects' responses. For example, if an experimenter is carrying out a study on the difference in behavior with students of so-called master teachers compared with behavior with students of so-called novice teachers, and if observers are used to record behavior with students of both types of teachers, the observers should not know which teachers have been classified as master or novice. If the observers were aware of which group the students were in (master or novice teacher), this knowledge may influence what the observers notice in the classrooms. In most research that involves the use of researchers as a part of the study, it is best to keep them unaware of the specifics of the research. They need to have only enough information to carry out the research objectively and to collect the information.

Treatment Replications   In an experiment, the treatment is supposed to be repeated so that each of the members of one group receives the same treatment separately and independently of the other members of the group. Thus, if the researcher is testing a new method of instruction with a whole class, there is really only one replication of the treatment; that is, the treatment is conducted once. Each class is like one subject, and hence several classes are needed to do the research properly. **Treatment replications** are a threat to internal validity to the extent that the reported number of subjects in the study is not the same as the number of independent replications of the treatment.

ALERT!   Be wary of research in which whole classes receive an intervention.

This threat is a particularly troublesome limitation for educational research because it is so difficult to use multiple groups of students. Often a study will compare two treatments: one given to one class, the other to a different class. While this type of design usually results in a technical sample size of two, rather than the number of students in the classes, the threat of treatment replications does not mean the results are completely invalid. Rather, what needs to be recognized is that whatever the results, interpretations and conclusions should be made with great caution. Some experimental treatments are given to students as a group assignment, but the actual treatment condition, such as a particular type of homework assignment, is individualized. In this circumstance, treatment replication is not a threat to internal validity.

Subject Effects   In ideal research, the subjects behave and respond naturally and honestly. However, when people become involved in a study they often change their behavior simply because they understand they are subjects, and sometimes these changes affect the results. **Subject effects** refer to subject changes in behavior initiated by the subjects themselves in response to the research situation. If subjects have some idea of the purpose of the study or the motivation for doing well, they may alter their behavior to respond more favorably. Subjects will pick up cues from the setting and instructions, which will motivate them in specific ways. These cues are called **demand characteristics.**

Subjects in most studies will also want to present themselves in the most positive manner. Thus, there may be positive self-presentation, social desirability, or a belief that certain responses are expected, which may affect the results. For instance, most people want to appear intelligent, competent, and emotionally stable, and they may resist treatments that they perceive as manipulating them in negative ways or they may fake responses to appear more positive. Some subjects may increase positive or desirable behavior simply because they know they are receiving special treatment. (This is termed the *Hawthorne effect,* considered by some researchers as a threat to external validity; see the section on ecological external validity.) Control group subjects may try harder because they see themselves in competition with a treatment group or may be motivated because they did *not* get the treatment. (This may be termed the *John Henry effect* or *compensatory rivalry.*) Other subjects, when they realize that they were not selected for what they believe is a preferred treatment, may become demotivated (i.e., *resentful demoralization*). Finally, many individuals will react positively, with increased motivation or participation because they are doing something new and different. (This is termed the *novelty effect.*) As you can see, there are many possible subject effects.

Construct Validity

Research almost always involves making inferences about unobservable mental states (e.g., intelligence, motivation, aggression, and happiness) and experimental interventions. The inference is drawn from what is measured and/or treated pertaining to these mental states. Construct validity refers to inferences that are made from the nature of the measurement and interventions used to the constructs they purportedly represent. Suppose a researcher is studying the effect of curriculum alignment with high-stakes testing on student achievement. The test of student achievement is given to make inferences about what students know and can do, and the specifics of the intervention are used to make inferences about curriculum alignment. Construct validity concerns the efficacy of using the test as a measure of what students know and can do, as well as the representativeness of the intervention as an illustration of curriculum alignment. There are many ways of measuring student achievement and doing curriculum alignment, so if only one test is used and only one model of curriculum alignment is proposed, construct validity will be weak.

Shadish, Cook, and Campbell (2002) list 14 threats to construct validity, some of which were considered earlier as subject effect threats to internal validity. The three threats with the greatest relevance for education research include the following:

1. **Inadequate explication of the constructs**   Failure to adequately explain the nature of the construct may lead to inaccurate inferences.
2. **Mono-operation bias**   A single example of the intervention or the dependent variables limits inferences (e.g., one method of showing humor in an intervention or using only observation to measure the effect of the humor on attentiveness; humor could be presented by both men and women; observations could use a single format for recording behavior).
3. **Mono-method bias**   Use of a single method in implementing the intervention and/or measuring the dependent variable (e.g., humor could be in writing or presented orally; humor could be measured with a paper-and-pencil questionnaire or observations).

Construct validity is closely related to generalizability, since using a weak conceptualization or single method of measurement will limit inferences about the details of the conceptualization and method. Suppose student achievement is limited to how students score on a multiple-choice test. Other ways of measuring achievement might give different results. Thus, what is meant by student achievement is limited to the method of measurement.

External Validity

External validity refers to the generalizability of the results. For quantitative designs there are two general categories of external validity that need to be considered when designing studies or in evaluating research findings: population external validity and ecological external validity.

Research Navigator.com

6.2 External Validity
Accession No.: 6814382

Population External Validity   The subjects used in an investigation have certain characteristics and can be described with respect to such variables as age, race, sex, and ability. Strictly speaking, the results of a study can be generalized only to other people who have the same, or at least similar, characteristics as those used in the experiment. The extent to which the results can be generalized to other people is referred to as **population external validity.**

Consider the prevailing situation in much psychological research. Because of time, money, and other constraints, psychologists often use college students as subjects in research. The results of such research, strictly speaking, are limited in generalizability to other similar college students. In other words, what might be true for certain college students may not be true for sixth-grade students. Similarly, research conducted with elementary students should not be generalized to secondary students, nor males generalized to females, nor Hispanic Americans generalized to African Americans, and so forth. A treatment might be effective with one type of student and be ineffective with another. If subjects are volunteers for research, the findings may be limited to characteristics of the volunteers.

Ecological External Validity   **Ecological external validity** refers to the conditions of the research and the extent to which generalizing the results is limited to similar conditions. The conditions of the research include such factors as the nature of the independent and dependent variables, physical surroundings, time of day or year, pretest or posttest sensitization, and effects caused by the presence of an experimenter or treatment. Included in these factors is the well-known **Hawthorne effect:** the tendency for people to act differently simply because they realize they are subjects in research. (It is called the Hawthorne effect because the original study was conducted at the Western Electric Hawthorne Plant in Chicago. Although some research has questioned the validity of the original study, the label *Hawthorne effect* endures.) Much as with threats of subject effects, subjects may become anxious, fake responses in order to look good, or react in many other ways because of their knowledge of aspects of the research.

A variation of external validity is to be careful not to conclude that what may be true for an entire group of subjects is also true for subgroups of subjects. For example, if research with a large high school shows a positive relationship between amount of time spent with homework and achievement for all students, it does not necessarily follow that this same relationship holds for high-ability students or low-ability students or that it is just as true for sophomores as for seniors. This is called generalizing *across* a population and can lead to erroneous interpretations.

It is possible to be so strict with respect to external validity that practically all research is useful only in specific cases. While it is necessary to consider the external validity of studies, we need to be reasonable, not strict, in interpreting the results. It is common, for example, for researchers to cite in the discussion or conclusion section of the article the limitations of generalizing their results.

ETHICAL AND LEGAL CONSIDERATIONS

Since most educational research deals with human beings, it is necessary to understand the ethical and legal responsibilities of conducting research. Often, researchers face situations in which the potential costs of using questionable methods must be balanced by the benefits of conducting the study. Questionable methods come about because of the nature of the research questions and methodology designed to provide valid results. The costs may include injury and psychological difficulties, such as anxiety, shame, loss of self-esteem, and affronts to human dignity, or they may involve legal infringement on human rights. Such costs, if a potential result of the research, must be weighed against the benefits for the research participants, such as increased self-understanding, satisfaction in helping, and knowledge of research methods, as well as more obvious benefits to theory and knowledge of human behavior.

It is ultimately the responsibility of each researcher to weigh these considerations and to make the best professional judgment possible. To do this, it is necessary for the researcher to be fully aware of the ethical and legal principles that should be addressed. We present these principles with a discussion of the implications.

Ethics of Research

Ethics generally are considered to deal with beliefs about what is right or wrong, proper or improper, good or bad. Naturally, there is some degree of disagreement about how to define what is ethically correct in research. But it is a very important issue, one of increasing concern for private citizens, researchers, and legislators. Many professional and governmental groups have studied ethical issues in depth and published guidelines for planning and conducting research in such a way as to protect the rights and welfare of the subjects. Most relevant for educational research are the ethical principles published by the American Educational Research Association. Another useful source is the American Psychological Association.[1] The principles of most concern to educators are discussed here:

1. *The primary investigator of a study is responsible for the ethical standards to which the study adheres.*
2. *The investigator should inform the subjects of all aspects of the research* that might influence willingness to participate and answer all inquiries of subjects on features that may have adverse effects or consequences.

3. *The investigator should be as open and honest with the subjects as possible.* This usually involves a full disclosure of the purpose of the research, but there are circumstances in which either withholding information about the research or deceiving the subjects may be justified. Withholding information means that the participants are informed about only part of the purpose of the research. This may be done in studies where full disclosure would seriously affect the validity of the results. For example, in research on students' racial attitudes, it may be sufficient to inform students that the research is investigating attitudes toward others.

   A more volatile issue involves research in which, to put it bluntly, the researcher deliberately misleads the subjects. A good example is the classic study on teacher expectations by Rosenthal and Jacobson (1968). The researchers informed the teachers that certain students had been identified as "bloomers" on a test designed to predict intellectual gain. In fact, the test was a measure of intelligence, and the students were identified at random. In this design, it was necessary to tell the teachers an untruth. Is such deception justified? After all, in this case the students would only benefit from the misinformation, and the results did have very important implications.

   From one perspective, the deception may be justified on the basis of the contribution of the findings. On the other hand, it is an affront to human dignity and self-respect and may encourage mistrust and cynicism toward researchers. It seems that deception should be used only in cases where (1) the significance of the potential results is greater than the detrimental effects of lying; (2) deception is the only valid way to carry out the study; and (3) appropriate debriefing is used, in which the researcher informs the participants of the nature of and reason for the deception following the completion of the study. Deception does not mean that the subjects should not have a choice whether to participate at all in the study.

4. *Subjects must be protected from physical and mental discomfort, harm, and danger.* If any of these risks is possible, the researcher must inform the subjects of these risks.

5. *Many studies require the investigator to secure informed consent from the subjects before they participate in the research.* **Informed consent** is achieved by providing subjects with an explanation of the research, an opportunity to terminate their participation at any time with no penalty, and full disclosure of any risks associated with the study. Consent is usually obtained by asking subjects (or the parents of minor subjects) to sign a form that indicates understanding of the research and consent to participate. Almost all data gathering in public schools that requires student participation beyond normal testing requires parental as well as school district and principal permission.

   Informed consent implies that the subjects have a choice about whether to participate. Yet there are many circumstances when it seems acceptable that the subjects never know that they have been participants. Sometimes, it is impractical or impossible to locate subjects; sometimes, knowledge of participation may invalidate the results. Some educational research is quite unobtrusive and has no risks for the subjects (e.g., the use of test data of students over the past 10 years in order to chart achievement trends). Still, the researcher infringes on what many believe is the ethical right of participants to make their own decisions about participation. In general, the more the research inconveniences subjects or creates the potential for harm, the more severe the ethical question in using them as subjects without their consent.

   Certainly, people should never be coerced into participating. Coercion is enacted in different degrees. At one extreme, teachers can insist that their students participate, or employers can strongly suggest that their employees cooperate as subjects. Less obvious subtle persuasion is exerted by convincing subjects that they are benefiting science, a program, or an institution. The researcher may indicate freedom of choice to participate or not participate, but the implicit message, "you're

Research Navigator.c⊕m

6.3 Informed Consent
Accession No.: 8699738

letting us down if you don't participate" may also be clear, resulting in partial coercion. In other cases, subjects are simply bribed. Where does freedom of choice end and coercion begin? It is often difficult to know, but it is the responsibility of the researcher to be aware of the power of subtle coercion and to clearly maintain the freedom of the potential participant to decide whether or not to be a subject in the research. Whenever possible, participation should be voluntary and invasion of privacy should be minimized.

6. *Information obtained about the subjects must be held confidential* unless otherwise agreed on, in advance, through informed consent. This means that no one has access to individual data or the names of the participants except the researcher(s) and that the subjects know before they participate who will see the data. Confidentiality is ensured by making certain that the data cannot be linked to individual subjects by name. This can be accomplished in several ways, including (1) collecting the data anonymously; (2) using a system to link names to data that can be destroyed; (3) using a third party to link names to data and then giving the results to the researcher without the names; (4) asking subjects to use aliases or numbers; and (5) reporting only group, not individual, results. Boruch and Cecil (1979) provide details of many different procedures for ensuring confidentiality.

7. *For research conducted through an institution, such as a university or school system, approval for conducting the research should be obtained from the institution before any data are collected.* Typically, this involves obtaining permission from the institution's **internal review board (IRB),** a committee that prepares guidelines for obtaining permission, conducts reviews of proposals for research, and approves studies. An IRB weighs the potential benefits of the research with possible risks to the participants and may suggest additional procedures to better protect their rights. The IRB process can be very time consuming, so advanced planning is required. It is important for the IRB to make decisions about what must be approved, including research conducted by students. At the very least, students should not go out and collect data without obtaining permission from a professor or administrative head. IRB approval is needed for any research that may be disseminated in a formal manner or in public. This suggests that informal class projects may be exempt from IRB approval, as long as there is assurance that the findings will not be more widely disseminated in the future. All doctoral dissertations require IRB approval, as do many program evaluations.

8. *The investigator has a responsibility to consider potential misinterpretations and misuses of the research* and should make every effort to communicate results so that misunderstanding is minimized.

9. *The investigator has the responsibility of recognizing when potential benefits have been withheld from a control group.* In such situations, the significance of the potential findings should be greater than the potential harm to some subjects. For example, a new program that purports to enhance achievement of children with learning disabilities may be withheld from some of these children in the belief that an experiment is necessary to document the effectiveness of the program. In the process, the controls who may have benefited are denied participation in the program.

10. **The investigator should provide subjects with the opportunity to receive the results of the study in which they are participating.**

Some research (e.g., studies of the effects of drugs), obviously has potential danger that must be considered carefully by the investigator. While much educational research may not seem to involve any ethical problems, the investigator's view may be biased. It is best to seek the advice and approval of others. Consulting with others provides an impartial perspective and can help the researcher identify procedures for protecting participants from harm.

There is also an interesting, if not frustrating, interaction between being ethical, on the one hand, and designing the research to provide the best, most objective data, on

TABLE 6.5   Keys to Conducting Ethical Research
• Be knowledgeable about ethical principles, professional guidelines, and legal requirements.
• Maximize potential benefits.
• Minimize potential risks.
• Obtain needed permission.
• Minimize potential misinterpretations and misuses of results.
• Obtain informed consent.
• Protect the privacy and confidentiality of the subjects.

the other. It is relatively easy, for example, to observe behavior unobtrusively, such that the subjects might never know they were in an experiment. As previously noted, the Hawthorne effect can reduce the validity of the study. To maximize both internal and external validity, therefore, it seems best for subjects to be unaware that they are being studied. Suppose, for instance, that a researcher planted a confederate in a class in order to record unobtrusively the attending behavior of college students. Does the researcher have an obligation to tell the students that their behavior is being recorded? If the students are aware of being observed, will this awareness change their behavior and invalidate the results? Such situations present ethical dilemmas, and the researcher must weigh the criteria listed above in order to determine the best course of action.

See Table 6.5 for a summary of key points for conducting ethical research.

Legal Constraints

Most of the legal constraints placed on researchers since 1974 have focused on protecting the rights and the welfare of the subjects. These requirements are generally consistent with the ethical principles summarized earlier, and are in a constant state of reinterpretation and change by the courts.

The Family Educational Rights and Privacy Act of 1974, known as the Buckley Amendment, allows individuals to gain access to information pertaining to them, such as test scores, teacher comments, and recommendations. The act also provides that written permission of consent is legally necessary with data that identify students by name. The consent must indicate the information that will be disclosed, the purpose of the disclosure, and to whom it will be disclosed. Exceptions to this requirement are granted for research using school records in which the results are of "legitimate educational interest" and when only group data are reported. It should be noted that data gathered in a study can usually be subpoenaed by the courts, even if confidentiality has been promised to the participants by the researcher.

The National Research Act of 1974 requires review of proposed research by an appropriate group in an institution (school division or university) to protect the rights and welfare of the subjects. While most research involving human subjects must be reviewed by such a group, there are some exceptions, such as research using test data that result from normal testing programs and analyzing existing public data, records, or documents without identifying individuals. These regulations were expanded and modified in 1991 with publication of the *Code of Federal Regulations for the Protection of Human Subjects*. The code was further updated in 2003.

SUMMARY

This chapter introduced the fundamental characteristics of designing quantitative research. It focused particular attention on selecting subjects and instruments and on variables that should be considered in designing and interpreting the research. Key points include the following:

1. Research design refers to the way a study is planned and conducted.
2. The purpose of a good research design is to enhance the credibility of the results by taking into account three sources of variability: systematic, error, and extraneous.
3. Probability sampling is used to be able to generalize to a larger population.
4. Probability sampling is done through simple random sampling, systematic sampling, stratified random sampling, and cluster sampling.
5. Nonprobability sampling includes purposeful, convenience, and quota types. While available and easily obtained, the use of such samples limits generalizability.
6. The size of the sample should be as large as possible without reaching a point at which additional subjects contribute little or no new information.
7. In order to have acceptable reliability and validity for the subjects used in the study, instruments should be

chosen carefully. Validity is an estimate of the appropriateness of the use of scores, and reliability is an indication of the consistency of the scores.

8. Researchers should try to locate existing instruments before developing their own.
9. Statistical conclusion validity is concerned with whether there is an actual relationship.
10. Threats to the internal validity of quantitative studies include selection, history, statistical regression, pretesting, instrumentation, subject attrition, maturation, diffusion of treatment, experimenter effects, treatment replications, subject effects, and statistical conclusion.
11. Construct validity considers the match between theoretical constructs and actual interventions and measures.
12. Threats to the external validity of quantitative studies that limit generalizability are classified as population characteristics or ecological conditions.
13. The procedures section of a study should show how the information was collected in detail sufficient to allow other researchers to replicate or extend the study.
14. Researchers should be aware of ethical responsibilities and legal constraints that accompany the gathering and reporting of information.

RESEARCH NAVIGATOR NOTES

Reading the following articles will help you understand the content of this chapter. Go to the education database (included in the EBSCO database) in Research Navigator; use the Accession Number provided to find the article.

6.1   *Sampling*

What size sample would you recommend for the class project that is described? Accession Number: 8752465.

6.2   *External Validity*

See how different methods of sampling affect the generalizability of developmental studies. Accession Number: 6814382.

6.3   *Informed Consent*

This study examined the capacity of children and adolescents to understand their rights in research. Accession Number: 8699738.

CHECK YOURSELF

Multiple-choice review items, with answers, are available on the Companion Website for this book:

www.ablongman.com/mcmillanschumacher6e.

APPLICATION PROBLEMS

1. For each case described here, list potential threats to internal and external validity:

   a. Two researchers designed a study to investigate whether physical education performance is affected by being in a class with students of the same sex only or in a class with students of both sexes. A college instructor is found to cooperate with the researchers. Three sections of the same tennis class are offered: an all-male section, an all-female section, and a mixed section. The researchers control the instructor variable by using the same person as the instructor for each section, informing the instructor about the study and emphasizing to the instructor the need to keep instructional activities the same for each section. One section is offered in the morning, one at noon, and one in the afternoon. Students sign up for the course by using the same procedure as for all courses, although there is a footnote about the gender composition in the schedule of courses. A pretest is given to control for existing differences in the groups.

   b. In this study, the effect of day care on children's prosocial behavior is examined. A group of volunteer parents agree to participate in the study. (The investigators pay part of the day-care fees.) Children are assigned randomly from the pool of volunteers either to attend a day care of their choice or not to attend. Observers measure the degree of prosocial behavior before and after attending day care for nine months by observing the children on a playground.

   c. A superintendent wishes to get some idea of whether or not a bond issue will pass in a forthcoming election. Records listing real estate taxpayers are obtained from the county office. From this list, a random sample of 10 percent of 3,000 persons is called by phone two weeks before election day and asked whether they intend to vote yes or no.

   d. The Green County School Board decided that it wanted a status assessment of the ninth-graders' attitudes toward science. A questionnaire was designed and distributed in January to all ninth-grade science teachers. Each teacher was told to give the questionnaire within six weeks, to calculate mean scores for each question, and to return the questionnaires and results to the district office. The instructors were told to take only one class period for the questionnaires in order to minimize interference with the course. Sixty percent of the questionnaires were returned.

NOTE

1. Consider these sources:
American Educational Research Association. (1992). Ethical standards of the American Educational Research Association, *Educational Research, 21*, 23–26.
American Educational Research Association. (2002). Ethical principles of psychologists and code of conduct. *American Psychologist, 47* [Special insert].

American Psychological Association. (1982). *Ethical principles in the conduct of research with human participants*. Washington, DC: APA.
Strike, K. A., Anderson, M. S., Curren, R., van Geel, T., Pritchard, J., & Robertson, E. (2002). *Ethical standards of the American Educational Research Association: Cases and commentary*. Washington, DC: AERA. Available online: www.aera.net/about/policy/ethics.htm

Descriptive Statistics

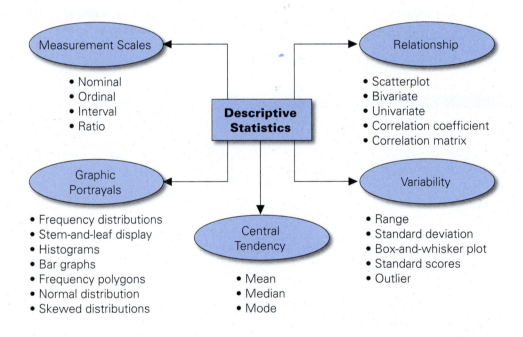

Measurement Scales

- Nominal
- Ordinal
- Interval
- Ratio

Relationship

- Scatterplot
- Bivariate
- Univariate
- Correlation coefficient
- Correlation matrix

Descriptive Statistics

Graphic Portrayals

- Frequency distributions
- Stem-and-leaf display
- Histograms
- Bar graphs
- Frequency polygons
- Normal distribution
- Skewed distributions

Central Tendency

- Mean
- Median
- Mode

Variability

- Range
- Standard deviation
- Box-and-whisker plot
- Standard scores
- Outlier

KEY TERMS

statistics	normal distribution
descriptive statistics	skewed
inferential statistics	positively skewed
measurement scales	negatively skewed
nominal	measures of variability
ordinal	range
interval	standard deviation
ratio	percentile rank
univariate	variance
bivariate	box-and-whisker plot
frequency distribution	standard scores
stem-and-leaf display	z-score
histogram	outlier
bar graph	scatterplot
frequency polygon	positive relationship
measures of central tendency	negative relationship
mean	correlation coefficient
median	intercorrelation matrix
mode	

This chapter explains the tools that are essential for understanding quantitative research (something many students find hard to get excited about). The procedures represent parsimonious ways to summarize and organize data that have been collected. The most frequently used descriptive statistical procedures (i.e., those that describe phenomena) are presented, including frequency distributions, measures of central tendency, measures of variability, and measures of relationship. The reasons for using each procedure are discussed and examples from published articles are provided to illustrate how results are reported.

INTRODUCTION TO DESCRIPTIVE STATISTICS

Quantitative research relies heavily on numbers in reporting results, sampling, and providing estimates of instrument reliability and validity. The numbers are usually accompanied by unrecognized strange words and even stranger symbols and are manipulated by something called *statistics*. Like magic, statistics lead to conclusions. Often, readers of research simply prefer to skip over anything related to statistics. In the words of a prominent specialist in educational measurement: "For most educators, mere contemplation of the term 'statistics' conjures up images akin to bubonic plague and the abolition of tenure" (Popham, 1981, p. 66).

Even though some statisticians may like the image just described, in truth, the fundamental concepts and principles of statistics are readily comprehensible. Advanced skills in mathematics are not a prerequisite to understanding statistics, and there is no need to memorize complex formulas. In fact, learning about statistics can actually be fun! (Consider the great new words learned that will be perfect for impressing friends and family.)

More seriously, there are important reasons for all educators to gain a functional command of statistical principles:

1. To understand and critique professional articles (for example, were appropriate statistical tools used?)
2. To improve evaluation of student learning

3. To conduct, even in modest and informal ways, research studies (for example, how should the results be analyzed?)
4. To understand evaluations of programs, personnel, and policies
5. To become better equipped as a citizen and consumer, making decisions based on quantitative data or arguments
6. To upgrade the education profession by providing standard skills to communicate, debate, and discuss research that has implications for educational practice

Types of Statistics

Statistics are methods of organizing and analyzing quantitative data. These methods are tools designed to help the researcher organize and interpret numbers derived from measuring a trait or variable. The mere presence of statistical procedures does not ensure high quality in the research. While the contribution of some results does depend on applying the correct statistical procedure, the quality of the research depends most on proper conceptualization, design, subject selection, instruments, and procedures. Statistics is an international language that only manipulates numbers. Statistics and numbers do not interpret themselves, and the meaning of the statistics is derived from the research design. Of course, the improper use of statistics invalidates the research, but the interpretation of statistical results depends on carefully designing and conducting the study—that is, it depends heavily on producing high-quality quantitative data.

There are two broad categories of statistical techniques: descriptive and inferential. **Descriptive statistics** transform a set of numbers or observations into indices that describe or characterize the data. Descriptive statistics (sometimes referred to as *summary statistics*) are thus used to summarize, organize, and reduce large numbers of observations. Usually, the reduction results in a few numbers, derived from mathematical formulas to represent all observations in each group of interest. Descriptive statistics portray and focus on *what is* with respect to the sample data—for example, What is the average reading grade level of the fifth graders in the school? How many teachers found the in-service valuable? What percentage of students want to go to college? and What is the relationship between socioeconomic status of children and the effectiveness of token reinforcers? The use of descriptive statistics is the most fundamental way to summarize data, and it is indispensable in interpreting the results of quantitative research.

Inferential statistics, on the other hand, are used to make inferences or predictions about the similarity of a sample to the population from which the sample is drawn. Since many research questions require the estimation of population characteristics from an available sample of subjects or behavior, inferential statistics are commonly used in reporting results. Chapter 11 discusses in greater detail the function and types of inferential statistics. Inferential statistics depend on descriptive statistics. Without a complete understanding of descriptive statistics, therefore, inferential statistics make very little sense. Figure 7.1 illustrates the relationship between descriptive and inferential statistics. It shows how a researcher would first take a sample from a population, use descriptive statistics to

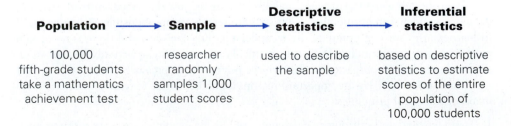

Population	Sample	Descriptive statistics	Inferential statistics
100,000 fifth-grade students take a mathematics achievement test	researcher randomly samples 1,000 student scores	used to describe the sample	based on descriptive statistics to estimate scores of the entire population of 100,000 students

FIGURE 7.1 **Relationship of Descriptive to Inferential Statistics**

describe the sample, and then use inferential statistics to estimate the true value of the test score for the population.

Researchers may choose from many types of descriptive statistics in characterizing a set of data. The choice usually depends on three factors: the type of measurement scale employed, assumptions about the data, and the purpose of the research. The purpose of the research, or *research problem,* actually depends on a knowledge of different statistical techniques, since each technique offers information for answering particular kinds of questions. Hence, each of the common descriptive techniques is presented here, with examples of the research problems it addresses.

Scales of Measurement

Measurement in education usually involves assigning numbers to things in order to differentiate one thing from another. Unlike the measurement of physical phenomena, however, such as weight, density, and length, researchers can use numbers in different ways for investigating problems. These different ways are based on four properties of numbers: (1) numbers can be distinct from one another (e.g., 10 is different from 13; 0 is different from −5); (2) numbers are relative to one another (e.g., 13 is larger than 10; −3 less than 0); (3) numbers can be related to each other in identified units (e.g., 10 is five units greater than 5); and (4) numbers can be related proportionately (e.g., 10 is twice as large as 5; 25 is to 5 as 30 is to 6).

These properties, in turn, determine what psychometricians refer to as **measurement scales,** or levels of measurement. There are four measurement scales: nominal, ordinal, interval, and ratio. These terms are often used to describe the nature of the measure, indicating, for example, that a nominal measure or nominal measurement was used.

Nominal   The first and most rudimentary level of measurement is called **nominal,** *categorical,* or *classificatory.* The word *nominal* implies *name,* which describes what this scale accomplishes—a naming of mutually exclusive categories of people, events, or other phenomena. Common examples of nominal levels include classifying on the basis of eye color, gender, political party affiliation, and type of reading group. The groups are simply names to differentiate them; no order is implied (i.e., one group does not come before or after another), and there is no indication of the way the groups differ from each other. Often, researchers assign numbers to the different groups (for example, yes = 1, no = 2, maybe = 3), but this is only for convenient coding of the groups in analyzing the data. Nominal data result in categorical variables, and results are reported as frequencies in each category.

Ordinal   The second type of measurement scale is called **ordinal,** and as the name implies, measurement of this type assumes that categories of the variable can theoretically be rank ordered from highest to lowest. Each value can thus be related to others as being equal to, greater than, or less than. In other words, there is an inherent order to the categories. Examples of ordinal measurement include ranking class members by means of grade-point average, ranking ideas from most important to least important, and using percentile ranks in achievement tests.

Interval   Interval measures share characteristics of ordinal scales and indicate equal intervals between each category. Interval scales give meaning to the difference between numbers by providing a constant unit of measurement. The difference or interval between 5 and 6, for example, is the same as the difference between 18 and 19. Percentile scores associated with the normal curve, for example, are not interval because the distance between percentile points varies depending on the percentiles compared. There is a greater difference between extreme percentiles (e.g., 2nd and 3rd or 95th and 96th) than between percentiles near the middle of the distribution. Examples of interval scales include Fahrenheit and Centigrade temperatures and most standardized achievement test scores.

Ratio   **Ratio** scales represent the most refined type of measurement. Ratio scales are ordinal and interval, and the numbers can be compared by ratios: that is, a number can be compared meaningfully by saying it is twice or three times another number or one-half or one-fourth of a number. Such observations as distance attained, strength expressed as weight lifted, or times in the mile run are ratio scale measurements. Most measurements in education, however, are not expressed as ratios. Educators think in terms of less than or greater than, not multiples (e.g., a student is more cooperative or less cooperative, not twice as cooperative or half as cooperative).

While it is not always easy to identify the scale of measurement of some variables, it is important to distinguish between nominal and higher levels. The use of many of the more common statistical procedures, such as the mean and variance, usually requires an interval or ratio scale of measurement, although an ordinal scale is often acceptable. The choice of other more advanced statistical procedures depends on whether the data are nominal or in the higher levels. If, for example, a researcher wants to compare minority and nonminority students on the basis of their choices of careers, the data are nominal and certain statistical procedures would be appropriate for analyzing them. If, on the other hand, these same students were being compared on achievement or attitudes toward school, a different set of statistical procedures would be appropriate because the scale of the achievement and attitude data are ordinal or interval. These differences will be discussed further in Chapter 11.

Figure 7.2 summarizes the characteristics and provides further examples of the four scales of measurement.

Types of Descriptive Analysis

There are several different ways to describe data, many of which will be familiar to you. One way to classify the methods is to determine whether they are univariate or bivariate. **Univariate** analysis is done to summarize data on a single characteristic or variable, usually the dependent variable. You probably already have an understanding of the univariate techniques, including the mean, median, and frequency distributions. Univariate analysis is especially important for descriptive studies.

Scale	Scale Characteristics	Examples
RATIO	Numbers represent equal amounts from an absolute zero. Scores can be compared as ratios or percentages.	Age, dollars, time, speed, class size
INTERVAL	Equal differences between numbers represent equal differences in the variable or attribute being measured.	Year (A.D.), °F, °C, IQ score
ORDINAL	Numbers represent rank order of the variable being measured.	Any ranked variable, percentile norms, social class, attitude scales
NOMINAL	Numbers distinguish among the categories. Numbers do not represent quantity or degree. Assignment of numbers to groups is arbitrary.	Sex, ethnicity, political party, personality type

FIGURE 7.2   **Measurement Scales**
Source: From Glass, G. V., & Hopkins, K. D. (1996). *Statistical Methods in Education and Psychology,* 3rd ed. Published by Allyn and Bacon, Boston, MA. Copyright © 1996 by Pearson Education. Reprinted by permission of the publisher.

TABLE 7.1 Types of Descriptive Analysis	
Univariate	**Bivariate**
Frequency distribution	Correlation
Histogram	Comparing frequencies
Frequency polygon	Comparing percentages
Stem-and-leaf display	Comparing means
Percentage	Comparing medians
Mean	
Median	
Mode	
Range	
Standard deviation	
Box-and-whisker plot	

Bivariate analysis is used when there is a correlation among variables or when different groups are compared. Thus, two variables are used for correlation (e.g., age and strength), and two or more categories are used for comparisons (e.g., males compared to females on self-concept; differences in achievement among African American, European American, and Hispanic American students; or trends in graduation rates for several school districts). The most common univariate and bivariate procedures are listed in Table 7.1.

GRAPHIC PORTRAYALS OF DATA

When data are collected, the observations must be organized so that the researcher can easily and correctly interpret the results. This section presents three common methods of representing group data.

Frequency Distribution or Count: A Picture of a Group

In most studies, there are many different scores, and if these scores are arrayed (arranged) without regard to their values, as in Table 7.2, it is difficult to make sense out of the data. The simplest organization of the scores is to list them from highest to lowest and create what is called a *rank-order distribution*. The rank-order distribution is transformed to a **frequency distribution** by indicating the number of times each score was attained, as indicated in Table 7.3.

It is also common to combine scores into class intervals and tally the number of scores in each interval, as indicated in Excerpt 7.1. Intervals are especially useful for data in which few of the numbers are the same (e.g., ranking of states on median income).

Frequency distributions indicate quickly the most and least frequently occurring scores, the general shape of the distribution (e.g., clusters of scores at certain places or scores spread out evenly), and whether any scores are isolated from the others (i.e., outliers).

Along with the frequency of scores, researchers often summarize results by the percentage of responses for each score or interval (see Excerpt 7.1) and for subjects that provide different answers. The latter use is illustrated in Excerpt 7.2, which shows the

TABLE 7.2 Unorganized Examination Scores of 50 Students

47	37	41	50	45
39	49	44	43	40
42	43	42	46	40
44	45	47	45	45
36	45	46	48	44
42	48	40	43	37
46	45	45	44	42
43	43	42	43	41
44	45	42	44	36
44	38	44	46	42

TABLE 7.3 Frequency Distribution of Scores in Table 7.2

Scores in Rank Order	Tallies	Frequency (f)
50	1	1
49	1	1
48	11	2
47	11	2
46	1111	4
45	1111 111	8
44	1111 111	8
43	1111 1	6
42	1111 11	7
41	11	2
40	111	3
39	1	1
38	1	1
37	11	2
36	11	2
		$n = 50$

EXCERPT 7.1 Frequency Distribution

During an academic year, new clients at a university counseling center were recruited to participate in this study. All new clients requesting individual counseling services were eligible to participate. Ninety-four new clients (the majority of new clients at the center) agreed to participate. . . . The ages of participants ranged from 18 years to 47 years ($Mdn = 21.00$, $M = 22.4$ . . .).

Table 2 presents a frequency distribution of counseling duration. Participants completed from 1 to 28 sessions ($Mdn = 3.0$, $M = 4.6$ . . .). As evident in the table, most participants completed a relatively small number of sessions.

TABLE 2 Frequency Distribution of Counseling Duration

No. of Sessions Completed	f	%	Σ%
1–3	54	57.4	57.4
4–6	22	23.4	80.8
7–9	8	8.5	89.3
10–12	4	4.3	93.6
14–17	3	3.2	96.8
18–28	3	3.2	100.0

Note. $Mdn = 3$, Mode = 1, $M = 4.6$

EXCERPT 7.2 Use of Percentages to Report Results

TABLE 2 Percentages of Elementary Teachers' Responses to Selected Items for Mathematics Assessment Practices and Grading

Question	Not at all	Very Little	Some	Quite a bit	Extensively	Completely
Factors Contributing to Grades						
Improvement of performance since the beginning of the year	13	17	38	21	7	2
Student effort—how much students tried to learn	6	14	44	27	7	2
Ability levels of students	10	13	31	24	19	4
Academic performance compared with other factors	2	3	12	29	44	10
Types of Assessments Used						
Objective assessments	2	8	28	36	21	5
Performance assessments	14	23	38	17	7	1
Cognitive Level of Assessments						
Assessments that measure student reasoning	0	2	25	44	25	4

Source: From McMillan, J. H., Myran, S., & Workman, D. (2002). Elementary teachers' classroom assessment and grading practices. *Journal of Educational Research, 95*(4), 203–213.

percentages of responses to different points on a scale. Actual frequencies can be calculated by multiplying each percentage by the total n.

ALERT! Be careful with percentages. The actual number of cases can increase but show a lower percentage.

Stem-and-Leaf Displays

Another technique for showing the distribution of scores is called a **stem-and-leaf display.** The "stem" is shown on a vertical column and represents the first number of each score. The "leaf" contains the last digit(s) of each score in the stem. Excerpt 7.3 presents an example of a stem-and-leaf display. It shows that there is one score in the distribution with a value of 0.78 (i.e., 0.7 stem and 8), one score that is 0.53, one that is 0.54, and two scores with values of 0.34.

Histograms and Bar Graphs

Frequency data are often effectively displayed pictorially. One type of illustration uses columns in a two-dimensional graph to represent the frequency of occurrence of each

TABLE 3 Stem and Leaf Display of Unweighted Achievement Effect Sizes

Stem	Leaf
+.7	8
+.5	34
+.4	3
+.3	2448
+.2	22359
+.1	002223
+.0	3479
−.0	033446779
−.1	00
−.2	014
−.3	7
−.4	
−.5	6

Note. Effect sizes (*d* indexes) are based on each district as an independent sample (*n* = 39). The dotted line represents the value zero; the wavy line indicates a break in the distribution (there is no +.6 value in the stem column).

Source: From Cooper, H., Valentine, J. C., Charlton, K., & Melson, A. (2003). The effects of modified school calendars on student achievement and on school and community attitudes. *Review of Educational Research, 73*(1), 1–52. Copyright © 2003 by the American Educational Research Association. Reproduced with permission of the publisher.

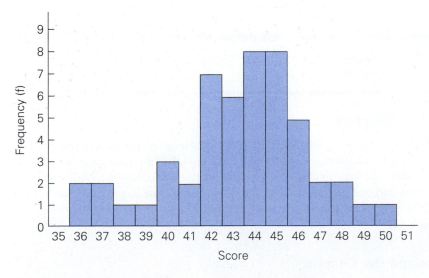

FIGURE 7.3 Histogram of Scores from Table 7.2

score or interval. This way of presenting a frequency distribution is called a **histogram.** The data from Tables 7.2 and 7.3 are presented as a histogram in Figure 7.3. In this example, the vertical dimension on the graph lists the frequencies of the scores, and the horizontal dimension rank orders the scores from lowest to highest. The columns are drawn in the graph to correspond with the results. In similar fashion, Excerpt 7.4 shows how histograms can depict results in an article.

A **bar graph** looks very much like a histogram, with columns that present an image of the findings. In a bar graph, however, the ordering of the columns is arbitrary, whereas in a histogram, there is an order from least to most. Bar graphs are used, then, with nominal variables such as gender, state, political party affiliation, and similar categorical variables that have no implied order. A bar graph is illustrated in Excerpt 7.5.

Histograms are effective because they provide an easily comprehended image of results. However, the image may be distorted by manipulating the spacing of numbers along the vertical dimension of the graph. The intervals between score frequencies can vary, and the size of the units that are used can be changed to give different images. For example, a crafty researcher can make a very small difference appear great by increasing the space between measurement units. Consider the two graphs in Figure 7.4. Each graph has summarized the same data, but the visual results are different.

Frequency Polygons

Another way to illustrate a frequency distribution is to use a **frequency polygon.** A frequency polygon is very similar to a bar graph except that single points rather than bars, are graphed and these points are then connected by a line. Figure 7.5 shows the example data in a frequency polygon. Notice that this representation is very similar to Figure 7.3.

Finally, it is also useful to represent the distribution graphically by curving the straight lines of a frequency polygon. The well-known normal curve, discussed later in this chapter, is an example of using this technique.

EXCERPT 7.4 Histogram

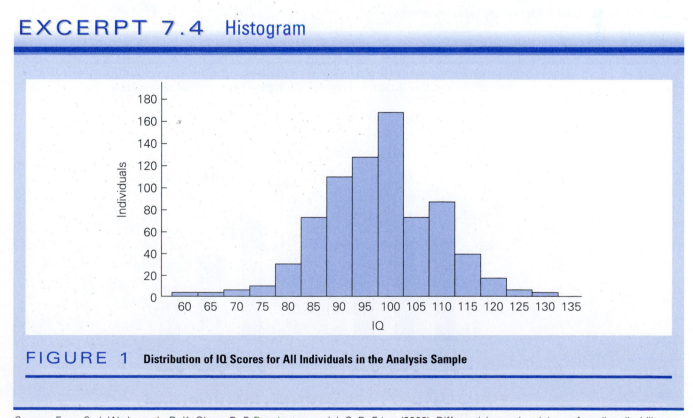

FIGURE 1   **Distribution of IQ Scores for All Individuals in the Analysis Sample**

Source: From S. J. Wadsworth, R. K. Olson, B. F. Pennington, and J. C. DeFries. (2000). Differential genetic etiology of reading disability as a function of IQ. *Journal of Learning Disabilities. 33*(2), p. 195. Copyright © 2000 by PRO-ED, Inc. Adapted with permission.

EXCERPT 7.5 Bar Graph

High School Grades of College Freshmen

The high school grade point averages of students entering four-year colleges and universities of all types continue to increase, according to an annual survey of freshmen by the University of California, Los Angeles. Overall, a record high of 45.7 percent of freshmen reported earning A averages in high school in the fall 2002 survey. Students entering private universities reported the highest grades.

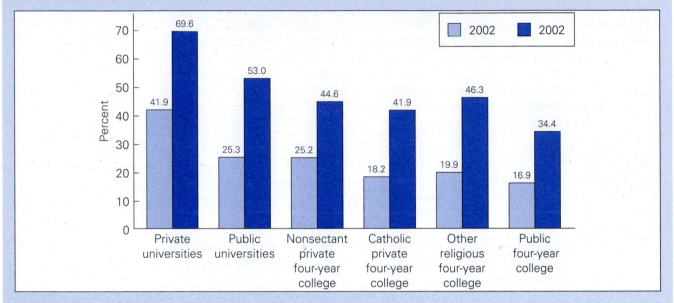

Entering Freshmen with A Averages by Type of Institution

Source: From "The American Freshman: National Norms for Fall 2002," Higher Education Research Institute, UCLA Graduate School of Education and Information Studies, 3005 Moore Hall, Box 951521, Los Angeles, CA 90095-1521. Reprinted by permission.

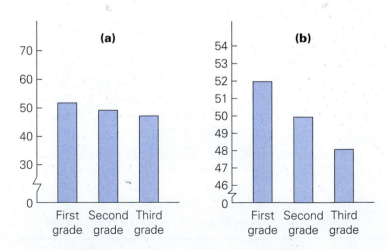

FIGURE 7.4 **Graphs of Reading Scores of First-, Second-, and Third-Graders**

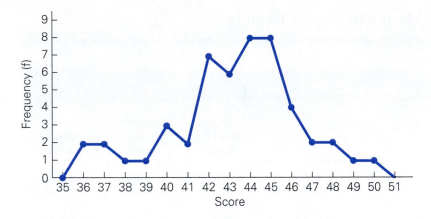

FIGURE 7.5   **Frequency Polygon of Scores from Table 7.2**

MEASURES OF CENTRAL TENDENCY

For most sets of data, it is useful to get some idea of the typical or average score or obser-vation in addition to knowing the frequency distribution. While the word *average* has many connotations, in research, only the *mean* refers to the average score. Two other indices, the *median* and the *mode*, also provide information about typical scores of a group. Together, these three indices are referred to as **measures of central tendency.** Each pro-vides a numerical index of the typical score of a distribution. (Calculations for these and other descriptive statistics can be found in Appendix D.)

Mean

The **mean** (symbolized by $\bar{X}$ or M) is simply the arithmetic average of all the scores. It is calculated by summing all the scores and then dividing the sum by the number of scores. If, for example, we have a distribution of 5, 8, 9, and 2, the mean is 6 (5 + 8 + 9 + 2 = 24; 24 ÷ 4 = 6). The mean is the most frequently used measure of central tendency because every score is used in computing it. The weakness of the mean is that when a distribution contains extremely high or low scores (i.e., outliers), those very untypical of the rest of the distribution, the mean is pulled toward the extreme score. If, for example, a distribu-tion contained scores of 4, 5, 7, and 40, the mean would be 14. Since in this case, most of the scores are considerably lower than 14, the mean is somewhat misleading with respect to central tendency.

The mean is very frequently reported in quantitative research reports and is essential to the interpretation of results in which groups are compared with each other. While some researchers and statisticians maintain that the mean should only be calculated when the data are at interval or ratio level and scores in the population are normally distributed, these assumptions routinely are not met in published articles, where only ordinal level data are provided and the size of the sample is large. Excerpt 7.6 illustrates the use of means in an article. In this use of bivariate statistics, Russian and American student attitudes, per-ceptions, and tendencies toward cheating are compared.

Median

The **median** (symbolized by Mdn) is that point that divides a rank-ordered distribution into halves that contain an equal number of scores. Fifty percent of the scores thus lie below the median and 50 percent of the scores above it. The median is unaffected by the actual values of the scores. This is an advantage when a distribution contains atypically

EXCERPT 7.6 Use of Means to Report Results

TABLE 2 American and Russian Business Students' Beliefs about Cheating

	Overall Mean	American Students n = 443	Russian Students n = 174
Percentage of students believed to cheat on exams	36.53	24.18	69.59*
Most students cheat on exams	3.45	2.80	5.12*
Most students cheat on out-of-class assignments	4.09	3.88	4.64*
Cheating on one exam is not so bad	2.90	2.34	4.36*
OK to tell someone in later section about an exam	4.71	4.07	6.36*
Giving someone your past exams is cheating	2.26	2.02	2.87*
Using an exam from a prior semester is cheating	2.65	2.23	3.02*
Instructor must make sure students do not cheat	3.68	3.88	3.18*
Instructor discussing issues tied to cheating reduces amount of cheating	3.92	4.27	3.01*

Note: The first item in the table is a percentage (e.g., 36.53%). All other items are mean ratings using a seven-point scale, where 1 = Strongly disagree and 7 = Strongly agree.
*t = test of mean differences between nationalities significant at $p < 0.000$.

Source: From Lupton, R. A., & Chapman, K. J. (2002). Russian and American college students' attitudes, perceptions, and tendencies towards cheating. Educational Research, 44, 17–27. Reprinted by permission.

large or small scores. For example, the median of the set of scores 10, 15, 16, 19, and 105 is 16, since half the scores are above 16 and half below. Sixteen would thus be a better indicator of central tendency than the mean, which is 33. If a distribution contains an even number of scores, the median is the midpoint between the two middle scores (e.g., for the scores 2, 2, 4, 7, 8, and 12, the median is 5.5).

Since the value of the median is based only on the percentages of scores higher than and lower than the midpoint, the median is the preferred measure of central tendency when describing highly skewed data. The median is used to describe data that may have extreme scores, such as income level in the United States. Medians also are often employed to divide one group of respondents into two groups of equal numbers. A researcher may, for example, get an indication of perceived degree of success from each respondent on a 7-point scale (extreme success = 7, extreme failure = 1). If the researcher wanted to divide the group of subjects into those with high and low self-perceptions of success, the median could be used. This procedure is called a *median-split technique*.

Mode

The **mode** is simply the score that occurs most frequently in a distribution. As such, it is a crude index of central tendency and is rarely used in educational research. It is useful only when there is an interest in knowing the most common score or observation or when the data are in nominal form. The word *mode* is used more frequently, perhaps, to describe a distribution by indicating that the distribution is bimodal (two modes) or trimodal (three modes). These terms are used even when, technically, there is only one mode but at least two scores that have definitely higher frequencies than the rest.

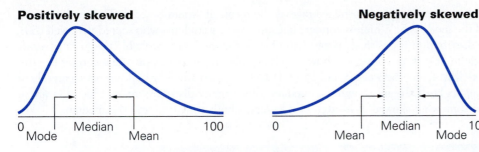

Positively skewed

0 Mode Median Mean 100

Negatively skewed

0 Mean Median Mode 100

FIGURE 7.6   **Skewed Distributions**

Relationships among Measures of Central Tendency

As long as a distribution of scores is relatively symmetrical, the mean, median, and mode will be about the same. In what is referred to as a **normal distribution,** these indices are exactly the same. The normal distribution (see Figure 7.11 on page 169) forms a bell-shaped symmetrical curve. The normal curve is the theoretical distribution that is used to transform data and calculate many statistics. While many educational variables—for example, large numbers of achievement scores—are normally distributed, the data from a single research study may be distributed unevenly; that is, the distributions are unsymmetrical, and the scores tend to bunch up at one end of the distribution or the other.

Such distributions are called **skewed,** and with skewed distributions, the choice of measure of central tendency becomes more important. Distributions are **positively skewed** if most of the scores are at the low end of the distribution with a few high scores and **negatively skewed** if most scores are located at the high end. To remember the difference between positive and negative skew, think of the curved shape of the distribution forming an arrow or a pointer. If it forms an arrow that points in a positive or higher direction, the distribution is positively skewed, and if it points in a negative or lower direction, the distribution is negatively skewed. That is, using the median or mode as a reference point, the mean is higher in a positively skewed distribution and lower in a negatively skewed distribution. Actually, you can think of the mean as being either positively or negatively skewed in relation to the median. In Figure 7.6, positively and negatively skewed distributions are illustrated with corresponding means, medians, and modes. Notice that the mean in each distribution is farther toward the tail of the distribution than the median or mode, and the mode is farthest from the tail.

To further illustrate this relationship, consider the following example. Suppose a teacher wants to report an average reading score for his class. He has a reading score for each of 20 students, ranging from 5 to 80. The distribution of scores is represented in Table 7.4.

TABLE 7.4   Frequency Distribution of Reading Scores

Scores	(f)
5	8
10	4
12	2
15	2
80	4
	$n = 20$

If the teacher reports the average as the mean, it would be 22.7. The median is 10, and the mode is 5. Which is correct? Because of a few students who scored very well (80), the distribution is positively skewed and hence the median is probably the most accurate single indicator. In such cases, however, it is probably best to report the mean for the students who scored between 5 and 15 (8.4) and to report the four high scores separately or to report both the mean and the median. Since many distributions in education are at least somewhat skewed, it is often best to report both the mean and the median.

MEASURES OF VARIABILITY

Central tendency is only one index that can be used to represent a group of scores. In order to provide a full description, a second statistical measure is also needed. This statistic is referred to as a measure of variability. **Measures of variability** show how spread out the distribution of scores is from the mean of the distribution or how much, on the average, scores differ from the mean. Variability measures are also referred to in general terms as measures of *dispersion, scatter,* and *spread.*

The need for a measure of dispersion is illustrated in Figure 7.7. This figure shows how two classrooms with the same mean score can actually be very different. In Class B, the students are rather homogeneous, or similar to each other, with few high- or low-achieving students. In Class A, however, the teacher has a great range of achievement, or a heterogeneous group of students whose scores spread from 55 to 100.

As another example, suppose Ernie is going to bet on Saturday's basketball game between the Bombers and the Dunkers. The sports section of the newspaper lacks the statistics on individual players, but the sports writer reports that both teams have approximately equal height: the average height is 6' 6½" and 6' 7½", respectively, for the Bombers and Dunkers. With only the mean to help decide, Ernie places a bet on the Dunkers. When Ernie sees the program with the heights of the players, he discovers a shortcoming of the mean.

Bombers	Dunkers
Gerber, guard—6'0"	Regen, guard—6'5"
Bosher, guard—6'3"	Lambiotte, guard—6'6"
Davis, forward—6'5"	Hambrick, forward—6'8"
Gallagher, forward—6'7"	Lang, forward—6'9"
Robinson, center—7'3"	Wergin, center—6'10"
$\bar{X} = 6'6\frac{1}{2}"$	$\bar{X} = 6'7\frac{1}{2}"$

As the Bombers' offense proceeds to take advantage of Robinson's height over Wergin's to score, Ernie realizes that the mean fails to tell about the characteristics of the distribution. The Dunkers have little variability, while the Bombers have high variability, and so Ernie loses the bet!

Variability, then, tells us about the difference between the scores of the distribution. While we can use such words as *high, low, great, little,* and *much* to describe the degree of variability, it is necessary to have more precise indices. Two common measures of variability are *range* and *standard deviation.*

Range

The **range** is the most obvious measure of dispersion. It is simply the difference between the highest and lowest scores in the distribution. If, for example, the lowest of 30 scores on a test was 65 and the highest score 90, the range would be 25 (90 − 65 = 25). Since

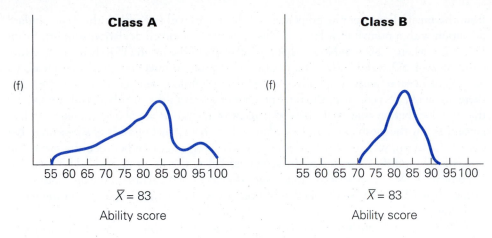

Class A

(f)

55 60 65 70 75 80 85 90 95 100

$\bar{X} = 83$

Ability score

Class B

(f)

55 60 65 70 75 80 85 90 95 100

$\bar{X} = 83$

Ability score

FIGURE 7.7   **Score Dispersion**

there are only two scores involved in calculating the range, it is very simple to obtain. However, it is also a very crude measure of dispersion and can be misleading if there is an atypically high or low score. The range also fails to indicate anything about the variability of scores around the mean of the distribution. Sometimes, researchers will use the *interquartile range*, which indicates the dispersion among the middle half of the scores.

Standard Deviation

The **standard deviation** is a numerical index that indicates the average variability of the scores. It tells us, in other words, about the distance, on the average, of the scores from the mean. A distribution that has a relatively heterogeneous set of scores that spread out widely from the mean (e.g., Class A of Figure 7.7) will have a larger standard deviation than a homogeneous set of scores that cluster around the mean (Class B of Figure 7.7). The first step in calculating the standard deviation (abbreviated SD, σ [sigma], or s) is to find the distance between each score and the mean (see Figure 7.8), thus determining the amount that each score deviates, or differs, from the mean. In one sense, the standard deviation is simply the average of all the deviation scores, the average distance of the scores from the mean.

For any set of scores, then, a standard deviation can be computed that will be unique to the distribution and indicates the amount, on the average, that the set of scores deviates from the mean. (Appendix D reviews the steps for computing the standard deviation, which are not complex.) The most common convention in reporting the standard deviation is to indicate that one standard deviation is equal to some number (e.g., $SD = 15.0$; $\sigma = 3.40$). One standard deviation added to and subtracted from the mean has a special meaning; it tells us about the distance that most but not all of the scores are

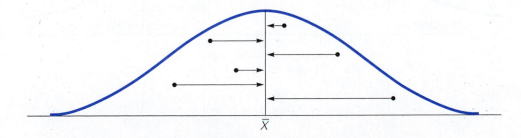

$\bar{X}$

FIGURE 7.8   **Illustration of Distance of Each Score from the Mean**

from the mean. For example, 68 percent of the scores will fall within the first standard deviation with a normal distribution. This property of standard deviation is illustrated in Figure 7.9, where 1 *SD* = 5. Notice that on both sides of the mean (15), there is a line that designates –1 *SD* and +1 *SD*. The negative and positive directions from the mean are equivalent in score units (i.e., both – and +1 *SD* = 5 units), and between –1 and +1 *SD*, there are about 68 percent of the total number of scores in the distribution. If we assume that the distribution is normal, then 50 percent of the scores are above the mean and 50 percent below the mean. Now, since we know there is an equal number of scores on either side of the mean, we know that 34 percent of the scores must be between the mean and – or + 1 *SD*, and if 50 percent of the scores are below the mean and we add 34 percent by going up +1 *SD*, then we know that about 84 percent of the scores of the distribution are below +1 *SD*. Similarly, if we subtract 34 from 50, we know that 16 percent of the scores are below –1 *SD*.

When we indicate that a certain percentage of the scores is at or below a particular score, we are referring to the **percentile rank** of the score. If, for example, a score of 38 is at the 87th percentile, it means that 87 percent of the scores are the same as or lower than 38. In other words, only 12 percent of the scores are higher than 38. With normal distributions, +1 *SD* is always at the 84th percentile and –1 *SD* is at the 16th percentile.

The interpretation of 1 *SD* is always the same with regard to the percentages of scores within certain points of a normal distribution. Because the numerical units used to represent scores change, however, the standard deviation can equal 15 in one distribution and 0.32 in another distribution. Or in a circumstance with the same numerical units but two different distributions, the standard deviations will be unique to each distribution. That is, one *SD* has a meaning that is constant for any distribution regardless of the actual value of 1 *SD* for each distribution. For example, in Figure 7.10, two distributions are illustrated. Distribution A has a large standard deviation and

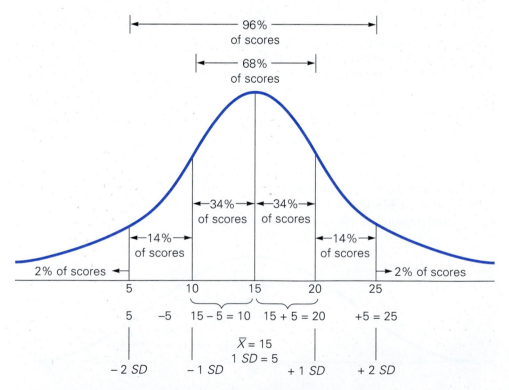

FIGURE 7.9   **Relation of Standard Deviation to Percentile Rank in a Normal Distribution**

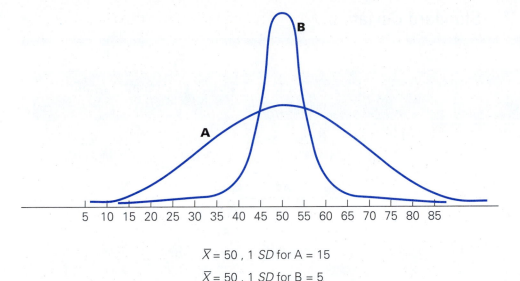

$$\bar{X} = 50 \text{ , } 1 \text{ } SD \text{ for A} = 15$$
$$\bar{X} = 50 \text{ , } 1 \text{ } SD \text{ for B} = 5$$

FIGURE 7.10   **Comparison of Distributions with Different Standard Deviations**

distribution, B a small one; a score of 65 in distribution A has the same percentile rank as 55 in distribution B.

Along with the mean, the standard deviation is an excellent way to indicate the nature of the distribution of a set of scores. Standard deviation is typically reported in research with the mean. A measure of dispersion related to the standard deviation is termed the **variance** of a distribution (noted by σ^2 or s^2; thus, the standard deviation is equal to the square root of the variance). The term *variance*, however, is usually used as a general term in regard to dispersion (e.g., in stating that the variance is large or small) and is rarely reported as a specific number to indicate variability.

ALERT!   The term *variance* can refer either to a specific number or to a description of one aspect of a set of scores.

Excerpts 7.7 and 7.8 are examples of the ways that standard deviations can be reported. Standard deviations are almost always reported along with means. In Excerpt 7.7, for each of several factors used in grading students, there is a mean and standard deviation for middle school teachers, a mean and standard deviation for high school teachers, and means and standard deviations for the total sample. Notice how the values of standard deviation range from 0.76 to 1.32, showing different degrees of variance. Means at the ends of the scale are associated with smaller standard deviations. In Likert-type scales such as this one, standard deviations about 1 are typical. In Excerpt 7.8, the standard deviations are in parentheses.

Box-and-Whisker Plot

The **box-and-whisker plot** is used to give a picture or image of the variability. A "box" is formed for each variable. The size of this rectangular box is determined by the first and third quartiles of the distribution (i.e., 25th to 75th percentiles). The "whiskers" are lines drawn from the ends of the rectangle to the 10th and 90th percentiles. Sometimes additional points are included to show extreme high or low scores. The box-and-whisker plot in Excerpt 7.9 shows how U.S. student achievement in mathematics compares with Japanese student achievement. Notice the wider variation of the achievement of U.S. students.

EXCERPT 7.7 Standard Deviation

TABLE 12 Means and Standard Deviations of Items of Factors Used in Grading Practices by Secondary Teachers[1]

Factors	Middle (N = 630) Mean	SD	High (N = 846) Mean	SD	Total (N = 1476) Mean	SD
Disruptive student performance	1.50	.83	1.60	.91	1.56	.88
Improve since the beginning of the year	2.86	1.14	2.83	1.12	2.85	1.13
Student effort—how much the student tried to learn	3.31	1.13	3.16	1.10	3.23	1.11
Ability levels of the students	3.38	1.33	3.43	1.28	3.41	1.30
Work habits and neatness	2.80	1.07	2.68	1.06	2.73	1.07
Academic performance as opposed to other factors	4.37	1.08	4.34	1.09	4.35	1.08
Specific learning objectives mastered	4.38	.92	4.35	.91	4.37	.92
Degree to which the student pays attention and/or participates in class	3.12	1.11	3.20	1.12	3.17	1.12
Inclusion of 0s in determining final percentage correct	3.61	1.29	3.90	1.32	3.77	1.12
Extra credit for academic performance	2.66	1.18	2.54	1.06	2.60	1.11

[1]A six point scale was used, where 1 = not at all and 6 = completely.

Source: McMillan, J. H., & Workman, D. (1998). Teachers' Classroom Assessment and Grading Practices. Richmond, VA: Metropolitan Educational Research Consortium and Virginia Commonwealth University.

Standard Scores

You may have observed that it is cumbersome to analyze several distributions if the means and standard deviations are different for each distribution. To alleviate this problem and expedite interpretation, the raw score distributions are often converted to standard scores. **Standard scores** have constant normative or relative meaning. They are scores that are obtained from the mean and standard deviation of the raw score distribution.

Because, as we have seen, a normal distribution has certain properties that are useful for comparing one person's score with the score of others, by converting to normalized standard scores, the normal curve properties can be assumed. Thus, raw score distributions with different means and standard deviations that are difficult to compare can be transformed to the same standard scores and compared easily. Since standard scores are linear transformations, it is conceivable that a small raw score difference is exaggerated when converted to standard scores. For example, the SAT has a standard score mean of 500 and standard deviation of 100, while the raw scores are much lower. Thus, a raw score difference of 2 or 3 questions may result in a standard score difference of 10 to 20 points.

EXCERPT 7.8 Standard Deviation

Means and Standard Deviations for All Variables

Dependent Variables

Any science career	4.40	(1.55)
Physical science professions[1]	4.24	(1.79)
Health science professions	4.56	(2.01)
Human services professions	4.22	(1.77)

Independent Variables

Science GPA[2]	3.66	(.48)
Friends' support	5.69	(1.08)
Number of science/math activities[3]	1.73	(1.32)
Number of nonscience activities[4]	9.74	(3.67)
Mothers' perceptions of child's science ability	6.10	(1.05)
Mothers' valuing of science for females	4.57	(1.04)
Adolescents' interest in biology	5.10	(1.43)
Adolescent's interest in physical science	4.75	(1.40)

[1]Professional includes jobs requiring bachelor's degrees and advanced degrees. [2]Range = 1–4. [3]Range = 0–5. [4]Range = 2–21.

Source: From Jacobs, J. E., Finken, L. L., Griffin, N. L., & Wright, J. D. (1998). The career plans of science-talented rural adolescent girls. *American Educational Research Journal, 35*(4), 681–704. Copyright © 1998 by the American Educational Research Association. Reproduced with permission of the publisher.

The **z-score** is the most basic standard score, with a mean of 0 and a standard deviation of 1. Thus, a z-score of 11 is at the 84th percentile for a normal distribution, 21 is at the 16th percentile, and 22 is at the 2nd percentile. Other standard scores are linear transformations from the z-score, with arbitrarily selected means and standard deviations. That is, it is possible to choose any mean and any standard deviation. Most IQ tests, for example, use 100 as the mean and 15 to 16 as the standard deviation. The resultant IQ score is a standard score. (The ratio IQ, mental age divided by chronological age × 100, is rarely used today.) Figure 7.11 shows a normal distribution, standard deviations, percentiles, and some common standard scores.

Research Navigator.com

7.1 Connections
among Values
Accession No.: 11650478

Outliers

An **outlier** (or fringelier) refers to a data point that falls far outside the main distribution of scores. Depending on how extreme it is and the total number of scores in the distribution (i.e., the fewer the scores, the bigger the impact), an outlier can distort statistical analyses that include actual values of all the scores, such as the mean and standard deviation. Although some researchers rely on a visual display to identify extreme scores, outliers are typically identified as data points that are three standard deviations from the mean. Osborne and Overbay (2004) point out three deleterious effects of outliers: (1) they increase the standard deviation, which exaggerates variance; (2) they cause the

EXCERPT 7.9 Box-and-Whisker Plot

Given the differences in the patterns of coverage of algebra between these U.S. course types, what happens when U.S. achievement in algebra is disaggregated by course type?

Figure 3 presents such a disaggregation for class-level posttest scores—extended to include the parallel posttest achievement for Japan—and shows a striking pattern.

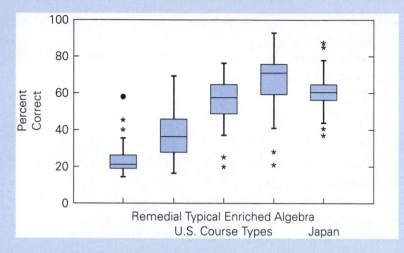

FIGURE 3 United States and Japan: Posttest achievement in Population A Algebra (*Note:* In boxplots like those found in [this figure] . . . , the length of the box, the rectangle bounded by the "hinges," represents the proportion of the distribution that falls between the 25th and 75th percentiles. The line across the box represents the median. The length of the "whiskers" represents the min and the max or the adjacent outermost value,

$$1.5 = (pctile_{75} - pctile_{25}),$$

If this is less than the min and the max. The * and the • represent extreme values.

distribution to decrease normality (which is an assumption for using many statistics); and (3) they can bias results, leading to erroneous conclusions.

Outliers are like bad apples: One in a basket of good apples spoils the whole bunch. What do we do with them? If it's clear on further investigation that the scores are invalid (e.g., a mistake in scoring or recording), then they should be corrected or dropped. When an outlier is valid, however, there is no consensus on what to do. Some researchers maintain that valid outliers should be dropped, while others believe that they should be included. A reasonable compromise to these choices is to conduct the statistical analyses twice—once with the outlier and once without it.

ALERT! Always check your data set for outliers.

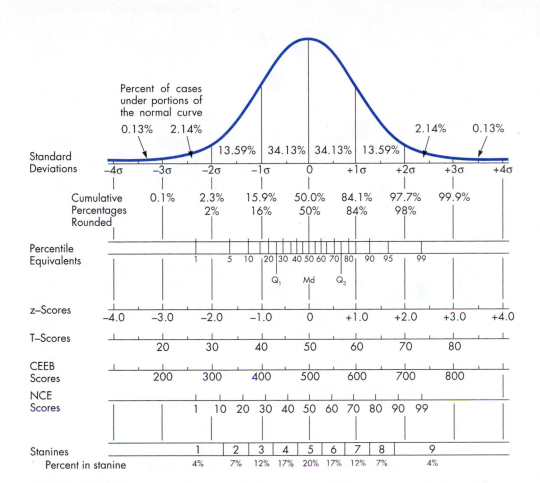

FIGURE 7.11   **Normal Curve, Standard Deviations, Percentiles, and Selected Standard Scores**

Source: Seashore, Harold G. (1980). Methods of expressing test scores, in *Test Service Notebook 148.* New York: The Psychological Corporation. Reproduced from Test Service Bulletin No. 148, January 1955, updated 1980. Courtesy of Harcourt Assessment, Inc.

MEASURES OF RELATIONSHIP

Up to this point, we have been discussing descriptive statistics that are used to summarize or give a picture of groups on one variable at a time. There are, however, many questions of interest that depend on the way two or more variables are related to each other—for instance, are brighter students more motivated? If we increase the frequency of reinforcement, will the reinforced or target behavior also increase? Is there a relationship between self-concept and achievement? If students exert more effort in studying, will they feel better about their achievement? In each instance, two variables are measured for each subject in the group.

Scatterplot

The most fundamental measure of relationship is called a *scatterplot, scatter diagram,* or *scattergram.* The **scatterplot** is a graphic representation of the relationship, achieved by forming a visual array of the intersection of each subject's scores on the two variables. As illustrated in Figure 7.12, one variable is rank ordered on the horizontal axis (age, in this example) and the second variable is rank ordered on the vertical axis (weight). Each subject's scores are indicated next to the graph in random order, and the intersections are

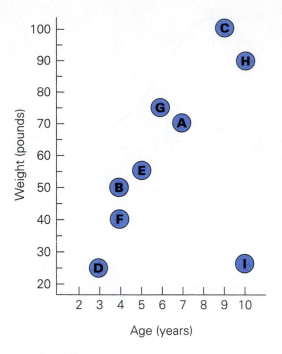

Subject	Age	Weight
Ryann (A)	7	70
Jessica (B)	4	50
Amanda (C)	9	100
Meghan (D)	3	25
Katie (E)	5	55
Cristina (F)	4	40
Emma (G)	6	75
Jan (H)	10	90
Helen (I)	10	25

FIGURE 7.12 Scatterplot

Research Navigator.com

7.2 Curvilinear Scattergrams
Accession No.: 4781122

noted by the letter assigned each subject. Together, the intersections form a pattern that provides a general indication of the nature of the relationship. Obviously, as children grow older their weight increases, and in such cases, the relationship is said to be positive or direct. Thus, with a **positive relationship,** as the value of one variable increases, so does the value of the second variable. Conversely, as the value of one variable decreases, the value of the other variable also decreases.

Scatterplots are useful in identifying outliers. For instance, in Figure 7.12, Helen was 10 years old and reported a weight of 25 pounds, which is very different from what is represented in points A through H. Scatter diagrams also provide a first hint about whether the relationship is linear or curvilinear (see Figure 7.13). (The usual approach in graphing relationships is to use dots, not circles, within the graph at the intersections.)

Several different types of patterns can emerge in scatterplots. When one variable decreases as the other increases (e.g., the number of miles on a tire and the depth of remaining tread), there is a **negative** (or *inverse*) **relationship.** If there is no pattern at all in the graph, there is no relationship. Figure 7.13 illustrates different scatter diagrams. Notice the curvilinear relationship in Figure 7.13(d). Curvilinear relationships are not uncommon but are usually detected only by plotting the scores. An example of a curvilinear relationship might be anxiety level and test performance. Performance could often be low during either high- or low-level anxiety and high for medium-level anxiety.

The direction of the pattern in the scatterplot, then, indicates whether there is a relationship and whether the relationship is positive, negative, or curvilinear. If a line is drawn through the plotted dots to minimize the distance of each dot to the line, then the degree of clustering around the line indicates the strength of the relationship. Plots that have mostly scattered dots have weak or low relationships, while dots clustered near the line indicate a strong or high relationship. The strength of the relationship is independent of its direction. Dots clustered so tightly as to form a straight line represent a perfect relationship (maximum strength). Correlations thus indicate three things: whether there is any relationship at all, the direction of the relationship, and the strength of the relationship.

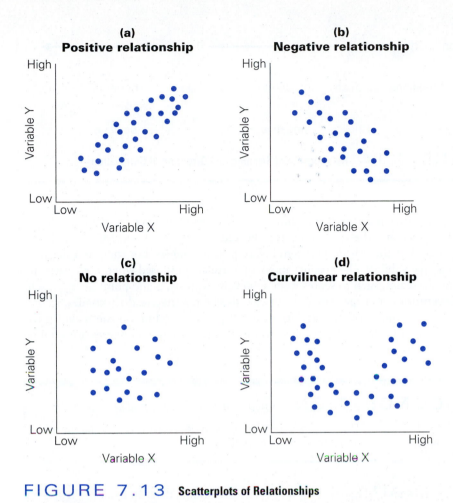

FIGURE 7.13   Scatterplots of Relationships

ALERT!   Always prepare a scatterplot when investigating a bivariate correlation.

Bivariate Correlation

Even though scatterplots are indispensable tools for evaluating the relationship between two variables, researchers rarely report such graphs in published articles. The typical convention is to calculate a number to represent the relationship, called a **correlation coefficient.**[1] There are many types of correlation coefficients, and the choice of the one to use is determined by the scale used in data collection and the research question and the number of variables. When there are two variables and the purpose is to examine the relationship between them, the procedure used is a *bivariate* or *zero-order correlation*. Bivariate correlations are also used to investigate the many relationships that exist when there are many variables and a coefficient is calculated for each pair. The interpretation of the number used, however, is basically the same. The number that represents the correlation can range from −1.00 to +1.00. A high positive value (e.g., .85, .90, .96) represents a high positive relationship; a low positive value (.15, .20, .08) a low positive relationship; a moderate negative value (−.40, −.37, −.52) a moderate negative relationship, a value of 0 no relationship, and so on. Thus, the strength of the relationship becomes higher as the correlation approaches either +1 or −1 from zero. This is illustrated in Figure 7.14. Note that strength is independent of direction.

Correlation coefficient: -1 ⟵———— $-.5$ ————— 0 ————— $+.5$ ————⟶ $+1$

Strength of relationship: high   moderate   low   low   moderate   high

Direction: negative   positive

FIGURE 7.14   **Relationship of Strength and Direction of Correlations**

The most common correlation technique is the Pearson product-moment coefficient (represented by r), and the correlation is indicated by $r = 0.65$, $r = 0.78$, $r = 0.03$, and so on. (Notice that there is no plus sign before positive values, but there is a negative sign for negative values.) The product-moment correlation is used when both variables use continuous scales, such as scores from achievement tests, grade-point average, self-concept inventories, and age. Since scores can also be reported as dichotomies, in several categories, or ranks, other correlation techniques, depending on the scale for the variables, are used to measure the relationship. Some of these techniques are summarized in Table 7.5.

> **MISCONCEPTION**   A negative correlation is bad or undesirable.
>
> **EVIDENCE**   The term *negative correlation* describes the direction of the relationship. It has nothing to do with desirability.

Excerpts 7.10 and 7.11 show how to report correlational data. In Excerpt 7.10, there is a list of all correlations of interest in the study. In Excerpt 7.11 there is an **intercorrelation matrix,** in which many variables are correlated with each other. The numbers in a row on top of the table correspond to the variables listed vertically on the left. The correlation of teachers' disapproval and criticism with teachers' encouragement is -0.54; the correlation of engagement with teachers' long-term expectations is 0.44. In Chapter 9, we will discuss important principles of interpretation of correlation coefficients.

TABLE 7.5   **Types of Correlation Coefficients**

Type of Coefficient	Symbol	Types of Variables
Pearson product-moment	r	Both continuous
Spearman	r_s	Both rank ordered
Biserial	r_b	One continuous, one an artificial dichotomy
Point-biserial	r_{pb}	One continuous, one a true dichotomy
Tetrachoric	r^t	Both artificial dichotomies
Phi coefficient	ϕ	Both true dichotomies
Contingency coefficients	C	Both two or more categories
Correlation ratio, eta	η	Both continuous (used with curvilinear relationships)

EXCERPT 7.10 Pearson Product-Moment Correlation

Pearson product-moment correlations were computed between all demographic variables (i.e., percentage White; low income; attendance rate; percentage mobility; high school dropout rate; high school graduation rate; average class size; average teacher experience in years; pupil–teacher ratio; average teacher salary; average per-pupil expenditure) and the achievement scores (i.e., scores in reading and mathematics). The 1994 correlations (see Table 2) were similar across grade levels and subject matter within the 1994 data.

To summarize, we detected statistically significant relationships (or associations) between the school demographic variables and the achievement scores. The strongest relationships occurred for the following variables: low income, percentage White, high school graduation, and dropout rate. Moderate relationships existed for attendance, mobility, and high school pupil–teacher ratio. The weakest relationships occurred for average class size, elementary pupil–teacher ratio, teacher salary, teacher experience, and expenditure per pupil.

TABLE 2 Correlations of Attitude Measures with Achievement Scores

Variable	Grade 3		Grade 10	
	Reading	Mathematics	Reading	Mathematics
Percentage White	.78	.66	.75	.67
Low income	−.79	−.72	−.79	−.75
Attendance	.59	.53	.82	.72
Mobility	−.52	−.46	−.54	−.49
Dropout	—	—	−.69	−.61
High school graduation	—	—	.76	.69
Average class size, Grade 3	−.09**	−.06**	—	—
Average class size, high school	—	—	−.18	−.11**
Teacher experience	−.14	−.13	−.05	.00
Elementary pupil–teacher ratio	−.26	−.22	−.32	−.24
High school pupil–teacher ratio	—	—	−.32	−.24
Teacher salary	−.20	−.08	−.05	.07
Expenditure per pupil	−.31	−.19	.10*	−.01

Note: Grade 3, n = 2,307; Grade 10, n = 644. Correlations are statistically significant at the .001 level unless otherwise noted. $*p < .05$. $**p < .01$.

Source: From Sutton, A., & Soderstrom, I. (1999). Predicting elementary and secondary school achievement with school-related and demographic factors. *Journal of Educational Research, 92*(6), 330–338. Reprinted by permission.

SUMMARY

This chapter introduced the fundamental principles of descriptive statistics. The statistical procedures are used in one way or another in nearly all quantitative research studies. The major points covered are summarized below:

1. Descriptive statistics are indices that summarize or characterize a large number of observations.

2. Measurement scales (i.e., nominal, ordinal, interval, and ratio) and the purpose of the research suggest the descriptive statistics that are appropriate.

3. Descriptive statistical procedures can be classified as univariate (i.e., one variable) or bivariate (i.e., two variables).

EXCERPT 7.11 Correlation Matrix

Zero-order correlations among the motivational context variables and behavioral signs of alienation are depicted in Table 2. All correlations were in the expected direction. Students' disciplinary problems were most strongly related to their reports of teachers' disinterest and criticism and teacher expectations. The strongest relation to emerge was between students' perceptions of teacher's expectations and student engagement. Peers' academic aspirations and their perceptions of the economic limitations of education were related to both disciplinary problems and engagement.

TABLE 2 Zero-Order Correlations between Perceived Motivational Context Variables and Indexes of Alienation

Motivation Context Variables	1	2	3	4	5	6	7	8	9	10
1. Teachers' disapproval and criticism	—									
2. Teachers' encouragement	−.54***	—								
3. Teachers' long-term expectations	−.39***	.34***	—							
4. Peers' academic aspirations	−.21***	.13**	.36***	—						
5. Peers' resistance to school norms	.27***	−.09	−.22***	−.47***	—					
6. Peers' academic support	−.32***	.31***	.29***	.47***	−.44***	—				
7. Economic limitations of education	.38***	−.24***	−.35***	−.38***	.27***	−.25***	—			
8. Economic benefits of education	−.12*	.21***	.32***	.32***	−.12*	.21***	−.36***	—		
Indexes of Alienation										
9. Discipline problems	−.35***	.15**	−.36***	−.26***	.17**	−.21***	.29***	−.11**	—	
10. Engagement	−.16**	.04	.44***	.27***	−.14**	.19***	−.22***	.11**	−.47***	—

*$p < .05$. **$p < .01$. ***$p < .001$.

4. Frequency distributions in the form of class intervals, histograms, bar graphs, frequency polygons, and stem-and-leaf displays provide an overview picture of all the data.

5. Measures of central tendency include the mean, median, and mode. Each measure provides a numerical index of the typical score in the distribution.

6. The mean is the best measure of central tendency for distributions that have no extremely high or low scores; the median is the best for highly skewed data. Often, both the mean and the median should be reported.

7. Measures of variability indicate the spread of scores from the mean of the distribution.

8. Measures of variation include the range, standard deviation, and box-and-whisker plots.
9. Outliers are extreme scores that can distort findings.
10. Standard deviation is a measure of variability unique to each distribution that indicates, on the average, how much a score deviates from the mean.
11. Standard scores are converted raw score distributions with common units to indicate the mean and the standard deviation.

12. A scatterplot is used to indicate the general direction and strength of a relationship between two variables in one group or sample.
13. A correlation coefficients is a number that represents the direction and strength of the relationship between two or more variables.

RESEARCH NAVIGATOR NOTES

Research Navigator.c⊕m Reading the following articles will help you understand the content of this chapter. Go to the education database (included in the EBSCO database) in Research Navigator; use the Accession Number provided to find the article.

7.1 *Connections among Values*
Shows and explains the connections among standard deviations, and normal distributions. Accession Number: 11650478.

7.2 *Curvilinear Scattergrams*
Scattergrams are used to illustrate curvilinear relationships between teacher disapproval and pupil on-task behavior. Accession Number: 4781122.

CHECK YOURSELF

Multiple-choice review items, with answers, are available on the Companion Website for this book:

www.ablongman.com/mcmillanschumacher6e.

APPLICATION PROBLEMS

1. For each case below, choose the most appropriate statistical procedure:
   a. A teacher of a low-level reading group is interested in what the average score is for the group of 25 students.
   b. An administrator wants to find out if there is a relationship between teacher absences and student achievement.
   c. A math teacher wants to know how many ability groups should be formed within a class of 30 students.
   d. A student teacher is interested in finding out the number of students who rate his performance as good, excellent, average, or poor.

2. Identify the scale of measurement in each of the following:
   a. attitudes toward school
   b. grouping students on the basis of hair color
   c. asking judges to rank order students from most cooperative to least cooperative
3. For the following set of scores, prepare a frequency distribution, a histogram, and a stem-and-leaf display for each variable. Also calculate the mean, the median, and the standard deviation of each score. Are there any outliers in the distribution? If so, what is the result if these scores are removed from the data set? Draw a scatterplot that illustrates the relationship between the two variables.

Subject	Variable A: Attitude toward descriptive statistics (1 = low and 20 = high)	Variable B: Achievement on test of knowledge of descriptive statistics
Sam	12	80
Sally	10	60
Frank	19	85
Bob	8	65
Colleen	2	55
Isaiah	15	75
Felix	1	95
Dan	20	82
Robert	6	70
Jim	11	88
Michelle	3	59
Jan	7	60

4. If you have access to SPSS (Statistical Package for the Social Sciences), create a dataset that can be used for calculating descriptive statistics and making graphs. When you open SPSS, the title of the page will be *Untitled SPSS Data Editor*. The tab at the bottom (*Data View*) tells you that you are in the right screen to enter your data. The variables are named across the top, and each number on the left corresponds to a different subject. Once you have entered the scores, it is best to open the tab named *Variable View* and specify characteristics of each variable. Click on *Analyze* to see a number of different procedures. Select *Descriptive Statistics* and then *Descriptives* and *Explore*. To do the correlation, click on *Correlate* and then *Bivariate*. Click on *Graphs* to find *Histogram* and *Scatterplot*. Use these procedures to do the calculations in problem 3 and confirm your work.

NOTE

1. This discussion is limited to simple correlation. More advanced correlational procedures—such as multiple correlation, partial correlation, discriminant function analysis, and canonical correlation—are based on these principles to examine the combined relationships of several variables.

Quantitative Data Collection Techniques

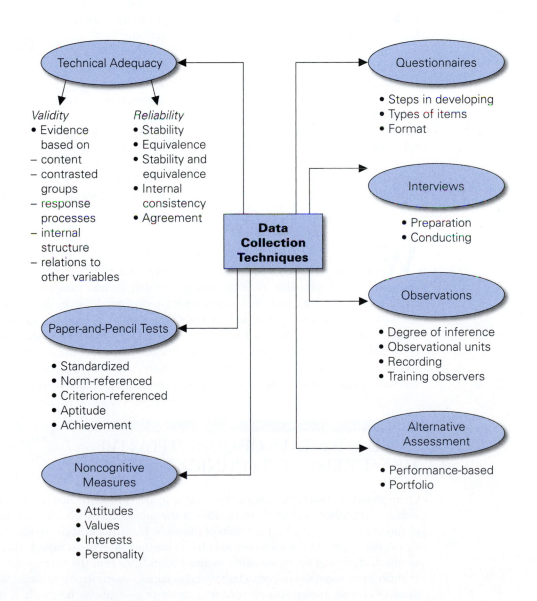

Technical Adequacy

Validity
- Evidence based on
- content
- contrasted groups
- response processes
- internal structure
- relations to other variables

Reliability
- Stability
- Equivalence
- Stability and equivalence
- Internal consistency
- Agreement

Data Collection Techniques

Questionnaires
- Steps in developing
- Types of items
- Format

Interviews
- Preparation
- Conducting

Observations
- Degree of inference
- Observational units
- Recording
- Training observers

Paper-and-Pencil Tests
- Standardized
- Norm-referenced
- Criterion-referenced
- Aptitude
- Achievement

Alternative Assessment
- Performance-based
- Portfolio

Noncognitive Measures
- Attitudes
- Values
- Interests
- Personality

KEY TERMS

construct underrepresentation
construct irrelevant variance
evidence based on test content
evidence based on contrasted groups
evidence based on response
    processes
evidence based on internal structure
evidence based on relations to other
    variables
reliability
stability
equivalence
internal consistency
split-half reliability
Kuder-Richardson
Cronbach alpha
agreement
standardized tests
norm-referenced interpretation
criterion-referenced interpretation
standards-based interpretation
aptitude test
achievement test
alternative assessments
performance-based assessment
portfolio

noncognitive instruments
social desirability
questionnaire
double-barreled questions
closed form
open form
scale
Likert scale
semantic differential
checklist
contingency questions
structured questions
semistructured questions
unstructured questions
leading questions
probing
complete observer
high inference
low inference
duration recording
frequency-count recording
interval recording
continuous observation
time sampling
nonreactive
unobtrusive measures

We are now ready to consider how instrumentation plays a vital role in quantitative research. This chapter elaborates on principles of validity and reliability and presents the characteristics of five major techniques for gathering quantitative data: tests, question-naires, interviews, observation, and unobtrusive measures. The advantages and disadvan-tages of each type are discussed in relation to the objectives of research problems and procedures employed with each technique. Once the purpose of the research and the con-straints of the research situation are clear, a particular technique is chosen to fit the research design. No single technique is best, easiest, or most convenient.

FUNDAMENTALS OF QUANTITATIVE MEASUREMENT: TECHNICAL ADEQUACY

Quantitative measurement uses some type of instrument or device to obtain numerical indices that correspond to characteristics of the subjects. The numerical values are then summarized and reported as the results of the study. Consequently, the results depend heav-ily on the quality of the measurement. If the measure is weak or biased, then so are the results. Conversely, strong measures increase confidence that the findings are accurate. It is imperative, then, to understand what makes measurement strong or weak. Whether you need to choose instruments to conduct a study or to evaluate results, it is necessary to understand what affects the quality of the measure. In this section, two technical concepts of measurement, validity and reliability, are discussed as important criteria for determin-ing quality.

Validity

As indicated in Chapter 6, test *validity* is the extent to which inferences made on the basis of numerical scores are appropriate, meaningful, and useful. Validity is a judgment of the appropriateness of a measure for specific inferences or decisions that result from the scores generated. In other words, validity is a situation-specific concept: It is assessed depending on the purpose, population, and environmental characteristics in which measurement takes place. A test result can therefore be valid in one situation and invalid in another. Consequently, in order to assure others that the procedures have validity in relation to the research problems, subjects, and setting of the study, it is incumbent on the investigator to describe validity in relation to the instruments used to collect data.

This conceptualization of test validity implies much more than simply determining whether a test "measures what it is supposed to measure." The most recent *Standards for Educational and Psychological Testing* (2000) make it clear that it is an *inference, use,* or *consequence* that is valid or invalid, not a test. That is, "Validity refers to the degree to which evidence and theory support the interpretations of test scores entailed by specific uses of tests" (*Standards*, 2000, p. 9).

To assure validity, then, the researcher needs to identify assumptions or make arguments to justify an inference or use for a specific purpose (e.g., concluding that students in one group have more knowledge or have a stronger self-concept than students in another group) and then collect evidence to support these assumptions (Shepard, 1993). This emphasis is consistent with the idea that validity is a single, unitary concept that requires evidence for the specific use that is cited. It follows, then, that a test by itself is not valid or invalid because the same test can be used for different purposes. For example, a college entrance test may lead to valid inferences about a student's future performance as an undergraduate but to invalid inferences about the quality of his or her high school program.

Two kinds of inferences are typically used in educational research. The first is related to assessing achievement, which depends primarily on how well the content of a test or other assessment represents a larger domain of content or tasks. For this kind of inference, evidence based on the content of the assessment is needed to support inferences that are made. A second kind of inference, one that is even more common in educational research, is about traits or characteristics that are more abstract than clearly defined content. These traits or characteristics are often called *constructs* and include, for example, intelligence, creativity, reading ability, attitudes, reasoning, and self-concept.

When inferences involve these constructs, it is important to have a clear theoretical conceptualization about what is being measured as well as evidence that there are no viable rival hypotheses to challenge the intended interpretation. Two types of rival hypotheses can be considered: *construct underrepresentation and construct irrelevant variance*. **Construct underrepresentation** occurs if the assessment fails to capture important aspects of the construct. For example, if a self-concept measure did not include items on social as well as academic areas, it would measure less than the proposed construct of self-concept. **Construct irrelevant variance** refers to the extent to which a measure includes materials or factors that are extraneous to the intended construct. An example of this kind of factor would be measuring mathematical reasoning ability with story problems. Since reading comprehension is needed to understand the problems, this ability is important to success, as well as mathematical reasoning. Thus, the measure is influenced to some extent by factors that are not part of the construct.

Whether the inference involved in research is primarily content or construct, six major types of evidence can be used to both support intended interpretations and eliminate any rival hypotheses about what is being measured: evidence based on content, on contrasted groups, on response processes, on internal structure, on relations to other variables, and on consequences. We will consider the first five, which have the greatest relevance for research.

Evidence Based on Test Content   In general, **evidence based on test content** demonstrates the extent to which the sample of items or questions in the instrument is representative of some appropriate universe or domain of content or tasks. This type of evidence is usually accumulated by having experts examine the content of the instrument and indicate the degree to which it measures predetermined criteria or objectives. Experts are also used to judge the relative criticality, or importance, of various parts of the instrument. For example, to gather evidence for a test of knowledge for prospective teachers, it is necessary to have experts examine the items and judge their representativeness (e.g., Is a question about Piaget representative of what needs to be known about child development?) and whether the percentage of the test devoted to different topics is appropriate (e.g., 20 percent of the test is on classroom management, but maybe it should be 40 percent). Evidence based on test content is essential for achievement tests. Also, the domain or universe that is represented should be appropriate to the intended use of the results.

Unfortunately, evidence based on test content for validity is often not reported in research articles, usually because there is no systematic effort to obtain such evidence for locally devised instruments. When standardized instruments are used, it is important to refer to previous research, reviews of the instrument, and technical manuals.

Evidence based on content is similar to *face validity*, but face validity is a less systematic appraisal between the measure and the larger domain. Face validity is a judgment that the items appear to be relevant, while content validity evidence establishes the relationship empirically.

Evidence Based on Contrasted Groups   A straightforward approach to establishing validity is to see if groups that should be different respond as predicted. Usually, this is done with groups that clearly contrast one another with respect to what is being measured. For example, a measure of teaching effectiveness should give very high results from individuals who have been recognized for their teaching (e.g., teachers of the year), while teachers who are judged by principals to be marginally effective should receive low scores. Excerpt 8.1 provides an example of how **evidence based on contrasted groups** is used.

Evidence Based on Response Processes   **Evidence based on response processes** is focused on an analysis of performance strategies or responses to specific tasks and whether these strategies and responses are consistent with what is intended to be measured. For example, if students are to be involved in mathematical reasoning, it would be possible to ask them about their thinking in relation to solving problems to assure that reasoning, not rote application of an alogrithm, is used. Similarly, observers or judges can be asked to indicate criteria used for their judgments to be sure appropriate criteria are being applied.

Evidence Based on Internal Structure   The *internal structure* of an instrument refers to how items are related to each other and how different parts of an instrument are related. **Evidence based on internal structure** is provided when the relationships between items and parts of the instrument are empirically consistent with the theory or intended use of

EXCERPT 8.1   Evidence Based on Contrasted Groups

The validation approach used both contrasted groups and correlational analysis. Contrasted groups are groups for whom there is prior expectation of different values and where we would therefore expect a valid instrument to produce significant inter-group differences. Thus, Israeli Druz students are expected to differ from Israeli Jewish students owing to cultural differences; Special Education students and school counselors are expected to hold more democratic beliefs than student-teachers in a regular programme, owing to differences in educational background and perhaps also to different vocational interests. Finally, effective teachers are expected to hold more democratic beliefs compared with non-effective teachers, given the evidence on the links between democratic beliefs and classroom effectiveness.

Source: From Schechtman, Z. (2002). Validation of the democratic teacher belief scale (DTBS). *Assessment in Education, 9*(3), 363–377.

EXCERPT 8.2   Evidence Based on Internal Structure

Factor analysis was used to examine the internal structure of the inventory. The method of principal factors with oblique rotation produced three factors with eigenvalues of more than 1.0. . . . Using a factor loading of .50 or higher as the criterion, Items 1, 2, 3, and 13 loaded on Factor 1.

Using the same criterion, Items 6, 7, and 15 loaded on Factor 2. Items 8, 9, and 10 loaded on Factor 3. . . . The three factor loadings represented a Technique Confidence (TC) dimension, an Interpersonal Confidence (IC) dimension, and a Competition Confidence (CC) dimension.

Source: From Park, J. (2004). A conceptual model of coaching confidence: Development of a reliable and valid Coaching Confidence Scale. *International Journal of Sport Psychology, 35,* 37–59.

the scores. Thus, if a measure of self-concept posits several types of self-concept (e.g., academic, social, athletic), then the items measuring the academic component should be strongly related to each other and not as highly related to the other components. A procedure called *factor analysis* is often used to provide internal structure evidence, as illustrated in Excerpt 8.2.

Evidence Based on Relations to Other Variables   The most common way that validity of interpretations is established is by showing how scores from a given measure relate to similar as well as different traits. There are several ways this can be done. When scores from one instrument correlate highly with scores from another measure of the same trait, we have what is called *convergent* evidence. *Discriminant* evidence exists when the scores do not correlate highly with scores from an instrument that measures something different. Thus, we would expect that scores from a measure of self-concept would correlate highly with other measures of self concept and show less correlation to related but different traits, such as anxiety and academic performance. In many research articles, this type of evidence will be referred to as *construct validity.*

Another approach to gathering **evidence based on relations to other variables** pertains to the extent to which the test scores or measures predict performance on a criterion measure (i.e., test-criterion relationships). Two approaches are used to obtain test-criterion evidence: predictive and concurrent. With *predictive evidence,* the criterion is measured at a time in the future, after the instrument has been administered. The evidence pertains to how well the earlier measure can predict the criterion behavior or performance. For instance, in gathering evidence on a new measure to select applicants for leadership positions, the scores on the instrument would be correlated with future leadership behavior. If persons who scored low on the test turned out to be poor leaders and those who scored high were good leaders, predictive test-criterion evidence would be obtained. Excerpt 8.3 shows how predictive evidence is used to establish validity. With *concurrent*

Research
Navigator.c○m

8.1 Discriminant Validity
Accession No.: 7409893

EXCERPT 8.3   Predictive Test-Criterion Evidence for Validity

The predictive validity of this instrument is reflected in the findings that three of the four beliefs have predicted different aspects of learning. Belief in quick learning predicted comprehension monitoring, quality of summarizing, and test performance for social science and physical science passages. . . . Belief in certain knowledge predicted inter-

pretation of tentative information. . . . Belief in simple knowledge predicted comprehension and monitoring of comprehension in mathematical passages. . . . Belief in fixed ability predicted students' appreciation of the value of education.

Source: From Schommer-Aikins, M., & Hutter, R. (2002). Epistemological beliefs and thinking about everyday controversial issues. *Journal of Psychology, 136*(1), 5–20.

EXCERPT 8.4 Concurrent Test-Criterion Evidence for Validity

Concurrent validity was assessed by correlating raters' scores of parents on the two dimensions with the scores provided by their children on the PBI. The correlations for this measure ranged from .78 for the care scale to .48 for overprotection. The low correlation found for overprotection is thought to stem from the ambiguity of the factor and the fact that it is so closely related to a lack of care (Parker et al., 1979).

Source: From Judy, B., & Nelson, E. S. (2000). Relationship between parents, peers, morality, and theft in an adolescent sample. *High School Journal, 83*(3), 31–42.

evidence, the instrument and the criterion are given at about the same time. Criterion-related evidence is often reported in research by indicating that a measure correlates with criteria that assess the same thing. An example of concurrent evidence is presented in Excerpt 8.4. In this study, raters' scores are correlated to scores from children.

Validity is clearly the single most important aspect of an instrument and the findings that result from the data. The quality of the evidence judged by the users of the findings varies a lot in educational research. If standardized tests are used, there will be sophisticated evidence, while locally developed questionnaires may have little systematic evidence. In either case, good researchers always ask Are the inferences appropriate? What evidence supports my conclusion? The components of test validity are summarized in Table 8.1.

Effect of Validity on Research   Because validity implies proper interpretation and use of the information gathered through measurement, it is necessary to judge the degree of validity that is present based on available evidence. In this sense, validity is a matter of degree, not an all-or-nothing proposition. Investigators should show that for the specific

TABLE 8.1   Components of Test Validity

Component	Description	Procedure
Evidence based on content	Extent to which the items or factors represent a larger domain	Examine the relationship between content in the items and content in the domain.
Evidence based on contrasted groups	Whether groups that should be different are different in predicted direction	Examine the differences between the groups.
Evidence based on response processes	Whether thinking and response processes are consistent with intended interpretation	Examine the respondent explanations and patterns of responses.
Evidence based on internal structure	Extent to which items measuring the same trait are related	Correlate items measuring the same trait.
Evidence based on relations to other variables	Whether the measure is related to similar or predicted variables and unrelated to different variables	Correlate the measure to other measures of the same trait and to measures of different traits.

inferences and conclusions made in their study, there is evidence that validity exists. Consumers need to make the same decision based on their use of the results. Does this suggest that validity must be established for each research situation and possible use? Such a requirement would add a considerable amount of data collection and analysis to each study and is therefore impractical. In practice, it is necessary to generalize from other studies and research that interpretation and use are valid. That is one reason that already established instruments, for which some evidence on validity has probably accumulated, usually provide more credible measurement. On the other hand, it would be a mistake to assume that just because an instrument is established, its results are valid.

ALERT!   *Inferences* are valid or invalid, not tests, surveys, and other instruments.

Locally devised instruments, which have no history of use or reviews by others, need to be evaluated with more care. When researchers develop new instruments, it is more important to gather appropriate evidence for validity and then report this evidence in the study.

Whether a locally prepared or established instrument is used, it is best to gather evidence for validity before the data for a study are collected. This is a major reason for a pilot test of the instrument and procedures for administering it.

Reliability

Reliability refers to the consistency of measurement—the extent to which the results are similar over different forms of the same instrument or occasions of data collection. Another way to conceptualize reliability is to determine the extent to which measures are free from error. If an instrument has little error, then it is reliable, and if it has a great amount of error, then it is unreliable. We can measure error by estimating how consistently a trait is assessed.

Think for a minute about tests you have taken. Were the scores you received accurate, or was there some degree of error in the results? Were some results more accurate than others? In measuring human traits, whether achievement, attitude, personality, physical skill, or some other trait, you will almost never obtain a result that does not have some degree of error. Many factors contribute to the less than perfect nature of our measures. There may be ambiguous questions, the lighting may be poor, some subjects may be sick, guessing on an achievement test may be lucky or unlucky, observers may get tired, and so on. What this means is that even if a trait remained the same when two tests were given a week apart, the scores would not be exactly the same because of unavoidable error.

According to classical test theory, the obtained score may be thought of as having two components, a *true* or *universe score*, which represents the actual knowledge or skill level of the individual, and *error*, sources of variability unrelated to the intent of the instrument:

$$obtained\ score\ =\ true\ or\ universe\ score\ +\ error$$

Common sources of error are listed in Table 8.2. The objective in selecting or evaluating instruments, then, is to look for evidence that error has been controlled as much as possible.

The actual amount of error variance in test scores, or the reliability, is determined empirically through several types of procedures.[1] Each type of reliability is related to the control of a particular kind of error and is usually reported in the form of a reliability coefficient. The reliability coefficient is a correlation statistic comparing two sets of scores from the same individuals. The scale for a reliability coefficient is from .00 to .99. If the coefficient is high, for example .90, the scores have little error and are highly reliable. The opposite is true for the correlation near .20 or .35. An acceptable range of reliability for coefficients for most instruments is .70 to .90.

TABLE 8.2 Sources of Measurement Error	
Conditions of Test Administration and Construction	**Conditions Associated with the Person Taking the Test**
Changes in time limits	Reactions to specific items
Changes in directions	Health
Different scoring procedures	Motivation
Interrupted testing session	Mood
Race/ethnicity of test administrator	Fatigue
Time the test is taken	Luck
Sampling of items	Fluctuation in memory or attention
Ambiguity in wording	Attitudes
Misunderstood directions	Test-taking skills (test wiseness)
Effects of heat, light, ventilation in testing situation	Ability to comprehend instruction
Differences in observers	Anxiety

The five general types of reliability estimates are stability, equivalence, stability and equivalence, internal consistency, and agreement. Each is addressed in a following section, and all five are summarized in Table 8.3.[2]

Stability   A coefficient of **stability** is obtained by correlating scores from the same test on two different occasions of a group of individuals. If the responses of the individuals are consistent (i.e., if those scoring high the first time also score high the second time, and so on), then the correlation coefficient and the reliability are high. This *test-retest* procedure assumes that the characteristic measured remains constant. Unstable traits, such as mood, should not be expected to yield high stability coefficients. Furthermore, stability usually means that there is a long enough time between measures (often several months) so that the consistency in scores is not influenced by a memory or practice effect. In general, as the time gap between measures increases, the correlation between the scores becomes lower. Excerpt 8.5 shows how stability estimates are reported.

Equivalence   When two equivalent or parallel forms of the same instrument are administered to a group at about the same time and the scores are related, the reliability that results is a coefficient of **equivalence.** Even though each form is made up of different items, the score received by an individual would be about the same on each form. Equivalence is one type of reliability that can be established when the researcher has a relatively large

EXCERPT 8.5   Stability Evidence for Reliability

Test-retest reliability over a 2 month time period was obtained for a subsample of 55 randomly selected participants, yielding a stability coefficient of .78 for the total POB scale scores and stability coefficients of .72 and .68 for the Career-Related and Educational subscales, respectively.

Source: From Luzzo, D. A., & McWhirter, E. H. (2001). Sex and ethnic differences in the perception of educational and career-related barriers and levels of coping efficacy. *Journal of Counseling and Development, 79*(1), 61–67.

number of items from which to construct equivalent forms. Alternative forms of a test are needed in order to test initially absent subjects who may learn about specific items from the first form or when an instructor has two or more sections of the same class meeting at different times.

Equivalence and Stability   When a researcher needs to give a pretest and posttest to assess a change in behavior, a reliability coefficient of equivalence and stability should be established. In this procedure, reliability data are obtained by administering to the same group of individuals one form of an instrument at one time and a second form at a later date. If an instrument has this type of reliability, the researcher can be confident that a change of scores across time reflects an actual difference in the trait being measured. This is the most stringent type of reliability, and it is especially useful for studies involving gain-scores or improvement.

Internal Consistency   **Internal consistency** is the most common type of reliability, since it can be estimated from giving one form of a test once. There are three common types of internal consistency: split-half, Kuder-Richardson, and the Cronbach alpha method. In **split-half reliability,** the items of a test that have been administered to a group are divided into comparable halves, and a correlation coefficient is calculated between the halves. If each student has about the same position in relation to the group on each half, then the correlation is high and the instrument has high reliability. Each test half should be of similar difficulty. This method provides a lower reliability than other methods, since the total number in the correlation equation contains only half the items (and we know that other things being equal, longer tests are more reliable than short tests). (The Spearman-Brown formula is used to increase split-half reliabilities to estimate what the correlation would be for a whole test.) Internal consistency techniques should not be used with speeded tests. This is because not all items are answered by all students, a factor that tends to increase spuriously the intercorrelation of the items.

Research
Navigator.com

8.2 Coefficient Alpha
Accession No.: 5542030

TABLE 8.3   Types of Reliability

Type	Description	Procedure	Common Examples*
Stability (test-retest)	Consistency of stable characteristics over time	Administer the same test to the same individuals over time.	Aptitude tests
IQ tests
Equivalence	Comparability of two measures of the same trait given at about the same time	Administer different forms to the same individuals at about the same time.	Achievement tests
Equivalence and stability	Comparability of two measures of the same trait given over time	Administer different forms to the same individuals over time.	Assessments of changes over time
Personality assessment
Internal consistency (split-half; KR; Cronbach alpha)	Comparability of halves of a measure to assess a single trait or dimension	Administer one test and correlate the items to each other.	Most measures except for speeded tests
Attitude questionnaires
Agreement	Consistency of ratings or observations	Two or more persons rate or observe.	Observations and interviews

*These examples are not meant to suggest that forms of reliability other than those indicated are inappropriate (e.g., achievement tests also use test-retest reliability).

EXCERPT 8.6 Internal Consistency Evidence for Reliability

The internal reliability of each factor was tested using Cronbach's α coefficient. The enjoyment subscales showed high reliability, all between .74 and .87, except the truth procedures scale (factor 7), for which α was .66. It is likely that this factor elicited a lower α value because of the small number of items (3) on this scale. The first four goal factors also showed high internal reliability (between .69 and .86), but self-esteem (factor 5) and competitive achievement (factor 6) subscales, each with a low number of items, yielded lower alphas of .59 and .62, respectively.

Source: From Breen, R., & Lindsay, R. (2002). Different disciplines require different motivations for student success. *Research in Higher Education, 43*(6), 693–725.

A second method for investigating the extent of internal consistency is to use a **Kuder-Richardson (KR)** formula in order to correlate all items on a single test with each other when each item is scored right or wrong. KR reliability is thus determined from a single administration of an instrument but without having to split the instrument into equivalent halves. This procedure assumes that all items in an instrument are equivalent, and it is appropriate when the purpose of the test is to measure a single trait. If a test has items of varying difficulty or measures more than one trait, the KR estimate would usually be lower than the split-half reliabilities.

The **Cronbach alpha** also assumes equivalence of all items. It is a much more general form of internal consistency than the KR, and it is used for items that are not scored right or wrong. The Cronbach alpha is generally the most appropriate type of reliability for survey research and other questionnaires in which there is a range of possible answers for each item. Internal consistency estimates are used extensively in educational research. Two examples are provided in Excerpts 8.6 and 8.7.

Agreement   The fifth type of reliability is expressed as a coefficient of **agreement.** It is established by determining the extent to which two or more persons agree about what they have seen, heard, or rated. That is, when two or more observers or raters independently observe or rate something, will they agree about what was observed or rated? If they do, then there is some consistency in measurement. This type of reliability is commonly used for observational research and studies involving performance-based assessments in which professional judgments are made about student performance. It will be reported as *inter-rater* reliability, *intercoder agreement,* or *scorer agreement* and will be expressed either as a correlation coefficient or as percentage of agreement. However, this type of analysis does not indicate anything about *consistency* of performance or behavior at different times. (Ironically, internal consistency estimates don't either.) This means that it is one thing to obtain high inter-rater agreement, which is relatively easy to do, and quite another to obtain data that show that the behavior or trait is consistent over time. In Excerpt 8.8, observer agreement is used to provide reliability evidence.

EXCERPT 8.7 Internal Consistency Evidence for Reliability

To assess the internal consistency of the Parent Survey, Cronbach's alpha statistic was calculated for each treatment group and the control group. . . . Cronbach's alpha for the treatment group that received tangible non-reading related incentives was .89, while the Cronbach alpha for the treatment group that received books as incentives was .87.

Source: From Edmunds, K. M., & Tancock, S. M. (2003). Incentives: The effects on the reading motivation of fourth-grade students. *Reading Research and Instruction, 42*(2), 17–38.

EXCERPT 8.8   Agreement Evidence for Reliability

Videotaped observations were coded by two raters using the CBRS and MBRS. Each had a master's degree in developmental psychology and had completed approximately 30 hours of training until they had attained interrater agreement of 90% on each of the two scales. Reliability was computed based on interrater agreement for 70% if the observations used for the final study. . . . For the CBRS, overall exact agreement was 81%. . . . For the MBRS, overall exact agreement was 81%.

Source: From Kim, J., & Mahoney, G. (2004). The effects of mother's style of interaction on children's engagement: Implications for using responsive interventions with parents. *Topics in Early Childhood Special Education, 24*(1), 31–38.

These five types of reliability estimates are summarized in Table 8.4 according to when different forms of an instrument are given.

Interpretation of Reliability Coefficients   Several factors should be considered in interpreting reliability coefficients:

1. The more heterogeneous a group is on the trait that is measured, the higher the reliability.
2. The more items there are in an instrument, the higher the reliability.
3. The greater the range of scores, the higher the reliability.
4. Achievement tests with a medium difficulty level will result in a higher reliability than either very hard or very easy tests.
5. Reliability, like validity, when based on a norming group, is demonstrated only for subjects whose characteristics are similar to those of the norming group.
6. The more that items discriminate between high and low achievers, the greater the reliability.

Researchers often ask how high a correlation should be for it to indicate satisfactory reliability. This question is not answered easily. It depends on the type of instrument (personality questionnaires generally have lower reliability than achievement tests), the purpose of the study (whether it is exploratory research or research that leads to important decisions), and whether groups or individuals are affected by the results (since action

TABLE 8.4   Procedures for Estimating Reliability*

	Time 1		Time 2
Stability	A		A
Equivalence	A	B	
Stability and Equivalence	A		B
Internal Consistency	A		
Agreement	R1	R2	

*A and B refer to different forms of the same test; R1 and R2 refer to rater 1 and rater 2, though more than two raters or observers can be used with agreement.

Source: Adapted from James McMillan; *Educational Research: Fundamentals for the Consumer,* 4th ed. Published by Allyn and Bacon, Boston, MA. Copyright © 2004 by Pearson Education. Reprinted by permission of the publisher.

affecting individuals requires a higher correlation than action affecting groups). However, a good rule of thumb is to be wary of reliabilities below .70.

Effect of Reliability on Research   As with validity, the reliability of scores should be established before the research is undertaken and the type of reliability should be consistent with the use of the results. If you will use the results for prediction or selection into special programs, stability estimates of reliability are necessary. If you are interested in programs to change attitudes or values, equivalency estimates are needed. Reliability should also be established with individuals who are similar to the subjects in the research. If previous studies report good reliability with middle school students and you intend to use the results with elementary school students, the reliability may not be adequate. More commonly, reliability is reported with the subjects used in the study. Failure to report reliability would be cause to interpret the results with caution, although there are some simple measures for which reliability coefficients are not needed (see below).

You will read some research in which reliability is not addressed, yet the results of the research show what are called "significant differences." This is an interesting situation in research because it is more difficult to find differences between groups with instruments that have resulted in scores that have low reliability. It is as if the differences were observed despite what may have been low reliability. Of course, it is possible that the measurement was reliable, even though no reliability estimates were reported. This situation is likely to occur in research in which the subjects are responding to questions so straightforward and simple that reliability is assumed. For example, in studies of students' perceptions of success or failure following performance on a test, the subjects may be asked to indicate on a scale from 1 to 10 (1 being a high degree of failure and 10 being a high degree of success) their feelings of success or failure. In much research, the subjects report information such as age, sex, income, time spent studying, occupation, and other questions that are relatively simple. For these types of data, statistical estimates of reliability are generally not needed.

ALERT!   *All* data collection instruments and procedures include some degree of error.

Reliability is a function of the nature of the trait being measured. Some variables, such as most measures of achievement, provide highly reliable scores, whereas scores from personality measures have lower reliabilities. Consequently, a reliability of 0.80 or above is generally expected for achievement variables, whereas estimates of 0.70 may be acceptable for measuring personality traits. By comparison, then, a personality instrument reporting a reliability coefficient of 0.90 would be judged to have excellent reliability, and an achievement test with a reliability of 0.65 may be seen as weak. We need a much stronger reliability if the results will be used to make decisions about individuals. Studies of groups can tolerate a lower reliability. Measures of young children are usually less reliable than those of older subjects.

To enhance reliability, it is best to establish standard conditions of data collection. All subjects should be given the same directions, have the same time frame in which to answer questions at the same time during the day, and so on. Error is often increased if different persons administer the instruments. It is important to know whether there were any unusual circumstances during data collection, because they may affect reliability. The instrument needs to be appropriate in reading level and language to be reliable, and subjects must be properly motivated to answer the questions. In some research, it is difficult to get subjects to be serious—for instance, when students are asked to take achievement tests that have no implications for them. Reliability can also suffer when subjects are asked to complete several instruments over a long time. Usually, an hour is about all any of us can tolerate, and for younger children, less than a half hour is the maximum. If several instruments are given at the same time, the order of their administration should not be the same for all subjects. Some subjects should answer one instrument first, and other subjects should answer the same instrument last. This is called *counterbalancing* the instruments.

Finally, reliability is a necessary condition for validity. That is, scores cannot be valid unless they are reliable. However, a reliable measure is not necessarily valid. For example, we can obtain a very reliable measure of the length of your big toe, but that would not be valid as an estimate of your intelligence!

The remainder of this chapter will consider methods of data collection that are commonly used in quantitative research. While the basic principles of validity and reliability apply to all five types of data collection, note that each data collection technique has unique characteristics that affect the way validity and reliability are established.

PAPER-AND-PENCIL TESTS

The term *paper-and-pencil test* means that a standard set of questions is presented to each subject in writing (on paper or computer) that requires completion of cognitive tasks. The responses or answers are summarized to obtain a numerical value that represents a characteristic of the subject. The cognitive task can focus on what the person knows (achievement), is able to learn (ability or aptitude), chooses or selects (interests, attitudes, or values), or is able to do (skills). Different types of tests and their uses in research are summarized briefly in this chapter, but it is important to stress that all tests measure current performance. Tests differ more in their use than in their development or actual test items, particularly when comparing achievement and aptitude tests. In fact, it would be more accurate to say that there are different types of inferences and uses. It is what we do with the test results that creates distinctions such as achievement and aptitude.

Research Navigator.c⊛m

8.3 Establishing Reliability and Validity
Accession No.: 2943418 and 3701198

Standardized Tests

Standardized tests provide uniform procedures for administering and scoring them. The same questions are asked each time the test is used, with a set of directions that specifies how the test should be administered. This would include information about qualifications of the person administering the test and conditions of administration, such as time allowed, materials that can be used by subjects, and whether questions about the test can be answered during testing. The scoring of responses is usually objective, and most but not all standardized tests have been given to a norming group. The *norm group*, as it is called, allows comparison of a score with the performance of a defined group of individuals.

Most standardized tests are prepared commercially by measurement experts. This generally means that careful attention will be paid to the nature of the norms, reliability, and validity. This results in instruments that are objective and relatively uninfluenced or distorted by the person who administers the instrument. Because most standardized tests are prepared commercially, they are intended to be used in a wide variety of settings. Consequently, whatever is tested is typically defined in broad and general terms. This may mean that for some research purposes, a standardized test may not be specific enough to provide a sensitive measure of the variable. For instance, if you were conducting a study to investigate the effect of general education at a university on students' knowledge in social science or humanities, a standardized test that you might use would be intended as a measure of social science and humanities outcomes at nearly *all* universities. This means that what is taught at one particular university may not be well represented on the test. This illustrates a trade-off in using standardized tests in research. On the one hand, you have a carefully constructed instrument, with established reliability, directions, and scoring procedures. On the other hand, the test may not focus directly on the variable of interest in the study, may have inappropriate norms, or may cost too much. The alternative is to develop your own instrument; it will measure the variable more directly, but it may have questionable technical qualities.

> **MISCONCEPTION** Achievement of U.S. students, as measured by standardized tests, declined significantly from 1970 to 1990 (punctuated by *A Nation At Risk* in 1983).
>
> **EVIDENCE** Longitudinal standardized test data for both achievement and aptitude tests show that student achievement dropped in the mid to late 1970s but then rose again to surpass levels of the early 1970s.

Norm- and Criterion-Referenced Interpretation

A major distinction between tests is whether they are norm or criterion referenced. The purpose of a **norm-referenced interpretation** is to show how individual scores compare with scores of a well-defined reference or norm group of individuals. The interpretation of results, then, depends entirely on how the subjects compare with others, with less emphasis on the absolute amount of knowledge or skill. That is, what matters most is the comparison group and the ability of the test or instrument to distinguish between individuals. The goal is to know, for example, whether the subjects know more or less than the norm group, and the score is often reported to indicate specifically where the subject stands in relation to others (e.g., the 67th percentile or upper quartile).

Researchers need to keep two characteristics of norm-referenced interpretations in mind. First, because the purpose of the test is to differentiate between individuals, the best distribution of scores is one that shows a high variance. To achieve a high variability of scores, the items must discriminate between individuals. To accomplish this, the test items, particularly in standardized norm-referenced tests, are fairly difficult. It is not uncommon for students at the 50th or 60th percentile to answer slightly more than half the items correctly. Easy items, ones that almost everyone gets correct, are used sparingly. (Obviously, if all the items are easy, everyone gets a high score, and there is no differentiation between individuals.) Thus, important content or skills may not be measured, which will affect the meaning you give to the results. On the positive side, the large variability helps in establishing relationships. The highest correlations are often found with two variables that have large variability.

Second, researchers should attend carefully to the characteristics of the norm or reference group. Perhaps you have had the same experience as we have, being enrolled in a class of bright, hard-working students with an instructor who graded by the curve. You could learn a lot but still get low marks. The interpretation of norm-referenced scores makes sense only when we understand what we are being compared against. Many standardized norm-referenced tests indicate that national norms are used. Despite the fact that the term *national* is subject to different interpretations, if you are studying gifted students and compare their scores with the national norm, the chances are good your students will all score very high and show little variability. This gives you what is called a *ceiling effect* and a restricted range, which in turn may lead to nonsignificant results.

In a **criterion-referenced** or **standards-based interpretation** an individual's score is interpreted by comparing it with a professionally judged standard of performance. The comparison is between the score and a criterion or standard, rather than the scores of others. The result is usually expressed as the percentage of items answered correctly or as pass-fail in the case of minimum competency testing. There is a focus on *what* the subjects are able to do, with a comparison of that with standards of proficiency. Most criterion-referenced tests result in a highly skewed distribution, which lessens variability. Despite this limitation, criterion-referenced tests are good to use for diagnosis and for categorizing subjects into pass-fail groups. A related type of test, *domain referenced*, is used to show how much of a specifically defined larger domain of knowledge is demonstrated by those being tested. For example, if the domain is knowledge of addition with three-digit numbers, the test will sample this domain, and the researcher will make a professional judgment using the percentage of correctly answered items to judge the mastery of the domain.

ALERT!   Standards are set on the basis of professional judgment. However, the types of individuals setting the standards and the ways that the standards are set can vary considerably.

The recent emphasis on high-stakes testing with state accountability systems and passage of the 2001 No Child Left Behind (NCLB) Act have resulted in the extensive use of standards-based tests for educational research. It should be noted that these tests are rarely diagnostic. They typically cover a lot of material and provide a single total score and some subscale scores. Moreover, the tests are usually specific to each state, so state-to-state comparisons are not possible. This is true even for NCLB data, since each state sets a beginning level of achievement as well as the difficulty of the test. So while each state indicates what percentage of students is proficient, the meaning of *proficient* is not standardized across the states.

Often, high-stakes tests are used for longitudinal research. This requires the tests used from year-to-year to be *equated* or *linked* so that comparisons across years are meaningful. When new standards are adopted, new test results should not be compared to previous results.

Aptitude Tests

The purpose of an **aptitude test** is to predict future performance. The results are used to make a prediction about performance on some criterion (e.g., grades, teaching effectiveness, certification, or test scores) prior to instruction, placement, or training. The term *aptitude* refers to the predictive use of the scores from a test, rather than the nature of the test items. Some terms, such as *intelligence* and *ability*, are used interchangeably with *aptitude*.

Intelligence tests are used to provide a very general measure, usually reporting a global test score. Because they are general, intelligence tests are useful in predicting a wide variety of tasks. Intelligence is measured by an individual or group test. For most research, group tests of intelligence are adequate and cost much less than individual tests. Most group tests are designed so that researchers need training to administer and score them. Usually, these tests produce three scores: a verbal language score, a nonverbal or performance score, and a combined score. The scores are often used to adjust for ability differences in intact groups of subjects. Some of the common individual and group aptitude tests are listed in Table 8.5.

Many measures assess multiple aptitudes or specific kinds of aptitudes. Multifactor aptitude tests are used to provide separate scores for each skill or area assessed. Some would argue that this makes more sense than using a single score because relative strengths and weaknesses can be identified. Multifactor aptitude tests have become increasingly popular in vocational and educational counseling. However, the usefulness of factor scores in research is more problematic. Because just a few items may measure one factor, the reliability of the scores may be questionable. Total single scores, while more general, are often more stable and reliable. Special aptitude tests are good for research, since the focus is on an accurate indication of ability in one area. Table 8.5 contains examples of both multiple aptitude and special aptitude tests.

Achievement Tests

It is not always evident how achievement tests differ from aptitude tests. Often very similar items are used for both types of tests. In general, however, **achievement tests** have a more restricted coverage, are more closely tied to school subjects, and measure more recent learning than aptitude tests. Also, of course, the purpose of achievement tests is to measure what has been learned, rather than to predict future performance.

There are many standardized achievement tests. Some are diagnostic, which isolate specific areas of strength and weakness; some are concerned with measuring achievement in a single content area, while others (survey batteries) test different content areas; some

TABLE 8.5 Examples of Standardized Tests

Aptitude	Achievement
Group Intelligence or Ability	**Diagnostic**
Cognitive Abilities Test	Stanford Diagnostic Mathematics Test
Otis-Lennon School Ability Test	Woodcock Reading Mastery Test
Scholastic Assessment Test	Key Math Diagnostic Arithmetic Test
Individual Intelligence	California Diagnostic Reading Test
Stanford-Binet Intelligence Scale	**Criterion-referenced**
Wechsler Scales	Objectives-Referenced Bank of Items and Tests
Kaufman Assessment Battery for Children	Skills Monitoring System
McCarthy Scales of Children's Abilities	Writing Skills Test
Multifactor	**Specific Subjects**
Differential Aptitude Test	Metropolitan Readiness Tests
General Aptitude Test Battery	Gates-MacGinitie Reading Tests
Armed Services Vocational Aptitude Battery	Modern Math Understanding Test
Special	**Batteries**
Minnesota Clerical Test	Terra Nova Comprehensive Tests of Basic Skills
Law School Admissions Test	California Achievement Tests
Medical College Admission Test	Metropolitan Achievement Tests
Bennett Mechanical Comprehension Test	Iowa Test of Basic Skills
Torrance Test of Creative Thinking	Stanford Achievement Test Series
Watson-Glaser Critical Thinking Appraisal	

are norm referenced and others are criterion referenced; some emphasize principles and skills, rather than knowledge of specific facts. The choice of achievement test depends on the purpose of the research. If the research is concerned with achievement in a specific school subject, then it would be best to use a test that measures only that subject, rather than using a survey battery. If comparisons between several schools will be made, it is best to use norm-referenced tests.

It is very important to assess content validity with a standardized achievement test before using it in research. This is because the curriculum in some schools may be different from the content of standardized tests that are designed for use in most schools. The best way to assess evidence for content validity is to examine the items of the test and make professional judgments of the match between what the item tests and the curriculum. Finally, those choosing a test should consider the difficulty level of the test and the abilities of the students. The desired goal is to have a fairly normal distribution of test scores. If results are skewed by a test that is too easy for bright students or too difficult for slow students, it will be difficult to relate the scores to other variables (e.g., measuring gain in achievement over a year or more with gifted students). Table 8.5 lists some popular standardized achievement tests.

Alternative Assessments

In contrast to traditional testing formats that rely on written, objective items, **alternative assessments** are designed to provide different ways of demonstrating student performance and achievement, often in more authentic contexts and relying on having students construct responses. While there are many kinds of alternative assessments, including demonstrations and exhibitions, we will consider the two most often encountered in research: performance based and portfolio.

Performance-Based Assessments   With **performance-based assessment,** the emphasis is on measuring student proficiency on cognitive skills by directly observing how a student performs the skill, often in an authentic context. Contexts are *authentic* to the extent that they reflect what students will actually do with what they are learning. For example, asking students to complete an oral history project based on a synthesis of interviews and written sources, write letters of inquiry about a job, complete a music recital, or prepare a portfolio of artwork could be considered performance-based assessments.

Performance-based assessments have the advantage of providing a direct, holistic measure of thinking skills that are indirectly assessed in written tests. These assessments also provide a better measure of skill performance in contexts more like those students will encounter outside of school. Performance-based assessments are typically criterion referenced, without the sometimes unrealistic, arbitrary time constraints of written tests. Also, performance-based assessments are closely tied to instruction. This means that research on the relationships of instructional practices to dependent variables measured by performance-based assessments will be very sensitive, unlike more general standardized tests. However, the major drawback of performance-based assessments is the dependence on subjective ratings or observations of teachers, which often results in low reliability. This is most likely a problem when there is reliance on a single rating or observation. In addition, performance-based assessments are time consuming to develop, administer to students, and score. Typically, teachers evaluate students singly or in small groups. Thus, from a research perspective, while these assessments can be very helpful in providing a direct measure of skills, careful planning is necessary to be certain that sufficient resources are allocated to provide reliable results.

Portfolio Assessment   A **portfolio** is a purposeful, systematic collection and evaluation of student work that documents progress toward meeting learning objectives. Portfolios have been used for years in fields such as architecture, art, and journalism as the primary method of evaluating learning and accomplishment. In education, portfolios are being used with increasing frequency, especially with the assessment of reading and writing skills.

ALERT!   Performance-based and portfolio assessments often have weak evidence for reliability.

While portfolios have the advantage of providing many examples of student work over time, which can be used to evaluate growth or change, from a psychometric perspective, the reliability is often weak. The scoring of portfolios is done subjectively according to scoring guidelines or rubrics, and it is difficult to obtain high inter-rater reliability. This may result from scoring criteria that are too general and inadequate training of raters, even in national and statewide programs. If classroom teachers are scoring locally developed portfolios, even more scoring error can be expected.

Finally, evidence for validity needs to be carefully considered, since there is usually a desire to generalize from the examples to broader learning traits and objectives. For example, if judgments are being made about the ability of the student to communicate by writing and the only types of writing in the portfolio are creative and expository, then the validity of the inference to writing more generally is weak (i.e., construct underrepresentation).

PERSONALITY, ATTITUDE, VALUE, AND INTEREST INVENTORIES

Aptitude and achievement tests are types of cognitive measures. Affective or **noncognitive instruments** measure traits such as interests, attitudes, self-concept, values, personality, and beliefs. Most agree that these traits are important in school success, but measuring them accurately is more difficult than assessing cognitive traits or skills, for a number of reasons.

First, noncognitive test results may be adversely affected by response set, which is the tendency of a subject's answer to be influenced by a general set when responding to items. There are several types of response sets, including responding with all positive or negative answers regardless of the content of the items, guessing, and sacrificing speed for accuracy. Response set is particularly prevalent with ambiguous items or items that use a continuum such as agree-disagree or favorable-unfavorable. Second, noncognitive items are susceptible to faking. While there are some techniques that help reduce faking, such as using forced-choice questions, disguising the purpose of the test, and establishing a good rapport with subjects, faking is always conceivable. One of the most serious types of faking is **social desirability,** in which subjects answer items in order to appear most normal or most socially desirable, rather than responding honestly. Third, the reliability of noncognitive tests is generally lower than that of cognitive tests. Fourth, in most noncognitive tests, we are interested in evidence of construct validity, which is difficult to establish. Finally, noncognitive tests do not have "right" answers like cognitive tests. The results are usually interpreted by comparison with other individuals, so the nature of the comparison group is particularly important. Despite these limitations, noncognitive traits are used in research because they are an integral part of the learning process.

Personality tests include a wide range of checklists, projective tests, and general adjustment inventories. Most are self-report instruments containing a structured question-response format, and they require specialized training for interpretation. Because of psychometric weakness in most personality tests, the results should be used for groups of subjects rather than individuals.

Attitude and interest inventories are used extensively in educational research. Most are self-report instruments and are subject to faking and response set. Interest inventories measure feelings and beliefs about activities in which an individual can engage. Attitude inventories measure feelings and beliefs about something other than an activity, such as an object, group, or place. Both are concerned with likes and dislikes, preferences, and predispositions.

A complete discussion of these types of inventories, is beyond the scope of this book, although we discuss questionnaires as one way to assess attitudes later in this chapter. Table 8.6 lists examples of personality, attitude, interest, and value inventories.

QUESTIONNAIRES

For many good reasons, the questionnaire is the most widely used technique for obtaining information from subjects. A **questionnaire** is relatively economical, has the same questions for all subjects, and can ensure anonymity. Questionnaires can use statements or questions, but in all cases, the subject is responding to something written for specific purposes. In this section of the chapter, information about questionnaires is presented by following the sequence of steps researchers use in developing them. The steps are summarized in Figure 8.1.

Justification

A questionnaire is one of many ways information can be obtained. However, before using one, the researcher should ask, Are there other more reliable and valid techniques that

TABLE 8.6   Examples of Noncognitive Instruments

Personality	Attitude	Value	Interest
Adjustment Inventory	Survey of Study Habits and Attitudes	Study of Values	Strong-Campbell Interest Inventory
Minnesota Multiphasic Personality Inventory	Survey of School Attitudes	Rokeach Value Survey	Minnesota Vocational Interest Inventory
California Psychological Inventory	Minnesota School Affect Assessment	Gordon's Survey of Values	Kuder Occupational Interest Survey
Personality Inventory for Children	Children's Scale of Social Attitudes	Work Values Inventory	Kuder General Interest Inventory
Omnibus Personality Inventory	Learning Environment Inventory		Vocational Preference Inventory
Rorschach Inkblot Test	Student Attitude Inventory		
Thematic Apperception Test	Revised Math Attitude Scale		
Tennessee Self-Concept Scale			
Piers-Harris Children's Self-Concept Scale			
Coopersmith Self-Esteem Inventory			

FIGURE 8.1   **Steps in Developing a Questionnaire**

could be used? Answering this question requires knowing the strengths and weaknesses of each technique (which is addressed later in the chapter by comparing several commonly used techniques). Researchers should carefully consider whether they should develop new questionnaires. In many cases, existing instruments can be used or adapted for use instead of preparing a new one. If the researcher can locate an existing questionnaire, time and money will be saved and an instrument with established reliability and validity may be located.

Defining Objectives

The second step in using a questionnaire is to define and list the specific objectives that the information will achieve. The objectives are based on the research problems or questions, and they show how each piece of information will be used. They need not be strict behavioral objectives, but they must be specific enough to indicate how the responses from each item will meet the objectives. By defining objectives, the researcher is specifying the information that is needed. Unfortunately, many researchers include questions that have not been thought through properly, and the results are never used. Time and energy are wasted, and interested audiences are disenchanted.

Writing Questions and Statements

It is best to write the items by objective and to be aware of the way the results will be analyzed once the data have been collected. There are two general considerations in writing the items: comply with rules for writing most types of items, and decide which item format is best.

Babbie (1998) suggests the following guidelines for writing effective questions or statements:

1. **Make items clear.** An item achieves clarity when all respondents interpret it in the same way. Never assume that the respondent will read something into the item. Often, the perspectives, words, or phrases that make perfect sense to the researcher are unclear to the respondents. The item may also be too general, allowing different interpretations. The question "What do you think about the new curriculum?" for example, would probably evoke counter questions: for example, "Which curriculum? What is meant by 'think about'?" Finally, vague and ambiguous words like *a few*, *sometimes*, and *usually* should be avoided, as should jargon and complex phrases.

2. **Avoid double-barreled questions.** A question should be limited to a single idea or concept. **Double-barreled questions** contain two or more ideas, and frequently the word *and* is used in the item. Double-barreled questions and statements are undesirable because the respondent may, if given an opportunity, answer each part differently. If, for instance, a respondent is asked to agree or disagree with the statement "School counselors spend too much time with recordkeeping and not enough time with counseling of personal problems," it would be possible to agree with the first part (too much recordkeeping) and disagree with the second part (not enough time with counseling).

3. **Respondents must be competent to answer.** It is important that the respondents be able to provide reliable information. Some questions that ask teachers to recall specific incidents or to reconstruct what they did several weeks earlier, for example, are subject to inaccuracy simply because the teachers cannot reliably remember the incidents. Similarly, it would be of little value to ask college professors who teach the historical foundations of education to judge the adequacy of a minimum competency test of reading readiness skills that prospective teachers should demonstrate knowledge of for certification. In many instances, the subjects are unable to make a response they can be confident of, and in such circumstances, it is best to provide in the response options something like *unsure* or *do not know* in order to give the subjects an opportunity to state their true feelings or beliefs.

4. **Questions should be relevant.** If subjects are asked to respond to questions that are unimportant to them or are about things they have not thought about or care little about, they will likely respond carelessly and the results will be misleading. This may occur, for instance, when teachers are asked their preferences in standardized tests when they rarely if ever use the results of these tests in teaching. Their answers might be based on an expedient response, rather than a careful consideration of the tests.

5. **Short, simple items are best.** Long and complicated items should be avoided because they are more difficult to understand, and respondents may be unwilling to try to understand them. Assume that respondents will read and answer items quickly and that it is necessary to write items that are simple, easy to understand, and easy to respond to.

6. **Avoid negative items.** Negatively stated items should be avoided because they are easy to misinterpret. Subjects will unconsciously skip or overlook the negative word, so their answers will be the opposite of the intended. If researchers use negative items, they should boldface, underline, or capitalize these items (e.g., <u>not</u>, or NO).

7. **Avoid biased items or terms.** The way in which items are worded, as well as the inclusion of certain terms, may encourage particular responses more than others. Such items are termed *biased* and, of course, should be avoided. There are many ways to bias an item. The identification of a well-known person or agency in the item can create bias. "Do you agree or disagree with the superintendent's recent proposal to . . . ?" is likely to elicit a response based on an attitude toward the superintendent, not the proposal. Some items provide biased responses because of the social desirability of the answer. For example, if you ask teachers whether they ever ridicule their students, you can be fairly sure, even if the responses are anonymous, that the answer will be *no* because good teachers do not ridicule students. Student responses to the same question or observations of other teachers might provide different information.

Researchers may also give a hint of what response they are hoping for. This occurs if the respondents want to please the researcher and provide responses they think the researcher wants, or it may occur if the subjects know the consequences of the responses. It has been shown, for example, that student evaluations of college professors are more favorable if the professor tells the students before they fill out the forms that the results will have a direct bearing on their (the teachers') tenure and salary raises. The students presumably feel less negative because of the important consequences of the results. Finally, items are ambiguous if the respondent thinks "Well, sometimes I feel this way, sometimes I feel that way" or "It depends on the situation." Many items fail to specify adequately the situational constraints that should be considered, leading to inaccurate responses. If asked, for instance, to agree or disagree with the statement "The discovery method of teaching is better than the lecture method," a teacher would likely respond, "It depends on the student."

Given these general guidelines, how do you know if the items are well written? One approach is to ask friends, colleagues, and experts to review the items and look for any problems. Beyond this subjective method, a good way to demonstrate empirically that items are unbiased, unambiguous, and clear is to construct two equivalent forms of each item and give them to random groups. If the two groups' responses are nearly the same on each pair of items, then the items are probably good. If not, then the items need to be rewritten.

Types of Items

There are many ways in which a question or statement can be worded and several ways in which the response can be made. The type of item should be based on the advantages, uses, and limitations of these options.

Open and Closed Form   The first consideration is to decide whether the item will have a **closed form,** in which subjects choose between predetermined responses, or an **open form,** in which the subjects write in any response they want. The choice of form to use depends on the objective of the item and the advantages and disadvantages of each type. Closed-form items (also called *structured, selected response,* or *closed ended*) are best for obtaining demographic information and data that can be categorized easily. Rather than ask "How many hours did you study for the test?" for example, a closed-form question would provide categories of hours and ask the respondent to check the appropriate box, as indicated below:

Check the box that indicates the number of hours you spent studying for the test.

- ☐   0–2
- ☐   3–5
- ☐   6–8
- ☐   9–11
- ☐   12+

Obviously, it is much easier to score a closed-form item, and the subject can answer the items more quickly. It is therefore best to use closed-form items with a large number of subjects or a large number of items.

There are certain disadvantages to using structured items, however. With the question "How many hours did you study for the test?" for example, if every subject checks a response labeled *3 to 5 hours*, the researcher has lost accuracy and variability (i.e., no spread of responses across all response categories) with this factor. In other words, if categories are created that fail to allow the subjects to indicate their feelings or beliefs accurately, the item is not very useful. This occurs with some forced-choice items. Another disadvantage is that a structured item cues the respondent with respect to possible answers. If asked, for example, "Why did you do so poorly on the test?" students might, if an open-ended format was used, list two or three factors that were relevant—things that they thought were important. A structured format could, however, list 25 factors and have the student check each one that was important (such as *I didn't study hard enough; I was sick; I was unlucky*); the student may check factors that would have been omitted in the open-ended mode. One approach to the case in which both the open and the closed form have advantages is to use open-ended questions first with a small group of subjects in order to generate salient factors and then to use closed-ended items, based on the open-ended responses, with a larger group. Open-ended items exert the least amount of control over the respondent and can capture idiosyncratic differences. If the purpose of the research is to generate specific individual responses, the open-ended format is best; if the purpose is to provide more general group responses, the closed form is best.

Scaled Items   A **scale** is a series of gradations, levels, or values that describes various degrees of something. Scales are used extensively in questionnaires because they allow fairly accurate assessments of beliefs or opinions. This is because many of our beliefs and opinions are thought of in terms of gradations. We believe something very strongly or intently, or perhaps we have a positive or negative opinion of something.

The usual format of scaled items is a question or statement followed by a scale of potential responses. The subjects check the place on the scale that best reflects their beliefs or opinions about the statement. The most widely used example is the **Likert scale** (pronounced "Lick-ert"). A true Likert scale is one in which the stem includes a value or direction and the respondent indicates agreement or disagreement with the statement. Likert-type items use different response scales; the stem can be either neutral or directional. The following are examples of true Likert scales:

Science is very important:

Strongly agree	Agree	Neither agree nor disagree (undecided or neutral)	Disagree	Strongly disagree

Disagree	Tend to disagree	Tend to agree	Agree

It should be pointed out that while the agree-disagree format is used widely, it can also be misleading. We might, for example, disagree with the statement "Mrs. Jones is a good teacher" because we feel she is an outstanding teacher.

Likert-type scales provide great flexibility since the descriptors on the scale can vary to fit the nature of the question or statement. Here are examples:

Science is:

Critical	Very important	Important	Somewhat important	Very unimportant

How often is your teacher well organized?

Always	Most of the time	Sometimes	Rarely	Never

How would you rate Cindy's performance?

Very poor	Poor	Fair	Good	Excellent

Indicate the extent to which your performance was a success or failure.

Extreme success	Success	OK	Failure	Extreme failure

Indicate how you feel about your performance:

Immense pride	Some pride	Neither pride nor shame	Some shame	Immense shame

Very happy	Somewhat happy	Neither sad nor happy	Somewhat sad	Very sad

Researchers sometimes wonder whether the undecided or neutral choice should be included in a true Likert scale. While both forms are used, it is generally better to include the middle category. If the neutral choice is not included and that is the way the respondent actually feels, then the respondent is forced either to make a choice that is incorrect or not to respond at all. The forced-choice format may lead to some frustration by respondents. However, the argument for deleting the undecided or neutral choice has merit in instances in which respondents have a tendency to cluster responses in that middle category.

A variation of the Likert scale is the **semantic differential.** This scale uses adjective pairs, with each adjective as an end or anchor in a single continuum. On this scale, there is no need for a series of descriptors; only one word or phrase is placed at either end. The scale is used to elicit descriptive reactions toward a concept or object. It is an easily constructed scale and can be completed quickly by respondents. The examples that follow illustrate typical uses:

Math

Like ____ ____ ____ ____ ____ ____ ____ Dislike
Tough ____ ____ ____ ____ ____ ____ ____ Easy

My teacher

Easy ____ ____ ____ ____ ____ ____ ____ Hard
Unfair ____ ____ ____ ____ ____ ____ ____ Fair
Enthusiastic ____ ____ ____ ____ ____ ____ ____ Unenthusiastic
Boring ____ ____ ____ ____ ____ ____ ____ Not Boring

Reading

Unimportant ____ ____ ____ ____ ____ ____ ____ Important

Or for young children:

Ranked Items   One problem with using a Likert scale or a semantic differential is that all the answers can be the same, making it difficult to differentiate between items. If a Likert scale is used to investigate the importance of each of five ways of spending money by a university department, for instance, a respondent can mark *very important* for each one. This result would do little for the researcher's efforts to prioritize expenditure of funds. If, however, the respondents are asked to *rank order* the five ways in sequential order, from most to least important, then the researcher can gather more valuable information on ways to spend the money. A rank-order assessment of the above example might look like this:

Rank order the following activities with respect to their importance as to ways our research fund should be allocated this year. Use 1 = most important, 2 = next most important, and so forth until 5 = least important.

_____ Annual colloquium	_____ Computer software
_____ Individual research projects	_____ Student assistantships
_____ Invited speakers	

Respondents should not be asked to rank order more than about eight statements, however.

Checklist Items   A **checklist** is simply a method of providing the respondent with a number of options from which to choose. The item can require a choice of one of several alternatives (e.g., "Check one: The biology topic I most enjoy is _____ ecology, _____ botany, _____ anatomy, _____ microbiology, or _____ genetics."), or the item can ask respondents to check as many words as apply—for instance:

Check as many as apply. The most enjoyable topics in biology are

_____ botany	_____ ecology
_____ comparative anatomy	_____ microbiology
_____ genetics	_____ zoology

Checklists can also be used in asking respondents to answer *yes* or *no* to a question or to check the category to which they belong—for example:

Are you married? _____ yes _____ no

If no, check the appropriate category:

_____ single	_____ separated
_____ never married	_____ divorced
	_____ widowed

Item Format

There are several ways to present items and answers to items. The clearest approach is to write the item on one line and to place the response categories below, not next to, the item. It is also advisable to use boxes, brackets, or parentheses, rather than a line, to indicate where to place the checkmark—for example:

Have you ever cheated?
☐   yes
☐   no

is better than

Have you ever cheated? _____ yes _____ no

With Likert and semantic differential scales, using continuous lines or open blanks for checkmarks is not recommended, since check marks may be entered between two options.

Sometimes when a researcher asks a series of questions, answering one question in a certain way directs the respondent to other questions. These are called **contingency questions** and are illustrated below:

Have you used the Mathematics Curriculum Guide?

☐   yes
☐   no

If yes: How often have you used the activities suggested?

☐   0–2 times
☐   3–5 times
☐   6–10 times
☐   more than 10 times

Did you attend the State Conference on Testing?
- ☐   yes (please answer questions 17–20)
- ☐   no (please skip to question 21)

If several questions will use the same response format, as is typical with Likert scale items, it is often desirable to construct a matrix of items and response categories. An example of a matrix is illustrated in Figure 8.2.

General Format

The general layout and organization of the questionnaire are very important. If it appears to be carelessly done or confusing, respondents are likely to set it aside and never respond. A well-done format and appearance provide a favorable first impression and will result in cooperation and serious, conscientious responses. The following rules should be adhered to:

1. Carefully check grammar, spelling, punctuation, and other details.
2. Make sure printing is clear and easy to read.
3. Make instructions brief and easy to understand.
4. Avoid cluttering the questionnaire by trying to squeeze many items onto each page.
5. Avoid abbreviated items.
6. Keep the questionnaire as short as possible.
7. Provide adequate space for answering open-ended questions.
8. Use a logical sequence, and group related items.
9. Number the pages and items.
10. Use examples if the items may be difficult to understand.
11. Put important items near the beginning of a long questionnaire.
12. Be aware of how the positioning and sequence of the questions may affect the responses.
13. Print the response scale on each new page.

When surveying a large number of respondents, a *scantron form* is typically developed so that the answers can be accurately and quickly scored by a computer and entered into a database. While in the past the format of scantron forms was standard, forms are now typically individualized for particular studies. An example of items on a scantron form is illustrated in Figure 8.3.

For questions 1–8 use the following response scale:

1	2	3	4	5	6
Not At All	Very little	Some	Quite a bit	Extensively	Completely

To what extent were the final first semester grades of students in your class based on:

1. including 0s in the determination of final percentage correct   1 2 3 4 5 6
   if students failed to complete an assignment?
2. disruptive student behavior?   1 2 3 4 5 6
3. laudatory behavior of the student?   1 2 3 4 5 6
4. student attitudes toward learning?   1 2 3 4 5 6
5. improvement of performance since the beginning of the   1 2 3 4 5 6
   semester?
6. low student effort to learn?   1 2 3 4 5 6
7. high student effort to learn?   1 2 3 4 5 6
8. degree of effort of low-ability students?   1 2 3 4 5 6

FIGURE 8.2   Question Matrix

76. Your state-mandated testing program influences the amount of the time you spend on. . .

Strongly Agree | Agree | Disagree | Strongly disagree

- Whole group instruction
- Critical thinking skills
- Individual seat work
- Basic skills
- Students working together in small groups (cooperative learning)
- Concept development using manipulatives or experiments
- Problems that are likely to appear on the state-mandated test

Background Information

77. How many year of teaching experience do you have, including this year?

- 1
- 2–3
- 4–8
- 9–12
- 13–20
- Over 20

78. What is your gender?
- Female
- Male

79. Please mark the appropriate range for your age?

- 20–30
- 31–40
- 41–50
- 51–60
- 61+

80. Mark ALL of the following categories that best describe you.

- African American
- American Indian or Alaskan Native
- Asian
- White
- Pacific Islander
- Hispanic
- Other, please specify:

FIGURE 8.3 **Example of Questionnaire Items on Scantron Form**

Source: From *Teacher Survey on the Impact of State Mandated Testing Programs,* 2000, Boston, MA: National Board on Educational Testing and Public Policy, Boston College. Copyright © 2000 by National Computer Systems, Inc. All rights reserved. Reprinted by permission.

Pilot Testing

It is highly recommended that researchers conduct pilot tests of their questionnaires before using them in studies. To do so, it is best to locate a sample of subjects with characteristics similar to those that will be used in the study. While the size of the sample should be greater than 20, it is better to have only 10 subjects than to have no pilot test. The administration of the questionnaire should be about the same as that to be used in the study, and the pilot test respondents should be given space to write comments about individual items and the questionnaire as a whole. The researcher wants to know whether it takes too long to complete, whether the directions and items are clear, and so on. If there are enough pilot test subjects, an estimate of reliability may be calculated, and some indication will be given of whether there is sufficient variability in the answers to investigate various relationships. There are thus two steps in getting feedback about the questionnaire before it is used in the study: an informal critique of individual items as they are prepared and a pilot test of the full questionnaire.

Table 8.7 summarizes the do's and don'ts of writing questionnaires.

TABLE 8.7   Do's and Don'ts of Writing Questionnaires

Do	Don't
• Use short, simple, clear directions and items.	• Use open-ended items.
• Label all points on a scale.	• Use "Other" as a category.
• Make the questionnaire professional looking.	• Use double-barreled questions.
• Use "Almost always" rather than "Always."	• Use negative items.
• Spell out acronyms.	• Use more than six or seven points on a scale.
• Ask only for information you will use.	• Clutter the questionnaire.
• Draw attention to important terms (e.g., use bold type).	• Use ranking items with a long list.
• Put items into logically coherent sections.	• Use jargon.
• Put important items near the beginning.	• Squeeze as much as possible on each page.
• Number all items and pages.	• Use terms that are biased.
	• Use leading questions.

INTERVIEW SCHEDULES

Interviews in quantitative studies are essentially vocal questionnaires. The major steps in constructing an interview are the same as in preparing a questionnaire: justification, defining objectives, writing questions, deciding general and item format, and pretesting. The obvious difference is that the interview involves direct interaction between individuals, which has both advantages and disadvantages as compared with the questionnaire.

The interview technique is flexible and adaptable. It can be used with many different problems and types of persons, such as those who are illiterate or too young to read and write, and responses can be probed, followed up, clarified, and elaborated to achieve specific accurate responses. Nonverbal as well as verbal behavior can be noted in face-to-face interviews, and the interviewer has an opportunity to motivate the respondent. Interviews result in a much higher response rate than questionnaires, especially for topics that concern personal qualities or negative feelings. For obtaining factual and less personal information, a questionnaire is preferable.

The primary disadvantages of the interview are its potential for subjectivity and bias, its higher cost and time-consuming nature, and its lack of anonymity. Depending on the training and expertise of the interviewer, the respondent may be uncomfortable in the interview and unwilling to report true feelings; the interviewer may ask leading questions to support a particular point of view; or the interviewer's perceptions of what was said may be inaccurate. Because interviewing is labor intensive, it is costly and time consuming (with the possible exception of telephone interviews), which usually translates to sampling fewer subjects than could be obtained with a questionnaire. Since an interview involves one person talking with another, anonymity is not possible. Confidentiality can be stressed, but there is always the potential for faking or for being less than forthright and candid, because the subjects may believe that sharing certain information would not be in their best interest.

To mitigate potential bias, the interviewer should be thought of as a neutral medium through which information is exchanged. If this goal is attained, then the interviewer's presence will have no effect on the perceptions or answers of the respondent. In other words, if the interview is done correctly, it does not matter who the interviewer is; any number of different interviewers would obtain the same results. This aspect of interviewing is essentially one of reliability. If two or more interviewers agree on the way most of the responses to the questions should be classified, then the process will be reliable, as assessed by inter-rater agreement.

A good approach that can be used to increase the accuracy of the interview is to allow the respondent an opportunity to check the interviewer's perceptions. This can be accomplished if the interviewers write their perceptions of the answer to each question and send these written perceptions to the respondents. The respondents can then read the answers and make additions and corrections where appropriate. An additional advantage to this approach is that it helps build a positive relationship between the interviewer and respondents. This is helpful if the interviewer will be following up initial interviews or will be involved in a continuing evaluation or study.

Preparing the Interview

Once the researcher has made the decision to use an interview to collect data, an interview schedule is constructed. The schedule lists all the questions that will be asked, giving room for the interviewer to write answers. The questions are related directly to the objectives of the study and follow a given sequence that will be adhered to in each interview. In most cases, the written questions are exactly what will be asked orally, with appropriate probing questions. The questions are usually in one of three forms: structured, semistructured, or unstructured.

Structured questions (also called *limited-response* or *selected-response* questions) are followed by a set of choices, and the respondent selects one of the choices as the answer—for example, "Would you say the program has been highly effective, somewhat effective, or not at all effective?" **Semistructured questions** have no choices from which the respondent selects an answer. Rather, the question is phrased to allow for individual responses. It is an open-ended question but is fairly specific in its intent—for example, "What has been the most beneficial aspect of your teacher training program?" **Unstructured questions** allow the interviewer great latitude in asking broad questions in whatever order seems appropriate. In quantitative educational studies, most interviews use a combination of structured and semistructured questions. This provides a high degree of objectivity and uniformity yet allows for probing and clarification.

After the questions have been written, a pilot test is necessary as a check for bias in the procedures, the interviewer, and the questions. During the pilot test, the procedures should be identical to those that will be implemented in the study. The interviewer should take special note of any cues suggesting that the respondent is uncomfortable or does not fully understand the questions. After the interview, the respondent can evaluate the questions for intent, clarity, and so on. The pilot test provides a means of assessing the length of the interview and will give the researcher some idea of the ease with which the data can be summarized.

ALERT! Most interviewing is now done as a qualitative method, not a quantitative method.

It is important to remove or rephrase **leading questions,** which are worded so that the respondent is more aware of one answer than another or contain information that may bias the response (as summarized earlier for questionnaire items). If, for example, the researcher asks "Given the expense of adopting a new reading series, should we make the adoption this year?" the wording obviously makes it easy and desirable to answer *no.* Or consider the question "Do you favor hot lunches in school?" It is more likely to elicit a *yes* than *no* response. As in the case of questionnaires, the best way to avoid leading questions in an interview is to solicit feedback from other experts and to pilot test the questions.

A final consideration in preparing the interview is to think about the way personal characteristics of the interviewer may influence the responses (see Table 8.8). Many educational studies use naive or inexperienced interviewers. In this situation, not only will the personal characteristics of the interviewer provide possible bias, but there will be a potential for error simply because the interviewer is unskilled at handling interviews. If

TABLE 8.8 Interviewer Characteristics

Variable	Effect on the Interview
Age of interviewer	• Rapport is high for young interviewers with middle-aged respondents. • The least inhibition in responding occurs with young persons of the same sex. • Most inhibition in responding occurs with persons of the same age but different sexes. • Interviewers between 26 and 50 years of age generally do the best job of interviewing.
College major	• Interviewers trained in the behavioral sciences are rated as being more accurate than those in physical sciences; lowest rated are those who majored in fine arts, business, law, and the humanities.
Experience in interviewing	• Interviewers' accuracy increases as their experience in interviewing increases.
Racial background	• Responses of blacks differ depending on whether they are interviewed by whites or blacks.
Gender	• Male interviewers tend to obtain fewer responses than do females.

novices are used, it is best to provide training and supervision. This can be expensive and time consuming but will increase the validity and reliability of the study. For details on training interviewers, see Babbie (1998), Gall, Gall, and Borg (2003), and the *Interviewer's Manual* (1999).

During the Interview

Appearance is very important. It is best for the interviewer to dress according to existing norms or in a fashion similar to the respondents, not in a way that may lead the respondent to think that the interviewer represents a particular point of view. The interviewer should be friendly, relaxed, and pleasant, and he or she should appear interested in the welfare of the respondents. To provide honest answers to questions, the respondent must feel comfortable with the interviewer. Appropriate appearance and demeanor provide a basis for establishing a comfortable relationship and rapport. The interviewer should spend a few minutes with "small talk" in order to establish a proper relationship.

Before asking specific questions, the interviewer should briefly explain the purpose of the interview and ask whether the respondent has any questions or concerns. The questions should then be addressed as indicated on the interview schedule. The questions should be read without error or stumbling in a natural, unforced manner. To accomplish this, the interviewer should be very familiar with the questions and should practice asking the questions aloud.

As the subject responds to the questions, the interviewer needs to record the answers. The recording is usually done in one of two ways: by tape recording or by means of written notes. Taped answers can be analyzed by several judges and used to estimate reliability. Tape recording the answers is generally most useful with open-ended questions. A tape recorder will obviously collect the information more completely and objectively than notes, but the mere presence of a recorder may disrupt the interview and affect the responses, especially if personal questions are asked. If the questions are highly structured, there is little need for recorded responses.

EXCERPT 8.9 Using Probes in Interviews

The "funnel" interview technique was used, in which initial broad questions encourage students to make extended statements about a topic. . . . Probing then begins with follow-up questions asking (if necessary) for clarification or elaboration of these initial statements. Finally, more specific questions are asked (if necessary) to call students' attention to aspects of the topic that they did not address spontaneously. . . . Interviews typically lasted 20–30 minutes. They were conducted in small offices or other locations outside the students' classrooms. To facilitate rapport and make sure that responses were preserved verbatim, the interviews were tape-recorded.

Source: From Brophy, J., & Alleman, J. (2002). Primary-grade students' knowledge and thinking about the economics of meeting families' shelter needs. *American Educational Research Journal, 39*(2), 423–468.

The most common method used to record responses is taking notes based on the answers. There are two extremes with notetaking. At one extreme, the interviewer can try to write the exact response as it is given, and at the other, the interviewer can wait until the interview is over and then reconstruct the answer to each question. The problem with taking verbatim notes is that it takes much time during the interview; on the other hand, information is lost when interviewers rely solely on their memories to write answers after the interview. Most interviewers compromise between these extremes and during the interview take abbreviated notes that can be expanded on after the interview is completed.

Probing for further clarification of an answer is a skill that, if misused, can lead to incomplete or inaccurate responses. The interviewer should allow sufficient time for the respondent to answer and should avoid anticipating and cuing a potential answer. Probes should also be neutral so as not to affect the nature of the response. If the initial question usually results in probing, then it is useful to list some probes next to the question. This allows time to develop the best probe and standardizes the probes for all interviews. A good example of using probes is illustrated in Excerpt 8.9. In this study, K–grade 3 students were individually interviewed to determine their understanding of economics and cultural universals.

Table 8.9 lists do's and don'ts for using interviews to collect quantitative data.

TABLE 8.9 Do's and Don'ts of Interviewing

Do	Don't
• Assure the respondent of confidentiality.	• Ask the complex questions first.
• Build rapport.	• Talk more than the respondent.
• Explain the benefits of the study.	• Dress in an intimidating manner.
• Ask questions that contain single ideas.	• Hint at expected responses.
• Use simple probes.	• Cross-examine the respondent.
• Be friendly and nonthreatening.	• Waste the respondent's time.
• Dress in an appropriate professional manner.	• Make respondents feel anxious.
• Conduct the interview in a quiet place.	• Be inflexible.
• Make respondents feel comfortable and relaxed.	• Rephrase questions too much.
• Listen more than talk.	• Use leading questions.
• Keep respondents focused.	• Interrupt the respondent.
• Tolerate silence.	• Debate the respondent.

OBSERVATION SCHEDULES

In a sense, all techniques of gathering data involve observation of some kind. As a general term, then, the word *observation* is used to describe the data that are collected, regardless of the technique employed in the study. Observational research methods also refer, however, to a more specific method of collecting information that is very different from interviews or questionnaires. As a technique for gathering information, the observational method relies on a researcher's seeing and hearing things and recording these observations, rather than relying on subjects' self-report responses to questions or statements.

The role of the observer in most quantitative research is to remain detached from the group or process and thus act as a **complete observer.** A researcher may, for example, want to study the adjustment of college freshmen to campus life by observing their behavior in various settings as an outsider, not participating but simply recording information.

A good example of a recent quantitative study that used observation focused on the self-regulatory behaviors of second-grade students (Stright & Supplee, 2002). In this study, the observers recorded the frequency of such behaviors as "seeking assistance" and "fails to follow instruction" and used a three-point scale (i.e., "Not at all," "slightly," "moderately") for rating listening, reading, and organization. Excerpt 8.10 is taken from this article. In reviewing it, note the careful attention to establishing intercoder agreement for reliability.

The role of observer also depends on the degree of inference or judgment that is required. At one extreme, the observer makes **high-inference** observations, which are judgments or inferences based on observed behaviors. What is recorded with high-inference observations is the judgment of the observer. For example, a high-inference observation of a teacher would be a rating made by the principal on factors such as classroom management and enthusiasm. The principal would observe the class and make a rating of excellent, good, fair, or poor in each of the two areas. **Low-inference** observations on the other hand, require the observer to record specific behaviors without making judgments in a more global sense. Thus, the principal might record the number of rebukes or cues used by the teacher as information that is used subsequently to judge classroom management. Low-inference observation usually is more reliable, but many would argue that it is necessary to make judgments, based on the complexity and multitude of variables in a classroom, for valid observations. An in-between role for the observer is to make judgments (high inference) and then record the specific behaviors and context that led to the inference implied in the judgment.

EXCERPT 8.10   Observation

We trained two educational psychology doctoral students (observers) with experience as elementary school classroom teachers to use the classroom coding system over a 2-month period by coding together in third-grade classrooms not participating in the study. The coders were blind to the purpose of the study. Only one coder observed in a classroom unless data for intercoder agreement was being collected. . . . The headphones and the observers' manner minimized attempts by students and teacher to interact with the observers and to reduce disruptive effects of their presence. . . . The observers coded each child in his or her third-grade classroom for 12 five-min observation periods spaced evenly throughout the school year. . . . The observers immediately coded each child's self-regulatory behaviors after observing for a 5-min interval. . . . Data were collected for each child using at least four classroom visits. . . . To assess the intercoder agreement for the coding system, once data collection began, the two coders observed together and then independently coded 155 of the 624 5-min intervals of data collected (25%). Observations to assess agreement were spaced out equally across the school year. For the three codes assessed during a 3-point rating scale, Pearson's correlations of the two coders ranged from .94 to .98, and a version of Cohen's Kappa designed for ratings . . . ranged from .85 to .95.

Source: From Stright, A. D., & Supplee, L. H. (2002). Children's self-regulatory behaviors during teacher-directed, seat-work, and small-group instructional contexts. *Journal of Educational Research, 95*(4), 235–244.

Justification

The primary advantages of using observational methods are that the researcher does not need to worry about the limitations of self-report bias, social desirability, and response set and that the information is not limited to what can be recalled accurately by the subjects. Behavior can be recorded as it occurs naturally. This advantage is very important for research designed to study what occurs in real life, as opposed to in highly contrived or artificial settings. However, observational research is expensive and difficult to conduct reliably for complex behavior. It is relatively easy and straightforward to record simple behavior objectively, but most studies focus on more complex behavior that is difficult to define and assess through observation. There is also the problem of how the observer affects the behavior of subjects by being present in the setting.

Defining Observational Units

The first step in developing an observational study is to define in precise terms what will be observed. Beginning with the research problem or question, the variables that need to be observed are ascertained. If the problem or question is general, such as "How long are students engaged academically?" then the researcher must narrow the purpose to obtain specific, measurable units that can be observed. Since it is impossible to observe everything that occurs, the researcher must decide on the variables or units of analysis that are most important and then define the behavior so that it can be recorded objectively.

Recording Observations

Once the researcher has defined the behavior to be observed, the recording procedure is selected. There are five types: duration recording, frequency-count recording, interval recording, continuous observation, and time sampling.

Duration Recording   In **duration recording,** the observer indicates the length of time a particular kind of behavior lasts. Often a stop watch is used to keep track of the duration of the behavior. The researcher thus simply looks for a type of behavior (e.g., out of seat, talking to other students) and records the length of time this type of behavior occurs within a given time span.

Frequency-Count Recording   **Frequency-count recording** is used when the observer is interested only in the frequency with which the behavior occurs, not the length of time it persists. Generally, the observer has a list of several kinds of behavior that will be recorded and keeps a running tally to indicate how often each occurs. Obviously, this type of recording is best when the duration of the behavior is short (i.e., from one to five seconds).

Interval Recording   In **interval recording,** a single subject is observed for a given time and the behaviors that occur are recorded. The observer may indicate that each kind of behavior either does or does not occur, or he or she may record how many times it occurs within each interval.

Continuous Observation   In **continuous observation,** the observer provides a brief description of the behavior of the subject over an extended period. The description is written in chronological order, and the observer must decide which kind of behavior is important.

Time Sampling   In **time sampling,** the observer selects, at random or on a fixed schedule, the time periods that will be used to observe particular kinds of behavior. This procedure is used in conjunction with each of the four previously mentioned procedures. If possible, it is best to locate existing observational schedules that have been standardized to some degree. Virtually hundreds of schedules have been developed, and because they have been pilot tested and used in previous studies, they are more likely than new schedules to demonstrate good validity and reliability.

EXCERPT 8.11 Interobserver Agreement

Interobserver agreement on the ESI was assessed on a randomly selected 38% of all 326 assessment tapes. Agreement was checked by a second person who independently recorded the same videotaped session simultaneously with the primary observer. The two observers' frequency counts for key elements and composite scores were examined for interobserver agreement and measurement reliability. Pearson *r* was used to calculate the correlation between observers' estimates and the paired *t*-test was used to test for mean differences. Strong to very strong correlation and the lack of a statistically significant difference between two observers' estimates served as evidence of reliability and agreement.

Source: From Carta, J. J., Greenwood, C. R., Luze, G. J., Cline, G., & Kuntz, S. (2004). Developing a general outcome measure of growth in social skills for infants and toddlers. *Journal of Early Intervention, 26*(2), 91–114.

Training Observers

The most important limitation of complete observation is with the person who records what is seen and heard—the observer. The difficulty lies in obtaining observations that are objective, unbiased, and accurate in the sense that the observer has avoided influencing the behavior of the subjects. The objectivity of the observer depends to some degree on the specificity of the behavior. That is, a kind of behavior described as "teasing other students" is much less specific and subject to error in interpretation than something as specific and objective as "raises hand" or "leaves chair."

Bias is a factor in observational research to the extent that the idiosyncratic perceptions and interpretations of the observer, influenced by previous experiences, affect the recording of behavior. While it is next to impossible to eliminate bias, it can be controlled. One way to control bias is by carefully choosing observers. Obviously, it would be a bad idea to choose as an observer of the effects of authentic assessment an advocate of that kind of education, just as it would be unfair to choose a known opponent, since his or her preconceived notions could easily bias his or her observations. A second approach to controlling bias is to use carefully trained observers, comparing their observations with each other's in similar and different situations. Third, bias can be mitigated by using two observers in each setting during the study. As long as the observers agree independently, there is less chance that bias will be a confounding factor. A final type of bias that needs to be considered is contamination, which may occur if the observer is knowledgeable about the specifics of the study. For example, in a study of the differences between so-called good and poor teachers if the observer knows before making the observations which teachers are supposedly good and which poor, this knowledge is likely to bias the observations. It is thus best for the observers to have little or no knowledge of the purpose of the study. Their job is to observe and record in an objective, detached manner.

Excerpt 8.11 shows how researchers typically report interobserver agreement, and Excerpt 8.12 illustrates how observation as the instrument is described.

EXCERPT 8.12 Using an Observational Rating Scale

To evaluate and determine the level of counseling skill development of the study participants, a team of six counselor educators was trained to use The Global Scale for Rating Helper Responses. . . . The instrument requires observers to score participants' counseling responses on a 4-point scale indicating that the counseling response was the following: 1 = *not helpful: harmful,* 2 = *not helpful: ineffective,* 3 = *helpful: facilitative,* 4 = *helpful: additive.* This scale has been widely used in research studies as a measure of interpersonal communication skills.

Source: From Hayes, B. G., Taub, G. E., Robinson III, Ed. H., & Sivo, S. A. (2003). An empirical investigation of the efficacy of multimedia instruction in counseling skill development. *Counselor Education and Supervision, 42*(3), 177–188.

UNOBTRUSIVE MEASURES

Questionnaires, interviews, and direct observation are intrusive or reactive in the sense that the participants realize they are being questioned or watched. A major difficulty with subjects' awareness that they are participants is that their behavior may be affected by this knowledge. A type of measurement that is considered to be **nonreactive,** in which subjects are asked or required to do nothing out of the ordinary, is called *unobtrusive.* **Unobtrusive measures** provide data that are uninfluenced by subjects' awareness that they are participants or by an alteration in the natural course of events. The major types of unobtrusive measures include physical traces, such as worn floors, books, and computers; documents, reports, and letters; and observations in which the subject is unaware of being researched (see Webb, Campbell, Schwartz, & Sechrest, 2000).

There are both strengths and weaknesses with each of the five major types of data collection techniques discussed in this chapter, as summarized in Table 8.10. Researchers need to consider these in selecting appropriate methods of gathering information.

SUMMARY

This chapter introduced several techniques that are commonly used to collect descriptive, quantitative data. These techniques are used in basic, applied, and evaluation research and can be used in experimental or nonexperimental research. The major points in the chapter are the following:

1. Evidence to establish valid inferences from test scores should be appropriate to the use of the results.

2. Evidence for validity is based on five components: content, contrasted groups, response processes, internal structure, and relations to other variables.

3. Five major types of reliability are used to judge the consistency of scores: stability, equivalence, stability and equivalence, internal consistency, and agreement.

4. Standardized tests provide uniform procedures for administration and scoring.

5. Norm-referenced test results are based on comparing a score with the scores of a reference or norming group.

6. Criterion-referenced test results compare a score with an established standard of performance.

7. Aptitude tests predict behavior.

8. Achievement tests measure prior learning.

9. Alternative assessments, which include performance-based and portfolio assessments, provide a direct, constructed-response measure of skills.

10. Noncognitive instruments measure personality, attitudes, values, and interests.

11. Written questionnaires are economical, can ensure anonymity, and permit use of standardized questions.

12. Existing questionnaires probably have better reliability and validity than those developed by a researcher.

13. Items in a questionnaire should be based on specific objectives and be clear, relevant, short, and uncluttered. Biased items and terms should be avoided.

14. Items are in a closed or open format, depending on the objectives and nature of the information desired.

15. Scaled items, such as Likert and semantic differential items, use gradations of responses.

16. Questionnaires are economical and can be anonymous.

17. Interview schedules provide flexibility and the ability to probe and clarify responses; they note nonverbal as well as verbal behavior. They provide high response rates but are costly and more susceptible to bias.

18. Interview questions are structured, semistructured, or unstructured. Each type has advantages and disadvantages.

19. Observational procedures can record naturally occurring behavior and avoid some of the disadvantages associated with questionnaires and interviews.

20. Establishing and maintaining reliability and validity in observational research is difficult.

21. Low-inference observations stress objective recording of behavior, while high-inference observations require greater subjective judgments of observers.

22. Recording procedures in direct observation include duration, frequency, interval, continuous, and time sampling.

23. Unobtrusive measures are nonreactive and can be used to collect data without disruption of a naturally occurring event.

TABLE 8.10	Strengths and Weaknesses of Data Collection Techniques	
Technique	**Strengths**	**Weaknesses**
Paper-and-pencil tests	Economical	Norms may be inappropriate
	Standard questions	Standardized tests may be too broad and general
	Commercial tests strong in technical qualities	Standard scores may distort differences
	Objective tests easy to score	Standardized tests may give false sense of validity
	Standardized tests provide uniform procedures for all subjects and standard scores	Locally developed tasks often technically weak
		Test anxiety
		Restricted to subjects who can read
Alternative assessments	Provides direct, holistic measure of skills	Subjective ratings result in low reliability
	Closely aligned to instruction	Poor sampling of larger domain of skills
	Uses more authentic contexts	Costly
		Time consuming
Questionnaires	Economical	Response rate of mailed questionnaires
	Can be anonymous	Inability to probe and clarify
	Standard questions and uniform procedures	Scoring open-ended items
	Usually easy to score	Faking and social desirability
	Provides time for subjects to think about responses	Restricted to subjects who can read and write
		Biased and ambiguous items
		Response set
Interviews	Flexible	Costly
	Adaptable	Time consuming
	Ability to probe and clarify	Interviewer bias
	Ability to include nonverbal behavior	Not anonymous
	High response rate	Subject effects
	Used with nonreaders	Effect of interviewer characteristics
		Requires training
		Leading questions
Observations	Captures natural behavior	Costly
	Mitigates social desirability, response set, and subject effects	Time consuming
	Relatively unobstrusive	Effect of observer on subjects
	Reliable for low-inference observations	Observer bias
		Requires training
		Reliability difficult for complex behavior and high-inference observations
		Inability to probe and clarify
		Usually not anonymous
		Interpretation of high-inference observations

RESEARCH NAVIGATOR NOTES

Reading the following articles will help you understand the content of this chapter. Go to the education database (included in the EBSCO database) in Research Navigator; use the Accession Number provided to find the article.

8.1 *Discriminant Validity*
This article illustrates how discriminant validity is established. Accession Number: 7409893.

8.2 *Coefficient Alpha*
This article provides a detailed explanation of how to use coefficient alpha. Accession Number: 5542030.

8.3 *Establishing Reliability and Validity*
Two investigations show procedures for establishing validity and reliability. Accession Numbers: 2943418 and 3701198.

8.4 *Use of Likert Scale*
A Likert scale is used in this study of mentor teachers' attitudes. Accession Number 11984470.

CHECK YOURSELF

Multiple-choice review items, with answers, are available on the Companion Website for this book:

www.ablongman.com/mcmillanschumacher6e.

APPLICATION PROBLEMS

1. For each of the following cases, indicate whether the questionnaire, interview, or observation technique would be most appropriate and justify your answer.
   a. Reasons that 1,500 couples believe they have problems in their marriages
   b. The attitudes of seventh-grade students toward mainstreamed children
   c. Knowledge of parents regarding the school curriculum
   d. Average age and experience of school principals
   e. The effects of watching violent TV programs on aggressive behavior
   f. College students' perceptions of the effectiveness of residence hall advisors
   g. Attitudes of preschool children toward their parents
   h. Attitudes of teachers toward competence-based instruction
2. Indicate what is wrong with each of the following questionnaire items:
   a. What do you think about open education?
   b. Rank the statements from most important to least important.
   c. Senior and junior high school teachers need more training in ways to motivate students.

_____	_____	_____	_____
Strongly agree	Agree	Disagree	Strongly disagree

   d. Mrs. Jones is a good teacher.

_____	_____	_____	_____
Strongly agree	Agree	Disagree	Strongly disagree

3. It is important for teachers to observe and record indications that their students are studying and trying to learn assigned material. If a third-grade teacher came to you and asked how such observations could be made with the least amount of disruption to the normal routine, what suggestions would you have?
4. Search the literature in your field and identify a study that has a section on the reliability and validity of an instrument. Identify the types of evidence that are presented, and evaluate whether the evidence is sufficient for the types of inferences that are made based on the results. What additional evidence could have been gathered to strengthen validity and/or reliability?
5. Construct a short questionnaire that could be used to measure college students' attitudes toward research. What type of item and item format will you use? How will you score the results? What will be a good plan for collecting evidence for validity and reliability?

NOTES

1. Most of the procedures are based on the assumption that there will be a sufficient dispersion or spread in the scores to calculate correlation coefficients. Some types of tests (e.g., criterion-referenced) do not provide much score variability, and traditional correlational indicators of reliability may be inappropriate. For such tests, researchers examine percentages of test takers who are classified in the same way after taking the test twice or after taking different forms of the same test, or the percentage of answers that are the same at different times, rather than the correlation coefficient. The presentation of reliability in this chapter will focus on traditional correlational procedures, since these are the ones most frequently used in the literature.

2. According to the *Standards for Educational and Psychological Testing* (2000) these traditional indices of reliability are special cases of a more general classification called *generalizability theory*. Generalizability theory has the ability to combine several sources of error into a single measure of variability. Although it is not reported frequently in the literature, it does provide a more accurate indication of the degree of error.

Nonexperimental Research Designs and Surveys

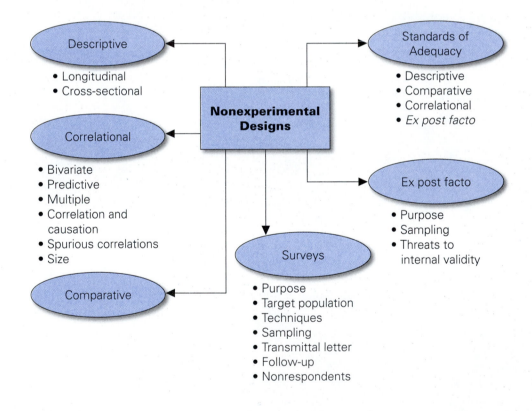

KEY TERMS

descriptive designs
developmental studies
longitudinal
cross-sectional
comparative research
bivariate
prediction studies
predictor variable
criterion variable
bivariate regression
multiple regression
regression coefficient

beta weights
coefficient of multiple correlation
logistic regression
odds ratio
path analysis
structural equation modeling
spurious correlation
attenuation
restriction in range
coefficient of determination
survey research
ex post facto research

In Chapter 2, an important distinction was made between *experimental* and *nonexperimental* research designs. This chapter will consider four common types of nonexperimental designs in greater depth, along with survey research.

SIMPLE DESCRIPTIVE DESIGNS

Descriptive designs are used to summarize the current or past status of something. This type of research simply describes achievement, attitudes, behaviors, or other characteristics of a group of subjects. A descriptive study asks *What is?* or *What was?* It reports things the way they *are* or *were*. There is no intervention.

Simple descriptive designs provide very valuable data, particularly when first investigating an area. For example, there has been much research on the nature of classroom climate and its relationship to student attitudes and learning. A first step in this research was to describe adequately what is meant by *classroom climate*. Climate surveys—which assess characteristics such as how students talk and act toward one another, how they feel about the teacher, and feelings of openness, acceptance, trust, and respect—are used to understand the atmosphere of the classroom. Once this descriptive understanding has been achieved, various dimensions of climate can be related to student learning and teacher satisfaction, and ultimately climate can be controlled to examine causal relationships. For many teachers, simply describing the climate can be very useful in understanding the nature of the class. Suppose you want to study the relationship between leadership styles of principals and teacher morale. Again, a first step is to describe principal leadership styles. The appropriate descriptive question might be "What are the leadership styles of principals?" Here are some additional examples of descriptive research questions:

How much do college students exercise?
What are the attitudes of students toward mainstreamed children?
How often do students cheat?
What do teachers think about merit pay?
How do students spend their time during independent study?
What are the components of the gifted program?

Excerpt 9.1, which is from a study of student bullying, illustrates the importance of simple descriptive research. Note how the authors indicate the need to develop a measure that adequately documents the dimensions of student bullying.

Partial results from a descriptive study of parental involvement with homework are shown in Excerpt 9.2. In this study, middle school students completed homework with

EXCERPT 9.1   Simple Descriptive Research

We began the exploration of bullying in schools by attempting to develop empirical indicators of student bullying. Thus, we report the results of two pilot studies. The first study maps the domain of the construct of student bully-

ing and the second study refines the measure and meaning of bullying and examines teacher and school characteristics related to bullying.

Source: From Smith, P. A., & Hoy, W. K. (2004). Teachers' perceptions of student bullying: A conceptual and empirical analysis. *Journal of School Leadership, 14,* 308–324.

parents and then answered questions about how much they enjoyed working with parents and whether they believed they did better in school if they worked on their homework with parents. The results are presented by indicating the number of students who gave different answers.

ALERT!   Some researchers use the term *descriptive* to describe anything other than experimental research.

Once a phenomenon has been described adequately, developmental, difference, and relationship questions can be addressed. **Developmental studies** investigate changes of subjects over time. The same group or similar groups of subjects may be studied over some length of time on factors such as cognitive, social–emotional, or physical variables. For example, a **longitudinal** developmental study of adult development would begin by identifying a group of adults as subjects; measure dependent variables such as interests, goal satisfaction, friendship patterns, and the like; and then continue to measure these variables for the same subjects every five years. Actually, there are variations of longitudinal designs, depending on the subjects who are samples or are used to make up the groups. In a *trend* study, a general population is studied over time, although the subjects are sampled from the population each year or other time of data collection. In a *cohort* longitudinal study, the same population is studied over time, and in a *panel* study, the same individuals are surveyed each time data are collected. A good example of the procedures used in a recent longitudinal study is presented in Excerpt 9.3. The study was a panel investigation in which the same 50 teachers were interviewed over three years. Developmental studies can also be **cross-sectional,** in which different groups of subjects are studied at the same time—for example, as in our study of adult 20-, 25-, 30-, 35-, 40-, and 45-year-old groups.

Research Navigator.c⊕m

9.1 Longitudinal Study
Accession No.: 8974008

EXCERPT 9.2   Simple Descriptive Design Results

Answers to Question 3 found that a significant number of students (40) perceived they do better in school if their parent(s) help them with homework. . . . Twenty-two students reported that they believe they sometimes do better in

school when their parents help them with homework. Three students reported that parental involvement with homework does not help them do better in school.

Source: From Balli, S. J. (1998). When mom and dad help: Student reflections on parent involvement with homework. *Journal of Research and Development in Education, 31,* 142–147.

EXCERPT 9.3   Panel Longitudinal Study

Overall, the round of interviews that we conducted in 1999 revealed how many factors come into play as teachers consider whether to remain in teaching, and the data underscored the role of school-site conditions in teachers' ultimate career decisions. Follow-up interviews conducted during the summer of 2001 enabled us to track these new teachers' experiences and choices and to explore how they weighed various factors in deciding whether to stay in public school teaching, remain in their schools, or move to new ones.

Source: From Johnson, S. M., and Birkeland, S. E. (2003). Pursuing a "sense of success": New teachers explain their career decisions. *American Educational Research Journal, 40*(3), 581–617.

MISCONCEPTION   Fourth-grade reading achievement in the United States dropped beginning in 1970 and then improved in the 1990s.

EVIDENCE   Scores from the National Assessment of Educational Progress (NAEP) show that reading scores were essentially flat from 1971 to 1999 (http://nces.ed.gov/nationsreportcard/naepdata).

An obvious advantage of a panel study is that since the same group is studied over time, comparability of subjects is assured. Another advantage is that the subjects respond to present circumstances, attitudes, beliefs, and so on, rather than trying to recollect the past. A disadvantage of trend studies is that the population of interest may change from one year to the next, which could affect the results. A good example of this is the trend analysis of Scholastic Assessment Test (SAT) scores. While it is true that from 1975 to 1990, the average SAT score for all students taking the test declined, this decline was more a function of who took the test than the performance of the students. As illustrated in Figures 9.1 and 9.2,

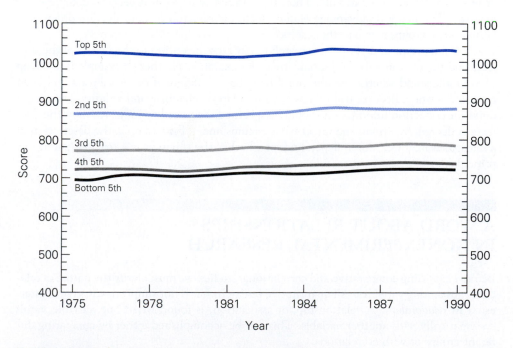

FIGURE 9.1   **Average SAT by High School Class Rank**

Source: Perspectives on Education in America, 1991, Albuquerque, NM: Sandia National Laboratories. Reprinted by permission.

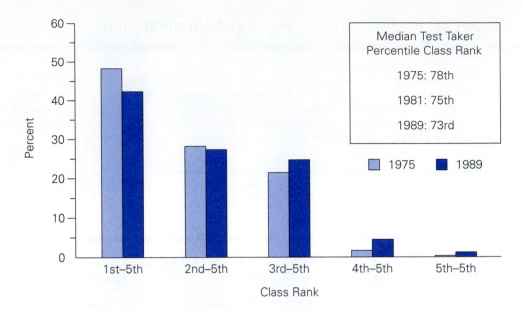

FIGURE 9.2   **Percentage of Students Taking SAT by Class Rank**

Source: Perspectives on Education in America, 1991, Albuquerque, NM: Sandia National Laboratories. Reprinted by permission.

the so-called "decline" was really caused by more students who were less able taking the test. The actual finding, when SAT scores were analyzed for different levels of high school performers, was that the scores remained relatively stable; they clearly did not show a decline.

Major disadvantages of longitudinal research are that it takes a long time to complete and that it involves significant commitments of the researcher's time, money, and resources. It is also difficult to keep track of subjects and maintain their cooperation for an extended period. Researchers involved in cross-sectional studies can study larger groups at less cost, all at the same time. Thus, they do not need to wait years to complete the research. The major disadvantage of cross-sectional research is that selection differences between the groups may bias the results.

It is important in descriptive research to pay close attention to the nature of the subjects and the instruments. You should know, for example, whether the sample is made up of volunteers and whether results could have been different if other subjects had been included. Data collection techniques need to address reliability and validity, and procedures for collection information should be specified. You need to indicate when the data were collected, by whom, and under what circumstances. For example, the description of a classroom may well differ, depending on whether the observer is a teacher, parent, or principal.

A WORD ABOUT RELATIONSHIPS IN NONEXPERIMENTAL RESEARCH

Before examining comparative and correlational studies, we must clarify the nature of relationships among variables. All quantitative research that is not simply descriptive is interested in *relationships*. A relationship, or association, is found when one variable varies systematically with another variable. This can be accomplished either by comparing different groups or with correlations.

A relationship established by comparing different groups is illustrated in Figure 9.3, where the variables of interest are grade level and self-concept. There is a relationship between grade level and self-concept because there are progressively fewer students with

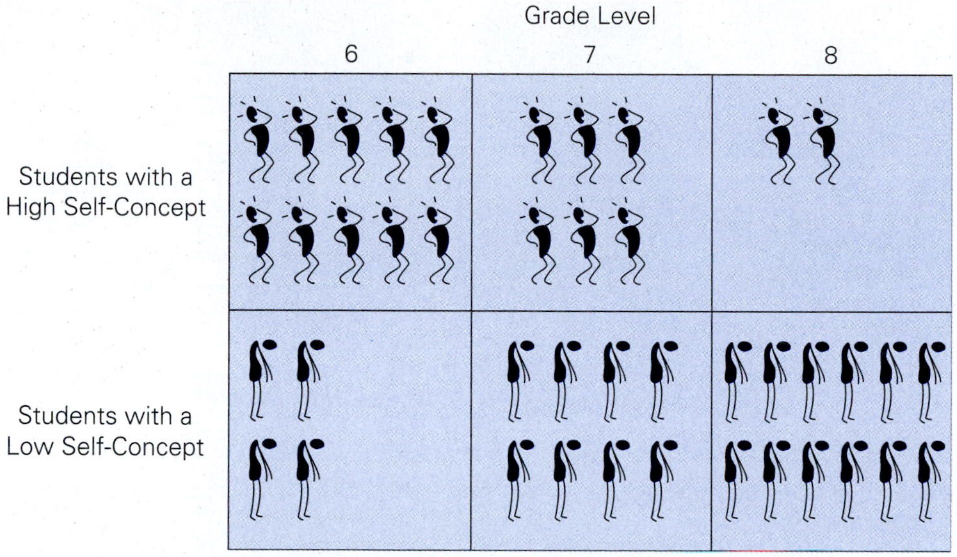

Grade Level

FIGURE 9.3   **Relationship between Grade Level and Self-Concept**
Source: From James McMillan, *Educational Research: Fundamentals for the Consumer,* 4th ed., (p. 179). Published by Allyn and Bacon, Boston, MA. Copyright © 2004 by Pearson Education. Reprinted by permission of the publisher.

a high self-concept as grade level increases. In this case, the relationship is negative, since as grade level increases, the number of high-self-concept students decreases. This same research question could be examined by computing a correlation coefficient between grade level and self-concept score.

Relationships are important in our understanding of teaching and learning for several reasons. First, relationships allow us to make a preliminary identification of possible causes of important educational outcomes. Second, relationships help us identify variables that need further investigation. Third, relationships allow us to predict one variable from another. As we will see later in this chapter, prediction is needed for a variety of purposes.

COMPARATIVE DESIGNS

The purpose of comparative studies is to investigate the relationship of one variable to another by simply examining whether the value of the dependent variable in one group is different from the value of the dependent variable in the other group. In other words, **comparative research** examines the differences between two or more groups on a variable. Here are some examples of difference questions:

Is there a difference between eighth-grade and ninth-grade attitudes toward school?
What are the differences between students attending private schools and students attending public schools?
How are new teachers different from experienced teachers?
Is there a difference between second-, third-, and fourth-grade self-concept scores?

In each case, the researcher makes a comparison based on descriptive data.

A simple example of comparative research is a study of the relationship between gender and school grades. A sample of female students' grades could be compared to the grades of a sample of male students. The results would show how differences in one variable, gender, relate to differences on another variable, grades. If the results showed that females have a higher grade-point average (not surprising!), this would indicate that there

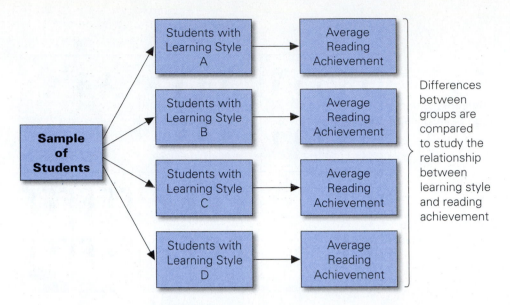

FIGURE 9.4 **Diagram of a Relationship Study Comparing Different Groups**

Source: From James McMillan, *Educational Research: Fundamentals for the Consumer*, 4th ed. (p. 180). Published by Allyn and Bacon, Boston, MA. Copyright © 2004 by Pearson Education. Reprinted by permission of the publisher.

is a relationship between the two variables. Note, however, that this would not be a *causal* relationship. While we can predict grades by knowing gender, we do not know why being male or female affects grades.

Another example is a study of the relationship between learning style and achievement. Suppose there are four types or categories of learning styles and a measure of reading achievement. A sample of students representing each learning style can be obtained, and the average reading score for each group can be compared. If we find that some styles are associated with higher reading achievement, then there is a relationship, although as in the example of gender and grades, it cannot be concluded that the styles caused the achievement. This hypothetical study is diagramed in Figure 9.4.

A good example of a published study that uses comparisons is an investigation that examined differences between American and Russian business college students' attitudes, perceptions, and tendencies toward cheating (see Excerpt 9.4). A single independent variable, student nationality, had two levels, and there were several dependent variables. This is very typical of comparison studies. Samples of students from each country were given scenarios about different aspects of cheating and the percentages of possible responses were compared. For example, 68.5 percent of American students responded yes to the question

EXCERPT 9.4 Comparative Research Design

[The table] highlights the significant differences in self-reported cheating behaviour. . . . A larger share of the Russian students reported cheating at some point. While 55% of the American students reported they had cheated at some point during college, 64% of the Russian students reported having cheated. Russian students also were much more likely to report cheating in the class in which the data were collected. In fact, only 2.9% of the American students acknowledged cheating in the class where the data were collected, whereas 38.1% of the Russian students admitted to cheating in the class.

Source: From Lupton, R. A., & Chapman, K. J. (2002). Russian and American college students' attitudes, perceptions, and tendencies towards cheating. *Educational Research, 44,* 17–27.

EXCERPT 9.5   Comparative Research Design

Do male and female teachers perceive bullying differently? To begin to answer this question, we compared the mean scores of men and women teachers on our measures of bullying. There were no significant differences between men ($n = 40$) and women ($n = 53$) on the two measures. For student bullying, men had a mean of 3.36 and women a mean of 3.59 ($t = -.15$, ns) and for teacher protection, men had a mean of 3.62 and women 3.79 ($t = -.76$, ns).

Source: From Smith, P. A., & Hoy, W. K. (2004). Teachers' perceptions of student bullying: A conceptual and empirical analysis. *Journal of School Leadership, 14,* 308–324.

"Have you given a student in a later section information about an exam?", while 91.9 percent of Russian students responded yes to the same question. (*Note:* As you might surmise, selecting the samples from each country was critical to the credibility of this study.)

Excerpt 9.5 is from the study about teachers' perceptions of student bullying that also compared male to female teachers.

Excerpt 9.6 shows how the term *comparative* is used to describe the research and Excerpt 9.7 is an example of how descriptive and comparative data are reported in journals. This study summarized children's responses to the question why they succeeded or failed in school. Essentially, this is a description of children's responses. Since both success and failure conditions are used to generate the responses, the research also examines differences of success compared to failure conditions.

Like descriptive studies, comparative research needs to provide a clear description of subjects, instrumentation, and procedures. Also like descriptive research, causal conclusions cannot be made. The best that can be concluded is that there is a difference or relationship. This principle is easily overlooked because some comparative studies seem to logically establish a causal connection between the independent and dependent variables. For example, suppose it is reported that students from private charter schools outperform students from public schools. It is tempting to conclude that the reason, or cause, of the difference is the nature of the school. However, there are many other possible explanations, such as differences in parental involvement or socioeconomic status of the students.

Often, comparative research results are presented in graphs. As pointed out in Chapter 7, sometimes a visual image does not match well with the actual data. When interpreting such graphs, be sure to examine the actual numbers or scales on which the graph is based and be alert to distortions.

CORRELATIONAL DESIGNS

Chapter 7 described the correlation coefficient. This chapter uses the basic idea of correlation as a way to conceptualize research problems and report results. Simple relationship

EXCERPT 9.6   Comparative Research

The purpose was to identify variables that can promote effective science learning environments for all students. Specifically, comparisons were made between the perceptions of male and female students and of black and white students within the same classes. In addition, perceptions of the learning environment were compared for students in classes taught by male and female teachers as well as black and white teachers.

Source: From Huffman, D., Lawrenz, F., & Minger, M. (1997). Within-class analysis of ninth-grade science students' perceptions of the learning environment. *Journal of Research in Science Teaching, 34,* 791–804.

EXCERPT 9.7 Descriptive and Comparative Results

The data in Table 1 indicate that the children were able to identify the variables that affect their success and failure. Their initial attributions were primarily task attributions (46% to 58% said the words were easy). Their own effort was the next most common cause of their success (40% of the responses). When asked for a second response, the subjects evenly divided their answers among the four types of attributions. From the total responses, when they succeeded in reading a word, they were most likely to attribute their success to their effort (33%) or to task difficulty (37%). When they failed to read a word they were most likely to attribute their failure to task features (40%).

TABLE 1 Percentages of Children Who Named Various Attributes in Response to Why They Succeeded (S) or Failed (F)

| Types of Attributions | Question Condition | | | | | |
| | Initial[a] | | Second[b] | | Total | |
	S	F	S	F	S	F
Ability	.10	.02	.22	.05	.16	.03
Effort	.40	.12	.25	.15	.33	.14
Task Difficulty	.46	.58	.28	.22	.37	.40
Luck	.02	.15	.15	.20	.08	.18
Other[c]	.02	.12	.10	.38	.06	.25

[a]*Initial* includes those children who responded spontaneously and those who were given a choice of responses if they did not respond spontaneously.
[b]*Second* is a second attribution the children gave.
[c]Other is composed of "don't know's," "I guessed," and no response.
Note: N = 40.

Source: From Cauley, K. M., & Murray, F. B. (1982). Structure of Children's Reasoning About Attributes of School Success and Failure. *American Educational Research Journal, 19,* 473–480. Copyright © 1982 by American Educational Research Association, Washington, DC. Reproduced with permission of the publisher.

studies are presented first, then more complex multifactor prediction research, and finally cautions in interpreting correlations.

Bivariate Correlational Studies

In a bivariate correlational study, researchers obtain scores from two variables for each subject and then use the pairs of scores to calculate a correlation coefficient. The term **bivariate** or *zero-order* means that two variables are correlated. The variables are selected because theory, research, or experience suggests that they may be related. Then a sample is selected and data are collected from the sample.

It is important in correlational studies that researchers select the subjects to provide a range of responses on the variables. If the subjects are homogeneous with respect to either variable, a relationship between the variables is unlikely. Similarly, it is important to select instruments that are reliable and will provide a range of responses. Various methods of instrumentation can be used, including tests, questionnaires, interviews, and observations. Regardless of the type of instrumentation, it is best to conduct a pilot test or have previous data from similar subjects to ensure reliability and variability in responses. For instance, it is often difficult to relate student ratings of professors to other variables because of a ceiling effect in such ratings, which results in most professors being rated high. Similarly, norm-referenced achievement scores of gifted students are unlikely to correlate with other variables because the scores may have a restricted range. (We will discuss restricted range in more detail later in the chapter.)

In some relationship studies, bivariate correlations of several variables may be reported. In fact, an advantage of correlational research is that it permits the simultaneous study of several variables. However, it is possible for some researchers, without reasonable justification, to measure a large number of variables to find some significant relationships. This is called the *shotgun* approach, and it is used inappropriately in the hope that some of the many correlations calculated will indicate significant relationships.

An example of how the results from a bivariate correlational study are presented is illustrated in Excerpt 9.8. In this study, bivariate correlations were calculated to explore relationships between adolescents' and mothers' attitudes toward science, intrinsic value of science, peer support, available science activities, grades, science grade-point average, and preference for future science careers.

EXCERPT 9.8 Presentation of Bivariate Correlation Results

Zero-Order Correlations between Perceived Motivational Context Variables and Indexes of Alienation

Independent Variables	1	2	3	4	5	6	7	8	9
1. Science GPA	1.0								
2. Grade in school	.02	1.0							
3. Friends' support	.16	.05	1.0						
4. Number of science/math activities	.21*	−.15	.20*	1.0					
5. Number of nonscience activities	.21*	.02	.08	.23**	1.0				
6. Mothers' perceptions of child's science ability	.56**	−.05	.10	.17*	.07	1.0			
7. Mothers' valuing of science for females	.13	−.01	.09	.19*	.03	.30**	1.0		
8. Adolescents' interest in biology	.28**	.02	.19*	.36**	.14	.29**	.16	1.0	
9. Adolescents' interest in physical science	.29**	.08	.08	.29**	.23**	.39**	−.24**	.47**	.10

*$p < .05$. **$p < .01$.

Source: From Jacobs, J. E., Finken, L. L., Griffin, N. L., & Wright, J. D. (1998). The career plans of science-talented rural adolescent girls. *American Educational Research Journal, 35*(4), 681–704. Copyright © 1998 by the American Educational Research Association. Reproduced with permission of the publisher.

Prediction Studies

There are many situations in education when we need to make predictions. Teachers predict student reactions in making certain assignments. Principals predict teacher behavior on the basis of the criteria used for evaluation of teacher effectiveness. Teachers counsel students to focus on particular majors on the basis of occupational interest or aptitude tests. Students are selected for special programs because teachers predict that they will do better than other students.

We conduct **prediction studies** to provide a more accurate estimation of prediction. Suppose you are the director of admissions at a small, selective college. A large number of students apply to the college each year, many more than can be admitted. How will you decide which students will be admitted? You could draw names from a hat randomly, but then some students will be admitted who may flunk out, while some well-qualified students will be rejected. You decide that it would be best if you could *predict,* on the basis of already established characteristics, which students are most likely to succeed. Since it seems reasonable that prior achievement will predict later achievement, you see whether there is a correlation between high school grade-point average (GPA) (prior) and college GPA (later achievement). When you discover that these two variables correlate .70, then you have information that can be used to select students. Other things being equal, high school students with high GPAs are more likely to have high college GPAs than high school students with low GPAs.

In this case, high school GPA is a **predictor variable** and college GPA is a **criterion variable.** The predictor variable is determined *before* the criterion variable. Thus, in prediction studies, outcomes such as grade-point average, dropping out, success as a leader or manager, effectiveness of a drug to cure a disease, and the like are related to behaviors that occurred prior to the criterion. To do this, it is necessary to have data on the subjects that span some length of time. This can be done retrospectively through records on subjects, or it can be done longitudinally by first collecting predictor variable data, waiting an appropriate amount of time, and then collecting the criterion variable data.

For example, suppose you need to select the best new teachers for a school division. Essentially, you are predicting that the new teachers you choose will be effective. In your state, all prospective teachers take the Teacher Examinations (TE), so you are able to study the predictive relationship of the TE to teacher effectiveness (measured by principal and supervisor evaluations). Once you have established the predictive power of the TE with one group of teachers, you would test the predictive relationship with another group of new teachers. In testing the prediction, the researcher uses the values of the predictor variables from a new group of prospective teachers—in this example, actual scores on the TE—and then weights each score by a factor calculated from the original prediction equation. This will indicate how well the researcher can expect the TE to predict teacher effectiveness. The tested relationship will be lower than the one originally used to establish a prediction equation.

When researchers make predictions based on two variables, the statistical procedure that they use is called **bivariate regression.** Bivariate regression is similar to *bivariate correlation* in that both are used with two variables in the analysis. Whereas a simple correlation describes the relationship between variables, a regression determines how well scores from the independent variable predict scores on the dependent variable. Unlike simple correlation, bivariate regression establishes a regression equation that can be used to make predictions.

Excerpt 9.9 provides a good example of predictive research. In this study, student success in a gifted program was used as the criterion variable and scores from the Wechsler Intelligence Scale for Children–Revised, teachers' recommendations, grades, and achievement test scores were used as predictor variables. Notice that one group of students is used to establish the predictive relationship and another group of students is used to test it.

It may occur to you that by having several predictor variables, you would be able to make a more accurate prediction. Suppose that in our example of predicting effective teaching, we also had information such as college GPA, references, results of an interview,

EXCERPT 9.9 Prediction Research

This study was conducted in two phases. The initial phase of the study involved 120 elementary school students aged 6 through 11 years. These students had different degrees of success in a gifted program. . . . The second phase of the investigation involved random selection of an additional 41 subjects from the same gifted program. . . . In phase two, an attempt was made, using the results of phase one data, to predict the students who were known to have been either marginally or highly successful in the program.

Source: From Lustberg, R. S., Motta, R., & Naccari, N. (1990). A model using the WISC-R to predict success in programs for gifted students. *Psychology in the Schools, 27,* 126–131.

and a statement by each applicant in addition to the TE scores. Each subject would receive a score for each variable. (The references, results of the interview, and statement would be judged and scored according to a rating system.) All of the predictor variables could be combined to form what is called a **multiple regression** prediction equation. This equation adds together the predictive power of several independent variables. Each predictor variable could be represented by X_1, X_2, X_3, and so on, and the criterion variable by Y. Thus, in our example:

$$Y = X_1 + X_2 + X_3 + X_4 + X_5$$

where

$$
\begin{aligned}
Y &= \text{teaching effectiveness} \\
X_1 &= \text{TE score} \\
X_2 &= \text{college GPA} \\
X_3 &= \text{rating on references} \\
X_4 &= \text{rating on interview} \\
X_5 &= \text{rating on applicant's statement}
\end{aligned}
$$

To obtain a predicted teacher effectiveness score, values on each of the five predictor variables would be placed in the equation and each would be weighted by a number, called a **regression coefficient,** to determine the contribution of each factor to predicting teacher effectiveness. Since the units of each predictor variable are different (i.e., ratings might range from 0 to 10, GPA from 0 to 4), the regression coefficients in the equation cannot be compared directly. To compare the predictive power of the variables, the regression coefficients are converted to **beta weights,** which can be compared directly. Thus, in our example, the relative contribution of each variable can be compared. If the beta weight for TE is .32 and the beta weight for GPA is .48, then GPA is contributing more than the TE in predicting teaching effectiveness. The combined effect of the independent variables, in terms of predictive power, to the dependent variable is represented by R, the coefficient of multiple correlation. The **coefficient of multiple correlation** can be thought of as a simple correlation of all the independent variables together with the dependent variable.

When planning a predictive study, the researcher should keep in mind several factors that will affect the accuracy of the prediction. One is the reliability of the measurement of the predictor and criterion variables. More reliable measures will result in more accurate predictions. Another factor is the length of time between the predictor and criterion variables. In most cases, predictions involving short time spans (e.g., weeks or months) are more accurate than those in which there is a long time between the predictor and criterion variables (e.g., years). This is because of the general principle that the correlation between two variables decreases as the amount of time between them increases; also, with more time, there is more opportunity for other variables to affect the criterion variable, which would lower the prediction. Finally, some criterion variables, such as success in college, leadership, and effective teaching, are more difficult to predict because they are influenced by so many factors. Relatively simple criterion variables, such as success on the next mathematics test and being admitted to at least one college, are much less difficult to predict.

It should be pointed out that multiple regression is a versatile data analysis procedure that is used for many different kinds of studies not just prediction research. It can be used with comparative and even experimental studies and with variables that are nominal, ordinal, or interval in nature. Regression is often used to explain *why* subjects have different scores on the dependent variable. For example, if you were interested in what variables explain why students differ in their level of motivation to learn science, several independent variables—such as past success in science, parental support and involvement, motivation of peers, and self-efficacy—could be used in a regression for explanation. However, it is important in such studies to differentiate between *why* and *what caused* something. Regressions are excellent for explaining, but causal conclusions may not be warranted. For example, showing that parental support and involvement explains some of a student's motivation does not necessarily mean that this support actually caused the motivation. At the same time, parental support may indeed be causally linked to motivation. It's just that other variables, some not included in the design, may be the actual causal agents.

ALERT!   Many researchers use terms *effect* and *impact* when describing regression results, but they do not imply *cause and effect* as is the case with an experiment.

One of the most useful features of multiple regression is that it allows researchers to control for selected variables to determine the relationship between the remaining independent variables and the dependent variable. For example, if a study is investigating the relationship between class size and achievement, a measure of socioeconomic status could be entered first in the regression so that it is controlled, allowing a conclusion about the relationship without having to worry about socioeconomic status being confounded with class size (e.g., smaller classes have higher-socioeconomic-status students). It is as if variability in achievement due to socioeconomic status is removed, allowing the remaining variability in achievement to be related to class size. Excerpt 9.10 shows how student background variables are controlled in a study of the relationship between after-school activities and academic achievement.

A further example of the use of regression in research is shown in Excerpt 9.11. In this study, an experimental design is used to determine which of several factors explains different aspects of reading.

A third kind of regression increasingly used in educational regression is called **logistic regression.** Like other types of regression, it involves one dependent variable, and typically two or more independent variables. In contrast to bivariate and multiple regression, in logistic regression, the dependent variable is dichotomous. For example, logistic regres-

Research Navigator.com

9.2 Logistic Regression.
Accession No.: 7255159

EXCERPT 9.10   Multiple Regression Analyses to "Control" for Selected Variables

Each regression used one of the three measures of achievement as the criterion variable. In all three analyses, five student background variables were entered simultaneously as the first group of variables predicting one of the achievement measures. The background variables were the students' gender, grade level, ethnicity, free-lunch eligibility, and whether or not an adult was home after school. As the second step of the hierarchical multiple regression analysis, all five after-school activity variables were added as a group to determine if they explained a significant amount of variability in the achievement measures beyond that explained by the background variables alone.

Source: From Cooper, H., Valentine, J. C., & Nye, B. (1999). Relationships between five after-school activities and academic achievement. *Journal of Educational Psychology, 91*(2), 369–378.

EXCERPT 9.11   Multiple Regression

We performed regression analyses using hierarchical entry of independent variables to test a sequence of hypotheses about the factors influencing reading engagement, attitude, and learning. . . . The three independent variables were entered in separate steps to test their relative contributions in accounting for the outcome measures. At Step 1, topic interest was entered. At Step 2, situational interest was entered. Finally, at Step 3, choice was added to the equation to determine whether it made any additional contribution to prediction of the outcome over and above the effects of the two interest measures.

Source: From Flowerday, T., Schraw, G., & Stevens, J. (2004). The role of choice and interest in reader engagement. *Journal of Experimental Education, 72*(2), 93–114.

sion could be used to predict whether a student drops out of high school or passes or fails a test. A unique aspect of logistic regression is in the nature of the findings. Central to reporting results is the concept of odds ratios. The **odds ratio** allows the researcher to show for each independent variable the probability that it will be related to determining the difference in the dependent variable. Suppose you are studying high school dropouts and find that the number of failing grades is related to whether a student does or does not drop out. The results would allow you to conclude something like "Students who fail three classes are twice as likely to drop out than students who do not fail any classes." Language such as "half as likely," "five times more likely," and "less likely" is used, which is more easily interpreted by many in comparison to other statistical findings. Odds ratios are calculated for each independent variable.

Excerpt 9.12 shows how logistic regression results are reported. In this study, the dependent variable was high or low participation in sports in young adulthood.

Although the vast majority of correlational research is concerned only with relationships, some statistical techniques use multiple correlations to investigate cause-and-effect questions. One technique, **path analysis,** uses the correlations of several variables to study causal patterns. A causal model is established, based on theory, which shows by arrows the cause sequences that are anticipated. The correlations between the variables in the model provide empirical evidence of the proposed causal links.

A relatively new technique that investigates relationships among many variables is called **structural equation modeling (SEM).** SEM is a powerful and increasingly popular analysis that suggests causal effects from the nature of relationships obtained that test a theoretical model. Typically, a factor that is called a *latent trait* or *latent variable* is used. The latent trait results from combining multiple measures, which enhances reliability. One extensively used SEM procedure is called LISREL. Excerpt 9.13 uses LISREL in a study of

EXCERPT 9.12   Logistic Regression

The first logistic regression model examined sports participation in young adulthood as the dependent variable with the following independent variables: gender, sports participation in childhood, family structure, parental education, young adult education level, young adult SES, young adult marital status, young adult parental status, and sports participation in adolescence. Gender and sports participation in adolescence were found to be significant predictors of sports participation in young adulthood. . . . According to the odds ratio, men have twice the odds of participating in sports as young adults than women. . . . Those who participated in a medium amount of sports as adolescents are 3.67 times more likely to participate in sports as young adults than those who rated their adolescent sports participation low.

Source: From Perkins, D. F., Jacobs, J. J., Barber, B. L., & Eccles, J. (2004). Childhood and adolescent sports participation as predictors of participation in sports and physical fitness activities during young adulthood. *Youth and Society, 35*(4), 495–520.

EXCERPT 9.13　Use of LISREL Structural Equation Modeling

I formulate a LISREL model to gauge the ultimate impact of college racial composition on blacks' self-esteem and self-efficacy. The model assumes that the racial makeup of colleges potentially influences post-college self-esteem and efficacy both directly and indirectly. College racial composition in turn is deemed a correlate of institutional selec-

tivity and a likely function of attributes of the individual's background and personality. These attributes include socioeconomic background, standardized test performance, quality of the high school, and pre-college attitudes toward self.

Source: From St. Oates, G. L. (2004). The color of the undergraduate experience and the black self-concept: Evidence from longitudinal data. Social Psychology Quarterly, 67(1), 16–32.

the impact of institutional racial composition on African American students' self-concept by first controlling for various precollege attributes and institutional selectivity.

Although these techniques are useful for examining causal relationships, they are sophisticated statistically and are difficult to use. Also, they have the same fundamental limitations as all correlational data. Unmeasured variables related to both the independent and dependent variables are always a source of potential alternative causal explanations, and the direction is not always clear.

Interpreting Correlational Research

Correlation coefficients are widely used in research and appear to be simple, straightforward indices of relationship. There are, however, several limitations with the use of correlation that need to be understood fully. Most concern an overinterpretation—making too much of a measured relationship. In this section, we present some important principles that will help you understand the meaning of results of correlational research.

Correlation and Causation　You may be familiar with the well-known injunction "Never infer causation from correlation." This principle is virtually drilled into the minds of students and for good reason, since it is probably the most violated principle of measures of relationship.

There are two reasons correlation does not infer causation: First, a relationship between X and Y may be high, but there is no way to know whether X causes Y or Y causes X; and second, there may be unmeasured variables that are affecting the relationship. With respect to the direction of possible causation, consider this example: A researcher finds a high positive correlation between self-concept and achievement. Does this mean that improving self-concept will cause an improvement in achievement? Perhaps, but it would be equally plausible for improved achievement to result in a higher self-concept. If we find that school dropout rates are negatively associated with teacher salaries, should we assume that higher teacher pay will cause fewer dropouts?

Unaccounted-for variables are also important to consider in interpreting correlations. Let us say that there is a positive relationship between attending church-related schools and honesty. Although the schools may help cause greater honesty, there are many other variables, such as family beliefs, parental attitudes, and methods of discipline, that would be more plausibly related in a causal way. Or what about the finding that schools that spend more per pupil have higher achievement? It would be a mistake to pump money into poor schools with the expectation that this will cause better achievement, because family background, an unmeasured variable, would more likely be a much larger factor in achievement than per pupil expenditure.

These two limitations seem straightforward enough, but correlations are still misinterpreted. Consider the *fact* that there is a strong positive relationship between body weight and reading achievement. Unbelievable? Examine the explanation that follows (adapted from Halperin, 1978).

1. Plot the body weight and scores of a group of first-graders.

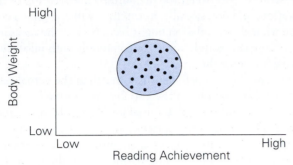

2. Next, add the scores of second-graders.

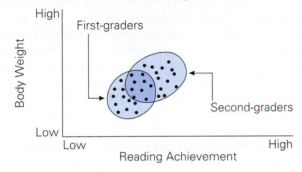

3. Finally, add the scores of pupils in grades three through six.

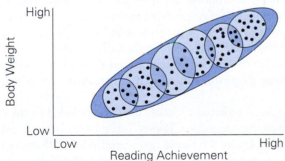

Voilà! We now have a positive relationship between body weight and reading achievement by stringing together a series of near-zero correlations. Why? Because a third variable that was not included, age, happens to be related to body weight, and obviously, there is a positive relationship between age and reading achievement. If the reader believes that *correlation* did mean *causation*, then reading achievement could be improved by fattening up students! (Or improving reading achievement would lead to fatter students.)

Spurious Correlations   When a correlation overrepresents or underrepresents the actual relationship, it is called a **spurious correlation.** Spurious correlations that overestimate relationships are obtained if there is a common variable that is part of both the independent and the dependent variables. For example, if a researcher has pretest and posttest data and measures the relationship between posttest scores and the gain scores from pretest to posttest, the correlation would be spuriously high because the posttest score would be included in both variables. Obviously, when something is correlated with itself the relationship will be very high! Similarly, if there were a third unmeasured variable that is common to both variables, as with our example of reading achievement and body weight, the correlation would be spuriously high. Such a result would occur when height was correlated with weight, since a third factor, age, would be common to both.

Correlations obtained from two measures that are imperfectly reliable will result in coefficients lower than the true relationship between the measures. This lowering of the coefficient is referred to as **attenuation,** and occasionally, researchers will compute a correction for attenuation to estimate what the correlation might have been if the measures were more reliable. A researcher will use this correlation most commonly with pilot studies in which the measures used have low reliability.

Another situation in which the correlation coefficient is lower than the actual relationship is one in which the range of scores on one of the variables is confined to a representation of only a part of the total distribution of that variable. This problem is called **restriction in range,** and it results in a lowering of the correlation. Suppose, for example, that a researcher wants to investigate the relationship between aptitude test scores and achievement of students in a program for the gifted. Figure 9.5 shows why the researcher would probably find only a small positive relationship between these two variables. Note that the figure illustrates the hypothetical aptitude and achievement scores for all students (A and B), along with the sample of students in the gifted program (B).

In this case, the range of aptitude scores is thus limited or restricted to a small part of the total range of aptitude scores. If the full range of scores is utilized, then the correlation is highly positive. Restriction in range explains in part the usually modest relationship between college admissions tests and achievement in college: The range is restricted to students who have high test scores on the admissions tests. Under certain conditions, a correction for restriction in range can be applied in these cases in order to indicate what the correlation might have been if a large sample had been available.

Another situation that can lead to spurious correlations is one in which the sampling procedures result in a more heterogeneous or more homogeneous sample than is actually present in the population. This sampling bias would lead to either a high spurious correlation, if the sample were more heterogeneous, or a low spurious correlation, if the sample were more homogeneous. For example, if a researcher investigating the relationship between effective teaching behavior and student achievement for all students oversampled high achievers, resulting in a more homogeneous group than the population, the correlation would be spuriously low. If, however, the population had mostly gifted students but the procedures undersampled these gifted students, then the correlation would be spuriously high.

Finally, spurious correlations may be reported if outlier data are included in the calculations. The concept of outliers was introduced in Chapter 7 in relation to the need to create scatterplots of relationship data. Figure 9.6 shows two scatterplots to illustrate the effect an outlier can have on either increasing or decreasing the correlation coefficient so

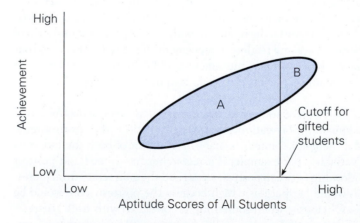

FIGURE 9.5 **Restriction of Range**

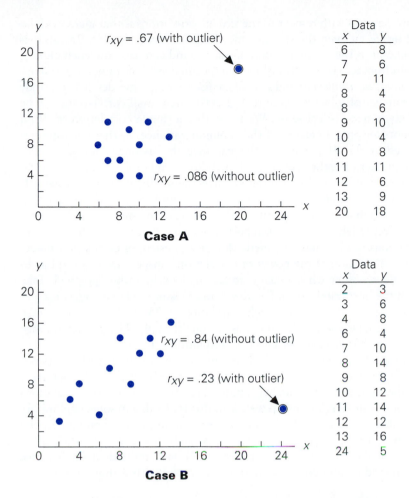

Data (Case A)

x	y
6	8
7	6
7	11
8	4
8	6
9	10
10	4
10	8
11	11
12	6
13	9
20	18

Data (Case B)

x	y
2	3
3	6
4	8
6	4
7	10
8	14
9	8
10	12
11	14
12	12
13	16
24	5

FIGURE 9.6 **The Effect of Outliers on Correlation Coefficients**
Source: From *Applied Multivariate Statistics for the Social Sciences*, 3rd ed. (p. 16), by J. Stevens, 1996, Mahwah, NJ: Lawrence Erlbaum Associates. Reprinted by permission.

that the correlation misrepresents the data. Correlations have been calculated both with and without the outliers. As you can see, the difference in results obtained is dramatic with a relatively low number of subjects.

Size of Correlation Coefficients   It was already pointed out in Chapter 7 that correlations such as .86, .95, and −.89 are high; .43, −.35, and .57 are moderate; and .07, −.01, and .12 are small, but these words only hint at the magnitude of the relationship. Because correlation coefficients are expressed as decimals, it is easy to confuse the decimal with a percentage. The coefficient is a mathematical way of expressing the degree to which there is covariance between the variables, not an indication of the degree to which the variables share common properties or characteristics. To obtain an estimate of the proportion of the variance that the two measures share or have in common, the coefficient must be squared. A correlation of .40, squared, for example, indicates that the variables have 16 percent of their variance in common. In other words, 84 percent is left unexplained or unpredicted by the .40 correlation. Even for some high correlations, such as .70 and .80, the square of the correlations thus results in a moderate degree of common variance (49 and 64 percent, respectively, out of a total of 100 percent, which would be a perfect relationship). The index that results from squaring the correlation is called the **coefficient of determination.**

Another consideration with respect to the size of correlations is that many correlations are termed *significant* even though they may be quite low (.15, .08). Researchers use the word *significant* in the context of correlations to indicate that the coefficient is *statistically* different from zero (no relationship) at a specified level of confidence. (Chapter 11 discusses *statistical significance* and *level of confidence* in greater detail.) If a study has a very large number of subjects (more than 1,000), then small correlations can be significant but only in a statistical sense. We know that a simple correlation of .30, if significant, accounts for only 9 percent of the common variance, so that our interpretation needs to reflect the 91 percent of the variance that is unaccounted for. For research in which prediction is the primary goal, such low correlations, even though statistically significant, are of little practical significance. Generally, in studies investigating relationships only, correlations as low as .30 or .40 are useful, but in prediction studies or estimates of reliability and validity, higher correlations are needed. In educational research, if a very high correlation is reported, such as .99, or .98, then the reader should suspect spurious results caused by methodological, design, or calculation inadequacies. As a final illustration of the power of correlations, inspect the scatterplots in Figure 9.7. These figures show what actual correlations look like when graphed. Take the score of 5.5 on the horizontal axis in Figure 9.7 and look at the large range of scores it predicts. For scatterplot (a), which is a high correlation of .75, predicted scores range from 3 to 8. This isn't nearly as precise, then, as .75 might imply. The predicted range for scatterplot (b) (r = .35) is wider because the correlation is lower.

Finally, with respect to interpretation, the usefulness of correlations varies, depending on whether the investigation is focusing on groups or on individuals. Generally, a much larger correlation is needed for use with individuals than groups. For correlations below about .35, only a small relationship is shown; this is of value in some exploratory research but has little value in predictions concerning individuals or groups. In the middle range, from .35 to .75, crude group predictions can be made, and if several moderate correlations can be combined, they can be used with individual predictions. Above .75 both individual and group predictions are useful with a single measure of correlation.

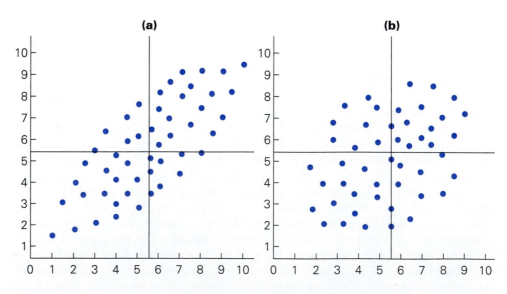

FIGURE 9.7 **Scatterplots Indicating Different Correlations (*N* = 50)**

SURVEY RESEARCH

What Is Survey Research?

In **survey research,** the investigator selects a sample of respondents from a larger population and administers a questionnaire or conducts interviews to collect information on variables of interest. Questionnaires are distributed by mail, in person to a captive group of subjects, or via the Internet. Interviews are conducted either by phone or face to face. Surveys are used to learn about people's attitudes, beliefs, values, demographics, behavior, opinions, habits, desires, ideas, and other types of information. They are used frequently in business, politics, government, sociology, public health, psychology, and education because accurate information can be obtained for large numbers of people with a small sample.

Most surveys describe the incidence, frequency, and distribution of the characteristics of an identified population. In addition to being descriptive, surveys can also be used to explore relationships between variables, or in an explanatory way. Consider these examples of topics in each of the three categories:

Descriptive

What is the average length of time that teachers take to prepare a lesson?
What are the most popular counseling techniques used by high school counselors?
What do principals think about inclusion of students with disabilities?

Exploring a Relationship

Do teachers who favor tenure try innovations less often than teachers who disapprove of tenure?
Is there a relationship between teacher attitude toward discipline and student satisfaction with the class?

In an Explanatory Way

Why do some principals send regular letters to parents and other principals rarely send letters?
Why are the students in one school achieving better than similar students in another school?

Survey research is very popular in education, primarily for three reasons: versatility, efficiency, and generalizability (Schutt, 1996). Surveys are versatile because they can be used to investigate almost any problem or question. Many doctoral dissertations use surveys; state departments of education use surveys to determine levels of knowledge and to ascertain needs in order to plan programs; schools use surveys to evaluate aspects of the curriculum or administrative procedures; governmental agencies use surveys to form public policy.

Surveys are popular because credible information from a large population can be collected at a relatively low cost, especially if the survey is distributed and collected by mail, during a phone interview, or through the Internet (as long as the response rate is good). Surveys are also efficient because data on many variables can be gathered without substantial increases in time or cost. Surveys are also popular because small samples can be selected from larger populations in ways that permit generalizations to the population. In fact, surveys are often the only means of being able to obtain a representative description of traits, beliefs, attitudes, and other characteristics of the population. Surveys also allow for generalizability across the population, in which subgroups or different contexts can be compared.

A good example of survey research is shown in Excerpt 9.14, which is from a study that used a survey with both descriptive and explanatory objectives. The survey was

EXCERPT 9.14   Descriptive and Explanatory Survey Research

A fictitious-annotated-titles survey was used to determine reading preferences in ten fiction and eleven nonfiction categories, and to determine the effect of gender of main characters on reading preference. A sample stratified by type of school district was randomly selected from the elementary schools in Ohio.

Source: From Harkrader, M. A., Moore, R. (2002). Literature preferences of fourth-graders. *Reading Research and Instruction, 36,* pp. 325–339.

designed to describe the literature preferences of fourth-grade students and to investigate the effect of the gender of the main characters on reading selections.

ALERT!   Conducting good survey research is neither simple nor easy.

Conducting Survey Research

The following sequence of steps is used to conduct survey research:

1. ***Define purpose and objectives.*** The first step is to define the purpose and objectives of the research. This should include a general statement and specific objectives that define in detail the information that needs to be collected. The objectives should be as clearcut and unambiguous as possible. This is not always as easy as it sounds. An objective such as "The purpose of this research is to determine the values of college students" is quite vague. What is meant by *values?* Which college students are included? Another way to evaluate the objectives is to ask whether there are specific uses for the results. Often data are collected with the idea that either "It would be nice to know" or "Let's see what the results are and then decide how to use the data." Either notion is a weak reason to collect data. The researcher needs to know before the data are collected exactly how the results will be used. Careful consideration of objectives also helps in determining what to emphasize and what to treat in a more cursory way.

2. ***Select resources and target population.*** It is necessary to make decisions about the total amount of time, money, and personnel available before designing the specific methodology to gather the data. A locally developed questionnaire might be best, for example, but financial constraints may make it necessary to use an instrument that has established reliability and validity. The amount of money available will also affect the size of the sample that can be drawn. The objectives of the study may also need to be modified to reflect the financial constraints. It is better to do a small study well than a large study poorly.

It is also important to define the population or target group to which the researcher intends to generalize. The definition is a list of characteristics or boundaries to clarify external validity and specify the group from which the data are collected. If the population is too broad, such as "all teachers" or "all students," then it will be difficult and expensive to obtain a representative sample. If the population is too narrow, such as "male special education teachers with between five and ten years' teaching experience," then the external validity of the study will be weak.

3. ***Choose and develop techniques for gathering data.*** The written questionnaire, telephone interview, and personal interview reviewed in Chapter 8 are the most frequently used techniques for collecting data, although Internet-based surveys are becoming increasingly popular. Consider the advantages and disadvantages of each technique for reaching the objectives, and then select the approach that will provide the most credible information given available resources.

4. *Instructions.* It is important to develop clear instructions for the respondent. There can be no ambiguity about how, where, and when participants will respond. For example, does the respondent check a box, circle the correct answer, or make checks on a continuum? If there is a separate answer sheet (which generally is not recommended; if you intend to use a scantron form it is best to have the questions printed right on the form), be clear about "bubbling," using a pencil if needed (some scantron forms only need a darkened area, not necessarily in pencil), and administer the survey in person rather than via the mail. Instructions should also clearly indicate how the participant should return the questionnaire. You can point this out in the letter of transmittal, at the beginning of the survey, or at the end of the survey. The best policy is to have the instructions for completing and returning the survey on the survey itself.

5. *Sampling.* The basic principles of sampling were presented in Chapter 6. Most surveys use probability sampling in order to ensure adequate representation of the population. The random sampling is often stratified on some variables, such as sex, grade level, ability level, and socioeconomic status. When researching a relationship, be sure that the sample will provide variation in responses. Use the largest possible number of subjects for probability sampling that resources will allow.

6. *Letter of transmittal.* In the case of mailed and Internet-based questionnaires, the nature of the cover letter or letter of transmittal is crucial in determining the percentage of subjects who return completed forms. The letter should be brief and establish the credibility of the researcher and the study. This is accomplished by including the following: the names and identifications of the investigators; the purpose and intention of the study without complete details; the importance of the study for the respondent and profession; the importance of the respondent for the study; the protection afforded the respondent by keeping the identities of the respondents confidential; a time limit for returning a written survey that is neither too long nor too short (usually a week or less); endorsements for the study by recognized institutions or groups; a brief description of the questionnaire and procedure; mention of an opportunity to obtain results; a request for cooperation and honesty; and thanks to the respondent. Naturally, if the letter is neat, professional in appearance, and without grammatical and spelling errors, the respondent will be more likely to cooperate. It is best if the letter establishes that the research is being conducted by an organization that is recognized by the respondent as credible. If possible, letters of transmittal should be personalized. Figures 9.8 and 9.9 show sample letters illustrating these points.

7. *Pilot test.* It is critical to pilot test both the instructions and the survey before distributing them to the identified sample. This pilot should be done with respondents similar to those in the sample. Generally, the pilot can be successful in identifying needed changes if as few as 10 individuals are willing to complete it and provide suggestions to improve clarity and format. The pilot test also gives you an estimate of the amount of time it will take to complete the survey. Finally, the pilot test provides an initial idea of the pattern of responses that are likely and whether revisions need to be made to avoid ceiling or floor effects. Occasionally, an initial informal pilot test will be conducted, followed by a more formal pilot test with a larger sample.

8. *Mail survey follow-up.* The initial mailing of the letter of transmittal, questionnaire, and stamped return-addressed envelope will usually result in a response rate of from 40 to 60 percent—that is, 40 to 60 percent of the sample will typically return the questionnaires. This rate is higher for short questionnaires of obvious importance and lower for long questionnaires on an obscure or highly personal topic. The standard procedure for follow-up is to first send a reminder postcard about 10 days to two weeks after receipt of the initial mailing. For nonrespondents, a follow-up letter is sent about three to four weeks after the initial mailing, which includes another copy of the survey. If the return rate is still low and resources permit, a certified letter with yet another copy of the survey is sent six to eight weeks after the initial mailing. In the case of surveys that have assured anonymity, it is impossible to know who has or has not returned the questionnaire. In this case, researchers can use one of several procedures: They can send a follow-up letter or postcard to everyone, indicating that those who did return the questionnaire may ignore

FIGURE 9.8   Letter of Transmittal

Dear Parent Association Executive Board Member,

Your position in education is an important one.

Your concern for your children and their school is demonstrated by the position that you hold in the Parent Association. As an executive board member you are a key person in many ways. You listen to the parents and speak for them. You listen and speak to the principal and work with him or her. You are an important link between school and community. Your decisions have great importance for your children and their school. — **Importance of respondent**

The elementary principal's position is also important. You are well aware of the serious responsibilities that he or she has. His or her decisions affect your children daily, and may very well affect them for the rest of their lives. — **Importance of study**

I am doing a doctoral study at St. John's University, New York City, that is concerned with Parent Association executive board members and elementary principals. As an executive board member, you, and your executive role, are of particular interest to this study.

This is a nationwide study. You, and all of the participants, have been randomly selected. Permission has been secured from the superintendent to request your cooperation. — **Identify investigator; purpose of study; importance of respondent**

We share a common interest and concern for the problems under investigation. It is on this basis of a common goal of increased knowledge about education that I am requesting your cooperation in filling out the enclosed questionnaire. — **Request cooperation**

The questionnaire contains three parts. The first two parts are concerned with your perceptions of the principal and the third part requests personal information about you. — **Description of questionnaire**

The questionnaire has been carefully studied and evaluated by professionals and Parent Association executive board members.

The executive board members were asked to complete the questionnaire. They unanimously reported that it took no more than twenty minutes to fill it out. — **Endorsement of study**

You need not sign the questionnaire and you are assured that your response will remain anonymous and confidential. Your participation is, of course, voluntary. — **Protection afforded respondent**

Please answer all of the questions and return the completed questionnaire to me in the enclosed envelope as soon as possible. — **Description of procedure (time limit)**

If you wish a summary of the study, please check the appropriate box at the end of the questionnaire and send your name and address on the enclosed postal card. — **Opportunity to obtain results**

Thank you for your cooperation. — **Thank respondent**

Yours truly,

Stanley Cogan
Assistant Principal
New York City Public Schools

Source: From *The Relationship of the Social Class and Personal Characteristics of Parent Association Executive Board Members to the Role Expectations and Personal Characteristics Which They Advocate in the Selection of Elementary Principals in Selected American Cities,* doctoral dissertation by Stanley Cogan, 1982. Reprinted by permission of Stanley Cogan.

the follow-up; they can code the questionnaires without the knowledge of the subjects in order to identify respondents; or the subjects can send separate postcards when they return their questionnaires. The postcard follow-up usually brings 10 to 30 percent more returns, and a second follow-up will add another 10 to 20 percent to the return rate. If the researchers can obtain a total return rate of 70 percent or better, they are doing very well.

9. **Nonrespondents.** In most survey studies, there will be a percentage of subjects who fail to return the completed questionnaire. These subjects are called *nonrespondents*, and the researcher may need to make additional efforts to check whether the inclusion of these subjects would have altered the results. For most surveys with a large sample (e.g., 200 or more), the nonrespondents will probably not affect the results in an appreciable way if the return rate is at least 70 percent. If the results are to be used for important deci-

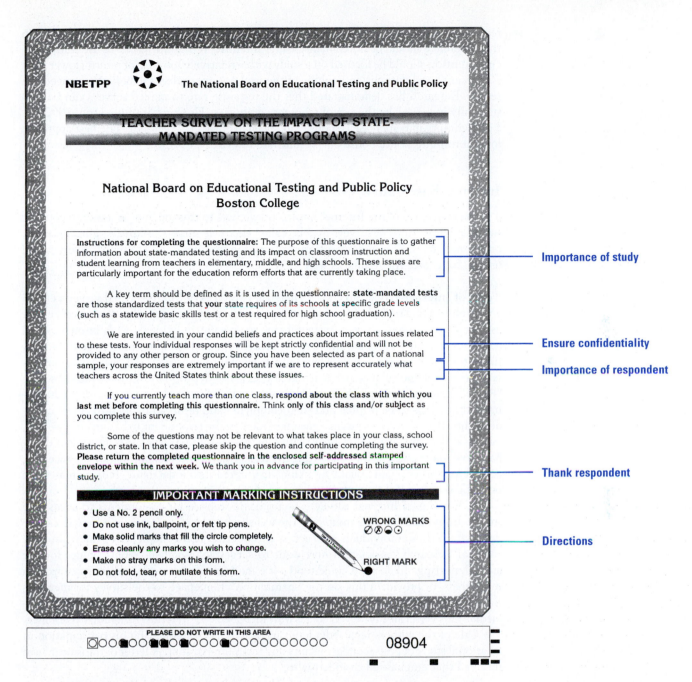

FIGURE 9.9   Letter of Transmittal

Source: From Teacher survey on the impact of state-mandated testing programs, National Board on Educational Testing and Public Policy, Boston: Boston College Press. Reprinted by permission.

sions or if the nature of the questions might cause a certain type of subject not to respond, then the nonrespondents should be checked. The suggested approach for investigating the possibility of a biased group of respondents is to somehow obtain a random sample of the nonrespondents. If possible, these individuals should be interviewed and their responses compared with those of the subjects who completed written questionnaires. If the responses are the same, then the researcher is safe in concluding that the obtained written questionnaires represent an unbiased sample. If it is impossible to interview the randomly selected nonrespondents, the next best procedure is to compare them with the subjects who did respond with respect to demographic characteristics. If either the responses or the demographic characteristics of the nonrespondents are different, then this difference should be noted in discussing and interpreting the results of the study. Special attention should be focused on a study with a relatively low rate of return (lower than 70 percent) and without an analysis of the way nonrespondents may have changed the results. Research has demonstrated that the response rate to mailed surveys can be substantially increased by the use of monetary gratuities (Hopkins & Gullickson, 1992). A $1.00 gratuity may increase response rate by an average of 20 percent. The best approach for determining nonresponse bias is illustrated in Excerpt 9.15.

Internet-Based Surveys

The pervasiveness of the Internet has led researchers to this medium as a way to conduct surveys. These kinds of surveys may be called *electronic surveys, e-surveys, e-mail surveys,* or *Internet surveys.* The common feature is that the Internet is used to send the survey and usually to receive the results, as well.

Types of Internet-Based Surveys   There are two types of Internet-based surveys: e-mail and Web based. The initial kind of Internet survey used e-mail to send the survey, either as part of the e-mail or as an attachment, to specific individuals with known e-mail addresses. E-mail surveys are the least expensive type and have the advantage of looking like a traditional paper survey. They are also simple to construct and distribute, particularly when all the subject needs to do is check the appropriate responses and use the "Reply" function to return the completed survey. E-mail can also be used with an attachment that needs to be printed and then completed and returned by mail to assure confidentiality. (Of course, this places a greater burden on the respondent to obtain an envelope, address it, and mail it.) Following up with e-mail is easy and inexpensive. The major drawback to e-mail surveys is that tabulating the results may be problematic, since the received, completed surveys must usually be manually entered into a database. This increases not only the cost but also the possibility of introducing errors.

A Web-based Internet survey uses a specific website for respondents to access the survey. Individuals may be invited to the website by e-mail or letter, or a sample can be drawn from those individuals who access the website. For example, the American Educational Research Association may want to survey its members about themes for the annual meeting. To do so, it could send out e-mail to members, solicit their participation in journals, or provide a link on the organization's homepage to the survey for members to access it. Web-based surveys can have more advanced graphics and can utilize multimedia. This versatility, however, comes with increased cost in terms of technical assistance.

One of the authors received a letter in January 2004, requesting his participation in a national study of postsecondary faculty and instructional staff. A letter of transmittal was received that emphasized confidentiality:

> Your responses will be secured behind firewalls and will be encrypted during Internet transmission. All identifying information is maintained in a separate file for follow-up purposes only. Your responses . . . [will] not be disclosed, or used, in identifiable form for any other purpose.

EXCERPT 9.15   Determining Nonresponse Bias

Additionally, we contacted 20 nonrespondents by telephone and asked them to complete the inventories. All of the individuals agreed to complete the inventory. . . . Comparative analysis on the composite scale scores of each of the inventories . . . revealed that there were no statistically significant differences in the mean responses of respondents and nonrespondents.

Source: From Nelson, J. R., Maculan, A., Roberts, M. L., & Ohlund, B. J. (2001). Sources of occupational stress for teachers of students with emotional and behavioral disorders. *Journal of Emotional and Behavioral Disorders, 9*(2), 123–130.

The letter also gave simple directions to find the questionnaire on the Web:

- Go to: https://surveys.nces.ed.gov/nsopf/.
- Type in the study ID and password (see below) on the Home/Login page.
- Press "Enter" or "Login" to begin the questionnaire.

Advantages and Disadvantages of Using Internet-Based Surveys   Internet-based surveys offer a number of advantages compared to paper, telephone, or personal interview techniques, and in the right circumstances, these advantages far outweigh the associated disadvantages. The main advantages are obvious: reduced cost and time, quick response, easy follow-up, and the ability to survey a large population. The main disadvantages are also obvious: limited sampling (i.e., those with computer access), lack of confidentiality and privacy, and response rate. These disadvantages are less serious when the samples are Internet savvy, such as teachers, principals, and college faculty, and the nature of the topic is professional, not personal.

Depending on the topic and sample surveyed, response rates for Internet-based surveys can fluctuate widely, from rates in single digits to higher rates comparable to those of mail surveys. E-mail response rates are better than Web-based response rates, but in either case, obtaining a sufficient response rate is difficult. Research has shown that mail surveys typically result in about a 20 percent higher return rate but nearly a 40 percent cost savings with simple surveys that do not require much technical expertise (Schonlau, Fricker, & Elliott, 2002). However, the nature of the sample and the questions can significantly affect the return rate and cost. The response rate can be improved by making follow-up contacts with nonrespondents, by making personalized contacts, and by using a preliminary contact prior to receiving the survey (Cook, Heath, & Thompson, 2000). Table 9.1 provides a comprehensive list of the advantages and disadvantages of using Internet-based surveys.

Internet-Based Survey Design   Many of the suggestions in Chapter 8 about effective questionnaire design are also appropriate for Internet-based surveys; however, there are additional considerations related to the technology. Essentially, you want to have a simple, clear layout of easily answered questions. These further guidelines for the design of Internet-based surveys are provided by Best and Krueger (2004) and Dillman (2000):

- Use a few short items that are simple and direct.
- Show one or just a few items per screen.

Research
Navigator.c⊛m

9.3 Mail- versus Internet-
Based Surveys
Accession No.: 6282924

TABLE 9.1 Advantages and Disadvantages of Internet-Based Surveys	
Advantages	**Disadvantages**
Cost savings	Low response rate and response bias
Time savings	Lack of incentive
Increased accuracy	Authenticity of respondent
Direct participant entry of data	Security and confidentiality
Enhanced presentation	Potential for information overload
Immediate respondent feedback	Visual differences with different browsers and monitors
Increased convenience	
Design flexibility	Lack of computer expertise
Fast creation and delivery	Difficulty obtaining a random sample

Source: From Terry Anderson and Heather Kanuka, *E-Research Methods, Strategies, and Issues,* Published by Allyn and Bacon, Boston, MA. Copyright © 2002 by Pearson Education. Reprinted by permission of the publisher.

- Avoid excessive scrolling.
- Use simple graphics.
- Limit the use of matrix questions.
- Use specific error/warning messages.
- Password protect Web surveys.
- Indicate progress in completing the survey.
- Use hypertext and color to enhance presentation and understanding.

Most likely, Internet-based surveys will become more prevalent as the technology improves and this application becomes more universal and accepted. With the right sample, there is no question that this kind of survey can offer a reasonable alternative to a mail or interview survey. While many software products are already available for use in designing surveys, such as CreateSurvey (www.createsurvey.com), further development and research on effective design and implementation will result in greater understanding and use as well as greater credibility of findings and conclusions.

Before leaving the topic of surveys, we need to emphasize that survey research is not simple to prepare and conduct. There are many factors related to item format, positioning of questions, wording, sampling, and other variables that need to be considered. For an excellent review of these problems, see Schuman and Presser (1996), and for additional information on developing and conducting surveys, see *The Survey Kit* (i.e., a series of volumes published by Sage Publications that covers question development, conducting surveys, data analysis, and reporting).

Because most surveys use closed-form items that are computer analyzed, it is essential for researchers to consult with experts who can assist in properly designing the survey for easy and accurate data entry. Such experts are also very helpful in reviewing wording, directions, layout, and other technical aspects of the survey.

EX POST FACTO DESIGNS

In descriptive and correlational designs, it is almost always the case that causal relationships are not studied. However, certain nonexperimental designs are used to investigate causal relationships. One of these is termed *ex post facto*. In these studies, the purpose of the research is to examine how an identified independent variable affects the dependent variable, but the circumstances of conducting the research do not allow for an experimental design. Consider the following list of research questions. In each case, the implied cause-and-effect relationship rules out experimental manipulation of the independent variable:

What is the effect of attendance at day care on the social skills of children?
What is the effect of single parenting on achievement?
Do teachers who graduate from liberal arts colleges have greater longevity in the teaching field than teachers who graduate from colleges of education?
What is the relationship between children's participation in extracurricular activities and self-concept?

Characteristics of *Ex Post Facto* Research

It is simply impossible, unethical, and infeasible to manipulate variables such as single or couple parenting, day-care attendance, and choice of college by students, as well as many other variables such as race, socioeconomic status, and personality. A researcher would probably have some difficulty assigning children on a random basis to either attend or not attend day care!

Although it is desirable to study cause-and-effect relationships in such situations, the circumstances of the research are such that manipulation of the independent variable cannot be carried out. The type of design most frequently used in these situations is called *ex post facto*, or *causal comparative*. The purpose of **ex post facto research** is to investigate whether one or more pre-existing conditions have possibly caused subsequent differences in the groups of subjects. In other words, the researcher identifies conditions that have already occurred (*ex post facto* is Latin for "after the fact") and then collects data to investigate the relationship of these varying conditions to subsequent behavior. In *ex post facto* research, the investigator attempts to determine whether differences between groups (the independent variable) have resulted in an observed difference on the dependent variable.

Ex post facto designs are easily confused with experimental designs because they both have a similar purpose (to determine cause-effect relationships), group comparisons, and the use of similar statistical analyses and vocabulary in describing the results. In experimental and quasi-experimental studies, however, the researcher deliberately controls the effect of some condition by manipulation of the independent variable, while in ex post facto research, there is no manipulation of conditions because the presumed cause has already occurred before the study is initiated. In ex post facto designs, therefore, there is usually a *treatment* and a *control* group—a factor that can further confuse the research with experimental approaches. *Ex post facto* designs are also confused with comparative and correlational research, because all three involve no manipulation and there are similar limitations in interpreting the results.

Conducting *Ex Post Facto* Research

Several procedures are used in planning *ex post facto* research that enhance control and limit plausible rival hypotheses. The first step is to formulate a research problem that includes possible causes of the dependent variable. The choice of possible causes is based on previous research and on the researcher's interpretation of observations of the phenomena being studied. Suppose, for example, the researcher wants to investigate the effect of class size on achievement, and it is impossible to assign students randomly to different size classes to conduct a true experiment. The researcher's interest may be based on correlational research that shows a negative relationship between class size and achievement and observations that students in smaller classes seem to do better. The research problem, then, is this: What is the effect of class size on achievement?

A second step is to identify plausible rival hypotheses that might explain the relationship. For instance, the researcher might list as possible causes of better achievement in smaller classes several factors such as the following: smaller classes have better teachers; students with higher ability are in smaller classes; students with stronger motivation are in smaller classes; more students from high socioeconomic backgrounds attend smaller classes than do students from low socioeconomic backgrounds; and perhaps teachers of smaller classes use a different type of instruction than those of larger classes use. Each of these factors might be related to the reason students in smaller classes achieve more than students in larger classes.

The third step is to find and select the groups that will be compared. In our example of class size and achievement, the researcher will first need to define operationally *large* and *small* class size as well as *achievement*. A *small* class could have fewer than 15 students and a *large* class more than 25. *Achievement* could be defined as the gain in knowledge of the students while in the class. The researcher also needs to identify grade levels and locations. Suppose in this case, the researcher is interested in elementary grade levels and the accessible population is a single school district. Once the variables have been defined, groups must be selected that are as homogeneous as possible in the characteristics that constitute rival hypotheses and that are different with respect to the independent variable. In our example, then, the researcher will select groups that differ with respect to class size but that are similar in such factors as ability, socioeconomic background, teaching methods, quality of teachers, and student motivation. Matching is a good approach to forming groups that will be as homogeneous as possible in factors affecting the dependent variable. For example, in our study of class size, the researcher could match and select students on the basis of initial ability so that only students with about the same level of ability are included in the analysis, even though other students would be contained in the classes.

The fourth step is to collect and analyze data on the subjects, including data on factors that may constitute rival hypotheses. Since *ex post facto* research is after the fact, most of the data that are needed have already been collected, and only the data from appropriate sources need to be gathered. Data analysis is very similar to procedures used for experimental and quasi-experimental studies in that groups are compared on the variables of interest. In our proposed study of class size, for example, all achievement scores in the small classes would be averaged and compared with the average achievement in large classes. Data from the extraneous variables would also be compared and incorporated into the statistical analyses to help make judgments about plausible rival hypotheses.

In interpreting the results of *ex post facto* research, cause-and-effect statements can be made only cautiously. In our example of large and small classes, if a difference in achievement is found between the groups, then the researcher can conclude that there is a relationship between class size and achievement. The results do not mean, unequivocally, that being in either a small or large class had a causative effect on achievement. There may be a cause-and-effect relationship, but this depends on the researcher's ability to select comparison groups homogeneous on all important variables except being in small or large classes and by the confidence with which other plausible rival hypotheses can be ruled out. If, for example, it turned out that all the small classes came from one school and large classes from another, then policies or procedures unique to the schools and unrelated to class size (e.g., stress on basic skill attainment or a special training program for teachers) may constitute plausible rival hypotheses.

A good example of *ex post facto* research is a study investigating the effect of same-age and mixed-age preschool classrooms on play. As pointed out in Excerpt 9.16, modes of play and social interaction of children in four same-age classrooms were compared with those of children in two mixed-age classrooms. Notice that the researchers summarize in the second paragraph of the excerpt how the same-age and mixed-age classrooms were comparable with respect to physical layout, materials, teacher-child ratio, socioeconomic

EXCERPT 9.16 *Ex Post Facto* Research

Method

Subjects

The social-cognitive modes of play and peers' responses to them were observed in two classrooms of 3-year-olds ($N = 40$), two classrooms of 4-year-olds ($N = 32$), and two mixed-age classrooms of 3- and 4-year-olds ($N = 36$). The classrooms were considered mixed-age if at least 40% of the children were 3-year-olds and at least 40% of the children were 4-year-olds. Children considered 3-year-olds ranged from 2 years, 9 months to 3 years, 8 months, and 4-year-olds ranged from 3 years, 9 months to 4 years, 8 months at the beginning of the study. To assure equal opportunities for same-sex and cross-sex activities, classrooms were selected in which at least 40% of the children were boys and at least 40% were girls. These criteria for classifying classrooms as mixed-age were similar to those of previous research (e.g., Goldman, 1981; Roopnarine, 1984). These criteria were used because we wanted to study similar age groups of children in order to make comparisons with the findings of previous studies (e.g., Goldman's).

All classrooms assumed a child-centered orientation and were comparable in terms of physical layout, play and instructional materials, and teacher-child ratio (1:9). The children were from middle-income backgrounds as assessed by the Hollingshead Four Factor Index of Social Position (Hollingshead, undated). Preliminary analyses revealed no significant differences in sociodemographic factors between children in same-age and mixed-age classrooms. In addition, children in both classroom arrangements were enrolled for approximately the same length of time in the mixed-age classrooms prior to observations (same-age classrooms $\bar{x} = 6$ months; mixed-age classrooms $\bar{x} = 5$ months).

Source: From "Social-Cognitive Play Patterns in Same-Age and Mixed-Age Preschool Classrooms" by N. S. Mounts and J. L. Roopnarine, 1987, *American Educational Research Journal*, 24, pp. 463–476. Copyright © 1987 American Educational Research Association, Washington, DC.

factors of the children, and the amount of time the children had been in the classroom. Presumably, these characteristics were identified before data were collected to rule out these plausible rival hypotheses. Of course there may be other differences between the groups besides the same-age/mixed-age variable that could affect the results. For instance, a difference in instructors could affect play and social interaction.

STANDARDS OF ADEQUACY

In judging the adequacy of the descriptive, comparative correlational, survey, and *ex post facto* research designs it will be helpful to keep the following questions in mind. The questions are organized to focus your attention on the most important criteria in designing and evaluating these types of research:

Descriptive Designs
1. Is the research problem clearly descriptive in nature?
2. Is there a clear description of the sample, population, and procedures for sampling?
3. Will the sample provide biased or distorted results?
4. Are the scores resulting from the instrumentation reliable and valid?
5. Do graphic presentations of the results distort the findings?
6. Are inappropriate relationships or causal conclusions made on the basis of descriptive results?
7. If cross-sectional, do subject differences affect the results?
8. If longitudinal, is loss of subjects a limitation?
9. Are differences between groups used to identify possible relationships?

Comparative Designs
1. Does the research problem clearly indicate that relationships will be investigated by comparing differences between groups?
2. Is the description of subjects, sampling, and instrumentation clear?
3. Do sampling procedures bias the results?
4. Is there sufficient evidence for reliability and validity?
5. Are inappropriate causal inferences made?

Correlational Designs
1. Does the research problem clearly indicate that relationships will be investigated?
2. Is there a clear description of the sampling? Will the sample provide a sufficient variability of responses to obtain a correlation?
3. Are the scores resulting from the instrumentation valid and reliable?
4. Is there a restricted range on the scores?
5. Are there any factors that might contribute to spurious correlations?
6. Is a shotgun approach used in the study?
7. Are inappropriate causal inferences made from the results?
8. How large is the sample? Could sample size affect the significance of the results?
9. Is the correlation coefficient confused with the coefficient of determination?
10. If predictions are made, are they based on a different sample?
11. Is the size of the correlation large enough for the conclusions?

Survey Research
1. Are the objectives and purposes of the survey clear?
2. Is it likely that the target population and sampling procedure will provide a credible answer to the research question(s)?
3. Is the instrument clearly designed and worded? Has it been pilot tested? Is it appropriate for the characteristics of the sample?

4. Is there an assurance of confidentiality of responses? If not, is this likely to affect the results?
5. Does the letter of transmittal establish the credibility of the research? Is there any chance that what is said in the letter will bias the responses?
6. What is the return rate? If low or borderline, has there been any follow-up with non-respondents?
7. Do the conclusions reflect the return rate and other possible limitations?

Ex Post Facto Designs
1. Was the primary purpose of the study to investigate cause-and-effect relationships?
2. Have the presumed cause-and-effect conditions already occurred?
3. Was there manipulation of the independent variable?
4. Were the groups being compared already different with respect to the independent variable?
5. Were potential extraneous variables recognized and considered as plausible rival hypotheses?
6. Were causal statements regarding the results made tenuously?
7. Were threats to external validity addressed in the conclusions?

SUMMARY

This chapter has provided a review of descriptive, correlational, survey, and *ex post facto* research, stressing design principles that affect the quality of the research. The main points in the chapter include the following:

1. Descriptive research is concerned with current or past status of something.
2. Developmental studies investigate changes of subjects over time and are longitudinal or cross-sectional.
3. Comparative relationship studies examine differences between groups.
4. Correlational relationship studies use at least two scores that are obtained from each subject.
5. Comparative and correlational studies should clearly define sampling, instrumentation, and procedures for gathering data.
6. The selection of subjects and instruments in correlational research should ensure a range of responses on each variable.
7. In predictive research, the criterion variable is predicted by a prior behavior as measured by the independent variable.
8. Bivariate regression predicts the dependent variable from a single independent variable.
9. Multiple and logistic regression allow several independent variables to combine in relating to the dependent or criterion variable.
10. Correlation should never infer causation because of third nonmeasured variables and the inability to assess causal direction between the two variables.
11. Spurious correlations overrepresent or underrepresent the actual relationship between two variables.

12. The coefficient of determination is the square of the correlation coefficient, and it estimates the variance that is shared by the variables.
13. Correlation coefficients should be interpreted carefully when they are statistically significant with low relationships and a large number of subjects.
14. Decisions for individuals require higher correlations than do decisions for groups.
15. Survey research uses questionnaires and interviews to describe characteristics of populations.
16. Surveys are used for descriptive, relationship, and explanatory purposes.
17. The nature of the letter of transmittal in a mail survey is crucial to obtaining an acceptable response rate of 60 percent or greater.
18. Internet-based surveys can be one of two types: e-mail or Web based.
19. With the right kind of sample and purpose, an Internet-based survey is more economical than a paper survey or interview.
20. Low response rates and lack of confidentiality are significant disadvantages of Internet-based surveys.
21. *Ex post facto* designs are used to study potential causal relationships after a presumed cause has occurred.
22. In *ex post facto* research, subjects are selected on the basis of the groups they were in at one time; there is probably no random assignment of subjects to different groups; and there is no active manipulation of the independent variable.

RESEARCH NAVIGATOR NOTES

Reading the following articles will help you understand the content of this chapter. Go to the education database (included in the EBSCO database) in Research Navigator; use the accession number provided to find the article.

9.1   *Longitudinal Study*
Here is an example of a study using a longitudinal design with 28 schools over three years. Accession number: 8974008.

9.2   Logistic Regression
Provides guidelines for what to expect in studies using logistic regression. Accession number: 7255159.

9.3   Mail-versus Internet-Based Surveys
This is a study examining the usefulness of the Internet in survey research. Accession number: 6282924.

CHECK YOURSELF

Multiple-choice review items, with answers, are available on the Companion Website for this book:

www.ablongman.com/mcmillanschumacher6e/

APPLICATION PROBLEMS

1. In a study of motivation and learning, a teacher employed the following research strategy: Students were asked what teaching methods were most motivating. The teacher then looked back at her test scores to investigate whether the test scores were higher for the more motivating sessions compared with the less motivating sessions. The teacher found that, indeed, student achievement rose as the teacher used more and more motivating methods. From this result, she decided to use the more motivating methods all the time. Was her decision to use more motivating methods correct? Why or why not?

2. For each description below, indicate whether the research is descriptive, comparative, correlational, predictive, or *ex post facto*.
   a. A researcher finds that there is a positive relationship between grades and attendance.
   b. A researcher finds that students who are more lonely have more permissive parents than students who are less lonely.
   c. The dean of the school of education uses SAT scores to identify students who may have trouble with National Teacher Examinations.
   d. Children in supportive, loving homes have a higher self-concept than children in rejecting homes.
   e. The majority of faculty at U.S.A. university favor abolishing tenure.
   f. Researchers find that graduate students who attended small colleges have stronger writing skills than students from large universities.

3. Identify a topic in your area of study that would be appropriate for an Internet-based survey. Write out some questions for the survey as well as a letter of transmittal. Design the screen pages, at least in the form of rough sketches. Considering the advantages and disadvantages of using Internet-based surveys, would your proposed survey be best done on the Internet? Why or why not?

4. On the Research Navigator, access the article "Principal self-efficacy and effective teaching and learning environments" (accession number: 12252517). Read the article and then answer the following questions:
   a. Is this correlational, comparative, or ex post facto research?
   b. Is this survey research? If so, are principles of effective survey research evident?
   c. Are the relationships presented credible? Why or why not?
   d. Does the instrument provide sufficient variation of responses?
   e. Does the sampling provide sufficient variation of responses?
   f. What is your judgment about the overall quality of the research? What are your reasons?

5. Read the study presented in Excerpt 9.17 (Barbee, Scherer, & Combs, 2003) for understanding and analysis. What kind of nonexperimental research is this study? What are the independent and dependent variables? Judge the research according to the standards of adequacy presented in this chapter, as well as the criteria for judging the research question and review of literature. Do the regression results make more sense with or without outliers? Do the conclusions seem warranted? What could be done to improve the research?

EXCERPT 9.17 Example of a Nonexperimental Study

Prepracticum Service-Learning: Examining the Relationship with Counselor Self-Efficacy and Anxiety

Phillip W. Barbee, David Scherer, & Don C. Combs

Prepracticum service-learning is an integral part of the curriculum for counselor education students at a large southwestern university. Service-learning is accomplished by placing novice students in school or community agency settings to acquire early, práctical, field-based experience. Activities are more structured and supervised than in an internship or practicum. Analysis indicated that prepracticum service-learning had a positive significant relationship with counselor self-efficacy and a significant negative relationship with student anxiety. However, substantial counseling course work and experience with counseling-related work both had a stronger Influence than did prepracticum service-learning, indicating that the latter is more appropriate for novice students.

Service-learning, an instructional method for integrating community service experiences into the learning environment, was first proposed by John Dewey and William Kirkpatrick at the beginning of the 1900s (Conrad & Hedin, 1991). These prominent educators believed that both academic development and social development were stimulated by service toward others and that learning was enhanced by nontraditional classroom experiences such as community service work. Service-learning is still prominent in higher education today and is increasingly used in graduate-level training (Berson, 1993, 1994; Gose, 1997). Indeed, because of the potential benefits to counselors-in-training, the Association for Counselor Education and Supervision (ACES; 1990) recommended that counseling programs incorporate service-learning into their curricula by means of collaborative partnerships between universities, community agencies, and public schools.

Service-Learning for Counselor Preparation

Some counselor preparation programs have incorporated service-learning in the training of beginning and intermediate school and community agency counseling students (Arman & Scherer, 2002; Hayes, Dagley, & Horne, 1996). A primary reason for this "innovation" is the opportunity that service-learning provides for counselor educators to create an immediate linkage between concepts presented in the classroom and early field experiences. Consequently, service-learning projects are distinct from internship and practicum training. The latter generally occur near the end of a student's training and are capstone courses designed

to provide a transition for the student into professional life. Prepracticum service-learning, on the other hand, occurs at the beginning stages of student training and provides the first glimpse of counseling-related activities, either through direct participation or observation.

As an example, the Traverse Outreach Project, the focus for this study. is the prepracticum service-learning model used in the preparation of novice counseling students at a large southwestern university. The Traverse project is a collaborative partnership between the university's counselor education program, local public schools, and community agencies. The counselor education students who participate in the Traverse project are required as part of their course work to complete a minimum of 30 clock hours in either school or community agency work settings. Training varies at each site and includes activities such as mentoring; cofacilitating groups providing prevention and intervention services for divorce, separation, grief and loss, assertiveness, and other developmentally appropriate topics; giving psychoeducational presentations; and/or observing a counselor perform duties specific to comprehensive guidance. On-site supervisors, doctoral students, and faculty provide supervision (Traverse Outreach Project: Program Updates, 1998).

Service-Learning, Educational Outcomes, and Counselor Preparation

The preliminary findings from studies regarding the influence of service-learning on student development are positive. In the general student population, students who participated in service-learning indicated increased levels of personal and professional growth (Berson, 1993), whereas other students have reported an increased sense of self-efficacy (Conrad & Hedin, 1991). Several studies of student outcomes that were done after a service-learning experience have indicated significant increases in problem-solving abilities, enhanced social and psychological development, and a more positive attitude toward others (Conrad & Hedin, 1982, 1991).

However, only a few studies exist on the effects of service-learning for novice students in counselor preparation. Sprinthall and Sprinthall (1977) found that undergraduate students who had service-learning types of experiences as tutors and peer counselors developed counseling skills that were on a par with those of more ad-

Source: From Barbee, P. W., Scherer, D., & Combs, D. C. (2003). Prepracticum service-learning: Examining the relationship with counselor self-efficacy and anxiety. *Counselor Education & Supervision, 43,* 108–119. Reprinted by permission.

vanced counseling graduate students. Two studies—both qualitative in nature and both involving the Traverse project—examined counselor education service-learning at the graduate level to determine the potential benefits of service-learning for counselor preparation. The first study used end-of-course surveys from the initial group of students participating in the project (Arman, Barbee, Carlin, & Salazar-Lohar, 1996). A major theme that emerged was the value and effectiveness that students attributed to their service-learning experiences. This theme was also noted in a second study, in which counselor education students who were enrolled in a school counseling class expressed a belief that service-learning was effective in integrating theory with the actual practice of school counseling (Arman & Scherer, 2002). The participants in this study also had reported an increased awareness of the day-to-day realities of school counseling after the service-learning experience.

These preliminary studies indicated that service-learning may have a positive influence on the preparation of novice student counselors. Our aim was to continue to investigate the effects of prepracticum service-learning on novice counselor education students. Consistent with previous studies of service-learning and the literature on optimal methods for training counselors, we examined the relationship between participation in service-learning and counselor self-efficacy and student anxiety.

Counselor Self-Efficacy, Student Anxiety, and Counselor Preparation

Counselor self-efficacy is described as the counseling student's expectation and confidence to successfully master those skills specific to the effective practice of counseling (Johnson, Baker, Kopala, Kiselica, & Thompson, 1989). Various training factors have shown an influence on the self-efficacy of counseling students (Larson & Daniels, 1998). Several studies supported the hypothesis that a positive relationship existed between level of counselor training/development and counselor self-efficacy (Leach, Stoltenberg, McNeill, & Etchenfield, 1997; Melchert, Hays, Wiljanen, & Kolocek, 1996; Sipps, Sugden, & Faiver, 1988). Leach et al. related counselor self-efficacy to both the degree of anticipation of working with particular types of clients and the level of counselor development. Using the Supervisee Levels Questionnaire-Revised (McNeill, Stoltenberg, & Romans, 1992) as a measure of developmental level and the Counseling Self-Estimate Inventory (COSE; Larson et al., 1992) as a measure of counselor self-efficacy, Leach et al., in a multivariate analysis of variance, found a significant positive relationship between the independent variables of trainee developmental level, client type, and counseling experience and the dependent vari-

able of counselor self-efficacy. Melchert et al., using the Counselor Self-Efficacy Scale (CSES) and a multiple regression analysis, demonstrated a significant positive relationship between levels of training and years of clinical experience (the independent variables) and counselor self-efficacy (the dependent variable).

Other training variables, such as role playing and role modeling, have also shown a positive significant relationship with counselor self-efficacy. Johnson et al. (1989) reported that students experienced a significant increase in counselor self-efficacy after observing counseling sessions with role-playing graduate students. Larson et al. (1999) looked at both role playing and video counseling presentations, along with associated changes in the self-efficacy of prepracticum trainees. Using the COSE as a measure of counselor self-efficacy before and after either viewing a video presentation of a counseling session or conducting a role-playing counseling session with a pseudoclient, Larson et al. (1999) found that role-playing interventions could either increase or decrease counseling self-efficacy scores, depending on how the trainee judged the level of success of the counseling session. These authors further concluded that in some instances this type of intervention might do more harm than good, especially for novice trainees. They suggested that a video presentation of a successful counseling session may be more appropriate for beginning counseling students than is role playing.

Bandura (1977) concluded that an inverse relationship exists between counselor self-efficacy and anxiety. Other studies have led to a similar conclusion, showing that counselor self efficacy and anxiety have an inverse relationship (Larson & Daniels, 1998). Friedlander, Kelley, Peca-Baker, and Olk (1986), in a study on anxiety generated from supervisor-supervisee conflict, noted a significant negative relationship between anxiety and the self-efficacy of the student participants.

Recalling Larson et al.'s (1999) findings that training protocols requiring student participation, such as role playing, may in some cases lower a novice counseling student's self-efficacy, we decided it was vital to empirically evaluate the effects of service-learning, which also requires student participation. This study investigated whether the responses of prepracticum counseling students who had been trained with a service-learning model varied significantly on a measure of perceived counselor self-efficacy and a measure of anxiety from prepracticum students who had not experienced service-learning. We hypothesized that prepracticum service-learning would have a positive relationship with counselor self-efficacy and a negative relationship with student anxiety, particularly for those students with limited counselor training or counseling-related work experiences.

(continued)

e x c e r p t   9 . 1 7 *(c o n t i n u e d)*

Method

Participants

For this study, 113 prepracticum counseling students were recruited over a two-semester period from counseling programs at a university with prepracticum service-learning and at another regional university without similar training. Not all study participants at the university that offered service-learning had participated in such activities. However, this study focused on service-learning participants and nonparticipants, not on university counseling programs. Sampling was completed during the first third of each respective semester. Of the 113 participants, 77 were prepracticum counseling students at the university with service-learning, and from this sample 39 had reported participating in service-learning activities. The 77 counseling students were enrolled in one of the following courses: school counseling, group counseling, career counseling, counseling practicum, or counseling internship. The 36 participants at the university without service-learning were enrolled in either school counseling or group counseling. For the total sample, 85 (75%) of the respondents were women and 28 (25%) were men. The age of the participants ranged from 22 to 66 years ($M = 34.7$). The majority (58%) of participants identified their ethnicity as Anglo, followed by Hispanic (31%), Native American (4%), and other (7%), which included African Americans and students who identified with more than one ethnic group. The majority (92%) of the participants had completed at least one counseling course, and more than half (56%) had reported some type of previous counseling-related work experience.

Procedure and Measures

After they indicated their consent, participants were given a packet containing three instruments: a demographic questionnaire, the CSES (Melchert et al., 1996), and the State-Trait Anxiety Inventory (STAI; Spielberger, Gorusch, & Lushene, 1970). Students completed these measures in their respective classes. In addition to personal information on the demographic questionnaire, students were also queried on the number of completed counseling courses (hours) to determine the level of counselor training/development, previous counseling-related work experience (months), and total service-learning experience (clock hours).

The CSES is a reliable and validated 20-item instrument designed to measure the participants' level of confidence to gain the skills necessary to provide both individual and group counseling. The CSES has a reported Cronbach alpha internal consistency of .93 and a test-retest reliability of .85 (Melchert et al., 1996). In examining convergent construct-related validity, the CSES has a reported .83 correlation with a self-efficacy inventory prepared by Friedlander et al. (1986). The CSES requires participants to respond to questions using one of five options on a Likert scale

ranging from *strongly disagree* (1) to *strongly agree* (5). The instrument provides an indication of the degree of perceived counselor self-efficacy. We decided to use the CSES because the counseling knowledge and skills represented on the instrument are basic and similar to those that the participants in this study were observing or performing during their prepracticum service-learning activities in the field. We conjectured that the CSES would indicate variations in students' levels of confidence to successfully counsel clients between counseling students with and counseling students without service-learning.

The STAI is a well-known, reliable, and validated instrument designed to measure anxiety. The STAI comprises two forms, each having 20 items. The inventory differentiates between state anxiety (Form Y-1), which is considered more temporary, such as the apprehension a student may experience with the prospect of doing actual counseling, and trait anxiety (Form Y-2), which is more enduring and associated with individual personality traits (Spielberger et al., 1970).

Results

Outcome of Measures

All 113 participants completed the CSES instrument. The scores, based on a 5-point Likert scale, ranged from a low of 2.10 to a high of 5.00, with a mean of 3.85. Higher scores suggest an increased sense of counselor self-efficacy. Scores were relatively normal in distribution and consistent with Melchert et al.'s (1996) study on levels of training and clinical experience in which the mean score for 2nd-year, master's-level counseling psychology students was 3.82. This score was remarkably similar to the mean score for the participants in this study.

The 113 participants also completed the State-anxiety scale (Form Y-1) on the STAI. However, 3 participants did not complete the Trait-anxiety scale on the reverse side (Form Y-2), resulting in incomplete data for trait anxiety. This was not a problem because this study used only State-anxiety scale results. State-anxiety scores ranged from a low of 20 to a high of 69 ($M = 32.44$). This mean score was markedly lower than the mean score for the normative sample of college students enrolled in a psychology course (Spielberger et al., 1970).

Statistical Analysis

An independent samples *t* test ($N = 113$), a simple analysis designed to evaluate the effects of one independent variable on a dependent variable, revealed a significant difference in self-efficacy between those participants who took part in service-learning versus those who did not engage in service-learning ($p < .030$). The participants with service-learning experience indicated higher levels of counselor self-efficacy. There was a negative correlation (–.298) between counselor self-efficacy and state anxiety, which was consistent with similar study results. Because the *t* test showed a significant positive relationship between service-learning participation and counselor self-efficacy, a similar analysis was undertaken using state anxiety as the dependent variable. The independent samples *t* test ($N = 113$) indicated a significant positive relationship ($p < .038$) between lower state anxiety levels and service-learning participation. Participants with service-learning experience had lower levels of state anxiety than did participants without service-learning experiences.

We conducted a more complex multiple regression analysis, which enables an evaluation of multiple independent variables on a dependent variable, to determine the effects of service-learning, previous counseling-related work experience, and level of counselor training/development on counselor self-efficacy, the dependent variable. A multiple regression analysis shows the researcher the degree of unique variance that each independent variable has with the dependent variable and provides a significance test of these individual variable contributions. The results indicated an overall significant positive relationship, $F(3, 107) = 16.75$, $p < .001$, between counselor self-efficacy and the independent variables of service-learning, previous counseling-related work experience, and counselor training/development, together accounting for 37% of the variance (R^2, see Table 1).

An analysis of the coefficients revealed the effect of each independent variable on counselor self-efficacy. Individually, the independent variables for counselor training/development ($R^2 = 21.8\%$) and previous counseling-related work experience ($R^2 = 8.5\%$) each showed a significant positive relationship with counselor self-efficacy ($p < .001$ for both). The variable for service-learning did not show a positive significant relationship with counselor self-efficacy ($R^2 = 2.5\%$). In view of the results of the independent samples *t* test, which indicated a significant positive relationship between service-learning and counselor self-efficacy, we undertook a more detailed analysis.

Pedhazur (1997) stressed the importance of identifying outliers in research studies. Standardized residual values greater than 2 should be scrutinized, along with the degree of influence each case has on the results. Some researchers are reluctant to report analysis with outliers removed, because this may be viewed as being less than honest. However, to ignore outliers and the possible influence they may have is in itself misleading. The prudent course, according to Pedhazur, is to report analysis both with outliers included and with them removed and then let the reader determine the validity of the results presented. With this in mind, we conducted a case-by-case diagnostic review to identify any cases with standardized residual values greater than 2. We followed this review with a Cook's Distance procedure to check for the degree of influence of any potential outliers. The case-by-case diagnostic review identified six outliers with standardized residuals greater than 2 in absolute value. These six outliers were then checked for the degree of influence each had using a Cook's Distance procedure. The mean Cook's *D* for the total sample ($N = 113$) was .009. We removed the three outliers with the greatest divergence from the mean, with values of .07, .09, and .14, from the sample. This represented 2.7% of the total sample.

A multiple regression analysis on the sample; with outliers removed ($n = 110$), showed a positive significant relationship between counselor self-efficacy and the independent variables of service-learning availability, previous counseling-related work experience, and counselor training/development, $F(3, 104) = 24.35$, $p < .001$. Analysis of the availability of service-learning, with the outliers removed, revealed a positive significant relationship ($p < .025$) with counselor self-efficacy (see Table 2).

TABLE 1   Multiple Regression Analysis for All Participants

Variable*	SS	df	MS	F	Sig
Regression	13.08	3	4.36	16.75	.001
Residual	27.85	107	0.26		

*Dependent variable is the Counselor Self-Efficacy Scale and independent variables are service-learning availability, counselor training/development (i.e., number of graduate counseling credits), and previous counseling-related work experience.

TABLE 2   Multiple Regression Analysis of Coefficients with Outliers Removed

Variable*	B	t	Sig
Constant		33.42	.001
Service-learning	0.17	2.28	.025
Counselor development	0.50	6.63	.001
Experience	0.28	3.68	.001

*Dependent variable is the Counselor Self-Efficacy Scale, and independent variables are service-learning availability, counselor training/development (i.e., number of graduate counseling credits), and previous counseling-related work experience.

(continued)

Discussion

The major focus of this study was to determine if novice counseling students who were trained using a service-learning model varied significantly in counselor self-efficacy and student anxiety from students who were not trained in this way. As mentioned previously, research on service-learning in counselor preparation has been inadequate, with only a handful of studies investigating the effects of this form of experiential training. This study purported to address this limitation with an examination of the relationship between service-learning and its relationship with counselor self-efficacy and student anxiety.

The major finding of this study indicated that prepracticum service-learning does seem to have a positive relationship with counselor self-efficacy and a negative association with student anxiety. However, the level of counselor training/development and previous counseling-related work experience, accounted for more variance in counselor self-efficacy than did service-learning. A closer examination revealed that each variable had varying degrees of association with counselor self-efficacy. Each is presented in decreasing order of significance, which coincides with the decreasing amounts of unique variance that each variable shared with the dependent variable.

The most pronounced relationship was identified between level of counselor training/development and counselor self-efficacy. This finding supported conclusions drawn by other studies on the positive relationship between level of counselor training/development and counselor self-efficacy (Leach et al., 1997; Melchert et al., 1996). In our study, 92% of the respondents had completed various numbers of counseling courses. This measure of completed number of counseling courses was scaled in credit hours and then used to establish the level of development for each prepracticum student. This method of establishing the level of development was more precise than using the number of completed semesters of course work. The number of completed counseling credits, with the strong association with counselor self-efficacy, provided an indication of the degree of increasing levels of confidence that counseling students have of being able to complete counseling tasks successfully.

The prominence of the association of counselor training/development level with counselor self-efficacy was not only evidenced by the degree of significance but also by the amount of shared variance between these two variables. Counselor training/development accounted for 22% of unique variance with counselor self-efficacy, out of a total of 37% of the unique variance that all three independent variables shared with the dependent variable.

The variable previous counseling-related work experience also showed a strong positive relationship with counselor self-efficacy. Surprisingly, almost 56% of the participants in this study reported some type of work experience in a counseling-related job. The data strongly suggested that students who experienced counseling-related work also had an increased sense of confidence in their ability to be successful counselors. This increase in self-efficacy was consistent with Bandura's (1977) description of *direct mastery experiences,* wherein he contended that an individual's drive to successfully complete a given task is influenced by the experience with that particular task. The degree of unique shared variance of previous counseling-related work experience, although not as prevalent as counselor training/development, still accounted for 8.5% of the 37% of the shared variance with counselor self-efficacy.

The unique shared variance between service-learning and counselor self-efficacy was less than what each of the other two independent variables had with self-efficacy. Of the collective 37% unique variance for all independent variables, service-learning accounted for 2.59% Both counselor training/development and previous counseling-related work experience accounted for the majority of the shared unique variance with counselor self-efficacy.

Novice counseling students without previous counseling-related work experience and/or with few completed counseling courses may find prepracticum service-learning an experience that would help them to increase levels of confidence and decrease the anxiety associated with counselor training. Counseling students with substantial course work or previous counseling-related work experience, or both, seem to have already acquired these characteristics.

Study Limitations and Recommendations for Future Research

The low number of participants who had service-learning experience was considered a major, unexpected limitation of this study. Out of the 77 participants from the institution that offered service-learning, only 39 reported participation in service-learning. What we did not know at the time of the study was that several basic counseling classes from which participants were recruited had been taught by adjunct faculty members who had not required student participation in service-learning. Because the counseling department has now made prepracticum service-learning a departmental requirement, we strongly recommend repeating this study. Another recommendation indicated by the results of this study is to collect data using repeated measures, such as in a single-subject design, for analyzing the impact of prepracticum service-learning in counseling programs. Participants enrolled in classes with service-learning could be sampled at the beginning and at the end of each semester to note changes in counselor self-efficacy and student anxiety.

excerpt 9.17 (continued)

Coordinating the appropriate activity with the level of counselor training/development is an important component of prepracticum service-learning. Certain service-learning activities may be more or less effective with counseling students, depending on the point they have reached in their training. More advanced students or those with experience in counseling-related professions may find prepracticum service-learning too basic. Conversely, some service-learning activities may be too advanced for novice counseling students. With this in mind, the placement of students at sites offering training opportunities matched to the level of counselor training/development or previous experience may well be the most important recommendation for programs considering integrating prepracticum service-learning into counselor preparation.

Conclusion

As evidenced in this study, both the level of counselor training/development and previous counseling-related work experience have a strong significant relationship with counselor self-efficacy. For students with low self-efficacy, as found in novice counseling students or those without previous counseling-related work experience, prepracticum service-learning may help to increase counselor self-efficacy and decrease student anxiety sufficiently so that specific counseling training goals are more readily attainable.

References

Arman, J. F., Barbee. P. W., Carlin, M. J., & Salazar-Lohar, C. (1996). *Traverse Outreach Project.* Unpublished research report, University of New Mexico, Albuquerque.

Arman, J. F., & Scherer, D. (2002). Service learning in school counselor preparation: A qualitative analysis. *Journal of Humanistic Counseling, Education and Development, 41,* 69–86.

Association for Counselor Education and Supervision. (1990). Standards and procedures for school counselor training and certification. *Counselor Education and Supervision, 29,* 213–215.

Bandura, A. (1977). Toward a unifying theory of behavioral change. *Psychological Review, 84,* 191–215.

Berson, J. S. (1993). Win/win/win with a service-learning program. *Journal of Career Planning and Employment, 53*(4), 30–35.

Berson, J. S. (1994). A marriage made in heaven: Community colleges and service-learning. *Community College Journal, 64(6),* 14–19.

Conrad, D., & Hedin, D. (1982). The impact of experiential education on adolescent development. *Child & Youth Services, 4,* 57–76.

Conrad, D., & Hedin, D. (1991). School-based community service: What we know from research and theory. *Phi Delta Kappan, 72,* 743–749.

Friedlander, M. L., Keller, K. E., Peca-Baker, T. A., & Olk, M. E. (1986). Effects of role conflict on counselor trainees' self-statements, anxiety level, and performance. *Journal of Counseling Psychology, 33,* 73–77.

Gose, B. (1997, November 14). Many colleges move to link courses with volunteerism. *The Chronicle of Higher Education,* pp. 45–46.

Hayes, R. L., Dagley, J. C., & Home, A. M. (1996). Restructuring school counselor education: Work in progress. *Journal of Counseling & Development, 74,* 378–384.

Johnson, E., Baker, S. B., Kopala, M., Kiselica, M. S., & Thompson, E. C., III. (1989). Counseling self-efficacy and counseling in prepracticum training. *Counselor Education and Supervision, 28,* 205–218.

Larson, L. M., Clark, M. P., Wesley, L. H., Koraleski, S. F., Daniels, J. A., & Smith, P. L. (1999). Videos versus role plays to increase counseling self-efficacy in prepractica trainees. *Counselor Education and Supervision, 38,* 237–248.

Larson, L. M., & Daniels, J. A. (1998). Review of the counseling self-efficacy literature. *The Counseling Psychologist, 26,* 179–218.

Larson, L. M., Suzuki, L. A., Gillespie, K. N., Potenza, M. T., Bechtel, M. A., & Toulouse, A. L. (1992). Development and validation of the Counseling Self-Estimate Inventory. *Journal of Counseling Psychology, 39,* 105–120.

Leach, M. M., Stoltenberg, C. D., McNeill. B. W., & Eichenfield, G. A. (1997). Self-efficacy and counselor development: Testing the integrated development model. *Counselor Education and Supervision, 37,* 115–124.

McNeill, B. W., Stoltenberg, C. D., & Romans, J. S. C. (1992). The integrated developmental model of supervision: Scale development and validation procedures. *Professional Psychology: Research and Practice, 23,* 504–508.

Melchert, T. P., Hays, V. L., Wiljanen, L. M., & Kolocek, A. K. (1996). Testing models of counselor development with a measure of counseling self-efficacy. *Journal of Counseling & Development, 74,* 640–644.

Pedhazur, E. J. (1997). *Multiple regression in behavioral research: Explanation and prediction* (3rd ed.). Fort Worth, TX: Harcourt Brace College Publishers.

Sipps. C. J., Sugden, C. J., & Faiver, C. M. (1988). Counselor training level and verbal response type: Their relationship to efficacy and outcome expectations. *Journal of Counseling Psychology, 35,* 397–401.

Spielberger. C. D., Gorusch, R. I., & Lushene, R. E. (1970). *Manual for the State-Trait Anxiety Inventory.* Palo Alto, CA: Consulting Psychologists Press.

Sprinthall, R. C., & Sprinthall, N. A. (1977). *Educational psychology: A developmental approach.* Reading, MA: Addison-Wesley.

Traverse Outreach Project: Program updates. (1998). Unpublished manuscript. University of New Mexico, Albuquerque, College of Education.

10 Experimental and Single-Subject Research Designs

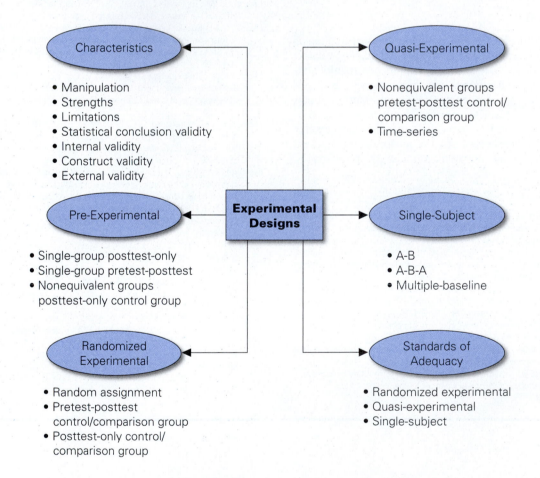

Experimental Designs

Characteristics

- Manipulation
- Strengths
- Limitations
- Statistical conclusion validity
- Internal validity
- Construct validity
- External validity

Pre-Experimental

- Single-group posttest-only
- Single-group pretest-posttest
- Nonequivalent groups posttest-only control group

Randomized Experimental

- Random assignment
- Pretest-posttest control/comparison group
- Posttest-only control/comparison group

Quasi-Experimental

- Nonequivalent groups pretest-posttest control/comparison group
- Time-series

Single-Subject

- A-B
- A-B-A
- Multiple-baseline

Standards of Adequacy

- Randomized experimental
- Quasi-experimental
- Single-subject

KEY TERMS

randomized experimental research
experimental or treatment group
control or comparison group
treatment fidelity
pre-experimental designs
single-group posttest-only
   design
single-group pretest-posttest
   design
pretest-posttest design
nonequivalent groups posttest-only
   control group design
randomized pretest-posttest control
   group design
randomized posttest-only control
   and comparison group design

quasi-experimental designs
nonequivalent groups pretest–
   posttest control and
   comparison group design
time-series design
single-group interrupted
   time-series design
control group interrupted
   time-series design
single-subject designs
baseline
A-B design
A-B-A design
reversal or withdrawal design
multiple-baseline designs

Experiments are making a comeback in educational research! For the past 20 years, there has been a steady, justified emphasis on qualitative methods. Now, due to changes in policy at the U.S. Department of Education, experimental designs must be employed, where possible, when investigating cause-and-effect relationships.

In Chapter 2, the concepts of experiment and experimental modes of inquiry were introduced. This chapter considers the conduct of experiments in greater detail. It focuses on four major categories of experimental designs that are used to make causal inferences about the relationship between independent and dependent variables: pre-experimental, randomized experimental, quasi-experimental, and single-subject designs.

Throughout this chapter, we summarize the purpose, strengths, and limitations of experimental research in general as well as more specific designs. In addition, we stress the point that in any study in which causation is inferred, the investigator must rule out *plausible rival hypotheses* that may explain the results. Standards of adequacy for evaluating the designs are summarized at the end of the chapter.

INTRODUCTION TO EXPERIMENTAL RESEARCH

The term *experiment*, like many other terms, can have different meanings. Defined in a general way, an experiment is simply a way of learning something by varying some condition and observing the effect on something else. In other words, we change something and watch for the effect. As humans, we use natural experiments constantly to learn—for instance, young children experiment with a host of tactics to see which one will affect Mom or Dad most; teachers try a new approach to discipline to see whether it works; and students vary study techniques to see which ones seem to result in the best grades. Each of these simple trial-and-error behaviors is an attempt to show causation, which is the primary purpose of an experiment. The difference between these casual experiments and highly sophisticated experiments is the extent to which the researcher can be certain that the varied conditions caused the observed effect. It is the interpretation of *causation*, then, that is a key element in experimental research.

Characteristics of Experimental Research

Traditionally defined experimental research—that is, the type of research that is now presented as the "gold standard" for determining cause and effect in educational research—has six distinguishing characteristics:

1. theory-driven research hypotheses
2. statistical equivalence of subjects in intervention and control and/or comparison groups (achieved through random assignment)
3. researcher-controlled interventions independently and uniformly applied to all subjects
4. measurement of each dependent variable
5. use of inferential statistics
6. rigorous control of conditions and extraneous variables

These characteristics are usually present in physical and biological science experimental research, but as we noted in Chapter 2, such conditions can rarely be achieved completely in educational research. This does not, however, diminish the importance of the experimental method for education. Much research in education approximates most of these characteristics, and we need to understand the way different methods of conducting research that investigates causal relationships affect the interpretation of the results. That is what Campbell and Stanley (1963) had in mind in writing their classic and influential chapter "Experimental and Quasi-Experimental Designs for Education." The following quotation leaves little doubt about their perspective at that time:

> This chapter is committed to the experiment: as the only means for settling disputes regarding educational practice, as the only way of verifying educational improvements, and as the only way of establishing a cumulative tradition in which improvements can be introduced without the danger of a faddish discard of old wisdom in favor of inferior novelties. (p. 2)

We need to distinguish, then, between what can be labeled **randomized experimental research** (sometimes called *true* or *pure experimental research*), in which the previous six characteristics are completely present, and the experimental method of research more broadly, in which the characteristics are partially present. This is particularly important given that so many agencies and organizations now have an increased interest in conducting experiments. The attention has been focused on research that contains the six characteristics mentioned earlier. Here are some terms commonly used to communicate the nature of the experiment:

Randomized trials of uniform treatment
Randomized controlled experiment
Randomized controlled trials (RCTs)
Random trials
Experimental research
Randomized experiments

Clearly, the emphasis is on the design feature of being *randomized*, but there is also an intent to have more rigorous designs from which cause-and-effect relationships can be established. While in the broader literature all of these terms are used, we will define *research* in which the six characteristics are present as *randomized experiments*.

ALERT!   Some researchers interpret the word *experiment* to include random assignment of subjects.

The first characteristic, having theory-driven research hypotheses, explains why there are cause-and-effect findings and provides a clear indication of how the findings should be generalized. Because specific hypotheses are postulated, the range of possible outcomes is restricted and the likelihood that chance is a factor is reduced.

Achieving statistical equivalence of individuals in groups that are compared, the second characteristic, is essential for ruling out the many possible variables that could invalidate causal conclusions. That is, the researcher wants to make the groups under comparison as similar as possible, so that no subject characteristics or experiences can be said to explain the results.

ALERT! Do not confuse the *random assignment* of subjects in an experiment with the *random selection* of subjects from a larger population.

Whether or not randomization is implemented in educational research depends on many factors, including the willingness to use students as subjects and to expose them to alternate interventions that might have a negative impact, or a control group. It would not be ethical to withhold a treatment known to have a positive impact. Randomization should be implemented when the demand for a program or service outstrips the supply and when a program or service cannot be introduced to all subjects at the same time (e.g., perhaps for financial reasons).

Researcher-controlled interventions, or direct manipulation of a treatment, is perhaps the most distinct feature of experimental research. *Manipulation*, in this sense, means that the researcher decides on and controls the specific intervention, treatment, or condition for each group of subjects. The independent variable is manipulated in that different values or conditions (levels) of the independent variable are assigned to groups by the experimenter. Suppose, for example, that a research team is interested in investigating whether the order of difficulty of items in a test makes a difference in student achievement. The study might have one independent variable, order of items, with two levels: items ordered from easiest to most difficult and items ordered from most difficult to easiest. These are the conditions that are manipulated by the researchers, who would probably divide a class into two groups, randomly, and give all students in each group one of two types of item order. It should be pointed out that there are many variables in education that can never be manipulated, such as age, weight, gender, and socioeconomic status.

The fourth characteristic, measurement of dependent variables, means that experimental research is concerned with things that can be assigned a numerical value. If the outcome of the study cannot be measured and quantified in some way, then the research cannot be experimental.

Another characteristic that involves numbers is the use of inferential statistics. Inferential statistics are used to make probability statements about the results. This is important for two reasons: (1) because measurement is imperfect in education and (2) because we often want to generalize the results to similar groups or to the population of subjects. (See Chapter 11 for details concerning inferential statistics.)

The final characteristic of experimental research is perhaps the most important from a generic point of view because the principle of control of extraneous variables is not unique to experimental research. What is unique to experimental research is that there is a determined effort to ensure that no extraneous variables provide plausible rival hypotheses to explain the results. We control extraneous variables either by making sure that they have no effect on the dependent variable or by keeping the effect the same for all groups.

Strengths and Limitations of Experimental Research

The experimental method is clearly the best approach for determining the causal effect of an intervention. This is primarily because of the potential for a high degree of control of extraneous variables and the power of manipulation of variables. The careful control that characterizes good experimental research becomes a liability for the field of education, however. Control is most easily achieved with research on humans only in restrictive and artificial settings. This is a weakness in education for two reasons. Humans react to artificially restricted, manipulated conditions differently from the way they react to naturally occurring conditions, and if the research is conducted under artificial conditions, then the generalizability of the results (i.e., external validity) is severely limited.

Here is an example of this dilemma: Suppose that the problem to be investigated is whether an individualized approach or a cooperative group discussion is the best method for teaching science concepts to fourth-graders. The objective is to find the method of teaching that gives the best results in achievement. An experimental approach is selected because the problem is clearly one of causation, and presumably the method of instruction—the independent variable—can be manipulated easily. To maximize control of extraneous variables, the experiment might be arranged as follows: At the beginning of one schoolday, all fourth-graders report to a special room, where they are randomly divided into individualized and cooperative groups. To remove any effect the present teachers might have, graduate assistants from the universities act as the teachers. To remove any effect of different rooms, all of the groups of students are taken to similar rooms in different locations. To control possible distractions, these rooms have no windows. To ensure that directions are uniform, the teachers read from specially prepared scripts. The science material selected has been carefully screened so that it will be new information for all students. After studying the material for an hour, the students are tested on the concepts. The results compare the achievement of the groups, and since the design has controlled for most extraneous variables, this difference can be attributed to the independent variable: method of instruction.

What do we do with this knowledge? Because one approach seemed best in this experiment, does it mean that Mr. Jones—in his class, with his style of teaching, in his room, with students that may have particular learning strengths and weaknesses—should use the supposedly proven method? Perhaps, but the difficulty that is illustrated is one of generalizability, a common problem for experiments that are able to exhibit tight control over extraneous variables—that is, internal validity. On the other hand, if we want to maximize external validity, then we need to design the experiment right in Mr. Jones's class, as well as in the classes of other teachers, and somehow design the study to control as many variables as possible without disrupting the natural environment of the class. The researcher would need to select the variables most likely to affect achievement, such as aptitude, time of day, and composition of groups, and control these as much as possible. This approach makes it more difficult to show that one or the other method of teaching is more effective, but the results will be more generalizable to normal classrooms. The real challenge is in designing the procedures so that the results obtained can be reasonably generalized to other people and environments—that is, balancing internal and external validity in a design. This task is difficult but not impossible, and one of the objectives of this chapter is to introduce various designs and procedures that allow reasonable cause-and-effect conclusions to be made in the context of natural settings.

We hope the use of the word *reasonable* is not confusing. The simple fact is that we approximate randomized experimental designs as well as we can because such designs convincingly determine causation. In the final analysis, however, since we are working with human beings in complex situations, we must almost always use professional judgment, or reason, in making conclusions on the basis of observed results. Knowledge of the designs covered in this chapter and threats to internal and external validity help us in applying this judgment.

Finally, it should be pointed out that experimental research is not appropriate for all educational research; it is appropriate only for some investigations seeking knowledge about cause-and-effect relationships. The experimental method would be inappropriate for many educational problems, such as descriptive studies (for example, "What is the attitude or level of achievement?") or studies of relationship (for example, "Is there a relationship between age and self-concept?"). In some situations, a qualitative approach would be more valid for explaining events, and in evaluation studies, experiments are frequently used with other approaches to investigate questions about a single practice.

The American Educational Research Association (AERA) unanimously adopted a resolution in 2003 in which there is recognition for the importance of randomized designs.

The resolution also stressed that research questions should guide the selection of method of inquiry from many alternatives. The resolution states:

> Council recognizes randomized trials among the sound methodologies to be used in the conduct of education research and commends increased attention to their use. . . . However, the Council of the Association expresses dismay that the Department of Education . . . is devoting singular attention to this one tool of science, jeopardizing a broader range of problems best addressed through other scientific methods. (www.aera.net/meeting/councilresolution03.htm)

Planning Experimental Research

The first steps in planning experimental research are to define a research problem, search the literature, and state clear research hypotheses. It is essential that experimental research be guided by research hypotheses that state the expected results. The actual results will either support or fail to support the research hypotheses.

Next, the researcher selects subjects from a defined population and, depending on the specific design used, usually assigns subjects to different groups. A simple experimental study involves two groups, one called the **experimental** or **treatment group** and the other called the **control** or **comparison group.** Each group is then assigned one level (intervention) of the independent variable. Technically, a control group receives no treatment at all (e.g., when comparing people who smoke with people who do not), but in most educational research, it is unproductive to compare one group receiving a treatment with another group receiving nothing. It would be like comparing children who received extra individual tutoring with children who did not and then concluding on the basis of the results that children need individual tutoring. It is also unrealistic in school settings to expect that a group will be doing nothing while another group receives a special treatment. For these reasons, it is most common to conceive of the two groups in experimental research as the treatment and comparison groups or as a design with two interventions.

In assigning the treatments, as indicated by levels of the independent variable, the researcher determines the nature of the value, forms, or conditions each group receives. This could be a simple assignment, such as lecture versus discussion, loud reprimands versus soft reprimands, or an autocratic versus a participatory leadership style; or there could be more than two levels, with varying degrees of the condition in each level of the independent variable. For example, if a researcher were interested in the effect of different types of teacher feedback on student attitudes, then feedback, the independent variable, could be represented in four levels: grade only, grade plus one word only, grade plus one sentence, and grade plus three sentences. Hence, the researcher would form four levels by randomly assigning subjects into four groups. The researcher would arrange appropriate control so that any difference in attitude could be explained as caused by different types of feedback.

One of the difficulties in planning experimental research is knowing whether the interventions will be strong enough—that is, if the treatment condition is providing feedback to students, will the feedback make enough of an impact to affect student attitudes? Would feedback given over several consecutive days make a difference? Maybe the feedback has to be given for a month or more. In other words, either the treatment should be tested in advance to ensure that it is powerful enough to make an impact or sufficient time should be allocated to give the treatment a chance to work. This can be an especially difficult problem in much educational research because many factors (e.g., achievement, attitudes, motivation, and self-concept) may affect the dependent variables, and it is hard to single out a specific independent variable that will have a meaningful, unique effect, given all other influences. Finally, experimental treatments are sometimes insufficiently distinct from treatments given comparison groups for a statistical difference to be possible. In a study of different counseling techniques, for example, if the only difference between the experimental and control conditions was the distance the counselor sat from the clients (say, four feet or six feet), it is unlikely, given all the other influences, that a researcher will obtain a difference in results.

EXCERPT 10.1 Treatment Fidelity

Three lessons . . . were filmed in each intervention classroom to obtain data on the fidelity of implementation of the treatment at each site. The tapes were subsequently coded to reflect the degree to which the teacher correctly implemented the key elements of the lesson plan. . . . They were summed per lesson per teacher to provide a single score indicating fidelity of implementation. Six of the nine teachers implemented over 70% of key lesson elements over the three weeklong observations. . . . The three teachers with the highest fidelity enhanced the implementation with additional elements that were consistent with its design, and none of the six high implementers committed any errors of implementation.

Source: From Carp, M. S., August, D., McLaughlin, B., Snow, C. E., Dressler, C., Lippman, D. N., Lively, T. J., & White, C. E. (2004). Closing the gap: Addressing the vocabulary needs of English-language learners in bilingual and mainstream classrooms. *Reading Research Quarterly, 39*(2), 188–215.

Another important consideration in designing an experiment is to be sure that the treatment or intervention has occurred as planned, which is called **treatment fidelity.** The lack of treatment fidelity results in the *unreliability of treatment implementation*, a threat to statistical conclusion validity (see the following section). Note how in Excerpt 10.1, the authors specifically address this issue in their study.

Once treatment conditions have been established, it is necessary to specify the design that will be employed. This chapter summarizes most of the basic designs used in experimental educational research. The designs include the procedures for subject assignment, the number of groups, and when treatments are given to each group. The primary concern of the researcher in choosing a design is to maximize internal validity, a concept that is reviewed in the next section.

EXPERIMENTAL VALIDITY

In Chapter 6, four types of experimental validity were introduced: statistical conclusion, internal, construct, and external. Each of these is considered in a following section with particular implications for experimental designs.

Statistical Conclusion Validity

Five of the seven threats to statistical conclusion validity address why a study may not provide valid conclusions of "no difference" or "no relationship." In an experiment, this may mean that a conclusion such as "The intervention of technology did not significantly affect achievement" may be wrong if there are plausible threats to statistical conclusion validity. This is one of two ways in which a research hypothesis is considered against the findings: Either it is or is not supported by the data. When it is not supported by the data, the researcher must be sure that none of the five threats is present. The threat of "fishing" and the error rate problem is one in which support for the research hypothesis can be found because of doing many statistical tests (i.e., one of which is significant). The threats to statistical conclusion validity presented in Chapter 6 are summarized in Table 10.1.

Internal Validity

Chapter 6 discussed the concept of internal validity. The internal validity of a study is a judgment that is made concerning the confidence with which plausible rival hypotheses can be ruled out as explanations for the results. It involves a deductive process in which the investigator must systematically examine how each of the threats to internal validity, which constitute rival alternative hypotheses, may have influenced the results. If all the

TABLE 10.1 Summary of Threats to Statistical Conclusion Validity

Threat	Description
Low statistical power	The design does not have enough subjects or a powerful enough treatment to detect a difference.
Violated assumptions of statistical tests	Assumptions such as having a population with a normal distribution and equal variances are not met, leading to incorrect support or incorrect nonsupport of the research hypotheses.
"Fishing" and the error rate problem	A statistically significant difference has been found with one of many statistical tests on the same data.
Unreliability of measures	The presence of measurement error makes it difficult to obtain a significant difference.
Restriction of range	Small variances or ranges makes it difficult to obtain significant relationships.
Unreliability of treatment implementation	Differences in the administration of an intervention to different individuals or groups result in underestimating the effect of the treatment.
Extraneous variance in the experimental setting	Differences in the settings in which the treatments took place inflate the error rate, making it more difficult to find a relationship or difference.

threats can be reasonably eliminated, then the researcher can be confident that an observed relationship is causal and that the difference in treatment conditions caused the obtained results.

Internal validity is rarely an all-or-none decision. Rather, it is assessed as a matter of degree, depending on the plausibility of the explanation. As will be pointed out, some designs are relatively strong with respect to internal validity because most rival hypotheses can be ruled out confidently, while designs that lend themselves to a host of plausible rival explanations are weak in internal validity. It cannot be stressed too much that, in the final analysis, researchers must be their own best critics and carefully examine all threats that can be imagined. It is important, then, for consumers of research, as well as for those conducting research, to be aware of the common threats to internal validity and of the best ways to control them.

A useful way to think about threats to internal validity is to distinguish what is *possible* from what is *plausible*. A possible threat is clearly not controlled by the design, but to be considered seriously, the possible threat needs to be plausible in two respects. First, the factor needs to be something that affects the dependent variable. For example, there can be differences between compared groups in eye color, but that is not likely to be related to the dependent variable! Second, the factor needs to be systematically related to one group. That is, it needs to affect one group more than the other group. If a factor affects both groups equally, then generally it is not a threat to internal validity.

The threats to internal validity discussed in Chapter 6 are summarized in Table 10.2 in order to help you commit each one to memory. They will be discussed again in the context of each of the designs summarized in the chapter, both in the text and in Tables 10.3 through 10.5, which provide overviews of the threats that are controlled by each design.

Construct Validity

Chapter 6 introduced the notion of the construct validity in research design. In experiments, the term *construct validity* describes how well measured variables and interventions

TABLE 10.2   Summary of Threats to Internal Validity

Threat	Description
History	Unplanned or extraneous events that occur during the research may affect the results.
Selection	Differences between the subjects in the groups may result in outcomes that are different because of group composition.
Statistical regression	Scores of groups of subjects take on values closer to the mean due to respondents' being identified on the basis of extremely high or low scores.
Pretesting	The act of taking a test or responding to a questionnaire prior to the treatment affects the subjects.
Instrumentation	Differences in results are due to unreliability, changes in the measuring instrument, or observers.
Attrition	The systematic loss of subjects affects the outcome.
Maturation	An effect is due to maturational or other natural changes in the subjects (e.g., being older, wiser, stronger, tired).
Diffusion of treatment	Subjects in one group learn about treatments or conditions for different groups.
Experimenter effects	Deliberate or unintended effects of the researcher influence subjects' responses.
Treatment replications	Number of replications of the treatment is different from the number of subjects.
Subject effects	Changes in behavior result in response to being a subject or to being in an experiment.

represent the theoretical constructs that have been hypothesized (i.e., construct validity of the *effects* and *causes*, respectively). That is, how well is the theory supported by the particular measures and treatments? Table 10.3 lists three threats to construct validity that may, if not controlled, invalidate or at least restrict causal conclusions.

ALERT!   The determination of cause (i.e., internal validity) is separate from interpreting the nature of the cause (i.e., construct validity).

TABLE 10.3   Summary of Threats to Construct Validity

Threat	Description
Inadequate explication of the constructs	Invalid inferences are made about the constructs because they have not been sufficiently described and supported by theory.
Mono-operation bias	Only a single type of intervention or dependent variable is used when using multiple types would lead to more assurance that the more abstract theory is supported.
Mono-method bias	Implementing the treatment or measuring the dependent variable in only one way restricts inferences to just those methods as well as to the hypothesized theoretical relationships.

External Validity

External validity is the extent to which the results of an experiment can be generalized to people and environmental conditions outside the context of the experiment. That is, if the same treatment or experimental conditions were replicated with different subjects, in a different setting, would the results be the same? We conclude that an experiment has strong external validity if the generalizability is relatively extensive and has weak external validity if we are unable to generalize very much beyond the actual experiment. Table 10.4 summarizes the sources of threats to external validity.

It is difficult to view external validity in the same way that we view internal validity because most experiments are not designed specifically to control threats to external validity. Researchers consciously control some threats to internal validity by using a particular design, but most threats to external validity are a consideration regardless of the design. In only a few designs can it be concluded that sources of external validity are controlled. Under the ecological category, for example, such threats as description of variables, novelty effect, setting/treatment interaction, and time of measurement treatment interaction, are not controlled with any particular experimental design. These threats are more a function of procedures and definitions than of design, and in most studies, the reader decides whether any of the threats are reasonable.

TABLE 10.4   Summary of Threats to External Validity

Threat	Description
Population	
Selection of subjects	Generalization is limited to the subjects in the sample if the subjects are not selected randomly from an identified population.
Characteristics of subjects	Generalization is limited to the characteristics of the sample or population (e.g., socioeconomic status, age, location, ability, race).
Subject/treatment interaction	Generalization may be limited because of the interaction between the subjects and treatment (i.e., the effect of the treatment is unique to the subjects).
Ecological	
Description of variables	Generalization is limited to the operational definitions of the independent and dependent variables.
Multiple-treatment interference	In experiments in which subjects receive more than one treatment, generalizability is limited to similar multiple-treatment situations because of the effect of the first treatment on subsequent treatments.
Setting/treatment interaction	Generalization is limited to the setting in which the study is conducted (e.g., room, time of day, others present, other surroundings).
Time of measurement/treatment interaction	Results may be limited to the time frame in which they were obtained. Treatments causing immediate effects may not have lasting effects.
Pretest-posttest sensitization	The pretest or posttest may interact with the treatment so that similar results are obtained only when the testing conditions are present.
Novelty or disruption effect	Subjects may respond differently because of a change in routine, and generalization may be limited to situations that involve similar novelty or disruption (e.g., an initially effective treatment may become ineffective in time as novelty wears off).

Two of the ecological threats—multiple treatment interference and pretest–posttest sensitization—are present only in particular designs. Multiple treatment interference is a consideration only if more than one intervention is applied in succession. Pretest sensitization is a serious threat when investigating personality, values, attitudes, or opinions, since taking the pretest may sensitize the subject to the treatment. For example, if a study investigating the effect of a workshop on attitudes toward the use of the Internet in education gave a pretest measure of attitudes, the pretest itself might affect subsequent attitudes regardless of or in interaction with the workshop. Pretest–treatment interaction is minimized in studies conducted over a relatively long time, such as several weeks or months, and in studies of small children. Posttest sensitization occurs only if the posttest sensitizes the subject to the treatment and affects the results in a way that would not have occurred without the posttest.

Educational researchers are often confronted with the difficult dilemma that as internal validity is maximized, external validity may be sacrificed. High internal validity requires strict control of all sources of confounding and extraneous variables, a type of control that may mean conducting the study under laboratory-like conditions. The more the environment is controlled, however, the less generalizable the results will be to other settings. This is a constant dilemma for educators. While research that cannot be used with other populations in other settings contributes little to educational practice, there must be sufficient control for making reasonable causal conclusions. Without internal validity, of course, external validity is a moot concern. Most research strives to balance the threats of internal and external validity by using sufficient rigor to make the results scientifically defensible and by conducting the study under conditions that permit generalization to other situations. One good approach to solving the dilemma is to replicate tightly controlled studies with different populations in different settings.

PRE-EXPERIMENTAL DESIGNS

The three designs summarized in this section are termed **pre-experimental designs** because they are without two or more of the six characteristics of experimental research listed earlier. As a consequence, few threats to internal validity are controlled. This does not mean that these designs are always uninterpretable, nor does it mean that the designs should not be used. There are certain cases in which the threats can be ruled out on the basis of accepted theory, common sense, or other data. Because they fail to rule out most rival hypotheses, however, it is difficult to make reasonable causal inferences from these designs alone. They are best used, perhaps, to generate ideas that can be tested more systematically.

It should be noted that all of the designs in this chapter use a *single* independent variable, and that many studies, if not most, use *more than one* independent variable. The designs of these latter studies are called *factorial*, and they will be explained more fully in Chapter 11.

Notation

In presenting the designs in this chapter, we will use a notational system to provide information for understanding the designs. The notational system is unique although similar to that used by Campbell and Stanley (1963), Cook and Campbell (1979), and Shadish, Cook, and Campbell (2002). Our notational system is as follows:

R	Random assignment
O	Observation, a measure that records observations of a pretest or posttest
X	Treatment conditions (subscripts 1 through n indicate different treatments)
A, B, C, D, E, F	Groups of subjects, or for single-subject designs, baseline or treatment conditions

Single-Group Posttest-Only Design

In the **single-group posttest-only design,** the researcher gives a treatment and then measures the dependent variable, as is represented in the following diagram, where A is the treatment group, X is the treatment, and O is the posttest.

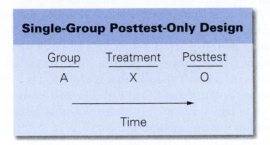

While not all threats to internal validity are applicable to this design because there is no pretest and no comparison with other treatments, valid causal conclusions are rare. Without a pretest, for example, it is difficult to conclude that behavior has changed at all (e.g., when testing a method of teaching math to students who know the answers to the final exam before receiving any instruction). Without a comparison or control group, it is also difficult to know whether other factors occurring at the same time as the treatment were causally related to the dependent variable. Even though only five of the threats to internal validity are relevant to this design, the above weaknesses are so severe that the results of research based on this design alone are usually uninterpretable (see Table 10.5). The only situation in which this design is reasonable is when the researcher can be fairly certain of the level of knowledge, attitude, or skill of the subjects before the treatment and can be fairly sure that history is not a threat. For example, let's say that an instructor in research methods wants to conduct a study of how much students have learned about statistical regression from his or her class. It seems reasonable to conclude that they did not know much about regression before the course began and that it is unlikely that they will

TABLE 10.5 Threats to Internal Validity of Pre-Experimental Designs

Design	History	Selection	Statistical Regression	Pretesting	Instrumentation	Attrition	Maturation	Diffusion of Treatment	Experimenter Effects	Treatment Replications	Subject Effects
Single-group posttest only	–	–	?	NA	?	?	–	NA	?	?	?
Single-group pretest–posttest	–	?	?	–	?	?	–	NA	?	?	?
Nonequivalent groups posttest only	?	–	?	NA	?	?	?	?	?	?	?

Note: In this table, and in Tables 10.6 and 10.7, a minus sign means a definite weakness, a plus sign means the factor is controlled, a question mark means a possible source of invalidity, and NA indicates the threat is not applicable to this design (and is also, then, not a factor).

learn about it in other ways—say, during party conversations! Consequently, the single-group posttest-only design may provide valid results.

Single-Group Pretest-Posttest Design

This common design is distinguished from the single-group posttest-only design by one difference—the addition of an observation that occurs before the treatment condition is experienced (pretest).

In the **single-group pretest-posttest design,** one group of subjects is given a pretest (O), then the treatment (X), and then the posttest (O). The pretest and posttest are the same, just given at different times. The result that is examined is a change from pretest to posttest. (This design is popularized as the so-called **pretest-posttest design.**) While the researcher can at least obtain a measure of change with this design, there are still many plausible rival hypotheses that are applicable.

Single-Group Pretest-Posttest Design			
Group	Pretest	Treatment	Posttest
A	O	X	O

Time

Consider this example: A university professor has received a grant to conduct inservice workshops for teachers on the topic of mainstreaming. One objective of the program is to improve the attitudes of the teachers toward mainstreaming children with disabilities. To assess this objective, the professor selects a pretest-posttest design, administering an attitude pretest survey to the teachers before the workshop and then giving the same survey again after the workshop (posttest). Suppose the posttest scores are higher than the pretest scores. Can the researcher conclude that the cause of the change in scores is the workshop? Perhaps, but several threats to internal validity are plausible, and until they can be ruled out, the researcher cannot assume that attendance at the workshop was the cause of the change.

The most serious threat is history. Because there is no control or comparison group, the researcher cannot be sure that other events occurring between the pretest and posttest did not cause the change in attitude. These events might occur within the context of the workshop (e.g., a teacher gives a moving testimonial about exceptional children in a setting unrelated to the workshop), or they might occur outside the context of the workshop (e.g., during the workshop an article about mainstreaming appears in the school paper). Events like these are uncontrolled and may affect the results. It is necessary for the researcher, then, to make a case either that such effects are implausible or that if they are plausible, that they did not occur. Data are sometimes used as evidence to rule out some threats, but in many cases, it is simply common sense, theory, or experience that is used.

Statistical regression could be a problem with this design if the subjects are selected on the basis of extremely high or low scores. In our example with the workshop, for instance, suppose the principal of the school wanted only those teachers with the least favorable attitudes to attend. The pretest scores would then be very low and, because of regression, would be higher on the posttest regardless of the effect of the workshop.

Pretesting is often a threat to research carried out with this design, especially in research on attitudes, because simply taking the pretest can alter the attitudes. The content of the questionnaire might sensitize the subjects to specific problems or might raise the general awareness level of the subjects and cause them to think more about the topic. Instrumentation can also be a threat. For example, if the teachers take the pretest on Friday afternoon and the posttest the next Wednesday morning, the responses could be different simply because of the general attitudes that are likely to prevail at each of these times of the day and week.

Attrition can be a problem if, between the pretest and posttest, subjects are lost because of particular reasons. If all the teachers in a school begin a workshop, for example, and those with the most negative attitude toward mainstreaming drop out because they do not want to learn more about it, then the measured attitudes of the remaining subjects will be high. Consider another example. To assess the effect of a schoolwide effort to expand favorable attitudes toward learning, students are pretested as sophomores and posttested as seniors. A plausible argument—at least one that would need to be ruled out—is that improvement in attitudes is demonstrated because the students who have the most negative attitudes as sophomores never make it to be seniors; they drop out. Attrition is especially a problem in cases with transient populations, with a long-term experiment, or with longitudinal research.

Maturation is a threat to internal validity of this design when the dependent variable is unstable because of maturational changes. This threat is more serious as the time between the pretest and posttest increases. For instance, suppose a researcher is investigating self-concept of middle school students. If the time between the pretest and posttest is relatively short (two or three weeks), then maturation is probably not a threat, but if there is a year between the pretest and posttest, changes in self-concept would probably occur regardless of the treatment because of maturation. Maturation includes such threats as being more tired, bored, or hungry at the time of test taking, and these factors might be a problem in some pretest-posttest designs. In the example of the workshop on mainstreaming, it is unlikely that maturation is a serious threat, and it would probably be reasonable to rule out these threats as plausible rival hypotheses.

Treatment replications may be a threat, depending on the manner in which the treatment is administered. Experimenter effects, subject effects, and statistical conclusion threats are possible in any experiment, and these would need to be examined.

From this discussion, it should be obvious that there are many uncontrolled threats to the internal validity of single-group pretest-posttest design. Consequently, this design should be used only under certain conditions that minimize the plausibility of the threats (e.g., use reliable instruments and short pretest-posttest time intervals) and when it is impossible to use other designs that will control some of these threats.

Several modifications can be made to the single-group pretest-posttest design that will improve internal validity, including the following:

- Adding a second pretest
- Adding a second pretest and posttest of a construct similar to the one being tested (i.e., to show change in the targeted variable and no change in the other variable)
- Following the posttest with a second pretest/posttest with the treatment either removed or repeated and determining if the pattern of results is consistent with predictions

Excerpt 10.2 is an example of a study that used a single-group pretest-posttest design. Note how the targeted students suggest that regression to the mean may be a plausible rival hypothesis.

EXCERPT 10.2   Single-Group Pretest-Posttest Design

An eight-week summer program was designed and implemented to prevent high-risk adolescents from dropping out of school. Identified by their high school counselors as being at high risk for dropping out, participants were provided a total immersion curriculum that included academic and vocational instruction, as well as personal counseling services. . . . The results of the two administrations of the Coopersmith Self-Esteem Inventory . . . [revealed] significant differences . . . between pretest and posttest self-esteem total scores.

Source: From Wells, D., Miller, M., Tobacyk, J., & Clanton, R. (2002). Using a psychoeducational approach to increase the self-esteem of adolescents at high risk for dropping out. *Adolescence, 37,* 431–434.

Nonequivalent Groups Posttest-Only Design

This design is similar to the single-group posttest-only design. The difference is that in a **nonequivalent groups posttest-only control group design,** a group that receives no treatment or a different treatment is added to the single-group posttest-only design. The design is diagrammed below.

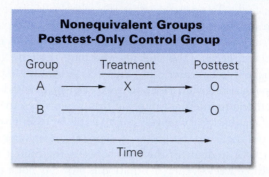

The procedure followed in this design is to give the treatment to one group and then assess the dependent variable (via the posttest) and then to give only the posttest to another group at the same time the posttest is administered to the first group. The term *nonequivalent groups* is used as the name for the design because selection is the most serious threat to the internal validity of the results.

Notice that there is no random assignment of subjects to each group. Differences in the groups of subjects may therefore account for any differences in the results of the posttests. The more different the groups are, the more plausible selection becomes as a reason for the results. Suppose, for example, the professor conducting the mainstreaming workshop wanted to get a comparison group and located a school willing to help. Even if the posttest scores of the treatment group were better than the scores of the comparison group, it is untenable to conclude that the better scores were due to the workshop. It may be that the teachers in the treatment school had more favorable attitudes to begin with and that the workshop had little effect on the attitudes of teachers there.

There are also other less serious threats to the internal validity of research based on this design. These threats occur when the basic design includes alternate treatments, as indicated below.

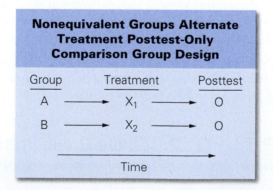

This design is used when a researcher wants to compare two or more treatments but cannot give a pretest or randomize the assignment of subjects to each group. In this case, internal or within-group history is a threat, since what might occur within each group, unrelated to the treatments, could affect the posttest. External history is not usually a threat, unless selection differences expose subjects outside the context of the study to different conditions that affect the results. Regression may be a threat even though only one observation is made. Pretesting is not a threat because there is no pretest, but instrumentation could be a threat if there are differences in how the posttest assessments are made for each group (e.g., an observer's being more alert for one group than the other). Attrition is a threat because subject loss, due either to the initial characteristics of the subjects (selection) or to different treatments, may cause certain subjects to drop out. Maturation may also be a threat, depending on selection characteristics. If the subjects in each group are aware of the treatment given the other group, it is possible for diffusion of treatment to be a threat. Experimenter effects, subject effects, treatment replications, and statistical conclusion threats are also possible.

The nonequivalent groups posttest-only design is relatively weak for testing causation. If the design is used, a researcher should make every effort to use comparable groups in order to decrease the selection threat.

The possible sources of invalidity for research carried out by the three pre-experimental designs are summarized in Table 10.5. Since different designs control different factors and also have unique weaknesses, the researcher chooses the best design on the basis of the research conditions. If, for example, the researcher can reasonably argue that two groups are about the same with respect to important variables (e.g., socio-economic status, achievement, age, experience, motivation), then the strongest design will be the posttest-only with nonequivalent groups. In any event, all these designs are relatively weak for use in testing causal relationships, but with sufficient foresight, they usually can be modified slightly to permit more reasonable causal inferences. (See Shadish, Cook, and Campbell [2002] for ways to improve nonequivalent groups posttest-only designs.)

RANDOMIZED EXPERIMENTAL DESIGNS

This section presents two designs that have been called *randomized experimental designs*. Both include procedures for ruling out intersubject differences through randomization of subjects to groups. These designs represent what is now called the "gold standard" for educational research and evaluation.

Randomized Pretest-Posttest Control Group Design

The **randomized pretest-posttest control group design** is an extension of the single-group pretest-posttest design in two ways: A second group is added, called the *control group*, and subjects are assigned randomly to each group. This design is represented below. Group A is the experimental group, and R represents randomization of subjects.

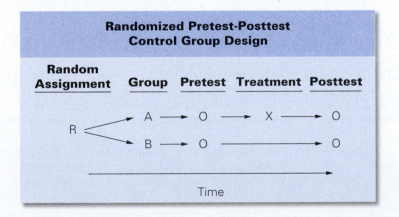

The first step is random assignment of the subjects to the experimental group and the control group. In studies with a relatively small number of subjects, it is usually best to

EXCERPT 10.3   Checking for Statistical Equivalence between Randomized Treatment and Control Groups

The participants were assigned to one of two study conditions (i.e., experimental and control) for the purposes of the study using stratified, random sampling. . . . Cross-tabs were conducted to analyze categorical equivalency across the experimental and control groups. The analysis revealed statistically non-significant relations across the groups for all variables [e.g., gender, teacher rating] except language.

Source: From Gaskill, P. J., & Murphy, P. K. (2004). Effects of a memory strategy on second-graders' performance and self-efficacy. *Contemporary Educational Psychology, 29,* 27–49.

Research Navigator.com

Conducting Randomized Experiments
Accession No.: 9688642

rank order the subjects on achievement, attitudes, or other factors that may be related to the dependent variable. Then, in the case of a two-group design, pairs of subjects are formed; the researcher randomly assigns one subject from each pair to the experimental group and the other subject to the control group.

The purpose of random assignment is to enable the researcher to reasonably rule out any differences between the groups that could account for the results. With a small group of subjects, it is less likely that the groups will be the same. If only 10 subjects are randomly assigned to two groups, for example, there is a good chance that even though the assignment is random, there will be important differences between the groups. If 200 subjects are randomly assigned, however, there is a very small chance that the groups will differ. Generally, educational researchers like to have at least 15 subjects in each group in order to assume statistical equivalence, and they have more confidence in the results if there are 20 to 30 subjects in each group. Excerpts 10.3 and 10.4 illustrate how researchers check for statistical equivalence even though there has been random assignment. Note, too, how the researchers used stratification before random assignment. Note in Excerpt 10.5 how random assignment is made by class and not by student. This would be considered a pre-experimental posttest-only design, which means there would be many potentially serious threats to internal validity. Students are not, as implied, randomly assigned to treatments. In Excerpt 10.6, matching is used with random assignment to ensure the statistical equivalence of the groups being compared.

The second step is to pretest each group on the dependent variable. (In some designs, the pretest is given first, followed by random assignment.) The third step is to administer the intervention to the experimental group but not to the control group, keeping all other conditions the same for both groups so that the only difference is

EXCERPT 10.4   Checking for Statistical Equivalence between Randomized Treatment and Control Groups

The participants were randomly assigned to either an experimental treatment group receiving advance planning strategy instruction or a comparative treatment group receiving a modified version of process writing instruction. Separate *t*-tests were performed to determine if there were significant differences between the two groups with respect to chronological age, IQ, reading and writing achievement, or number of years enrolled in special education. No significant differences between the groups were found.

Source: From Troia, G. A., & Graham, S. (2002). The effectiveness of a highly explicit, teacher-directed strategy instruction routine: Changing the writing performance of students with learning disabilities. *Journal of Learning Disabilities, 35*(4), 290–305.

EXCERPT 10.5   Random Assignment of Intact Groups

Students from three classrooms at a local elementary school participated in this study. Each of the three intact classrooms was randomly assigned to one of the three classroom evaluations structure conditions. Twenty-five fifth-grade students were assigned to the token economy condition, 18 fourth-grade students to the contingency contract condition, and 28 fifth-grade students to the control condition.

Source: From Self-Brown, S. R., & Mathews, II, S. (2003). Effects of classroom structure on student achievement goal orientation. *Journal of Educational Research, 97*(2), 106–111.

the manipulation of the independent variable. Each group is then posttested on the dependent variable.

Randomized Pretest-Posttest Comparison Group Design

In the diagrammed control group design, there is no treatment at all for the control group. As indicated previously, it is more common and usually more desirable to have comparison rather than control groups. A comparison design uses two or more variations of the independent variable and can use two or more groups. Suppose, for example, that a teacher wants to compare three methods of teaching spelling. The teacher randomly assigns each student in the class to one of three groups, administers a pretest, tries the different methods, and gives a posttest. The design would look like this, with R representing random assignment of subjects:

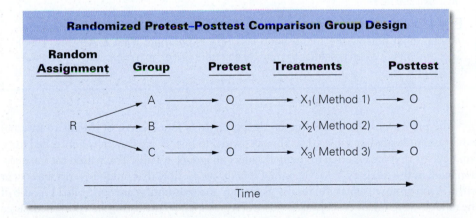

EXCERPT 10.6   Random Assignment with Matching

Within each class, the remaining students were matched in terms of abilities and then randomly assigned to three experimental conditions: (a) mastery learning only, (b) accuracy-oriented overlearning, and (c) fluency-oriented overlearning.

Source: From Peladeau, N., Forget, J., & Gagne, F. (2003). Effect of paced and unpaced practice on skill application and retention: How much is enough? *American Educational Research Journal, 40*(3), 769–801.

It would also be possible to combine several different treatments with a control group, as shown below:

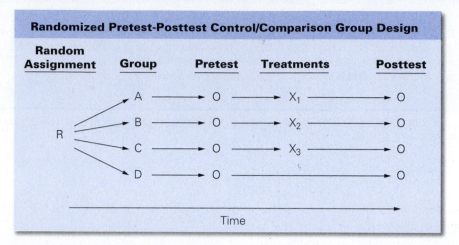

Excerpt 10.7 illustrates the preceding design.

ALERT!   Random assignment of *individuals* is much different than random assignment of *groups of individuals* (as is often done with classes of students).

MISCONCEPTION   Credible experiments are not feasible in educational research.

EVIDENCE   There are many good examples of credible educational experiments, most notably the Tennessee Class Size Experiment (Finn & Achilles, 1990). Cooperation between practitioners and researchers will enable more such experimental studies.

The pretest-posttest control group design controls four sources of threats to internal validity, as indicated in Table 10.6. Threats related to history are generally controlled insofar as events that are external to the study affect all groups equally. The reason for the question mark in the category, however, is that it is always possible that unique events may occur within each group to affect the results. Selection and maturation are controlled because of the random assignment of subjects. Statistical regression and pretesting are controlled, since any effect of these factors is equal for all groups. Instrumentation is not a problem when

EXCERPT 10.7   Randomized Comparison Group Design

In the instructional experiment, 96 second graders with low reading achievement were randomly assigned to one of four conditions: (a) explicit and reflective word recognition, (b) explicit and reflective reading comprehension, (c) combined explicit word recognition and explicit reading comprehension, or (d) treated control that only practiced reading skills without any instruction.

Source: From Berninger, V. W., Vereulen, K., Abbott,. R. D., McCutchen, D., Cotton, S., Cude, J., Dorn, S., & Sharon, T. (2003). Comparison of three approaches to supplementary reading instruction for low-achieving second-grade readers. *Language, Speech, and Hearing Services in Schools, 34*(2), 101–117.

TABLE 10.6   Threats to Internal Validity of Randomized Experimental Designs

Design	History	Selection	Statistical Regression	Pretesting	Instrumentation	Attrition	Maturation	Diffusion of Treatment	Experimenter Effects	Treatment Replications	Subject Effects
Pretest-posttest control and/or comparison group	?	+	+	+	?	?	+	?	?	?	?
Posttest-only control and/or comparison group	+	+	NA	NA	?	?	+	?	?	?	?

Note: In this table, and in Tables 10.5 and 10.7, a minus sign means a definite weakness, a plus sign means the factor is controlled, a question mark means a possible source of invalidity, and NA indicates the threat is not applicable to this design (and is also, then, not a factor).

the same standardized self-report procedures are used, but studies that use observers or raters must be careful to avoid observer or rater bias (e.g., knowing which students are receiving which treatments, or different observers or raters are used for each group). Attrition is not usually a threat unless a particular treatment causes systematic subject dropout.

Diffusion of treatments may be a source of invalidity in experiments in which subjects in one group, because of close physical proximity or communication with subjects in another group, learn about information or treatments not intended for them. Because the conditions that were intended for one group, then, are transmitted to other groups, the effect of the intervention is dispersed. For example, if a researcher compares two methods of instruction, such as cooperative group instruction and individualized instruction, and conducts the experiment within a single fourth-grade class by randomly assigning half the class to each method, it is likely that students in one group will know what is occurring in the other group. If the students in the individualized group feel left out or believe they have a less interesting assignment, they may be resentful and may not perform as well as possible. Diffusion might also occur if students in the cooperative group learn to help others and then assist students in the individualized group.

Experimenter effects comprise another threat, depending on the procedures of the study. If the individuals who are responsible for implementing the treatments are aware of the purpose and hypotheses of the study, they may act differently toward each group and affect the results. If a teacher is involved in a study to investigate the effect of differential amounts of praise on behavior (i.e., more praise, better behavior) and understands what the hypothesized result should be, then he or she may act more positively toward the students receiving more praise (e.g., be closer physically, give more eye contact, offer less criticism) and thus contaminate the intended effect of amount of praise.

Similarly, subject effects could be important if subjects in different groups respond differently because of their treatment. For example, subjects who know they are in the control group may try harder than they otherwise would, or they may be demotivated because they were not selected for the special treatment, or those in the special treatment may feel an obligation to try harder or give better responses. Treatment replications may be a threat, depending on how the treatments were administered, and statistical conclusion is always a possibility.

Randomized Posttest-Only Control and Comparison Group Designs

The purpose of random assignment, as indicated previously, is to equalize the experimental and control groups before introducing the intervention. If the groups are equalized through randomization, is it necessary to give a pretest? While there are certain cases in which it is best to use a pretest with random assignment, if the groups have at least 15 subjects each, the pretest may not be necessary—that is, it is not essential to have a pretest in order to conduct a true experimental study. The **randomized posttest-only control and comparison group designs** are the same as the randomized pretest-posttest control and comparison group designs except that there is no pretest on the dependent variable. The posttest-only control group design can be depicted as follows, with R representing the pools of subjects:

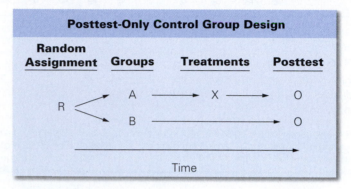

Here is the same type of design using comparison groups. (See also Excerpt 10.4 for an example of a comparison group design.)

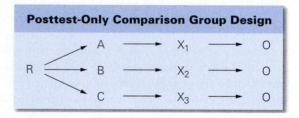

The randomized posttest-only group design is used when it is unfeasible or inconvenient to give a pretest and in situations in which the pretest might have an effect on the treatment. There are four disadvantages to using a randomized posttest-only rather than a randomized pretest–posttest design:

1. If there is any chance that randomization has not controlled for initial group differences or the lack of a pretest makes it difficult either to check whether differences exist or control statistically those differences that may be found.
2. The researcher is unable to form subgroups on the basis of the pretest for investigating effects of the treatment on different subgroups.
3. The researcher is unable to determine whether differential attrition has occurred.
4. The statistical analysis is less precise and less likely to show a difference between the groups.

The pretest–posttest design may be preferable in these situations:

1. There are subtle, small differences between treatment conditions
2. Differential mortality is possible
3. Subgroup analysis is desirable
4. Anonymity is unnecessary
5. Pretesting is a normal part of the subjects' routine.

The advantages of the posttest-only design are that it allows experimental evidence when it is impossible to give a pretest, it avoids the reactive effect of pretesting, and it makes ensuring anonymity easier. This design is especially good, then, for attitude research for two reasons: The use of an attitude questionnaire as the pretest may well affect the treatment, and attitudes are generally reported more honestly if anonymity can be ensured.

EXCERPT 10.8 Randomized Posttest-Only Control and Comparison Group Design

We randomly assigned the 84 participants to one of six experimental conditions or a practice-only control group, with 12 girls in each group. The experimental conditions were based on the three types of goal setting (process goal, outcome goal, and shifting process-outcome goal), and two variations in self-recording (present or absent). . . . As a check for effectiveness of random assignment, we com-

pared the NEDT English usage of girls in the six experimental groups at baseline and found no significant differences. . . . All girls were posttested in order for attributions, self-efficacy, writing skill, self-reaction, and intrinsic interest. The experimenter began and terminated each section of the study and recorded the posttest scores.

Source: From Zimmerman, B. J., & Kitsantas, A. (1999). Acquiring writing revision skill: shifting from process to outcome self-regulatory goals. *Journal of Educational Psychology, 91*(2), 244–245.

The posttest-only control group design controls for almost the same sources of invalidity as the pretest-posttest control group design. Table 10.6 summarizes the sources of invalidity.

In Excerpt 10.8, a randomized posttest-only control/comparison design is used to investigate the effect of several sentence-combining revision strategies on writing skill, self-motivation, and intrinsic interest in writing. There were six experimental conditions and a control group.

Occasionally, a contingency arises in which the researcher needs to rule out the effect of the pretest on the treatment. The design used for this purpose is a combination of the posttest-only control group and pretest–posttest control group design and is called the *Solomon four-group design.* Although this design controls for the effects of mortality and pretest-treatment interactions, it is difficult to carry out in education because it requires twice as many subjects and groups as other designs.

QUASI-EXPERIMENTAL DESIGNS

True experimental designs provide the strongest, most convincing arguments of the causal effect of the independent variable because they control for the most sources of internal invalidity. There are, however, many circumstances in educational research in which it is not feasible to design randomized experiments or in which the need for strong external validity is greater than the need for internal validity. The most common reasons that true experimental designs cannot be employed are that random assignment of subjects to experimental and control groups is impossible and that a control or comparison group is unavailable, inconvenient, or too expensive.

Fortunately, there are several good designs that can be used under either of these circumstances. They are termed **quasi-experimental designs** because, while not true experiments, they provide reasonable control over most sources of invalidity and are usually stronger than the pre-experimental designs. Although there are many quasi-experimental designs (Cook & Campbell, 1979; Shadish, Cook, & Campbell, 2002), we will discuss only the most common ones.

Nonequivalent Groups Pretest-Posttest Control and Comparison Group Designs

Nonequivalent groups pretest-posttest control and comparison group designs are very prevalent and useful in education, since it is often impossible to randomly assign subjects. The researcher uses intact, already established groups of subjects, gives a pretest, administers the treatment condition to one group, and gives the posttest. The only difference between this design, then, and the randomized pretest-posttest control group design is the lack of random assignment of subjects. The design is represented below:

Nonequivalent Groups Pretest–Posttest Control Group Design

Group	Pretest	Treatment	Posttest
A	O	X	O
B	O		O

Time

As shown in Table 10.7 (p. 278), the most serious threat to the internal validity of research conducted with this design is selection. Because the groups may differ in characteristics that affect the dependent variable, the researcher must address selection and provide reasonable arguments that this threat is not a plausible rival hypothesis. Suppose a researcher is interested in studying the effect of three different methods of changing the attitudes of student teachers toward computer-assisted instruction. The researcher has three classes of student teachers to work with, and it is impossible to assign students randomly within each class to each of the three methods. The researcher therefore uses each class intact and gives each class a different treatment. The design would be as follows:

Class	Pretest	Method	Posttest
A	O	X_1	O
B	O	X_2	O
C	O	X_3	O

Time

The interpretation of the results will depend largely on whether the groups differed on some characteristic that might reasonably be related to the independent variable. This decision is made by comparing the three groups on such characteristics as gender, time the groups meet, size of groups, achievement, aptitude, socioeconomic status, major, and pretest scores. For instance, if Class A comprises all elementary majors and Classes B and C secondary majors and the results showed that Class A gained more than B and C, the gain may be attributable to the values and backgrounds of elementary majors compared with those of secondary majors. On the other hand, if the classes are about the same in most characteristics, then it would be reasonable to assume that selection differences probably would not account for the results. Consequently, if the researcher knows in advance that randomization is impossible, the groups should be selected to be as similar as possible. The pretest scores and other measures on the groups are then used to adjust the groups statistically on the factor that is measured. Another approach to controlling selection when intact groups such as classrooms must be used is to use a large number of groups and then randomly assign entire groups to either control or treatment conditions. This procedure then changes the study to a true experimental design. This is, in fact, the preferred approach when diffusion of treatment or local history threats are viable.

The threats of maturation and statistical regression are the only other differences between this design and the pretest-posttest control group design. Regression is a problem if one of the groups happens to have extremely high or low scores. For example, if a study

EXCERPT 10.9 Quasi-Experimental Pretest-Posttest Comparison Group Design

A nonequivalent control group quasi-experimental design (Campbell & Stanley, 1966) involving 16 intact classes was adopted. Random assignment of students to new classes is not likely in Taiwan's educational system; intact class set was the unit of the experimental design. Eight intact classes ($n = 319$) were randomly assigned to the inquiry-group instruction; eight classes ($n = 293$) were assigned randomly to the traditional lecture group. The participants in both groups were tested and surveyed before and after the 4-week intervention.

Source: From Chang, C., & Mao, S. (1999). Comparison of Taiwan science students' outcomes with inquiry-group versus traditional instruction. *Journal of Educational Research, 92*(6), 342.

to assess the impact of a program on gifted children selected gifted children who score low and normal children who score high as comparison groups, then statistical regression will make the results look like a difference in posttest scores when nothing has actually changed. Maturation effects (e.g., growing more experienced, tired, bored) will depend on the specific differences in characteristics between the groups.

In Excerpt 10.9, a nonequivalent groups pretest-posttest quasi-experimental design is employed by using students in intact classes as subjects. Notice how even though there is random assignment of classes, the researchers properly indicate that this is not a true experimental design because students were not randomly assigned to classes. The study has a single independent variable with two levels and measures of achievement and attitude as dependent variables.

Quasi-experimental designs that use either control or comparison groups can be strengthened by taking the following measures:

- Adding a second pretest
- Replicating the treatment with another group at another time with the same pretest
- Using a comparison group that reverses the effect of the targeted intervention

The plausibility of threat to internal validity for quasi-experimental nonequivalent groups designs depends in part on the pattern of pretest differences between the groups, predicted outcomes, and posttest differences. Figure 10.1 shows four possible patterns of findings. In pattern (a), the treatment group's pretest score is higher than the control group's pretest score, and the results suggest that the treatment group is simply maturing at a different rate. In (b), it is possible that the treatment group's posttest score will be higher, since its pretest score was initially higher than that of the control group. Patterns (c) and (d) show relatively strong findings, since improvement is demonstrated for the treatment group even though its pretest score was lower.

Time-Series Designs

In the single-group pretest-posttest design, a single group of subjects usually receives only one pretest and one posttest. If the group is repeatedly measured before and after the treatment, rather than once before and once after, a different design, called a *time series*, is created. **Time-series designs** are especially useful when there are continuous, naturally occurring observations of the dependent variable over time and there is a sudden or distinct treatment during the observations. These designs offer significant improvement over the pretest-posttest design because with a series of preobservations and postobservations, patterns of stability and change can be assessed more accurately.

Single-Group Interrupted Time-Series Design The **single-group interrupted time-series design** requires one group and multiple observations or assessments before and after the treatment. The observations before the treatment can be thought of as repeated

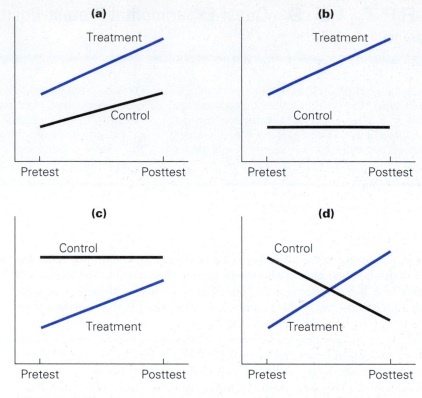

FIGURE 10.1 **Possible Outcomes of Two-Group Quasi-Experimental Pretest-Posttest Designs**

pretests, and those after the treatment can be thought of as repeated posttests. The single-group interrupted time-series design can be diagrammed as follows:

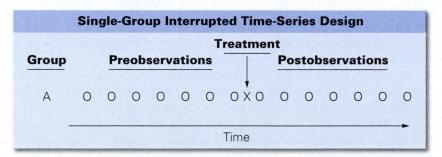

Several conditions should be met in employing this design. First, the observations should be made at equal time intervals and conducted with the same procedures in order to reduce the threat of instrumentation. Second, the treatment introduced should be a distinctive, abrupt intervention that is clearly new to the existing environment. Third, there should be some evidence that the subjects involved in each observation are the same (i.e., have low attrition). A variation of using the same subjects for each measurement is to use different but very similar groups. A new curriculum could be assessed very well in this manner. For example, sixth-grade student achievement could be plotted for several years with the old curriculum, and then achievement scores could be recorded for several years after the new curriculum was introduced. The key element in this design is that the characteristics of the sixth-grade students must be about the same year after year. Obviously, if there is an immigration of brighter students over the years, achievement will increase regardless of the curriculum.

Some possible outcomes for the study are indicated in Figure 10.2. If Outcome A is achieved, then the researcher may conclude that the curriculum had a positive effect on achievement. Outcome B indicates a steady improvement of scores, so it is difficult to

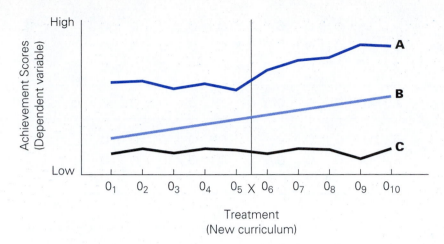

FIGURE 10.2 **Possible Outcome Patterns of Achievement over Time for Time-Series Designs**

interpret the effect of the curriculum, and Outcome C indicates little change over the time span. In interpreting these results, however, the researcher should look for alternate explanations. If there happened to be a change in the student population, such as migration from city to suburban schools, then the observations would be expected to change. The testing instrument would need to be the same (e.g., there should be no change in the norming group). Perhaps the most serious threat to validity is history. It is possible that events other than the treatment—in this case, the curriculum—occurred at about the same time and affected the posttest observations; for example, maybe in the same year the curricula were changed, the teachers also changed. Other threats include seasonal variation (e.g., self-concept scores may be lower in winter than in spring) and pretesting (e.g., the effect of the pretesting on the treatment).

Control Group Interrupted Time-Series Design   In this design, a control or comparison group is added to the single-group interrupted time series. The addition of a control group strengthens the design considerably, since the major threat of history is eliminated. Instrumentation is also a less likely explanation, and if random assignment is included, then selection is not a threat to validity. Since a control group is present, however, diffusion of treatment becomes a threat. The **control group interrupted time-series design** is represented below:

Control-Group Interrupted Time-Series Design								
				Treatment				
Group	**Preobservations**				**Postobservations**			
A	O	O	O	O X O	O	O	O
B	O	O	O	O	O	O	O	O

Time

There are many variations of the basic time-series design. A treatment can be removed rather than added, for example, and multiple treatments can be compared, either with one group or several groups. Some variations are illustrated in the next diagram. In Situation 1, three different treatments are compared and three groups of subjects are used. In Situation 2, only one group of subjects is used and two treatments are compared, and in Situation 3, the same treatment is compared in two groups at different points in time.

Situation 1	A	O	O	O	O	O X₁O	O	O	O	O	
	B	O	O	O	O	O X₂O	O	O	O	O	
	C	O	O	O	O	O X₃O	O	O	O	O	

$$\text{Situation 1} \quad A \quad O \; O \; O \; O \; O\,X_1O \; O \; O \; O \; O$$
$$B \quad O \; O \; O \; O \; O\,X_2O \; O \; O \; O \; O$$
$$C \quad O \; O \; O \; O \; O\,X_3O \; O \; O \; O \; O$$

Situation 2   A   O   O   O   O X_1O   O   O   O X_2O   O   O   O

Situation 3   A   O   O   O X_1O   O   O   O   O   O   O

           B   O   O   O   O   O   O   O X_1O   O   O

Time

The quasi-experimental designs that have been introduced in this chapter are simple, basic designs that are usually expanded in actual studies, and there are several designs that have not been mentioned. The choice of design will depend on the variables studied, the circumstances of the setting in which the research is conducted, and the plausibility of threats to internal validity. The important point is that there are weaknesses in all research designs, and it is necessary for the investigator and the reader of research to search out and analyze plausible rival hypotheses that may explain the results. Table 10.7 summarizes threats to the internal validity of quasi-experimental designs.

SINGLE-SUBJECT DESIGNS

The experimental designs that have been discussed thus far are based on a traditional research concept that behavior is best investigated by using groups of subjects. We are

TABLE 10.7 Threats to Internal Validity of Quasi-Experimental Designs

Design	History	Selection	Statistical Regression	Pretesting	Instrumentation	Attrition	Maturation	Diffusion of Treatment	Experimenter Effects	Treatment Replications	Subject Effects
Nonequivalent groups pretest-posttest design	?	−	?	+	?	?	−	?	?	?	?
Single-group interrupted time-series	−	?	+	?	?	?	+	NA	+	?	?
Control group interrupted time-series	+	?	+	+	?	?	+	?	?	?	?

Note: In this table, and in Tables 10.5 and 10.6, a minus sign means a definite weakness, a plus sign means the factor is controlled, a question mark means a possible source of invalidity, and NA indicates the threat is not applicable to this design (and is also, then, not a factor).

typically interested, for example, in fourth-grade students' attitudes in general or in whether a particular method of reading is generally best. There are, however, many circumstances in which it is either undesirable or impossible to use groups of subjects, such as when examining instructional strategies to be used with individual students. In these situations, **single-subject designs** are often employed to provide rigorous causal inferences for the behavior of one, two, or a few individuals. The term *single subject* actually refers to the way the results are presented and analyzed—that is, by individual subject—as contrasted with group designs, which use average scores. The basic approach is to study individuals in a nontreatment condition and then in a treatment condition, with performance on the dependent variable measured continually in both conditions.

The design characteristics that achieve high internal validity with single-subject designs are somewhat different from those covered previously in the context of group designs. The most important characteristics of single-subject designs can be summarized as follows:

1. *Reliable measurement* Single-subject designs usually involve many observations of behavior as the technique for collecting data. It is important that the observation conditions, such as time of day and location, be standardized; that observers be well trained and checked for reliability and bias; and that the observed behavior be defined operationally. Consistency in measurement is especially important as the study moves from one condition to another. Because accurate measurement is crucial to single-subject designs, the researcher typically reports all aspects of data collection so that any threat to validity can be reasonably ruled out.

2. *Repeated measurement* A distinct characteristic of single-subject designs is that a single aspect of behavior is measured many times, in the same way, throughout the study. This is quite different from measurement in many group studies, in which there is a single measure before or after the treatment. Repeated measurement controls for normal variation that would be expected within short time intervals and provides a clear, reliable description of the behavior.

3. *Description of conditions* A precise, detailed description of all conditions in which the behavior is observed should be provided. This description allows application of the study to other individuals in order to strengthen both internal and external validity.

4. *Baseline and treatment condition; duration and stability* The usual procedure is for each condition to last about the same length of time and contain about the same number of observations. If either the length of time or number of observations varies, then time and number of observations become confounding variables that complicate the interpretation of the results and weaken internal validity. It is also important that the behavior be observed long enough for the establishment of a stable pattern. If there is considerable variation in the behavior, then it will be difficult to determine whether observed changes are due to natural variation or to the treatment. During the first phase of single-subject research, the target behavior is observed under natural conditions until stability is achieved. This period of time is called the **baseline.** The treatment phase occurs with a change in conditions by the researcher and also must be long enough to achieve stability.

5. *Single-variable rule* It is important to change only one variable during the treatment phase of single-subject research, and the variable that is changed should be described precisely. If two or more variables are changed simultaneously, the researcher cannot be sure which change or changes caused the results.

A-B Design

In order to distinguish single-subject designs from traditional group designs, a unique notational convention is used. In it, the letters stand for conditions instead of groups of subjects. That is, A stands for the baseline condition and B for the treatment condition.

The **A-B design** is the most simple and least interpretable single-subject design. The procedure in using it is to observe the target behavior until it occurs at a consistent, stable rate. This condition is the baseline, or A condition. A treatment is then introduced into the environment in which baseline data have been collected, and that condition is labeled B. The design can be diagrammed as follows:

A-B Single-Subject Design

Intervention

Baseline Data A	Treatment Data B
	X X X X X X
O O O O O O	O O O O O O

Time →

The interpretation of the results is based on the premise that if no treatment were introduced, the behavior would continue as recorded in the baseline. If the behavior does change during the treatment condition, it may be attributed to the intervention introduced by the researcher. Other factors, however, such as testing and history, often cannot be ruled out reasonably in this design, so it is relatively weak in internal validity.

A-B-A Design

A more common design in single-subject research is the **A-B-A design,** also called a **reversal** or **withdrawal design,** in which a second baseline period is added after the treatment. In this design, which is represented below, the researcher establishes a baseline (A), introduces the treatment (B), and then removes the treatment to re-establish the baseline condition (A).

A-B-A Single-Subject Design

Baseline A	Treatment B	Baseline A
	X X X X X	
O O O O O	O O O O O O	O O O O O

Time →

This design allows strong causal inference if the pattern of behavior changes during the treatment phase and then returns to about the same pattern as observed in the first baseline after the treatment is removed. As a hypothetical example, suppose a teacher is interested in trying a new reinforcement technique with John, one of the fifth-graders, in the hope that the new technique will increase the time John spends actually engaged in study (i.e., time on task). The teacher first records the average amount of time on task for each day until a stable pattern is achieved. Then the teacher introduces the reinforcement technique as the intervention and continues to observe time on task. After a given length of time, the teacher stops using the reinforcement technique to see whether the on-task behavior returns to the baseline condition. Figure 10.3 illustrates the results of this hypothetical study, which provides good evidence of a causal link between the reinforcement technique and greater time on task.

Further evidence of a change in behavior that is caused by the treatment may be obtained if the A-B-A design is extended to reinstitute the treatment, or become A-B-A-B. Not only does the A-B-A-B design provide stronger causal inference than the A-B-A design, but it also ends with the treatment condition, which, for ethical reasons, is often more favorable for the subject. If the pattern of results fails to support the effect of the treatment, then the interpretation is less clear. If the behavior is changed during the treatment

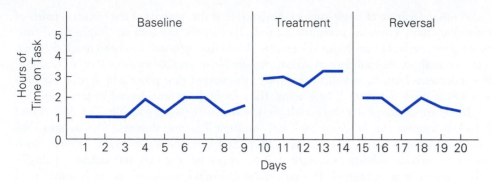

FIGURE 10.3   **Results from a Hypothetical Study Using an A-B-A Design**

but fails to return to the baseline condition once the treatment is ended, the researcher does not know whether factors other than the treatment caused the change, or perhaps the treatment was so effective that it could be removed and still have an impact on behavior.

Multiple-Baseline Designs

When it is impossible or undesirable to remove a treatment condition or when the effects of a treatment condition extend into a second baseline phase, strong causal inference can be made by using **multiple-baseline designs,** rather than by a simple A-B design. Multiple-baseline designs employ the A-B logic, but rather than using one subject and one kind of target behavior, the researcher collects data on two or more actions, subjects, or situations or some combination of actions, situations, and subjects.

Multiple-Baselines across Behavior   In this design, baseline measurements are recorded on two or more discrete, independent behaviors for one subject. After a stable baseline has been established for all behaviors, the treatment is first applied to one behavior and then, after a constant time interval, it is applied to the second behavior, and so forth until all have received the treatment.

Strong causal inference can be made as to the effect of the treatment if performance shows consistent change only after the treatment has been introduced for each type of behavior. To provide a meaningful comparison, it is necessary to begin the treatments at different times for each one. In this way, behavior remaining at the baseline condition provides control for that receiving the treatment condition. The most troublesome problem with this design occurs when using two or more behaviors that are so similar that the first time the treatment is introduced, it affects both.

Multiple-Baselines across Situations   In this design, a single type of target behavior of one individual is observed in two or more settings. A teacher might, for example, be interested in investigating whether a student will respond the same way to individualized feedback in math, science, and English. The basic design is the same as in the multiple-baselines-across-behaviors design except that situation replaces types of behavior as the condition that is varied (e.g., learning behavior in both a classroom and a grocery store or a classroom and cafeteria).

Multiple-Baselines across Individuals   This design uses two or more individuals and holds the behavior and the situation constant. After a stable baseline has been observed for one subject, the treatment is introduced for that subject only. After a given interval, the second subject receives the treatment and so forth. This design is effective as long as the subjects involved are uninfluenced by one another because one of them has received the treatment (e.g., with students in the same class or with siblings). A good use of this type of design would be to have a teacher employ the same treatment procedure with individual students in four different classes.

A unique feature of single-subject designs is that the analysis of the results consists of a visual analysis. There are no statistical tests. Essentially, the data are graphed and conclusions are reached by analyzing the graphs. While this approach has been much debated, behavior analysts are confident in making reasonable interpretations based on its findings. The judgments have been validated through the peer-review process in journal publication. Effect size is determined by whether the new findings are adopted by practitioners.

Many variations of the three multiple-baseline designs are possible. The A-B-A and A-B-A-B formats can be combined with multiple-baseline designs. The designs that involve removal, reversal, or reinstatement of the treatment are generally strongest with respect to internal validity. As might well be suspected, the external validity of single-subject designs is quite limited. The generalizability of the results of one study is increased primarily by replication with other subjects and different settings.

STANDARDS OF ADEQUACY

In judging the adequacy of the designs that have been presented in this chapter, you should focus your attention on a few key criteria. These criteria are listed here in the form of questions that should be asked for each type of design.

Randomized Experimental Designs

1. Was the research design described in sufficient detail to allow for replication of the study?
2. Was it clear how statistical equivalence of the groups was achieved? Was there a full description of the specific manner in which subjects were assigned randomly to groups?
3. Was a true experimental design appropriate for the research problem?
4. Was there manipulation of the independent variable?
5. Was there maximum control over extraneous variables and errors of measurement?
6. Was the treatment condition sufficiently different from the comparison condition for a differential effect on the dependent variable to be expected?
7. Were potential threats to internal validity reasonably ruled out or noted and discussed?
8. Was the time frame of the study described?
9. Did the design avoid being too artificial or restricted for adequate external validity?
10. Was an appropriate balance achieved between control of variables and natural conditions?
11. Were appropriate tests of inferential statistics used?

Quasi-Experimental Designs

1. Was the research design described in sufficient detail to allow for replication of the study?
2. Was a true experiment possible?
3. Was it clear how extraneous variables were controlled or ruled out as plausible rival hypotheses?
4. Were all potential threats to internal validity addressed?
5. Were the explanations ruling out plausible rival hypotheses reasonable?
6. Would a different quasi-design have been better?
7. Did the design approach a true experiment as closely as possible?
8. Was there an appropriate balance between control for internal validity and for external validity?
9. Was every effort made to use groups that were as equivalent as possible?
10. If a time-series design was used, (a) Was there an adequate number of observations to suggest a pattern of results? (b) Was the treatment intervention introduced distinctly at one point in time? (c) Was the measurement of the dependent variable consistent? (d) Was it clear, if comparison groups were used, how equivalent the groups were?

Single-Subject Designs
1. Was the sample size one or just a few?
2. Was a single-subject design most appropriate, or would a group design have been better?
3. Were the observation conditions standardized?
4. Was the behavior that was observed defined operationally?
5. Was the measurement highly reliable?
6. Were sufficient repeated measures made?
7. Were the conditions in which the study was conducted fully described?
8. Was the baseline condition stable before the treatment was introduced?
9. Was there a difference between the length of time or number of observations between the baseline and the treatment conditions?
10. Was only one variable changed during the treatment condition?
11. Were threats to internal and external validity addressed?

SUMMARY

The purpose of this chapter has been to introduce designs that permit investigation of the causal effect of one variable on another. The challenge to most researchers is using the design that, given the conditions of the research, is best suited to their goal. The major points of the chapter can be summarized as follows:

1. Experimental research involves manipulating experimental variables in order to investigate cause-and-effect relationships.
2. Classic experimental research is characterized by random assignment of subjects to treatment and control groups, manipulation of independent variables, and tight control of extraneous variables.
3. Strict control of extraneous variables in experimental educational research may lead to limited generalizability of results.
4. Planning experimental research involves the creation of experimental and comparison groups, manipulation of

the factor of the group to receive the treatment, and assessment of the effect of the treatment on behavior.
5. The key element in interpreting experimental studies is to rule out plausible rival hypotheses.
6. Pre-experimental designs control for very few threats to internal validity.
7. Randomized experimental designs control the threats to internal validity, but some threats, such as local history and diffusion of treatment, may still constitute plausible rival hypotheses.
8. Quasi-experimental designs are often employed because of the difficulties in conducting randomized experiments.
9. Time-series designs, in which many observations are made before and after the treatment, are especially useful in cases where periodic testing is a natural part of the environment.
10. Single-subject designs provide techniques for making strong causal inferences about the effect of a treatment on a single individual or group.

RESEARCH NAVIGATOR NOTES

Reading the following articles will help you understand the content of this chapter. Go to the education database (included in the EBSCO database) in Research Navigator; use the Accession Number provided to find the article.

10.1 *Conducting Randomized Experiments*
The article reviews the reasons for using randomized experiments, which are difficult to implement in field settings. Accession Number: 9688642.

10.2 *Single-Subject Studies*
These two studies illustrate how single-subject designs are implemented. Accession Numbers: 12848683 and 7355607.

CHECK YOURSELF

Multiple-choice review items, with answers, are available on the Companion Website for this book:

www.ablongman.com/mcmillanschumacher6e.

APPLICATION PROBLEMS

For each of the following cases, identify the design that is being used and represent it graphically using the notation system discussed in the chapter.

1. A researcher wants to test the effectiveness of three methods of teaching typing to a group of eleventh-grade students. The researcher locates a school willing to cooperate and a teacher who says that the researcher can use three of his classes. The researcher administers a pretest to all students, each class receives a different method of teaching for two weeks, and then the researcher gives all students a posttest.

2. A teacher is interested in determining the effect of using a point system with students in order to control misbehavior. The teacher decides to record the amount of misbehavior of two students, a boy and a girl who seem to have more problems than the other students. For two weeks, the teacher records the misbehavior of the students. At the end of the second week, the teacher begins using the point system with the boy and at the same time continues to record misbehavior for another two weeks. The girl does not receive the point treatment until the end of the third week.

3. A researcher is interested in whether the order of questions in a multiple-choice test affects the number of items answered correctly. The researcher makes three forms of the test: one with easy items first and difficult items last; another with easy items last, difficult first; and a third with no order at all, easiest and difficult mixed together. The test is given to a class of 60 students. The tests are organized into 20 piles, with each pile containing Forms 1, 2, and 3. The 20 piles are then put together, and the tests are passed out to the students. The researcher then compares the average scores of students taking each form of the test.

4. Using the Research Navigator, retrieve this article: "Effect of Difficulty Levels on Second Grade Delayed Readers Using Dyad Reading" (Accession Number: 3806085). For this article, identify the research hypotheses, if there are any; whether randomization of subjects is present; what type of experimental design is used; the independent and dependent variables; and procedures for implementing the intervention. Use the standards of adequacy presented at the end of this chapter to evaluate the credibility of the study (see pp. 282–283). What, if anything, about the design could be changed to enhance the credibility of the findings?

5. Use the standards of adequacy presented in this chapter to evaluate the article in Excerpt 10.10, a study of the effect of a specific type of cooperative learning on students' self-concept and achievement.

EXCERPT 10.10   Example of an Experimental Study

Cooperative Small-Group Instruction Combined with Advanced Organizers and Their Relationship to Self-Concept and Social Studies Achievement of Elementary School Students

Jeanie A. Box and David C. Little

Research has shown that the use of small-group instruction in the classroom may positively affect student self-concept, as well as academic achievement. The purpose of this study was to determine if the use of the Jigsaw cooperative learning approach incorporated with social studies materials presented in the form of advance organizers could positively affect the self-concept and academic achievement of elementary school students. Five third-grade social studies classes served as the subjects of the study, four experimental and one control. Three assessment instruments were used: the Piers-Harris Children's Self-Concept Scale, the Teacher Inferred Self-Concept Scale, and a researcher developed social studies test based on information contained within the third-grade textbook. The students' self-concepts increased in three of the experimental classes and in the control class; however, a significant decline occurred in teacher perceptions of student self-concept in the control class, as opposed to the experimental classes. Finally, the social studies test scores revealed considerable gains in all five classes. In conclusion, the researchers believe that teachers should consider the use of cooperative small groups with advance organizers as a method of improving self-concepts and social studies achievement of their students.

Numerous articles have explored the relationship between academic achievement and the self-concept of children. A study by Aspy and Buhler (1975) supports the influence of general self-concept in learning situations. A study by Lyon (1993) also reveals data in support of academic self-concept as a powerful predictor of academic achievement.

excerpt 10.10 *(continued)*

Research has shown that the use of small-group instruction in the classroom may affect student self-concept. Aronson, Blaney, Rosenfield, Sikes, and Stephan (1977) conducted an experiment using a cooperative form of small grouping along with regular classroom instruction. Results of the study indicated that students who received only small-group instruction gained in self-esteem. A decrease in self-esteem occurred in the control groups.

Aronson and his associates (Aronson, Blaney, Sikes, Snapp, and Stephan 1975) developed a method of classroom instruction that incorporated the beneficial aspects of small-group cooperation and peer teaching into the tightly structured environment of the traditional classroom. With this Jigsaw approach, teachers are no longer the major source of instruction within the classroom. In time, students, through teaching and listening in cooperative learning situations, depend on each other for instruction. Peer teaching is essential to the concept of cooperative learning. Aronson has indicated that four to six students form into small groups to study assigned *instructional* material. Members of each group are assigned questions or activities about the material being studies. Then each student is placed in a subgroup composed of members from each of the other groups who are responsible for studying the same material. After completing their specific questions in subgroups, all members return to their regular groups to share the answers to the assigned questions.

Ausubel (1963), in his theory of meaningful verbal learning, advocated the use of advance organizers to facilitate the learning of written material. Ausubel reasoned that advance organizers presented students an overview of the more detailed material being studied. This could facilitate learning when presented before the actual presentation of material to be learned. Advance organizers, as defined by Barnes and Clausen (1975), are written materials that serve the function of facilitating the incorporation and retention of reading material. The use of chapter summaries, outlines, key terms, and chapter questions, as introductions to more detailed text are examples of advance organizers.

The purpose of this study was to determine if the use of the Jigsaw cooperative learning approach coupled with social studies materials presented in the forms of advance organizers could positively affect the self-concept and academic achievement of elementary school students. Also measured within this study was the effect of the two treatments on teacher-inferred self-concept toward the students being taught.

Methodology

The subjects of the study included members of five third-grade social studies classes at a suburban elementary school located in the Southeast. Third grade was chosen because developmentally third grade is when children's self-regulatory skills become more proficient (Alexander, Cart, & Schwanenflugel, 1995). Approximately twenty-five students were assigned to each class and were heterogeneously grouped.

Three assessment instruments were used in the study. The Piers-Harris Self-Concept Scale (Harris & Piers, 1969) measured student reported self-concept with a pretest to posttest design. The Teacher Inferred Self-Concept Scale measured the pre- to post assessments of students' self concepts' as reported by their classroom teachers (McDaniel, 1973). The researchers developed a social studies test based on information contained within the third-grade textbook used in the study to assess the pre- to posttest social studies achievement of the students.

Four experimental third-grade classes received social studies instruction in small groups instructionally designed according to Aronson's Jigsaw cooperative learning approach. In addition, one of the four types of advance organizers used in the study was randomly assigned to each experimental group.

A fifth third-grade class served as the control group. In this class, the teacher taught using traditional, large-group instruction techniques. Small groups or advance organizers were not included in the *instructional* design of the control group.

Data Analysis

The raw scores from the self-concept scales and the social studies test were analyzed by using a two-way analysis of variance (ANOVA). Analyses of the simple main effects and Tukey's KSD test results were conducted to determine if significant differences existed between pre- and posttest mean scores on the three assessment instruments. An alpha level of $p < .05$ represented the criterion for statistical significance.

Results

The results of the study were varied. Observation on the differences between pre- and post evaluation mean scores for the Piers-Harris Children's Self Concept Scale revealed gains in three of the experimental classes concerning students' self ratings of self concept. The evaluation of the mean scores for the fourth experimental group showed a decline in the Piers-Harris Children's Self-Concept Scale scores from pre- to posttest. On the other hand, significant gains in self-concept occurred in the control class.

Observations of the differences between pre- and post evaluations mean scores for the Inferred Self-Concept Scale revealed significant gains in three of the experimental classes concerning teacher rating of self-concept. A fourth experimental class revealed a slight decline in the mean scores from pre- to posttest. In the control class, a significant decline occurred in teacher perceptions of student self-concept.

Observations of the differences between pre- and post evaluation mean scores for the social studies test

(continued)

excerpt 10.10 (continued)

revealed significant gains in the four experimental classes. A significant gain was also reported for the social studies scores of the control class.

Discussion

The advantages of the Jigsaw Small-Group Approach combined with advance organizers could be placed in two categories: Academic and psychological. First, the researchers noted that the use of the Jigsaw approach combined with advance organizers was effective in improving the self-concepts of students as measured by the Piers-Harris Children's Self-Concept Scale. The teacher-inferred self-concept as measured by the Inferred Self-Concept Scale was also found to be effective.

Second, the researchers noted that the *instructional* procedures used in all five classrooms were effective in improving the social studies achievement of the third-grade students. While no clear cause for this outcome is evident, the researchers believe that the results may indicate that the students and teachers who participated in the study possessed a high level of motivation.

Third, of major concern is the significant decline in scores for the control group on the Inferred Self Concept Scale. The question could be asked if the continuous teaching of students in large groups could negatively affect how the teacher views the self-concepts of the students in the class.

Overall, the researchers believe that the results of the study support the use of cooperative small-group instruction and advance organizers in teaching classes. It should be emphasized, however, that the use of such small groups and advance organizers should serve as a supplement to conventional instruction, rather than an alternative to it.

References

Alexander, J. M., Cart, M., & Schwanenflugel, P. J. (1995). Development of metacognition in gifted children: Directions for future research. *Developmental Review, 15,* 1–37.

Aronson, E., Blaney, N., Sikes, J., Snapp, M., & Stephen, C. (1975). Busing and racial tension: The jigsaw route to learning and liking. *Psychology Today, 8*(9), 43–50.

Aronson, E., Blaney, N. T., Rosenfeld, D., Sikes, J., & Stephan, C. (1977). Interdependence in the classroom: A field study. *Journal of Educational Psychology, 69*(2), 121–128.

Aspy, D. N., & Buhler, J. H. (1975). The effect of teachers' inferred self concept upon student achievement. *Journal of Educational Research, 68,* 386–389.

Ausubel, D. P. (1963). *The psychology of meaningful verbal learning.* New York: Grune and Stratton.

Barnes, B. R., & Clauson, E. U. (1975). Do advance organizers facilitate learning? Recommendations for further research based analysis of 32 studies. *Review of Educational Research, 45,* 637–659.

Harris, D. B., & Piers, E. V. (1969). *The Piers-Harris children's self-concept scale.* Los Angeles: Western Psychological Services.

Lyon, M. (1993). Academic self concept and its relationship to achievement in a sample of junior high students. *Educational and Psychological Measurement, 53,* 201–209.

McDaniel, E. L. (1973). *Inferred self-concept scale.* Los Angeles: Western Psychological Services.

Source: From Box, J. A., & Little, D. C. (2003). Cooperative small-group instruction combined with advanced organizers and their relationship to self-concept and social studies achievement of elementary school students. *Journal of Instructional Psychology, 30*(4), 285–288. Reprinted by permission.

NOTE

1. Several sources provide further detail on these designs: Barlow and Hersen (1984), Kazdin (1982), Franklin, Allison, and Gorman (1997), and Bailey and Burch (2002).

Inferential Statistics

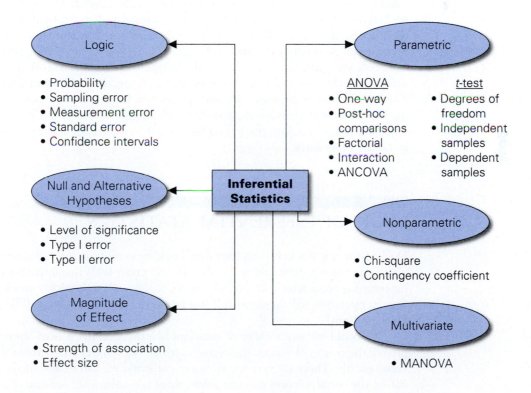

KEY TERMS

probability	degrees of freedom
sampling distribution	independent samples *t*-test
standard error	dependent samples *t*-test
confidence interval	analysis of variance (ANOVA)
statistical hypothesis	post hoc comparisons
null hypothesis	planned comparisons
alternative hypothesis	factorial ANOVA
level of significance	interaction
alpha level	analysis of covariance (ANCOVA)
Type I error	parametric
Type II error	nonparametric
statistically significant	chi-square
effect magnitude measures	independent samples chi-square test
effect size	multivariate
t-test	

This is the part of research books that many readers dread. The term *inferential statistics* can send waves of anxiety and fear into students already concerned about the so-called more simple descriptive data analysis procedures! While it is true that the actual mathematical computations associated with inferential statistics are complicated, you do not need to learn equations nor complete calculations to understand and use the results of these procedures. (Some calculations are presented in Appendix D.) Learning the principles of inferential statistics requires study and application, but it is more a matter of understanding logic than of mathematical calculations. This chapter presents the logic on which inferential statistics are based, the principles of hypothesis testing, and a few commonly used statistical procedures.

LOGIC OF INFERENTIAL STATISTICS

In some ways, it would be very nice if we could be certain in predicting outcomes. When we go see a movie, how sure are we that we will enjoy it? When a teacher uses a particular grouping procedure, how sure is he or she that it will work? How confident is a patient that an operation will be successful? Are farmers certain that there will be sufficient rain for their crops?

We could ask any number of questions like this because it is in our nature to try to predict the future. However, the degree to which we can be certain about the predictions varies greatly. There are very few things in our world we can be absolutely certain about, and in the social sciences and education, there is usually a fair amount of uncertainty. In making statements about investigated phenomena, we use language that reflects the probabilistic nature of the case. The numbers, concepts, and terms used in inferential statistics provide this language. Although there are a great number of inferential statistical procedures, many quite complicated, the purpose is always the same: to determine in a precise way the probability of something.

Probability

Probability is a scientific way of stating the degree of confidence we have in predicting something. Consider dice rolling as an example. With one die, there is a total of six possible cases. If the favorable case is rolling a four, the probability of actually rolling a four would be 1/6, or .17; that is, if a die is rolled 100 times, about 17 fours will be rolled. If we have two dice, what is the probability of rolling a seven? Since there is a total of 36 different combinations for throwing two dice (1 and 1; 1 and 2; 1 and 3, and so on) and only six of these equal 7 (1 and 6; 2 and 5; 3 and 4; 6 and 1; 5 and 2; and 4 and 3), the probability of rolling a seven is 6/36, or .17. What about throwing boxcars (two sixes)? There is only one combination of numbers that will give you boxcars, so the probability is 1/36, or .03.

This logic is applied to more complicated situations in research. How sure, for example, can pollsters be that their predictions are accurate? What is the probability of being right or wrong? When teachers use positive reinforcement, how sure are they that the desired behavior will increase in frequency? In these situations, we make probability statements that are influenced by the amount of error possible in measuring and sampling events.

Error in Sampling and Measurement

Sampling was discussed in Chapter 6 as a technique for studying a portion from the population of all events or observations under consideration. The *population* is the larger group to which the researcher intends to generalize the results obtained from the sample. As a subgroup of the population, the *sample* is used to derive data, and then inferential statistics are used to generalize to the population. Let us assume, for example, that a researcher is interested in assessing the self-concept of fourth-graders in a school district. The researcher could measure the self-concept of every fourth-grader, but that would be time consuming, expensive, and probably unnecessary. Rather, the researcher should take a *sample* of the fourth-graders and measure each child's self-concept. Then the researcher could *infer* what the self-concept of all fourth-graders is from the results of the sample chosen. The group of all fourth-graders is the population, and the researcher uses descriptive statistics (i.e., mean and standard deviation) from the sample to estimate the characteristics of the population.

Where does probability enter this process? When a sample is drawn, the resulting statistics represent an imperfect estimate of the population. There is error in drawing the sample, and probability relates to our confidence in the fact that the sample accurately represents the population. Even if the researcher uses a random sample, the mean and variance of the particular sample drawn would be slightly different from those of another sample. A third sample would also be different, as would a fourth, a fifth, and so on. The sample descriptive statistics only estimate the population values, so the inferences made must take into account what possible sample statistics could have been generated.

Consider the following example (see Figure 11.1). Let us say that a researcher is interested in determining the reading level of ninth-graders of a school district. A random sample is selected and the mean of the sample is, say, 65, with a standard deviation of 2.5 (Figure 11.1a). Now let us say the researcher draws another random sample, and this time the mean is 66. Now there are two means (Figure 11.1b). Which one is correct? He or she decides to take five more samples and gets means of 64, 63.5, 64.5, 65.7, and 65.2 (Figure 11.1c). Now which one is correct? The researcher decides to really find out and takes 30 more samples. Surely that will do it! Different sample means are drawn, but when the means are put together, they begin to look like something familiar—a normal curve (Figure 11.1d).

In fact, if 100 samples were drawn, the sample means, when put together, would constitute a normal curve, with its own mean and standard deviation. The resulting distribution is called the **sampling distribution,** and the standard deviation of this distribution is termed the **standard error.** Thus, when we imagine that multiple samples are extracted from the population and scored, the standard error is the standard deviation of this sampling distribution. That is, the standard error is the measure of variability when multiple samples are drawn from the population. The *mean of means*, then, and the standard error of the sampling distribution can be calculated. The researcher can use this information to know not what the population mean is but what the probability is of its having a certain value based on the properties of the normal curve. That is, about two-thirds of the means

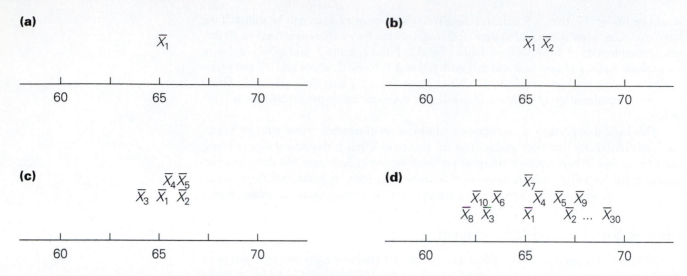

FIGURE 11.1   Random Sample with (a) One Mean, (b) Two Means, (c) Several Means, and (d) the Means Showing a Normal Curve

drawn would be within one standard error of the mean of means, and 96 percent of the means would be within two standard errors. This allows the researcher to describe a range of probable means and be fairly certain of the range, even though individual sample means will be slightly different.

In reality, researchers only take one sample, but from the mean and variance of that sample, the range of population means that could be drawn, if possible, can be calculated. Here, then, is where probability is integrated with inferential statistics. Inferential statistics are used to estimate the probability of a population mean's being within a range of possible values. The researcher is able to say, to infer, that 68 times out of 100, the population mean will be within one standard error of the mean of means and that 96 times out of 100, it will be within two standard errors.

An important related concept is that of *confidence interval*. The **confidence interval** is a range of numerical values in which the actual value of the population probably lies. The upper and lower boundaries of the confidence interval are called the *confidence limits*. Typically, researchers report a 95 or 99 percent confidence interval, which means that the probability of the population value being between the confidence limits is 95 or 99 percent, respectively. For example, if it is reported that the 99 percent confidence interval from a statewide poll is .435 to .492, this means that from the sample it can be inferred that there is a 99 percent chance that between 43.5 and 49.2 percent of the population is in favor of a particular proposal. Thus, it is highly likely that the majority of the population is against the proposal. If the 99 percent confidence interval was completely above .50, then a majority would probably favor the proposal.

Suppose a researcher is not interested in taking a sample from a population but rather includes the entire population as the sample. Would this mean that the researcher could ignore the principles of sampling error and inferential statistics in obtaining a result that represents the entire group? While sampling error is not a concern, measurement error is. Recall from Chapter 8 that whenever we assess variables in education, the measurement is never perfect. There is always some degree of error, summarized statistically as the standard error of measurement. Thus, we *infer* a real or true value on a variable from the imperfect measure. This could be thought of as a type of sampling error in the sense that the one measure obtained is a sample estimating the true value. Consequently, in all educational research, there is definitely measurement error, and in some research, there is also sampling error.

In most research, however, we are interested in much more than estimating populations from samples. We usually want to compare population means with each other or with some established value. The next section discusses how these comparisons are made.

NULL AND ALTERNATIVE HYPOTHESES

Let us assume that a researcher wants to compare the attitudes of sixth-graders toward school to those of fourth-graders. The researcher randomly selects samples of sixth- and fourth-graders and finds the mean of each group. The mean is 30 for fourth-graders and 37 for sixth-graders. Can the researcher then assume that sixth-graders have more positive attitudes than fourth-graders? Perhaps, but this conclusion must take into account sampling and measurement error. The population means are thus estimated and compared to find the probability that the possible population means of each group are different. The probabilities are formalized by statements that are tested. These statements are referred to as *hypotheses*. Research hypotheses have already been introduced as the research prediction that is tested. (In this example, the research hypothesis might be that sixth-graders have more positive attitudes than fourth-graders.)

When we refer to probability in terms of sampling and measurement error, the statement used is called the **statistical hypothesis.** Statistical hypotheses are stated in either the *null* or *alternative* form. The **null hypothesis** states that there is no difference between the population means of the two groups. That is, the population means are the same. The researcher employs an inferential statistical test to determine the probability that the null hypothesis is untrue. If the null is false, then there is a high probability that there is a difference between the groups. The null hypothesis in our example would be that attitudes of sixth- and fourth-graders toward school are the same. If we can show that there is a high probability of being correct in rejecting the null, then we have found evidence of a difference in the attitudes.

The null hypothesis is indicated by the symbol H_0, which is followed by population means that are compared. The population means are symbolized by u. Thus, a typical null hypothesis would be $H_0: u_1 = u_2$, where u_1 is the mean of one population and u_2 is the mean of a second population. If four populations are compared, the null hypothesis will be $H_0: u_1 = u_2 = u_3 = u_4$.

Theoretically, we know that the population range of means of both groups can be estimated, and if there is little overlap in those ranges, then it is likely that the population means are different. This case is diagramed in Figure 11.2. Note that there is virtually no overlap between the two normal curves. This means that we can be confident of being correct in rejecting the null hypothesis.

The reason null hypotheses are used with inferential statistics is that we never prove something to be true; we only fail to disprove it. Failure to disprove is consistent with the reality of probability in our lives. If we cannot find compelling evidence that they are different, the most plausible conclusion is that they are the same.

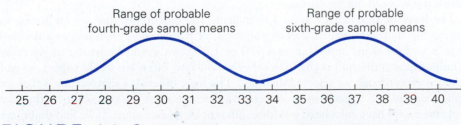

Range of probable
fourth-grade sample means

Range of probable
sixth-grade sample means

25 26 27 28 29 30 31 32 33 34 35 36 37 38 39 40

FIGURE 11.2   **Range of Population Means of Two Groups**

EXCERPT 11.1   Null Hypothesis

To further explore attitudinal differences between the two groups, a hypothesis test of the difference between the two group means was performed between users and nonusers for each of the seventeen attitudinal variables.

The null hypothesis for each variable was that the mean score answers for the two groups were identical: $H_0 : u_{users} = u_{nonusers}$.

Source: From Bee, R. H., & Usip, E. E. (1998). Differing attitudes of economics students about web-based instruction. *College Student Journal, 32*(2), 258–269.

It should be pointed out that failure to reject the null hypothesis does not necessarily mean that the null is true. It is especially difficult to accept null hypotheses as reality in studies that use a small number of subjects or that use instruments with low reliability. The fact that the null hypothesis was not rejected may be because of a large sampling error or measurement error. In Excerpt 11.1, a null hypothesis is described.

ALERT!   The null hypothesis is not undesirable or negative.

The **alternative hypothesis,** which is designated as H_a or H_1, is the opposite of the null hypothesis. It states the research or experimental hypothesis in statistical terms. The alternative hypothesis can be either directional or nondirectional. A *directional* alternative hypothesis states that one population mean is either greater than or less than the other population mean (e.g., $H_a: u_1 > u_2$). A *nondirectional* alternative hypothesis states that the means are not the same (e.g., $H_a: u_1 \neq u_2$). Because the directional alternative hypothesis postulates one outcome, it is often referred to as *one tailed* or *one sided*. The nondirectional alternative hypothesis, which is used much more frequently than the directional one, only predicts a difference without specifying whether one mean is greater than or less than another mean. This is called a *two-tailed* or *two-sided alternative hypothesis*. The directional/nondirectional nature of the alternative hypothesis is used to make decisions about whether the null hypothesis can be rejected.

LEVEL OF SIGNIFICANCE

Since the basis of inferential statistics is the probability of estimation, then rejecting the null hypothesis is also related to probability or chance, rather than being a dichotomous decision. That is, because of error in sampling and measurement, we can only give the probability of being correct or incorrect in rejecting or not rejecting the null. To put it differently, we can be fairly sure that a certain number of times out of 100, the sample means we *could* draw would not be the same.

The **level of significance** is used to indicate the probability that we are wrong in rejecting the null. Also called *level of probability*, or *p* level, it is expressed as a decimal and tells us how many times out of a 100 or 1,000, we would be wrong in rejecting the null assuming the null is true. (In other words, how often we would expect no real difference even though we rejected the null.) The logic of level of significance is that we assume that the null hypothesis is correct, and then see what the probability is that the sample means we have calculated would be different by chance alone. If we find that there is a probability of only 1 in 100 that we would find a particular difference in the means by chance or random fluxations, ($p = .01$), then we would probably reject the null because it is quite probable that the null is false. In other words, the level of significance tells us the chance probability of finding differences between the means. The smaller the level of significance, therefore, the more confidence we have that we are safe in rejecting the null. After all, for example, if we find a difference of five points between two means that, through our null hypothesis, we assume to be the same, and our statistics tell us there is only 1 chance in 1,000 of finding a five-point difference by chance ($p = .001$), then it is only logical to assume that the null hypothesis is false and reject it (or say we are very, very lucky!). We reject the null hypothesis in favor of the research, or alternative, hypothesis.

Some researchers will use a slightly different approach to hypothesis testing, in which a given level of significance is determined prior to data collection to act as a criterion for accepting or failing to accept the null hypothesis. This critical value is called the **alpha level** (α), and it determines the conclusion based on the numbers generated from the results.

Errors in Hypothesis Testing

The purpose of using inferential statistics, null hypotheses, and levels of significance is to make a decision, based on probability, about the nature of populations and real values of variables. It is possible that the decision is wrong. When the decision is to reject the null hypothesis when in fact the null hypothesis is true, the researcher has made what is called a **Type I error.** The probability of making this type of error is equal to the level of significance: that is, with a significance level of .05, there is a probability of 5 times out of 100 that the sample data will lead the researcher to reject the null hypothesis when it is in fact true. A researcher consequently avoids a Type I error to the degree that the level of significance is high. (That is, a .001 level is better than .01 for avoiding Type I errors.)

Another type of wrong decision occurs when the null hypothesis is not rejected when, in fact, the null hypothesis is actually wrong. This is referred to as a **Type II error.** While there is no direct relationship between the level of significance and the probability of making a Type II error, as the level of significance increases, the likelihood of Type II error decreases. A level of significance of .10 is thus better for avoiding a Type II error than .05 or .01. Figure 11.3 shows how error type is related to types of decisions.

Interpreting Level of Significance

The interpretation of rejecting or failing to reject a null hypothesis depends on whether the researcher is interested in avoiding a Type I or Type II error and in whether a predetermined alpha level is set. If a predetermined value is stated, such as .05 or .01 for a Type I error, then the researcher rejects the null by comparing the computed level of

	State of Nature	
	Null hypothesis is true	Null hypothesis is false
Reject null hypothesis	Type I error	Correct decision
Fail to reject null hypothesis	Correct decision	Type II error

FIGURE 11.3 **Relationship of State of Nature, Decisions, and Error in Hypothesis Testing**

significance with the predetermined level. If the calculated significance is less than the predetermined level (for example, .01 < .05), then the null hypothesis is rejected.

In many research studies, there is no predetermined alpha level. In these studies, statisticians use a general rule for rejecting a null hypothesis. If the *p* value is the same as or less than .05, then the null is rejected and the statement is made that there is a **statistically significant** difference (though more accurately, it is always a difference at some level of confidence). A *p* value between .05 and .10 is usually thought of as *marginally* significant, and anything greater than .10 is labeled a nonsignificant difference. We are saying, then, that if there is more than 1 chance out of 10 of being wrong in rejecting the null (1 chance in 10 that the means are the same), then that is too much risk to take in saying that the means are different. The results may be due more to error than to a treatment or real difference.

It is best to report the *p* level for each statistical test because the conventions for rejecting the null hypothesis are general rules of thumb. Individual researchers and consumers, depending on the circumstances, may differ with respect to what constitutes a statistically significant difference. A level of .05, for example, generally agreed to be statistically significant, would probably be unacceptable if the test concerned usage of a drug that might cause death (i.e., 5 times out of 100, the researcher is wrong in saying no death will occur).

Another important point in interpreting *p* levels and corresponding conclusions is that while it is common for researchers to fail to reject the null (e.g., *p* = .20), the failure to find a statistically significant difference or relationship does not necessarily mean that in *reality* there is no difference or relationship. Only when the circumstances of the research warrant (in which there is what is called *adequate power* in the test) is a nonsignificant finding taken as evidence that there is no relationship. The reason a nonsignificant finding is usually uninterpretable is that many factors, such as low reliability, diffusion of treatment, insufficient number of subjects, and so forth, can cause the nonsignificance. Thus, a significant finding indicates that a real relationship exists, but the opposite is not necessarily true. Recently, there has been considerable criticism of the use of null hypothesis significance testing. Most arguments focus on placing too much emphasis on using the so-called magical .05 level of significance to determine conclusions (as if there is a meaningful difference between .05 and .06). See Wainer and Robinson (2003) for a review of these criticisms.

MAGNITUDE OF EFFECT

One of the most important issues that creates confusion in interpreting statistics is the decision about whether the results are meaningful. That is, how much will the results make a difference in the real world? Are the results *educationally* significant, not just statistically significant? The statistical test tells only that there is a difference, but the worth or importance of a finding must also be judged. When a finding is reported to be statistically significant, the reader should examine the reported means to see how different they are and the magnitude of the correlations. Meaningfulness is related to the specifics of a situation. For example, there may be a statistically significant difference in reading achievement among first-graders who use curriculum X as opposed to curriculum Y, but that does not mean curriculum X should be purchased. It is possible that the difference represents only one percentile point and that curriculum X costs several thousand dollars more than curriculum Y. Only the reader can judge what is meaningful.

One of the reasons that statistically significant *p* values can be misleading is that the value that is calculated is directly related to sample size. Thus, it is possible to have a very large sample, a very small difference or relationship, and still report it as significant. For example, a correlation of .44 will be statistically significant at the .05 level with a sample as small as 20, and a sample of 5,000 will allow a statistically significant .05 finding with a correlation of only .028, which is, practically speaking, no relationship at all.

ALERT!   Statistical significance depends on three factors: (1) difference between the means, (2) variability, and (3) sample size.

MISCONCEPTION   If studies find no statistically significant results between two methods of teaching reading, then either method could be used to maximize student learning.

EVIDENCE   Useful results depend on practical significance.

The American Psychological Association (2001), and many research journals now strongly recommend or require that investigators report appropriate indicators that illustrate the strength or magnitude of a difference or relationship along with measures of statistical significance. These **effect magnitude measures,** as they are called, are either measures of strength of association or effect size. Measures of association are used to estimate proportions of variance held in common, such as the coefficient of determination, (r^2), R^2, eta-squared (η^2), or omega-squared (ω^2). **Effect size** (ES) is more commonly used. It is typically reported in a generalized form as the ratio of the difference between the group means divided by the estimated standard deviation of the population. This is referred to as the *standardized mean difference,* and it is represented by the following equation:

$$d = \frac{\bar{X}_1 - \bar{X}_2}{SD_p}$$

where

$\quad d$ = Cohen's ratio for effect size
$\quad \bar{X}$ = the mean
SD_p = the standard deviation of the population

According to Cohen (1988), the *effect size index* may then provide an indication of the practical or meaningful difference. Effect size indexes of about .20 are typically regarded as small effects, of about .5 as medium or moderate effects, and .8 and above as large effects. However, these interpretations are arbitrary. It is best to evaluate practical significance in the context in which the research is conducted and upon considering the intended use of the results.

Examples of reporting effect size in a journal are illustrated in Excerpts 11.2 and 11.3. Excerpt 11.4 shows how effect sizes are presented using graphs. Clearly, measures of effect magnitude, along with confidence intervals, provide much better information than a simple rejection of the null hypothesis.

Research Navigator.com

11.1 Effect Size
Accession No.: 12342701

ALERT!   Studies with small samples are less likely to show statistical significance than studies with large samples, even though very large samples can lead to statistically significant but impractical results.

EXCERPT 11.2   Reporting Effect Size

On the basis of Cohen's categories of small, medium, and large effect sizes (Buzz, 1995), a power analysis revealed that most of the effect sizes for sex differences in this study were small to medium (see Table 3).

TABLE 3   Summary of Sex Equity Findings

Dependent Measure	Males		Females		F	df	p	Effect Size	Cohen's Category
	M	SD	M	SD					
Instructor calling on students	0.2480	0.2425	0.2034	0.2608	0.71	1, 22	.4131	0.18	Small
Student volunteering	1.1000	1.0615	0.9548	1.3027	0.45	1, 22	.5081	0.12	Small
Instructor interacting with students	1.3274	1.2999	1.5623	1.6247	0.55	1, 22	.5078	0.11	Small
Students raising their hands	0.1835	0.1469	0.1334	0.1155	1.70	1, 22	.2055	0.38	Medium
Staying after class	0.1440	0.0534	0.1066	0.0612	3.18	1, 22	.0885	0.58	Medium
Seat location	1.2496	1.4105	0.3891	0.0571	1.65	1, 28	.2101	1.17	Large

Note: The means presented here are in ratio form. Each female student mean is based on averages of the female response divided by the number of women in the class. Each male student mean is based on averages of the male response divided by the number of men in class. Men and women are compared on the basis of their actual participation rates, taking into consideration the proportion of women to men in class.

Source: From Brady, K. L., & Eisler, R. M. (1999). Sex and gender in the college classroom: A quantitative analysis of faculty-study interactions and perceptions, *Journal of Educational Psychology, 91*(1), 127–145. Reprinted by permission.

EXCERPT 11.3   Reporting Effect Size

I found that practical as well as statistically significant differences existed on several variables when I made further comparisons between the control group and the experimental group. I calculated effect sized for four of the five dependent variables for which statistical significance was achieved. . . . The calculation for the effect size of achievement gain scordes was $d = 1.0$, which was indicative of a moderate effect size. The correlation coefficient revealed was $r = .45$. . . . With regard to the scores attained on the attitude scale, the calculations of $d = 1.4$ and $r = .6$ were indicative of a strong effect size and correlation. . . . The calculations for effect size and correlation coefficient for the gain scores in the empathy scale were $d = 1.2$ and $r = .5$. . . . Those findings were indices of a strong effect size. Finally, the effect size and correlation coefficient for the dependent variable transfer of skills . . . yielded the following statistics for effect size and correlation, respectively: $d = 3.4$ and $r = .9$. The findings suggest that the effect size for the dependent variable was strong.

Source: From Farkas, R. D. (2003). Effects of traditional versus learning-styles instructional methods on middle school students. *Journal of Educational Research, 91*(1), 42–51.

EXCERPT 11.4   Effect Size Comparisons

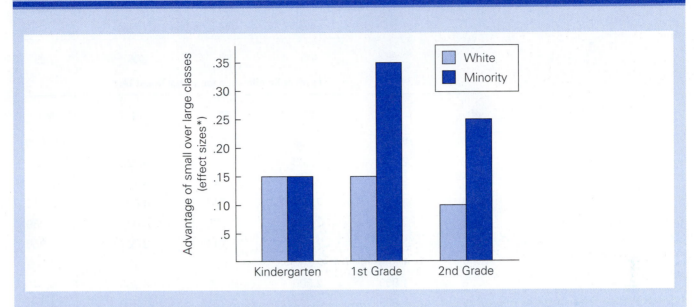

Significant Benefits in Reading from Attending Small Classes

*The effect size of an experiment is the extent to which the independent variable—class size—influences the outcome, in this case, student achievement in reading. The graph shows that in kindergarten there were significant and equivalent effects of small classes for both white and minority students. In the first and second grades, effects were even greater for minorities.

Figure adapted from Finn, J. D. (1998). *Class Size and Students at Risk: What Is Known? What Is Next?* Washington, DC: U.S. Department of Education.

Source: From *Research Points* (Fall, 2003). Washington D.C.: American Educational Research Association.

COMPARING TWO MEANS: THE *t*-TEST

There are many research situations in which a mean from one group is compared with a mean from another group to determine the probability that the corresponding population means are different. The most common statistical procedure for determining the level of significance when two means are compared is the **t-test.** The *t*-test is a formula that generates a number, and this number is used to determine the probability level (*p* level) of rejecting the null hypothesis.

What happens is that the sample means, standard deviations, and sizes of the samples are used in the *t*-test equation to obtain a *t* value (sometimes called *t* statistic). The formula for calculating the *t* value is

$$t = \frac{\bar{X}_1 - \bar{X}_2}{S}$$

where

$\bar{X}_1$ = mean of group 1
$\bar{X}_2$ = mean of group 2
S = amount of variation between and within the groups

S can be thought of as a measure of the amount of error in estimating the population mean from a sample mean. As the distance between X_1 and X_2 gets larger, then, and as the error

TABLE 11.1   *t* Distribution

	Level of Significance for a One-Tailed Test				
	.05	.025	.01	.005	.0005
	Level of Significance for a Two-Tailed Test				
df	.10	.05	.02	.01	.001
1	6.314	12.706	31.821	63.657	636.619
2	2.920	4.303	6.965	9.925	31.598
3	2.353	3.182	4.541	5.841	12.924
4	2.132	2.776	3.747	4.604	8.610
5	2.015	2.571	3.365	4.032	6.869
6	1.943	2.447	3.143	3.707	5.959
7	1.895	2.365	2.998	3.499	5.408
8	1.860	2.306	2.896	3.355	5.041
9	1.833	2.262	2.821	3.250	4.781
10	1.812	2.228	2.764	3.169	4.587
11	1.796	2.201	2.718	3.106	4.437
12	1.782	2.179	2.681	3.055	4.318
13	1.771	2.160	2.650	3.012	4.221
14	1.761	2.145	2.624	2.977	4.140
15	1.753	2.131	2.602	2.947	4.073
16	1.746	2.120	2.583	2.921	4.015
17	1.740	2.110	2.567	2.898	3.965
18	1.734	2.101	2.552	2.878	3.922
19	1.729	2.093	2.539	2.861	3.883
20	1.725	2.086	2.528	2.845	3.850
21	1.721	2.080	2.518	2.831	3.819
22	1.717	2.074	2.508	2.819	3.792
23	1.714	2.069	2.500	2.807	3.767
24	1.711	2.064	2.492	2.797	3.745
25	1.708	2.060	2.485	2.787	3.725
26	1.706	2.056	2.479	2.779	3.707
27	1.703	2.052	2.473	2.771	3.690
28	1.701	2.048	2.467	2.763	3.674
29	1.699	2.045	2.462	2.756	3.659
30	1.697	2.042	2.457	2.750	3.646
40	1.684	2.021	2.423	2.704	3.551
60	1.671	2.000	2.390	2.660	3.460
120	1.658	1.980	2.358	2.617	3.373
∞	1.645	1.960	2.326	2.576	3.291

Source: From Fisher, R. A., and Yates, F., (1974). Statistical Tables for Biological, Agricultural and Medical Research, Table III. 6th Ed. London: Pearson Education Limited. Copyright © 1974 by Pearson Education Limited. Reprinted by permission of the authors and publisher.

involved in estimating the means gets smaller, the *t* statistic is greater. The calculated *t* value is a three- or four-digit number with two decimal places, such as 2.30; 3.16; 8.72; 1.85. To determine the level of significance, the researcher compares this number with theoretical *t* values in a table. The table is called *distribution of t* or *critical values for the t-test* and is found in Table 11.1. The researcher uses the table by locating two numbers: the *degrees of freedom (df)* and the level of significance desired. The term **degrees of freedom** is a mathematical concept that denotes the number of independent observations that are free to vary. For each statistical test, there is a corresponding number of degrees of freedom that is calculated, and then this number is used to estimate the statistical significance of the test. In the distribution of a *t*-table, the number at the intersection of the degrees of freedom row and the level of significance column is the relevant theoretical value of *t*. If this critical *t* is less than the *t* value calculated by the *t*-test equation, it means that the observed difference in means is greater than could have been expected under the null hypothesis, so the hypothesis can be rejected at that level of significance.

Notice that at the top of the table, there are two rows: the top row for what is called a *one-tailed* and the other for a *two-tailed* test of significance. The *tails* refer to the ends of the normal sampling distribution that are used in the significance test. *One-tailed* means that one of the two ends of the distribution is used as the region of rejection, so that if the *p* value is .05 that 5 percent is all at one end of the distribution. In a two-tailed test, the region is divided between both ends of the distribution; for example, for a *p* value of .05, .025 percent is at each end of the distribution. The one-tailed test is more liberal and should be used only when the researcher is very confident that a result that is opposite the research hypothesis will not be obtained. Unless otherwise stated, significance tests can be assumed to be two-tailed.

The calculated *t* statistic and corresponding *p* level are reported in most studies. In Excerpts 11.5 and 11.6, the results sections of research studies show how *t*-tests are summarized. The number in parentheses following the *t* is the degrees of freedom.

There are two different forms of the equation used in the *t*-test: one for independent samples and one for samples that are paired, or dependent. *Independent samples* are groups of subjects that have no relationship to each other; the two samples have different subjects in each group, and the subjects are usually either assigned randomly from a common population or drawn from two different populations. Therefore, if a researcher is testing the difference between an experimental group and a control group mean in a posttest-only design, the **independent samples *t*-test** would be appropriate. Comparing attitudes of fourth- and sixth-graders would also utilize an independent samples *t*-test.

The second form of the *t*-test can be referred to by several different names, including *paired, dependent samples, correlated,* or *matched t-test.* This *t*-test is used in situations in which the subjects from the two groups are paired or matched in some way. A common example of this case is the same group of subjects tested twice, as in a pretest-posttest study. Whether the same or different subjects are in each group, as long as there is a systematic relationship between the groups, it is necessary to use the **dependent samples *t*-test** to calculate the probability of rejecting the null hypothesis.

The *t*-test can be used for purposes other than comparing the means of two samples. It can be used when a researcher wants to show that a correlation coefficient is significantly different from 0 (i.e., no correlation). The mean of a group can be compared with a number rather than another mean, and it is possible to compare variances rather than means. Because there are so many uses for the *t*-test, it is frequently encountered in reading research.

A more concrete explanation of using the *t*-test is the following example. Suppose a researcher is interested in finding out whether there is a significant difference between blue-eyed and brown-eyed sixth-graders with respect to reading achievement. The research question would be Is there a difference in the reading achievement (the dependent variable) of blue-eyed fourth-graders compared with brown-eyed fourth-graders (the independent variable)? The null hypothesis would be There is no difference between blue-eyed and brown-eyed fourth-graders in reading achievement. To test this hypothesis, the researcher would randomly select a sample of brown- and blue-eyed fourth-graders from the population of all fourth-grade students. Let us say that the sample mean of blue-eyed

EXCERPT 11.5 Independent Samples *t*-Test

Means, standard deviations, and obtained *t* statistics for distance education and on-campus course evaluation com-parisons are presented in Table 3.

TABLE 3 Means, Standard Deviations, and *t* Statistics for On-Campus and Distance Course Evaluation Comparisons

| | SPED 6126 | | | SPED 6127 | | |
| | Campus | Distance | | Campus | Distance | |
Evaluation Area	($n = 4$)	($n = 23$)	Obtained *t*	($n = 11$)	($n = 13$)	Obtained *t*
Overall rating						
M	3.69	3.94	−0.81	3.69	3.79	−0.48
SD	0.59	0.33		0.28	0.44	
Course						
M	3.56	3.88	−1.82	3.72	3.60	1.14
SD	0.33	0.31		0.29	0.22	
Instructor						
M	3.65	3.88	−0.75	3.65	3.65	0.00
SD	0.59	0.34		0.19	0.43	
Organization						
M	4.15	4.23	−0.44	3.83	4.25	−6.70*
SD	0.34	0.17		0.19	0.10	
Teaching						
M	3.48	3.62	−0.56	3.58	3.42	1.09
SD	0.47	0.44		0.44	0.23	
Communication						
M	3.49	3.79	−1.26	3.56	3.63	−0.54
SD	0.48	0.27		0.13	0.40	

*$p < .01$.

Source: From Spooner, F., Jordan, L., Algozzine, B., & Spooner, M. (1999). Student ratings of instruction in distance learning and on-campus courses. *Journal of Educational Research, 92*(3), 132–140. Reprinted by permission.

EXCERPT 11.6 Independent Samples *t*-Test

In terms of perspective of instructional planning, a post hoc independent *t*-test revealed that low performers tended to have a change in perspective more than the high performers ($M = .69$ vs. $M = .45$), $t = 2.08$, $p < .05$.

Source: From Baylor, A. L. (2002). Expanding preservice teachers' metacognitive awareness of instructional planning through pedagogical agents. *Educational Technology, Research and Development, 5*(2), 5–22.

students' reading achievement is 54, and the sample mean for brown-eyed fourth-graders is 48. Since we assume the null hypothesis—that the population means are equal—we use the t-test to show how often the difference of scores in the samples would occur if the population means are equal. If our degrees of freedom (i.e., total sample size minus 1) is 60 and the calculated t value 2.00, we can see by referring to Table 11.1 that the probability of attaining this difference in the sample means, for a two-tailed test, is .05, or five times out of 100. We reject the null hypothesis and say that there is a statistically significant difference between the reading achievement of blue-eyed and brown-eyed fourth-graders.

COMPARING TWO OR MORE MEANS: ANALYSIS OF VARIANCE (ANOVA)

One-Way Analysis of Variance

If a study is done in which three or more sample means are compared on one independent variable, then to test the null hypothesis, the researcher would employ a procedure called *one-way analysis of variance* (abbreviated ANOVA). ANOVA is simply an extension of the t-test. Rather than the researcher's using multiple t-tests to compare all possible pairs of means in a study of two or more groups, ANOVA allows the researcher to test the differences between all groups and make more accurate probability statements than when using a series of separate t-tests. It is called **analysis of variance** because the statistical formula uses the variances of the groups and not the means to calculate a value that reflects the degree of differences in the means. Instead of a t statistic, ANOVA calculates an F statistic (or F ratio). The F is analogous to the t. It is a three- or four-digit number that is used in a distribution of F table with the degrees of freedom to find the level of significance that the researcher uses to reject or not reject the null. There are two degrees of freedom. The first is the number of groups in the study minus one, and the second is the total number of subjects minus the number of groups. These numbers follow the F in reporting the results of ANOVA. For example, in reporting $F(4,80) = 4.25$, the degrees of freedom mean that there are five group means that are being compared and 85 subjects in the analysis.

ANOVA addresses the question Is there a significant difference between the population means? If the F value that is calculated is large enough, then the null hypothesis (meaning there is no difference among the groups) can be rejected with confidence; the researcher is correct in concluding that at least two means are different. Let us assume, for example, that a researcher is comparing the locus of control of three groups—high-, medium-, and low-achieving students. The researcher selects a random sample from each group, administers a locus of control instrument, and calculates the means and variances of each group. Let us further assume that the sample group means are A (low achievement) = 18, B (medium achievement) = 20, and C (high achievement) = 25. The null hypothesis that is tested, then, is that the population means of 18, 20, and 25 are equal or, more correctly, that these are different only by sampling and measurement error. If the F was 5.12 and $p < .01$, then the researcher can conclude that at least two of the means are different, and that this conclusion will be right 99 times out of 100.

The results of a one-way ANOVA are usually reported by indicating in the results section the groups that are different. A table of means and standard deviations will accompany the written information. In reporting results, occasionally the researcher will write two numbers in front of the ANOVA. This will be a number 1, a multiplication sign, and then another single digit number—for example, 1×3; 1×5; 1×2. This means that there is one independent variable (1) that has the number of groups or levels indicated by the second number. A 1×4 ANOVA is thus a one-way ANOVA that is comparing four group means.

Often, the results from an ANOVA are presented in a *summary table*, as illustrated in Excerpt 11.7.

EXCERPT 11.7 ANOVA and Post Hoc Tests

One way analysis of variance was used to analyze the achievement data. Where significant differences were found, SNK tests were used to determine which means differed significantly.

Our second hypothesis stated that the groups taught with the children's book would score significantly higher on the posttest than the group taught with the textbook only. These data supported the hypothesis, $F(2, 54) = 10.23$, $p = .0002$. The mean and standard deviation for the group taught with the children's book were 8.79 and 4.66 respectively. The mean and standard deviation for the group taught with the textbook and children's book were 7.17 and 3.40 respectively. The mean and standard deviation for the group taught with the textbook only were 3.80 and 2.07 respectively. Follow-up tests (SNK) indicated that the two groups taught with the children's book differed significantly from the group taught with the textbook only.

TABLE 3 Results of One-Way Analysis of Variance for the Subtest That Measured Content Contained Only in Children's Book

Source	D.F.	Sum of Squares	Mean Square	F Ratio	F Prob
Between	2	253.3526	126.6763	10.2272	.0002
Within	54	668.8579	12.3863		
Total	56	922.2105			

Source: From McKinney, C. W., & Jones, H. J. (1993). Effects of a children's book and a traditional textbook on fifth-grade students' achievement and attitudes toward social studies. *Journal of Research and Development in Education, 27*(1), 56–62. Reprinted by permission.

Post Hoc and Planned Comparison Procedures

When a researcher uses ANOVA to test the null hypothesis that three means are the same, the resulting statistically significant F ratio tells the researcher only that two or more of the means are different. Usually, the researcher needs to employ further statistical tests that will indicate those means that are different from each other. These tests are called **post hoc comparisons.** Other terms that are synonymous for post hoc comparisons include *a posteriori test, follow-up test,* and *multiple-comparison test.* Another procedure, called the *Bonferroni technique,* is also used as a post hoc test, although it is more commonly used when researchers are investigating many dependent variables to adjust the level of significance to reduce the chance of finding a significant difference because of multiple statistical tests.

Post hoc comparisons are designed to test each possible pair of means. There are five common multiple comparison tests: Fisher's LSD, Duncan's new multiple range test, the Newman-Keuls, Tukey's HSD, and the Scheffé's test. All of the tests are used in the same way, but they differ in the ease with which a significant difference is obtained; for some tests, that is, the means need to be farther apart than for other tests for the difference to be statistically significant. Tests that require a greater difference between the means are said to be *conservative,* while those that permit less difference are said to be *liberal.* The listing of the tests above is sequential, with Fisher's test considered most liberal and Scheffé's test most conservative. The two most common tests are Tukey (pronounced "too-key") and Scheffé, but different conclusions can be reached in a study depending on the multiple comparison technique employed.

Excerpts 11.7 and 11.8 are examples of using one-way ANOVA and post hoc tests.

Planned comparisons are similar to post hoc tests in that pairs of means are compared, but the procedure is used with specific comparisons that are identified prior to com-

EXCERPT 11.8   ANOVA and Post Hoc Tests

For each measure post hoc multiple comparisons were conducted using the Tukey method to identify significant differences among specific institutional types.

Source: From Peterson, M. W., & Einarson, M. K. (2001). What are colleges doing about student assessment? Does it make a difference? *Journal of Higher Education, 72*(6), 629–669.

pleting the research. Usually, a few of the possible pairs of means, those that are of particular interest, are included in the analysis. Because the pairs are identified before, rather than after the ANOVA, it may also be referred to as an *a priori test*.

Factorial Analysis of Variance

One-way ANOVA has been introduced as a procedure that is used with one independent variable and three or more levels identified by this variable. It is common, however, to have more than one independent variable in a study. In fact, it is often desirable to have several independent variables because the analysis will provide more information.

For example, if a group of researchers investigates the relative effectiveness of three reading curricula, they would probably use a 1×3 ANOVA to test the null hypothesis that there is no difference in achievement between any of the three groups (that is, $\bar{X}_1 = \bar{X}_2 = \bar{X}_3$). If the researchers were also interested in whether males or females achieved differently, gender would become a second independent variable. Then there would be six groups, since for each reading group, males and females would be analyzed separately. If X is the reading curriculum and M/F is gender, then the six groups are X_1M; X_1F; X_2M; X_2F; X_3M; and X_3F. This situation is diagrammed below:

First independent variable:
Reading curriculum groups X_1 X_2 X_3

Second independent variable: Gender   M   F   M   F   M   F

Another way to illustrate the study is to put each independent variable on one side of a rectangle, as follows:

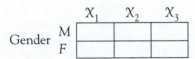

Reading curriculum

	X_1	X_2	X_3
Gender M			
F			

In this hypothetical situation, then, there are two independent variables analyzed simultaneously and one dependent variable (achievement). The statistical procedure that would be used to analyze the results would be a two-way ANOVA (*two-way* because of two independent variables). Since *factor* is another word for *independent variable*, *factorial* means more than one independent variable. **Factorial ANOVA,** then, is a generic term that means that two or more independent variables are analyzed together. The more specific term, such as *two-way* or *three-way* ANOVA, tells the exact number of independent variables. Researchers can be even more precise in indicating what the analysis is by including the levels of each independent variable. As pointed out earlier, *levels* refers to the subgroups or categories of each independent variable. In the example cited earlier, *reading curriculum* has three levels and *gender* two levels. The levels can be shown by numbers that precede the ANOVA abbreviation. In our reading example, it is a 2×3 ANOVA. (For a three-way

ANOVA, there would need to be three numbers, such as $2 \times 2 \times 3$ ANOVA. This means that there are two levels in two of the variables and three levels in one variable.)

Using this notation, a researcher can concisely communicate a lot of information. The number of factors is usually two or three, and the number of levels can be any number greater than one (though rarely above 5). Each number shows the number of levels in each dependent variable. In the hypothetical example above, if there were four reading curriculums and the researcher was interested in the way each curriculum affected high, low, and medium achievers, then the resulting analysis would be a 3×4 ANOVA. It would still be a two-way ANOVA, but the number of levels would be different. This situation can be illustrated with the following diagram:

Reading curriculum

		X_1	X_2	X_3	X_4
	High				
Ability level	Medium				
	Low				

Excerpt 11.9 is an example of the way researchers refer to two-way factorial designs and how results are reported.

Here is another hypothetical example to clarify the tests of significance that result from a two-way ANOVA: A teacher is interested in whether using specific techniques to aid retention are effective in improving the achievement of high-anxiety and low-anxiety students. The teacher has developed two techniques, one with mnemonics and the other with distributed practice in memorizing the material. The teacher also has a control group. Thus, there are two independent variables, one with two levels (anxiety: high and low), the other with three levels (treatment techniques: mnemonics, distributed practice, and control group). This would constitute a 2×3 ANOVA design, as illustrated in Figure 11.4.

Within each square in the diagram is a mean for that group. These squares are called *cells*. The number 50 in the upper-right-hand cell ($\overline{X}_5$) thus refers to the mean of highly anxious subjects who served as the control group. The 2×3 ANOVA tests three null hypotheses: that there is no difference between high- and low-anxiety students; that there is no difference between the treatment and control conditions; and that there is no

EXCERPT 11.9 Factorial ANOVA

We used a 2×2 (Program: Direct Instruction vs. Traditional Instruction × Mobility: Mobile Students vs. Stable Students) analysis of variance to analyze each total score and its component subscores.

For main effects, the direct-instruction students scored significantly higher than did the traditional students on mathematics computation. Also, stable students scored significantly higher than did mobile students on total reading, word attack, vocabulary, comprehension, and total battery. There were no significant differences in the total language scores or two of its components, mechanics and expression, nor was there a significant difference in the total mathematics scores.

There were also three significant interactions related to vocabulary, spelling, and mathematics concepts. A post hoc test using Tukey's HSD procedure revealed that the stable traditional students scored significantly higher than did the mobile traditional students on vocabulary and spelling. On mathematics concepts and applications, the stable traditional students scored significantly higher than did the traditional mobile students and the stable direct-instruction students.

An examination of the means for all groups reveals a similar pattern of significant differences. The pattern shows a similar level of achievement for both direct-instruction stable and mobile students. The stable traditional means are similar to both direct instruction groups. However, the mobile traditional students' means are lower than their stable counterparts and both direct-instruction groups.

Source: From Brent, G., & DiObilda, N. (1993). Effects of curriculum alignment versus direct instruction on urban children. *Journal of Educational Research, 86,* 335.

Treatment Techniques

		Mnemonics	Distributed practice	Control	
Anxiety	High	$\overline{X}_1 = 62$	$\overline{X}_3 = 50$	$\overline{X}_5 = 50$	$\overline{X}_7 = 54$
	Low	$\overline{X}_2 = 44$	$\overline{X}_4 = 59$	$\overline{X}_6 = 59$	$\overline{X}_8 = 54$
		$\overline{X}_9 \cong 53$	$\overline{X}_{10} \cong 55$	$\overline{X}_{11} \cong 55$	

FIGURE 11.4   Hypothetical 2 × 3 ANOVA

interaction between the two factors. (*Interaction* is defined in the next paragraph.) The first two hypotheses are similar in interpretation to one-way ANOVAs. They tell the researcher whether any differences occur for each of the factors independent of each other. These are termed *main* or *simple effects* in a factorial ANOVA. There is a main (not necessarily significant) effect for anxiety and another main effect for treatment technique. In computing the 2 × 3 ANOVA, there will be a separate F ratio for each main effect, with corresponding levels of significance. In our example, the main effect for anxiety is tested by comparing $\overline{X}_7$ with $\overline{X}_8$. These row means disregard the influence of the techniques and address anxiety only. Since $\overline{X}_7$ and $\overline{X}_8$ both equal 54, the null hypothesis that $\overline{X}_7 = \overline{X}_8$ would not be rejected; examining anxiety alone, that is, there is no difference in achievement between high- and low-anxiety students. For the main effect of technique, $\overline{X}_9$, $\overline{X}_{10}$, and $\overline{X}_{11}$ are compared. Again, it appears that there is little difference in achievement between the three technique groups. The first two null hypotheses could have been tested by using separate one-way ANOVAs, but the 2 × 3 ANOVA is more accurate, more powerful in detecting differences, and more parsimonious than using two one-way ANOVAs. In addition, the 2 × 3 ANOVA allows the researcher to test the third null hypothesis. This hypothesis is concerned with what is called an *interaction* between the independent variables.

An **interaction** is the effect of the independent variables together; that is, the impact of one factor on the dependent measure varies with the level of a second factor. Stated differently, it is the joint effect of the independent variables on the dependent variable. An interaction is evident if the differences between levels of one independent variable are inconsistent from one level to another of the other independent variable. In other words, an interaction exists if the effect of one variable differs across different levels of the second variable. In our example, if we look at the difference between $\overline{X}_1$ and $\overline{X}_2$ (62 – 44 = 18) and compare that difference with $\overline{X}_3 - \overline{X}_4$ (–9) and $\overline{X}_5 - \overline{X}_6$ (–9), we find that there is a large difference between high and low anxiety as we move across each of the treatment techniques. This is visual evidence of an interaction. Statistically, an F ratio is reported for the interaction with a corresponding level of significance. This statistical test is called the interaction effect.

Now it is clear how a factorial ANOVA can provide more information than one-way ANOVAs. In our example, it is evident that treatment techniques do make a difference for high- or low-anxiety students. High-anxiety students do better with mnemonics than distributed practice or with no treatment, while low-anxiety students do better with distributed practice or with no treatment than they do with mnemonics. This finding would be statistically significant even though neither of the main effects by themselves was significant. In Excerpts 11.9 and 11.10, significant interactions are reported.

It is common to present a graph of a statistically significant interaction, which shows the nature of the interaction more clearly than cell means do. The graph is constructed by placing values for the dependent variable along the vertical axis (ordinate) and the levels of one independent variable on the horizontal axis (abscissa); all the cell means are located within the graph and identified with the second independent variable. For our hypothetical example, the interaction is illustrated in Figure 11.5. In the figure, lines are used to connect the cells' means. If the lines are parallel, then there is no interaction. If the lines cross, the interaction is said to be disordinal.

EXCERPT 11.10 ANOVA Interaction

The analysis of variance showed a highly significant effect of experimental condition ($F = 10.59$, $p < .01$), a significant effect of school ($F = 3.35$, $p = < .05$), and an interaction between condition and school ($F = 5.01$, $p < .05$). . . . The motivational effect was the same for boys and girls and constant across grade levels, but it differed among schools. Figure 1 shows a very large effect at School A, a large effect at School C, and the control group somewhat higher than the experimental group at School B.

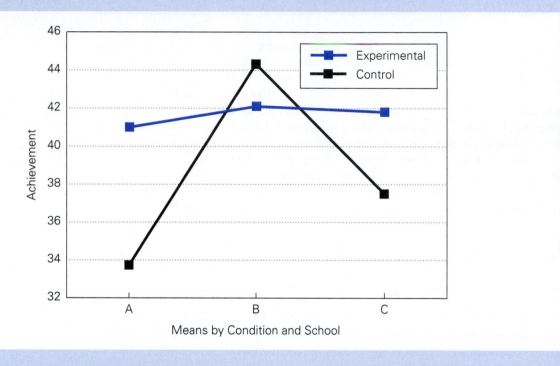

FIGURE 1 **Means by Condition and School**

Source: From Brown, S. M., & Walberg, H. J. (1993). Motivational effects of test scores of elementary students. *Journal of Educational Research, 86,* 134, 135. Reprinted by permission.

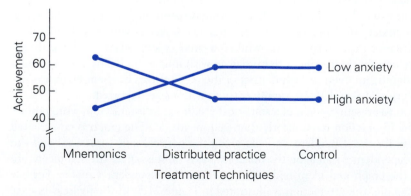

FIGURE 11.5 **Interaction for Hypothetical Study**

ALERT!   In the absence of a statistical test, lines that are not parallel do not necessarily indicate that the interaction is significant.

Analysis of Covariance

Analysis of covariance (ANCOVA) is a statistical procedure used in cases similar to ones in which a one-way or factorial ANOVA is used. ANCOVA has two major purposes: (1) to adjust initial group differences statistically on one or more variables that are related to the dependent variable but uncontrolled and (2) to increase the likelihood of finding a significant difference between group means.

For the first purpose, consider the following example. A researcher uses two classes to investigate whether cooperative or individualized instruction is most effective. On the basis of a pretest, the researcher knows that one class has greater knowledge of the dependent variable (achievement in mathematics) than the other group. (For example, the cooperative group pretest mean is 12 and the individualized group pretest mean is 10.) If a posttest is given and it is found that the cooperative group mean is 24 and the individualized group mean 20, the researcher might be tempted to conclude that the cooperative group achieved more than the individualized. This would be likely to happen if the pretest scores were ignored.

An alternative approach would be to look at pretest-posttest gain scores and use a t-test to determine whether the gain scores are significantly different. This approach would result in comparing 12 (24 − 12) to 10 (20 − 10). While this approach is theoretically better than not using the pretest scores, for reasons beyond the scope of this book, there are technical problems with comparing gain scores. The best method of analyzing the data in this circumstance is by using ANCOVA. ANCOVA would statistically adjust the posttest scores by the differences that existed between the groups on the pretest. In this example, the posttest score of the cooperative group would be lowered by one point, since this group's mean was higher by one point than the mean of both groups on the pretest. Similarly, because the individualized group pretest mean is one point lower than the mean of the two pretests, the posttest score of 20 would be raised by one point to 21. Instead of comparing 20 to 24, ANCOVA would thus compare 21 to 23.

The variable that is used in ANCOVA to adjust the scores (in the above example, the pretest) is called the *covariate* or *concomitant variable*. Covariates are often pretest scores or results from achievement, attitude, or aptitude tests that would be related to the dependent variable. IQ scores and scores on prior standardized achievement tests, for instance, are commonly used as covariates.

The second purpose of covariance analysis is to increase what is called the *power* of the statistical test to find differences between groups. A full explanation of the concept of power is beyond the scope of this book. Briefly, power is the probability of detecting a significant difference. It is useful to increase power when the sample size is low or when the researcher has reason to believe that the differences between the groups will be small.

ANCOVA can be used in several situations: with two groups and one independent variable in place of a t-test; with one independent variable that has more than two groups in place of one-way ANOVA; and with factorial analysis of variance. Studies can also use more than one covariate in a single ANCOVA procedure. The reporting of ANCOVA is very similar to the reporting of ANOVA. Excerpts 11.11 and 11.12 show how covariance analysis was used in two actual studies to adjust initial group differences.

Since ANCOVA is used frequently with intact groups, without random assignment, it should be noted that the interpretation of results should weigh the possibility that other uncontrolled and unmeasured variables are also related to the dependent variable and hence may affect the dependent variable. In other words, while statistical adjustment of the effect of the covariate can be achieved, the researcher cannot conclude that the groups are equal in the sense of random assignment.

EXCERPT 11.11 Using ANCOVA to Adjust for Group Differences

There were 14 ANCOVAs performed that had group (experimental activity-oriented, experimental discussion-oriented, and control) as an independent variable. . . . The pretreatment group scores of school attendance, grade point average, number of disciplinary referrals, total score of the Piers-Harris scale, Behavior cluster of the Piers-

Harris scale, and the Happiness and Satisfaction cluster of the Piers-Harris scale were used as the covariates for the 14 ANCOVAs. Using ANCOVAs allowed the researchers to adjust for any pretreatment differences that existed between the experimental groups and the control group.

Source: From Page, R. C., & Chandler, J. (1994). Effects of group counseling on ninth-grade at-risk students. *Journal of Mental Health Counseling, 16,* 346.

NONPARAMETRIC TESTS

In our discussion of statistical tests up to this point, we have been concerned with procedures that use sample statistics to estimate characteristics of the population. These characteristics of the population are called *parameters*, and the statistical procedures are referred to as **parametric** procedures. In addition, parametric statistics are used when the researcher can assume that the population is normally distributed, has homogeneity of variance within different groups, and has data that are interval or ratio in scale.

As long as the assumptions upon which parametric statistics are based are met, for the most part, the researcher uses a *t*-test, ANOVA, ANCOVA, or some other parametric procedure. If these assumptions are not met—for example, if the data are not interval or ratio or are not distributed normally—the researcher should consider using a **nonparametric** analog to the parametric test. For most parametric procedures, there is a corresponding nonparametric test that can be used. The interpretation of the results is similar with both kinds of tests. What differs is the computational equation and tables for determining the significance level of the results. Both procedures test a hypothesis and report a level of significance for rejecting the null. In contrast to parametric tests, however, nonparametric tests do not test hypotheses about the characteristics of a population. Rather, nonparametric procedures test hypotheses about relationships between categorical variables, shapes of distributions, and normality of distribution. While parametric procedures use means, nonparametric techniques are concerned with frequencies, percentages, and proportions. The parametric tests are generally more powerful in detecting significant differences and are used frequently even when all assumptions cannot be met.

Table 11.2 gives the names of nonparametric tests that are analogous to parametric tests we have already discussed.

Chi-square (pronounced "kī square") is a common nonparametric procedure that is used when the data are in nominal form. This test is a way of answering questions about association or relationship based on frequencies of observations in categories. The frequen-

EXCERPT 11.12 Using ANCOVA to Adjust for Group Differences

An analysis of covariance (ANCOVA) resulted in an *F*-ratio of 13.0 and a *p*-value of < .001 for Total Utterances, an *F*-ratio of .37 and a *p*-value of .55 for Mean Length of Utter-

ance, and a *f*-ratio of 19.0 and a *p*-value of .0002 for Different Root Words.

Source: From Paulson, L. H., Kelly, K. L., Jepson, S., van den Pol, R., Ashmore, R., Farrier, M., & Guilfoyle S. (2004). The effects of an early reading curriculum on language and literacy development of head start children. *Journal of Research in Childhood Education, 18*(3), 169–178.

TABLE 11.2   Parametric and Nonparametric Procedures*

Parametric	Nonparametric
Independent samples *t*-test	Median test
Dependent samples *t*-test	Mann-Whitney *U* test
One-way ANOVA	Sign test
	Wilcoxon matched-pairs signed-ranks test
	Median test
	Kruskal-Wallis one-way ANOVA of ranks

*For further information on nonparametric tests, see Siegel (1956), Marascuilo and McSweeney (1977), and Gibbons (1993).

cies can be in most any form—people, objects, votes—and are simply counted in each category. The researcher thus forms the categories and then counts the frequency of observations or occurrences in each category. In the single sample chi-square test, the researcher has one independent variable that is divided into two or more categories. For example, a college administrator may be interested in the number of freshman, sophomore, junior, and senior students who attended the counseling center, or in other words, the relationship between year in college and use of counseling services. The independent variable is year in college, with four categories. The researcher might select a random sample of 50 students from each category and record the number of students in each category who attended the counseling center. The statistical test compares the reported, or observed, frequencies with some theoretical or expected frequencies. In our example, the college administrator might expect that the frequencies in each category would be the same. Then the null hypothesis that is tested is that there is no difference in the number of students attending the counseling center among the four categories. The following table illustrates this example.

	Freshmen	Sophomores	Juniors	Seniors
Observed	30	25	15	30
Expected	25	25	25	25

To obtain the level of significance, the researcher computes a formula to obtain a chi-square value (χ^2), uses the appropriate degrees of freedom, and refers to a chi-square table (see Appendix D) in order to determine the level of significance in rejecting the null. In our example, it appears that the test would be significant, showing that freshmen and seniors attend the counseling center more than sophomores and juniors and that juniors attend less than any other class.

If the researcher has more than one independent variable, the **independent samples chi-square test** can be used to analyze the data. In our example above, if the administrator was also interested in differences between males and females at each class level, then the analysis would be like a factorial ANOVA. In this case, it would be a 2 × 4 contingency table.

There are many uses for the chi-square test. It can be used in attitude research if the researcher categorizes responses to favorable and unfavorable; with high, low, and medium ability students displaying on-task behavior; in special education research with frequencies of appropriate behavior; and in many other problems. Researchers may report a generic measure of relationship with the chi-square results. These measures would be termed *phi coefficient* or *contingency coefficient* and would be interpreted in about the same way as a Pearson product-moment correlation coefficient. Excerpt 11.13 is an example of reporting chi-square test results.

EXCERPT 11.13 Chi-Square

Chi-square analyses indicated statistically significant differences between athletes and nonathletes in reported use of 4 of the 12 substances. In terms of recreational drugs, significantly more nonathletes than interscholastic athletes have smoked cigarettes, χ^2 (1, $N = 520$) = .7.455, $p < .01$. Nonathletes also reported using cocaine, χ^2 (1, $N = 59$) = 11.491, and psychedelics, χ^2 (1, $N = 171$) = 18.382, $p < .001$, with greater frequency. One ergogenic aid, creatine, was used significantly more by athletes than nonathletes (1, $N = 115$) = 7.455, $p < .01$. Athletes were less likely to use marijuana, amphetamines, and barbiturates than were nonathletes, although the differences fell just short of being statistically significant.

Source: From Naylor, A. H., Gardner, D., & Zaichkowsky, L. (2001). Drug use patterns among high school athletes and nonathletes. *Adolescence, 36*(144), 627–639.

MULTIVARIATE ANALYSES

Our discussion of inferential statistics would be incomplete if we did not introduce *multivariate analyses*. Social scientists have realized for many years that human behavior in complex situations can be understood best by examining many variables simultaneously, not by dealing with one or two variables in each study. The statistical procedures for analyzing many variables at the same time have been available for many years, but it has only been since computers were available that researchers have been able to utilize these procedures. Today, these more complex statistics are commonly reported in journals.

The term **multivariate** refers to methods that investigate patterns among many variables or to studies that involve two or more related dependent variables for each subject. Many researchers will refer to *multiple regression* as a multivariate procedure, and some researchers use the term *multivariate* to describe the analysis in any study of many variables. In contrast, designs that employ *t*-tests, ANOVA, and ANCOVA with a single dependent would clearly be classified as *univariate*.

All of the statistical procedures discussed to this point have had only one dependent variable. Yet there are many instances in which the researcher is interested in more than one dependent variable. For example, if a researcher is studying attitudes toward science, many aspects of a general attitude toward science would be of interest, such as enjoying science as well as valuing science, for chemistry as well as biology, for dissection as well as field trips, and so on. In fact, many attitude instruments have subscales that more specifically and accurately reflect feelings and beliefs than one general score can. The researcher could combine all these different aspects and consider the attitude as a general disposition, but it is usually better to look at each aspect separately. Why not use a separate univariate analysis for each dependent variable? That is, why not compute as many ANOVAs or *t*-tests as there are dependent variables? The reason is that as long as the dependent variables are correlated, the use of separate univariate analysis will increase the probability of finding a difference simply because so many tests are employed. It is similar to the reason that in ANOVA, we use post hoc tests rather than many *t*-tests. Multivariate analyses are also more parsimonious—that is, more direct, quicker, with fewer separate calculations.

Although the computation and interpretation of multivariate tests are quite complex, the basic principle of rejecting null hypotheses at some level of significance is the same as for all inferential statistics. The difference is that all the dependent variables are considered together in one analysis. For most of the procedures previously discussed that have one dependent variable, a multivariate analog can be used when there is the same independent variable or variables but more than one dependent variable.

Table 11.3 summarizes some multivariate tests that correspond to procedures used with one dependent variable. Excerpt 11.14 illustrates use of a 1 × 3 MANCOVA to analyze the effects of single-sex education.

TABLE 11.3	Multivariate Analogs
Univariate Test	**Multivariate Test**
t-test	Hotelling's T^2
ANOVA	MANOVA (Multivariate analysis of variance)
ANCOVA	MANCOVA

EXCERPT 11.14   Multivariate ANCOVA

The first set of analyses compared post-intervention achievement and course enrollments in math and science for each of the three groups (coeducational boys, coeducational girls, and single-sex girls). A multivariate analysis of covariance (MANCOVA) was run for the four achievement and course-enrollment outcomes . . . with class condition entered as the grouping variable and with parental education, perceived parental expectations, perceived teacher effectiveness, school, and pre-high school math achievement entered as covariates. . . . The effect of class condition for this MANCOVA was significant. . . . In all of the four univariate follow-up analyses, it was also significant. That is, achievement in math, achievement in science, and average course enrollment in math and science differed as a function of educational group.

Source: From Shapka, J. D., & Keating, D. P. (2003). Effects of a girls-only curriculum during adolescence: Performance, persistence, and engagement in mathematics and science, *American Educational Research Journal, 40*(4), 929–960.

SUMMARY

This chapter has introduced the logic of inferential statistics and described some of the more common statistical procedures researchers use to analyze data. The following points summarize the concepts presented:

1. Inferential statistics are used to make inferences based on measured aspects of a sample about the characteristics of a population.
2. In conducting research, probability is a concern because of the error involved in sampling and measurement.
3. Sample statistics represent imperfect estimates of the population.
4. Inferential statistics estimate the probability of population characteristics being within a certain range of values. Confidence levels are commonly reported.
5. The null hypothesis is used to test the assumption that there is no difference between population values.
6. Researchers attempt to reject the null hypothesis by using inferential statistics to indicate the probability of being wrong in rejecting the null.
7. The level of significance of the statistical test tells the researcher the probability of making a Type I error in rejecting the null hypothesis.

8. Most researchers use a p level of .05 or less (< .05) to indicate statistical significance.
9. Effect magnitude measures, such as effect size, indicates the magnitude of differences and relationships and should be reported with statistical significance.
10. The t-test is used to compare two means, and depending on the nature of the research, it uses an independent samples equation or a dependent samples equation to calculate the t value.
11. One-way ANOVA tests the difference between levels of one independent variable, while factorial ANOVA examines more than one independent variable.
12. Post hoc and planned comparison tests are designed to locate significant differences among pairs of means in ANOVA.
13. An interaction is examined in factorial ANOVA as the unique effect of the independent variables acting together to affect the dependent variable results.
14. Parametric tests assume ratio, interval, or ordinal data, homogeneity of variance, and a normal distribution. Nonparametric tests can be used in cases in which the assumptions are violated and the test is not robust for that violation.

15. Analysis of covariance is used to adjust differences between groups on a covariate variable that is related to the dependent variable.

16. Chi-square is a frequently encountered nonparametric test that is used when the researcher is examining frequencies of occurrences.

17. Multivariate analyses are used in cases in which there are several related dependent variables.

RESEARCH NAVIGATOR NOTES

Research Navigator.com

Reading the following articles will help you understand the content of this chapter. Go to the education database (included in the EBSCO database) in Research Navigator; use the Accession Number provided to find the article.

11.1   *Effect Size*
Practical guide for reporting different types of effect size estimates. Accession Number: 12342701.

CHECK YOURSELF

Companion Website

Multiple-choice review items, with answers, are available on the Companion Website for this book:

www.ablongman.com/mcmillanschumacher6e.

APPLICATION PROBLEMS

For each of the examples below, select the statistical procedure that would best analyze the data.

1. A researcher is interested in the way three different approaches to discipline work with fifth-graders. Student teachers were assigned randomly to one of three groups. Each group received instruction in a different approach to handling discipline problems. Each student teacher was then observed over a three-week period, and the frequency and duration of discipline problems were recorded.

2. A teacher is interested in whether her sixth-graders' attitudes toward sex will change following a four-week sex-education course. To assess the impact of the program, the teacher measures the students' attitudes before and after the course.

3. The teacher in problem 2 now decides to test her program more thoroughly and is able to assign each of her students randomly to one group that receives a control condition. The teacher also analyzes the effects on boys and girls.

4. A counselor wants to know if there is a relationship between self-esteem of eleventh-graders and frequency of visits to the counseling center.

5. A doctoral student is interested in studying the attitude differences between high- and low-achieving students who receive different kinds of teacher feedback following

performance on tests. Four types of teacher feedback are designed for the study, and there are eight attitudes, such as attitude toward teacher, toward the subject studied, toward learning, and so on.

6. Calculate the approximate effect size for each of the following:
   a. The difference between two means is 14 and the standard deviation of the population is 7.
   b. The mean for Group A is 32 and that for Group B is 22. The standard deviation of the population is 10.
   c. The group that received individualized counseling obtained a mean score of 76 on the measure of self-concept, while the group that received no counseling obtained a mean score of 52. The standard deviation of the population was 15.
   d. Group A showed the following scores: 4, 5, 7, 7, 8, 10. Group B had scores of 12, 12, 13, 13, 14, 16. The standard deviation of the population was 6.

7. Summarize in words each of the following findings:
   a. Group A = 52, Group B = 63, $t = 4.33$, $p < .02$.
   b. Group A's mean SAT score was 558; Group B's was 457; Group C's was 688; $F = 4.77$, $p < .001$.
   c. The Tukey test was significant at .01 for two groups (A and E).

QUALITATIVE RESEARCH DESIGNS AND METHODS

*E*ducators frequently ask questions such as these: How do researchers design a qualitative study? How does one address the issues of rigor, validity, subjectivity, and use of the study? When does one employ participant observation and/or in-depth interviews? Should a variety of data collection strategies be employed in a single study? How is systematic data analysis done in qualitative research? Are there guidelines for presenting narrative findings? How does a reader judge the credibility of the findings in a qualitative study?

Qualitative research was classified in Chapter 2 as *interactive research* or *noninteractive research* termed *analytical research*. Qualitative interactive research is addressed in Part III, and analytical research is addressed in Part V. In Part III, Chapter 12 describes qualitative research design and criteria, and Chapter 13 looks at multiple data collection strategies. Chapter 14 describes qualitative data analysis processes, including manual and electronic data analysis. Interactive data collection strategies are used primarily in the study of current social happenings, social scenes, and processes. Inductive data analysis uses descriptive data of the meanings people derive from or ascribe to particular events and processes. Qualitative research can suggest grounded propositions, provide explanations to extend understanding of phenomena, or promote opportunities for informed social action. Qualitative research contributes to theory, educational practice, policy-making, and social consciousness.

12 Designing Qualitative Research

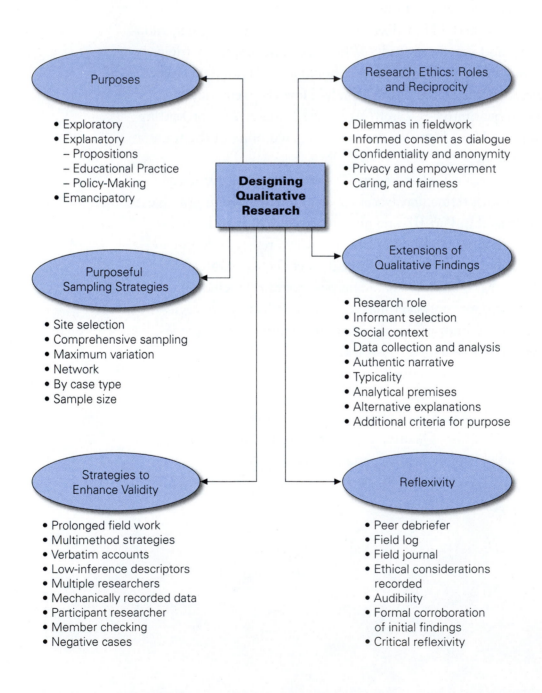

KEY TERMS

interactive strategies

field research

case study design

emergent design

purposeful sampling

site selection

comprehensive sampling

maximum variation sampling (quota sampling)

network sampling (snowball sampling)

validity of qualitative designs

reflexivity

positionality

audibility

extension of the findings

authenticity

typicality

Q*ualitative research* is inquiry in which researchers collect data in face-to-face situations by interacting with selected persons in their settings (e.g., field research). Qualitative research describes and analyzes people's individual and collective social actions, beliefs, thoughts, and perceptions. The researcher interprets phenomena in terms of the meanings that people assign to them. Qualitative studies are important for theory generation, policy development, improvement of educational practice, illumination of social issues, and action stimulus.

In this chapter, we introduce qualitative design and relate it to the general research question and potential contributions of the study. We explain purposeful sampling strategies, data collection and analysis phases, research ethics, and design standards. A variety of ways to demonstrate evidence-based findings are discussed: strategies to enhance validity, techniques to minimize research bias (reflexivity), and design components to generate extension of results. We point out the differences between traditional and critical approaches to inquiry.

PURPOSES, RESEARCH QUESTIONS, AND CASE STUDY DESIGN

Five of the interactive research approaches (i.e., modes of inquiry) discussed in Chapter 2 were ethnographic, phenomenological, case study, grounded theory, and critical studies. These inquiry modes share assumptions about and goals for research that influence design.

Research Approach and Orientation

Here, we review the research orientation shared among these inquiry modes because it provides a rationale for many design decisions.

Assumptions Qualitative research is based on a constructivist philosophy that assumes that reality is a multilayer, interactive, shared social experience that is interpreted by individuals. Reality is a *social construction;* that is, individuals and groups derive or ascribe meanings to specific events, persons, processes, and objects. People form constructions to make sense of their world and reorganize these constructions as viewpoints, perceptions, and belief systems. In other words, people's perceptions are what they consider real and thus what directs their actions, thoughts, and feelings.

Goal Qualitative research is first concerned with *understanding* social phenomena from participants' perspectives. That understanding is achieved by analyzing the many contexts of the participants and by narrating participants' meanings for these situations and events.

Participants' meanings include their feelings, beliefs, ideas, thoughts, and actions (see Excerpt 12.1). Some qualitative research aims for more than understanding the phenomena and also generates theory or empowerment.

Multimethod Strategies   Qualitative researchers study participants' perspectives with **interactive strategies:** participant observation, direct observation, in-depth interviews, artifacts, and supplementary techniques. Research strategies are flexible, using various combinations of techniques to obtain valid data. Most researchers adjust decisions about data collection strategies during the study. The multiple realities are viewed as so complex that one cannot decide a priori on a single methodology.

Research Role   Qualitative researchers become immersed in the situations and the phenomena studied. The research role varies from the more traditional neutral stance to an active participatory role, depending on the selected research approach.

Context Sensitivity   Other features of qualitative research are rooted in the belief that human actions are strongly influenced by the settings in which they occur. The study is **field research;** that is, the researcher collects data over a prolonged time at a site or from individuals without interfering with the natural events.

Purpose and Research Questions

Historically, qualitative researchers cited two major purposes of a study: *to describe and explore* and *to describe and explain*. Similar terms could be *to examine* or *to document, to understand*, and *to discover or generate*.

Exploratory studies add to the literature by building rich descriptions of complex situations and by giving directions for future research. Other qualitative studies are explicitly explanatory. They show relationships between events and meanings as perceived by participants. These studies increase readers' understanding of the phenomena. Other purposes address action, advocacy, or empowerment, which are often the ultimate goals of critical studies (critical, feminist, postmodern, and participatory research). Although researchers can claim empowerment and taking action as part of the study purpose, realistically, they can only note how the inquiry may offer opportunities for informed empowerment (see Table 12.1).

Case Study Design

In a **case study design,** the data analysis focuses on *one phenomenon*, which the researcher selects to understand in depth regardless of the number of sites or participants for the study.[1] The *one* may be, for example, one administrator, one group of students, one program, one process, one policy implementation, or one concept.

An initial plan is necessary to choose sites and participants for beginning data collection. The plan is an **emergent design,** in which each incremental research decision depends

EXCERPT 12.1   Goal of Understanding

More specifically, these narratives can enrich understanding of the culture and daily lives of minority female faculty members. Readers can hear the pain, can see the struggles, and can note the barriers. For example, these voices can help an administrator understand that support and monitoring are critical to minority females in their teaching and scholarship. These voices can help majority faculty members understand. (p. 63)

Source: From Medina, C., & Luna, G. (2000). Narratives from Latina professors in higher education. *Anthropology and Education Quarterly, 31*(1), 47–66.

TABLE 12.1   Research Purpose and Illustrative Research Questions

Research Purpose	Illustrative Research Questions
Descriptive Exploratory	
To examine new or little understood phenomena	What is occurring in this social situation?
To discover themes of participant meanings	What are the categories and themes of participants' meanings?
To develop in detail a concept, model, or hypotheses for future research	How are these patterns linked for propositions/assertions?
Descriptive Explanatory	
To describe and explain the patterns related to the phenomena	What events, beliefs, attitudes, and/or policies impact on this phenomenon?
To identify relationships influencing the phenomena	How do the participants explain the phenomenon?
Emancipatory	
To create opportunities and the will to initiate social action	How do participants describe and explain their problems and take positive action?

Source: Adapted from Marshall & Rossman, 1999, p. 33.

on prior information. The emergent design, in reality, may seem circular, as processes of purposeful sampling, data collection, and partial data analysis are simultaneous and intertwined rather than discrete sequential steps.[2]

Qualitative researchers investigate in-depth small, distinct groups, such as all the faculty in an innovative school, all the students in a selected classroom, or one principal's role for an academic year. These are single-site studies, in which there is a natural sociocultural boundary and face-to-face interaction encompassing the person or group. A study may also focus on individuals who have had a similar experience but may not be interacting with each other, such as families of children who have been physically abused.

Contrasting subunits may also be a focus, such as demographic groups (male/female or black/white) or programmatic groups (dropout/graduates), but the purpose is to understand the *one* phenomenon: the entity or process. Subunits are contrasting groups who are likely to be informative about the research foci.[3] These groups are not viewed as statistically comparative or as mutually exclusive; they often are selected to investigate the extent or diversity of the phenomenon. The researcher examines the first group thoroughly and then selects another group to contrast with or to corroborate findings about the first group.

In the case study design of Excerpt 12.2, the researcher selected one science teacher, Sarah, for a collaborative study. The purpose was to understand Sarah's behaviors and the actions of her students, her colleague teachers, and the school administrators in "terms of what she believed and how she constructed the various contexts in which she taught" (Tobin & LaMaster, 1995, p. 227).

Significance and Justification

To plan a case study design involves selecting the general research question and incorporating components that add to the potential contributions and significance of the study.

EXCERPT 12.2 Case Study Design

The research methodology employed in the study was interpretive and endeavored to make sense of the culture of the [two] classes taught by Sarah in terms of the actions of the participants (Sarah, students, colleague teachers, and school administrators). Accordingly, one rationale of the study was to make sense of Sarah's actions by describing her behaviors, and endeavoring to make sense of them in terms of what she believed and how she constructed the various contexts in which she taught. Our view of collaborative research required that we listen to the voices of Sarah and other participants in the study and also to assign a clear "signature" (Clandinin & Connelly, 1994) to what we learned in terms of interpretation that reflected the perspectives of both authors. (p. 227)

Source: From Tobin, K., & LaMaster, S. (1995). Relationships between metaphors, beliefs, and actions in a context of science curriculum change. *Journal of Research in Science Teaching, 32*(3), 225–242.

Qualitative research can be designed to contribute to theory, practice, policy, and social issues and action. We describe each of these in addition to other justifications.

Contributions to Theory   Case study design is appropriate for exploratory- and discovery-oriented research. An *exploratory study*, which examines a topic about which there has been little prior research, is designed to lead to further inquiry. The purpose is to elaborate a concept, develop a model with its related subcomponents, or suggest propositions. Some studies provide an understanding of an abstract concept, such as school-based management, from the participants' social experience. Other studies link participants' perceptions to social science and suggest propositions about humans in general, rather than link the findings to an educational concept. The concepts, models, or hypotheses are *grounded theory* because they are based on observations, rather than deduced from prior theories.

Contributions to Practice   Qualitative studies can provide detailed descriptions and analyses of particular practices, processes, or events. Some studies document happenings, and other studies increase participants' own understanding of a practice to improve that practice. A series of qualitative studies over a span of years may contribute to knowledge through the preponderance of evidence accumulated. Specific areas of education for which *quantitative* designs have proven inadequate have begun to accumulate case study evidence. Until quantitative design difficulties can be resolved, knowledge based on a preponderance of evidence cannot easily be ignored.

Contributions to Policy   Qualitative research employing a case study design also contributes to policy formulation, implementation, and modification. Some studies focus on the informal processes of policy formulation and implementation in settings with diverse cultural values to explain the outcomes of public policy. These studies frequently identify issues that suggest the need to modify statutes or regulations and to help policy-makers anticipate future issues.

Contributions to Social Issues and Action   Critical studies often aim at historical revision and transformation, erosion of ignorance, and empowerment. Some studies focus on the lived experiences of racial and ethnic groups, social classes, and gender roles. Researchers examine qualities such as race, ethnic group, social class, homosexual, and female in a more holistic social context to critique their ideological aspects and the political/economic interests that benefit from a given situation. Studies frequently express the so-called culture of silence experienced by various groups; others describe forms of resistance and accommodation of groups that develop their own values as a force for cohesion and survival within the dominant culture.

Other Justifications   *Feasibility issues* related to obtaining valid data can justify a qualitative case study design. Qualitative research is typically done when the nature of the sit-

Research
Navigator.c⊕m

12.1 Qualitative Challenges
Accession No.: 4783379

uation or the individuals do not permit use of an instrument. Qualitative strategies, for example, are appropriate with persons who are extremely busy, are expressive nonverbally, or use a second language. When the topic is controversial or confidential or occurred within an institution that has maintained minimal documentation, qualitative inquiry should be chosen. In some situations, an experimental study cannot be done for practical or ethical reasons.

PURPOSEFUL SAMPLING STRATEGIES

Purposeful sampling, in contrast to *probabilistic sampling,* is "selecting information-rich cases for study in-depth" (Patton, 2002, p. 242) when one wants to understand something about those cases without needing or desiring to generalize to all such cases. Purposeful sampling is done to increase the utility of information obtained from small samples. It requires that information be obtained about variations among the subunits before the sample is chosen. The researcher then searches for *information-rich* key informants, groups, places, or events to study. In other words, these samples are chosen because they are likely to be knowledgeable and informative about the phenomena the researcher is investigating.

The power and logic of purposeful sampling is that a few cases studied in depth yield many insights about the topic, whereas the logic of probability sampling depends on selecting a random or statistically representative sample for generalization to a larger population. Probability sampling procedures such as simple random or stratified sampling may be inappropriate when (1) generalizability of the findings is not the purpose; (2) only one or two subunits of a population are relevant to the research problem; (3) the researchers have no access to the whole group from which they wish to sample; or (4) statistical sampling is precluded because of logistical and ethical reasons.

Types of purposeful sampling include site selection, comprehensive sampling, maximum variation sampling, network sampling, and sampling by case type (see Table 12.2).

Site Selection

Site selection, by which a site is selected to locate people involved in a particular event, is preferred when the research focus is on complex microprocesses. A clear definition of the criteria for site selection is essential. The criteria are related to and appropriate for the research problem and purpose. For example, if the initial problem is phrased to describe and analyze teachers' decision making regarding learning activities or students' perspectives regarding classroom management, then the site selected should be one in which these viewpoints or actions are likely present and can be studied.

> **MISCONCEPTION**   Self-report surveys of principals' attitudes, behaviors, opinions, and demographic characteristics implied that a principal's job is orderly, routine, and predictable.
>
> **EVIDENCE**   When an ethnography focused on a selected principal's daily professional life, a different image emerged: expedient, rapid problem solving and constant engagement in multitasking with complex human interrelationships to contain any type of conflict immediately.

Comprehensive Sampling

Comprehensive sampling, in which every participant, group, setting, event, or other relevant information is examined, is the preferred sampling strategy. Each subunit is

TABLE 12.2 Purposeful Sampling Strategies

Sample Strategy	Description
Site selection	Select site where specific events are expected to occur.
Comprehensive sampling	Choose entire group by criteria.
Maximum variation sampling	Select to obtain maximum differences of perceptions about a topic among information-rich informants or group.
Network sampling	Each successive person or group is nominated by a prior person as appropriate for a profile or attribute.
Sampling by case type	
Extreme case	Choose extreme cases after knowing the typical or average case—e.g., outstanding successes, crisis events.
Intense case	Select cases that are intense but not extreme illustrations—e.g., below-average students.
Typical case	Know the typical characteristics of a group and sample by cases—e.g., selection of a typical high school principal would eliminate women, persons too young or too old, single males.
Unique case	Choose the unusual or rare case of some dimension or event—e.g., the implementation of a new federal policy mandate.
Reputational case	Obtain the recommendation of knowledgeable experts for the best examples—e.g., principal nominates "competent" teachers or state officials identify "effective" schools.
Critical case	Identify the case that can illustrate some phenomenon dramatically—e.g., the "real test" case or the "ideal" case.
Concept/theory-based	Select by information-rich persons or situations known to experience the concept or to be attempting to implement the concept/theory—e.g., school implementing site-based management, teacher "burnout."
Combination of purposeful sampling strategies	Choose various sampling strategies as needed or desired for purposes, especially in large-scale studies and lengthy process studies.

manageable in size and so diverse that one does not want to lose possible variation. For example, a study of mainstreaming autistic children in one school division would probably require observation of all autistic children. Suppose a study of high school student interns in an external learning program had 35 different sites. Each work setting was so diverse—a hospital speech clinic, a community newspaper, a labor union, two legislative offices, an animal shelter, and others—that comprehensive selection would be necessary. Because groups are rarely sufficiently small and resources are seldom plentiful, researchers use other sampling strategies.

Maximum Variation Sampling

Maximum variation sampling, or **quota sampling,** is a strategy to illuminate different aspects of the research problem. For instance, a researcher may divide a population of elementary school teachers by number of years of service into three categories and select key informants in each category to investigate career development. This is *not* a representative sample because the qualitative researcher is merely using this strategy to describe in detail different meanings of teacher career development for individuals with different years of service. See Excerpt 12.3 for a combination of purposeful sampling strategies.

EXCERPT 12.3 Purposeful Sampling: Nomination and Maximum Variation

The participants in this study were parents of students who graduated from a medium-size Mid-western city school district's program for individuals with cognitive disabilities between 1989 and 1993. The sample included parents whose children attended three of the four high schools in the city and had mild, moderate and severe cognitive disabilities. Using *purposeful sampling,* . . . participants were selected to represent three schools, presence of socio-economic disadvantage, degree of severity of child's disability and the child's current school status. A sample frame . . . was developed with the assistance of special education administrators in the school district. Parents without phone numbers were eliminated from the sampling frame. Twenty-four names . . . were selected, contacted by the researchers, and asked to participate in the study. The number of participants was based on considerations of time and feasibility. Of the 24 families contacted, 19 agreed to participate. (p. 5)

Source: From Hanley-Maxwell, C., Whitney-Thomas, J., & Pogoloff, S. M. (1995). The second shock: A qualitative study of parents' perspectives and needs during their child's transition from school to adult life. *JASH: Journal of the Association for Persons with Severe Handicaps, 20*(1), 3–15.

Network Sampling

Network sampling, also called **snowball sampling,** is a strategy in which each successive participant or group is named by a preceding group or individual. Participant referrals are the basis for choosing a sample. The researcher develops a profile of the attributes or particular trait sought and asks each participant to suggest others who fit the profile or have the attribute. This strategy may be used in situations in which the individuals sought do not form a naturally bounded group but are scattered throughout populations. Network sampling is frequently used for in-depth interview studies, rather than participant observation research.

Sampling by Case Type

Other sampling strategies are used when a study requires an examination of a particular type of case. Remember, *case* refers to an in-depth analysis of a phenomenon and not the number of people sampled. Examples of sampling by case type are extreme-case, intensive-case, typical-case, unique-case, reputational-case, critical-case, and concept/theory-based sampling. Each of these sampling strategies is defined in Table 12.2. A researcher may choose combinations of case types as needed, especially in large-scale studies and lengthy process studies. (See Patton [2002] for additional case-type sampling.)

Purposeful sampling strategies employed in a study are identified from prior information and are reported in the study to enhance data quality. In addition, the persons or groups who actually participated in the study are reported in a manner to protect confidentiality of data. Historical and legal researchers specify the public archives and private collections used and frequently refer to each document or court case in explanatory footnotes. In this manner, researchers using noninteractive techniques to study the past reduce threats to design validity.

Research
Navigator.c○*m*

12.2 Design Issues
Accession No.: 10609946

Sample Size

Qualitative inquirers view sampling processes as dynamic, ad hoc, and phasic rather than static or a priori parameters of populations. While there are statistical rules for probability sample size, there are only guidelines for purposeful sample size. Thus, purposeful samples can range from 1 to 40 or more. Typically, a qualitative sample seems small compared with the sample needed to generalize to a larger population.

The logic of the sample size is related to the purpose, the research problem, the major data collection strategy, and the availability of information-rich cases. The insights generated from qualitative inquiry depend more on the information richness of the cases and the analytical capabilities of the researcher than on the sample size.

The following are guidelines for determining sample size:

1. *Purpose of the study* A case study that is descriptive/exploratory may not need as many persons as a self-contained study that is description/explanatory. Further, a phenomenological study usually has fewer informants than are needed in grounded theory to generate dense concepts.
2. *Focus of the study* A process-focused study at one site may have fewer participants than an interview study using network sampling.
3. *Primary data collection strategy* Qualitative researchers are guided by circumstances. For instance, a study may have a small sample size, but the researcher may be continually returning to the same situation or the same informants, seeking confirmation. The number of days in the field is usually reported.
4. *Availability of informants* Some informants are rare and difficult to locate; others are relatively easy to identify and locate.
5. *Redundancy of data* Would adding more individuals or returning to the field yield any new insights?
6. *Researchers submit the obtained sample size to peer review* Most qualitative researchers propose a *minimum* sample size and then continue to add to the sample as the study progresses.

ALERT! There are no easy rules for determining sample size. It depends on what you want to know, the purpose of the inquiry, what is at stake, what will be credible, and the available time and resources.

PHASES OF DATA COLLECTION AND ANALYSIS STRATEGIES

The qualitative phases of data collection and analyses are interwoven and occur in overlapping cycles. They are not called *procedures* but *strategies*—that is, techniques that depend on each prior strategy and the resulting data. Figure 12.1 illustrates the five research phases: planning (Phase 1), data collection (Phases 2, 3, 4), and completion (Phase 5). Each phase will be discussed in this section.

Phase 1: Planning Analyzing the problem statement and the initial research questions will suggest the type of setting or interviewees that would logically be informative. In Phase 1, the researcher locates and gains permission to use the site or network of persons.

ALERT! Obtaining permission may take considerable time if you are a complete stranger to the site or the participants, unless someone can vouch for you.

Phase 2: Beginning Data Collection This phase includes the first days in the field, in which the researcher establishes rapport, trust, and reciprocal relations with the individuals and groups to be observed (Wax, 1971). Researchers obtain data primarily to become oriented and to gain a sense of the totality for purposeful sampling. Researchers also adjust their interviewing and recording procedures to the site or persons involved.

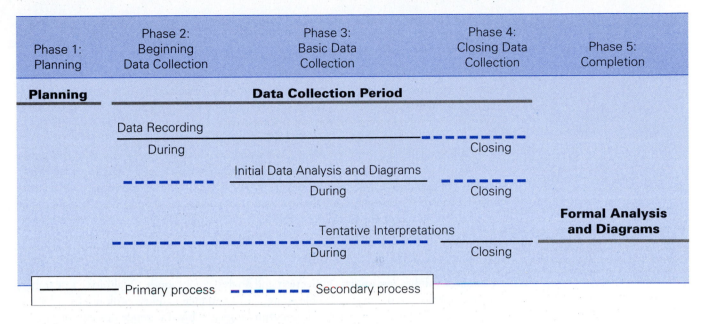

| Phase 1: Planning | Phase 2: Beginning Data Collection | Phase 3: Basic Data Collection | Phase 4: Closing Data Collection | Phase 5: Completion |

Planning   **Data Collection Period**

Data Recording
During   Closing

Initial Data Analysis and Diagrams
During   Closing

Formal Analysis and Diagrams

Tentative Interpretations
During   Closing

———————— Primary process   ▬ ▬ ▬ ▬ ▬ ▬ Secondary process

FIGURE 12.1   **Phases of Qualitative Research**

Phase 3: Basic Data Collection   The inquirer begins to *hear* and *see* what is occurring, which goes beyond just *listening* and *looking*. Choices of data collection strategies and informants continue to be made. Tentative data analysis begins as the researcher mentally processes ideas and facts while collecting data. Initial descriptions are summarized and identified for later corroboration.

Phase 4: Closing Data Collection   The researcher "leaves the field," or conducts the last interview. Ending data collection is related to the research problem and the richness of the collected data. More attention is given to possible interpretations and verifications of the emergent findings with key informants, remaining interviews, and documents. The field may yield more data but *not* yield more insights relevant to the research problem (see Excerpt 12.4).

Phase 5: Completion   Completion of active data collecting blends into formal data analysis and construction of meaningful ways to present the data. Integrative diagrams, time charts, frequency lists, process figures, and other graphics can synthesize a sense of the relationship of the parts to the whole. Data analysis and diagrams are essential for interpretations.

EXCERPT 12.4   When to Stop Collecting Data

Eventually, three categories reached theoretical saturation, a point at which, according to Strauss (1987), "additional analysis no longer contributes to discovering anything new about a category" (p. 21). The categories were the roles of religion, poverty, and ethnicity in relationship to second language learning. (p. 130)

Source: From Case, R. (2004). Forging ahead into new social networks and looking back to past social identities: A case study of a foreign-born English as a Second Language teacher in the United States. *Urban Education, 39*(2), 125–148.

VALIDITY OF QUALITATIVE DESIGNS

Validity refers to the degree of congruence between the explanations of the phenomena and the realities of the world. Although there is broad agreement to use pertinent research terms for qualitative research, disagreement occurs over the names of specific concepts. We will use general terms—that is, *validity, reflexivity,* and *extension of findings*—as the most common criteria for evidence-based inquiry in qualitative research.

Validity addresses these questions: Do researchers actually observe what they think they see? Do inquirers actually hear the meanings that they think they hear? In other words, **validity of qualitative designs** is the degree to which the interpretations have *mutual meanings* between the participants and the researcher. Thus, the researcher and participants agree on the description or composition of events, and especially the meanings of these events.

Strategies to Enhance Validity

Claims of validity rest on data collection and analysis techniques. Qualitative researchers use a combination of any 10 possible strategies to enhance validity: prolonged field work, multimethod strategies, participant verbatim language, low-inference description, multiple researchers, mechanically recorded data, participant researcher, member checking, participant review, and negative data.

Qualitative researchers typically use as many strategies as possible to ensure design validity. Choosing from strategies involves issues of feasibility and ethics. Strategies are added as appropriate to maintain the least amount of intrusion while increasing the quality of the data (see Table 12.3).

ALERT!   *Essential strategies* include prolonged field work, multimethods, verbatim accounts, low-inference descriptions, and negative case searches.

TABLE 12.3   Enhancing Design Validity: Data Collection Strategies to Increase Agreement on the Description by Researcher and Participants

Strategy	Description
Prolonged and persistent field work	Allows interim data analysis and corroboration to ensure match between findings and participant reality
Multimethod strategies	Allows triangulation in data collection and data analysis
Participant language; verbatim accounts	Obtain literal statements of participants and quotations from documents
Low-inference descriptors	Record precise, almost literal, and detailed descriptions of people and situations
Multiple researchers	Agreement on descriptive data collected by a research team
Mechanically recorded data	Use of tape recorders, photographs, and videotapes
Participant researcher	Use of participant recorded perceptions in diaries or anecdotal records for corroboration
Member checking	Check informally with participants for accuracy during data collection; frequently done in participant observation studies
Participant review	Ask participant to review researcher's synthesis of interviews with person for accuracy of representation; frequently done in interview studies
Negative or discrepant data	Actively search for, record, analyze, and report negative or discrepant data that are an exception to patterns or that modify patterns found in data

Prolonged and Persistent Field Work   Participant observation and in-depth interviews are conducted in natural settings to reflect lived experience. The lengthy data collection period provides opportunities for interim data analyses, preliminary comparisons, and corroboration to refine ideas and to ensure the match between evidence-based categories and participant reality.

Multimethod Strategies   Most qualitative researchers employ several data collection techniques in a study but usually select one as the central method—either participant observation or in-depth interviews. To some extent, participant observation, open observation, interviewing, and documents are an interwoven web of techniques. How each of these strategies is used varies with the study. Multimethod strategies permits *triangulation* of data across inquiry techniques. Different strategies may yield different insights about the topic of interest and increase the credibility of findings. In its broad sense, *triangulation* also can refer to use of multiple researchers, multiple theories, or perspectives to interpret the data; multiple data sources to corroborate data (see Chapter 13), and multiple disciplines to broaden one's understanding of the method and the phenomenon of interest (Janesick, 1998). For an example of selecting strategies to enhance design validity, see Excerpt 12.5.

Participant Language and Verbatim Accounts   Interviews are phrased in the informant's language, not in abstract social science terms. Researchers are also sensitive to *cultural translators*—that is, informants who translate their words into social class terms. For example, when "tramps" were asked "Where is your home? What is your address?" they interpreted the question as referring to a middle-class residence and said "I have no home." However, an ethnographer found that men labeled as *homeless* by social scientists did, in fact, have "*flops*," which functioned for them as "homes" (Spradley, 1979).

ALERT!   Recording verbatim accounts of conversations and transcripts is essential. Direct quotations from the data illustrate participants' meanings and thus ensure validity.

Low-Inference Descriptors   Concrete, precise descriptions from field notes and interview elaborations are the hallmarks of qualitative research and the principal method for identifying patterns in the data. *Low inference* means that the descriptions are almost literal and that any important terms are those used and understood by the participants. Low-inference descriptions stand in contrast to the abstract language of a researcher.

**Research
Navigator.c⊕m**

12.3 Verification Strategies
Accession No.: 10614549

EXCERPT 12.5   Enhancing Validity

The study employed an interpretive design (Erickson, 1986) that followed a hermeneutic cycle whereby what was learned was informed by what was already known, reading of the literature, experience in the field, and continuous data framing, analyses, and interpretations. A number of procedures, such as triangulation, were undertaken to ensure that the study had what Guba and Lincoln (1989) referred to as confirmability [validity]. Triangulation, involving the use of numerous data sources, maximized the probability that the emergent assertions were consistent with a variety of data. Because we were in the field for a prolonged time, the tendency of the participants in the study to exhibit contrived behaviors for the benefit of researchers was minimized. Furthermore, researchers were able to see whether given behaviors were typical or atypical. (pp. 227–228)

Source: From Tobin, K., & LaMaster, S. U. (1995). Relationships between metaphors, beliefs, and actions in a context of science curriculum change. *Journal of Research in Science Teaching, 32*(3), 225–242.

EXCERPT 12.6   Mechanically Recorded Data, Participant Researcher, and Member Checking

Data collection . . . occurred over a 10-month period by the first two authors and Millie, Jeffrey's mother. The procedures included semi-structured interviews and an audiojournal. The first two authors conducted five of the six . . . interviews with Millie, Bob, and Chris. Millie conducted the final interview with her husband, Bob. . . . Millie maintained a audiojournal where she recorded her feelings and perceptions of the support process and subsequent changes in Jeffrey's behavior and family functioning. . . . Establishing credibility occurred with member checks, . . . periodically offering Millie the opportunity to respond to the accuracy of the data and . . . coding. (p. 200)

Source: From Fox, L., Vaughn, B., Dunlap, G., & Bucy, M. (1997). Parent-professional partnership in behavioral support: A qualitative analysis of one family's experience. *JASH: Journal of the Association for Persons with Severe Handicaps, 22*(4), 198–207.

Multiple Researchers   The use of multiple researchers is one method to enhance validity. The use of more than one researcher is handled in different ways: (1) extensive prior training and discussion during field work to reach agreement on meanings, (2) short-term observations for confirmation at different sites, and (3) more commonly, an arrangement by which each field observer is independently responsible for a research site and periodically meets with the team to share emerging ideas and strategies. Qualitative research based on a large group team approach, however, is infrequently done; most studies involve only two researchers as a team.

Mechanically Recorded Data   Tape recorders, photographs, and videotapes provide accurate and relatively complete records. For the data to be usable, situational aspects that affected the data record are noted—for instance, failure of equipment, angles of videotaping, and effects of using technical equipment on the social scene (see Excerpt 12.6).

Participant Researcher   Many researchers obtain the aid of an informant to corroborate what has been observed and recorded, interpretations of participant meanings, and explanations of overall processes. Participants may keep diaries or make anecdotal records to share with the researcher.

Member Checking   Researchers who establish a field residence frequently confirm observations and participants' meanings with individuals through casual conversations in informal situations. Member checking can also be done within an interview as topics are rephrased and probed to obtain more complete and subtle meanings.

Participant Review   Researchers who interview each person in depth or conduct a series of interviews with the same person may ask the person to review a transcript or synthesis of the data obtained from him or her. The participant is asked to modify any information from the interview data for accuracy. Then, the data obtained from each interviewee are analyzed for a comprehensive integration of findings.

Negative and/or Discrepant Data   Researchers actively search for, record, analyze, and report negative cases or discrepant data. A *negative case* is a situation, a social scene, or a participant's view that contradicts the emerging pattern of meanings. *Discrepant data* present a variant to the emerging pattern. For example, a school ethnographer may find that faculty interact freely among themselves in six situations. No negative situations are found. Discrepant data, however, may suggest that faculty interactions are free in five situations and only semi-free in the sixth situation, depending on who is present.

REFLEXIVITY IN QUALITATIVE RESEARCH

Reflexivity is a broad concept that includes rigorous examination of one's personal and theoretical commitments to see how they serve as resources for selecting a qualitative approach, framing the research problem, generating particular data, relating to participants, and developing specific interpretations (Altheide & Johnson, 1998; Fine; 1998, Mason, 1996; Marcus, 1998; Schwandt, 2001; MacBeth, 2001). Further, all data are processed through and reconstructed in the researcher's mind as the report is written.

In other words, **reflexivity** is rigorous self-scrutiny by the researcher throughout the entire process. The researcher's very act of posing difficult questions to himself or herself assumes that he or she cannot be neutral, objective, or detached. Reflexivity is an important procedure for establishing credibility. Qualitative researchers thus do not deny human subjectivity, but rather take it into account through various strategies.

Interpersonal Subjectivity and Reflexivity

Qualitative research depends to a great extent on the interpersonal skills of the inquirer, such as building trust, keeping good relations, being nonjudgmental, and respecting the norms of the situation. Researchers use all their personal experiences and abilities of engagement, balancing the analytical and creative through empathetic understanding and profound respect for participants' perspectives. Interpersonal emotions in field work are essential in data collection activities because of the face-to-face interaction. Feelings serve several useful functions throughout the research process (Kleinman & Copp, 1993).

The progress of the study often depends primarily on the relationship the researcher builds with the participants. The interactive process is relatively personal; no two investigators observe, interview, or relate to others in exactly the same way. These issues are handled primarily within the actual study to enhance reflexivity.

Data obtained from informants are valid even though they may represent particular views or have been influenced by the researcher's presence. Such data are problematic only if they are claimed to be representative beyond the context. Potential researcher bias can be minimized if the researcher spends enough time in the field and employs multiple data collection strategies to corroborate the findings. Providing sufficient details about the design, including reflexivity strategies, is necessary.

What exactly is *reflexivity?* Pillow (2003) suggests these four validated strategies of reflexivity:

1. Reflexivity as recognition of self—personal self-awareness
2. Reflexivity as recognition of the other—capturing the essence of the informant, or "let them speak for themselves"
3. Reflexivity as truth gathering—the researcher's insistence on getting it right or being accurate
4. Reflexivity as transcendence—the aim that the researcher, through transcending her own subjectivity and cultural context, can be released from the weight of (mis)representation for accuracy in reporting

Reflexivity also involves discomfort, as researchers seek to minimize predispositions through self-questioning. Patton (2002) suggests this questioning focus on several screens that the researcher uses for self, audience, and participants (see Figure 12.2).

Some critical studies may require the use of additional strategies. Critical researchers are wary that their empirical work will be viewed as an ideological discourse and fearful of duplication of social, racial, ethnic, and gender biases in their studies. For example, one difficult question relates to *voice:* Were all the voices allowed to emerge, especially those of the socially silenced, whose perspectives are often counter to the situation?

Research Navigator.com

12.4 Reflexivity
Accession No.: 9756739

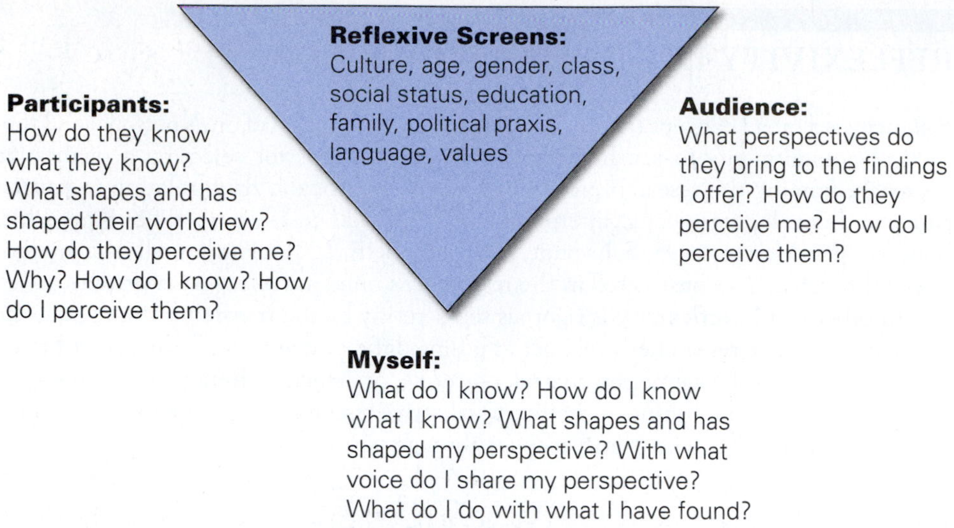

Reflexive Screens:
Culture, age, gender, class,
social status, education,
family, political praxis,
language, values

Participants:
How do they know
what they know?
What shapes and has
shaped their worldview?
How do they perceive me?
Why? How do I know? How
do I perceive them?

Audience:
What perspectives do
they bring to the findings
I offer? How do they
perceive me? How do I
perceive them?

Myself:
What do I know? How do I know
what I know? What shapes and has
shaped my perspective? With what
voice do I share my perspective?
What do I do with what I have found?

FIGURE 12.2 Reflexive Questions

Adapted from M. Q. Patton. (2002). *Qualitative research and evaluation methods,* 3rd ed. Thousand Oaks, CA: Sage (p. 66).

Another reflex strategy is **positionality,** which assumes that only texts in which researchers display their own positions (standpoints) and contextual grounds for reasoning can be considered good research (Lincoln, 1995; Lather, 1991; J. K. Smith, 1993). Critical researchers often write in the introduction their individual social, cultural, historical, racial, and sexual location in the study (see Excerpt 12.7). However, positionality statements can be only a gesture.

In participatory research, the inquirer writes into the data his or her own actions. The complicated dual role of researcher and participant requires scrutiny of both the role and the resulting data. This is not an easy task nor should it be taken lightly.

Strategies to Enhance Reflexivity

Qualitative researchers combine any of seven possible strategies to monitor and evaluate the impact of their subjectivity (see Table 12.4). The most important strategies are keeping a field log and a field (reflex) journal and documenting for audibility. Other strategies are added as needed to obtain valid data.

Peer Debriefer   A *peer debriefer* is a disinterested colleague who discusses the researcher's preliminary analysis and next strategies. Such a discussion makes more

EXCERPT 12.7   The Researcher's Stance

My status as a White, European American, male college professor would play an important role as a researcher in Mr. Wilson's class. . . . I hoped to break down the hegemonic relationships that form when a White, European American male college professor enters the classroom of a Black, African American male teacher. I began keeping a reflexive journal before I started the study in which I recorded my reactions to readings I had completed on the experience of Muslims and Africans in United States. This was the first step. (p. 131)

Source: From Case, R. (2004). Forging ahead into new social networks and looking back to past social identities: A case study of a foreign-born English as a Second Language teacher in the United States. *Urban Education, 39*(2), 125–148.

TABLE 12.4	Strategies to Enhance Reflexivity: Strategies to Monitor and Evaluate Researcher Subjectivity and Perspective
Strategy	**Description**
Peer debriefer	Select a colleague who facilitates the logical analysis of data and interpretation; frequently done when the topic is emotionally charged or the researcher experiences conflicting values in data collection
Field log	Maintain a log of dates, time, places, persons, and activities to obtain access to informants and for each datum set collected
Field (reflex) journal	Record the decisions made during the emerging design and the rationale; include judgments of data validity
Ethical considerations recorded	Record the ethical dilemmas, decisions, and actions in field journal, and self-reflections
Audibility	Record data management techniques, codes, categories, and decision-rules as a "decision trail"
Formal corroboration of initial findings	Conduct formal confirmation activities such as a survey, focus groups, or interviews
Critical reflexivity	Self-critique by asking difficult questions; positionality

explicit the tacit knowledge that the inquirer has acquired. The peer debriefer also poses searching questions to help the researcher understand his or her own posture and its role in the inquiry. In addition, this dialogue may reduce the stress that normally accompanies field work.

Field Log   A *field log* documents the persistent field work and provides a chronological record by date and time spent in the field, including getting access to sites and participants. The field log also contains, for each entry, the places and person involved.

Reflex Journal   A *reflex journal* is a continuous record of the decisions made during the emergent design and rationale. This allows for justification, based on the available information at the time, of the modifications of the research problem and strategies. The reflex journal also contains assessments of the trustworthiness of each data set. A reflex journal traces the researcher's ideas and personal reactions throughout the field work.

Ethical Considerations Recorded   Researchers make strategy choices in the field, some of which are based primarily on ethical considerations. A record of ethical concerns helps to justify choices in data collection and analysis.

Audibility   Audibility is the practice of maintaining a record of data management techniques and decision rules that document the chain of evidence or decision trail. That record includes the codes, categories, and themes used in description and interpretation as well as drafts and preliminary diagrams. Thus, the chain of evidence will be available for inspection and confirmation by outside reviewers.

Audibility criteria can be met with or without an outside reviewer—that is, an *auditor* who submits a reviewer's appraisal. An alternative is to place a list of files, codes, categories, and decision rules in an appendix for readers' perusal.

ALERT!   An auditor must be knowledgeable about *both* the methodology and the topic.

Formal Corroboration of Initial Findings   Surveys, focus groups, and in-depth interviews with those not selected originally may be used for formal confirmation, especially when the findings depend on a few informants. As a corroboration activity, the data must be completely analyzed first. Confirmation activities ensure that the patterns found have not been unduly contaminated by the researcher.

EXTENSION OF QUALITATIVE FINDINGS

Qualitative researchers provide for the logical **extension of findings,** which enables others to understand similar situations and apply the findings in subsequent research or practical situations. Knowledge is produced by the preponderance of evidence found in separate case studies over time.

    Authenticity is the faithful reconstruction of participants' perceptions. In other words, readers can relate to or connect with informants and situations. Some studies, such as grounded theory, cite the theoretical frameworks for other researchers. Other studies are more contextual for practical implications. A study that is idiosyncratic and has a minimum of design description has limited usefulness for future inquiry.

Design Components to Generate Extension of Findings

Ten design components can affect logical extensions; those actually employed should be described. The components are research role, informant selection, social context, data collection strategies, data analysis strategies, authentic narrative, typicality, analytical premises, alternative explanations, and other criteria associated with a particular research purpose (see Table 12.5).

Research Role   The importance of the inquirer's social relationship with the participants neccessitates a description of his or her role and status within the group or site. The preferred research role is that of a person who is unknown at the site—in other words, an *outsider*. Researchers often cite personal or professional experiences that enable them to empathize with the participants—that is, they recognize more readily the observed processes and subtle participant meanings than those who lack such experiences. Participatory research requires planning the dual role of participant and researcher, which usually limits extension of the findings.

Informant Selection   The rationale and decision-making process for choosing the participants is described. Future studies will require researchers to contact individuals similar to those used in the prior study. If a particular person is not cooperative or not available, researchers will search for other informants until a pattern emerges. Increasing the number of sites or persons does not aid in extension of findings; the criterion is information-rich individuals or social scenes (see Excerpt 12.8).

Social Context   The social context influences data content and is described physically, socially, interpersonally, and functionally. Physical descriptions of the people, the time, and the place of the events or the interviews all assist in data analysis. The purpose of group meetings, such as inservice training or official business, requires other researchers to find similar social contexts for further study.

TABLE 12.5   Design Components to Generate Extension of Findings

Strategy	Adequate Description in the Study
Research role	The social relationship of the researcher with the participants
Informant selection	Criteria, rationale, and decision process used in purposeful sampling
Social context	The physical, social, interpersonal, and functional social scenes of data collection
Data collection strategies	The multimethods employed, including participant observation, interview, documents, and others
Data analysis strategies	Data analysis process described
Authentic narrative	Thick description presented as an analytical narrative
Typicality	Distinct characteristics of groups and/or sites presented
Analytical premises	The initial theoretical or political framework that informs the study
Alternative explanations	Retrospective delineation of all plausible or rival explanations for interpretations
Other criteria by research approach (after study completed)	
Ethnography	Comprehensive explanation of complexity of group life
Phenomenology	Understand the essence of lived experience; generates more research questions
Case study	Understand the practice; facilitates informed decision making
Grounded theory	Concepts or propositions relate to social science; generates verification research with more structured designs
Critical traditions	Informs or empowers participants about their situation and opportunities; generates further research; action stimulus

EXCERPT 12.8   Informant Selection

Participants: Richness of professional background and willingness to participate in a series of personal in-depth interviews were the primary considerations in identifying participants for the study. . . . A male superintendent, who had supervised two women principals at different times and in different districts, suggested their names to the first author. A family friend of the first author suggested a third choice. . . . This study included 3 participants, all African American women who had been principals in urban school settings. (p. 149)

Source: From Bloom, C., & Erlandson, D. (2003). African American women principals in urban schools: Realities, (re)constructions, and resolutions. Educational Administration Quarterly, 39(3), 339–369.

Data Collection Strategies   Using the study for future inquiry will be impossible without precise descriptions of data collection techniques: the varieties of observational and interviewing methods and data recording techniques used. How different strategies were employed is noted, as well. For example, if the primary interest was observing a group process, then individual interviews and documents would be corroborative data collection strategies.

Data Analysis Strategies   Simply asserting that data analysis was done carefully or citing that a certain software program was used is insufficient. The researcher must provide retrospective accounts of how data were synthesized and identify the general analytical strategies used. Frequently, the categories used in data analysis and their decision rules are listed in an appendix.

Authentic Narrative   Most qualitative studies contain thick description in the narrative, interspersed with brief quotations representing participants' language. A good narrative is one that may be read and lived vicariously by others. A narrative is authentic when readers connect to the story by recognizing particulars, by visioning the scenes, and by reconstructing them from remembered associations with similar events (Connelly & Clandinin, 1990). It is the particular, not the abstract, that triggers emotions and moves people. Stories stand between the abstract and the particular by mediating the basic demands of research along with the personal aspects.

Typicality   Another design component is the extent of **typicality** of the phenomenon (Wolcott, 1973)—that is, the degree to which it may be compared or contrasted along relevant dimensions with other phenomena. Qualitative researchers' virtual obsession with describing the distinct characteristics of groups studied is, in fact, an appreciation of the importance of this information for extension of findings. The attributes of groups and sites can include socioeconomic status, educational attainment, age range, racial or ethnic composition, time period, and contextual features of the location. Unique historical experiences of groups and cultures may limit extension, but few groups' experiences are totally ethnocentric (see Except 12.9). Once typicality has been established, a basis for extension will be evident and can be used to provide insights across time frames and situations.

Analytical Premises   The choice of conceptual framework made by one researcher for a given study will necessitate other researchers to begin from similar analytical premises (see Excerpt 12.10). Because one major outcome of qualitative research is the generation and

EXCERPT 12.9   Typicality of Site and Persons Related to the Research Problem

To explore the authenticity dilemma confronting Asian ethnics, . . . ninety-five third, fourth, and fifth generation Chinese and Japanese ethnics living in northern and southern California [have been interviewed.] . . . All the participants are well-educated and from urban areas; many are white collar professionals. . . . Those who are not included are housewives, small business owners, students and a few artists. The youngest participants were in their early 20s while the oldest were into their 70s. . . .

The fact that this study was conducted in California is of special significance. . . . California has remained the state with the largest concentration of Asian-Americans. . . . Whether their numbers and long history have promoted greater social acceptance or the reverse—greater hostility—is not at all clear [even though] . . . they are well integrated into its social fabric. . . . In addition, the general climate towards immigrants, both legal and illegal, is decidedly less hospitable today. (pp. 106–107)

Source: From Tuan, M. (1999). Neither real Americans nor real Asians? Multigeneration Asian ethnics navigating the terrain of authenticity. *Qualitative Sociology, 22*(2), 105–125.

EXCERPT 12.10   Analytical Premises and Prior Research

Not surprisingly, then, the girls whose families were *not* like the television families thought the television families were more unrealistic. Following McRobbie's (1991) culturalist approach, the girls were interpreting and assessing media based on their own lived experiences. Greenberg and Reeves (1996) also find that children's personal experiences affect their perceptions of reality on television. Children in general do not have multiple reference points regarding family life, so the girls in this study saw any family as deviating from those they know as unrealistic. This data also empirically supports Greenberg and Reeves's prediction that television content is perceived as more like real life if the child's attitudes and behaviors, or in this case, family dynamics, are consistent with the television content. (pp. 398–399)

Source: From Fingerson, L. (1999). Active viewing: Girls' interpretations of family television programs. *Journal of Contemporary Ethnography, 28*(4), 389–418.

refinement of concepts, inquirers contrast their findings to those of prior research. When discrepancies are presented, researchers cite the attributes of the group, time period, and settings. This alerts other researcher when they use these same findings. Much qualitative research, however, is nontheoretical.

Alternative Explanations   During data analysis, qualitative researchers search for negative evidence and discrepant data to challenge or modify emerging patterns. Negative and discrepant data are useful for identifying alternative explanations. Observers and interviewers actively search for informants and social scenes that appear to vary from or disagree with prior data. A major pattern becomes an explanation only when alternative patterns do not offer reasonable explanations related to the research problem. Major and alternative explanations are discussed in the study because both might generate further research.

Other Criteria by Research Approach (After Study Completed)   In addition to providing adequate descriptions of the general components mentioned, specific qualitative approaches may emphasize additional criteria. For example, phenomenology, grounded theory, and critical studies have slightly different effects on research communities, readers, and participants. An *ethnography* provides a comprehensive understanding of the complexity of group life, which leads to further case studies. A *phenomenological study* increases the understanding of lived experiences by readers and others. A *case study* promotes better understanding of a practice or issue and facilitates informed decision making. A *grounded theory study*, however, usually leads to more structured designs to test a concept or to verify a proposition. Some forms of critical traditions not only inform through historical revisionism but also empower and stimulate action. Thus, the researcher frequently has a meeting with the major informants or all participants, reviews the findings, and initiates a dialogue. The researchers also may provide additional resource information to foster personal and group empowerment.

When qualitative researchers appropriately address the issues of design validity, reflexivity, and extension of findings, as noted previously, their work is regarded as credible by other qualitative investigators. Many design issues are handled by planning and conducting studies based on the appropriate criteria for evidence-based research.

RESEARCH ETHICS: ROLES AND RECIPROCITY

Qualitative research is more likely to be personally intrusive than quantitative research. Thus, ethical guidelines include policies regarding informed consent, deception, confidentiality, anonymity, privacy, and caring. Field workers, however, must adopt these principles in complex situations.

Ethical Dilemmas in Fieldwork

A credible research design involves not only selecting informants and effective research strategies but also adhering to research ethics. Qualitative researchers need to plan how they will handle the ethical dilemmas in interactive data collection. Some qualitative researchers, for example, have collected data after gaining the confidence of persons potentially involved in illegal activities. Other researchers have investigated controversial and politically sensitive topics. When researchers study, say, drugs on campus, lesbian and gay youth, and violence in schools or families, profound ethical dilemmas arise.

Researchers may also be drawn unexpectedly into morally problematic situations. Some typical questions that a qualitative inquirer may face are Do I observe this abuse, or do I turn away from it? Do I record this confession, and if I do record it, do I put it in a public report? If I see abuse or neglect, do I report it to the officials? Am I really seeing abuse or projecting my own values into the situation? If I promised confidentiality when I entered the field, am I breaking my bargain if I interfere? These questions suggest that it is difficult to separate research ethics from professional ethics and personal morality.

Most qualitative researchers devise roles that elicit cooperation, trust, openness, and acceptance. Sometimes, researchers assume helping roles, dress in a certain manner, or allow themselves to be manipulated. When people adjust their priorities and routines to help a researcher or even tolerate his or her presence, they are giving of themselves. A researcher is indebted to these persons and should devise ways to reciprocate, within the constraints of research and personal ethics. Some researchers prefer to collaborate with their informants and share authorship. Reciprocity can be the giving of time, feedback, attention, appropriate token gifts, or specialized services. Some inquirers, upon completion of the report, become advocates for a particular group in the larger community, including policy-making groups.

Research Ethics in Fieldwork

Most qualitative researchers use discussion and negotiation to resolve ethical dilemmas in fieldwork. Negotiations revolve around obtaining consensus on situational priorities.

Informed Consent as a Dialogue   In gaining permission, most researchers give participants assurances of confidentiality and anonymity and describe the intended use of the data. Institutional review boards (IRBs) require a protocol for informed consent to be signed by each participant. As Malone (2003) demonstrates, the typical protocol is usually not accurate for most qualitative research because one cannot anticipate what will be intrusive for each participant.[4]

Many researchers (L. M. Smith, 1990) view informed consent as a dialogue with each new participant. However, in some situations, such a dialogue is impossible—for instance, in a sudden and unexpected trauma that brings persons to the scene during the observation or the observation of public behavior in a crowd. Usually, the time required for participation and the noninterfering, nonjudgmental research role is explained. Informants select interview times and places. Because researchers need to establish trusting relationships, they plan how to handle the dialogue. Most participants can detect and reject insincerity and manipulation.

Confidentiality and Anonymity   The settings and participants should not be identifiable in print. Thus, locations and features of settings are typically disguised to appear similar to several possible places, and researchers routinely code names of people and places (see Excerpt 12.11). Officials and participants should review a report before it is finally released. Researchers have a dual responsibility: to protect the individuals' confidences from other persons in the setting and to protect the informants from the general reading public.

Research Navigator.c⊛m

12.5 Reciprocity
Accession No.: 4783375

Research Navigator.c⊛m

12.6 Consent Strategies
Accession No.: 11985252

EXCERPT 12.11   Anonymity of School and Persons

Most of the data . . . were collected . . . in several urban communities in San Diego . . . and in one urban high school. . . . We refer to this school by the pseudonym, Aux-ilio High School. The names of all the participants are also pseudonyms. (p. 235)

Source: From Stanton-Salazar, R. D., & Spina, S. U. (2003). Informal mentors and role models in the lives of urban Mexican-origin adolescents. *Anthropology and Education Quarterly, 34*(3), 231–254.

However, the law does *not* protect researchers if the government compels them to disclose matters of confidence. The report, the field notes, and the researcher can all be subpoenaed. For example, one researcher was asked to be an expert witness in a school desegregation case. The researcher initiated the "ethical principle of dialogue" (L. M. Smith, 1990, p. 271) in presenting the dilemma to several school officials for mutual problem solving. Finally, a top official said the lawyer would not call the researcher as a witness because it violated the confidentiality commitments. Spradley (1979) suggests that one should consider an alternative project if protecting informants is not possible.

Privacy and Empowerment   Deception violates informed consent and privacy. Although some well-known ethnographers have posed as hobos, vagrants, and even army recruits (Punch, 1994), they claim that no harm to informants resulted from their research. However, even informed persons who cooperate may feel a sense of betrayal upon reading the research findings in print.

Field workers negotiate with participants so that they understand the power that they have in the research process. This power and the mutual problem solving that results from it may be an exchange for the privacy lost by participating in a study (Lincoln, 1990).

Feminist researchers may focus on communitarian ethics, rather than the normal research ethics (Denzin, 1997). The mission of social science is to enable community life to transform itself. From this perspective, qualitative research is "authentically sufficient when it fulfills three conditions: represents multiple voices, enhances moral discernment, and promotes social transformation" (Christians, 2000, p. 145). These inquirers focus more on general morality rather on than professional ethics per se.

Caring and Fairness   Although physical harm to informants seldom occurs in qualitative research, some persons may experience humiliation and loss of trust. Justifying the possible harm to one individual because it may help others is unacceptable. A sense of caring and fairness must be part of the researcher's thinking, actions, and personal morality.

Many inquirers argue for *committed relativism* or *reasonableness* in particular situations. Open discussions and negotiation usually promote fairness to the participants and to the research inquiry.

STANDARDS OF ADEQUACY

Qualitative designs are judged by several criteria. Following are the questions readers typically ask about a qualitative design before accepting the study as evidence-based inquiry:

1. Is the one phenomenon investigated clearly articulated and delimited?
2. Are the qualitative approach (i.e., ethnographic, grounded theory, critical) and the purpose of the study stated?

3. Are the research questions focused and phrased to discover and describe the how's and why's of the phenomenon?
4. Which purposeful sampling technique(s) were selected to obtain information-rich informants or sites? Are the informants described and is the type of site obtained identified? If potentially useful groups were not selected, is a rationale presented?
5. Did the sample size seem logical, given the research purpose, time, and resources?
6. Is the design presented in sufficient detail to enhance validity? That is, does it specify essential strategies such as prolonged field work, collection of verbatim accounts with descriptive data, and negative case search? If the design was modified during data collection, is justification presented for the change?
7. Which multimethod data collection strategies were employed to ensure agreement between the researcher and informants? Did the researcher have knowledge and experience with the primary strategy used? How were different data collection strategies employed?
8. If multiple researchers or participant researchers collected data, how were issues of data quality handled?
9. Which strategies did the researcher employ to enhance reflexivity? Did these seem appropriate to the study?
10. Which design components were included to encourage the usefulness and the logical extensions of the findings? Could others have been incorporated into the study? If so, which ones?
11. Does the researcher specify how informed consent, confidentiality, and anonymity were handled? Was any form of reciprocity employed? If any design decisions were made due to ethical considerations, is the justification reasonable?

SUMMARY

The following statements summarize the major aspects of qualitative research design:

1. Qualitative researchers study participants' perspectives—feelings, thoughts, beliefs, ideals—and actions in natural situations.
2. Qualitative researchers use interactive strategies to collect data for exploratory, explanatory, and emancipatory studies.
3. Qualitative researchers employ emergent designs.
4. A case study design focuses on one phenomenon to understand in depth, regardless of the number of persons or sites in the study.
5. Case studies are significant for theory, practice, policy, and social action stimulus.
6. Purposeful sampling is selecting small samples of information-rich cases to study in depth without desiring to generalize to all such cases.
7. Types of purposeful sampling include site selection, comprehensive sampling, maximum variation sampling, network sampling, and sampling by case type.
8. Sample size depends on the purpose of the study, the data collection strategies, and the availability of information-rich cases.
9. Data collection and analysis are interactive and occur in overlapping cycles.

10. The use of research strategies rather than procedures allows for flexibility to study and corroborate each new idea as it occurs in data collection.
11. The five phases of qualitative research are planning, beginning data collection, basic data collection, closing data collection, and formal data analysis and diagrams.
12. The validity of a qualitative design is the degree to which the interpretations and concepts have mutual meanings between the participants and researcher.
13. Qualitative researchers enhance validity by making explicit all aspects of their designs.
14. Data collection strategies to increase validity are a combination of the following strategies: prolonged field work, multimethod, verbatim accounts, low-inference descriptors, multiple researchers, mechanically recorded data, participant researcher, member checking, participant review, and negative case reporting.
15. Qualitative researchers employ interpersonal subjectivity to collect data and reflex strategies or evidence-based inquiry.
16. Qualitative studies aim at extension of findings, rather than generalization of results. Generalizability is usually not the intent of the study.
17. Design components that enhance the extension of findings are specification of the researcher role, informant selection, the social context, data collection and

analysis strategies, authentic narrative, typicality, analytical premises, and alternative explanations.

18. Field researchers employ dialogue and reciprocity while following ethical and legal principles with participants.

RESEARCH NAVIGATOR NOTES

The following articles will help you understand the content of this chapter. Go to the education database (included in the EBSCO database) in Research Navigator; use the Accession Number provided to find the article.

12.1   Qualitative Challenges
Pilcher, J. (2001). Engaging to transform: Hearing black women's voices. *International Journal of Qualitative Studies in Education*, 14(3), 283–304. Accession Number: 4783379.

12.2   Design Issues
Lloyd-Jones, G. (2003). Design and control issues in qualitative case study research. *International Journal of Qualitative Methods*, 2(2), 1–19. Accession Number: 10609946.

12.3   Verification Strategies
Morse, J. M., Barrett, M., Mayan, M., Olson, K., & Spiers, J. (2002). Verification strategies for establishing reliability and validity in qualitative research. *International Journal of Qualitative Methods*, 1(2), 1–19. Accession Number: 10614549.

12.4   Reflexivity
Pillow, W. (2003). Confession, catharsis, or cure? Rethinking the uses of reflexivity as methodological power in qualitative research. *International Journal of Qualitative Studies in Education*, 16(2), 175–197. Accession Number: 9756739.

12.5   Reciprocity
Zigo, D. (2001). Rethinking reciprocity: Collaboration in labor as a path toward equalizing power in classroom research. *International Journal of Qualitative Studies in Education*, 14(3), 351–366. Accession Number: 4783375.

12.6   Consent Strategies
Malone, S. (2003). Ethics at home: Informed consent in your own backyard. *International Journal of Qualitative Studies in Education*, 14(3), 283–304. Accession Number: 11985252.

CHECK YOURSELF

Multiple-choice review items, with answers, are available on the Companion Website for this book:

www.ablongman.com/mcmillanschumacher6e.

APPLICATION PROBLEMS

1. The director of an inner-city preschool program wants to obtain parent perspectives of the program. She is especially interested in this year's innovation in one class: a parent education program. Materials are sent home twice a week for a parent or guardian to work with the child, and records of teacher/parent contacts are made. There are twelve children in the preschool class. Four children live with a single parent, six live with both parents, and two children live with one parent and their grandparents.
   a. What type of sampling is appropriate and why? (probability or purposeful)
   b. How should the sampling be done?
   c. Which qualitative strategies would be appropriate?

2. A researcher is interested in how principals make decisions about retention of elementary schoolchildren. How would you design this study?

3. A researcher wants to understand the concept of site-based school management. He has located a school district that has spent one year in planning and writing guidelines for site-based management at six selected schools. The researcher is primarily interested in how a site-based management team operates and whether this affects the role of the principal and the school's relationship to the district central management. A site-based management team consists of six members from the community and three teachers plus the principal as an ad hoc

member. A central office facilitator frequently attends the monthly meetings after conducting six orientation sessions. How would you design the study?

a. Which type of sampling is appropriate and why? (probability or purposeful)
b. How should the sampling be done?
c. Which qualitative methods would be appropriate?

4. For Problem 1 above, which research strategies could increase design validity, enhance reflexivity, and encourage extension of findings?
5. For Problem 3 above, which research strategies could enhance design validity, enhance reflexivity, and foster extension of findings?

NOTES

1. *Case study design* does not refer to a *case study*—that is, a study that may employ both qualitative and quantitative researcher techniques without comparison groups and not an in-depth study.
2. See Bogdan and Biklen (2003), Giesne and Pushkin (1992), Marshall and Rossman (1999), Strauss and Corbin (1999), Stake (1995), Le Compte and Preissle (1993), and Lincoln and Guba (1985).

3. Bogan and Biklen (2003) call an examination of subunits a *multicase study*. A multicase study is *not* a multisite study, which uses a modified analytical induction approach, frequently with multiple researchers.
4. Malone (2003) rewrote an informed consent letter to represent what actually occurred in interviews from her study and concluded that no one would have signed the revised version.

Qualitative Strategies

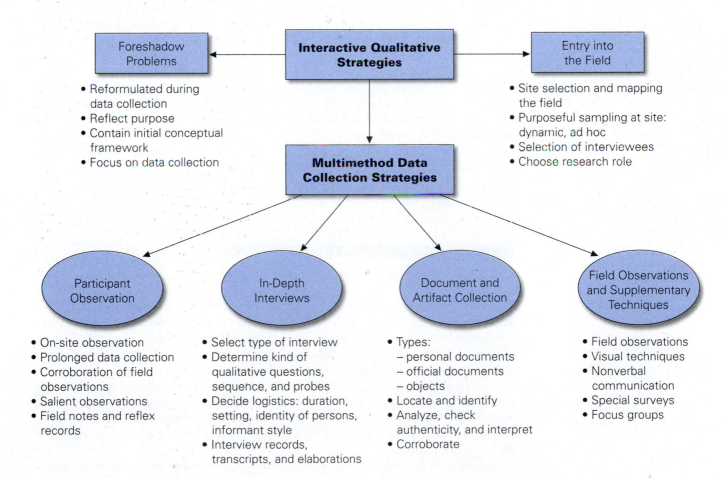

Interactive Qualitative Strategies

Foreshadow Problems
- Reformulated during data collection
- Reflect purpose
- Contain initial conceptual framework
- Focus on data collection

Entry into the Field
- Site selection and mapping the field
- Purposeful sampling at site: dynamic, ad hoc
- Selection of interviewees
- Choose research role

Multimethod Data Collection Strategies

Participant Observation
- On-site observation
- Prolonged data collection
- Corroboration of field observations
- Salient observations
- Field notes and reflex records

In-Depth Interviews
- Select type of interview
- Determine kind of qualitative questions, sequence, and probes
- Decide logistics: duration, setting, identity of persons, informant style
- Interview records, transcripts, and elaborations

Document and Artifact Collection
- Types:
  – personal documents
  – official documents
  – objects
- Locate and identify
- Analyze, check authenticity, and interpret
- Corroborate

Field Observations and Supplementary Techniques
- Field observations
- Visual techniques
- Nonverbal communication
- Special surveys
- Focus groups

KEY TERMS

multimethod	informal conversation interview
strategies	interview guide approach
foreshadowed problems	standardized open-ended interview
holistic emphasis	key informant interviews
mapping the field	career and life history interviews
research role	elite interviews
participant observation	phenomenlogical interviews
field residence	interview probes
field notes	interview elaborations
reflex records	artifact collections
in-depth interview	focus group interview

Many of us are familiar with using conversations and observations as ways of acquiring useful information about our students, our colleagues, the organizations in which we work, and even our friends and families. We interpret our observations and share with others brief stories about what we learned. Forms of conversations and observations are also the primary data collection strategies in qualitative research.

Qualitative research is interactive, face-to-face research, which requires a relatively extensive amount of time to systematically observe, interview, and record processes as they occur naturally. Data collection strategies focus on what the phenomenon means to *participants*. Despite considerable variation among qualitative studies, common methodological strategies distinguish this style of evidenced-based inquiry: participant observation, in-depth interviews, and artifact collection. Most qualitative studies are exploratory or explanatory and aim to understand people's views of their world. Other studies in the critical traditions employ the same techniques but for an emancipatory purpose. This chapter presents entry into the field, selecting an appropriate research role, interactive research strategies, supplementary techniques, and standards for appraising qualitative methods.

MULTIMETHOD STRATEGIES

Most qualitative research depends on the use of multimethod strategies to collect data. **Multimethod** means that multiple strategies are used to collect and corroborate the data obtained from any single data collection strategy and/or to confirm data within a single strategy. Qualitative researchers, called *field workers*, assume that any data can be corroborated during data collection. For example, data from the direct observation of elementary classes could be confirmed with casual interviews of teachers and pupils and more formal interviews with the principal and central supervisor. A study of a school system's politics and bureaucracy could corroborate the data with interviews, observations of meetings and hearings, press coverage of events, newsletters of interest groups, and reports of the board of education.

Qualitative researchers think of participant observation, interviewing, artifact analysis, field observation, and supplementary techniques as *strategies*. Researchers prefer strategies, rather than rigid step-by-step procedures. **Strategies** are sampling and data collection techniques that are continually being refined throughout the data collection process to increase data validity. The use of strategies permits the research design to emerge or to be partially shaped as data are collected and analyzed.

Researchers usually select one primary data collection strategy, such as participant observation or interviews, and use other strategies to verify the most important findings before completely leaving the field. How each strategy is employed is stated in the final report. Researchers determine the most practical, feasible, efficient, and ethical methods for collecting data as the research progresses. Use of multimethod strategies also enhances the credibility of the study.

We will discuss each of the following strategies in this chapter: participant observation, in-depth interviews, artifact collection, field observation, and supplementary strategies.

FORESHADOWED PROBLEMS AND REFORMULATIONS

Qualitative researchers begin with **foreshadowed problems:** anticipated research problems that will be reformulated in the field during data collection. Foreshadowed problems are typically broadly phrased research questions about the participants (e.g., time, place, events), such as *What* happens? *Why* does it happen? and *How* does it happen? Such questions can focus on the structure and the processes operating in different social scenes and experiences.

Qualitative research problems can be derived from several possible sources: common, recurring everyday events in education or personal experiences; ideologies and philosophies; theories; prior research; and problems and ideas identified by others in the setting. In other words, empirical problems exist all around, in varying forms, and for the most part they need only to be recognized for their possibilities. There is almost an intuitive feel for research problems in the form of such questions as I wonder what will happen now that . . . ? and What does this event really mean to the participants? Recognizing a possible research problem is a cognitive skill. Researchers have their curiosity aroused or are puzzled about the *whys* and *hows* of what they observe and experience. Qualitative researchers study theory and previous research as much as other researchers do, but they purposely put aside this knowledge until their experience in the field suggests its relevance.

The statement of foreshadowed problems indicates that the researcher has tentatively decided the research purpose, research questions, and focus of data collection strategies. Most foreshadowed problems have a descriptive emphasis.

Question Reformulations

Discovering participant meanings necessitates problem reformulation in the field. Foreshadowed problems are *not* preconceived ideas but represent a working knowledge of facts, issues, concepts, and theories that guide the decisions made during data collection. Qualitative research has an eclectic approach toward the use of theories in a study. In general, theories can influence research questions in two ways: by generating research questions and by providing conceptual frameworks in phrasing initial questions. Researchers who enter the field with several conceptual frameworks can recognize more easily the events that will lead to expanding the latent meanings.

Focus of Data Collection Strategies

Foreshadowed problems indicate the focus for data collection. This is particularly important for selecting the sites for participant observation and for selecting participants for in-depth interviews.

MISCONCEPTION   Interviewing is easy. After all, it's just talking to someone.

EVIDENCE   Researchers report difficulty in gaining the trust of some people and in adjusting to their individual communication styles while recording data.

EXCERPT 13.1 Foreshadowed Problems Reformulated

This study began in a similar vein [to prior disability research], attempting to identify specific educational practices that contribute to the success of a model inclusion program in an urban elementary school . . . in a culturally diverse community. During the year-long . . . [data collec-tion], it became apparent . . . that educational practices were one aspect of a larger school culture that was wholly supportive of inclusion. By identifying the characteristics of the "inclusive school culture," we hope to inform future efforts to implement inclusion programs. (p. 157)

Source: From Zollers, N. J., Ramanathan, A. K., & Yu, M. (1999). The relationship between school culture and inclusion: How an inclusive culture supports inclusive education. *International Journal of Qualitative Studies in Education, 12*(2), 157–174.

Foreshadowed problems do *not*, however, restrict the research because more research questions evolve during the lengthy field work (see Excerpt 13.1).

ENTRY INTO THE FIELD

Careful analysis of the foreshadowed problems will suggest criteria for site and/or social scene for participant observation. A similar analysis will suggest the profiles of individuals to be sampled for in-depth interviews. We discuss each of these strategies for entrance into the field. In the negotiations to obtain formal permission to conduct qualitative study, the researcher also makes explicit the research role to be assumed for data collection.

Site Selection and Mapping the Field

Choosing a site is a negotiation process to obtain freedom of access to a site that is *suitable* for the research problems and *feasible* for the researcher's resources of time, mobility, and skills. The field researcher usually obtains information in advance through informal channels. Useful information includes the identities, power alignments, and interests of the principal actors; the general history, routines, and social system of the site; and the activities of the site. Information regarding the site and its potential suitability is obtained from a variety of sources: documents, present and prior associates, and public information. Much depends on the researcher's good judgment, timing, and tact in gathering information informally.

After the researcher identifies a possible site, contact is made with a person who can grant permission for the research. Some researchers make a formal contact after informal confirmation that the research proposal will be positively reviewed (see Excerpt 13.2). Most prepare a brief written statement that specifies the site, the participants and activities, the length of time for the entire study, and the research role. The statement also provides information about the researcher, the sponsor or organizational affiliation, and the general uses of the data, including the protection of the rights of human subjects. Access to the site and the people are crucial at this time. Formal authorization is essential for research ethics and for proceeding to enter the field and establish a research role. Once authorization has been granted, the researcher disengages himself or herself from the leadership of the site to map the field, conduct purposeful sampling, and establish a research role.

Qualitative research describes and interprets any subset of context-bound data within the larger context of the site. This characteristic is often referred to as a **holistic empha-sis:** Subcases of data are related to the total context of the phenomenon studied. Although all that occurs within a setting is a potential source of data, participant observers cannot and do not need to observe *everything*, but they can obtain sufficient data for a holistic emphasis. By using mapping strategies, the researcher gains a sense of the totality and is in a better position to do purposeful sampling of information-rich cases.

EXCERPT 13.2   Gaining Access to Mr. Wilson's Class and Reciprocity

I prepared a full-length research proposal for Mr. Wilson and the principal . . . describing my data collection methods, my questions and the literature review. . . . Both were concerned about how Mr. Wilson would be represented in the final report and what mechanism would be in place for Mr. Wilson to review the findings. . . . In exchange for Mr.

Wilson's participation, I provided the following at the end of the study: (a) a three-week unit of instruction tailored to his students' needs that I would teach, (b) a full report disclosing the findings prior to any publication, and (c) and opportunity to present the findings of the study at a major conference. (pp. 131–132)

Source: From Case, R. E. (2004). Forging ahead into new social networks and looking back to past social identities: A case study of a foreign-born English as a second language teacher in the United States. *Urban Education, 39*(2), 125–148.

Mapping the Field   Gaining entry into the field requires establishing good relations with all individuals at the research site. Research permission comes without a guarantee that the participants will behave naturally before an outsider who takes field notes or that the participants will share their perceptions, thoughts, and feelings with the observer. The inquirer's skill is reflected in whether the participants see the researcher as an interested, respectful, nonjudgmental observer who maintains confidentiality or whether as a rude, disruptive, critical observer who cannot be trusted. The researcher must attend to maintaining the trust and confidentiality of the participants constantly throughout the data collection period. At any time, the participants may decline to share their perceptions, feelings, and thoughts with the ethnographer.

Research Navigator.com

13.1 Mapping the Site
Accession No.: 7532962

   Mapping the field is acquiring data of the social, spatial, and temporal relationships in the site to gain a sense of the total context (see Excerpt 13.3). A *social map* notes the numbers and kinds of people, the organizational structure, and the activities people engage in. A *spatial map* notes the locations, the facilities, and the specialized services provided. A *temporal map* describes the rhythm of organizational life, the schedules, and the unwritten routines.

Purposeful Sampling at Site   Once researchers have initially mapped the field, they selectively choose the persons, situations, and events most likely to yield fruitful data about the evolving research questions. Initially, researchers search for information-rich informants, groups, places, and events from which to select subunits for more in-depth study. Remember, purposeful sampling is a strategy to choose small groups or individuals likely to be knowledgeable and informative about the phenomenon of interest. Furthermore, most researchers do not know in advance whether potentially information-rich cases will yield valid data until they have completed an interim data analysis. Thus, comprehensive sampling is usually planned initially, followed by additional strategies. As new questions emerge during data collection, participant observers change (through additional purposeful sampling) the observation times and locations in order to collect valid data (see Excerpt 13.4).

EXCERPT 13.3   Mapping the Field

I attended Barton School on a daily basis between February 1997 and June 1998, after first obtaining permission. . . . During the initial phase of the study (February–June 1997)

I became acquainted with the school and its routines, and the students and staff also gradually became used to my presence around the school and corridors. (p. 52)

Source: From Olivo, W. (2003). "Quit talking and learn English!": Conflicting language ideologies in an ESL classroom. *Anthropology and Education Quarterly, 34*(1), 50–71.

EXCERPT 13.4   On-Site Participant Observer, Additional Purposeful Sampling

I observed the class over 30 times, interviewed the teachers both individually and together, and attended a number of related school events. I soon became aware that their collaboration was connected to school wide efforts to enhance sensitivity to diversity, this in response to a wave of neo-Nazi hate literature on campus. . . . I broadened my investigation, attending committee meetings related to diversity (the Multicultural Advisory Committee, the Multi-cultural Non-Sexist Committee, etc.) and asking questions about these efforts in interviews with administrators and teachers.

Data collection spanned the fall semester. . . . [I conducted] 19 hour-long interviews, observed 53 school events, gathered school and community artifacts, and maintained the fieldwork log and journal. (p. 308)

Source: From DiPardo, A. (2000). What a little hate literature will do: "Cultural Issues" and the emotional aspect of school change. *Anthropology and Education Quarterly, 31*(3), 306–332.

Field workers view selection and sampling strategies as dynamic and ad hoc rather than static or a priori parameters of populations for a research design. Thus, purposeful sampling is a process conducted simultaneously as one collects data. The specification of the selection criteria and the purposeful sampling strategies chosen are reported in a study to reduce threats to design validity. In addition, the person or groups who actually participated in the study are reported in a manner to protect confidentiality of data.

Selection of Interviewees

Selecting persons for in-depth interviews begins with describing the desired attributes or profile of persons who would have knowledge of the topic. An *attribute* is that each person has had a similar experience, such as voluntary resignation from an administrative position, experience with the death of a child, or former participation in a program.

Locating possible interviewees can be done by using records, an informal network, or nomination. Examples of records are memberships and required registrations, such as an application for a program or special service. When each person does not interact in face-to-face situations with others known to have similar experiences, *snowball sampling* is essential (see Chapter 12). Interviewees may also be nominated by reputation, such as the best teacher or coach.

Researchers screen each potential interviewee by the attribute or profile developed for the study. Only individuals who meet the criteria are interviewed in depth.

Research Role

Field workers choose a **research role**—a relationship acquired by and ascribed to the researcher in interactive data collection—appropriate for the purpose of the study. Possible roles are *complete observer, full participant, participant observer, insider observer, interviewer,* and the dual role of *participant-researcher* (see Table 13.1). These roles vary in terms of the way the researcher's presence affects the social system and the persons under study. The roles of complete observer or of full participant are seldom if ever assumed.

The roles of participant observer and interviewer are the typical research roles for most forms of qualitative inquiry. The field worker in each instance receives permission to create the role for the sole purpose of data collection. The participant observer obtains permission from the organization or cultural group; the field worker then has to establish his or her research role with each person or group selected for study. In contrast, the interviewer begins to establish the research role in the first contact with the person

TABLE 13.1   Possible Interactive Research Roles

Role	Description	Use	Research Approach
Complete observer	Researcher is physically and psychologically absent	Inappropriate	Other types of research
Full participant	Researcher lives through an experience and recollects personal insight	Inappropriate	None
Participant observer	Researcher creates role for purpose of study	Typical role	Ethnography Case study Some critical studies
Insider observer	Researcher has a formal position in organization	Inappropriate	Extremely rare (depends on topic)
Interviewer	Researcher establishes a role with each person interviewed	Typical role	Phenomenological studies Grounded theory Some critical studies
Participant researcher	Researcher establishes a dual role for purpose of study	Very difficult to do both roles simultaneously	Critical studies: participatory action research, action inquiry

when requesting an appointment and explaining the purpose and confidentiality. The interviewee selects the time and place for the interview. In phenomenological studies, interviewers may return three or more times to each person to acquire an understanding of his or her lived experience.

More questionable roles are those of the insider observer and participant researcher. The insider observer is a person who already has a role in the site in which he or she intends to study. The role (i.e., supervisor, counselor, teacher) exists whether or not the study is conducted. Even studies on highly sensitive topics, which probably could not have been done otherwise, have difficulty being accepted as credible research (see Excerpt 13.5). Some critical studies employ the dual role of participant researcher. This role is conducted simultaneously and requires the researcher to have constant self-awareness and be especially conscious about whose voice is being recorded as data. Because the data contain the researcher's reflections on his or her experience as well as those of the real participants, the dual-role researcher must be exceedingly sensitive regarding which voice is represented in the study.

EXCERPT 13.5   Research Role Variation, Personal Experience Insights

An ethnographic [study] is informed by relationships . . . best characterized as that between a researcher and subject. In other instances, I was first a fellow student, tutor, mentor, classroom instructor, or friend, and only later took on the role of researcher. The variety of roles I occupied vis-a-vis the subjects of my study complicated, but also added insight to my work. . . . Finally, in terms of background and initial interest in the intellectual life of student athletes, my work bears the influence of my experiences as an intercollegiate athlete on a . . . NCAA Division 1 wrestling team. (p. 302)

Source: From Foster, K. M. (2003). Panopticonics: The control and surveillance of black female athletes in a collegiate athletic program. *Anthropology and Education Quarterly, 34*(3), 300–323.

ALERT! Even when experienced researchers assume the participant researcher role, their work is scrutinized thoroughly for credibility issues.

The research role is really many roles, as the field worker acquires language fluency with the participants, interacts to obtain data, establishes social relationships, and moves from role sets appropriate for one group (or person) to different role sets for other groups (or persons). Some degree of participation is usually necessary to develop trust and acceptance of the outsider and for reciprocity. In addition, the research role may vary with the degree of interaction and intensity. For example, in many ethnographic studies, case studies, and grounded theory approaches the interactions are quite widespread but the researcher is less intrusive in collecting data. In phenomenological studies, the interaction is more intrusive, close, and personal. Unlike mechanical recording devices, field workers are able to raise additional questions, check out hunches, and move deeper into the analysis of the phenomenon.

Valid data results when the events unfold naturally and the participants act in typical fashion in the reseacher's presence. Because the research role affects the type of data collected, the primary role and the various roles assumed in data collection are stated in the study.

PARTICIPANT OBSERVATION

Participant observation is really a combination of particular data collection strategies: limited participation, field observation, interviewing, and artifact collection. Limited participation is necessary to obtain acceptance of the researcher's presence, even though she or he is unobtrusive. Field observation is the researcher's technique of directly observing and recording without interaction. Interviewing may be in the form of casual conversations after an event with others or more formal interviews with one person. Documents and artifacts are collected when available. Typically, the researcher uses multiple strategies to corroborate data (see Excerpt 13.6).

Decisions regarding data collection strategies are usually revised after site selection, entry into the field, and initial mapping of the field. Initial plans are reviewed and refined. Information originally planned to be obtained by observation may be available primarily through interviewing; preliminary findings from interview data may have to be substantiated through researcher-constructed questionnaires or artifact analysis. Analysis of documents or unexpected events may suggest new directions for observing or interviewing. Choosing data collection strategies is a process of deciding among available alternatives

EXCERPT 13.6 Multiple Data Collection Strategies

Our year-long ethnography employed participant observation, formal and informal interviewing, and document review. . . . Participant observation in the school milieu allowed us to unobtrusively and systematically obtain data and interact socially with informants. . . . We visited the school at least once a week. On the days of our visits, we participated in the school, shadowing the principal, visiting classrooms, and talking to parents and staff in the halls. We observed teachers, students and staff during the regular course of the school day and during special events. (p. 161)

Source: From Zollers, N. J., Ramanathan, A. K., & Yu, M. (1999). The relationship between school culture and inclusion: How an inclusive culture supports inclusive education. *Qualitative Studies in Education, 12*(2), 157–174.

for collection and corroboration of data and of modifying one's decisions to capture the reality of the phenomena.

Onsite Participant Observation

The most elementary requirement of the methodology is **field residence,** in which the researcher is present in the field or site for an extensive time (see Excerpt 13.7). Field work is often viewed as a labor-intensive mode of inquiry. Many field studies focus on processes over time and note change.

Prolonged Data Collection

Data collection continues until the logical termination of a naturalistic event or until the situation changes so dramatically that the site is not relevant for the research focus. For instance, the natural boundary for data collection may be the entire three-week period of a state-sponsored summer school arts program. The natural boundary for a study of nursing clinical instruction will be the length of the rotation, or ten weeks. When the examined situation is no longer relevant to the research foci, the field residence terminates. Data collection might also end with the unexpected promotion or resignation of a key person, which, of course, would remove him or her from the site.

Intensive Observing and Listening

Participant observation enables the researcher to obtain people's perceptions of events and processes expressed in their actions and expressed as feelings, thoughts, and beliefs. These perceptions or constructions take three forms: verbal, nonverbal, and tacit knowledge. It is crucial that the researcher acquire the particular linguistic patterns and language variations of the individuals observed to record and to interact with them. Field observation is an active process that includes *nonverbal cues*—facial expressions, gestures, tone of voice, body movements, and other unverbalized social interactions that suggest the subtle meanings of language. *Tacit knowledge* is personal, intuitive knowledge that is difficult or impossible for the individual to articulate; instead, the person demonstrates this knowledge by actions or by created objects. Some cultures are called *expressive* because meanings are conveyed more in the nonverbal and tacit modes than in the verbal mode. Participants' stories, anecdotes, and myths—such as are found in the daily gossip in the teachers' lounge or among student groups in hallways—indicate the content of their world and how they perceive it.

Listening is also a demanding task; researchers listen with all their senses. Listening involves being able to take on the role of the other person, to see the world as the

EXCERPT 13.7   Prolonged Field Time

Data collection for my research began in November 1997 and ended in July 1999. My key informants included 65 students, 6 principals, 23 teachers, and 10 staff members (including counselors for minority students, resource specialists, family-school liaisons, a social worker, a support staff, and a security officer). I approached the individuals in my study with broad questions regarding the significance of race, their racial and ethnic identity, and race relations at Hope High. (p. 162)

Source: From Lei, J. L. (2003). (Un)necessary toughness? Those "loud Black girls" and those "quiet Asian boys." *Anthropology and Education Quarterly, 34*(2), 158–181.

participant does. The field worker listens for the words *is* and *because. Is* reveals perceptions of things, people, events, and processes that appear real or factual to a person. *Because* reveals the *whys* and *wherefores*, the beliefs, thoughts, feelings, and values—in essence, the logic about the content of a person's perceptions. To listen intently requires the researcher to put aside his or her own thoughts and seek first those of the participants.

Corroborating Field Observations

Although the field worker is noninterfering, he or she actively seeks different views of events from different participants for accuracy and for confirmation. By extended observation of different participants in many contexts, the researcher elicits data that are almost impossible to obtain with other approaches. Ethnographers can, for example, corroborate what a participant says in response to a comment or question, to other people, in different situations, or at different times; what the participant actually does; what the participant implies with nonverbal communication, such as tone of voice and body movements; and what he or she perceives others are feeling, saying, or doing about an activity. The core of seeking and corroborating different perceptions lies in obtaining data from multiple data sources—different persons in different contexts at various times.

In seeking to corroborate data, researchers frequently discover discrepancies between what people say and what they do in their observed actions. Participant observation allows corroboration between what individuals think they are doing and what the researcher thinks they are doing based on data.

Salient Field Observations

Because the interactive social scene is too complex and too subtle to observe or record everything, researchers do *not* seek to capture everything that happens. Rather, they rely on the prolonged field residences to develop skills in deciding what should be included and what can be excluded. Researchers observe and record the phenomena salient to the foreshadowed problems, their broader conceptual frameworks, and the contextual features of the interactions. These elements explain the diversity of field notes cited in ethnographies despite the commonalities on the methodology (see Excerpt 13.8).

What do field workers observe? Most record descriptive details about *who, what, where, how,* and *why* an activity or social scene occurred. This information then can be used to obtain more subtle information. See Table 13.2 for a participant observation grid. Although no one addresses all these questions at once in studying a group scene, the framework does indicate major areas of observation foci.

Field Notes and Reflex Records

Data are recorded as **field notes,** or observations of what occurs while the researcher is in the field. Field notes are dated and the context is identified. The notes are often filled with idiosyncratic abbreviations and are difficult for others to read without editing. Researchers record detailed descriptive fields that are not vague or judgmental. Following

EXCERPT 13.8 Salient Field Observations

In its early phases, the study focused on how district leaders and school principals thought about and led district-wide reform in elementary literacy. As the district added mathematics to its agenda, the study shifted to include interviews and observations with principals, district leaders, and teachers surrounding ways in which they saw the mathematics work as both similar and different from the literacy work. (p. 425)

Source: From Stein, M. K., & Nelson, B. S. (2003). Leadership content knowledge. *Educational Evaluation and Policy Analysis, 25* (4), 423–448.

TABLE 13.2   Participant Observation Grid

Observation	Description
1. *Who* is in the group or scene?	How many people are present? What are their kinds or identities? How is membership in the group or scene acquired?
2. *What* is happening here?	What are the people in the group or scene doing and saying to one another?
a. *What* behaviors are repetitive and irregular?	In what events, activities, or routines are people engaged? How are activities organized, labeled, explained, and justified?
b. *How* do the people in the group behave toward one another?	How do people organize themselves or relate to one another? What statuses and roles are evident? Who makes what decisions for whom?
c. *What* is the content of their conversations?	What topics are common and rare? What languages do they use for verbal and nonverbal communication? What beliefs do the contents of their conversations illustrate? What formats and processes do the conversations follow? Who talks and who listens?
3. *Where* is the group or scene located?	What physical settings form their contexts? What natural resources and technologies are created or used? How does the group allocate and use space and physical objects? What sights, sounds, smells, tastes, and feelings are found in the group contexts?
4. *When* does the group meet and interact?	How often and how long are these meetings? How does the group conceptualize, use, and distribute time? How do participants view their past and future?
5. *How* do the identified elements interrelate—from either the participants' or the researcher's perspective?	How is stability maintained? How does change originate, and how is it managed? What rules, norms, or mores govern this social organization? How is this group related to other groups, organizations, and institutions?
6. *Why* does the group operate as it does?	What meanings do participants attribute to what they do? What symbols, traditions, values, and worldviews can be found in the group?

are hypothetical examples of vague notes contrasted to the actual field notes in a study of adult beginning readers (Boraks & Schumacher, 1981, pp. 76, 86):

Vague Notes	Descriptive Field Notes
1. Bea misreads *wood* for *would.*	"(OBS: Intensity of Bea is demonstrated by her heavy breathing, even swearing during the reading. There is little doubt she is trying hard.) Sometimes she cues herself, when reading: 'Would you believe I would not do it again,' Bea read *would* as *wood.* The tutor says would. Bea tries again to reread, then says, 'Oh, I missed the point, would he.'"
2. June retells few parts of a story and only the parts that relate to herself. She elaborates on these parts.	"June is a tall, thin, talkative woman. A staff member said she was referred by a treatment center and was considered mentally retarded and emotionally disturbed. When asked to tell a story from the text cue, she had to be prompted. For example, her story about an accident:
	June: 'My hair caught on fire.'
	Tutor: 'How did your hair catch fire? Can you tell me more?'
	June: 'I was smoking a cigarette and my lighter went up. I had the lighter close to my ear and it carried to my hair and my whole head was in flames.'
	Tutor: 'Can you tell me anything more?'
	June: 'And they told me I looked like a Christmas tree all lit up.'"

EXCERPT 13.9   Reflex Notes: Self in Research

Rather than make a futile attempt to eliminate this subjectivity, Horvat engaged in a "formal systematic monitoring of self" throughout the course of the data collection which enabled her to manage her own subjectivity. . . . To this end she wrote self-reflective memos, shared manuscripts of analyzed data with study participants, and discussed emerging themes with colleagues familiar with the project.

Moreover we believe that our backgrounds shape our roles as researchers. Horvat is a married white woman in her early thirties who grew up in . . . the area. . . . She comes from a privileged background. . . . She attended a private secondary school similar to Hadley. The second author . . . is a Filipino male who was raised by immigrant parents. . . . Socioeconomically his upbringing is somewhat dissimilar from that of the majority of the informants in the study. . . . As research collaborators, we took advantage of our different backgrounds by actively engaging each other with challenges to possible biases. (p. 320)

Source: From Horvat, E. M., & Antonio, A. (1999). Hey, those shoes are out of uniform: African American girls in an elite high school and the importance of habitus. *Anthropology and Education Quarterly, 30*(3), 317–342.

Reflex records, written immediately after leaving the site, synthesize the main interactions and scenes observed and, more important, assess the quality of the data, and suggest questions and tentative interpretations. In both the field notes and reflex records, the tentative interpretations are separated from the actual observations (data). Sometimes, these insights have the quality of free associations: They may cite analogies, use metaphors and similes, or note theories and literature that may be useful in subsequent data analysis.

Typically, part of the reflex records is the researcher's critical self-monitoring for potential biases. Often stated as "Self in Research" in the study, the researcher reports biographical sources of subjectivity and strategies to minimize the influence on data collection and analysis (see Excerpt 13.9).

IN-DEPTH INTERVIEWS

In-depth interviews are open-response questions to obtain data of participant meanings—how individuals conceive of their world and how they explain or make sense of the important events in their lives. Interviewing may be the primary data collection strategy or a natural outgrowth of observation strategies. Field interviews vary in formats, specialized applications, question content, question sequence, and the logistics of conducting and recording interviews.

Types of Interviews and Specialized Applications

Qualitative interviews may take several forms: the informal conversational interview, the interview guide approach, and the standardized open-ended interview. These forms all

EXCERPT 13.10   Informal Conversation Interview

Finally, approximately 45 hours of spontaneous interactions among ESL students and their teacher or his assistants in the classroom, as well as interactions among ESL friendship groups inside and outside the school, were recorded on audiocassette. (p. 52)

Source: From Olivo, W. (2003). "Quit talking and learn English!": Conflicting language ideologies in an ESL classroom. *Anthropology and Education Quarterly, 34*(1), 50–71.

EXCERPT 13.11 Semi-Structured Interviews

Semi-structured interviews of 1–2 hours in length were conducted following a predetermined interview guide. [Sexually assaulted] women were asked to describe the nature of the attack that they endured, their immediate re-actions to the assault, and the negative effects that they continued to experience up to the time of the interview. (p. 174)

Source: From Regehr, C. R., Marziali, E., & Jansen, K. (1999). A qualitaitve analysis of strengths and vulnerabilities in sexually assaulted women. *Clinical Social Work Journal, 27*(2), 171–183.

vary in the degree of structure and planning and the comparability of responses in data analysis.

In the **informal conversation interview,** the questions emerge from the immediate context and are asked in the natural course of events; there is no predetermination of question topics or phrasing (see Excerpt 13.10). Informal conversations are an integral part of participant observation. In the **interview guide approach,** topics are selected in advance, but the researcher decides the sequence and wording of the questions during the interview (see Excerpt 13.11). Both the informal conversation and the interview guide approach are relatively conversational and situational. In the **standardized open-ended interview,** participants are asked the same questions in the same order, thus reducing interviewer flexibility; however, standardized wording of questions may constrain and limit the naturalness and relevancy of the response (see Table 13.3).

Selection of the interview strategy depends on the context and purpose: (1) to obtain the present perceptions of activities, roles, feelings, motivations, concerns, and thoughts; (2) to obtain future expectations or anticipated experiences; (3) to verify and extend information obtained from other sources; and/or (4) to verify or extend hunches and ideas developed by the participants or researcher. Specialized applications of the interview strategy are key informant interviews, career and life history interviews, elite interviews, and phenomenological interviews.

Key informant interviews are in-depth interviews of individuals who have special knowledge, status, or communication skills that they are willing to share with the researcher. They are usually chosen because they have access to observations unavailable to the ethnographer. They are often atypical individuals and must be selected carefully from among possible key informants.

Career and life history interviews, which elicit life narratives of individuals, are used by anthropologists to obtain data about a culture. Educational ethnographers use this interview technique to obtain career histories or narratives of professional lives. For example,

TABLE 13.3 Types of Interviews

Type of Interview	Description
Informal conversation	Questions emerge from the immediate context. There are no predetermined topics or wording.
Interview guide	Topics are outlined in advance. Researcher decides the sequence and wording during the interview. Interview probes can increase comprehensiveness.
Standardized open-ended	The exact wording and sequence of questions are predetermined. Questions are completely open-ended.

when an examination of female secondary school teachers' notion of *career* differed from prior research about male teachers' notion of *career*, the researcher suggested that the concept of career should be extended to encompass professional women. Career and life history research of educators frequently requires two- to seven-hour interviews and may take considerable time to locate the informants, if the shared social experience occurred years ago.

Elite interviews are a special application of interviewing that focus on persons considered to be influential, prominent, and well informed in an organization or a community. Elites are usually familiar with the overall view of the organization, its relations to other organizations, and especially the legal and financial structure of the organization. The researcher must rely on sponsorship, recommendations, and introductions to obtain appointments with elites. Frequently, elites prefer a more active interplay with the interviewer, and much variation will occur in the degree of interview control. Elites respond well to inquiries in broad areas of content and to provocative, intelligent questions that allow them freedom to use their knowledge. Elites often contribute insights and meaning because they are comfortable in the realm of ideas, policies, and generalizations.[1]

A **phenomenological interview** is a specific type of in-depth interview used to study the meanings or essence of a lived experience among selected participants (see Excerpt 13.12). The strategy may be a single long comprehensive interview with each person or three separate interviews with each of the individuals.[2] Phenomenological studies investigate what was experienced, how it was experienced, and finally the meanings that the interviewees assign to the experience. The experience studied is usually something that has affected the individual significantly, such as recalling a teenage pregnancy or childhood incest or acquiring a physical disability. Before interviewing, the researcher writes a full description of his or her own experience with the phenomenon of interest. Phenomenological interviews permit an explicit focus on the researcher's personal experience combined with the experiences of the interviewees. Educators frequently apply phenomenological interviewing in a general manner to obtain the multiple meanings of an experience.

Qualitative Questions, Probes, and Pauses

Question content varies because of different research purposes and problems, theoretical frameworks, and the selection of participants. Adopting questions from prior research will probably *not* produce valid interview data; however, the examination of different alternatives is essential in interview script construction. Interview questions can focus on experiences or behaviors, opinions and values, feelings, knowledge, sensory perceptions, and the individual's background or demographic information (see Table 13.4). Each of these question topics can be phrased in a present, past, or future time frame.

Qualitative interviewing requires asking truly open-ended questions. Novice researchers often begin with what data they want to obtain and phrase questions in a manner that enables interviewees to infer the desired responses. These are *dichotomous-response questions*, which elicit yes/no answers or short phrases in response. When these occur, the interview assumes an interrogative rather than a conversational tone.

EXCERPT 13.12 Phenomenological Interviews

Following a phenomenological perspective, we want to understand the insider's viewpoint. . . . Semistructured interviews were conducted. The semistructured format guaranteed that we asked each principal open-ended questions where the researchers had little control over the principals' responses. All interviews were audio taped with participants' permission, and transcribed. Data analysis was ongoing and iterative. (p. 477)

Source: From Goldring, E., Crowson, R., Laird, D., & Berk, R. (2003). Transition leadership in a shifting policy environment. *Educational Evaluation and Policy Analysis, 25*(4), 473–488.

TABLE 13.4   Types of Interview Questions

Type	Description and Illustration
Experience/behavior	To elicit what a person does or has done—descriptions of experiences, behaviors, actions, activities during the ethnographer's absence: "If I had been here that day, what experiences would I see you having?"
Opinions/values	To elicit what the person thinks about his or her experiences, which can reveal a person's intentions, goals, and values: "What would you like to see happen or what do you believe about . . . ?"
Feelings	To elicit how the person reacts emotionally to his or her experiences: "Do you feel anxious, happy, afraid, intimidated, confident about . . . ?"
Knowledge	To elicit factual information the person has or what the person considers as factual: "Tell me what you know about . . ."
Sensory	To elicit the person's descriptions of what and how he or she sees, hears, touches, tastes, and smells in the world: "What does the counselor ask you when you walk into her office? How does she actually greet you?"
Background/demographic	To elicit the person's descriptions of himself or herself to aid the researcher in identifying and locating the person in relation to other people: Routine information on age, education, occupation, residence/mobility, and the like.

Note: Questions may be phrased in past, present, or future tense. See Patton (2002).

Qualitative in-depth interviews are noted more for their *probes* and *pauses* than for their particular question formats. Establishing trust, being genuine, maintaining eye contact, and conveying through phrasing, cadence, and voice tone that the researcher hears and connects with the person elicit more valid data than a rigid approach. After a series of interviews, researchers usually feel at ease in adjusting the interview to each person.

Techniques to ensure good qualitative questions include interview script critiques by experienced interviewers, interview guide field testing, and revision of initial questions for final phraseology (see Excerpt 13.13). Following are examples of initial phrasing with the field-test responses and the final phrasing of an interview guide (Schumacher, Esham, & Bauer, 1985, pp. 150–153):

Initial Dichotomous-Response Questions	Final Qualitative Questions
Q: Did teachers have difficulty in seminars? *R:* Yes.	*Q:* What did you expect teachers to have difficulties with in the seminar?
Q: Did teachers change? *R:* Some of them did.	*Q:* How did participation in the seminar affect the teachers?
Q: Did you learn anything in teaching the seminars? *R:* Yes.	*Q:* What did you learn about the teaching strategies you presented to this group?
Q: Did you identify any problems the planning committee should address? *R:* Yes.	*Q:* What would you like to see the planning committee do?

Research Navigator.c⊕m

13.3 An Interview Study
Accession No.: 10849125

Although this is an extreme example of responses to initial dichotomous-response questions, it is obvious that the qualitative questions would (and did) generate different data, revealing multiple meanings of the seminars.

EXCERPT 13.13 Interview Protocol Piloted

A 17-page [interview] protocol was piloted. The protocol consisted of six sections: general information, general university climate, mentor relationships, other faculty relationships, peer relationships, and influential factors. . . . [We] used items which emerged consistently from the literature that validated the experiences of African Americans in graduate programs. (p. 277)

Source: From Kea, C. D., Penny, J. M., & Bowman, L. J. (2003). The experiences of African American students in special education master's programs at traditionally white institutions. *Teacher Education and Special Education, 26*(4), 273–287.

Dichotomous-response questions can be *leading questions*, which imply a preferred response. Such questions may frame a "devil's advocate" or a *presupposition question*, a query that implies a deliberate assumption designed to provoke a complex or elaborate response. In the examples that follow, those in the left column are dichotomous-response leading questions that were rephrased as presupposition leading questions in the right column (Schumacher, 1984, pp. 75–82):

Dichotomous-Response Leading Questions	Presupposition Leading Questions
Were inservice teachers enthusiastic about taking a class after school hours?	"What were the most difficult aspects [of the program] to implement?" (Presupposition: Many difficulties.)
Did you expect the teachers to be different from from having participated in the seminars?	"How did you expect the teachers to be different from having participated in the seminars?" (Presupposition: There was an immediate change.)
Do you know of any unexpected results or spill-over effects?	"How did the planning committee handle unanticipated opportunities?" (Presupposition: There were unexpected opportunities.)

Some researchers emphasize the general ineffectiveness of questions preceded with the interrogative *why*. *Why* questions are usually assumptive, frequently ambiguous, and often too abstract to elicit concrete data. In some situations, however, beginning with the interrogative *why* enables the researcher to elicit cause-and-effect processes or relationships that are potentially informative by revealing assumptions of the person.

Question Sequence

Effective interviewing depends on efficient probing and sequencing of questions, as suggested in these guidelines:

1. **Interview probes** elicit elaboration of detail, further explanations, and clarification of responses. Well-designed interview scripts are field tested to identify the placement and wording of probes necessary to adjust topics to the variation in individuals' responses. Broad questions are often phrased more specifically as probes. The researcher should talk less than the respondent; the cues the respondent needs can usually be reduced to a few words during the interview.

2. **Statements of the researcher's purpose and focus** are usually made at the outset. Assurances of protection of the person's identity and an overview of the possible discussion topics are also given at this time (see Excerpt 13.14). The information communicated is the importance of the data, the reasons for that importance, and the willingness of the

EXCERPT 13.14   Interview Protocol and Interviewee Language

The interview protocol with the Mexican mothers included open-ended questions to initiate the conversation and to explore the mothers' values and personal experiences in relation to the schools and their children's education. [Footnote 2: *I am a Puerto Rican, native speaker of Spanish and . . . conducted the interviews in Spanish.*] I asked: Have you had an experience in which you had to make a decision about the education of your children and you did not know what to do? How did you solve the problem? If you were to advise Mexican mothers newly arrived in Chicago about the education of their children, what would you advise them? Do you find that it is more difficult to raise your children here or in Mexico? (p. 378)

Source: From Olmedo, I. M. (2003). Accommodation and resistance: Latinas struggle for their children's education. *Anthropology and Education Quarterly, 34*(4), 373–395.

interviewer to explain the purpose of the interview out of respect for the interviewee. Researchers provide explanations or shifts in the interview focus for informants to adapt their thinking along new areas.

3. *Order of questions* varies, although most researchers make choices that enable them to obtain adequate data for each question from the informant efficiently. Rigid sequencing may ensure comprehensiveness, but it may also produce both informant and interviewer fatigue and boredom. Generally, questions are grouped by topic, but in many instances, interviewers ignore the script sequence as people voluntarily elaborate on earlier replies.

4. *Demographic questions* may be spread throughout the interview or presented in the concluding remarks. Some researchers prefer to obtain this data at the beginning of the interview to establish rapport and focus attention.

5. *Complex, controversial, and difficult questions* are usually reserved for the middle or later periods in the interview, when the informant's interest has been aroused. Some interviewers prefer to begin interviews with descriptive, present-oriented questions and move to more complex issues of beliefs and explanations.

Research
Navigator.com

13.4 An Interview Study
Accession No.: 3933327

Interview Logistics

Researchers choose interview topics and questions while planning the general logistics that influence an interview session. Five contingencies that affect an interview session are (1) *duration,* or length of session; (2) *number,* or how many separate interviews are required to obtain the data; (3) *setting,* or location of the interview; (4) *identity of the individuals* involved and the number present in the session; and (5) *informant styles,* or communication mores of the interviewees. Some research designs plan for periodically scheduled interviews, and other designs require interviewing only after important events.

Interviewers vary their interactive styles. The interactive mode can be adversarial, emotionally neutral but cognitively sophisticated, or empathetic. Specific techniques can be used for pacing, keeping control of the interview, and using support and recognition appropriately. Most qualitative interviewers prefer a conversational tone to indicate empathy and understanding while conveying acceptance to encourage elaboration of subtle and valid data.

Interview Records, Transcripts, and Elaborations

The primary data of qualitative interviews are verbatim accounts of what transpires in the interview session. Tape recording the interview ensures completeness of the verbal interaction and provides material for reliability checks. These advantages are offset by possible respondent distrust and mechanical failure. The use of a tape recorder does *not* eliminate the need for taking notes to help reformulate questions and probes and to record nonverbal

EXCERPT 13.15   Interview Transcripts—Selected Quotations

[Principals' experiences with shared governance in their schools]

- "You always wonder if you're really needed. . . . A lot of times you start to question, Could this place just run without me? Then a parent calls, one who wouldn't talk with the teacher anymore, and I know I'm needed."
- "I don't think the teachers always realize how much they need me; sometimes they think that if I was out of the picture, they wouldn't have all these limitations. Now I have more of a community relations role, and I spend more time on community involvement. . . ."
- "I'm growing. Learning to become more of a partner. . . . You get a lot more accomplished working with a group than trying to work by yourself. . . ."
- "Personally and professionally, [shared governance] has given me a great sense of satisfaction." (pp. 83, 85)

Source: From Blase, J., & Blase, J. (1999). Shared governance principals: The inner experience. *NASSP Bulletin, 83*(606), 81–90.

communication, which facilitates data analysis. In many situations, handwritten notes may be the best method of recording. Interviewer recording forces the interviewer to be attentive, can help pace the interview, and legitimizes the writing of research insights (i.e., beginning data analysis) during the interview. Neither notetaking nor tape recording, however, should interfere with the researcher's focusing his or her full attention on the person.

Immediately following the interview, the researcher completes and types the handwritten records or transcribes the tape. Typed drafts will need to be edited for transcriber/typist error and put into final form. The final record contains accurate verbatim data and the interviewer's notation of nonverbal communication with initial insights and comments to enhance the search for meaning. Interviewer notations and comments are usually identified by the interviewer's initials. The final form also includes the date, place, and informant identity or code. Excerpt 13.15 illustrates data obtained from in-depth interviews.

The researcher writes an **interview elaboration** of each interview session—self reflections on his or her role and rapport, the interviewee's reactions, additional information, and extensions of interview meanings. This activity is a critical time for reflection and elaboration to establish quality control for valid data. Many initial ideas developed at this time are subsequently checked out through other data collection activities. As a rule of thumb, for every hour of interviewing, a researcher usually allows three hours of further work to produce the final record or transcript and the additional elaborations.

DOCUMENTS AND ARTIFACT COLLECTION

Artifact collection is a noninteractive strategy for obtaining qualitative data with little or no reciprocity between the researcher and the participant. It is less reactive than interactive strategies in that the researcher does not extract the evidence. During field residence in school settings, for example, the ethnographer must interact with individuals—even if only nonverbally—and become, to some degree, a participant. This is *not* an impediment if the researcher notes the consequences of this interactive role. In contrast, artifact collection strategies are noninteractive but may require imaginative field work to locate relevant data.

Artifact collections are tangible manifestations that describe people's experience, knowledge, actions, and values. Qualitative researchers studying current groups have adopted the techniques of historians who analyze documents (see Chapter 16) and of archaeologists who examine objects created by ancient peoples.

Types of Artifacts

Artifacts of present-day groups and educational institutions may take three forms: personal documents, official documents, and objects (see Table 13.5).

TABLE 13.5	Documents and Artifact Collections	
Type	**Examples**	**Used For**
Personal documents	Diaries	Personal perspective
	Personal letters	
	Anecdotal records	
Official documents	Internal papers	Informal or official perspective within the organization
	External communication	Official perspective for the public
	Student records and personnel files	Institutional perspective on child or employee
	Statistical data (enumeration)	Suggests trends, raises questions, corroborates qualitative findings, describes rituals and values
Objects	Symbols	Suggests social meanings and values
	Objects	Suggests social meanings and values

Personal Documents   A personal document is any first-person narrative that describes an individual's actions, experiences, and beliefs. Personal documents include diaries, personal letters, and anecdotal records. These documents are usually discovered by the researcher, but sometimes, an ethnographer will ask a participant to make anecdotal records such as a log, a journal, notes on lesson plans, or a parent's development record of a child. Documents also can surface during an interview or participant observation.

Official Documents   Official documents are abundant in organizations and take many forms. Memos, minutes of meetings, working papers, and drafts of proposals are *informal* documents that provide an internal perspective of the organization. These documents describe functions and values and how various people define the organization. Internal documents can show the official chain of command and provide clues about leadership style and values. Documents used for *external communication* are those produced for public consumption: newsletters, program brochures, school board reports, public statements, and news releases. These documents suggest the official perspective on a topic, issue, or process. School board minutes from 1915 to 1980, for example, were an important source in the study of an innovative school 15 years after an ethnographic study, and the original job applications of the school staff provided demographic clues to locate these persons for interviews.

Existing archival and demographic collections may be located during field residence and are usually readily available to the researcher. Institutions also keep individual records on each student and employee; in order to gain access to these, parental, student, or employee permission is usually required. *Student and personnel files* can become quite elaborate over time and may contain a variety of records and reports. A student's file may have records of testing, attendance, anecdotal comments from teachers, information from other agencies, and a family profile. Researchers use a file *not* so much for what it tells about the student but rather for what it suggests about the people who make the records. The file represents different perspectives (e.g., psychologists', teachers', counselors', administrators') on the student.

Statistical data can be demographic information about a group or population, dropout rates, achievement scores, number of acts of violence and suspension, attendance records, number of students with handicapping conditions, student eligibility lists for certain federal programs, the number of athletic injuries, and other numerical computations. Qualitative researchers use statistical data in several ways: (1) to suggest trends, (2) to propose new questions, and (3) to corroborate qualitative data. Qualitative researchers are more interested in what the statistics tell about the assumptions of the people who use and compile the data—that is, how statistics reveal people's thinking and common-sense understandings. Routinely produced numerical data describe the rituals and social values of an organization. Field workers seldom take statistical data at face value but instead question the social process that produced the data and how the data have been used.

Objects   *Objects* are created symbols and tangible entities that reveal social processes, meanings, and values. Examples of symbols are logos and mascots of school teams and clubs; such as athletic letters and trophies, posters, and award plaques. In a study of institutional collaboration, a symbolic record was a newly created logo that combined parts of the emblems of the university and of the school system to represent a new relationship between the two organizations. Interactive data revealed the difficulties surmounted to obtain official approval to use institutional emblems in a new form. The data obtained the following year described the use of the new logo. Qualitative researchers may investigate teachers' value of students' work by periodically checking bulletin board displays in elementary classrooms and corroborate this finding with other field data.

Analysis and Interpretation of Artifact Collections

Collecting and analyzing artifacts requires the use of these five strategies:

1. **Location of artifacts** begins with entering the field and continues for the duration of the study. Researchers anticipate the artifacts and proceed to locate and obtain documents and objects. Participants also offer documents and artifacts.
2. **Identification of artifacts** requires placing the artifact in retrievable form and cataloging for access. Documents are photocopied, and objects are photographed, filmed, or taped. Identifications are made by noting the category of artifact, a brief description of the artifact, a history of its use and owners/successors, and data on frequency and representativeness.
3. **Analysis of artifacts** requires descriptive data about the production or acquisition of the artifact by the group. Important questions are who uses it, how is it used, where is it used, and the purpose of its use.
4. **Criticism of artifacts** is the determination of its authenticity and accuracy to identify the meanings of the artifact in the social setting.
5. **Interpretation of artifact meanings** must then be corroborated with observation and interview data. Artifact interpretation for subtle meanings depends on the social context and other data.

FIELD OBSERVATIONS AND SUPPLEMENTARY TECHNIQUES

A technique fundamental to all qualitative research is *field observation*—direct, eyewitness accounts of everyday social actions and settings that take the form of field notes. A variety of supplementary techniques are also employed in most studies. They are selected to help interpret, elaborate, and corroborate data obtained from participant observation, in-depth interviews, and documents and artifacts.

Field Observations

Qualitative field observations are detailed descriptive recordings, presented as field notes, of events, people, actions, and objects in settings. Field observation is an integral part of both participant observation and in-depth interviewing. In the former, the researcher relies on careful observation as he or she initially explores several areas of interest at a site, searching for patterns of behaviors and relationships. In some social scenes, the participant observer collects the data entirely by observing the scene as it occurs, such as a class lesson or a board meeting. The interviewer also makes field records that note nonverbal interviewee body language and facial expressions to help interpret the verbal data. Field records also include descriptions of the context of the interview—for instance, in an office, in a restaurant, in a home, or in another setting.

Supplementary Techniques

Supplementary techniques include visual techniques, analysis of nonverbal communication, special surveys, and focus groups. Each of these is a separate, specialized method with its own methodological literature. The qualitative researcher, however, selectively uses these techniques as a generalist to corroborate initial findings and to raise additional questions.

Visual Techniques   The use of films and photographs of a current social scene comprise visual techniques. Films are especially useful for validation, as they document nonverbal behavior and communication and can provide a permanent record. Films also can be problematic, however, in terms of interpretation. One must consider the technical intrusion, the selective lens view, and the expense. Excerpt 13.16 describes the use of photographs for documentation.

Analysis of Nonverbal Communication   This technique is very important in most qualitative studies. The study of body motion and its messages is called *kinesics*. The recording of facial expressions, gestures, and movements can be triangulated with verbal data. An interviewer can trust participants' responses more if their body language is congruent with their verbal statements. However, many gestures have different meanings in different cultures.

Another issue is personal space. The study of the people's use of space and its relationship to culture is called *proxemics*. Studies have been conducted on the use of interpersonal space in public places and the identification of territorial customs of certain cultures. Qualitative researchers may note how others react to space and invasion of privacy (i.e., personal territory), for example, in assigned classroom seats, functioning in a crowded work area, and selecting seats in a formal meeting. Caution must be used in interpreting nonverbal communication and always with other data.

EXCERPT 13.16   Creating a Photographic Archive

Between 1996 and 2001, I visited 30 field sites throughout Eastern Europe that have been designated as memorial spaces to commemorate violent acts against Jews both during the war and immediately after.... I chose photography as a means of data gathering at the Holocaust sites. Photography facilitated the construction of a portable database that could be transferred from the emotion-laden research setting (the Holocaust site) to the comparatively safe haven of my office in the [United States].... I videotaped the interior of concentration camps ... and I took photographs of ... displays and artifacts of women that I could analyze when I returned. (pp. 225, 227–228)

Source: From Jacobs, K. L. (2004). Women, genocide, and memory: The ethics of feminist ethnography in Holocaust research. *Gender and Society, 18*(2), 223–238.

Special Surveys   Survey instruments may take the forms of confirmation surveys, participant-constructed instruments, and even projective techniques using photographs, drawings, and games. Data on preservice teacher induction activities, obtained through nine months of participant observation, for example, could be corroborated with a questionnaire administered to principals and participant-constructed instruments administered during planning retreats and workshops (Schumacher & Esham, 1986).

Focus Groups   A variation of an interview is the **focus group interview (FGI),** which is used to obtain a better understanding of a problem or an assessment of a problem, concern, new product, program, or idea. Namely, a purposefully sampled group of people is interviewed, rather than each person individually. By creating a social environment in which group members are stimulated by one another's perceptions and ideas, the researcher can increase the quality and richness of data through a more efficient strategy than one-on-one interviewing.[3] Participant observers and in-depth interviewers use focus group interviewing as a confirmation technique. Case study research and critical studies may use focus groups as one of several techniques. Focus groups also can be the only evidence-based technique used in evaluation and policy studies.

Focus groups build on a *group* process. The group leader or facilitator should be skilled in both interviewing and group dynamics. The group typically consists of 8 to 12 persons who are relatively homogeneous but unknown to each other. For complex topics, smaller groups of 5 to 7 are recommended. A typical session lasts from 1½ to 2 hours. Noticeable differences in education, income, prestige, authority, and other attributes can lead to hostility and even withdrawal. The leader facilitates discussion by posing initial and periodic questions. Usually, an assistant observes body language, tape records the session, and assists in interpretating the data.

The addition of supplementary techniques to a study can increase not only the validity of the initial findings but also the credibility of the entire study. However, most qualitative researchers are not formally trained in each supplementary method and thus should not use these methods exclusively for obtaining their data.

STANDARDS OF ADEQUACY FOR QUALITATIVE STRATEGIES

Many qualitative studies are published as books or reports, rather than as journal articles. With the increasing acceptance of the methodology, more journals are publishing qualitative manuscripts. The studies published in journals are highly synthesized, or only one of many findings is reported to fit the journal format. The typical journal article may also reduce the methodological procedures that would be explicit in the full study. Considering the following questions will aid the reader in reviewing such studies:

Entry into the Field
1. Did the foreshadowed research problem provide sufficient selection criteria for the site to be observed or suggest a profile for the individuals to be interviewed?
2. Is the research role that has been assumed clearly articulated and appropriate for the research questions?
3. How did the research role affect data collection? How does the researcher address her or his potential influence?

Participant Observation
1. Is the rationale given for the purposeful sampling choices made during the field work a reasonable one?
2. How were the multiple strategies employed in data collection? What was the primary method and what others were employed to corroborate the data?

3. Was the length of data collection at the site detailed and reasonable?
4. Are descriptive field notes presented as data? Is there evidence of a reflex record?

In-Depth Interviewing

1. Are the purposeful sampling strategies that were used with obtained interviewees described and are they reasonable?
2. Was each person screened by the attribute or profile developed for the study before proceeding with the interview?
3. Was the type of interview selected appropriate for the research problem?
4. Do the data presented indicate the use of appropriate interview questions and probes?

Supplementary Techniques

1. Were the supplementary techniques employed appropriate for the study, and did they yield valid data?

SUMMARY

The following statements summarize the major characteristics of qualitative strategies:

1. Data collection involves multimethod strategies, but a primary method is selected for a given study, such as participant observation or in-depth interviewing.
2. Foreshadowed problems state the initial focus and conceptual framework; they guide the field work but do not limit observations because other research foci may develop at the site.
3. Foreshadowed problems are reformulated during data collection.
4. Site selection is guided by the criteria implied in the foreshadowed problems and by concerns of suitability and feasibility.
5. The participant observer first maps the field to obtain a sense of the total context and to ensure purposeful sampling, thereby producing a selection of information-rich informants and social scenes.
6. Participant observation involves conducting prolonged field work to obtain and corroborate salient observations of different perspectives, which are recorded as field notes and reflex records.
7. In-depth interviews vary in terms of format, the kinds of questions posed, the question sequence, and interview logistics.
8. Interview records include field notes, tape recordings, transcripts, and interview elaborations.
9. Artifact collections include personal documents, official documents, and objects, all of which must be corroborated with other evidence.
10. Supplementary techniques are used to verify data collected by participant observation and in-depth interviewing. Methods include visual techniques, nonverbal communication records, specialized surveys, and focus groups.

RESEARCH NAVIGATOR NOTES

Research Navigator.c⊕m

Reading the following articles will help you understand the content of this chapter. Go to the education database (included in the EBSCO database in Research Navigator; use the Accession Number provided to find the article.

13.1   *Mapping the Site*
Agee, J. (2002). "Winks upon winks": Multiple lenses on settings in qualitative educational research. *International Journal of Qualitative Studies in Education, 15*(5), 569–586. Accession Number: 7532962.

13.2   *Emotions in Field Work*
deMarrais, K., & Tisdale, K. (2002). What happens when researchers inquire into difficult emotions? Reflections on studying women's anger through qualitative interviews. *Educational Psychologist, 37*(2), 115–124. Accession Number: 6790643.

13.3   *An Interview Study*
Brookhart, S. M., & Bronowicz, D. L. (2003). "I don't like writing. It makes my fingers hurt": Students talk about their classroom assessments. *Assessment in Education: Principles, Policy and Practice, 10*(2), 221–243. Accession Number: 10849125.

13.4 *An Interview Study*
Cho, S., Singer, G. H., & Brenner, M. (2000). Adaptation and accommodation of young children with disabilities: A comparison of Korean and Korean American parents.

Topics in Early Childhood Special Education, 20(4), 236–250. Accession Number: 3933327.

CHECK YOURSELF

Multiple-choice review items, with answers, are available in the Companion Website for this book:

www.ablongman.com/mcmillanschumacher6e.

APPLICATION PROBLEMS

1. To help make a decision about implementing a new science curriculum across the school district, a superintendent asked a researcher to observe how one elementary school implemented the new curriculum. The researcher easily established rapport with the science supervisor and the principal at that school and observed the teaching of five of the school's six teachers. The sixth teacher, who seemed to oppose the innovation, only related her experiences with the new curriculum. She skillfully managed to avoid teaching the curriculum when the ethnographer was present. What should the ethnographer do?

2. A researcher is living in a student dormitory for the purpose of studying how high school students attending a state summer school program develop creativity through photography. Although the researcher originally thought observation of the photography classes and the evening program would be sufficient, she found that participating in student social activities during free time and extracurricular activities on the weekends influenced students' photographic productions. Should the researcher observe and record these informal happenings? Would student products (i.e., photographs) be a useful source of data?

3. During data collection, an adult education program director overhears negative remarks made by some adults about the program and sees the researcher recording them. The director explains to the researcher that such remarks, if made public, could create a poor image for the program and asks the researcher to destroy those particular field notes. How should the researcher handle this situation?

4. Rephrase the following interview guide questions to make them suitable qualitative questions, and then place the questions in a sequence that would be appropriate for eliciting teachers' perceptions regarding evaluation by their building principal.
   a. Do you think teachers, as professionals, should be evaluated by their principal?
   b. Did your principal visit your classroom several times before he or she did your annual evaluation?
   c. Does your principal hold a conference with you after each visit?
   d. Is the principal's evaluation of your teaching fair?

5. Read the following full-text qualitative study in the Research Navigator education database; search by using the Accession Number provided. Then answer the following questions:

   Brookhart, S. M., & Bronowicz, D. L. (2003). "I don't like writing. It makes my fingers hurt": Students talk about their classroom assessments. *Assessment in Education: Principles, Policy and Practice, 10*(2), 221–243. Accession Number: 10849125.
   a. Are the interview questions descriptive and open ended? Why or why not?
   b. Were probes used? If so, why?

NOTES

1. See Dexter (1970) and Gorden (1981).
2. See Moustakas (1994) and Seidman (1998).
3. Focus group interviews (FGIs) are used primarily in evaluation and policy studies; however, sociologists originally developed the approach. FGI is often done in marketing research and to some extent in health care services. See Krueger and Casey (2000).

Qualitative Data Analysis

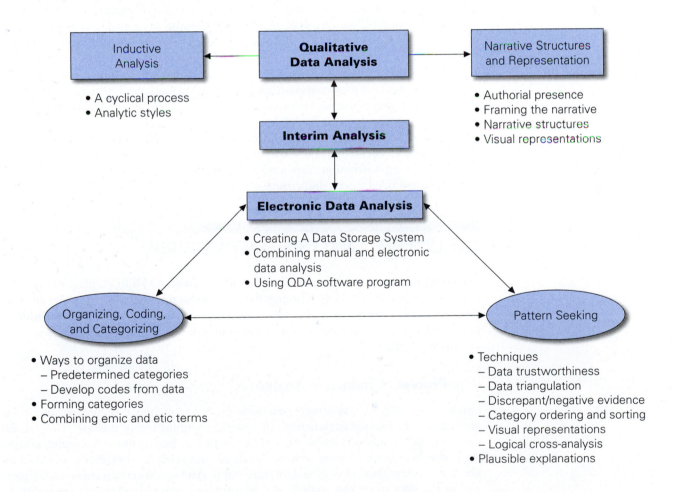

Qualitative Data Analysis

Inductive Analysis
- A cyclical process
- Analytic styles

Narrative Structures and Representation
- Authorial presence
- Framing the narrative
- Narrative structures
- Visual representations

Interim Analysis

Electronic Data Analysis
- Creating A Data Storage System
- Combining manual and electronic data analysis
- Using QDA software program

Organizing, Coding, and Categorizing
- Ways to organize data
  - Predetermined categories
  - Develop codes from data
- Forming categories
- Combining emic and etic terms

Pattern Seeking
- Techniques
  - Data trustworthiness
  - Data triangulation
  - Discrepant/negative evidence
  - Category ordering and sorting
  - Visual representations
  - Logical cross-analysis
- Plausible explanations

KEY TERMS

inductive analysis	etic
crystallization	pattern
interim analysis	triangulation
segment	visual representations
code	data management
category	context
emic	

Suppose you have carefully collected a series of field observations of teacher planning meetings in a school or gathered the concerns of principals about a controversial issue. How do you make sense of all of this evidence, which consists of many pages of field notes and/or interview transcripts and documents? Where do you start? How do you organize the information so you can locate the important findings? What techniques do researchers use? How can software packages assist in data management and analysis?

Qualitative data analysis is primarily an inductive process of organizing data into categories and identifying patterns (i.e., relationships) among the categories. While analytical styles vary among researchers, the general processes and techniques that they use are not universal.

This chapter introduces qualitative analysis as a process of interim analysis, coding and categorizing, and pattern seeking for plausible explanations. The data for evidence-based inquiry are managed electronically, whether partially or completely. Word-processing programs and specifically designed software packages for qualitative data analysis can assist in organizing numerous data sets (e.g., field notes, interview transcripts, and documents) and assembling coded data. Findings are presented as narratives. Narrative structures and representations vary moderately among ethnographic, phenomenological, case study, grounded theory, and critical studies.

INDUCTIVE ANALYSIS: AN OVERVIEW

Data analysis is an ongoing, cyclical process that is integrated into all phases of qualitative research (see Figure 14.1). Through the use of **inductive analysis,** categories and patterns primarily emerge from the data, rather than being imposed on them prior to collection. Computer programs can assist in this process but cannot replace the researcher's cognitive activities.

The Process of Inductive Analysis

Qualitative analysis is a relatively systematic process of coding, categorizing, and interpreting data to provide explanations of a single phenomenon of interest. The general process of data analysis is represented in Figure 14.1 as having four overlapping phases. As researchers move to more abstract levels of data analysis, they constantly double-check and refine their analysis and interpretation. And unless certain elements are present in the data, then the analysis will not proceed smoothly. Researchers negotiate permission to return to the field, if necessary, to seek additional data and to validate emerging patterns.

Most qualitative researchers have learned that there is no set of standard procedures for data analysis or for keeping track of analytical strategies. Making sense of the data depends largely on the researcher's intellectual rigor and tolerance for tentativeness of interpretation until the entire analysis is completed.

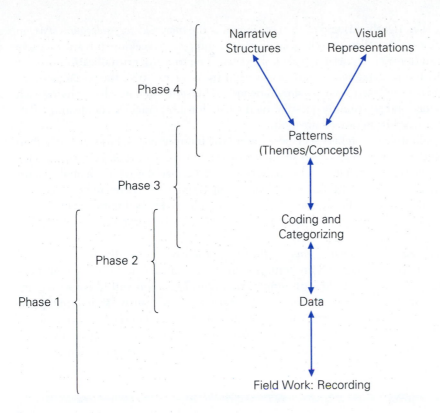

FIGURE 14.1   General Process of Inductive Data Analysis

Analytical Styles

Qualitative researchers develop analytical styles, but they rarely make explicit all of their data analysis strategies. Figure 14.2 shows a continuum of idealized analytic styles, from prefigured technical to emergent intuitive.

At the extreme objectivist (i.e., lefthand) end of the continuum is the *technical and quasi-statistical style*, in which the researcher decides the categories in advance. The categories are thus predetermined and rigid. This style is often used in linguistic analyses. A *template analysis style* logically applies derived sets of codes and categories to the data; however, these classifications are frequently revised during data analysis. The initial codes or categories may be derived from the research questions, the interview guide, or the data, and this initial set may or may not be retained in the final analysis. The *editing analysis style* is less prefigured; the interpreter searches the data for parts to illustrate categories of meaning and writes memos during the process. Although there is little or no use of codes, the analyst must group descriptive memos that illuminate major interpretations. At the

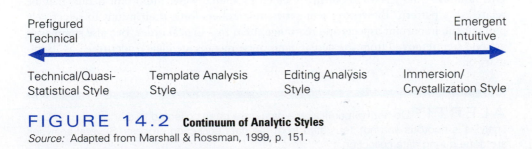

FIGURE 14.2   Continuum of Analytic Styles
Source: Adapted from Marshall & Rossman, 1999, p. 151.

subjectivist (i.e., righthand) end of the continuum is the *immersion/crystallization style*, in which the researcher collapses coding, categorizing, and pattern seeking into an extensive period of intuition-rich immersion within the data. The process of **crystallization** seeks to open the analyst to maximum experiences within the analytic style; the researcher may conduct intensive reflexive analyses simultaneously. This style often involves reliving each field experience and persistently questioning the data for subtle nuances of meaning. Patterns are identified by iterative reflection.

Most qualitative researchers lean more toward the interpretivist/subjectivist style than the technical/objectivist style. Even so, analyzing qualitative data is an eclectic activity. There is no one right way; data can be analyzed in any number of ways. Each analyst must find his or her own style of intellectual craftsmanship. And while there are no strict rules that must be followed mindlessly, the researcher is not allowed to be limitlessly inventive. Qualitative analysis should be done artfully, but it also demands a great amount of methodological knowledge and intellectual competence.

The technique of *comparing and contrasting* is used in practically all intellectual tasks during analysis. Categories are tentative in the beginning, and they remain flexible, not rigid. The goal is to identify similarities. Our discussion will illustrate a combination of template (i.e., use of codes and categories) and editing styles that many researchers use. The *template style* can be easily adapted to computer-assisted analysis. We have chosen to use more general qualitative data analysis terms, rather than the terminology of the five qualitative designs in Chapter 2. Several general principles guide most researchers.

MISCONCEPTION The use of qualitative data analysis (QDA) software makes a study more scientific.

EVIDENCE Published descriptions of individual and team uses of QDA programs say such programs are only tools. Researchers' intellectual skills must drive the analysis.

INTERIM ANALYSIS

Interim analysis occurs *during* data collection and serves two purposes: (a) to make data collection decisions and (b) to identify recurring topics. Several of the strategies that researchers employ while collecting data include the following:

1. Write many observer comments in the field notes and interview notes to identify possible themes, interpretations, and questions. Researchers' comments should *always* be separated from the actual data, typically by being enclosed in parentheses. A rule is to distinguish descriptive data from evolving ideas; data collection is descriptive, whereas researcher commentary is reflective.

2. After a field visit, write summaries of observations and of interviews by asking OK, now what did I learn about my research problem? What important details may be related to a pattern? By writing summaries, researchers force their minds to selectively pull out the important aspects and rearrange them in a logical order. Because summaries are one step removed from the actual data, these memos are clearly identified as "Summary of . . ."

ALERT! Do not wait until all the data have been collected to start analyzing. Data analysis is rigorous and not separated from the data collection process. Several analyses are done during data collection.

EXCERPT 14.1   Interim Data Analysis

[We] examined environmental features of the setting (i.e., lighting, seating) and how they seemed to support or detract from reading. . . . Therefore, our focus turned to an analysis of these features. Each observation was reviewed, and 17 environmental features were identified. Observations were then examined according to these attributes by three members of the research team, who had visited all . . . of the settings, and comparisons were made across communities through discussion. (p. 14)

Source: From Neuman, S. B., & Celano, D. (2001). Access to print in low-income and middle-income communities: An ecological study of four neighborhoods. *Reading Research Quarterly, 36*(1), 8–26.

Qualitative researchers do regular, frequent interim analysis throughout data collection to keep track of changes in data collection strategies and evolving ideas. Some of the analytical techniques that researchers use are:

1. Scan all data collected at that point for whatever possible ideas they may contain. The emphasis here is on describing what is happening or what people are saying.
2. Look for recurring ideas or meanings that may become themes. Themes come from conversations in the social setting, as well as from recurring activities and feelings. Research commentaries found in the observer comments, interview elaborations, and reflex records also suggest themes (see Excerpt 14.1).

ORGANIZING, CODING, AND CATEGORIZING

It is almost impossible to interpret data unless one is also organizing them. Qualitative researchers integrate the operations of organizing, analyzing, and interpreting data and call the entire process *data analysis*.

Organizing the Data

Where does a researcher get ideas for organizing data? More than likely, the researcher has some initial ideas for organizing the data from either his or her work in the field or preplanning. There are five sources that researchers use to get started:

1. The research question and foreshadowed problems or subquestions
2. The research instrument, such as an interview guide
3. Themes, concepts, and categories used by other researchers
4. Prior knowledge of the researcher or personal experience
5. The data themselves

Notice that the first four sources contain predetermined categories. All five can be used, but their usefulness will depend on the study.

Using Predetermined Categories   It is often easiest to use predetermined categories, especially with an interview guide, or the research questions or topics about which you are quite knowledgeable. These categories tend to be general and fairly broad. There are several kinds (Creswell, 2002; Bogdan & Biklen, 2003; Patton, 2002) from general knowledge that can be readily adapted to a particular study:

1. **An evaluator** might use categories such as the setting and context, program description, administrator's expectations of the program, participants' perceptions of the program, critical incidents, processes, and perceived outcomes and unanticipated effects. The categories might also be those topics about which the person authorizing the evaluation desires information.

2. **A study of a school or classroom** might use the setting and context, the situation, participants' perspectives, participants' ways of thinking about people, objects and activities, processes, activities/events, instructional strategies, relationships, and social structure.

3. **A study of small-group meetings** might use the setting and context, purpose of the meeting, discussions, decisions, processes, relationships, and social structure.

4. **An interview study** might use the topics embedded in the questions asked. An example is provided in Excerpt 14.2. Each category is then divided into subcategories as the data are analyzed. For example, the category "Participants' perspectives" could contain subcategories for each different perspective or person. However, the use of predetermined categories provides only a starting point; they are provisionally applied and refined.[1]

Developing a Coding System from Data   Another approach is to develop an organizing system from the data, beginning after one-fifth or one-fourth of the data (or at least three data sets) have been obtained. Researchers divide the data into parts—that is, smaller pieces of data containing some descriptive meanings. The data parts are called *segments, incidents,* or *units*. A data **segment** is comprehensible by itself and contains one idea, episode, or piece of relevant information. A segment can be of any size—a word, a few lines, a sentence, or several pages containing an entire event or participants' explanations, and several shorter units can be contained with the segment.

Each segment has two contexts. The first is the data set in which the part is embedded—that is, the particular field observation or interview. The second context is the category of meaning that each segment fits. How does a researcher develop an organizing system? He or she should follow these steps:

1. **Get a sense of the whole.** Read each of three data sets and write ideas about the data as you read. This will give you ideas about the data segments and about the larger phenomenon of interest.

2. **Generate codes from the data.** Read a data set and ask yourself What is this about? What were they doing or talking about? The descriptive name for the subject matter or topic is called the **code.** Each code is written in the margin of a copy of the data set. See Excerpt 14.3 for an illustration of the initial codes in three transcripts. Notice that some topics are recurring.

3. **Compare codes for duplication.** Make a list of the codes, with one column for each data set. Compare the codes for duplication and overlapping descriptions. See Figure 14.3 for a visual image of this process. Using a list of all the codes, check for duplication. Group similar codes and recode others to fit the description. At this point, some researchers write out a definition of the code. Make lists of the *major codes*, the *important codes*, and the *leftover codes*. Important codes may appear unique now but are necessary, in spite of their rarity. Leftover codes may become relevant later. In Figure 14.3, notice that Codes D and E are mentioned only once in the three data sets, but each is classified differently according to its importance in the study.

EXCERPT 14.2   Pre-Established Categories and Manual Coding

The six re-established categories [from interview topics]: general information, general university climate, mentor, faculty, university classroom experiences, and influential factors provided a frame for the next phase of data analysis. Each participant's typed comments were cut and pasted onto a 3 × 5 index card, coded and placed under one of seven categories. Next, repeated words, ideas, or phrases were used to develop themes and report experiences of the seven participants. (p. 278)

Source: From Kea, C. D., Penny, J. M., & Bowman, L. J. (2003). The experiences of African American students in special education master's programs at traditionally white institutions. *Teacher Education and Special Education, 26*(4), 273–287.

EXCERPT 14.3   Initial Topics in Transcripts of Elementary School Principals' Practices of Grade Retention

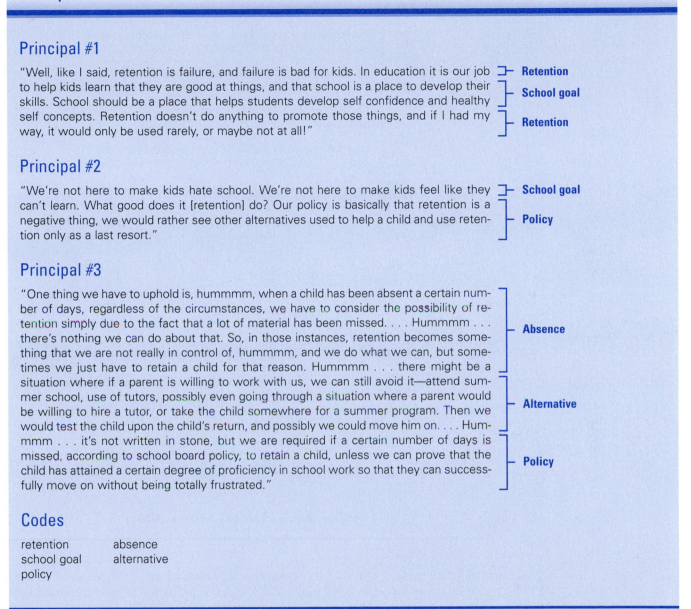

Principal #1

"Well, like I said, retention is failure, and failure is bad for kids. In education it is our job to help kids learn that they are good at things, and that school is a place to develop their skills. School should be a place that helps students develop self confidence and healthy self concepts. Retention doesn't do anything to promote those things, and if I had my way, it would only be used rarely, or maybe not at all!"

— Retention
— School goal
— Retention

Principal #2

"We're not here to make kids hate school. We're not here to make kids feel like they can't learn. What good does it [retention] do? Our policy is basically that retention is a negative thing, we would rather see other alternatives used to help a child and use retention only as a last resort."

— School goal
— Policy

Principal #3

"One thing we have to uphold is, hummmm, when a child has been absent a certain number of days, regardless of the circumstances, we have to consider the possibility of retention simply due to the fact that a lot of material has been missed. . . . Hummmm . . . there's nothing we can do about that. So, in those instances, retention becomes something that we are not really in control of, hummmm, and we do what we can, but sometimes we just have to retain a child for that reason. Hummmm . . . there might be a situation where if a parent is willing to work with us, we can still avoid it—attend summer school, use of tutors, possibly even going through a situation where a parent would be willing to hire a tutor, or take the child somewhere for a summer program. Then we would test the child upon the child's return, and possibly we could move him on. . . . Hummmm . . . it's not written in stone, but we are required if a certain number of days is missed, according to school board policy, to retain a child, unless we can prove that the child has attained a certain degree of proficiency in school work so that they can successfully move on without being totally frustrated."

— Absence
— Alternative
— Policy

Codes

retention	absence
school goal	alternative
policy	

Source: Reed, J. S. (1991). Ethnographic study of the practice of grade retention in elementary schools. Unpublished manuscript.

4. *Try out your provisional organizing system.* Using unmarked copies of each data set you have worked with so far, apply your organizing system. See Excerpt 14.4 for an illustration of recoded transcripts. Notice that some codes, such as "School goal" and "Retention," have gained subcomponents and that some initial codes have become categories. Notice that the single code of "Policy" is now two codes, "School policy" and "School Board policy," because the content of each differs. You can now tell how well the descriptive code name corresponds to the data and whether some codes in the data were initially overlooked on the first reading.

5. *Continue to refine your coding system.* As you collect more data, your initial system will be refined and perhaps more codes will be added. How many codes are essential? Consider that researchers have to remember all the codes as they later look for patterns. It is almost impossible to remember more than 25 to 35 individual codes, so they

Step 1: Identify the Segments in a Data Set

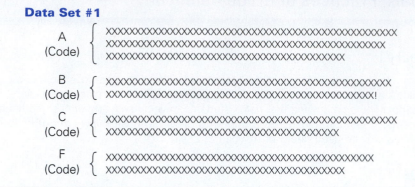

Step 2: List the Codes for Each Data Set

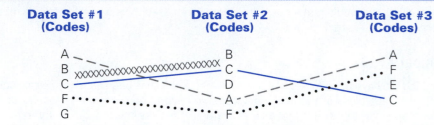

Step 3: Classify the Codes as Major, Important, and Leftovers

Major Codes	Important Codes	Leftover Codes
A	B	E
C	D	G
F		

Step 4: Apply the Coding System and Continue to Refine It

FIGURE 14.3 Developing a Coding System from the Data

will probably be grouped later into categories. If you started with predetermined descriptive categories (say, 6 to 10), it will initially be easier, unless you are an experienced user of qualitative data analysis software (see Excerpt 14.5).

Forming Categories

Forming categories from the coded topics forces researchers to think more abstractly. A **category** is a more general and abstract entity that represents the *meaning* of similar topics. Because the content of a topic may have different connotations, a topic may be part of more than one category.

Developing categories from topics requires researchers to look at data in different ways. Researchers debunk assumptions made by individuals to search for what people really mean, regardless of the terms they use. Here are some of the strategies that researchers use (Strauss & Corbin, 1998):

1. **Ask basic questions that will lead to more refined questions.** The basic questions are *Who? When? Where? What? How?* and *Why?* Giving provisional answers to these questions for each category will force the researcher to think with analytic depth.

Research Navigator.com

14.1 Evidence
Accession No.: 10614569

EXCERPT 14.4 Recoded Transcripts of Elementary School Principals' Practices of Grade Retention

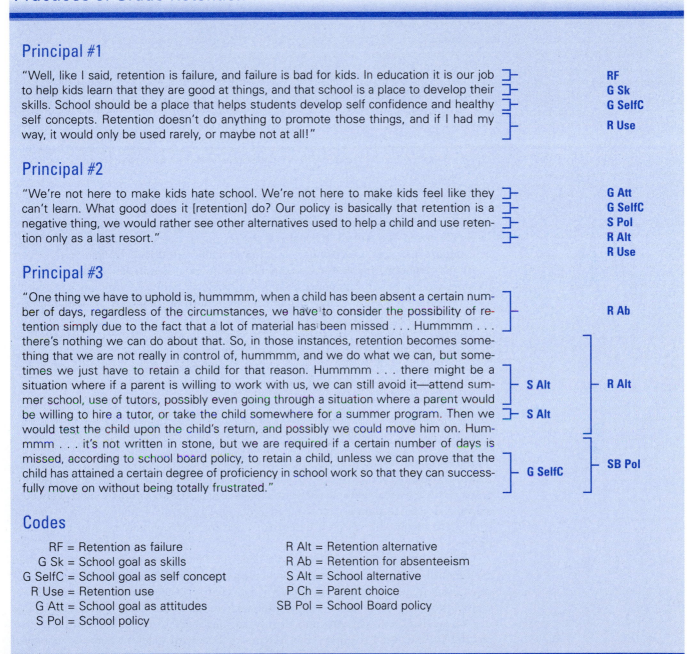

Principal #1

"Well, like I said, retention is failure, and failure is bad for kids. In education it is our job to help kids learn that they are good at things, and that school is a place to develop their skills. School should be a place that helps students develop self confidence and healthy self concepts. Retention doesn't do anything to promote those things, and if I had my way, it would only be used rarely, or maybe not at all!"

RF
G Sk
G SelfC
R Use

Principal #2

"We're not here to make kids hate school. We're not here to make kids feel like they can't learn. What good does it [retention] do? Our policy is basically that retention is a negative thing, we would rather see other alternatives used to help a child and use retention only as a last resort."

G Att
G SelfC
S Pol
R Alt
R Use

Principal #3

"One thing we have to uphold is, hummmm, when a child has been absent a certain number of days, regardless of the circumstances, we have to consider the possibility of retention simply due to the fact that a lot of material has been missed . . . Hummmm . . . there's nothing we can do about that. So, in those instances, retention becomes something that we are not really in control of, hummmm, and we do what we can, but sometimes we just have to retain a child for that reason. Hummmm . . . there might be a situation where if a parent is willing to work with us, we can still avoid it—attend summer school, use of tutors, possibly even going through a situation where a parent would be willing to hire a tutor, or take the child somewhere for a summer program. Then we would test the child upon the child's return, and possibly we could move him on. Hummmm . . . it's not written in stone, but we are required if a certain number of days is missed, according to school board policy, to retain a child, unless we can prove that the child has attained a certain degree of proficiency in school work so that they can successfully move on without being totally frustrated."

R Ab

S Alt
S Alt

R Alt

G SelfC

SB Pol

Codes

RF = Retention as failure
G Sk = School goal as skills
G SelfC = School goal as self concept
R Use = Retention use
G Att = School goal as attitudes
S Pol = School policy

R Alt = Retention alternative
R Ab = Retention for absenteeism
S Alt = School alternative
P Ch = Parent choice
SB Pol = School Board policy

Source: From Reed, J. S. (1991). Ethnographic study of the practice of grade retention in elementary schools. Unpublished manuscript.

EXCERPT 14.5 Rereading and Coding

Later, as I recursively reread and coded my notes and transcripts for pervasive themes, I was able to draw from multiple perspectives, both in identifying significant strands and in illustrating with relevant quotes, narrative, and description. (pp. 308–309)

Source: From DiPardo, A. (2000). What a little hate literature will do: "Cultural Issues" and the emotional aspect of school change. *Anthropology and Education Quarterly, 31*(3), 306–332.

EXCERPT 14.6   Recoding and Forming Categories

My coding of participants' statements went through many iterations. For example, at various times each team member spoke of personal relationships, professional development and mutual improvement of benefits of teaming. Each assessed his or her own ability to work closely with a colleague. . . . [These] initially were given general codes with tentative categories assigned to them and were progressively grouped and regrouped until a more specific category was established. For instance, the final categories of "teacher choice" and "influences on practice" were derived from analysis of earlier designations, such as "teachers' self-perceptions" and "teachers as risk takers," which I evaluated as either too vague or as reflecting too much of my own preferences. (p. 70)

Source: From Murata, R. (2002). What does team teaching mean? A case study of interdisciplinary teaming. *Journal of Educational Research, 96*(2), 67–77.

2. *Analyze a sentence, a phrase, or sometimes even a single word* that seems to be significant or of interest.

3. *Compare the data to a similar or an improbable situation.* By imagining a very similar situation, the researcher can identify more codes in his or her data. The same technique can be applied to an improbable situation. Making an imaginative comparison is merely a way to confirm that nothing new can be found in the data.

4. *Identify "red flags."* Examples of "red flag" phrases are "Never," "Always," "It couldn't possibly be," "Everyone knows that is the way it is done," "There is no need for discussion," and others. These phrases are signals to take a closer look and to ask more questions of the data. Researchers should seldom take anything for granted (see Excerpt 14.6).

Combining Emic and Etic Terms

Researchers use both emic and etic terms. **Emic** terms represent insiders' views, such as words, actions, and explanations that are distinctive to the setting or people. **Etic** terms provide a cross-cultural scientific view—that is, the researcher's views, concepts, and social science phrases. How much each type of term is employed in a specific study depends on the research design (i.e., the form of qualitative inquiry) and the purpose.

Researchers tend to emphasize emic topics and categories in the beginning, when they are still collecting data. Most researchers caution against the use of social science concepts (i.e., etic terms) in the early phases of data analysis because such terms often suggest connotations that participants did not intend. However, in the later, more abstract stages of data analysis, etic patterns and themes are necessary to communicate with other researchers and social scientists. See how researchers with different purposes employed emic and etic terms in Excerpt 14.7 and Excerpt 14.8.

EXCERPT 14.7   Emic Terms

Content analysis of the interview transcripts was carried out to see what themes and patterns existed in the responses, what types of conflicts the women identified, and what types of solutions they had found or would recommend to others. (p. 378)

Source: From Olmedo, I. M. (2003). Accommodation and resistance: Latinas struggle for their children's education. *Anthropology and Education Quarterly, 34*(4), 373–394.

EXCERPT 14.8   Etic Terms

As a critical ethnographic project, the underlying goal of the study was not to produce a familiar "emic" view of culture, but to provide a new and hopefully insightful perspective [using etic terms] on how class, race, ethnicity and gender forces play themselves out in the lives of urban minority teens. (p. 237)

Source: From Stanton-Salazar, R. D., & Spina, S. U. (2003). Informal mentors and role models in the lives of urban Mexican-origin adolescents. *Anthropology and Education Quarterly, 34*(3), 231–254.

DISCOVERING PATTERNS

The ultimate goal of qualitative research is to make general statements about relationships among categories by discovering patterns in the data. A **pattern** is a relationship among categories. Pattern seeking means examining the data in as many ways as possible. In searching for patterns, researchers try to understand the complex links among various aspects of people's situations, mental processes, beliefs, and actions.

Pattern seeking starts with the researcher's informed hunches about the relationships in the data. It demands a thorough search through the data, challenging each major hunch by looking for negative evidence and alternative explanations. The researcher then shifts to a deductive mode of thinking—moving back and forth among codes, categories, and tentative patterns for confirmation. The researcher determines how well the data illuminate the research problem and which data are central.

Patterns can take different forms and levels of abstraction, depending on the purpose and use of the study. Patterns also relate to the conceptual framework selected for the inquiry. The major pattern(s) serves as the framework for reporting the findings and organizing the reports. This process is schematically represented in Figure 14.4. Notice that

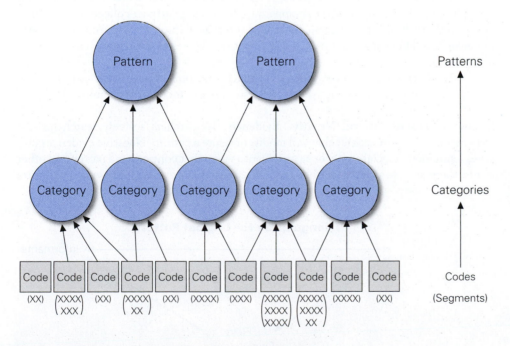

FIGURE 14.4   **Building Patterns of Meaning**
Source: Adapted from A. Vierra & J. Pollock. (1992). *Reading educational research,* 2nd ed., Scottsdale, AZ: Gorsuch Scarisbrick, p. 262.

the number of segments (the *x*'s) that a code represents varies. Some codes fit into more than one category, and other codes are not central to the research problem. Further, a category can fit into more than one pattern. This elasticity of code and category meanings allows for *patterns of meanings* to emerge. The meanings of categories and patterns depend on both the content of each and the comparison made with that content—other categories or other patterns.

The process is usually a circular one of returning to the data to validate each pattern and then modifying or recasting the idea as part of a larger abstraction. Although some of the process is tedious and time consuming, it also requires making carefully considered judgments about what is really important and meaningful in the data.

Techniques of Pattern Seeking

The following techniques are strategies that facilitate pattern seeking but are not intended to be exhaustive or prescriptive. Researchers must select strategies that illuminate the patterns. Qualitative researchers are obligated to monitor and report their own analytical techniques and processes as fully as possible.

Gauging Data Trustworthiness   Although gauging the trustworthiness of data is done at the time of each field experience and in reflex records, it is also important during intensive data analysis. The researcher should select trustworthy evidence for pattern seeking by qualitatively assessing solicited versus unsolicited data, subtle influences among the people present in the setting, specific versus vague statements, and the accuracy of the sources (e.g., an observant person? a thoughtful person? an emotional person? a biased person?). Selecting trustworthy data also involves an awareness of the researcher's assumptions, predispositions, and influence on the social situation.

Using Triangulation   Researchers use **triangulation,** which is the cross-validation among data sources, data collection strategies, time periods, and theoretical schemes. To find regularities in the data, the researcher compares different sources, situations, and methods to see whether the same pattern keeps recurring. A theme of *institutional collaboration*, for example, could be cross-checked by comparing data found in artifact collections (minutes, memos, official brochures, letters), informant interviews (project co-directors, teachers, principals), and field observations of project meetings. Figure 14.5 illustrates cross-method triangulation.

Researchers sense, however, that even though they only directly observed, heard, or recorded one instance, for some types of analysis, a single incident is meaningful.

Evaluating Discrepant and Negative Evidence   Researchers actively search for discrepant and negative evidence that will modify or refute a pattern. Negative evidence comprises a situation, a social scene, or a participant's views that contradicts a pattern. In other words, there are two patterns, rather than one. Discrepant evidence presents a variation

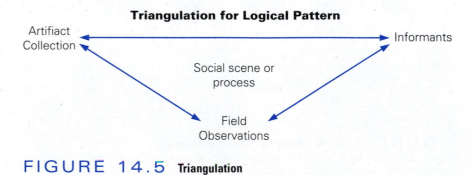

FIGURE 14.5   Triangulation

EXCERPT 14.9   Analysis of Discrepant Data

Not surprisingly, gender issues were sometimes more salient for Native women whose pueblos prohibited or limited severely the participation of women in the political lives of their tribes than they were for individuals such as Kari, who experienced few, if any, obstacles as women.

For example, contrast Kari's statement, above, with that of Karen, a pueblo activist: "I'm a woman caught between two worlds. I'm a professional outside but traditional and, I hate to use the word, submissive at home. For example, letting the men eat first, keeping your eyes down." (p. 603)

Source: From Prindeville, D-M. (2003). Identity and the politics of American Indian and Hispanic women leaders. *Gender and Society, 17*(4), 591–608.

of a pattern (see Excerpt 14.9). These exceptions are very useful because they make the original pattern more distinctive. For example, a pattern might be that a particular action occurs in most situations except this one.

Ordering Categories for Patterns   Ordering categories can be done several ways to discover patterns. One way is to place the categories in sequence of occurrence. Researchers might ask, Which situation or action came first? Did more than one belief accompany the event? What was the consequence or outcome? Arranging the categories in a sequence is useful for a process analysis to identify changes from one time to another time. A second way is to enlarge, combine, subsume, and create new categories that make empirical and logical sense—that is, they go together in meaning. The logical sense in pattern seeking is that the meaning of a category is influenced by its relationship to a pattern.

Sorting Categories for Patterns   Researchers group categories in several ways to identify meanings. In a study of principals and unsatisfactory teachers, for instance, the category "Unsatisfactory teachers" was sorted first by types of unsatisfactory teachers and then by types of resolution. Each category was rearranged to see whether there was a pattern between type of unsatisfactory teacher and type of resolution. When no pattern was found, another category—"Methods of identification of unsatisfactory teachers"—was sorted with types of resolution. This sorting led to a pattern that related methods of unsatisfactory teacher identification to types of resolution.

Constructing Visual Representations   Researchers construct a **visual representation,** an organized assembly of information, such as figures, matrices, integrative diagrams, and flowcharts, which assist in the analysis. There are many forms of visual representation. Figure 14.6 and Excerpt 14.13 are examples. Most researchers are cautious *not* to reach hasty closure in building integrative diagrams. Descriptive contextual data must accompany diagrams. Visual representations are *devices* and are not reality per se. Diagrams assist researchers in moving to a more abstract analysis by allowing them to ask different questions about the data. Researchers attempt to balance a respect for the complexity of reality with the need to simplify for analytical and communication purposes. Integrative diagrams, once finalized, serve as a visual representation of the entire study and are presented in the report.

Doing Logical Cross-Analyses   Usually presented in matrix format, categories are crossed with one another to generate new insights for further data analysis. These cross-categories reveal logical discrepancies in the already analyzed data and suggest areas in which data and patterns might be logically uncovered. However, the researcher should *not* allow these matrices to lead the analysis but rather should use them to generate hunches for further pattern seeking. In Figure 14.6, the six categories of teacher roles toward high school dropouts were first developed and then cross-analyzed, which allowed two dimensions of meaning to emerge: behaviors and beliefs.

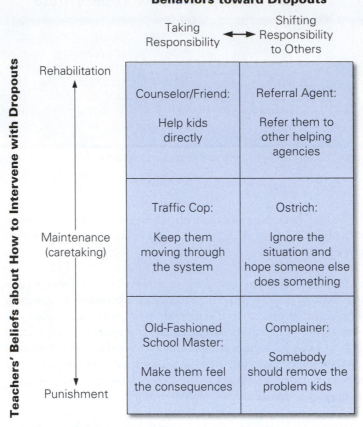

FIGURE 14.6 **An Empirical Typology of Teacher Roles with High School Dropouts**

Source: M. Q. Patton. (2002). *Qualitative evaluation and research methods,* 3rd ed. Newbury Park, CA: Sage, p. 469. Copyright © 2002 by Sage Publications. Reprinted by permission of Sage Publications, Inc.

Plausibility of Patterns

As researchers build their categories and search for patterns, they need to search for other plausible explanations for links among categories. Alternative explanations always exist, but they may not be reasonably supported by the data. A pattern becomes an explanation only when alternative patterns do not offer reasonable explanations central to the research problem. Plausibility is a matter of judgment about the quality of the data within the design limitations. Plausibility is demonstrated by the presentation of the data and the rigor of the analysis.

The following analogy illustrates plausibility: If a person is peeling an apple, she or he will first notice the whole apple—its size, shape, and other features. Initially, the skin is encountered; the skin also has distinctive characteristics. Underneath the skin is the flesh. Many people, at this point, will stop peeling the apple and be satisfied with their knowledge of the apple. Others will be more curious about why there is so much flesh. They will continue to probe and finally discover a membrane embedded in the flesh. Some people will wonder why there is a membrane. Careful cutting of the membrane will yield a seed. At this point, one has understanding—all the pieces fit together as a whole. There is an explanation for why the membrane, flesh, and skin surround the core of the apple—the seed.

At each phase of cutting the apple, alternative explanations can be found for the parts of the apple. However, in the last discovery (the seed), there is no other reasonable explanation for the real meaning of the parts of an apple. Notice that to discover the meaning of an apple, one must continue to ask questions and probe each layer to reach the core.

ELECTRONIC QUALITATIVE DATA ANALYSIS

Qualitative studies are noted for having mounds of data. Researchers have to manage this data for analysis and writing. **Data management** is a partially or totally electronic system to retrieve data sets (i.e., field notes and interview transcripts) and to assemble the coded data in one place. Researchers typically use one of two approaches: (1) to combine manual techniques and word-processing programs or (2) to use specially designed software for *qualitative data analysis (QDA)*, developed by researchers. Currently, there are over 25 QDA programs, although only a few provide advanced versions with support to the user. These are marketed on the Internet.

Following several steps of data management will enable one to make summary statements and conclusions:

1. Create a data storage system.
2. Decide how you will do data management—that is, partially or completely electronically.
3. If you decide to use a QDA software program, obtain the program and either training or a peer-support group until you are an experienced user.

Each of these steps will be discussed in the following sections.

Creating a Data Storage System

A data storage system provides a means of identifying and retrieving a specific set of original typed data. The purpose is the same, whether it is done partially or completely electronically. All pages are numbered sequentially to allow for locating data segments within each data set. In addition, each field note set or transcript set is identified on the first page by date, place, person(s), location, and event or social scene. Because working with data means extensive rearranging, several copies are made and a permanent copy is kept where it will not be disturbed, lost, or destroyed.

A data storage system contains each data set in a notebook, file folder, or computer file. One or more of the following methods can be adopted to retrieve a data set:

- By date of observation or interview, especially if the focus is process analysis
- By site, especially if the study includes more than one type of physical setting, as in a multisite study
- By person interviewed, frequently numbered as Interview 1, Interview 2, and so on, with a separate list to identify each number, especially if the focus is across individuals
- By type of social scene, especially if many types of social scenes occur for a small number of people, such as classrooms, parent/teacher conferences, faculty meetings, board meeting, and the like

Planning ahead by using color coding, numbering, and symbols or abbreviations will be invaluable in data analysis and writing the final report.

Some important considerations in deciding how to manage the data—partially or completely electronically—are as follow:

1. How experienced are you in the intellectual tasks of qualitative data analysis?
2. What is the size of your database? If your database is more than 100 pages, you should consider using a QDA program.
3. How important is your present research, and what will be your future needs?
4. What is your degree of comfort with computers, the Windows environment, and your file structure?

Research Navigator.com

14.3 Electronic or Not?
Accession No.: 10473857

5. How important is data "closeness" with the entire data set versus "distancing," or only seeing smaller parts at one time?
6. Can you afford the cost of a software purchase and the time needed for learning a new program, especially learning how to tailor it to your needs?
7. Is the selected program user friendly and flexible for recoding? What kind of support is available? Is there a peer group, an e-mail discussion group, or a technical advisor to assist?

Until you do a significant research project, you should combine manual and electronic data management.[2]

Combining Manual and Electronic Data Analysis

Most experienced researchers using this approach use a familiar word-processing program to type the original field notes, interview transcripts, and artifact content. Then, they manually code segments by using either the *cut-and-file technique* or the *index card technique* to group the coded segments. Then the researcher uses the word-processing program to write the drafts and final report (see Figure 14.7).

Two ways to manage data manually after the codes have been written on a copy of them are the *cut-and-file technique* and the *index card technique* (Bodgan & Biklen, 2003). There are many variations of these techniques.

The cut-and-file technique requires making multiple copies of each data set for cutting. Folders are labeled by code names. Upon going through the data, each coded segment is first marked to identify its source and page number. Only after each coded segment has such an identification label should the pages of data be cut and each code placed in the appropriate folder. If a data segment contains more than one code, then a copy is needed for each folder. One variation is to put the whole page of the data set containing the marked codes into the folder. Another variation is to paste or copy the coded data on 3" × 5" index cards and then to put the cards for each code in a pile. Each card must be marked for code and data set. Either way, the result is a box of file folders or cards that contains all the data segments relevant to each code. Figure 14.8 represents this process.

At this point, many researchers write up the content of each folder or set of cards and select illustrative quotable material. It does not matter which folder is selected to read first. By placing all the relevant topic folders together and reading through them, the researcher develops codes into categories. If there are many data segments in one folder or many index cards in one pile, then the content may indicate a category that needs to be broken into subcategories.

The second way to manage data is the index card technique, which is an indexing system for locating coded segments within the entire data bank. The researcher uses a photocopy of the data with the codes on each data set. The researcher also has his or her list of categories for the study. Each data set must be numbered, and both the pages and lines must be numbered. Thus, each topic has three methods of identification: the data set, the page, and the line(s). The researcher now reads the data, selects the category for each code (topic),

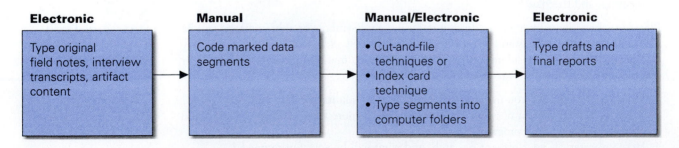

Electronic

| Type original field notes, interview transcripts, artifact content |

Manual

| Code marked data segments |

Manual/Electronic

| • Cut-and-file techniques or
• Index card technique
• Type segments into computer folders |

Electronic

| Type drafts and final reports |

FIGURE 14.7   **Combining Manual and Electronic Data Analysis**

Segments   **Codes**

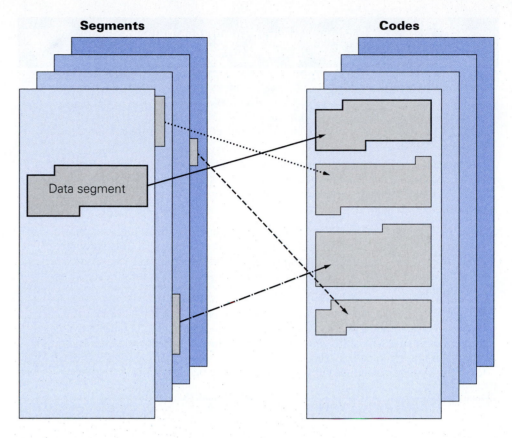

Data segment

FIGURE 14.8 **Assembling the Coded (Topic) Segments**

and writes on the index card three identifications: the data set, the page number, and the line number(s). The result of this process is an index of the data relevant to each category.

The advantage of this method is that it does not require cutting data pages and having bulky folders. Some disadvantages are (1) skimming the entire page to locate the particular coded segment if you did not number the lines, (2) retrieving all the coded segments to read when they are scattered throughout the entire data bank, and (3) returning each page to its former place in the filing system to make it accessible for pattern seeking. However, some researchers (using notebooks to store their data) prefer this technique.

Using QDA Software Programs

Perhaps the biggest advantage of using qualitative data analysis (QDA) software is that it saves time in the busy work of searching and retrieving text. But how does QDA software work? Two elements of QDA software differ from statistical software.

First, with a QDA program, much more researcher input is needed, compared to a statistical package. The analysis process is similar to the data analysis described earlier. The researcher goes through the text, codes it, and enters these codes into the computer. Programs may automatically indicate on each segment where the codes come from (i.e., page and line of data file). If the researcher prefers to work on hard copy, the program will print out all or part of the data. Many programs permit recoding of the data, as well.

Second, QDA programs vary a lot more than statistical packages do. Thus, the choice of a particular program requires knowing your research needs and which features the software provides.[3] Not all QDA software is available in both Macintosh and IBM formats. Some QDA programs may be used with text, photographs, audio, and video data.[4] A few programs allow importing data from a word-processing program. Some QDA programs

TABLE 14.1 Websites about Qualitative Data Analysis (QDA) Software
www.gtlasti.de.atlasneu.html Atlas.ti can process textual, graphic, audio, and video data. It has a variety of features for data analysis with a time-based backup mechanism that keeps data during power failures. It describes its approach as creative, unstructured, and systemic. Atlas.ti has an online listserv (i.e., an e-mail discussion group).
www.qualiresearch.com/ethnograph_software Ethnograph was one of the earliest QDA programs. It handles only text data and allows researchers to import their data from word-processing programs. Field notes, interview transcripts, and documents can all be coded.
www.researchware.com HyperRESEARCH 2.0, another earlier program, offers links to a demonstration download site and to an online help site. This software helps analyze text-based data, photographs, and videos. The researcher can code data, examine the data by coding category, and explore how different categories look together.
www.qsrinternational.com and **www.qsr.com.au** NUD*IST 5.0 (QRS N5) and NVIVO, developed by the QSR group, assist in data analysis but in different ways: the form and structure of the process. The websites provide downloaded demo models of both programs, which are also available on CD. N5 provides a QSR Merge for teams and multisite research. There is a listserv for each program.

prefer structured data (e.g., a structured interview schedule) better than others, and a few handle large data banks by merging two or more projects, as in team research or multi-site research.[5] Many programs can keep a record of the researcher's analysis for audibility purposes. Some support grounded theory analysis and concept mapping.

Table 14.1 identifies some of the most commonly used QDA programs and notes a few of their major distinctions and their Internet addresses. Table 14.2 provides selected websites for additional information and advice; QDA trainers can also be found through some of these websites.

VARIATIONS IN NARRATIVE STRUCTURE AND REPRESENTATION

A hallmark of most qualitative research is the narrative presentation of evidence and the diversity of visual representations of data. Data are presented as quotations of participants' actual language for an evidence-based inquiry. However, not all data are reported in a single study nor are they necessarily reported in the same format to all readers. There are four potential audiences: (1) academics, (2) participants in the study, (3) policy-makers, and (4) members of the general public. The narrative structure used will depend on the purpose of the research, the qualitative design, and the audience.

Qualitative authors recommend using an overall structure that does not blindly follow the standard quantitative introduction, methods, results, and discussion format (Richardson, 1998). Methods can be called *procedures* or *strategies*, and results can be called *findings*. Subheadings often use participants' expressive language, rather than social science rhetoric. The writing style might be personal, readable, and applicable for a broad audience, and the level of detail may make the narrative seem real and alive, carrying the reader directly into the world of the participants.

TABLE 14.2   Selected Internet Resources and E-Mail Discussion Groups (listservs) for Qualitative Data Analysis (QDA) Software
www.jiscmail.as.uk/lists.qual-software.htm;_qual-software   This website is the CAQDA (Computer-Assisted Qualitative Data Analysis Software) Project. Use this listserv if you need advice or want to make suggestions. The discussion focuses on a variety of software programs and their benefits and weaknesses.
www.yalberta,ca/_jrnorris/qda.html   Use this website for a list of QDA software programs. A double-click will send you to either the website for a given product or to a discussion of it. The products include data analysis software, software for dictating field notes, and qualitative content analysis software.
www.listserv.temple.edu, Visual Communications Discussion List   You can subscribe to this listserv by sending an e-mail to it.
www.Caqdas.soc.surrey.ac.uk/hews.htm   Use this website to find online articles about QDA programs.
www.bc.edu/offices/ats/rits/research/software/descriptions/qualitative   This university website compares NUD*IST, Ethnograph, and hyperRESEARCH.
www.audiencedialogue.org/soft-qual.html   Use this site to get a broader analysis of QDA programs and to learn about adapting word-processing programs for qualitative data analysis.

Audience and Authorial Presence

To write a report, the researcher must address issues such as encoding for specific audiences, preparing visual representations of findings, and acknowledging the author's presence (Creswell, 1998). *Encoding* is the use of literary devices to shape a report for a particular audience. For academic audiences and publications, it is appropriate to include the prominent display of academic credentials of the author; to include references, footnotes, and methodology sections; and to use academic metaphors. For moral/political audiences, it is appropriate to use highly connoted "in-group" words (e.g., *woman, women, feminist* in feminist writing), to provide the moral or active credentials of the author, and to use empowerment metaphors. For participants and policy-makers, there should be less literature and theory, an abbreviated methodological overview, and a detailed description of the practice, addressing practical concerns or issues and the use of common-sense metaphors.

The author's presence is acknowledged through various literary devices. First, the researcher's role is described. In addition, the author's presence can be acknowledged with reflective footnotes, interpretative commentaries, or an epilogue. In some critical studies, the researcher's political lense is usually stated in the introductory section.

Two aspects of a study are presented as data: the context and the quotations of participants. The researcher's task is to arrange these statements in a logical manner, making participants' meanings unmistakable to the reader.

Framing the Narrative and Presenting the Participants' Language

In most studies, framing the narrative is essential for readers to understand the study and for extending the findings to future research studies and practices. A study can be framed several ways: (1) in the naturalistic context, (2) in the phenomenological experience, (3) by using selected theories, or (4) by using a political orientation. The **context** of a study is the situational description of people and events in which the phenomenon of interest occurred. How the researcher frames a given study varies with the choice of qualitative design: ethnography, phenomenology, case study, grounded theory, or critical study.

In ethnographic studies and case studies, the context is the setting, the participants, and the data collection time period. The holistic context in case study research is considered an important finding; the naturalistic setting is described and used to identify contextual elements that influence the cultural life, or the case. In a study of the first year of operation of an innovative school, for example, the context is the floorplan and details of the new school building, the entirely new faculty, and the faculty mandate for the academic year. Part of the context is also how the innovative school fits into larger systems—that is, the school system, the community, and the state education system.

The frame for a phenomenological study is the type of experience that has happened—for instance, being a working single parent, a woman administrator who has voluntarily resigned, or a child who has experienced the death of a sibling. The naturalistic situation is used in descriptions of *what* happened and *how* the experience occurred.

Whereas the naturalistic context is very important in ethnographic and case study research, it is less important in grounded theory studies. In grounded theory, the identification of the theories that frame the study is crucial, and a brief description of the natural context (e.g., hospital wards, school playgrounds, cancer support groups) is part of the methodology. Because of the different types of critical studies, the narration may be framed by the naturalistic context or by a theoretical or political frame (e.g., the researcher's political orientation or standpoint).

Presentation of the participants' language is imperative because it is *the data*. Evidence can be presented in several formats: (1) using short, eye-catching quotations separated from the text, often bulleted or placed in a table; (b) embedding brief quotations within the narrative; and (c) including entire paragraphs of field notes and interview transcripts. The use of longer quotations requires guiding readers into and out of these quotations and focusing their attention on the controlling idea of the section. Lengthy quotations are usually set off from the narrative text and provide some identification of the original data set, such as the date or the interviewee number.

Narrative Structures and Visual Representations

Narrative structures and visual representations vary among qualitative designs. We will discuss each evidence-based design with an emphasis on substantive research manuscripts:

1. **Ethnographic studies** provide description, analysis, and interpretation of the culture-sharing group. The holistic "thick description" is presented in chronological order or narrative order. The analysis may focus on critical incidents or selected social scenes with dialogue, or it may tell the story from different perspectives. The analysis may also compare and contrast across groups within the culture. Data, transformed as patterns or themes, are summarized and provide a *cultural portrait*, or synthesis of all aspects of the group life illustrating its complexity (Wolcott, 1999). The overall interpretation or meaning is discussed with the findings in terms of how it relates to wider scholarly issues or to current issues (see Excerpt 14.10).

2. **Phenomenological studies** of a lived experience emphasize textual descriptions of what happened and how the phenomenon was experienced. Because the experience is one that is common to the researcher and the interviewees, data are drawn from both the researcher's written record of his or her experience and records of the interviewees. The report includes a description of each participant's experience, including the researcher's, followed by a composite description and the essence of the experience.

3. **Case studies,** similar to ethnographic studies, contain description, analysis, and naturalistic summaries. Case studies typically use a report format that includes vignettes to provide vicarious experiences for the reader (Stake, 2000). Case studies can be 60 to 40 percent or 70 to 30 percent in favor of description versus analysis and interpretation. An extensive description is given of the case and its context, based on a wide variety of data sources. A few key issues are presented so the reader can appreciate the complexity

Research Navigator.c⊕m

14.4 A Study
Accession N0.: 4052812

EXCERPT 14.10   Summary Statements and Recommendations

This study demonstrates that unshared sociolinguistic practices . . . are crucial aspects of communicative failure between hearing and deaf children in mainstream elementary school settings. . . . We suggest that just as deaf children are expected to develop skills for accommodating to hearing children, hearing children in classes with deaf children should be expected to develop comparable skills for interacting . . . to enrich peer interactions and enable the deaf students to have equal access to all learning opportunities. (p. 131)

Source: From Keating, E., & Mirus, G. (2003). Examining interactions across language modalities: Deaf children and hearing peers at school. *Anthropology and Education Quarterly, 34*(2), 115–135.

of the case. These issues are drawn from a collection of instances in the data to detect issue-relevant meanings. Finally, the researcher develops summaries (i.e., patterns) or "lessons learned," which are useful to participants or to readers when applied to similar cases (see Excerpt 14.11).

4. **Grounded theory studies** emphasize an analytic story; description is kept secondary to a theoretical scheme or concept density. The analytic story also specifies variations of the phenomenon and relevant conditions for multiple causes. A visual representation accompanies the culminating propositions of the grounded theory. Because of the emphasis on conceptual discussion and relating the grounded theory to theoretical literature, few readers fully appreciate the entire study (Charmaz, 2000). Other grounded theory studies present a descriptive narrative that connects the categories and advances concept density. Theoretical propositions can be presented in a narrative form or as a list of assertions (see Excerpt 14.12).

5. **Critical studies** include such diverse research methods as critical ethnography, feminist and ethnic research, narrative analysis, participatory action research, and action research. Most critical ethnographies and much feminist and ethnic research adopts the narrative structures of substantive research reports. However, researchers are particularly concerned about the multiple voices presented in the discourse, including that of the author. Visual representations may include tables, charts, and integrative diagrams. (Tables present verbatim statements.) Visual representations may also be matrices or models that identify context, causal conditions, and consequences. Directional arrows indicate the flow of initial events to consequences, as shown in Excerpt 14.13.

Research Navigator.com

14.5 Issues in Critical Studies
Accession No.: 5171609

A number of qualitative social scientists are writing experimental forms of *evocative representations.*[6] Some of these writings are narratives of self, ethnographic fictional representations, poetic representations, ethnographic dramas, and mixed genres. A number of scholarly qualitative journals have published studies employing experimental narrative structures. Many qualitative researchers have been influenced by experimental formats and

EXCERPT 14.11   Informing Educational Policy

In concluding, . . . [the] findings reported here might inform future educational policy. Judging from what second language researchers and those working with ESL students say about the importance of allowing language learners to practice speaking English, having a classroom environment that works to minimize opportunities for students to talk seems undesirable. (p. 67)

Source: From Olivo, W. (2003). "Quit talking and learn English!" Conflicting language ideologies in an ESL classroom. *Anthropology and Education Quarterly, 34*(1), 50–71.

EXCERPT 14.12   Grounded Theory Assertions

This study was a qualitative investigation of the knowledge and beliefs, roles, and guiding principles of two exemplary high school science teachers. . . . The findings of the study are summarized in the following assertions.

Assertion 1: The important knowledge and beliefs of each teacher are best represented as one cluster of teaching principles.

Assertion 2: Each teacher had multiple teaching roles, with each role described by a different role metaphor.

Assertion 3: The teaching roles of each teacher are consistent with his or her cluster of teaching principles.

Assertion 4: Each teacher had guiding principles that are overlying and constant.

Source: From Floyd, J. M. (1999). Knowledge and beliefs, roles, and guiding principles of two exemplary high school science teachers and model for teacher reflection. Unpublished doctoral dissertation, Virginia Commonwealth University, Richmond, VA.

EXCERPT 14.13   Concept Analysis: Visual Representation
Disability Domination

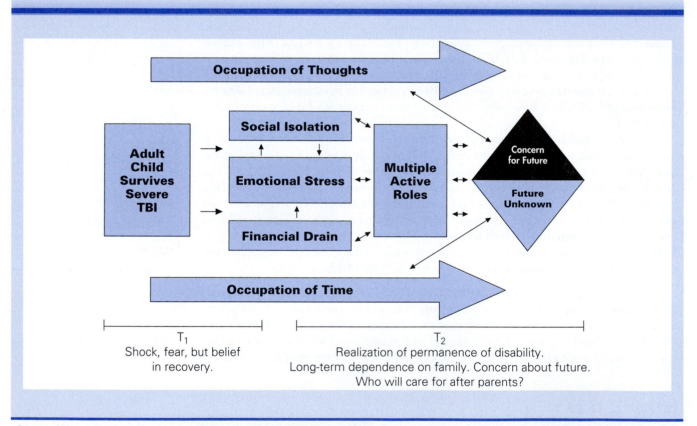

Source: Wood, W. M. (1993). Long-term consequences of severe traumatic brain injury on adults: A qualitative study of families' perceptions of impact and public policy. Unpublished doctoral dissertation, Virginia Commonwealth University, Richmond.

now write more reflexively and self-consciously; they also relate more deeply and complexly to their own texts while nurturing their own voices.

As a final example of qualitative research, a complete article is reprinted in Excerpt 14.14. The annotations provided throughout the article will assist readers in identifying the various elements of qualitative research employed in this study.

EXCERPT 14.14   Reading Qualitative Research

Parents as Professionals in Early Intervention: A Parent Educator Model

Peggy A. Gallagher, *Georgia State University*   Cheryl A. Rhodes, *Georgia State University*

Sharon M. Darling, *Boise State University*

One of the goals of a family-centered approach in early intervention is to equally involve family members as active partners with professionals. This article describes one state's model of family involvement using parents of young children with disabilities as parent educators in the Part C system. Qualitative focus group data were collected with the parent educators over 6 time periods and revealed their changing perceptions about their roles as parent educators, as well as their perceived challenges and successes. Parent educators ultimately came to see themselves as "professionals" working to bring a family perspective to the early intervention system.

Abstract

A hallmark of Part C of the Individuals with Disabilities Education Act (IDEA, 1990) is that parents of infants and toddlers with disabilities are partners with professionals in their children's development. The Part C Early Intervention (EI) system views family members as an integral component of the program through their participation in policy development, program implementation, training, and the Individualized Family Service Plan (IFSP) process. Bruder (2000) remarked that family-centered early intervention has become conceptualized around the values of family strengths (rather than deficits), the promotion of family choice, and the development of a collaborative partnership between the family members and the EI system and its professionals (Durst, Trivette, & Deal, 1994).

Legislative background

The goals of a family-centered philosophy are to equally involve parents as active partners and to recognize their central and long-term roles in the lives of their children with special needs (Mahoney et al., 1999). Controversy in the literature has focused on some of the terms used to involve families, such as "parent education," "parent involvement," and "parent support" (Durst, 1999). There has also been ongoing discussion of why family-centered care is not more easily implemented (Bruder, 2000). Bruder emphasized that parents must be given information in a supportive way so that they can parent their child with special needs and facilitate the child's learning without in any way threatening the family's self-confidence or cultural or religious traditions. McWilliam (2001) categorized these family supports as being emotional, informational, or instrumental/financial.

Winton and DiVenere (1995) outlined four ways that families of children with disabilities have been involved in early intervention to establish a broad base of parent support: parents as instructors, parents as practicum supervisors, parents as team participants in staff development, and parents as planners and policymakers. Winton and DiVenere stressed the value of having a wide variety of levels of involvement available because each family has unique circumstances and may (or may not) want to get involved at differing levels. Capone, Hull, and DiVenere (1997) described the partnerships that can develop between parents and professionals in EI systems. They suggested that parents are participating at both the preservice and inservice levels in various ways, including as members of task forces and advisory boards, as mentors for other families, as grant reviewers, as participants in quality improvement initiatives, and in personnel preparation.

Literature: Family-centered approach

A few empirical studies have validated the success of parents who were involved in EI programs beyond the traditional parenting role with their own children. Whitehead, Jesien, and Ulanski (1998) found that the consistent and regular presence of parents at planning and other meetings added a note of reality and shaped the entire complexion of the program in a more family friendly way. They recommended that programs include a parent of a child with a disability as a member of the core team. In doing so, program members would want to assure diverse representation in terms of ages of children, cultural backgrounds, and family composition of parents. Hanson, Randall, and Colston (1999)

Prior research

(continued)

e x c e r p t   1 4 . 1 4   *(c o n t i n u e d)*

described a process involving parents of children with disabilities as advisors to the Department of Defense systems of services and in medical education. These parents served
as advisors in many roles, such as making presentations at grand rounds or to service
providers, writing items for surveys to evaluate a program, and coteaching courses.
Bailey (2001) suggested that parent involvement and family support must be individualized, give parents every opportunity to be active partners in planning and working with
professionals, and be organized such that families feel competent to learn and to become
advocates for their child.   ⎤ **Prior research (continued)**
                                                                             ⎦

Building on Winton and DiVenere's (1995) model of parental involvement, Turnbull,
Blue-Banning, Turbiville, and Park (1999) discussed the idea of family members as educators of other professionals. They have viewed families from a strengths perspective (Allen
& Petr, 1996), in which the expertise of parents and other family members is valued as a   **Research needed**
critical resource for professionals. They have called for research that focuses on the efficacy of parents as providers of education to other parents and professionals and maintain
that if we truly value parents as resources, we need to help build an infrastructure that
supports parents taking on traditional educational roles. The purpose of this study is to
describe a model of parents as professionals in one state's EI system. Parent educators'
progress was documented through quantitative and qualitative methods, including sur-   **General purpose of article**
veys from the families and EI personnel with whom they worked and focus groups in
which parent educators shared their own perspectives.

Description of Model

The Parent Educator model began in December 1995 with the hiring of a parent of a child
with disabilities as the coordinator. Parent educators, parents of children who are or have
been in the Part C program, were then hired on a part-time, flexible schedule to develop
family-centered partnerships, collaborate with state and local EI staff and other agencies,
and promote cultural sensitivity throughout the state's Part C program, known as Babies
Can't Wait (BCW). The mission of the program is to actively promote family participation
in the BCW program by disseminating current information so that families of children with
disabilities have timely and easy access to needed resources and services.

The Parent Educator model is a component of Project SCEIs (Skilled Credentialed
Early Interventionists), a consortium of six universities created to implement the major   **Details of model**
components of Georgia's Comprehensive System of Personnel Development (CSPD) for
the Part C Early Intervention system. Parents have been instrumental in policy development since the beginning of the EI program, and family-centered principles are found
throughout SCEIs training activities including parents as authors of a handbook for other
parents about the EI system and parents paid as trainers at all SCEIs workshops required
for EI personnel. Thus, it was an easy progression to move to a Parent Educator model.

BCW parent educators develop and distribute parent education materials to families
new to BCW; provide information to BCW families on specific topics, as requested; work
with local EI personnel to plan and carry out activities and programs for families; serve on
and encourage other families to be involved in local and state interagency coordinating
councils and other policy committees; and work with EI personnel to publicize BCW in
the community. They also help to identify family needs and inform families about parent
resources available through BCW, including a parent handbook, a parent conference, and
lending libraries. Parent educators also develop materials in which parents have expressed
an interest, such as updates in local EI newsletters or information on specific issues such
as extended hospitalizations.

Recruitment of parent education specialists (the original job title used) began in December 1995 with an announcement and job description that was sent throughout Geor-   **Implementation process**
gia to EI coordinators, local interagency coordinating councils, and disability organizations.
The original job description specified overall job duties to "develop and conduct family

training activities and materials on BCW program and policies" and to "collaborate with local EI coordinators, public schools, parent groups, and other community agencies about BCW services to families." Although the original job name of "parent education specialist" was changed to "parent educator," the overall job responsibilities remained the same over time, though more specific duties, such as providing parents with a general introduction to the BCW system or maintaining monthly status reports, were added. The title "parent educator" was adopted in 1998 at parent educators' request because they thought it more clearly described their role in teaching other parents about and supporting parents in the BCW program than did the original title. "Parent educator" is consistent with the term used by Winton, Sloop, and Rodriguez (1999), who suggested its use in situations when parents are educating professionals.

A statewide interview committee—which included the parent educator coordinator, project SCEIs director, an early intervention coordinator; and in some cases, the parent of a child with a disability who was working as a graduate research assistant—interviewed all candidates who passed the initial screening. Prior to hiring, all references were checked, and the prospective parent educator had an interview with the local EI coordinator. In most cases, the EI coordinator already knew the parent from his or her district.

Six parent educators were hired in February 1996. All had children who either were currently in or who had participated in EI. All had at least a bachelor's degree, a job requirement, and had held various jobs, including attorney, community volunteer, and teacher. Since March 1996, Georgia has had 24 parent educators, with a maximum of 14 at any one time. The average length of stay has been 2 years 11 months, with the shortest tenure being 4 months and the longest 7 years; two of the original parent educators are still employed. All of the parent educators have had a strong desire to work within the EI system to help families maximize their time in early intervention and to give back to the program that has meant so much to them and their families.

Implementation process (continued)

Currently, there are 13 parent educators serving in Georgia, 11 covering 80% of the state's health districts and 2 serving as statewide resources, 1 in cultural diversity. Parent educators have many training opportunities, including a full-day orientation with Project SCEIs and BCW staff when they first begin. Parent educators receive a training manual containing BCW policies and procedures, definitions, a copy of the Parent Handbook for Success in Early Intervention, and resource and other useful materials. Specialized training also occurs at least once a year on such topics as IFSP development, transition planning, community resources, or natural environments. Parent educators also attend a service coordinator orientation and the six Project SCEIs training modules, which are designed for service coordinators and special' instructors.

Parent educators are paid a monthly salary that includes telephone and travel charges within their district. If they have expenses or are asked to come to activities outside of their district, they are reimbursed for those activities. Parent educators are supervised locally by the individual EI coordinators in their districts but are paid and directly supervised by the Project SCEIs parent educator coordinator, who is the parent of a child with disabilities and a licensed professional counselor and licensed marriage and family therapist. Parent educators work out of their homes; some are given office space in their local district office as well. All parent educators have access to a home computer.

Current status

Evaluation of the Parent Education Component

The evaluation is multifaceted, with data gathered from consumers (parents at an annual Parent Conference and parents selected through an independent evaluator); from supervisors, including EI coordinators and selected service coordinators; from Project SCEIs' parent educator coordinator (through annual university evaluations); and from the parent educators themselves through role surveys, focus groups, and monthly reports. Quantitative data summaries of ratings from EI coordinators and service coordinators have consistently indicated high levels of satisfaction with key aspects of the parent educators'

(continued)

e x c e r p t 1 4 . 1 4 (continued)

performance, including their assistance in getting information to families, their role in involving families in local inter-agency committees, and their responsiveness to requests from parents and EI personnel. Parents in the EI program, as well, have consistently reported that parent educators were helpful to them in giving information, answering questions, sharing resources, and making suggestions.

Monthly, quarterly, and annual reports show the number and type of parent educator contacts (telephone and in person), as well as the types of activities completed by the parent educators. As the number of parent educators has increased, so have their telephone contacts with families. In 1997 and 1998, approximately 450 calls were made to families, whereas the 1999 and 2000 data showed approximately 700 calls per year with Georgia families in BCW. Data from 2001 and 2002 showed contacts with more than 1,000 families annually. The focus of this article is to present the qualitative data from six focus groups held with parent educators to document the perspective of the parent educators regarding their roles, challenges, and successes across time. ⎤ **Purpose of *this* study**

Qualitative Methodology

The focus group component of the evaluation of the parent educators used a qualitative research paradigm (Bogdan & Biklen, 1982). Data were collected longitudinally) using a focus group format. A *focus group* is a "carefully planned discussion designed to obtain perceptions on a defined area of interest in a permissive and non-threatening environment" (Krueger, 1988, p. 18). The group interaction of a focus group is what differentiates it from other types of qualitative data collection (Morgan & Krueger, 1993). The ⎤ **Defined focus group interview**

qualitative data were gathered through a series of six focus groups held over a 5-year period. Themes and patterns emerged from the transcripts to reveal parent educators' perspectives on their evolving roles, challenges, and successes. ⎤ **Prolonged data collection**

Participants

Nine parent educators participated in the focus groups; two of them participated in all of the six focus groups, two more participated in five of the groups, one participated in four of the groups, and one participated in three, of the groups. The other three participated in one or two of the focus groups. The participants were all women; three of them were African American, and six of them were White. Their ages varied; three of the parent educators were from 25 to 30 years of age, four of them were in the 30- to 35-year age range, and two were older than 35 years of age at the beginning of the focus groups. All had a child with a disability; one of them was currently served in the BCW program, and seven of them had children with disabilities who were preschool age when the mother started as a parent educator. ⎤ **Informant selection**

Procedures

Questioning the Focus Group.   The appendix lists the focus group probe questions, which were designed from a review of the literature regarding parent involvement and parents as partners, as well as focus groups in general. The intent of the qualitative study was to understand the perspectives of parents on their roles as parent educators, as well as ⎤ **Source of questions**

factors that influenced their success as parent educators. To ensure consistency across time, the same questions were asked at each focus group meeting. The purpose of the study was outlined at the beginning of each session, and confidentiality discussed and informed consent obtained at the beginning of the study. ⎤ **Ethics**   ⎤ **Semi-structured interviews**

Conducting the Focus Groups.   Five focus groups with the parent educators were held over a 2-year time period. A follow-up focus group with the three parent educators from the original group was held 5 years after the program began. Focus groups lasted from 45 to 90 minutes and were always held in conjunction with a meeting in which parent educators were in attendance. The focus groups were always held before any ⎤ **Logistics**

excerpt 14.14 *(continued)*

training or meeting occurred so that any discussion did not influence the answers. Table 1 shows the dates and number of participants for each focus group session.

⊐ Logistics (continued)

The six focus group sessions were conducted by a two-member research team consisting of the moderator (first author) and an observer (second author). The moderator, who had been trained in focus group and structured interview methodologies, led each session based on the focus group questions, monitored discussion, probed for additional comments and insights, and kept field notes during the session and immediately afterwards. The observer audio-taped all of the sessions (with the permission of the participants), recorded extensive field notes during each session, and verified the field notes recorded by the moderator.

⊐ **Roles of leaders**

Data Collection and Analysis

Field notes and recordings were used to collect data from the sessions. The tape recordings of each session were transcribed verbatim. The narrative data from all six sessions were analyzed using two levels of qualitative methods (Johnson & LaMontagne, 1993; Krueger, 1988; Lederman, 1990; Morgan, 1997): postdiscussion reflection and a code-category-theme process.

⊐ **Tape-recorded data**

Immediate Postdiscussion The observer verified the moderator's field notes. The moderator and observer reviewed the field notes and documented the main themes at the end of each focus group session. They also discussed contextual elements, such as the overall tone and climate of the discussion, and noted any representative quotations from participants (Bogdan & Biklen, 1992).

⊐ **Interview elaborations/
Reflex record**

Code-Category-Theme Process. The content of the focus groups was analyzed using a code-category-theme process (McWilliam, Young, & Harville, 1996) in order to obtain comprehensive data analysis. At the end of the sessions, all transcripts and field notes were read at one sitting by the first author. Data reduction and content analysis procedures, as described later, were then conducted on each individual session, using each question as a separate entity. The first author then read and reread each individual question across the six time periods to check for accuracy of the original categories generated. For example, the October 1996 data were analyzed using Questions 1, 2, 3, and so forth; and then Question 1 was analyzed using the transcripts from October 1996, February 1997, August 1997, and so forth.

⊐ **Data analysis process**

TABLE 1 Dates and Participants in Focus Group Sessions

— **Field log**

Focus Group Date	Time on Job	Parent Educators Present
10/21/96	7 mo.	7
2/27/97	1 yr.	7 (4 for 1 year; 2 for 3 months; 1 for 1 month)
8/18/97	almost 18 mo.	5 (1 had resigned; 1 not present)
2/19/98	almost 2 yrs.	7 (1 for 1 month)
11/23/98	2½ yrs.	4 (1 home with baby; 1 resignation; 1 not present)
5/25/01	5 yrs.	3 (original parent educators)

(continued)

e x c e r p t   1 4 . 1 4   *(c o n t i n u e d)*

Data Reduction in Three Phases.   First, the lead author (and later a second rater, who was not the observer) looked at the individual narrative units (sentences) and reduced the narrative to a simple, descriptive content phrase. For example, the sentences "I've done numerous workshops. I started over the summer with the program for children who were hearing impaired. And worked with that agency and bringing in the Babies Can't Wait component of it" were reduced to "conducted workshops." Second, these descriptive content units were categorized according to their underlying focus Johnson & LaMontagne, 1993; Marchant, 1995; Morningstar, Turnbull, & Turnbull, 1996). For example "talking to parents on the phone" and "a lot of calling " and "call backs" were all used under the category of making and receiving phone calls. Representative quotations were also noted in the various response categories. Third, themes and patterns emerged from the data after additional reviews that looked at the data question by question, as well as by time period. This final phase, called "integrating categories and their properties," led to identifying themes by combining categories with similar properties (Glaser & Strauss, 1967, p. 105).

> **Generating themes in data analysis phases**

A second rater independently read and coded the data. This second rater was used to verify the first author's categorizing and coding system and to check the accuracy of the themes and patterns that emerged. On the few occasions when discrepancies occurred, the transcripts were reread and evaluated by both raters, as well as the observer, in order to reach consensus among the three researchers.

> **Verifying codes, categories, and themes**

Credibility

> **Enhance validity strategies**

The credibility of the findings was verified through data triangulation (Webb, Campbell, Schwartz, & Sechrest, 1965) by using several sources (field notes by two persons, verbatim transcripts), multiple raters (moderator, observer, second rater), member checks on the accuracy of notes, and stakeholder reviews (Brotherson, 1994; Brotherson & Goldstein, 1992; Morningstar et al., 1996; Patton, 2002).

> **Triangulation**
>
> **Member checks**

The data were verified through review with several of the parent educators during and after each session. Parent educators agreed with the data as presented after the sessions and clarified minor details, such as names specific to their districts. To further ensure credibility and accuracy of the data, a stakeholder review was conducted. A draft of the present article was sent to eight of the nine participating parent educators for review. One had moved out of the country with a military spouse and was not able to be contacted. Parent educators were asked to either send in comments or respond to a follow-up phone call made to each parent in an effort to gather feedback on the content, tone, and accuracy of the article through questions such as, "Does the summary reflect what you think the group said?" Three of the eight parent educators responded; fortunately, the respondents had each attended at least five of the sessions. All of the respondents agreed that the content of the article accurately portrayed their experiences as parent educators across time.

> **Participant review**

One of the respondents pointed out that she believed parent educators might be perceived differently in rural versus urban areas of the state, noting that rural parent educators have to travel long distances for meetings. Because data were not kept specific to respondents, this reply was noted as a limitation in the discussion section. She also noted that many of the focus groups had taken place in conjunction with the annual statewide parent conference.

Results

> **Directly related to research purposes**

Results are presented relative to the three overall purposes of the study: perceived roles, challenges, and successes of the parent educators across time.

Roles

> **Synthesis of Theme 1 with short quotations**

Four general themes emerged in response to the question describing roles and responsibilities. Parent educators described their roles as gathering, sharing, and disseminating information; linking families to resources, the EI system, and other families; representing the parent perspective at the local EI office and on local and state committees; and being sensitive to special issues such as cultural diversity, single parenting, or the special needs of teen mothers. At the beginning, parent educators responded to the question about their roles and responsibilities by describing their role as one of gathering and sharing information and trying to make the BCW process more parent friendly. Parent educators described themselves as a bridge, an information specialist, and a resource guide for parents and said, "We parents do have a bond—no one else understands."

Parent educators also talked about the value of communication and the linkages among EI coordinators, themselves, and the service coordinators. Parent educators saw their role as one of reassuring parents, with one woman stating that she had assured parents "they were not overreacting. As a parent, we have to make sure that we have explored every avenue in order to be able to sleep well at night." They also saw their role as one of educating the professionals regarding family issues. The value of communication and linkages was reiterated at several of the later focus groups when parent educators discussed how much they thought their role had changed; they were now seen as an integral part of the local Babies Can't Wait office, a "regular," if you will.

Parent educators also mentioned the importance of being a parent voice on committees, and one said, "I found that they really respect the parents' point of view." They described numerous ways they believed they represented the parent perspective through work at the local EI office and work on local and state committees, such as the finance committee or the cultural diversity committee of the state interagency coordinating council. Parent educators expressed the desire for more training in special issues such as cultural diversity, single parenting, or the special needs of teen mothers as they viewed themselves as needing to be sensitive to and educated on these issues.

In response to the question about what a typical day was like, parent educators listed making phone calls, attending meetings, helping with mailings to parents, and putting together materials as the major activities in fulfilling their roles. Making phone calls was overwhelmingly the number one activity across all sessions. One parent educator described part of her day as "brainwork . . . you think a lot when you are doing all these things—writing letters, getting resources together; answering questions." Several also mentioned copying materials and reading many materials on a typical day so that they could give more parent input "where you know parental input would be valuable." In later focus groups, participants also mentioned traveling as a predominant activity, indicating that they were serving on more state committees and traveling across the district to meetings with parents and providers. Parent educators in later groups also mentioned that they were spending quite a bit of time focusing on relationships. One woman mentioned that she was "trying to figure out where parents are coming from and then where everyone else is coming from and why some families might still feel alienated."

Several patterns emerged that outline the experiences of parent educators across time. Parent educators became.more specific in expressing the nature of their role and in valuing their role and its unique importance over time. In a cyclical fashion, as they came to value and express the importance of their role, they wanted more information to share and wanted to be sure the information they had was adequate and up to date. A second pattern was that parent educators increasingly saw themselves as a bridge or a link between the EI program and families, in helping professionals to understand the needs and perspectives of families. A third pattern was that parent educators saw themselves as having more and more public relations responsibilities. They expressed feeling successful in this role, and as they came to feel accepted as "professionals," they wanted to stay current on the information they were disseminating. Another pattern was that parent educators found it important to spend time connecting with the information and, increasingly, the people they saw so they could do "their job." This involved talking to others, gathering information, and building relationships with BCW and the community. Not surprisingly with the immense strides in technology over the time period of the focus groups, the parent educators expressed an increasing need for and appreciation of technology resources in their jobs.

(continued)

excerpt 14.14 *(continued)*

Challenges

Overall themes related to challenges included not being able to consistently connect with local families, due to either confidentiality issues or "gatekeeping" by professionals; the challenge of helping the local district become more friendly to families; and later, the challenge of balancing home and family life with the demands of being a parent educator. Participants had many questions at the beginning focus groups such as "Should we go into homes?" and "How do we get into homes and learn who the families are?"—suggesting that a challenge was getting to know and communicating with the families they would work with. Connecting with local parents in their district remained a challenge for parent educators due to confidentiality guidelines. Later, permission forms used during intake allowed a parent educator to contact a parent if the parent wished to be contacted. A challenge mentioned in the third session was that even with release forms now available, all service coordinators were not necessarily distributing them; thus, initial contact with parents was still difficult. Parent educators also worried that their roles were not understood or appreciated by service coordinators. For instance, one service coordinator told a parent educator, "What parent educators do would not be of interest to the parents I work with." Thus, service coordinators may have been serving a "gatekeeping" function. In a final focus group, a parent educator mentioned that she had probably depended too much on her relationship with the early intervention coordinator in the district and that she should have, instead, spent time building relationships with the service coordinators who had direct access to the families.

Making activities and materials from the district office more "family friendly" was also a challenge. As one parent educator noted, "It is not conducive for parents to have meetings always from 11:30 to 1:00. We are here to make it parent friendly." Balancing the role of a parent educator with home and family life was a third challenge. Several parent educators mentioned the challenge of trying to balance managing phone calls in the evening as well as during the day. One mentioned that having to work in the evenings and on the weekends (as some parents requested contacts during these times) was a challenge for her: "When you work in your home, you work all the time." Balance between job and family life was mentioned again by several parent educators during the last focus groups, with one reporting that balancing family life with the job was a constant challenge, and another saying, "I feel like I want to be mom, too." A related challenge to the balance of home and family life was one that emerged over time—that of storing and organizing information.

Successes

Themes related to parent educator success included helping fellow parents; facilitating positive public relations about the EI program; educating professionals on the needs and perspectives of families, which leads to gaining the respect of professionals; and finally, feeling success at a personal level through contributing to the family income and from one's own growth as a professional.

At all sessions, most participants mentioned the success they felt when they helped a fellow parent, especially when "a parent calls me back and thanks me." By the later focus groups, parent educators again expressed success in their work with families, in "being able to answer their questions," and in "telling families in baby steps how the system works." During the final focus group, parent educators expressed how they liked to "help parents get what they need" and how successful they felt when parents told them they appreciated them.

At the beginning focus group session, parent educators felt that their greatest success was sharing the parent educator and Babies Can't Wait programs with others, This feeling of success continued to be mentioned as parent educators discussed work with community resources such as childcare centers. Parent educators also expressed success in educating professionals on the needs and perspectives of families. By the second session, they felt that they had a successful and comfortable relationship with the EI

Synthesis of Theme 2 with direct quotations

Synthesis of Theme 3 with brief quotations

excerpt 14.14 *(continued)*

coordinator and could "walk in to the EI coordinator and say 'This is important and I think you need to know about it'." Later, parent educators discussed the importance of educating the professionals about parents and expressed feeling that they had gained the "respect of other members of the special needs community." Parent educators agreed that real success was being taken seriously and having the trust and respect of the professionals with whom they worked. One stated, "People seek me out to ask questions, from parents to professionals. They understand that I am legitimate, that I know what I am talking about." One mentioned that she now realized "we have valuable information to give . . . " and that she sees the "big picture" of EI.

A final theme of success was noted on a personal level. Participants mentioned the success that being a parent educator had been to them on a personal level, by helping with their family's income and helping learn to conduct themselves in a more professional manner. One summed up her success by saying, "We know the top people in the state [and] they appreciate our involvement."

Discussion

The Parent Educator model builds on a perspective of parental involvement in early intervention outlined by Winton and DiVenere (1995) and later by Turnbull et al. (1999), with a focus on family members as educators of other professionals. The model values the expertise of parents as a critical resource for professionals and for other parents. The progress of parent educators was documented through quantitative and qualitative methods, including surveys from the families and EI personnel they worked with and their own perspectives through focus groups. General themes emerged from the focus groups regarding the parent educators' perspectives on their roles, challenges, and successes.

The themes that emerged describing the roles and successes of the parent educators over time are consistent with the work of Capone et al. (1997) in documenting the partnerships that can develop between parents and professionals in an EI system. Interestingly, over time, parent educators asked for more for themselves, both financially, and emotionally (raises, retreats). This may be because they came to view themselves increasingly as "professionals" and reported that they were treated as such over time. According to Golin and Ducanis (1981), a *profession* is a group of people who have unique skills and knowledge that are established in stages, culminating in external recognition of the autonomy of the profession. In this study, parent educators came to value themselves more as professionals and were able to ask more for themselves and see the value they each had to offer. They came to view the expertise among the group members and began requesting teambuilding activities and retreats in an effort to grow and learn from each other. Across time, they continued to be optimistic and hopeful in working to meet their goals. Their tasks remained basically the same across time, although their challenges became more "personal," including balancing their own family and work issues, rather than issues of relationships with professionals or families in the BCW system. This points to the importance of building a model that is fluid and ever evolving for family participants.

Relates findings to literature

Qualitative research methodology inherently warrants some cautions (York & Tundidot; 1995). First is a limitation involving participants. The participants in this study came from only one state; thus, the results cannot be assumed to generalize to other parent populations. The parent educators hired in this model were all mothers; consequently, the perspective of a male parent educator was not available. Additionally, although two of the participants remained the same across focus groups, new parent educators were added as participants, changing the makeup and dynamics of the group and, thus, possibly affecting the outcomes. Changing focus group members over time might have influenced the themes discussed. Another possible limitation is that the data were not kept specific to the urban or rural category of residence of the participants. It may be that parent educators from different parts of the state had different perspectives specific to the nature

Limitation 1

(continued)

e x c e r p t   1 4 . 1 4 *(continued)*

search such as this brings a unique perspective of a critical stakeholder—to the parent— which is valuable (Johnson & LaMontagne, 1993) in generating future policy and research directions in EI. — **Limitation 1 (continued)**

Second, sampling bias may have occurred. Because participants had all voluntarily applied for the role of parent educator, this could have influenced their perceptions of their roles and responsibilities, challenges, or successes, or how they adapted to them. Other parents in such a position might react in a different manner. Facilitator bias can also be a — **Limitation 2**

limitation of focus group methodology. The first author (who also served as the focus group moderator) is a strong advocate of parents being fully involved and embedded in EI systems. She chose to study this issue to document the perceptions of the parent educators as they began a new role and followed them over time as they became more involved with families and professionals. It is possible that her biases might have affected the results. Although care was taken to optimize the reliability of the findings through the use of several sources and raters, the perspectives of the researchers involved are present and the potential exists for researcher bias during the data reduction phases. Finally, the same questions were used in each focus group session. It is possible that the repeated nature of the questions might have influenced the responses over time. — **Limitation 3**

As programs continue to look at a focus on family members as leaders in public policy and system improvement, it is important to have effective models in place to promote their growth and development and to continually expand the ways to involve family members at their level of comfort. Future research may look at what strategies are effective in achieving outcomes for varying types of families or whether geographic differences between parents in urban or rural areas play a role in parent education. This focus group data — **Future research**

provide a holistic understanding of the parent educator role from their own perspectives. Families of children in the program are the ultimate consumers of parent educator activities, and it is important to have their perspective in evaluating the overall program. In this case, families consistently rated the parent educators as being most helpful in the area of disseminating information, encouraging families to become involved in EI, and helping families feel like an important member of the EI team, supporting the perspectives of the parent educators regarding the value of their roles. The Parent Educator model brought families into the system at all levels, including locally with families and health district staff members and statewide in committees and policy development.

Authors' Note. Partial support for this project was provided by the Georgia Department of Human Resources, Division of Public Health, Babies Can't Wait Program. The opinions expressed herein do not necessarily reflect the policy of the granting agency, and no official endorsement by this agency should be inferred.

References

Allen, R. L., & Petr, C. G. (1996). Toward developing standards and measurements for family-centered practice in family support programs. In G. H. S. Singer, L. E. Powers, & A. L. Olson (Eds.), *Redefining family support: Innovations in public-private partnerships* (pp. 39–56). Baltimore: Brookes.

Bailey, D. B., Jr. (2001). Evaluating parent involvement and family support in early intervention and preschool programs. *Journal of Early Intervention, 24,* 1–14.

Bogdan, R. C., & Biklen, S. K. (1982). *Qualitative research for education: An introduction to theory and methods.* Boston: Allyn & Bacon.

Bogdan, R. C., & Biklen, S. K. (1992). *Qualitative research for education: An introduction to theory and methods* (2nd ed.). Boston: Allyn & Bacon.

Brotherson, M. J. (1994). Interactive focus group interviewing: A qualitative research method in early intervention. *Topics in Early Childhood Special Education. 14*(1),101–118.

Brotherson, M. J., & Goldstein, B. L. (1992). Quality design of focus groups in early childhood special education research. *Journal of Early Intervention, 16,* 334–342.

Bruder, M. B. (2000). Family-centered early intervention: Clarifying our values for the new millennium. *Topics in Early Childhood Special Education, 20,* 105–115.

excerpt 14.14 *(continued)*

Capone, A., Hull, K. M., & DiVenere, N. J. (1997). Partnerships in preservice and inservice education. In P. J. Winton, J. A. McCollum, & C. Catlett (Eds.), *Reforming personnel preparation in early intervention* (pp. 435–449). Baltimore: Brookes.

Dunst, C. J. (1999). Placing parent education in conceptual and empirical context. *Topics in Early Childhood Special Education, 19,* 141–147.

Dunst, C. J., Trivette, C. M., & Deal, A. G. (Eds.). (1994). *Supporting and strengthening families: Volume 1: Methods, strategies, and practices.* Cambridge, MA: Brookline Books.

Glaser, B. G., & Strauss, A. L. (1967). *The discovery of grounded theory strategies for qualitative research.* New York: Aldine.

Golin, A., & Ducanis, J. (1981). *The interdisciplinary team.* Rockville, MD: Aspen.

Hanson, J. L., Randall, V. F., & Colston, S. S. (1999). Parent advisors: Enhancing services for young children with special needs. *Infants and Young Children, 12*(1),17–25.

Individuals with Disabilities Education Act of 1990, 20 U.S.C. § 1400 *et seq.*

Johnson, L. J., & LaMontagne, M. J. (1993). Research methods: Using content analysis to examine the verbal or written communication of stakeholders within early intervention. *Journal of Early Intervention, 17,* 73–79.

Krueger, R. A. (1988). *Focus groups: A practical guide for applied research.* Newbury Park, CA: Sage.

Lederman, L. C. (1990). Assessing educational effectiveness: The focus group interview as a technique for data collection. *Communication Education, 38*(2),117–127.

Mahoney, G., Kaiser, A., Girolametto, L., MacDonald, J., Robinson, C., Safford, P., et al. (1999). Parent education in early intervention: A call for a renewed focus. *Topics in Early Childhood Special Education, 19*(3),131–140.

Marchant, C. (1995). Teachers' views of integrated preschools. *Journal of Early Intervention, 19,* 61–73.

McWilliam, R. A. (2001, April). *Early intervention programs changing to focus on natural environments.* Paper presented at the meeting of the Council for Exceptional Children, Kansas City, MO.

McWilliam, R. A., Young, H. J., & Harville, K. (1996). Therapy services in early intervention: Current status, barriers, and recommendations. *Topics in Early Childhood Special Education, 16,* 348–374.

Morgan, D. L. (1997). *Focus groups as qualitative research* (2nd ed.). Thousand Oaks, CA: Sage.

Morgan, D. L., & Krueger R. A. (1993). When to use focus groups and why. In D. L Morgan (Ed.), *Successful focus groups: Advancing the state of the art* (pp. 3–19). Newbury Park, CA: Sage.

Morningstar, M., Turnbull, A. P., & Turnbull, H. (1996). What do students with disabilities tell us about the importance of family involvement in the transition from school to adult life. *Exceptional Children, 62,* 249–260.

Patton, M. Q. (2002). *Qualitative research and evaluation methods* (3rd ed.). Thousand Oaks, CA: Sage.

Turnbull, A. P., Blue-Banning, M., Turbiville, V., & Park, J. (1999). From parent education to partnership education: A call for a transformed focus. *Topics in Early Childhood Special Education, 19,* 164–172.

Webb, E. J., Campbell, D. T., Schwartz, R. D., & Sechrest, L. (1965). *Unobtrusive measures.* Chicago: Rand McNally.

Whitehead, A., Jesien, G., & Ulanaki, B. K. (1998). Weaving parents into the fabric of early intervention interdisciplinary training: How to integrate and support family involvement in training. *Infants and Young Children, 10*(3), 44–53.

Winton, P. J., & DiVenere, N. (1995). Family-professional partnerships in early intervention personnel preparation: Guidelines and strategies. *Topics in Early Childhood Special Education, 15,* 296–313.

Winton, P. J., Sloop, S., & Rodriguez, P. (1999). Parent education: A term whose time is past. *Topics in Early Childhood Special Education, 19,*157–161.

York, J., & Tundidor, M. (1995). Issues raised in the name of inclusion: Perspectives of educators, parents, and students. *Journal of the Association for Persons with Severe Handicaps, 20*(1), 31–44.

Appendix: Focus Group Questions

1. Describe your role as a parent educator. What are your responsibilities?
2. What is a typical day like for you?
3. What has been your biggest challenge in being a parent educator so far?
4. What has been your greatest success as a parent educator so far?
5. What training needs do you have?
6. What do you wish you had more information on? What else do you need to know to be able to do your job?
7. What other resources and supports do you need?
8. If Georgia had just been given thousands of dollars to expand its parent education component for Part C or beyond, how would you suggest the money be spent?

Open-response questions

Source: From Gallagher, P. A., Rhodes, C. A., & Darling, S. M. (2004). Parents as professionals in early intervention: A parent educator model. *Topics in Early Childhood Special Education, 24*(1), 5–13. Adapted with permission.

SUMMARY

The following statements summarize the process and techniques of qualitative data analysis:

1. In inductive analysis, the categories and patterns emerge from the data, rather than being imposed on the data prior to data collection.

2. Analytic styles of qualitative data analysis include prefigured technical, template, editing, and crystallization styles.

3. Interim analysis, done while in the field, assists in making data collection decisions and identifying recurring topics.

4. Comparing and contrasting is used in practically all intellectual tasks during analysis.

5. Data must be organized in order to analyze them, using either predetermined categories or developing codes from the data.

6. Predetermined categories are derived from the research problem, an interview guide, literature, and personal or general knowledge.

7. A data segment (e.g., a word, sentence, paragraph, or page) is comprehensible by itself and contains one idea, episode, or piece of relevant information.

8. The term *code* is the descriptive name for the subject matter or topic.

9. Researchers refine their provisional organizing system of codes (topics) throughout the study.

10. A *category* is an abstract term used to describe the meaning of similar topics.

11. Some analysts develop no more than 25 to 35 codes, which are grouped later. Other analysts, using predetermined categories, begin with 6 to 10 categories and develop subcomponents (codes). In either approach, the initial codes or categories are continuously refined.

12. Techniques to develop categories include refining analytic questions, making mental comparison of similar and unlikely situations, and analyzing "red flags."

13. Emic terms represent the insider's or participants' view; etic terms represent a cross-cultural scientific view—that is, the researcher's views, concepts, or social science phrases. Emic terms are used at the beginning, and etic terms are applied later. Etic terms are necessary for communicating with other researchers and social scientists.

14. A *pattern* is a relationship among categories.

15. Techniques for pattern seeking include triangulation, ordering and sorting categories, analyzing discrepant or negative evidence, constructing visual representations, and conducting logical cross-analyses.

16. Patterns are plausible explanations when they are supported by data and alternative patterns are not reasonable.

17. Data management comprises the use of a partially or completely electronic system to retrieve data sets and to assemble coded data in one place. Researchers can combine manual techniques with word-processing programs or use specially designed qualitative data analysis (QDA) software.

18. Deciding to use a QDA program begins with assessing one's needs, computer skills, and other factors. Choosing a specific QDA program requires investigating the available choices and knowing your analytical style to taylor the program to your research.

19. Qualitative studies encode for different audiences, acknowledge authorial presence, and frame an appropriate narrative structure for the qualitative design or purpose.

20. Qualitative studies present the context and the quotations of participants' language as data.

RESEARCH NAVIGATOR NOTES

Reading the following articles will help you understand the content of this chapter. Go to the education database (included in the EBSCO database) in Research Navigator; use the Accession Number provided to find the article.

14.1   *Evidence*
Miller, S., & Fredericks, M. (2003) The nature of "evidence" in qualitative research methods. *International Journal of Qualitative Research Methods, 2*(1), 1–27. Accession Number: 10614569.

14.2   *Analytical Induction*
Morse, J. M., & Mitcham, C. (2002). Exploring qualitatively-derived concepts: Inductive-deductive pitfalls. *International Journal of Qualitative Research Methods, 1*(4), 1–18. Accession Number: 10614560.

14.3   *Electronic or Not?*
Basit, T. (2003). Manual or electronic? The role of coding in qualitative data analysis. *Educational Research, 45*(2), 143–155. Accession Number: 10473857.

14.4   *A Study*
Wasserstein-Warnet, M. M., & Klein, Y. (2000). Principals' cognitive strategies for changes of perspective in school innovation. *School Leadership and Management, 20*(4), 435–458. Accession Number: 4052812.

14.5 *Issues in Critical Studies*
Segall, A. (2001). Critical ethnography and the invocation of voice: From the field/in the field—single exposure, dou-

ble standard? *International Journal of Qualitative Studies in Education, 14*(4), 579–593. Accession Number: 5171609.

CHECK YOURSELF

Multiple-choice review items, with answers, are available at the Companion Website for this book:

www.ablongman.com/mcmillanschumacher6e.

APPLICATION PROBLEMS

1. Below are published paraphrases of teachers' beliefs about kindergarten readiness and practices (M. L. Smith & L. S. Shepard, 1988, pp. 316–319). Identify the line numbers for categories of the following:
   * Beliefs about child development
   * Beliefs about the possibility of catching up
   * Beliefs about the possibilities of influencing a child's preparation for school
   * Beliefs about what teachers can do

Also list any other categories you see in the data.

Mrs. Willis:

1 "Because development constitutes physiological unfolding, rates of
2 development are smooth, continuous, with no spurts or discontinuities. The
3 child who is 6 months behind in September will be 6 months behind in
4 June. . . . There is little likelihood that a child who is developmentally behind
5 his agemates would close the gap that separates them. . . . Intervention is
6 futile with a developmentally unready child. Extra help or remediation
7 causes pressure, frustration and compensation. Teachers cannot influence
8 psychomotor abilities, ability to attend, social maturity, and so
9 forth. . . . Teachers can provide the child with more time to mature; place the
10 child in developmental kindergarten or preschool, send him home another
11 year; place the child in a slow group in class; reduce instruction below
12 frustration level, lower expectations, boost self-concept, use
13 manipulatives; retain in kindergarten; providing academic assistance is
14 irrelevant and harmful."

Miss Johnson:

15 "Within broad limits of chronological age, children's readiness is a
16 function of their experience, learning program, and environment. . . . A child
17 who is less prepared than his peers can close the gap given the right
18 educational circumstances; academic assistance is required. . . . The teacher
19 can make a difference as can the parent and other aspects of environment;
20 within a broad range of pupil abilities, what the pupil learns is largely a
21 function of opportunities and experiences. . . . The teacher can provide
22 additional academic help; accommodate differences in achievement; hold high
23 expectations, reinforce and train; work hard and encourage the pupil to work
24 hard."

2. Now, go back and look at the meaning of each category. Do certain beliefs occur with other beliefs. That is, does one category relate to another category to suggest a pattern? State any patterns you see in the data.

NOTES

1. See Basit (2003) for a description of using predetermined categories in a project and developing codes from data in another project.
2. See Basit (2003) for a description of analyzing data manually and then electronically for two different studies.
3. For more information, go to www.audiencedialogue.org/soft-qual.htlm.
4. For more information, go to www.bc.edu/offices/ats/rits/research/software/descriptions/qualitative.
5. See Ryan and Bernard (2000) for information about data management and analysis methods and Weston et al. (2001) for a description of the process of team coding.
6. See Clandinin and Connelly (2000) and Richardson (1998, pp. 355–361) for cited examples and journals.

EMERGING METHODS OF RESEARCH

The methodologies of educational research are constantly evolving and changing. As we have already noted, qualitative designs became much more popular over the last 25 years, and experimental designs are making a comeback in popularity. In the past decade, three additional trends have emerged, and this part provides an introduction to each. The first and perhaps most significant trend is the use of mixed-method designs, which are studies that combine quantitative and qualitative features. The second trend, which is just under way among all researchers, is the use of secondary data analysis. (Some researchers have used secondary data analysis for many years.) This kind of study, which depends on being able to obtain electronic databases, uses data that have already been collected and analyzes them in new and different ways. Finally, conducting action research is becoming standard practice in some schools of education and local school districts, as teachers and administrators focus on researching local problems and questions.

Chapter 15 summarizes the essential characteristics of each of these emerging methods and provides examples from the literature. We hope this introduction will generate interest and further reading.

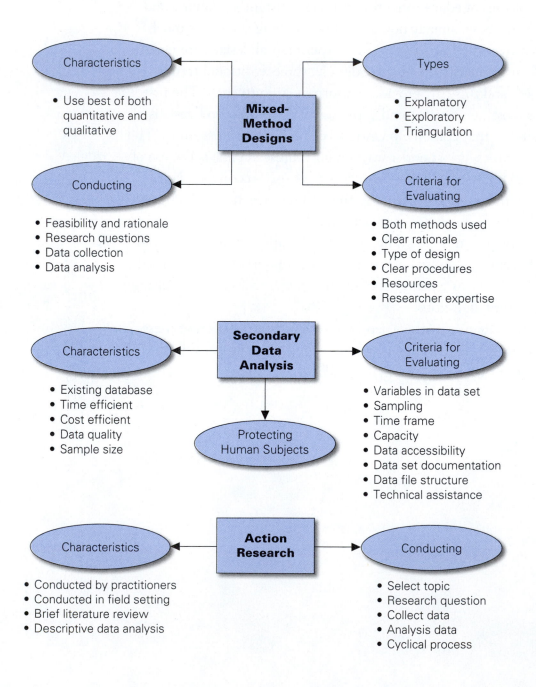

Mixed-Method Designs

Characteristics
- Use best of both quantitative and qualitative

Types
- Explanatory
- Exploratory
- Triangulation

Conducting
- Feasibility and rationale
- Research questions
- Data collection
- Data analysis

Criteria for Evaluating
- Both methods used
- Clear rationale
- Type of design
- Clear procedures
- Resources
- Researcher expertise

Secondary Data Analysis

Characteristics
- Existing database
- Time efficient
- Cost efficient
- Data quality
- Sample size

Criteria for Evaluating
- Variables in data set
- Sampling
- Time frame
- Capacity
- Data accessibility
- Data set documentation
- Data file structure
- Technical assistance

Protecting Human Subjects

Action Research

Characteristics
- Conducted by practitioners
- Conducted in field setting
- Brief literature review
- Descriptive data analysis

Conducting
- Select topic
- Research question
- Collect data
- Analysis data
- Cyclical process

KEY TERMS

mixed-method designs
explanatory design
exploratory design
triangulation design

secondary data
secondary data analysis
action research

This chapter introduces three approaches to educational research that have become increasingly common in the last 10 years: mixed-method designs, secondary data analysis, and action research. These designs are helpful for integrating qualitative and quantitative methods, for using existing databases, and for helping practitioners conduct research in school settings.

MIXED-METHOD DESIGNS

by Angela L. Snyder

The development and use of **mixed-method designs** (also called *mixed-mode*) have increased in recent years as researchers have realized that often the best approach to answering research questions is to use both quantitative and qualitative methods in the same study. For example, consider investigating whether there is a relationship between high-stakes testing and dropout rate when successful achievement is needed for graduation. On the surface, this question lends itself nicely to a nonexperimental, quantitative study, in which characteristics of students, including their scores on graduation tests, can be entered into a regression model to determine if performance on the tests predicts dropping out once other variables have been controlled. On a deeper level, it would also be helpful to understand *why* students did not perform better on the tests and how having graduation tests affects students' motivation. These issues could be studied most effectively using interviews with students, teachers, and parents. By combining quantitative data with qualitative data, a more complete understanding of the relationship between high-stakes testing and dropping out can be developed.

There are both advantages and disadvantages to using a mixed-method design. On the positive side, using both approaches allows the researcher to incorporate the strengths of each method. This provides for a more comprehensive picture of what is being studied, emphasizing quantitative outcomes as well as the process that influenced the outcomes. In addition, the nature of the data collected is not confined to one type of method, which encourages producing a more complete set of research questions as well as conclusions. It is also helpful to supplement a primarily quantitative or qualitative study with some data from the other method.

There are also some negatives to using mixed-method designs. First, combining qualitative and quantitative methods in a single study requires that the researcher have competence in each type. While it is relatively easy to gain an introductory understanding of both methodologies, greater depth of knowledge is needed to avoid less than credible findings. Second, a mixed-method study requires extensive data collection and more resources than many studies using only a quantitative or qualitative approach. This suggests that it may not always be feasible to conduct a mixed-method study. Finally, with the popularity of mixed methods, researchers may use one of the approaches superficially. For example, a researcher conducting a survey of school administrators about school climate could use both closed-ended (quantitative) and open-ended questions (presumably qualitative). Such a study would not be an example of a mixed-method design, however, since the "qualitative" part would not include characteristics of an actual qualitative investigation. Similarly, if a researcher used random sampling to identify a group of counselors and then conducted in-depth interviews, it would be misleading to call this a mixed-method study. There is a small trend toward using the term *mixed method* rather liberally to include any study that has some degree of each method in the research. We believe that it is best to use this term only for studies that include extensive aspects of both methodologies. It should not simply be a case of having more than one type of data collection or one type of data analysis.

A mixed-method study can be quickly identified by the title, methodology section, or research questions. Often, the title of the article will use the words *mixed method* or *quantitative and qualitative*. The title could also use the terms *mixed model*, *mixed approaches*, *combined*, and *integrated*. In the methodology section, there will be a clear indication of collecting both quantitative and qualitative data, usually in different sections or parts. Often, the research questions or purpose will include reference to using mixed methods or having both quantitative and qualitative purposes. Excerpt 15.1 shows how the methodology section of an article indicates the use of mixed methods.

Types of Mixed-Method Designs

Mixed-method designs can differ to a great extent, depending on the purpose of the research design as well as the sequence in which quantitative and qualitative methods are used and the emphasis given to each method. We will begin to examine these designs by discussing a notation system that helps clarify the nature of the study.

Notation System

Creswell (2002) describes the following notation system to represent different mixed-method designs:

- Uppercase letters (e.g., *QUAL* or *QUANT*) indicate a priority given to the method identified.
- Lowercase letters (e.g., *qual* or *quant*) show a lower priority given to the method.
- An arrow ($\longrightarrow$) indicates the sequence of the collection of data.
- A + indicates the simultaneous collection of both quantitative and qualitative data.

Explanatory Design In an **explanatory design,** quantitative and qualitative data are gathered sequentially, often in two phases, with the primary emphasis on quantitative methods. Initially, quantitative data are collected and analyzed. This is followed by qualitative data collection and analysis.

$$QUANT \longrightarrow qual$$

The qualitative data are needed to explain quantitative results or to further elaborate on quantitative findings.

An explanatory design is generally used when quantitative data collection is clearly warranted but further analysis—specifically, using qualitative methods—is necessary to

EXCERPT 15.1 Mixed-Method Study Identified by Methodology

Types of issues discussed and the impact of the support community on beginning teachers were examined using three data sources: messages generated by participants, follow-up phone interviews, and an online survey.

Source: From Helsel DeWert, M., Babinski, L., & Jones, B. (2003). Safe passages: providing online support to beginning teachers. *Journal of Teacher Education, 54*(4), 311–321.

elucidate the quantitative findings. For example, in a study comparing alternatively and traditionally prepared teachers, Miller, McKenna, and McKenna (1998) used three separate phases to answer their primary research question regarding differences in teaching practices between teachers who were traditionally certified and those who were alternatively certified (i.e., individuals who became teachers after having careers in other fields). The first two phases of the study were quantitative and utilized random sampling techniques and a 15-item rating scale to determine differences in teaching ability between the two groups. The last phase of the study used qualitative, in-person interviews to "gain insight into . . . teachers' perceptions of their teaching abilities" (p. 169). While this study focused primarily on quantitative data, the qualitative interviews provided a richer understanding of the teachers' perceptions of their own abilities and how their training and certification program provided them with preparation for their teaching careers.

Another example of a mixed-method explanatory study was conducted by McMillan (2000). In this study, a large sample of teachers (850) was surveyed to determine the extent to which they used different factors in classroom assessment and grading. This provided a general overview of the teachers' practices. In the second phase, teachers were selected who represented high or low scores on the factors. Qualitative interviews were conducted with these teachers to determine why certain factors were emphasized. Thus, the qualitative phase was used to augment the statistical data to provide explanations for the practices.

Research Navigator.com

15.1 Explanatory Mixed-Method Study
Accession No.: 12670776

Exploratory Design   A second type of mixed-method research is the **exploratory design,** in which qualitative data collection and analysis is followed by a quantitative phase. Generally, the purpose of an exploratory design is either to use the qualitative data exploring a particular phenomenon to develop a quantitative instrument to measure that phenomenon or to use the quantitative portion of the study to explore relationships found in the qualitative data. If the main purpose is to test out an instrument, there may be a greater emphasis on the quantitative part of the study:

$$Qual \longrightarrow QUANT$$

If the quantitative portion of the study is used to confirm, determine, or expand on qualitative findings, then the qualitative part of the study will be emphasized:

$$QUAL \longrightarrow quant$$

Using quantitative data to explore relationships found in qualitative studies allows the researcher to gather in-depth information from participants. This can be achieved by listening during interviews or focus groups and determining if any of the themes appear to be related and then following up with a quantitative measure to further explore those relationships, basically quantifying the connection established during the qualitative phase.

In developing a quantitative instrument from qualitative data, the researcher can use the language and emphasis of the participants in the wording of the items for the survey or scale. Doing so increases the validity of the scores from the newly developed instrument. For example, in a study by Rue, Dingley, and Bush (2002), the researchers utilized qualitative interviews and language from many different participants with chronic health conditions to develop a quantitative instrument to measure the inner strength of women. This study relied heavily on participant language and experiences with chronic conditions in order to develop items for a survey that could then quantitatively measure inner strength—a new concept in the field and one that had not previously been studied quantitatively.

Like explanatory designs, exploratory designs have both advantages and disadvantages. One advantage is that the quantitative portion of an exploratory study actually relies on the qualitative analysis to drive its direction, providing a greater understanding of the purpose of the quantitative data collection and analysis. However, like explanatory designs, exploratory designs require extensive data collection and analysis for both the qualitative and quantitative phases of the study. Moreover, it is sometimes difficult to indicate specifically how the qualitative findings were used to determine or influence the quantitative part of the study.

Triangulation Design   The third type of mixed-method study is a **triangulation design,** in which the researcher simultaneously gathers both quantitative and qualitative data, merges them using both quantitative and qualitative data analysis methods, and then interprets the results together to provide a better understanding of a phenomenon of interest. Approximately equal emphasis is given to each method, even though one can follow the other:

$$QUAL + QUANT \quad \text{or} \quad QUANT + QUAL$$

Or both can be conducted at the same time:

$$QUANT$$
$$+$$
$$QUAL$$

The interpretation of results is the key to this method, as it provides a convergence of evidence in which the results of both methods either support or contradict each other. When the results of different methods converge and support one another, researchers have *triangulated* the findings. In this case, the use of different methods results in very strong results. Often, the strengths of one method offset the weaknesses of the other, which allows for a much stronger overall design and thus more credible conclusions. Quantitative results enhance generalizability while qualitative results help explain context. For example, a recent study examined the relationship between working and family involvement in a child's education (Weiss et al., 2003). The researchers used concurrent quantitative and qualitative data collection and analysis to fully explore the relationship. They used data from an ongoing longitudinal study and also conducted interviews with working mothers and their children in order to determine the impact of working on family involvement in education. The researchers explain their methods in Excerpt 15.2.

While giving equal priority to both methods is great for validity, triangulation requires that researchers be able to conduct both qualitative and quantitative methods. It is also a challenge to merge the qualitative and quantitative data so that there is a single study, not two studies.

Table 15.1 summarizes the three major types of mixed-method designs.

EXCERPT 15.2 Triangulation Mixed-Method Design

For this study we employed a mixed-method approach, using both quantitative and qualitative analyses. The added value of mixed-method analysis has been well documented in the literature, allowing, for example, better data triangulation and expansion of findings. We conducted the quantitative analyses in two phases: (a) We estimated the associations between demographic characteristics of mothers and their work/school statuses and their levels of school involvement; and (b) we estimated the association between mothers' work/school statuses and their levels of school involvement. Qualitative techniques supporting description and interpretation included reviewing ethnographic field notes, writing analytic memos, and systematically coding interviews. . . . Presented separately in the results below, these quantitative and qualitative analyses occurred in part on "parallel tracks." However, we also employed a "cross-over tracks" approach—an iterative mixed-method process, such that emergent findings from one method helped to shape subsequent analyses.

Source: From Weiss, H. B., Mayer, E., Kreider, H., Vaughan, M., Dearing, E., Hencke, R., & Pinto, K. (2003). Making it work: Low-income working mothers' involvement in their children's education. *American Educational Research Journal, 40*(4), 879–901.

TABLE 15.1	Types and Purposes of Mixed-Method Designs	
Type	**Design**	**Purpose(s)**
Explanatory	Quantitative method followed by qualitative method	Qualitative data are used to elucidate, elaborate on, or explain quantitative findings (e.g., outliers or different groups). Qualitative data are used to develop a quantitative instrument or survey.
Exploratory	Qualitative method followed by quantitative method	Using qualitative data to establish groups to be compared. Using quantitative data to explore relationships found in qualitative data.
Triangulation	Quantitative and qualitative methods are concurrent	To provide a more comprehensive and complete picture of data by converging data analysis methods and offsetting strengths and weaknesses of each method.

Conducting Mixed-Method Research

Creswell (2002) identifies seven sequential steps in conducting mixed-method studies:

1. ***Determine the feasibility of doing a mixed-method study.*** Feasibility is a function of the adequacy of training of study personnel and resources to collect and analyze the data. Sufficient time is needed to complete the data collection and analysis, and researchers must have expertise in both quantitative and qualitative methods.

2. ***Determine the rationale.*** It is important to identify the reasons for conducting a mixed-method study and to determine whether these reasons provide sufficient justification. Researchers must be explicit about why a mixed-method study is preferable to one that is entirely either quantitative or qualitative.

3. ***Identify a data collection strategy and design.*** It is also important to identify the extent to which each of the two methods will be used, whether priority will be given to one method, and in what sequence the two methods will be used. This information will be used to identify the design as exploratory, explanatory, or triangulation. It is helpful at this point to construct a diagram to show data collection methods in the sequence used with assigned emphasis. Often, different *phases* are used to identify different stages of the design.

4. ***Determine research questions.*** While it is important to formulate a general purpose prior to establishing a design, at this point, specific research questions can be formulated. Both quantitative and qualitative questions should be developed (although in an explanatory study, it may not be possible to establish qualitative questions until the quantitative questions have been addressed). Quantitative research questions should state expected relationships, while qualitative questions should be nondirectional.

5. ***Collect the data.*** The sequence for collecting data is determined by the design (i.e., exploratory, explanatory, or triangulation). This stage of conducting the study will be lengthy, and appropriate principles for credible data collection for both the quantitative and qualitative phases should be followed.

6. ***Analyze the data.*** The data are analyzed depending on the nature of the design. Data analyses for exploratory and explanatory designs are done separately. With a triangulation design, the quantitative and qualitative data are analyzed concurrently in an integrated fashion.

7. **Write the report.** Like many aspects of planning and conducting mixed-method studies, the preparation of the report also depends on the nature of the design. The report can be constructed to reflect each phase by providing separate sections for each phase and then reflecting the synthesis of the results of each phase in drawing conclusions. Triangulation designs integrate the qualitative and quantitative findings for each research question.

The key to carrying out a credible mixed-method study is to ensure that both quantitative and qualitative methods are well executed and then to make reasonable interpretations. Given a clear rationale and appropriate resources, the quality of the conclusions rests on how well each method was conducted. The criteria for evaluating a mixed-method study include those identified earlier for both quantitative and qualitative results. The following questions should be considered (Creswell, 2002):

- Is it clear that both quantitative and qualitative methods were used?
- Is it identified as a *mixed-method study?*
- Is there a clear rationale that states a convincing case for doing a mixed-method study?
- Is the type of mixed-method design indicated?
- Is a priority stated for using different methods, and is an explanation made for the sequence of data collection used?
- Considering the available resources and the expertise of the researcher, is the study feasible?
- Are there both quantitative and qualitative research questions?
- Have data collection and analysis procedures been clearly described?
- Is the written structure consistent with the nature of the design?

SECONDARY DATA ANALYSIS

by Kirsten Barrett

Defining Secondary Data

Secondary data, simply put, are data that have already been collected. They are different from primary data in that the data user had no involvement in the data collection effort. When a researcher analyzes data that have been collected by some other organization, group, or individual at some prior time, the work is called **secondary data analysis**[1] (Kiecolt & Natham, 1985). Examples include a local school administrator analyzing decennial census data to better understand the socioeconomic status of parents in the community, a principal examining trends in high-stakes testing from a state database, and a parent analyzing achievement test scores across a number of schools to inform decisions about family relocation.

Reasons for Using Secondary Data

A researcher may choose to use secondary data for a number of reasons. Four of the most significant are the benefits of time efficiency, cost effectiveness, data quality, and increased sample size.

Using secondary data can save considerable time. The researcher does not need to spend time designing the research study and collecting primary data. When using secondary data, this work has already been done. Time savings can be a significant benefit when a person or an organization needs to make program or policy decisions within a short period of time. Also, students completing coursework, master's theses, or doctoral dissertations can often expedite their efforts by using secondary data.

Using secondary data also can be cost effective. Cost savings are realized because the researcher does not need to fund the primary data collection. Costs related to photocopy-

**Research
Navigator.c⊕m**

15.2 Secondary Data
Analysis
Accession No.: 7675348

ing, postage, telecommunication charges, personnel time, and data entry are minimized, as well. Also, many secondary data sets are freely available in electronic format from reputable organizations such as the Inter-University Consortium for Social and Political Research, the National Center for Education Statistics, the U.S. Census Bureau, and the National Center for Health Statistics. Further, state-level department of education websites often contain accessible, downloadable data pertaining to, among other things, achievement and accountability test scores, graduation rates, and disciplinary actions. Table 15.2 contains a listing of the key sources of secondary data and the Internet address for each.

A third benefit is data quality. Depending on the data set being used, the findings that result from secondary analyses may well have a high degree of validity and reliability. Reputable data collection organizations have the fiscal and human resources necessary to develop and extensively test surveys prior to implementing them. These organizations also have the resources necessary to field surveys using sampling methods and sample sizes that allow for reliable and valid population estimates.

ALERT!   The term *secondary* does not mean less important or significant in this context.

Finally, secondary data sets usually provide very large samples. With increased sample size comes greater flexibility in examining identified subgroups (especially small segments of the population), improved reliability, and generally credible results. However, large samples can also result in producing statistically significant findings that have little practical significance.

Considerations for Using Secondary Data

A number of factors should be considered when deciding if secondary data and secondary data analyses are appropriate to answer a research question or to test a research hypothesis:

1. *Does the data set contain variables that will allow the research question to be answered or the research hypothesis to be tested?* If the answer is *no* or *probably not*, then the data set is not appropriate. If the data set does contain the variables of

TABLE 15.2 Key Sources of Secondary Data	
Source	**Internet Address**
Inter-University Consortium for Social and Political Research (ICPSR)	www.icpsr.com
National Center for Education Statistics	http://nces.ed.gov
U.S. Census Bureau	www.census.gov
National Center for Health Statistics	www.cdc.gov/nchs
State-level departments of education	Examples: Virginia: www.pen.k12.va.us/VDOE/Publications Texas: www.tea.state.tx.us/research Maine: www.state.me.us/education/data/homepage.htm

interest, the researcher needs to determine how the data were collected. That is, how were the questions worded, and what response categories were made available to the respondents? In other words, the potential data user needs to determine how the variables of interest were operationally defined. Information about variables can usually be found in the technical documentation and code book that accompanies the data set. If these documents do not exist or exist only in part, the researcher should be wary about using the data set.

2. *Were data collected from the population of interest?* A survey may yield a data set containing the variables of interest, but the data may not have been collected from a sample that is representative of the population the researcher is interested in. For example, if a researcher is interested in children in a specific age bracket, the data set should contain data collected from children in the age bracket of interest. Similarly, if the researcher intends to generalize his or her findings to a specific geographic area, the data should have been collected from individuals living in the geographic area of interest.

3. *When were the data collected?* The researcher should consider the time period in which the data were collected. If the research has implications for current practice, the data used for the analyses should be relatively current. If the research is historical in nature or examines change over time, then the data set may be older or may contain data collected over a number of years. Also, the researcher should consider the timing of data collection relative to major social or political events. For example, data from a survey about attitudes toward women in sport conducted prior to the passage of Title IX should not be used to make inferences about current attitudes toward women in sport.

4. *Is there adequate computing capacity to work with the secondary data set?* This consideration relates both to computer software and computer storage capacity and processor speed. Many secondary data sets from reputable data repositories are derived from surveys that involved complex, multistage sampling designs. Some researchers may not have access to the statistical software necessary to analyze such data, or they may not have the expertise needed to use the software appropriately. Secondary data sets can range in size from less than one megabyte to many gigabytes. The larger the dataset, the greater the amount of free disk space needed. Also, as the size of the data set increases, so should the speed of the computer processor.

5. *Are the data easily accessible?* Some secondary data sets can be downloaded via the Internet, while others need to be ordered. If a data set needs to be ordered, it is important to determine how it will be provided to the end user. Will it be sent via electronic mail as an attachment or provided on a CD, DVD, or diskette? Also, in what format will the data file be provided? Does the end user have the skills to manipulate the data file? Data provided as hard copy (i.e., printed pages) can be useful but will require scanning or manual data entry. A final consideration with regard to accessibility is the extent to which the variables of interest are available. In some cases, certain variables may be removed from the data file due to issues of confidentiality. For example, if data are available for a number of cities within a specific state, city identifiers may be removed so that researchers cannot identify individuals by combining their demographic characteristics with their geographic information. Removal of the city identifier can be problematic if the research question is focused on an issue in specific city.

6. *Is documentation about the dataset available?* It is important for the researcher to have technical documentation that describes what data were collected through what method(s) and in what time interval(s). The technical documentation should provide the end user with the variable names, their locations in the data file, the associated survey question and response categories, and, ideally, the number of respondents for each response category. Figure 15.1 is an example of an entry from the technical documentation from the *Health Behavior in School-Aged Children Survey, 1997–1998* (WHO, 2002). The different elements in the entry can be explained as follows:

a. Q1 is the column heading in the data set for the variable denoting sex of the child.
b. "Are you a boy or a girl?" is the question that was asked of each respondent.

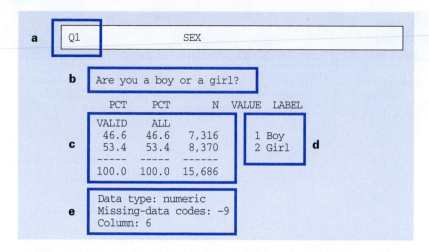

FIGURE 15.1 **Example of Technical Documentation**

c. These are the counts and percentages of respondents in the "Boy" and "Girl" categories. There were 7,316 boys and 8,370 girls for a total of 15,686 cases. The sample was 46.6 percent male and 53.4 percent female.

d. In the dataset, in the column identified as Q1, a value of 1 will indicate that the respondent was a boy and a value of 2 will indicate that the respondent was a girl.

e. The data are numeric in nature, rather than string. If a respondent did not answer this question, he or she would have a value of –9 in the Q1 field in the dataset. Finally, the variable is located in column 6 of the dataset.

Imagine receiving a dataset with a column labeled Q1 with respondent values of 1, 2, or –9. Without the technical documentation just described, the end user would not know what question Q1 corresponded to or what the values 1, 2, and –9 denoted.

7. **What is the structure of the data file?** This is an important and more technical consideration. Some secondary data sets contain data at different levels—say, an individual, a family, and/or a household. Figure 15.2 is an example of a data set that contains data at a number of different levels. In this example, although there are 10 records, only 5 unique households are represented (i.e., 100, 200, 300, 400, and 500). Household 100, comprised of three people (Person Numbers 1, 2, and 3), contains two families. This could be a husband and wife (Record IDs 1 and 2) and a nonrelated renter (Record ID 3). Contained within the dataset are two variables: age and household income. Age is a person-level variable, whereas Household Income is a household-level variable. As can be seen in the example, all people with a Household Number of 100 have the same household income. This distinction is important. Suppose that the researcher wants to report average household income by household. It would be incorrect to simply add all 10 household income values and divide by 10. If this were done, the average household income would appear to be $41,585. To determine the average household income by household, the researcher should add the household incomes of all the households and divide by 5, since there are 5 households in the file. The result would be an average household income of $40,970.

What is important with data file structures is to recognize that care needs to be taken to ensure that analysis is done at the appropriate level (household, family, and/or person) and that the interpretations are accurate based on the file structure and the variables used.

8. **Is technical assistance available relative to the data set and its use?** When working with secondary data, researchers may come across unanticipated problems, such as frequency counts that do not match those identified in the technical documentation, difficulty applying sample weights, or a lack of knowledge about how best to account for

FIGURE 15.2   Example of Data Set with Household, Family, and Person Records

Record ID	Household Number	Family Number	Person Number	Age	Household Income
1	100	1	1	42	$45,650
2	100	1	2	45	$45,650
3	100	2	3	32	$45,650
4	200	1	1	21	$32,000
5	300	1	1	35	$48,200
6	300	1	2	32	$48,200
7	400	1	1	54	$43,250
8	500	1	1	36	$35,750
9	500	2	2	42	$35,750
10	500	2	3	46	$35,750

a complex sample design. When such a situation arises, support from the individual or organization providing the data is needed. If support is not available, the researcher should find someone who has used the data set previously and seek his or her help.

Protecting Human Subjects

Secondary data that are publicly available, whether free or at cost, are usually coded so that the identification of any single individual is not possible. Thus, research involving the collection or study of existing data, documents, or records in which subjects cannot be identified—directly or through identifiers linked to them—is usually exempt from needing the subjects' informed consent. Regardless, most organizations and universities still require their researchers to submit their study protocols to the institutional review board (IRB), which allows a third party to review the proposed study and confirm that the criteria for exemption have indeed been met. As a general rule of thumb, users of secondary data should be familiar with the policies of their individual organizations with regard to human subjects' protection and IRB review requirements.

Not all secondary data sets are devoid of identifying information about participants. It is therefore important to look beyond the obvious identifiers, such as name, Social Security number, and address information. Sometimes, through a combination of variables in the data set, an individual can be identified. For example, consider a small data set of 200 individuals living in a small community. In the data set is information about individuals' jobs, types of cars, and numbers of people in households, as well as information about age, race, and marital status. This information, in combination, could be enough to allow for the identification of an individual person. Although no one variable would serve to identify an individual, combining variables could allow for identification. Reputable federal statistical agencies and data repositories address this issue by ensuring that there is an adequate number of respondents for key variables in the data set prior to its release.

Myths about Secondary Data

1. *Secondary data require manipulation before they can be useful.* One has to go no further than the U.S. Census Bureau website to realize that this statement is indeed a myth. Many data tables are available and ready for direct application to social issues without any data manipulation at all. Figure 15.3 is an example of a data table that is readily

PCT63. SEX BY COLLEGE OR GRADUATE SCHOOL ENROLLMENT BY AGE FOR THE
POPULATION 15 YEARS AND OVER [23] - Universe: Population 15 years and over
Data Set: Census 2000 Summary File 4 (SF 4) - Sample Data

NOTE: Data based on a sample. For information on confidentiality protection, sampling error, nonsampling error, and definitions see http://factfinder.census.gov/home/en/datanotes/expsf4.htm.

	United States
Total:	221,148,671
Male:	107,027,405
Enrolled in college or graduate school:	7,919,628
15 to 17 years	32,945
18 to 24 years	4,241,329
25 to 34 years	1,957,404
35 years and over	1,687,950
Not enrolled in college or graduate school	99,107,777
15 to 17 years	6,085,188
18 to 24 years	9,590,257
25 to 34 years	17,945,333
35 years and over	65,486,999
Female:	114,121,266
Enrolled in college or graduate school:	9,563,615
15 to 17 years	41,644
18 to 24 years	4,961,751
25 to 34 years	2,202,202
35 years and over	2,358,018
Not enrolled in college or graduate school	104,557,651
15 to 17 years	5,709,745
18 to 24 years	8,274,173
25 to 34 years	17,472,418
35 years and over	73,101,315

U.S. Census Bureau
Census 2000

FIGURE 15.3   Data Table from the U.S. Census Bureau

available that contains information about college and graduate school enrollment for individuals 15 years of age or older in the United States. Another agency, the National Center for Education Statistics, allows the user to build custom tables by selecting variables of interest for specified years and/or geographic areas. Figure 15.4 shows a custom table detailing the number of guidance counselors at various grade levels in Chesterfield, Virginia. As can be seen in this figure, the data can be downloaded in a variety of formats, including Excel. Furthermore, the data can be formatted for printing. The user can also reorder or resort the columns based on his or her needs.

2. *Secondary data files are analysis ready.* It would be convenient if secondary data files could be downloaded and opened with a statistical software package ready for statistical analyses. The process is not that simple, however. Often, expertise is required to manipulate data files of various formats, including .txt, .dat, and .xls. To do so requires an understanding of data file structure, knowledge of variable location, and skill at working with multiple computer files simultaneously. In addition, once a data file is in a statistical software package, a number of manipulations may be required, such as assigning variable names and value labels, recoding variables and collapsing response categories, and converting variables from string to numeric formats or vice versa.

3. *Research using secondary data is less rigorous than other types of research.* Although the researcher who uses secondary data is saving time and money by foregoing primary data collection, he or she still must have a sound theoretical basis for the research and the research questions must be clearly stated. Furthermore, the researcher needs to have a firm understanding of the research methodology that resulted in the data set being used. That includes an understanding of the target population, the sampling methods, the data collection methods, and the data management techniques. The operational definitions of the variables also need to be understood as well as the structure and characteristics of the data file. The researcher may spend months or longer identifying an appropriate

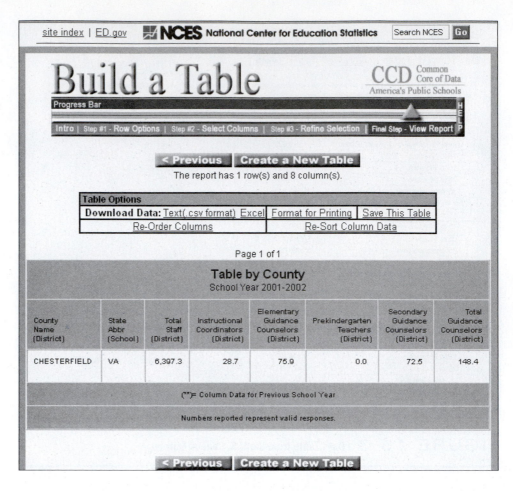

FIGURE 15.4 Custom Table from the National Center for Education Statistics

data set and deciding on the analysis plan once the data file has been selected and its characteristics are known.

Combining Secondary Data with Primary Data Collection

Using a combination of primary and secondary data can often strengthen research findings. Not only can analyzing existing data inform primary data collection efforts, but it can also lead to discovering new research questions, to refining existing research questions, and to informing primary data collection efforts. For example, if a researcher is analyzing secondary data and finds that a high percentage of the respondents refused to answer a particular question, he or she may use this information in developing new survey instruments.

Secondary data also can provide a context for interpreting the findings that result from primary data collection efforts. Consider the issue of school consolidation. When school leaders are making decisions about consolidating students and closing schools, they often solicit feedback from key stakeholders, including parents and teachers. School leaders could survey parents and teachers in order to learn about their attitudes about school consolidation, and the survey data could be augmented with data about student enrollment over time based on analysis of school administrative records. In this example, the survey data would be the primary data and the school administrative data would be the secondary data.

Secondary data can be used to help researchers identify where members of the target population are most likely to be located. An example would be a survey of households in which there are children under the age of 18. Decennial census data could be used to identify at very small levels of geography areas with the highest proportion of households with children under 18. Once this was determined, the sampling methods could be targeted so that these areas would be maximally surveyed and other areas would be surveyed to a lesser extent.

After data have been collected, there is a chance that the sample will be distributed in ways that are inconsistent with what is known about the target population. For example, in a hypothetical survey of a local community, 50 percent of the respondents have less than a high school education, 30 percent are married, and 20 percent have at least one child under the age of 18. However, through secondary analysis of decennial census data, you determine that the true percentages in the community in each of these categories are 35 percent, 50 percent, and 15 percent, respectively. The discrepancy identified through the secondary data analysis suggests that the researcher should apply statistical weighting procedures so that the sample will better represent the target population. This is one method of enhancing external validity.

Research Articles and Secondary Data

For the most part, journal articles written by researchers who have used secondary data follow the same form as journal articles written by researchers conducting primary data collection. However, when describing the sampling and data collection methods, researchers using secondary data write about what was done by the individual or group who initially collected the data. Researchers who conduct primary data collection write about what they did to collect the data used in the study yielding the findings being reported.

The following should be included in the research methods section of a journal article written by a researcher using secondary data:

- The name of the data set and its source should be clearly identified.
- If more than one data set is used and they are linked, the names of all data sets should be provided and their sources identified.
- The time period in which the data were collected should be identified. If the data were pooled over a number of years, this should be identified, as well.
- The sampling methods and the characteristics of the sample should be described.
- If the researcher is interested in a subset of cases in a data set, any procedures used to limit the data set to select cases should be identified in sequence.
- The key variables used in the analysis should be identified and, in some cases, the specific survey questions identified.

Excerpts 15.3 and 15.4 show examples from parts of secondary analysis research studies. In Excerpt 15.3, the researchers identify the source of data and how the sampling was

EXCERPT 15.3 Survey Identification and Sample Description in Secondary Analysis

The data for this study were drawn from the 1994 NAEP Trial State Data collection. Data from the 1998 NAEP had not been released when the study was completed and other recent data sets did not contain state-level data with student and teacher questionnaires on reading. In this assessment, a multistage sampling design was used to include the following: (a) selection of schools, both public and private and (b) selection of students within the identified schools. Sampling weights were computed to account for disproportionate representation of African American and Hispanic students from urban schools and lower sampling weights from very small schools. In the present analyses, the weighting was applied to the Maryland sample of 577 students used in HLM analyses, which allowed generalizations to the full population of Grade 4 students in Maryland.

Source: From Guthrie, J. T., Schafer, W. D., & Chun-Wei, H. (2001). Benefits of opportunity to read and balanced instruction on the NAEP. *Journal of Educational Research, 94*(3), 145–163.

EXCERPT 15.4   Description of Key Variables in Secondary Analysis

Two measures were used to determine demonstrated academic ability in grammar school, namely Grades and Repeat Grade. Respondents were asked what grades they received overall in the 8th grade. The measure Grades was coded such that 1 = Mostly B's or Better and 0 = Mostly C's or Worse. Respondents were also asked if they ever repeated a grade. Repeat Grade was coded such that those who reported that they repeated at least one grade in elementary school = 1, while others = 0.

Source: From Caputo, R. K. (2003). Early education experiences and school-to-work program participation. *Journal of Sociology and Social Welfare, 30*(4), 141–157.

done. Excerpt 15.4 shows how key variables were described and how they were coded for analytic purposes.

ACTION RESEARCH

Defining Action Research

With the current emphasis on data-driven decision making, educational professionals are increasingly asked to provide evidence that documents best practice. There is also an emphasis on *critical reflection* about practice that provides a systematic approach to gathering and analyzing information. It is the intersection, then, between systematic inquiry (i.e., research) and its use by practitioners that characterizes *action research*. **Action research** is the process of using research principles to provide information that educational professionals use to improve aspects of day-to-day practice. The research questions are rooted in practice, perhaps by K–12 teachers working in classrooms, administrators identifying and implementing guidelines, counselors practicing in schools and colleges, or faculty teaching at colleges and universities. It is simply a systematic approach to help professionals change practice, usually using a collaborative model that includes several individuals.

In K–12 education, the terms *teacher/researcher*, *teacher research*, *research practitioner*, and *teacher-as-researcher* are all used to focus on the action research of a single teacher. Action research is also completed in teams using a collaborative model and with entire schools (i.e., school-based action research). In other fields and at other levels of education, the broader term *applied* may be used to describe what is essentially action research. For example, teachers in a high school mathematics department may work together (or collaborate) to determine if a specific method of presenting a concept is effective, or the same question could be posed and answered by a single teacher.

Action research is not limited to a specific methodology (although in most cases, there is at least some use of qualitative methods), and typically quantitative data are used descriptively (with little or no emphasis on inferential statistics). The goal is to introduce a more systematic process than what is typically employed, be it qualitative, quantitative, or mixed method. One important difference is that the intent of action research is only to address specific actions in a single context, while applied research seeks to have implications for the field more generally. However, that does not mean that action research does not have implications for the overall field. Because practitioners are involved throughout the study, action research promotes change in classrooms and schools, greater collaboration among those with a vested interest in the results, an integration of research with practice, and a willingness to test new ideas.

Table 15.3 summarizes the differences between action research and traditional research. The reader should keep in mind, however, that there can be significant variability in the extent to which characteristics of traditional research are used in action research.

Research Navigator.c⊕m

15.3 Collaborative Action Research
Accession No.: 4783371

TABLE 15.3	Characteristics of Action Research versus Traditional Research	
Characteristic	**Action Research**	**Traditional Research**
Who identifies the research question(s) and conducts the research	Practitioners: teachers, principles, counselors	Trained researchers: university professors, scholars, graduate students
Where the research is conducted	Schools, universities, day cares, and other institutions where practice is implemented	Settings in which appropriate control can be implemented, from laboratories to field settings
Goal	Knowledge that is relevant to the local setting	Knowledge that can be generalized to the field
Literature review	Brief, with a focus on secondary sources	Extensive, with an emphasis on primary sources
Instrumentation	Use of instruments that are convenient and easy to administer and score	Measures are selected based on technical adequacy
Sampling	Convenient sampling of students or employees in the targeted setting	Tends to be random or representative
Data analysis	Descriptive	Descriptive and inferential
Dissemination	To the specific individual, classroom, or organization	To other professionals in different settings

Source: Adapted from Gall, Gall, & Borg (2003).

Conducting and Using Action Research

Action research is conducted in four phases: (1) selecting a focus, topic, or issue to study; (2) collecting data; (3) analyzing data; and (4) taking action based on the results. Each will be considered in more detail with some examples in a following section.

ALERT!   Action researchers must be careful not to let their biases or wishes influence their results or actions.

Selecting a Focus, Topic, or Issue to Study   The first step in any research endeavor is to determine the research question, goal, or purpose. A good topic is one that is important and relevant and that provides results that will immediately impact professional practice. Sometimes, an informal needs assessment is used to identify a topic; sometimes, a review of literature is used. Usually, the experiences of the researcher are used to identify topics. Research is often suggested because there is a problem in implementing practice, or something that is not going well.

Eventually, researchable questions need to be formulated to determine methods of data collection. Here are some examples of such questions:

- What is the effect of assigning greater responsibility to students in completing the yearbook on their attitudes toward writing?
- How effective is peer tutoring in the advanced placement (AP) history course?
- What teaching methods most motivate students to write detailed research proposals?
- Is there a difference in school climate after the introduction of more strict hall monitoring?

Collecting Data   The second phase of conducting action research is to collect data that will answer the research questions. Decisions need to be made about what type or types of data need to be collected and the sample from which data will be collected. Both quantitative and qualitative methods should be considered; using a variety of data collection tools usually strengthens the study by providing triangulation. Often, initial data gathering will lead to collecting additional data. For example, a teacher might begin to study the effectiveness of cooperative learning groups by first doing some informal observation while the groups are deliberating. From these data, a more structured observation could be developed, along with specific questions that students could be asked.

Typically, action researchers will use one of three approaches to data collection: experiencing, enquiring, and examining (Mills, 2003). *Experiencing* takes the form of observation, with a focus on understanding the variables, participants, and relevant phenomena. *Enquiring* occurs when the researcher needs to gather data that have not yet been obtained. This could involve interviews, questionnaires, and tests. *Examining* occurs when the researcher uses data that have already been conducted. Whatever the approach, one challenge is to decide what data really need to be collected. The researcher does not want to be swamped with so much data that it will be difficult to analyze and summarize them.

As in any research project, attention must be given to issues of credibility, transferability, dependability, validity, and reliability. While highly technical conceptualizations

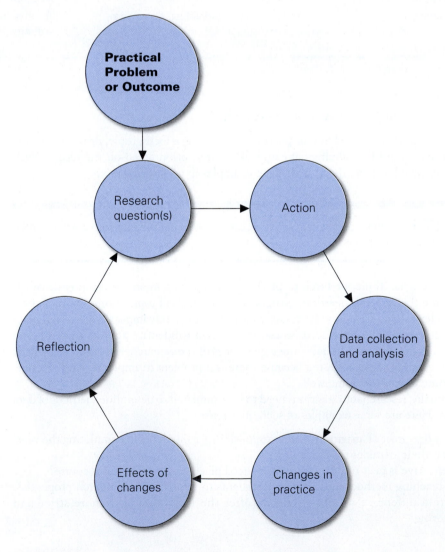

FIGURE 15.5 **Cyclical Nature of Action Research**

RESEARCH NAVIGATOR NOTES

Research Navigator.c⊕m

Reading the following articles will help you understand the content of this chapter. Go to the education database (included in the EBSCO database) in Research Navigator; use the Accession Number provided to find the article.

15.1 *Explanatory Mixed-Method Study*
This study is an example of using focus groups as a follow-up to an instructional intervention. Accession Number: 12670776.

15.2 *Secondary Data Analysis*
The author argues for greater use of secondary data. Accession Number: 7675348.

15.3 *Collaborative Action Research*
This article explores issues when collaborating with others to conduct action research. Accession Number: 4783371.

15.4 *Using Action Research*
Shows how to use action research in university classrooms. Accession Number: 9743990.

CHECK YOURSELF

Multiple-choice review items, with answers, are available on the Companion Website for this book:

www.ablongman.com/mcmillanschumacher6e.

APPLICATION PROBLEMS

1. For each of the following descriptions, indicate the type of design being used: mixed method, secondary data analysis, or action research.
   a. A researcher is interested in examining the correlation between high-stakes testing and grades. The test scores and grades are from 2000–2003.
   b. A doctoral student is interested in studying the effects of small-group counseling on students' self-esteem. Thirty students participate as subjects. The Coopersmith Self-Esteem Inventory is given as a pretest and a posttest, and interviews are used to follow up with students every month.
   c. Service learning is becoming very popular in both public schools and colleges and universities. However, relatively little is known about the perceptions of the beneficiaries of the services. A study is prepared to examine these perceptions using focus group interviews and a questionnaire to ask participants about the characteristics of effective volunteers.
   d. A principal is interested in knowing whether a new procedure for aligning classroom assessments with graduation requirements will result in more students graduating.
   e. To compare student achievement in the United States with that of students in other countries, a professor bought and used a CD containing three years of relevant data.

2. Give an original example of each of the three types of mixed-method designs.

3. A researcher has conducted a series of interviews about job stress and burnout with teachers of students with disabilities. Following the interviews, additional data could be collected to provide even more description of teachers' job stress and burnout as well as its effects on students. What procedures could be used to extend the study to be an exploratory design? What procedures could be used to extend the study to be a triangulation design?

4. For each of the following characteristics, indicate whether it is typical of action research or traditional research.
   a. Tends to use mostly secondary sources
   b. Is done in classrooms by teachers
   c. Uses inferential statistics or qualitative software
   d. Measures are selected to provide generalizability
   e. Involves limited dissemination
   f. Researcher bias is a particular concern
   g. Findings are relevant for the field in general

5. In your own field of work and study, suggest an action research study that uses a mixed-method design.

6. Suppose a teacher decides to study the impact of technology on the attention behavior of her fifth-grade students. She makes observations of students for three weeks before the technology is introduced and then continues her observations for the next three weeks while students use the technology. The results suggest that students pay

increased attention when they use technology, so the teacher decides to use it for the rest of the semester.

a. What should the teacher do to ensure credible results?

b. How can teacher bias be controlled?

c. Is this an example of cyclical research? Why or why not?

d. Using Table 15.3 (p. 415), explain how this could become an applied, more traditional study.

NOTE

1. Kiecolt, K. J. & Natham, L. E. (1985). *Secondary Analysis of Survey Data.* Beverly Hills, CA: Sage Publications.

V

ANALYTICAL RESEARCH

*E*ducators frequently ask questions such as Why is the history of schooling and educational practices important? What is a *concept* or *term*? How can knowledge about the past enlighten and inform current public discussions and decision-making processes about education?

Qualitative research was classified in Chapter 2 as *interactive research*, or *noninteractive research*, which was termed *analytical research*. We address qualitative research that is traditionally noninteractive in Part V.

Analytical research includes the analysis of concepts and historical events. Sources for historical research are documents, oral testimonies, and relics. Researchers use specialized techniques to search and locate documents in archives, manuscript repositories, libraries, and private collections. Some collections are now available on the Internet. Oral history involves interviewing eyewitness participants of past events for the purposes of historical reconstruction. Oral history provides empirical evidence about undocumented experiences hidden from history. Many oral history archives are online, as well.

Chapter 16 discusses briefly concept analysis and describes in more detail techniques for historical analysis and oral history. It also presents the credibility standards for this research tradition and illustrates the value of historical inquiry.

16 Concept Analysis and Historical Research

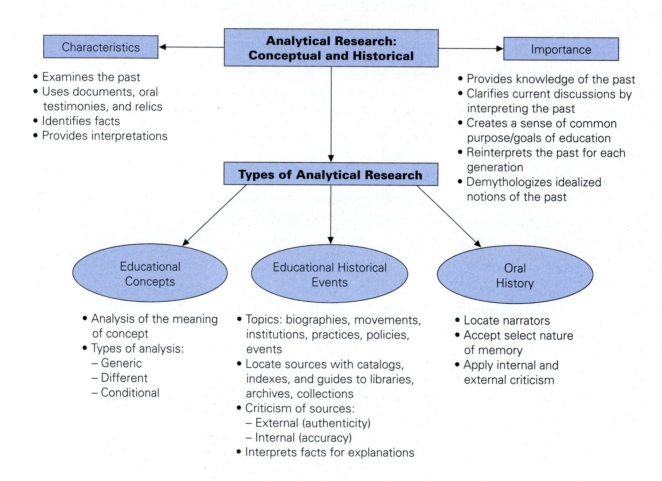

KEY TERMS

historiography
concept analysis
documents
oral testimonies
relics
primary source

secondary source
external criticism
internal criticism
facts
oral history

Understanding current educational policies and practices requires conducting an evidence-based inquiry that explains past events. How often have educators and non-educators made recommendations or justified decisions on the basis of what they assumed happened in the past? Explanations of past educational concepts and events provide insights into current educational events, issues, and policies.

Concept analysis and historical research are traditionally noninteractive document research. When in-depth interviews of knowledgeable persons about the past are recorded, oral history is preserved. Oral history research supplements these interviews with documents. Both historical research and oral history share characteristics of qualitative research: context-bound generalizations, a discovery orientation, emergent case study design, holistic emphasis (i.e., qualities of parts unify the whole phenomenon), noninterference in the natural setting, and inductive data analysis.

OVERVIEW AND PURPOSES OF ANALYTICAL RESEARCH

Several research techniques distinguish analytical studies from other kinds of educational research—namely, (1) selecting research topics related to the past, (2) applying internal and external criticism to primary sources, (3) identifying the facts, and (4) constructing interpretative explanations. The historical past may be as recent as the previous year or as distant as centuries ago. The evidence is usually written sources, many of which have been preserved in archives, manuscript collection repositories, and libraries. Sources include documents, oral testimonies, and relics.

Historiography is comprised of the techniques for discovering from records and accounts what happened during a past event or series of events, including revisions of prior history. Oral history, a form of historical research, records the spoken words and testimonies of eyewitnesses accounts to preserve a record before it is lost to future generations.

So, why study the past? What is the purpose of historical research? Why is so much time and money spent on preserving past records? Here are a few of the uses of analytical research:

1. *The analysis of educational concepts aids in the selection of research problems, designs, and methodologies.* The analysis of the concept of *teaching* as different types of teaching acts, for example, could suggest research questions and aid in designing either quantitative or qualitative research on teaching. Such concepts as *behavioral objectives, alternative schooling,* and *problem solving* are not merely terms but elements of a language system that constructs a framework for planning a study.

2. *Historical research provides knowledge about the so-called roots of educational ideas, institutions, leaders, policies, and practices.* Knowledge of the past informs educational professionals, policy-makers, and members of general society about education and its role in U.S. society. By examining the fates of past solutions to enduring problems, decision makers may become more realistic and moderate in their claims and more informed in their choices.

3. *Historical research clarifies present legal and policy discussions by interpreting the past with disciplined detachment and reasoned historical judgment.* Analytical research interprets the complexity of past collective educational, social, economic, legal, and political relationships. However, such research never claims that it *predicts* future actions.

4. *Historical research, in a broader and perhaps more philosophical sense, can create a sense of common purpose.* While historical research can demythologize idealized notions about past events, most interpretations of such events reflect the fundamental belief that public education in the U.S. has served and can serve a common good. The role of education in U.S. society is often neglected in fragmented empirical research. Implicit in the purpose of analytical research, however, is a concern that the goals of education and educational practices benefit both the individual and society.

5. *Historical research is a dynamic area of educational inquiry because each generation reinterprets its past.* Educational historians, especially those termed *revisionists*, ask new questions, use a greater variety of sources, analyze the past with a wider range of social science concepts, and apply quantitative procedures when appropriate.

ANALYSIS OF EDUCATIONAL CONCEPTS

Concept analysis involves clarifying the meaning of a concept by describing its essential meaning, different meanings, and appropriate use. By presenting an analysis of the concept, such an analysis helps us explain the way people think about education, for instance. The focus is on the meaning of the concept, not on the researcher's personal values or on factual information.

Three types of analysis may be used to analyze such concepts as *education, literacy, knowledge, teaching, learning,* and *equal opportunity:*

1. *Generic analysis* identifies the essential meaning of a concept, isolating the elements that distinguish that concept from others. To clarify the concept of *academic discipline,* one might make a comparison with history, mathematics, and physics as clear standard examples and contrast home economics, animal husbandry, and water skiing as counterexamples in order to arrive at the generic meaning of the concept of *academic discipline.*

2. *Differential analysis* distinguishes among the basic meanings of a concept and suggests the logical domain that it covers. Differential analysis is used when a concept seems to have more than one standard meaning. To analyze the concept of *subject matter,* the analyst intuitively classifies concrete examples, such as *Silas Marner,* solar system, school subjects, knowledge, and skills. The distinguishing characteristics of each type of subject matter are then ascertained to clearly separate them, and a topology is developed.

3. *Conditions analysis* identifies the conditions necessary for proper use of a concept. Conditions analysis begins by providing an example that meets the necessary conditions of the concept but can easily be made a noninstance by changing the context. This forces either revision or rejection of the condition and leads to formation of a set of necessary conditions for correct use of the concept.

Critical to the analysis of educational concepts is the selection of typical uses and counterexamples. Examples should be drawn from generally accepted common uses of a given concept. Because different sets of examples are used frequently, the analysis of educational concepts may lead to reanalysis and further conceptual clarity.

Analysis of educational concepts is applied in the study of educational concepts and in historical research. For example, a study of the public school movement or technology in education since 1970 would first have to determine the meaning of *public school* or *technology,* respectively.

ANALYSIS OF HISTORICAL EVENTS IN EDUCATION

Historiography requires the systematic application of techniques to phrase a historical problem, locate and criticize sources, and interpret facts for causal explanations. The historian often proceeds in a circular fashion because of the interrelationships among the research questions, sources, criticisms, analysis, and explanations (see Figure 16.1).

Topics and Justifications

Topics of Analysis   Topics of analysis include a wide range of new and recurring areas of interest. The following list illustrates the diversity of topics for historical investigation:

16.1 Biography
Accession No.: 10316767

1. Movements—progressive education, life-long learning
2. Institutions—public education, kindergarten, day care
3. Concepts—schooling, the child, literacy, professionalism
4. Biographies of educators—John Dewey, Phillis Wheatley, teachers
5. Comparative history of international education
6. Alternative forms of schooling—home instruction, distance education
7. Components of education—personnel, curriculum, administration, instruction
8. Cultural and minority education—gender, ethnic, minority, bilingual
9. Regionalism in U.S. education—geographic areas, state systems
10. Cultural influences—the family, professional associations, technology
11. Other topics—compilation (restoration) of documents with annotation

The historian begins with an initial subject, such as a historical period, person, idea, practice, institution, or policy. After initially reading widely for background knowledge, the historian will define the topic more exactly. Background knowledge will suggest the breadth of the subject, previous research on the problem, gaps in knowledge, and possible sources. The problem must be narrow enough to examine in detail but broad enough to allow identifying patterns for interpretation.

Background knowledge can be obtained from textbooks, monographs, encyclopedias and other reference works, dissertations, and specialized journals. General bibliographies cite secondary sources. Some bibliographies specifically useful to the historian, for example, are *A Guide to Historical Literature*, *The Historian's Handbook: A Descriptive Guide to Reference Works*, and *A Bibliography of American Educational History*.

Limiting a topic and phrasing a problem statement about it are continuing efforts. The problem statement is expressed most succinctly and clearly at the end of the research, when the sources have been collected, analyzed, and interpreted. Considerations in limiting a topic are the availability and accessibility of primary sources; the historian's interests, specialized knowledge, and time for completing the study; and the type of study to be done. The statement of a historical problem indicates the particular event, person, institution, or policy under examination. The problem is delimited by the time period, geographic location, and viewpoint

FIGURE 16.1   **The Process of Historical Research**

EXCERPT 16.1 The Historical Event and Selected Case

[Research examined] the story of how married women teachers gained tenure regardless of marital status. . . . While World War II saw the end of most hiring bans against married women, as the case of Rhode Island illustrated, legal discrimination in the form of denying them tenure survived until the mid 1960s. (p. 50)

Source: From Donahue, D. M. (2002). Rhode Island's last holdout: Tenure and married women teachers at the brink of the women's movement. *History of Education Quarterly, 42*(1), 50–74.

of the analysis (see Excerpt 16.1). Asking descriptive questions about the selected event is done in an effort to identify factual evidence, such as *who, what, where,* and *when.* Interpretations and explanations require evidence for how an event occurred and why (see Excerpt 16.2).

The significance of a historical topic is often stated in terms of completing the historical record, filling in gaps of knowledge about the past, exploring areas only alluded to in prior research, and opening a new field of inquiry. For instance, when the private papers of a well-known educator are made available for research years after his or her death, historians begin their task of understanding the person and his or her role in that era (see Excerpts 16.3 and 16.4). Moreover, when the interpretation of a prior study is seriously doubted, the topic is frequently re-examined from a revisionist viewpoint (see Excerpt 16.5).

Location and Criticism of Sources

Types of Sources Historical evidence usually takes the form of written sources, many of which have been preserved in archives, manuscript collections, libraries, and personal collections.

1. **Documents** are records of past events. They comprise both written and printed materials and may be official or unofficial, public or private, published or unpublished, prepared intentionally to preserve a historical record or prepared to serve an immediate practical purpose. As such, documents may be letters, diaries, wills, receipts, maps, autobiographies, journals, newspapers, court records, official minutes, proclamations, and regulations. Documents may also include statistical records (e.g., enrollment records).

EXCERPT 16.2 Historical Research Questions

To what extent were the town officials who hired teachers actually influenced by beliefs about the masculine nature of schoolteaching? How did their hiring practices reflect and reinforce gender differences in power in early colonial society? (p. 351)

Source: From Preston, J. A. (2003) "He lives as a Master": Seventeenth-century masculinity, gendered teaching, and careers of New England schoolmasters. *History of Education Quarterly, 43*(3), 350–371.

EXCERPT 16.3 Justification for a Little Known Topic

A noted but rarely explored axiom of the history of American education is that public school practices often originate in private sector settings. (p. 18)

Source: From Gold, K. M. (2002). From vacation to summer school: The transformation of summer education in New York City, 1894–1915. *History of Education Quarterly, 42*(1), 18–48.

EXCERPT 16.4   Problem Justification

Historians in recent decades have sought to recover the "lost voices" of teachers. . . . [This represents] a new field of inquiry . . . [as] predecessors . . . omitted frontline troops from the history of education. . . . Unless this gap could be filled, the historical record was incomplete and . . . very likely wrong-headed. (pp. 150–151)

Source: From Warren, D. (2004). Looking for a teacher, finding her workplaces. *Journal of Curriculum and Supervision, 19*(2), 150–168.

EXCERPT 16.5   Criticism of Prior Research

Footnote 58: Small, *Early New England Schools,* argues that schooldames sometimes served as the only town teacher as a cost-cutting measure. Since most of his evidence is derived from town records that can no longer be located, it is hard to verify the validity of his claim. (p. 371)

Source: From Preston, J. A. (2003) "He lives as a Master": Seventeenth-century masculinity, gendered teaching, and careers of New England schoolmasters. *History of Education Quarterly, 43*(3), 350–371.

2. **Oral testimonies** are records of the spoken word. The oral testimonies of persons who have witnessed events of educational significance are tape recorded, and verbatim transcripts are made. Oral testimonies relate to the event studied.

3. **Relics** are objects that provide information about the past. Although relics may not be intended to convey information directly about the past, the visual and physical properties of these objects can provide historical evidence. Relics may be such diverse items as textbooks, buildings, equipment, charts, and examinations (see Table 16.1).

TABLE 16.1   Types of Sources for Historical Research

Source	Historical Research	Source	Historical Research
Documents	Letters	Oral testimonies	Participants in a historical event
	Diaries		Relatives of a deceased person
	Bills and receipts		Persons who are knowledgeable about an event
	Autobiographies		
	Newspapers	Relics	Textbooks and workbooks
	Journals and magazines		Buildings
	Bulletins		Maps
	Catalogs		Equipment
	Films		Samples of student work
	Recordings		Furniture
	Personal records		Teaching materials
	Institutional records		
	Budgets		
	Enrollment records		
	Graduation records		

EXCERPT 16.6   Search for Sources

Footnote 23: Robert Patterson, "The Truth Cries Out," Association of Citizens' Council, Greenwood (MSU, Citizens' Council collection, folder 10); . . . Carroll, "Mississippi Private Education," 120–123; "How Can We Educate Our Children?," *The Citizen,* 10 (November, 1965), 7; William J. Simmons, "The Citizens' Councils and Private Education," *The Citizen,* 10 (February, 1966), 11. (p. 166)

Source: From Fuquay, M. W. (2002). Civil rights and private school movement in Mississippi, 1964–1971. *History of Education Quarterly, 42*(2), 159–180.

Classification of Sources   Sources can also be classified as primary and secondary. A **primary source** is the written or oral testimony of an eyewitness or participant or a record made by some mechanical device present at the event, such as a tape recorder, videotape, or photograph. Primary sources for a biography are the person's personal and public papers and the relics of his or her life (see Excerpt 16.6).

A **secondary source** is the record or testimony of anyone who was not an eyewitness to or a participant in the event. Thus, a secondary source contains information from someone who may or may not have lived through the event. Secondary sources include histories, biographies, and monographs that interpret other primary and secondary sources. As such, they provide insights and possibly facts for analysis.

The classification of a source as primary or secondary depends on the research problem. The number of primary sources necessary for a study varies with the topic. To obtain primary sources, the historian thinks of the sources that would yield information on the topic and then investigates whether the applicable records were preserved and are accessible. A single study may use different kinds of sources, but primary sources must serve as the basis for documentation. (*Documentation* is the process of providing proof based on any kind of source, whether written, oral, or object.)

The use of primary sources is essential, but secondary sources may be used selectively and as necessary. Both primary and secondary sources should be subjected to techniques of criticism. The sources for a study are cited in the bibliography, and usually each source, fact, and quotation is footnoted. Criticism of sources may be in the text of a study, the footnotes, or the appendices.

Research Navigator.c⊕m

16.2 Archives Online
Accession No.: 11435489

Location of Sources   The search for factual evidence begins with locating sources. The historian depends on sources that have been preserved; however, sources may or may not have been catalogued and identified for easy access. Locating sources is thus an exercise in detective work. It involves "logic, intuition, persistence, and common sense," (Tuckman, 1998, p. 258). The credibility of a study is determined partly by the selection of primary sources. The problem statement and limitations point to the necessary primary sources. For example, a study of the admissions policies of a university would be seriously flawed without institutional records (see Excerpt 16.7).

Documents can be located through specialized guides, catalogs, indexes, and bibliographies and through research centers. Examples of specialized reference works are *A Catalogue of Rare and Valuable Early Schoolbooks, Educational Periodicals during the Nineteenth Century, Selective and Critical Bibliography of Horace Mann,* and guides to national archives and private manuscript collections. *A Guide to Manuscripts and Archives in the United States* describes the holdings of 1,300 repositories, and the *Guide to Federal Records in the National Archives of the United States* (www.nara.gov/guide) indexes educational records of government agencies. The *National Union Catalogue of Manuscript Collections* (www.loc.gov./coll/nucmc/nucmc.html), published annually by the Library of Congress, cites the increasing number of educational collections made available to scholars. Archival research centers devoted to particular historical subjects often contain educational records, as well.[1] Some online archives are the Urban Archives (www.library.temple.edu/urbana), the Education

EXCERPT 16.7   Rationale for Choice of Primary Sources

Footnote 10: . . . The New York and Atlanta papers were chosen in particular because they represent . . . the closest to a "home town" paper available for Gibson and Coachmen. The black weeklies were selected . . . because of their prominence in the black community. (p. 249)

Source: From Lansbury, J. H. (2001). "The Tuskegee Flash" and "the Slender Harlem Stroker": Black women athletes on the margin. *Journal of Sports History, 28*(2), 233–252.

Policy Analysis Archives (www.epaa.asu.edu/epaa/.html), the Wilson Riles Archives and Institute for Education (WRAIE) (www.wredu.com/%7Ewriles/archive.html), and the Women's Studies Archives International Women's Periodicals (www.womensperiodicals. psmedia.com/html).

Research Navigator.com

16.3 Archival Facilities
Accession No.: 11435491

ALERT!   Do not decide on a historical research problem until you have located and have access to the necessary primary sources.

Conducting oral testimonies that are relevant to a topic requires preplanning. The researcher must decide which individuals are knowledgeable about the topic, and then locate them and collect data through interviews. The selection of informants for oral testimonies can be done with purposeful sampling procedures. Accessibility to the individuals, the importance of the presumed information, and feasibility (e.g., time, finances, and so on) are all considerations (see Excerpt 16.8).

Criticism of Sources   Techniques of *internal* and *external criticism* are applied to all sources: documents, oral testimonies, and relics. Even sources that are official publications or preserved in archives are subjected to criticism. As will be explained in detail later in this section, *external criticism* determines the authenticity of the source, and *internal criticism* determines the credibility of the facts stated by the source. Although the two types of criticism ask different questions about the source, the techniques are applied simultaneously. The criticism of sources may be covered in a methodological discussion, footnotes, or appendices (see Excerpt 16.9).

External criticism determines whether the source is the original document, a forged document, or a variant of the original document. Typical questions are Who wrote the document? and When, where, and what was the intention? The more specialized knowledge the analyst has, the easier it is to determine whether a document is genuine. The analyst needs knowledge about how the people in the era that produced the document lived and behaved, what they believed, and how they managed their institutions. An educational historian is less likely to deal with forged documents than is a social scientist

EXCERPT 16.8   Locating Oral Testimonies

Footnote 53: . . . I interviewed or corresponded with three teachers . . . who worked in Pawtucket in 1965. . . . [They] responded to my request . . . in the *Pawtucket Teachers Alliance* newsletter, for personal memories of the 1965 strike. (p. 67)

Source: From Donahue, D. M. (2002). Rhode Island's last holdout: Tenure and married women teachers at the brink of the women's movement. *History of Education Quarterly, 42*(1), 50–74.

EXCERPT 16.9 Limitations of Sources

Footnote 13: We know the highest level of education for hundreds more, but do not necessarily know what institution all attended. For example, we know of scores of the teachers who attended or graduated from a normal school or a normal course within a secondary school, but have not yet identified the institution. (p. 7)

Source: From Butchart, R. E. (2002). Mission matters: Mount Holyoke, Oberlin, and the school of southern blacks, 1861–1917. *History of Education Quarterly, 42*(1), 1–17.

who studies controversial political, religious, and social movements. Nonetheless, claims to a professional title or the date of an institution can be forged. Sometimes, it is impossible to determine the contribution of an individual to a government report or speech if there are multiple authors. The date and place of writing or publication can be established by means of the citation on the document, the date of the manuscript collection, and the contents of the document. However, working papers internal to an institution or a draft made by an individual may not contain any dates or may be insufficient for use if only the year is stated.

The educational historian is more likely to find *variant sources*—that is, two or more texts of the same document or two or more variant testimonies about the same event. For example, a newspaper account of the results of a state educational testing program may differ from the actual statistical report published by the State Department of Education, and both may differ from the separate drafts of the report (see Excerpt 16.10). In this situation, the newspaper account, the official report, and the separate drafts are all authentic sources of different texts. Oral testimonies by different individuals may also be authentic but variant sources.

Internal criticism determines the accuracy and trustworthiness of the statements in the source—for instance, How accurate are the statements, and are the witnesses trustworthy? *Accuracy* is related to a witness's chronological and geographical proximity to the event, his or her general competence, and his or her attention to the event. Obviously, not all witnesses equally close to the event are equally competent observers and recorders. *Competence* depends on expertness, state of mental and physical health, educational level, memory, narrative skill, and the like. It is well known that eyewitnesses under traumatic or stressful conditions remember selective parts of an event yet are convinced that because they were present, their accounts are accurate. Even though a witness may be competent, he or she may be an interested or biased party. Bias or preconceived prejudice causes a witness to habitually distort, ignore, or overemphasize incidents. The conditions in which the statements were made may influence accuracy, as well. Literary style, the laws of libel, the conventions of good taste, and a desire to please may lead to exaggerated politeness or expressions of esteem.

EXCERPT 16.10 Using Collections of Primary Documents in Archives

[The following are the archives listed in the footnotes of one study:]

"1. American Jewish Archives. . . . 6. Philadelphia Jewish Archives. . . . 15. Chicago Historical Society. . . . 32. American Jewish Historical Society. . . . 36. National Association of Jewish Social Workers Papers. . . . 46. Jewish Museum of Maryland. . . . 51. Chicago Jewish Archives. (pp. 24–31)

Source: From Klapper, M. (2002). "A long and broad education": Jewish girls and the problem of education in America, 1860–1920. *Journal of American Ethic History, 22*(1), 3–31.

EXCERPT 16.11   Need for Criticism of All Sources

Use oral history techniques and other personal memories, as I do, to help fill gaps left by the paucity of documents. Can memories be trusted? . . . All such sources require external evidence to establish plausibility. When contextualized, memory per se is not the problem. (p. 153)

Source: From Warren, D. (2004). Looking for a teacher, finding her workplaces. *Journal of Curriculum and Supervision, 19*(2), 150–168.

Several techniques can be used to estimate the accuracy and dependability of a statement. Statements by witnesses that are made as a matter of indifference, those that are injurious to the people stating them, and those that are contrary to the personal desires of the people stating them are less likely to be biased than others. Likewise, statements that are considered common knowledge or incidental are less likely to be in error. Finally, other credible sources can confirm, modify, and reject statements (see Excerpt 16.11).

In a qualitative analysis, however, the simple agreement of statements from independent witnesses can be misleading, since the research depends only on preserved sources. Agreement with other known facts and circumstantial evidence will increase the credibility of a statement. The historian may cite the source by stating something such as "According to the judge's opinion, . . ." "Horace Mann says, . . ." or "The Speaker of the House is our authority for the statement that . . ."

Applying internal and external criticism requires knowledge about the individuals, events, and behaviors of the period under study. The ability to put oneself in the place of historical individuals and to interpret documents, events, and personalities from their perspectives and standards is often called *historical mindedness*. Throughout the whole process, the researcher must remain skeptical of the sources and statements and not be easily convinced that the sources have yielded evidence as close to actual events as possible.

Facts, Generalizations, and Analytical Explanations

Historians analyze **facts,** the most accurate parts of accounts in the most trustworthy and authentic sources. Facts provide the basis for making generalizations, interpretations, and explanations. The process is not simple, however. Criticism of sources may lead to rephrasing the problem and conducting a further search for sources and facts. Consider the following:

1. *Facts describe the who, what, when, and where of an event.* Most historians go beyond obtaining the descriptive facts and ask the interpretative questions of *how* and *why* a historical event occurred. The questions asked of sources are crucial to the entire process (see Excerpt 16.12). The skills used in questioning are similar to those of a detective

EXCERPT 16.12   Short Quotations of Facts from Primary Sources

Referring to her as "the lithe and muscular Miss Gibson," a "lanky jumping jack of a girl," and "tall and leggy,"[30] . . . they often used such physical attributes to explain the masculine power with which she played the [tennis] game. Gibson is "lean and her long arms are muscular." . . . "Althea's service gains power from her height."[31] (p. 242)

Source: From Lansbury, J. H. (2001). "The Tuskegee Flash" and "the Slender Harlem Stroker": Black women athletes on the margin. *Journal of Sports History, 28*(2), 233–252.

EXCERPT 16.13   Interpretations

Overall, summer education in New York highlights a number of important patterns of the early vacation schools and represents a standard piece of progressive school reform. First, . . . a response to a perceived social problem of the cities: the idleness of children. . . . Second, . . . push the public systems to lengthen school time. . . . Finally, the changes in . . . management . . . represented a fundamental shift . . . to modern summer schools. (p. 48)

Source: From Gold, K. M. (2002). From vacation to summer school: The transformation of summer education in New York City, 1894–1915. *History of Education Quarterly, 42*(1), 18–48.

looking for evidence and a scientist testing evidence. Questions may be very specific, such as When did Henry Barnard die? or may be abstract, such as How did the scientific movement influence school administration practices? Methodological training and experience, both general and specialized knowledge, disciplined intuition, and logic all influence the analysis. The more questions asked of the sources about the topic, the more comprehensive and complex the analysis.

When statements and facts conflict, additional information is sought to resolve the apparent differences. Eventually, however, the researcher must make a decision based on the most accurate information available. Facts are weighed and judged by consistency, the accumulation of evidence, and other techniques.

2. *Interpretations of the relationships between facts are generalizations.* Each generalization is subjected to analysis and then usually modified or qualified. Elements that often appear as facts in research articles are frequently generalizations of those facts which cannot be presented in the limited space. A generalization summarizes the separate facts that assert that an event took place (see Excerpt 16.13).

3. *Analytical explanations are abstract syntheses of generalizations.* Explanations may be stated in the introduction as a thesis or in the closing as conclusions. Generalizations presented throughout the study are reanalyzed for context, internal consistency, documentation, accumulation of evidence, and logical induction. The process is cyclic, one of constantly returning to the facts and, if necessary, to the documents to derive meaning. A thesis stated in an introduction is a literary device of presenting an overview and not the researcher setting out to prove his or her personal notions. Consider that the introductory overview was probably the last section of the study to be written because the logic of the study must flow from it and the criteria for judging the quality of the study are derived from it. Conclusions synthesize generalizations that are previously documented in the study. In other words, conclusions are interpretative explanations. They may be stated in narrative form or as a brief list, followed by statements about the status of knowledge on the topic, identification of policy issues, and suggestions for further research.

When explanations are supported by facts stated in the study, the explanations are considered valid. A historian will say, "If you do not believe my explanation, take a closer look at the facts." Historians seldom claim, however, that they have all the facts. Instead, a given study contains a group of associated facts and ideas that leave no question unanswered *within* that presentation.

MISCONCEPTION   The 1954 Supreme Court decision that ruled against the doctrine of "separate but equal" educational facilities was based on the school expenditures of four public school systems.

EVIDENCE   In addition to the primary documentary evidence, G. Myrdal's report *The American Dilemma* and the testimonies of noted social scientists, sociologists, and psychologists were also provided as evidence.

ORAL HISTORY

Historians have noted how much history has been written from the viewpoints of those in authoritative positions and how little is known of the daily experiences of everyday people in all walks of life (Berg, 2004). Oral history strategies allow researchers to avoid the inherent limitations of residual and official evidence in documents. That is, researchers can reconstruct moderately recent history from the memories of individuals, giving access to the past for as long as 80 to 90 years. The oral collection of historical materials goes back to ancient times, but formal associations began in the 1940s.[2]

Conducting an **oral history** involves interviewing eyewitness participants in past events for the purposes of historical reconstruction (Grele, 1996). Oral histories provide empirical evidence about previously undocumented experiences and may empower social groups that have otherwise been hidden from history (Thompson, 1998). Oral history interviews are similar to other unstructured interviews and only differ in purpose. Oral history researchers proceed in much the same way as other historians but recognize that interviewing operates according to culturally specific communication norms.

Once the research topic has been selected and narrowed, the investigator locates individuals who have first-hand information on the subject. Such individuals can be located by several strategies: (1) advertising a description of the type of person needed, (2) asking knowledgeable people for recommendations, (3) using records to obtain names and addresses, and (4) using an existing oral history archive (see Excerpt 16.14).

An *oral history archive* is a collection of individuals' narrations of their lives and historical events. Countless archives of this nature are available. Some have materials available only on audiotape (e.g., the Columbus Jewish Historical Society, www.columbusjewishhistoricalsociety.org.html); others also have transcripts. There are numerous culturally related, religious, and political/economic oral history archives. Many of them can be accessed via the Internet and provide online audio versions of their materials and transcripts for downloading or printing. One of the most noted oral history archives is *Born in Slavery: Slave Narratives from the Federal Writers' Project, 1936–38*, which is housed at the Library of Congress and also available online. Many local and state oral history collections contain materials pertinent to research in education.

Some of the methodological issues involved in conducting oral histories are as follow:

1. ***Locating informed and willing narrators*** Few scholars know the total number of persons who fit the desired profile and therefore do not know what percentage of the total group they have located. Because only those persons who are willing to participate can be recorded, their stories are not statistically representative of the subject. Volunteers can be biased, as well.

2. ***Accepting that memories tend to be selective*** Researchers suggest that memory is best understood as a *social process*—that is, remembering in terms of experiences with others. Historians seek to understand how people's constructions of the past have been useful to them in the present.[3] Cognitive psychologists suggest that people remember best

Research Navigator.com

16.4 Oral History Issues
Accession No.: 10316757

EXCERPT 16.14   Oral History: Narrators

Footnote 4: I had forty-two responses from the newspaper/radio appeals, and found four other contributors by word of mouth. I interviewed twenty-seven people in all; the brief biographies . . . (names have been changed) are given. (p. 41)

Source: Clear, C. (2003). Hardship, help and happiness in oral history narratives of women's lives in Ireland, 1921–1961. *Oral History, 31*(2), 33–42.

what is normal, relevant, and consistent with their pre-existing knowledge. But in fact, individuals often remember best what is unexpected and bizarre. For a highly emotional event, the center is generally enhanced in memory while the peripheral detail is lost. Memory repeatedly edits and revises the stories of people's lives.

3. **Applying external and internal criticism** Although oral historians can detect authenticity during an interview, they often work with variant recollections of the same event. Thus, internal criticism becomes very important. Scholars look for internal consistency of the interview, agreement with other interviewees, and consistency with documentary evidence.

CREDIBILITY STANDARDS FOR ANALYTICAL RESEARCH

The research process suggests criteria for judging the credibility of historical research and oral history studies. Thus, the reader should judge a study in terms of the logical relationship among its problem statement, sources, facts, generalizations, and causal explanations. Implicit in the evaluation of a study is the question Did the analyst accomplish the stated purpose? If all the elements of the research are not made explicit, the study can be criticized as biased or as containing unjustifiable conclusions.

In evaluation credibility, consider these questions:

1. Does the topic focus on the past or recent past, and is it the problem justified?
2. Are primary sources relevant to the topic documented, authentic, and trustworthy? Was the selection and criticism of the sources appropriate?
3. Is factual evidence documented in detail? If conflicting facts are presented, is a reasonable explanation offered? If information is missing, is it noted and explained?
4. Are the generalizations reasonable and related logically to the facts?
5. Are the generalizations and explanations qualified or stated in a tentative manner?
6. Does the study address all the questions stated in the introduction—that is, does it fulfill the purpose of the study?

SUMMARY

The following statements summarize the major characteristics of analytical methodology and its application in studies of educational concepts, historical research, and oral histories:

1. Analytical research describes and interprets the past or recent past from relevant sources.
2. Historiography comprises the techniques for discovering from records and accounts what happened in the past.
3. Historical research provides knowledge of past educational events, clarifies present discussions with interpretations of the past with detachment, revises historical myths, and creates a sense of common purpose about education in U.S. society.
4. Concept analysis focuses on meaning within the language of education by describing the generic meaning, the different meanings, and the appropriate use of the concept.
5. Historical topics focus on biographies, movements, institutions, and practices. A historical problem is delimited

by the time period, the geographic location, the specific event studied, and the viewpoint of the analysis.

6. Historical problems are justified by gaps in the common knowledge and when new primary sources become available.
7. Sources include written documents, oral testimonies, and relics.
8. Primary sources are documents or testimonies of eyewitnesses to an event. Secondary sources are documents or testimonies of those who are not eyewitnesses to an event.
9. Specialized bibliographies and indexes locate the primary sources necessary for historical research; some catalogs of manuscripts and archives are online.
10. External criticism determines whether the source is the original document, a forged document, or a variant of the original document. Internal criticism determines the accuracy and trustworthiness of the statements in the source.

11. Oral testimonies are in-depth interviews of participants used to supplement documents.
12. Historical studies make generalizations of the facts (*who*, *what*, *where*, and *when*), about an event and state interpretations and explanations that suggest multiple causes for any single event.
13. Oral history involves interviewing eyewitness participants in past events for the purpose of historical reconstruction. Oral histories provide empirical evidence about undocumented experience and may empower social groups.
14. Credibility standards for historical and oral history studies emphasize the logical relationship among the problem statement, selection and criticism of sources, and facts, generalizations, and causal explanations.

RESEARCH NAVIGATOR NOTES

Reading the following articles will help you understand the content of this chapter. Go to the education database (included in the EBSCO database) in Research Navigator; use the Accession Number provided to find the article.

16.1 *Biography*
Martin, J. (2003). The hope of biography: The historical recovery of women educator activists. *History of Education, 32*(2), 219–233. Accession Number: 10316767.

16.2 *Archives online*
Potter, L. A. (2003). Online resources from the national archives. *Social Education, 67*(7), 390–394. Accession Number: 11435489.

16.3 *Archival Facilities*
Archival facilities across the nation. (2003). *Social Education, 67*(7), 397–401. Accession Number: 11435491.

16.4 *Oral History Issues*
Gardner, P. (2003). Oral history in education: Teachers' memory and teachers' history. *History of Education, 32*(2), 175–189. Accession Number: 10316757.

16.5 *Narrations of Teachers' Lives*
Cunningham, P. (2000). Narrative and text: Women, teachers and oral history. *History of Education, 29*(3), 273–281. Accession Number: 3613583.

CHECK YOURSELF

Multiple-choice review items, with answers, are available on the Companion Website for this book:

www.ablongman.com/mcmillanschumacher6e.

APPLICATION PROBLEMS

1. Suppose that a historian wants to study student discipline.
   a. How could this research problem be stated?
   b. State at least one specialized bibliography or index.
2. Suppose that a historian is studying the life of Dr. Henry Daniel, who served as the chief state school officer from 1959 to 1979. The following article appeared in a newspaper reporting the remarks of various speakers given at a dinner to honor Dr. Daniel after 20 years of service as the state superintendent of education:

   More than one hundred educational leaders throughout the state honored Dr. Henry Daniel last evening at the Hotel Johnson in the state capital. Following the remarks of several officials, an engraved plaque was presented to Dr. Daniel in recognition of his outstanding educational leadership to the state.

   The governor of the state noted that due solely to the efforts of Dr. Daniel, the state established a junior college system that has rapidly grown to meet important state needs in technical/vocational education for the state's industry, provided the only institutions of higher education in rural regions, and given a better general education to freshman and sophomores than four-year colleges and universities.

   The president of the state teachers' organization praised Dr. Daniel for his efforts to raise public school teachers' salaries and to maintain professionalism by expanding the requirements for certification of teachers. However, the president noted that salaries for public school teachers in the state still remained below the national average.

The president of the state association for curriculum development and supervision stated that the efforts of Dr. Daniel alone established the state minimum competency testing program. This innovation has raised standards for all high school subjects and proved to the public that the high school diploma represented a high level of "educational competency."

a. Why would the historian question the accuracy of the statements reported in this document?
b. How could the historian corroborate the reported statements?

NOTES

1. Examples of archives with documents relevant to education history are the Archives of the Industrial Society at the University of Pittsburgh, the Archives of the History of American Psychology at the University of Akron, the Ohio History of Education Project at the Ohio Historical Society, the Social Welfare Archives at the University of Minnesota, and state archives.
2. Examples of journals are *Oral History Review*, *Oral History*, and *International Journal of Oral History*. See also the North American Oral History Association.
3. Since the 1990s, the study of *historical memory*, an area of historical scholarship, has flourished. The subjects and sources for this history are typically the artifacts of public memory: monuments, battlefields, celebrations, Hollywood movies, and school textbooks. See Nord (1998) for more information.

EVALUATION AND POLICY RESEARCH DESIGNS AND METHODS

Most professionals recognize the increasing emphasis on evidence-based evaluation and policy analysis. Two trends have supported this emphasis: high-stakes testing and the federal policy to fund primarily research on program effectiveness. We present a broader view of evaluation to accommodate the different educational decisions and policies that require evidence in diverse programs and communities.

Educators frequently ask, What are the similarities and differences in evaluating a *program* and in evaluating a *policy*? How does one decide which designs and methods are most appropriate for use in a given situation? Can evaluation research and policy analysis also yield more general educational knowledge about specific practices common to many schools?

Part VI describes a variety of the approaches used in the evaluation of educational practice. Different approaches emphasize different questions regarding specific practices. Some evaluation and policy analyses are primarily quantitative, some are primarily qualitative, and some combine both quantitative and qualitative methods.

17 Evaluation Research and Policy Analysis

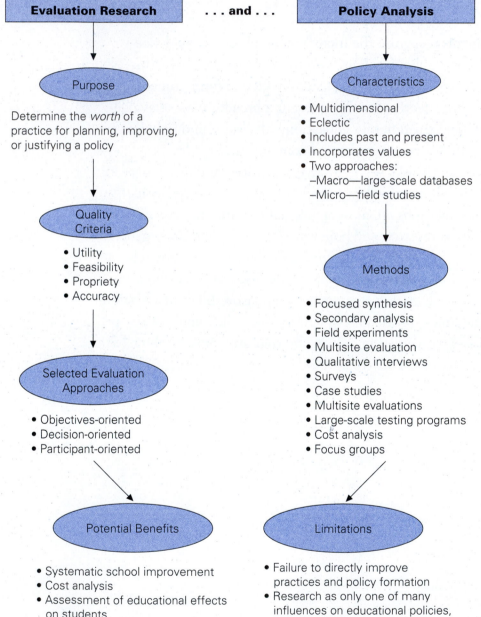

Evaluation Research . . . and . . . **Policy Analysis**

Purpose

Determine the *worth* of a practice for planning, improving, or justifying a policy

Quality Criteria

• Utility
• Feasibility
• Propriety
• Accuracy

Selected Evaluation Approaches

• Objectives-oriented
• Decision-oriented
• Participant-oriented

Potential Benefits

• Systematic school improvement
• Cost analysis
• Assessment of educational effects on students
• Appraisal of quality of education
• Reduction of uncertainty in innovative practices
• Legitimization of decisions
• Anticipation of policy issues
• Enlighten influential decision makers to anticipate issues

Characteristics

• Multidimensional
• Eclectic
• Includes past and present
• Incorporates values
• Two approaches:
  –Macro—large-scale databases
  –Micro—field studies

Methods

• Focused synthesis
• Secondary analysis
• Field experiments
• Multisite evaluation
• Qualitative interviews
• Surveys
• Case studies
• Multisite evaluations
• Large-scale testing programs
• Cost analysis
• Focus groups

Limitations

• Failure to directly improve practices and policy formation
• Research as only one of many influences on educational policies, practices, and decisions

KEY TERMS

evaluation	behavioral objectives
worth	decision-oriented evaluation
formative evaluation	participant-oriented evaluation
summative evaluation	responsive evaluation
evaluation approach	policy analysis
objectives-oriented evaluation	multisite evaluation
target group	cost-effectiveness analysis

This chapter draws on previous chapters about design, data collection, and data analysis. *Evaluation* is the application of research skills to determine the *worth* of an educational practice. Evidence-based evaluation aids in decision making at a given site and adds to the body of knowledge about a specific practice that is often relevant to the general public. Decisions to plan, to improve, or to justify widespread adoption of a practice need implementation and impact evidence. An *evaluator* is both a researcher and a concerned educator whose work is essential in the overall functioning of an educational organization. *Policy analysis* evaluates government policies to provide policy-makers with pragmatic recommendations from among policy alternatives. A *program* can be viewed as a specific means that is adopted to carry out a policy.

In this chapter, we summarize the purposes of evaluation, present an overview of evaluation approaches, and discuss three approaches to evaluation: objectives-oriented, decision-oriented, and participant-oriented evaluations. Policy analysis characteristics and methods, including cost analysis, are summarized, as well. We also cite the standards, potential uses, and limitations of evaluation research and policy analysis.

PURPOSES AND DEFINITION OF EVALUATION RESEARCH

Evaluation activities have always been an integral part of education. Professional judgments have frequently been made about modifications of programs. The need for formal evaluation increased as society allocated greater responsibilities and resources to education. Evaluation is used for accountability, in performance measures, and in so-called high-stakes testing programs. In 2002, 49 states had standards-based testing programs, and many states used the results to determine promotion and/or graduation.

The establishment of a National Center for Educational Evaluation and Regional Assistance (NCEE) in 2002 represented a significant federal policy shift. In the past, federal monies sponsored mostly implementation studies. Although implementation studies remain part of the federal mandate, most of the federal monies now will support evaluations that can provide evidence of program effectiveness using rigorous designs such as randomized trials.

Purposes and Roles of Evaluation

In brief, *evaluation research* is defined as the determination of the *worth* of an educational program, product, procedure, or objective. The three reasons most frequently given for conducting an evaluation study are (1) to judge the worth of a program, (2) to assist decision makers, and (3) to serve a political function. In any single report, these purposes will receive different degrees of emphasis.

Most educators recognize that evaluation can serve a formative purpose (e.g., to improve a program) or a summative purpose (e.g., to decide if that program should be continued). More specifically, evaluation can do the following:

1. Aid planning for the installation of a program
2. Aid decision making about program modification
3. Aid decision making about program continuation or expansion
4. Obtain evidence to rally support or opposition to a program
5. Contribute to the understanding of psychological, social, and political processes within the program as well as external influences on the program

Definition and Types of Evaluations

Evaluation requires a formal evaluation design and procedures to collect and analyze data systematically for determining the worth of a specific educational practice. To say that a practice or program has **worth** means to examine it and to judge its value according to standards that are applied relatively or absolutely. The *value* of an educational practice may be intrinsic to it (e.g., reading programs value reading comprehension) or within a given site (e.g., community culture and values). *Educational practice* refers to a program, a curriculum, a policy or administrative regulation, an organizational structure, or a product. Most of the examples in this chapter, however, will be drawn from curriculum and program evaluation.

A curriculum or program may be implemented at one site or at multiple sites within a single or many administrative units, such as school systems or cities. The number of sites in which the educational practice operates influences the evaluation questions and the design.[1]

Two types of evidence-based evaluation are formative and summative. The purpose of **formative evaluation** is to improve a curriculum in a developmental stage. Typical questions are What parts of the program are working? and What needs to be changed and how? The evaluation results may lead to a decision to revise the curriculum, to extend the field testing to gather more data, or to abort further development in order not to waste resources on a program that ultimately may be ineffective. These studies, which are often done by internal evaluators, should be timed to be useful and should focus on variables over which educators have some control.

Summative evaluation can be conducted once the program is fully developed—that is, when it functions well or does what it was intended to do with few detrimental side effects. **Summative evaluation** determines the effectiveness of a program, especially in comparison with other competing programs. A typical question may be Which of several programs achieves these objectives most effectively and efficiently? Summative studies, which are typically conducted by external evaluators, can aid in purchase or adoption decisions of programs, products, and procedures.

An external evaluator, however, may be engaged to conduct either formative and summative evaluations for credibility, a fresh outside perspective, and a neutral attitude toward the worth of the practice. Table 17.1 summarizes the distinctions between formative and summative evaluation.

Both formative and summative evaluations are essential because decisions are needed during the developmental stages of a program to improve it and then again when it has been stabilized to judge its effectiveness. Unfortunately, far too many educational agencies conduct only summative evaluations.

Standards for Judging the Quality of Evaluation Research

The second edition of *The Program Evaluation Standards*, released in 1994, indicated the continued professionalization and specialization of this type of research. The authoring group, the Joint Committee on Standards for Educational Evaluation, represented important national associations of people in education, research, evaluation, and measurement.

TABLE 17.1	Formative versus Summative Evaluation	
Characteristic	**Formative Evaluation**	**Summative Evaluation**
Purpose	To improve the program	To certify program utility
Audience	Program administrators and staff	Potential consumer or funding agency
Who should do it	Internal evaluator, supported by external evaluator	External evaluator
Data collection	Often multimethod, informal	Valid/reliable instruments
Sample	Purposeful and/or probability	Probability
Questions asked	What is working?	What are the results? For whom?
	What needs to be revised?	In what situations?
	How can it be improved?	Requiring what costs, materials, and training?

Source: Adapted from Fitzpatrick, J. L., Sanders, J. R., & Worthen, B. R. (2004). *Program evaluation: Alternative approaches and practical guidelines,* 3rd ed. Boston: Allyn & Bacon, p. 20.

The 30 standards they developed were intended to provide a conceptual framework for evaluation and a basis for self-regulation by professional evaluators.

The Joint Committee developed four criteria that a good evaluation study satisfies: utility, feasibility, propriety, and accuracy. Each criterion is described further in the following list, along with specific standards:[2]

1. *Utility standards* ensure that an evaluation will serve the practical and timely information needs of given audiences. Eight standards are audience identification, evaluator credibility, information scope and selection, valuation interpretation, report clarity, report dissemination, report timeliness, and evaluation impact.

2. *Feasibility standards* ensure that an evaluation will be realistic, frugal, and diplomatic. Three standards are practical procedures, political viability, and cost effectiveness.

3. *Propriety standards* ensure that an evaluation will be conducted legally, ethically, and with due regard for the welfare of those involved in the evaluation and those affected by its findings. These standards are formal obligation, conflict of interest, full and frank disclosure, public's right to know, rights of human subjects, human interactions, balanced reporting, and fiscal responsibility.

4. *Accuracy standards* ensure that an evaluation will state and convey technically adequate information about the features of the practice studied that determine its value. Eleven standards are object identification, context analysis, described purposes and procedures, defensible information sources, valid and reliable measurement, systematic data control, analysis of quantitative information, analysis of qualitative information, justified conclusions, and objective reporting.

ALERT!   Not all standards will be appropriate for a specific evaluation effort.

The standards are a compilation of commonly agreed on characteristics of good evaluation practice. In any specific formal evaluation situation, the choices and trade-offs relating to each standard are within the province of the evaluator. Furthermore, the standards serve as a guide to evaluators, officials who commission studies, and persons who use evaluation reports.

SELECTED APPROACHES TO EVALUATION

A broad array of educational entities are evaluated, including curriculum materials, programs, instructional methods, educators, students, organizations, and management. Crucial to evaluation is deciding on the entity to be evaluated: the group, product, method, organization, or management system. Careful delineation of the entity and all of its components will help the evaluator decide which aspects or components are most important for evaluation.

An **evaluation approach** is a strategy to focus the evaluation activities and to produce a useful report. Evaluation is multifaceted and conducted at different stages of program development. Evaluators have published schema that group various evaluation approaches. Each approach has prominent theorists, explicit rationales, discussions in the literature, a group of practitioners, actual evaluation studies, and critics (see Stufflebeam, Madeus, & Kellaghan, 2000). The major evaluation approaches are classified in this list:

1. *Objectives-oriented approaches,* in which the focus is on specifying goals and objectives and determining the extent to which they have been attained
2. *Consumer-oriented approaches,* in which the central issue is developing evaluative information on educational *products*, broadly defined, for use by educational consumers in choosing from among competing curricula, instructional products, and the like
3. *Expertise-oriented approaches,* which depend primarily on the direct application of professional expertise to judge the quality of educational endeavors, especially the resources and the processes[3].
4. *Decision-oriented approaches,* in which the emphasis is on describing and assessing an educational change process and resulting outcomes to provide information to a decision maker
5. *Adversary-oriented approaches,* in which planned opposition in points of view of different evaluators (pro and con) is the focus of the evaluation
6. *Participant-oriented approaches,* in which naturalistic inquiry and involvement of participants (i.e., stakeholders in the practice that is evaluated) are central in determining the values, criteria, needs, and data for the evaluation

Evaluators make eclectic uses of these approaches, combining alternative approaches or selectively combining the methods and techniques inherent within them. No evaluator, however, will mix evaluation approaches that are philosophically incompatible. Applying the approaches encourages evaluators to consider a number of critical components that are important in an evaluation effort.

Three of the approaches most frequently used are objectives-oriented evaluation, decision-oriented evaluation, and participant-oriented evaluation. Together, these approaches illustrate the diversity of evidence-based evaluation. The source of questions in an objectives-based study is the curriculum or instructional objectives; the source of questions in a decision-making approach is the decision maker; and the source of the questions in participant-oriented evaluation is the audience (i.e., the stakeholders, including the participants, affected by the practice).

Objectives-Oriented Evaluation

Objectives-oriented evaluation determines the degree to which the objectives of a practice were attained by the target group. In other words, the evaluation measures the outcomes of the practice. The discrepancy between the stated objectives and the outcomes is the measure of success of the practice. The practice may be a curriculum, inservice training, an inschool suspension program, parent education, or the like. The **target group,** or the group whose behavior is expected to change, may be students, parents, teachers, or others. We will illustrate the steps in conducting an objectives-oriented evaluation with curriculum evaluation (see Figure 17.1).

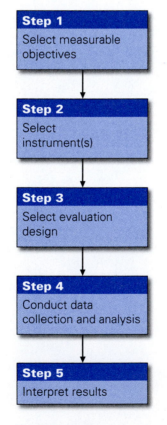

Step 1
Select measurable objectives

Step 2
Select instrument(s)

Step 3
Select evaluation design

Step 4
Conduct data collection and analysis

Step 5
Interpret results

FIGURE 17.1
Steps in Conducting an Objectives-Oriented Evaluation

Selection of Measurable Objectives   An evaluation study measures the objectives, not the abstract goals, of the practice. Curriculum *goals* are usually broad, general statements representing values in the society. *Objectives* are specific statements that are related logically to the goals and attainable through instruction.

Only student outcomes stated as **behavioral objectives** are evaluated. The term *behavioral objective* is synonymous with *performance* or *measured objective*. Behavioral objectives are either terminal student behaviors or student products (e.g., a research paper, clay figurine, oral presentation) but *not* the process leading to terminal behaviors. The criteria for achievement of the objective may or may not be stated in the objective. Four examples of behavioral objectives that differ in level of generality are these:

- A student, on request, will be able to spell and capitalize his or her name correctly.
- A student will be able to compute correctly the answer to any division problems chosen randomly from the review exercises.
- A student will produce a drawing that is judged by three raters as creative by the criteria of originality, flexibility, and elaboration developed by the raters.
- At least 90 percent of the students will be able to pass 70 percent of the questions in a competency test in mathematics.

The last example is a performance objective that states the minimal group performance of 90 percent and the minimal individual student performance of 70 percent. An analysis of the curriculum content coverage and emphasis will suggest the objectives that are the most important.

If the objectives are stated in terms other than behavioral, the evaluator has three choices: (1) reword the objectives in behavioral terms without changing the intent, (2) ignore the nonbehavioral objectives, or (3) communicate to the client the fact that nonbehavioral objectives will not be measured but that these objectives could be described or appraised with other procedures.

Research Navigator.com

17.1 Objectives-Oriented Evaluation
Accession No.: 9457666

Selection of Instruments and Design   Instruments may be tests, questionnaires and self-report devices, rating scales, observation systems, and interview schedules. The typical instrument is a standardized norm-referenced achievement test. Evaluators frequently use data from routine testing programs. Existing test data should be valid for the evaluation.

Content-related evidence for validity can be determined by a panel of local experts logically by comparing the curriculum content with the test items. The validity and reliability of a subtest may be considerably lower than that for the entire test and should be checked in *Mental Measurements Yearbooks*. Other considerations are the appropriateness of the norms for the target group and the type of information sought. Most standardized norm-referenced tests provide only general information about students compared with those in the norm group.

Criterion-referenced instruments may also be used to assess student outcomes. Criterion-referenced instruments must meet the requirements of any measurement procedure. If an evaluator or a local school system plans to develop a criterion-referenced instrument, knowledge of measurement and instrument development will be necessary. The instrument should be valid and reliable for the evaluation purposes, although the type of validity and reliability may differ from that associated with norm-referenced tests. Field testing is essential.

The most useful design in an objectives-based evaluation is a randomized or matched groups design; however, it may not be feasible. Quasi-experimental designs can also be used, such as the one-group pretest and posttest, time series, or counterbalanced designs. Because most programs have both cognitive and affective objectives, a comprehensive evaluation would measure the different types of objectives if valid and reliable instruments were available or could be developed.

Interpretation of Results   The evaluation assesses the percentage of the target group that achieved the predetermined objectives, or it assesses which program, compared with others having similar objectives, is more successful in achieving the objectives. When the evaluator looks more closely at the objectives, he or she often finds that they are stated at different levels of specificity and that not all objectives can be evaluated. The means for selecting the objectives for formal evaluation are often inconsistent. Because only terminal outcomes are actually assessed, process evaluation is omitted. The results may suggest modifications of a practice but provide no specific directions for intervention to improve a practice, or the results may not provide the complete information necessary for adopting a practice at other sites.

Objectives-based evaluation is probably the most frequently used approach for several reasons. Most educators would agree that the successful attainment of objectives indicates the worth of a practice. Educators can demonstrate accountability and the productive use of public funds when objectives are attained. Another advantage of the objectives-based approach is its highly definable methodology. The procedures for this approach have been worked out in great detail, a fact that appeals to many novice evaluators. No other approach has such an elaborate technology and scientific basis. Furthermore, the non-attainment of objectives or the attainment of only some objectives can lead to questioning programmatic components and a closer scrutiny of the practice.

MISCONCEPTION Teaching involves a set of behaviors that any-one can easily learn without training.

EVIDENCE Graduates of teacher preparation programs stay in the profession longer and are more competent in their instruction than those without such training.

Decision-Oriented Evaluation

Decision-oriented evaluation has a broad scope and implies a theory of educational change. Its purpose is primarily to collect and analyze the data needed to make decisions. The evaluator and the administrator identify decision alternatives, which can be routine maintenance decisions (e.g., staff policies) or incremental decisions leading to systemwide change. **Decision-oriented evaluation** studies may thus be done at any point in a change process: needs assessment, program planning, implementation, or process and outcome evaluation. The types of evaluation studies with their subsequent decisions are summarized in Table 17.2 and below:

1. *Needs assessment* compares the current status and values of an educational system with the desired outcomes. The evaluation identifies the context, provides baseline data on the accomplishments of the site, and identifies unmet needs. Needs can be stated by the students, the community, other groups, or society as a whole in relation to the system. Needs assessment leads to selection of a program to achieve specific objectives.

2. *Program planning and input evaluation* involves examining alternative strategies, such as adoption of an available program or development of a new program, to achieve the new objectives. Researchers study available programs for their practicality, cost, and ease of reproducing components to achieve objectives. Researchers also examine the feasibility of locally developing a program. Program planning and input evaluation leads to the selection of a plan, including procedures, materials, facilities, equipment, schedule, staffing, and budgets for program development or implementation.

3. *Implementation evaluation* assesses the extent to which a program is developed or implemented as planned, and it also identifies any defects in the program. Information with which to anticipate the changes necessary for continued program development and implementation is provided, as well.

Research Navigator.c⊛m

17.2 Implementation
Evaluation
Accession No.: 6943193

TABLE 17.2   Types of Decision-Oriented Evaluation

Needs Assessment

Evaluation	Current status contrasted with desired status—educational need
Decision	Problem selection

Program Planning and Input Evaluation

Evaluation	Kinds of programs that fit objectives derived from needs assessment and possible strategies
Decision	Program plan

Implementation Evaluation

Evaluation	Degree to which the program is implemented as planned
Decision	Program modification

Process Evaluation

Evaluation	Extent program achieves its objectives and products
Decision	Program modification and improvement

Outcome or Product Evaluation

Evaluation	Worth of program as reflected by process and outcomes
Decision	Program certification and adoption

Source: Based on Stufflebeam et al. (1971), pp. 215–239.

4. *Process evaluation* provides information on the relative success of the various components of a program and the extent to which the objectives and products are achieved. The evaluator plays the role of a so-called interventionist, collecting data that will lead to immediate program improvement. Data collection requires testing procedures and other methods. Process evaluation results in program modification.

5. *Outcome or product evaluation* assesses the extent to which the objectives were achieved. The data obtained include those from objectives-based evaluation and other information from earlier evaluations. This previously obtained information explains why the objectives were or were not achieved and helps the decision maker to eliminate, modify, retain, or expand the program for wider use. Outcome evaluation leads to program adoption.

Finally, the decision-oriented approach to evaluation focuses on gathering information by a variety of methods to aid in making decisions for program development and adoption or for wider use. Educational change is a logical, rational activity, and evaluation is an extension of it. Possible difficulties in using this type of evaluation lie in conflicting values and goal dissension within a complex educational system and between the educational organization and its constituencies. The decision-oriented approach assumes that the decision maker is sensitive to possible problems in bringing about educational change and is willing to obtain information regarding these realities. It is more difficult to specify and anticipate decisions to be served than it would first appear. Because the evaluator works closely with the decision maker, the impact of the evaluation effort depends as much on the skills of the evaluator as it does on the leadership of the decision maker.

Despite these difficulties, the decision-oriented approach allows for educational and methodological soundness in evaluation. Program evaluation is *not* based on an isolated outcome. The degree of program implementation is addressed before student outcomes are assessed. The approach is also flexible. It may be used for a formative purpose to guide decision making throughout an educational change process, or it may be used for a summative purpose to demonstrate accountability with a record of prior decisions and the rationale and record of the actual process, attainments, and recycling decisions.

Participant-Oriented Evaluation

Educators have often expressed concerns about many evaluations. Administrators have pointed out that (1) technically sophisticated instruments and reports often distract from what is really happening in education; (2) many large-scale evaluations are conducted without evaluators even once visiting some classrooms; and (3) report recommendations do not reflect an understanding of the phenomena behind the numbers, charts, and tables. Educators have further argued that the human element of everyday reality and the different perspectives of those engaged in education are missing. Hence, these approaches are called *participant-oriented evaluation.*

Participant-oriented evaluation is a holistic approach using a multiplicity of data to provide an *understanding* of the divergent values of a practice from the participants' perspectives (see Green, 2000; Guba & Lincoln, 1989). The literature and actual evaluation studies illustrate these commonalities:

1. Uses a *holistic approach,* which sees education as a complex human endeavor.
2. Accommodates and protects *value pluralism* by presenting or summarizing disparate preferences about the practice evaluated.
3. Reports a *portrayal,* as it has come to be called, of a person, classroom, school, district, project, or program that is placed in the broader context in which it functions.
4. Usually depends on *inductive reasoning,* which emerges from grass-roots observation and discovery.
5. Uses a *multiplicity of data* from several different sources, usually within a qualitative methodology or by combining qualitative and quantitative data.
6. Uses an *emergent design* to give an understanding of one specific practice with its contextual influences, process variations, and life histories.
7. Records *multiple realities,* rather than a single reality.

Stake (1975) notes that many evaluation studies are not used because the reports are irrelevant. According to Stake, "An educational evaluation is responsive evaluation if it orients more directly to program activities than to program intents; responds to audience requirements for information; and if the different value-perspectives present are referred to in reporting the success and failure of the programs" (p. 14). **Responsive evaluation** is an old alternative based on what people do naturally when they evaluate things: They observe and react. This approach responds to the natural ways in which people assimilate information and arrive at understanding. The evaluation design emerges from the issues and concerns expressed at the site.

Research Navigator.com

17.3 Responsive Evaluation
Accession Number: 3079524

Prominent Events: Informal Strategies   Responsive evaluation is cyclical, including events that recur. Again quoting Stake, "Any event can follow any event, many events occur simultaneously, and the evaluator returns to each event many times before the evaluation is finished" (1975, p. 18). In Figure 17.2, the prominent events are presented as the face of a clock, emphasizing the cyclic nature of the approach.

The events can be expressed as research phases. In Phase 1 (noon to 4 o'clock), the evaluator talks with clients, program staff, and audiences—anyone directly or indirectly connected with the program—to get a sense of the different perspectives and values of the program. The evaluator also observes the program in operation. From these activities, the evaluator discovers the meaning of the purposes of the program and conceptualizes the issues and problems. In Phase 2 (5 to 7 o'clock), the evaluator ascertains the data needs and selects data collection methods. Although Stake expects observers and judges to be the primary method of data collection, instruments may be appropriate. The data are organized as antecedents, transactions, and outcomes, including both intended and unintended out-

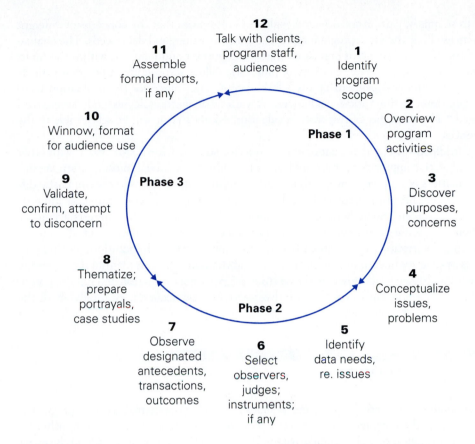

12
Talk with clients,
program staff,
audiences

11
Assemble
formal reports,
if any

1
Identify
program
scope

10
Winnow, format
for audience use

2
Overview
program
activities

Phase 1

Phase 3

9
Validate,
confirm, attempt
to disconcern

3
Discover
purposes,
concerns

8
Thematize;
prepare
portrayals,
case studies

4
Conceptualize
issues,
problems

Phase 2

7
Observe
designated
antecedents,
transactions,
outcomes

6
Select
observers,
judges;
instruments;
if any

5
Identify
data needs,
re. issues

FIGURE 17.2 **Prominent Events in Naturalistic and Participant-Oriented Evaluation**

Source: Adapted from Stake, R. E. (1975). *Program evaluation, particularly responsive evaluation.* Occasional Paper Series, No. 5, p. 19. Kalamazoo: Western Michigan University Evaluation Center. Reprinted by permission.

comes. In Phase 3 (8 to 11 o'clock), the evaluator is concerned with communicating the findings in natural ways. Portrayals can be embodied in the conventional research report, but they usually will take the form of descriptive case studies, artifacts, round-table discussions, newspaper articles, graphics, or videotapes, depending on the audience. Only the primary concerns of each audience are reported to that audience. Last, the evaluator assembles formal reports and other types of reports.

Evaluator's Role   Two aspects of participant-oriented evaluation—the evaluator's role and continuous feedback—distinguish this approach from the prior approaches discussed. The evaluator responds to audience concerns as they change throughout program development and stimulates ideas by trying out data-based insights and findings on the respondents. Negotiation and interaction are part of the method of ensuring accuracy and communication. Communication is a two-stage process, in which findings are tried out on different audiences. This may lead to the evaluator's returning to the field for additional data or altering the way findings are stated in order to communicate more effectively. The results presented in the final report should not surprise any audience, because its content should have been thoroughly criticized before release.

ALERT!   Participant-oriented evaluation is more useful for formative than summative evaluation.

In summary, participant-oriented evaluation recognizes that the concerns of different audiences about the same program represent different values and data needs. The evaluator must select the concerns and issues that are important and relevant, within the limits of time and resources. The discovery of pluralistic values surrounding a program is made by the evaluator independent of any administrator. The source for the evaluation focus and questions is the various audiences. A variety of methodologies and designs can be used.[4] The flexibility of responsive evaluation assures that it will be serviceable to the audiences.

Participant-oriented evaluation is usually a case study (Stake, 2000), and as with other semi-subjective approaches, there are issues of credibility. Although most case studies differ in matters of emphasis, rather than truth or falsity, different observers emphasize different events. Ensuring methodological consistency while representing diverse interests remains a problem. Some believe that evaluators should balance the interests according to their own sense of justice; other evaluators take a disinterested and neutral position, providing descriptions and analyses but not recommendations. In addition, writing portrayals or case studies requires skill, training, and the handling confidential data. Despite these difficulties, a well-constructed case study is a powerful evaluation and has the potential to be coherent, fair to people with diverse views, and accurate, especially about the inner workings of a program.

POLICY ANALYSIS

Policy analysis evaluates government policies to provide policy-makers with pragmatic, action-oriented recommendations. *Policy* is both what is intended to be accomplished by government action and the cumulative effort of the actions, assumptions, and decisions of people who implement public policy. School administrators and teachers, in a real sense, make policy as they carry out their day-to-day jobs.

Policy analysis can focus on (1) policy formulation, especially deciding which educational problems to address; (2) implementation of programs to carry out policies; (3) policy revision; and (4) evaluation of policy effectiveness and/or efficiency. A program can be analyzed as separate from a policy, or it can be defined as a specific means adopted for carrying out a policy.

Characteristics of Policy Analysis

Two distinctive approaches used in policy analysis are (1) a *macro approach*, which is based on economic models such as cost analysis and use of large-scale databases, and (2) a *micro approach*, which is field-based to getting the facts and emphasizes qualitative methods. Many policy studies are eclectic, combining both qualitative and quantitative methods. Depending entirely on statistical proof is seldom done in policy analysis for major policies.

Similar to evaluation research, policy analysis focuses on variables open to influence and intervention and is responsive to the users. The users may be numerous and vary in expectations, values, assumptions, and needs. The values of the users enter into the processes of defining the educational problem; formulating the research questions, design, and policy alternatives; and developing recommendations. Educational values are always embedded in the cultural context. These values often differ at the district level and at the state level. In addition, the normative values of society at large are considered.

Methods of Policy Analysis

Policy analysis incorporates a variety of methods to analyze problems of policy. These methods include focused synthesis, secondary analysis, field experiments, large-scale experimental or quasi-experimental evaluation, qualitative interviews, surveys, large-scale testing programs, case study analysis, cost analysis, and focus groups. The methods discussed in prior chapters and others are briefly defined here in the context of policy analysis:

- **Focused synthesis** is the selective review of written materials and prior research relevant to the policy question. A synthesis differs from a traditional literature review in that it discusses information obtained from a variety of sources beyond published articles—interviews with experts and stakeholders, records of hearings, anecdotal stories, personal experiences of the researcher, unpublished documents, staff memoranda, and published materials. An entire policy analysis study can employ this method.

- **Secondary analysis** is the analysis and reanalysis of existing databases. Rather than examine databases to determine the state of knowledge about an educational practice, secondary analysis generates different policy models and questions from which to examine the databases.

- **Field experiments** and quasi-experiments investigate the effect or change that results from policy implementation. Because experimental approaches explain existing educational conditions, the results are not useful in projecting into the future. Moreover, policy conditions may be so dynamic that the results are confined to that particular period of implementation.

- **Large-scale experimental or quasi-experimental evaluations** of major social and human services programs in the areas of health care, education, mental health, and public welfare can address several questions about the programs and sites. Large-scale quasi-experimental policy analysis of projects, usually funded for three to five years, is called **multisite evaluation.** Some reasons for conducting multisite evaluations include the following:

  - To determine the overall effect of the program after aggregating effects across all sites
  - To evaluate the program in a sample of representative sites to estimate the effect of the program across all sites
  - To determine if the program works under a variety of implementation conditions
  - To study how the program interacts with specific site characteristics
  - To compare program performance across sites to identify the most effective and ineffective ways of operating the program
  - To facilitate cross-site sharing of effective practices and others

Research Navigator.com

17.4 Multisite Studies
Accession No.: 7048403

Because multiple sites will have a number of different local administrative units, an effort must be made to do careful sampling and to standardize program implementation and procedures for collecting and analyzing data.[5] The most widely agreed upon purposes of multisite evaluations are to increase generalizability of findings, to maximize sample size to increase statistical power, and to respond to a variety of political and social concerns.

- **Qualitative interviews** of individual key informants help policy-makers anticipate the implications and consequences of proposed laws or policies. *Prospective studies* combine interviewing people who are knowledgeable in a field to solicit the latest and best thinking on a proposal with using existing government reports to identify trends.

- **Surveys** yield data on the present educational conditions of selected groups or situations. They can be in questionnaire or interview form and use purposeful or probability sampling.

- **Large-scale testing programs** at state and national levels reflect educational policies mandated by governments. Performance measurement and monitoring typically compares current performance with either past performance or some predetermined goal or standard. Most performance-monitoring programs assess outcomes. In K–12 education, standards-based education centers on student achievement.[6] These data, collected from multiple sites, can determine the overall effect of a program or policy when outcomes are aggregated. Examples include the reports to the nation on the status of U.S. education based on the National Assessment of Educational Progress program.

- *Case study analysis* is frequently used for policy research because it can be designed to give a more global analysis of a situation.[7] Case studies provide a more complete understanding of complex situations, identify unintended consequences, and examine the process of policy implementation, which is useful for future policy choices.[8]

- *Cost analysis* focuses on policy effectiveness (i.e., Does the policy produce the desired results?) and policy efficiency (i.e., Were those results obtained at the least amount of cost?). Four types of analysis are cost-benefit, cost-effective, cost-utility, and cost-feasibility analysis. The analysis typically done in education is cost-effective analysis. **Cost-effective analysis** compares program outcomes with the costs of alternative programs when the objectives of the different programs are similar and when common measures of effectiveness are used. *Effectiveness* could be measured by the results of standardized achievement test, psychological tests, or physical tests. Outcome measures need not be converted to monetary values, and the analysis is replicable. One drawback of cost-effective analysis, however, is that it fails to provide automatic policy choices between alternatives because nonquantifiable outcomes and constraints are not part of the analysis. It is difficult to incorporate multiple outcomes, rather than a single outcome, into the analysis.[9]

ALERT!   Expertise in cost analysis requires formal mastery of the underlying tools of both economic analysis and evaluation/policy.

- *Focus groups,* a method of obtaining qualitative data from a selected group of individuals, are frequently used for policy questions. The technique can be used to obtain reactions to planned or existing services, policies, or procedures or to learn more about the needs and circumstances of the participants. Focus groups can be employed in any phase of planning, implementation, or policy impact.

EDUCATIONAL EVALUATION AND POLICY ANALYSIS: POTENTIAL BENEFITS AND LIMITATIONS

Evaluation studies and policy analysis offer many potential benefits to education, although they are not a panacea for all of the ills of education. Education is a complex activity that occurs within a larger and everchanging society comprised of interdependent social, economic, and political systems. In this context, evaluation research and policy analysis bring a rational and empirical perspective to the arenas of educational decisions and policy-making.

Evaluation and policy studies are intended to be used. A study is considered utilized if the research is related to a discrete decision or enlightens decision makers about issues, problem definition, or new ideas for alternative actions. The latter type of research utilization—the psychological processing of a study—does not necessarily direct decisions or dictate action, however.

Some evaluators and analysts, with a realistic understanding of how policy is made, propose the types of research most likely to be used. For instance, studies using diverse criteria for worth and containing more comprehensive information, such as program context and implementation, have a good chance of being used. In addition, systematic, long-term studies are more likely to influence policy-makers, providing specifications of the full scope of issues and nontechnical summaries of findings.

Potential Benefits The list of potential benefits will increase as more educators gain experience in conducting and using evaluation and policy studies. The most frequently mentioned potential benefits are listed here:

1. Allows planning and implementing school improvements on a systematic basis. Evidence of what works is important in program justification. Evidence of what does *not* work allows decision makers and those with influence over policy to recast alternatives considered as solutions.
2. Tests several popular myths about the effects of education on student development
3. Demonstrates professional responsibility by appraising the quality of educational programs
4. Reduces uncertainty about educational practices when experience is limited
5. Satisfies external agencies' requirements for reports to legitimize decisions and improve public image
6. Conducts cost-effectiveness analysis of programs and practices that require large expenditures
7. Enlightens influentials in decision and policy arenas to enable them to better anticipate program and policy issues

Possible Limitations The limitations most often cited are as follow:

1. Failure of many studies to improve educational practices and educational policy formation. Studies frequently are conducted without first understanding the factors that affected the use of research information even when the studies were well done.
2. Lack of appreciation that research is only one of many influences on educational policies, practices, and decisions. Evaluation studies and policy analysis cannot *correct* problems, but they can identify strengths and weaknesses, highlight accomplishments, expose faulty areas, and focus on realistic policy alternatives. Correcting a problem is a separate step from using research results.

CREDIBILITY OF EVALUATION AND POLICY REPORTS

An evaluation or policy report is typically long and contains several chapters. The report consists of an introduction, stating the focus and design; the findings, organized by research questions or components of the practice; and a summary, which offers recommendations.

The criteria for judging the adequacy of a report emphasize two aspects: (1) the evaluation focus and design and (2) the findings, conclusions, and recommendations. Much of the report's credibility rests on proposing and conducting a study according to *The Program Evaluation Standards* (Joint Committee, 1994). The following questions illustrate typical criteria:

1. Is the evaluation focus stated, along with the context, objectives, and description of the practice or policy, the general purposes of the study, and the evaluation or policy approaches used?
2. Are the research questions stated and the data collection and analysis procedures specified? Are the procedures defensible?
3. Are the results reported in a balanced manner and with full and frank disclosure, including the limitations of the study?
4. Is the reporting objective to the extent that the findings are based on verified facts and free from distortion from personal feelings and biases?
5. Are the conclusions and recommendations justified and is sufficient information presented to determine whether these conclusions and recommendations are warranted? Are plausible alternative explanations presented for findings, when appropriate?

SUMMARY

1. Evidence-based evaluation requires a formal design and procedures to determine the worth of a practice. Evaluation studies are used to plan, improve, and justify (or not justify) educational practices.

2. The worth of a practice is determined by making a judgment of its value according to standards applied, whether relatively or absolutely.

3. Formative evaluation helps revise a practice in a developmental cycle. Summative evaluation, which is conducted when a practice is established, determines the effectiveness of a practice compared with other competing practices.

4. A credible evaluation study satisfies the standards of utility, feasibility, propriety, and accuracy.

5. Major evaluation approaches include objectives-oriented, consumer-oriented, expertise, decision-oriented, adversary, and participant-oriented approaches.

6. Objectives-oriented evaluation focuses on terminal behaviors, or the extent to which the measurable objectives of a practice are attained by the target group.

7. Decision-oriented evaluation—such as needs assessment, program planning, implementation, and process and outcome assessment—provides information to decision makers during program or system change processes.

8. Participant-oriented evaluation is based on the concerns of the various stakeholders. Multiplicity of data, inductive reasoning, and writing portrayals or a series of case studies characterize this approach.

9. Policy analysis evaluates government policies to provide policy-makers with pragmatic recommendations. Both macro (large-scale databases) and micro (field studies) approaches are employed.

10. Some policy analysis methods include focused synthesis, field experiments, large-scale multisite evaluations, qualitative interviews, surveys, large-scale testing programs, cost analysis, case studies, and focus groups.

11. The potential benefits of evaluation studies and policy analysis are systematic school improvements, cost analyses, assessment of educational effects on students, appraisal of the quality of education, reduction of uncertainty in innovative practices, legitimization of decisions, and enlightenment of policy-makers to better anticipate program and policy issues.

12. An evaluator, a client, and a user can each judge the adequacy of an evaluation proposal or report by using a checklist of criteria.

RESEARCH NAVIGATOR NOTES

Reading the following articles will help you understand the content of this chapter. Go to the education database (included in the EBSCO database) in Research Navigator; use the Accession Number provided to find the article.

17.1   *Objectives-Oriented Evaluation*
Hosen, R., & Solovey-Hosen, D. (2003). The instructional value of fostering social capital in the classroom. *Journal of Instructional Psychology, 30*(1), 84–93. Accession Number: 9457666.

17.2   *Implementation Evaluation*
Marshall, C., & Patterson, J. (2002). Confounded policies: Implementing site-based management and special education

policy reforms. *Educational Policy, 16*(3), 351–387. Accession Number: 6943193.

17.3   *Responsive Evaluation*
Nistler, R. J., & Maiers, A. (2000). Stopping the silence: Hearing parents' voices in an urban first-grade family literacy program. *Reading Teacher, 53*(8), 670–681. Accession Number: 3079524.

17.4   *Multisite Studies*
Peterson, C. A. (2002). Reflections on the challenges of program evaluation. *Topics in Early Childhood Special Education, 22*(2), 82–86. Accession Number: 7048403.

CHECK YOURSELF

 Multiple-choice review items, with answers, are available on the Companion Website for this book:

www.ablongman.com/mcmillanschumacher6e.

APPLICATION PROBLEMS

1. Analyze the following evaluation situation by identifying the problem and suggesting alternative procedures.

   A supervisor of instruction wanted to conduct an evaluation in order to compare a new independent study approach with the regular instructional approach in high school mathematics. A written formal agreement with the district evaluation staff stated the following arrangements:

   a. The evaluation was to help the high school mathematics department chairpersons decide whether to adopt the independent study approach districtwide.
   b. The procedures were to conduct a districtwide comparison of the two approaches, involving 20 percent of the high school's mathematics teachers and all of their students.
   c. Mathematics achievement, student attitude, and teacher enthusiasm would be assessed.
   d. Teachers would be randomly selected and assigned to the two different approaches.

   The supervisor later decided that the evaluation should provide feedback to improve the new approach, rather than to decide on adoption. She changed the procedure for assigning teachers and students to the project, which resulted in their not being assigned randomly. The evaluation staff—assuming that the evaluation focus and design, once agreed on, would remain the same—collected and analyzed data as originally planned.

   The evaluators found that student attitudes toward both approaches were similar but that student achievement and teacher enthusiasm were significantly greater for the independent study approach. The report judged this approach as superior and recommended it for adoption.

   The supervisor was disappointed that the report did not help improve the independent study approach. The department chairpersons complained that the findings were not dependable for two reasons: (1) Many of the teachers assigned to the independent study approach were biased in favor of it before the study began, and (2) the students in the independent study classes were generally high-achievers prior to entering the program.

   For each of the following items, read the following full-text evaluation study in the Research Navigator education database; search by Accession Number to locate each study. Then answer the following questions.

2. Box, J. A., & Little, D. C. (2003). Cooperative small-group instruction combined with advanced organizers and their relationship to self-concept and social studies achievement of elementary school students. *Journal of Instructional Psychology, 30*(4), 285–288. Accession Number: 12010631.
   a. Identify the two experimental treatments.
   b. What is the evidence of validity for the achievement test?
   c. How do the researchers explain the improvement in achievement for both the experimental and the control groups?
   d. Name the evaluation approach employed.

3. Ramsey, A. L., Rust, J. O., & Sobel, S. M. (2003) Evaluation of the gang resistance and training (GREAT) program: A school-based prevention program. *Education, 124*(2), 297–310. Accession Number: 11978670.
   a. What do you think limits the validity of this evaluation? What do the authors recommend if the study were to be replicated?

4. Wilcox, D. J., Putnam, J., & Wigle, S. E. (2002). Ensuring excellence in the preparation of special educators through program evaluation. *Education, 123*(2), 342–352. Accession Number: 9134806.
   a. Identify the limitations you think exist in this evaluation.
   b. The authors claim the value of the study lies in using the data to improve the program. Would you make program changes in two competency areas based on this data? Why or why not?

5. Brookhart, S. M., & Bronowicz, D. L. (2003). "I don't like writing. It makes my fingers hurt": Students talk about their classroom assessments. *Assessment in Education: Principles, Policy and Practice, 10*(2), 221–243. Accession Number: 10849125.
   a. Identify the major concepts and the academic discipline that provide the framework for the interview questions.
   b. Identify the design and describe in detail the three levels of purposeful sampling.
   c. What is the context of the study?
   d. Which evaluation approach does this study illustrate?

NOTES

1. We briefly discuss large-scale multisite studies as a policy analysis method.
2. See Joint Committee on Standards for Educational Evaluation (1994). *The program evaluation standards*, 2nd ed. Thousand Oaks, CA: Sage.
3. Examples are (1) accreditation and informal professional review systems and (2) ad hoc panel reviews, such as those by funding agencies and "blue ribbon" panels (e.g., the National Commission on Excellence in Education).
4. For recent variations of this approach, see Cousins and Whitmore (1998) and Patton (1996).

5. For a discussion of design issues, see Greenberg, Meyer, and Wiseman (1995); Rist (2000); and Fitzpatrick, Sanders, and Worthen (2004).
6. See the American Evaluation Association statement on high-stakes testing with links to references on this topic at www.eval.org/hstlinks.html.
7. See Yin (2004) for a variety of studies.
8. For recent variations, see Fetterman (2000) and House & Howe (2000).
9. For an example of cost-benefit analysis, see Reynolds, Temple, Robertson, and Mann (2000).

Answers to Application Problems

CHAPTER 1

1. A. The teacher is more aware that classroom misbehavior might be related to the home environment.
2. C. A new research question might concern whether the reading comprehension test is also valid for grades 3 and 4.
3. C. A new research problem would be to study the organization of schools since the 1954 Supreme Court rulings.
4. B. The principal decides to send an information letter to parents that explains the new report card and grading system.
5. B. The curriculum developer decides to revise the module to reflect the suggestion from the field testing of the pilot module.
6. C. The professor proposes a new study to investigate the degree and type of autonomous behavior of superintendents, principals, and teachers.

CHAPTER 2

1. a. nonexperimental
   b. experimental or nonexperimental
   c. nonexperimental or qualitative
   d. experimental
   e. nonexperimental
   f. nonexperimental
   g. nonexperimental
   h. experimental
   i. qualitative

CHAPTER 3

1. a. Need to specify population, "different ways of learning," and "effects." Example: Is there a difference between the SRA social studies achievement scores of eighth-graders who had an inquiry approach and those who had a lecture approach?
   b. Need to specify population and measures of two variables. Example: Do the attitudes toward learning of middle school students differ between those in cooperative instruction and those in competitive instruction?

   c. Need to specify which educational opinions of which parents (population). Example: What are the opinions of parents of Fox School pupils toward the proposed athletic eligibility regulations?
   d. Need to specify which family characteristics are to be measured or categorized and measurement for school attendance. Example: Is there a relationship between educational level of parents and number of siblings and their average daily school attendance?
   e. Need to specify type of validity sought, population, and criterion for validity. Example: Is there a relationship between the scores of the WISC and the CAT among primary-grade minority children?
2. Directional hypothesis: Low-achieving students reinforced with tangible rewards will demonstrate greater achievement in basic skills than low-achieving students reinforced with intangible rewards. Independent variable is type of reward (categorical), and dependent variable is achievement (continuous or measured).
3. a. High school students in an individualized curriculum will score higher on a social studies test than students in a structured curriculum.
   b. Teachers' use of positive task introduction compared to neutral task introduction will produce sustained student engagement in those tasks.
   c. Students who are retained have higher scores on a measure of personal adjustment than comparable students who are promoted.
   d. There are significant differences in the scores of a teacher burnout inventory among teachers of mildly retarded, moderately retarded, and nonretarded children, or the degree of teacher burnout increases as the students' level of intellectual ability decreases.
4. a. Female faculty members of an urban university
   b. The school board records of a suburban school system, 1950 to 1980
   c. Sue Olson's first year as a teacher in an elementary school
   d. A faculty implementing an innovative middle school program
5. a. Dependent variable: self-concept—Piers-Harris Children's Self-Concept Scale and Teacher Inferred Self-Concept Scale; dependent variable: researcher-developed social studies achievement test.

b. The two scales are well-established instruments, presumably with evidence of validity and reliability; the social studies achievement test has face validity only.

c. Yes, especially for the achievement variable.

6. a. The case was the role of speech-language pathologists (SLPs).

b. Five SPLs with 10 or more years of experience in five Wyoming schools.

c. Fifteen ancillary participants of two to four teachers in each of the five schools.

7. a. Independent variable: story impressions preview; dependent variable: passage recall.

b. Levels of independent variable: write a story using the phrases; list predictions from the phrases; read the narrative passage.

c. To include reading ability as a factor in the experiment.

8. a. Sixteen Korean mothers in Korea and sixteen Korean American mothers, all of whom had children with disabilities.

b. Cross-national/cross-cultural.

c. Parental understanding of child's disability, family stresses and social supports, benefits from children to parents, process of adaptation to child's disability.

d. Yes.

CHAPTER 4

1. Search *RIE* by type of document: curriculum guidelines and evaluation studies for Title I ESEA Act mathematics programs and by years desired. By using connecting identifiers with key terms, Chapter 1 (new terminology) can be located.

2. a. For a narrow search:
A and E and H and J

b. For a more thorough search:
Search 1: (A or B) and (E or F) and (H or I) and J
Search 2: (A or B) and (E or F) and (H or I) and (J or K)
Search 3: (A or B or C or D) and (E or F or G) and (H or I) and J
Search 4: (A or B or C or D) and (E or F or G) and (H or I) and (J or K)

3. The order of priority for presenting sources in a literature review is from the least related or most general to the most related literature. The sources would thus be organized as (d) theories, (e) studies on animal behavior, (b) program descriptions, (a) evaluations of instruction, and (c) evaluations of students.

4. a. MLA (Modern Language Association), APA (American Psychological Association), and CMS (Chicago Manual of Style).

b. Swadener, E. B., & Bloch, M. N. (1997). Children, families and change: International perspectives. Preface to the Special Issue. *Early Education and Development*, 8(3), 207–218.

c. (Swadener & Bloch, 1997) *or* Swadener & Bloch (1997).

d. VandenBos, G., Knapp, S., & Doe, J. (2001). Role of reference elements in the selection of resources by psychology undergraduates. *Journal of Bibliographic Research, 5*, 117–123. Retrieved July 23, 2005, from http://jbr.org/articles.html

CHAPTER 5

1. Internet Search tools and searches

a. Search Engine: Search for all of the key ideas (*Internet, guidelines or policies, Georgia*)

b. Subject Directory: Search for a category of Internet guidelines or policies; then look for listings by state or by setting. Search for listings of Georgia schools.

c. Known locations with probable links to policies and/or listings of websites for Georgia schools
a. Georgia Department of Education
b. Georgia Education Association
c. American Association of School Administrators

2. Evaluate each component of the citation, abstract, and bibliography, and address.

a. Author: Has Catherine Maloney published any other research on this topic? Is there really a Fairfield University? If so, is she listed as a member of the faculty?

b. Abstract and research methodology: This just sounds ridiculous.

c. Bibliography: Is there really a journal called *Western Musicology Journal?*

d. Address: This might look legitimate, but if you shorten the address to www.improb.com, you find that it hosts many spoofed websites.

3. Title: Private School Universe Survey, 1997–98
Internet address: http://nces.ed.gov/surveys/pss/
Summary: Survey data on the characteristics of K–12 private schools. Includes information on school size and religious orientation of school.
Statistic: The survey reported that 5.3 million students were enrolled in K–12 private schools in the fall of 2001.

CHAPTER 6

1. a. Evidently, the instructor knew about the study, and his or her bias could affect the results. Subjects choose the sections they will be in; hence, selection is a major threat. The time of day of the sections may affect selection and is itself a threat to internal validity. There is no assurance that the instructor will treat each section the same. Diffusion of treatment may be a problem if students from different sections interact. Some students may purposely score low on the pretest in order to show significant improvement in the course (instrumentation—the

results may be inaccurate). History may also be a threat, depending on the nature of the class groups. The generalizability is limited to the students taking the course in this particular college, the course itself (tennis), the instructor, and the methods used in the class.

b. Instrumentation is a potential threat, since details about the nature of the observations are lacking. Test validity could also be considered, since measuring prosocial behavior in a playground may not reflect the benefits of day-care attendance. Compensatory rivalry or resentment might be a factor, because mothers who were chosen as a control group might arrange other experiences for their children that would enhance prosocial behavior. External validity is limited because of the volunteer nature of the sample and the specific programs of the day-care institutions utilized. If many different day-care organizations are represented, it will be difficult to generalize about the cause of the difference. Each case will have to be examined individually.

c. The question here is whether the population that votes is the same as the population from which the sample is drawn; after all, those who rent can also vote, so depending on the percentage of renters in the district, sampling property owners alone may be misleading. In addition, not all property owners have children going to school, and only a portion of the population ever votes. The generalizability of the results thus would be suspect. Depending on the nature of the issue at hand, some respondents may provide less than honest information. They may also change their minds within the two weeks before voting.

d. The major threat is selection, since only 60 percent of the poulation returned questionnaires, and teachers could withhold information if they want to. Instrumentation may be a threat, depending on the way the questionnaire was designed (validity and reliability, and the standardization of the way it is administered—that is, its directions). There is a chance for scoring error, since each instructor does his or her own scoring. Subject attrition might be a problem. Since the questionnaire was given only once, students who were absent would be excluded. The generalizability of the results would be limited by the nature of the sample that returned questionnaires and the time of year the study was done.

CHAPTER 7

1. a. mean
   b. Pearson product-moment correlation
   c. standard deviation (the wider the dispersion, the greater the number of groups)
   d. frequencies and percentages

2. a. interval or ordinal
   b. nominal
   c. ordinal

3.

	Variable A	Variable B
Mean	10.09	74.09
Median	10.00	75.00
Standard deviation	6.20	13.07

The correlation is .31. Felix is an outlier; when his scores are removed, the correlation is .76.

4. (Use SPSS to confirm answers to question 3.)

CHAPTER 8

1. a. Questionnaire, to enhance confidentiality of sensitive topics and keep expenses low
   b. Observation, since self-report measures would be susceptible to social desirability
   c. Phone interview, to ensure representative responses
   d. Questionnaire, because the information is simple and easily obtained
   e. Observation, to keep the situation as natural as possible
   f. Interview since there would be a need to probe
   g. Interview; most small children are honest and are unable to respond to questionnaires
   h. Questionnaire or interview, depending on the specificity of the information needed. An interview is useful for generating specific items that can then be used on a questionnaire.

2. a. Ambiguity of the term *open education*
   b. No information about how to rank; is 1 or 10 most important?
   c. Use of both senior and junior high teachers creates ambiguity; should ask about either senior or junior high teachers but not both
   d. Ambiguity permitting a respondent who thinks "she's not just good, she's great" to answer "strongly disagree"

3. a. Alternate individual work sessions and group activities, and observe during individual work sessions
   b. Teach students to observe themselves (i.e., record time taken to complete assignments)
   c. Use unobtrusive measures, such as number of requests from students for help, pencil shavings in pencil sharpener, detail and care in assignments, and amount of eraser that is used

4. (individual student answer)
5. (individual student answer)

CHAPTER 9

1. Her decision may have been correct, but her inference that the methods caused the achievement is incorrect

because it is possible that other events occurred at the same time as the methods to cause greater achievement. This is an example of inferring causation from correlation.

2. a. correlational
   b. comparative
   c. predictive
   d. comparative
   e. descriptive
   f. ex post facto

3. (individual student answer)

4. a. Correlational (multiple correlation)
   b. Yes, this is survey research. More information is needed to know if principles of effective survey research were followed. From what is presented, it does not appear that principles were followed (e.g., no indication of pilot; population; follow-up; nature of sample).
   c. Correlational findings are not credible because they appear to be inconsistent with the logic that principals in smaller schools and schools with fewer students of low socioeconomic status would have more involvement in instruction.
   d. There is insufficient information to know if the variability of responses was adequate.
   e. Very little information is given about sampling. As a result, it is not known if the sample would give sufficient variability. Given that variables such as size and low socioeconomic status were used and that there were significant correlations, it would be reasonable to conclude that there probably was sufficient variability in the sample.
   f. This study looks very suspect, although a full report might show otherwise.

5. This is an example of both a comparative and a correlational study. The independent variables were participation/no participation in service learning, previous work experience, and level of training. The dependent variables were self-efficacy and state anxiety. The description of the sample was not complete, since characteristics of each group were not documented. This is a serious limitation, since other differences between the groups, in addition to whether they did service learning, could account for the findings. The group that did not participate in service learning was small. The measures are fairly well described, although more detail would help evaluate the information. Reliability and validity are addressed, although it would be best to have evidence from their subjects. There is good range of scores. Correlation and coefficient of determination, here reported as R^2, are reported separately. A shotgun approach was not used. Spurious correlations could easily result if other factors at the schools affected self-efficacy and anxiety. Causal conclusions are not presented. Overall credibility is not strong.

CHAPTER 10

1. Nonequivalent groups pretest–posttest comparison group design

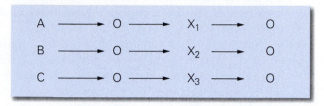

2. Multiple baseline across subjects design

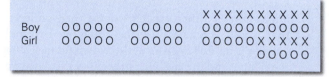

3. Randomized posttest-only comparison group design

Randomization	Group	Treatment	Posttest
60 students	A	X_1	O
	B	X_2	O
	C	X_3	O

4. There is a research hypothesis: namely, that there will be a difference in reading achievement based on different levels of difficulty in dyad learning. This is nondirectional research hypothesis. There is randomization of students to the three comparison groups. A true or randomized groups design is used, with three levels of the experimental variable (i.e., difficulty in dyad learning) and several achievement-related dependent variables. Procedures for implementing the experiment are clearly presented and sufficiently detailed. A good description is provided of procedures for random assignment of students to the three groups. There was clearly a manipulation of the independent variable. An experimental design is appropriate. The procedures indicate good control of extraneous variables. It was an excellent idea to use different levels of dyad difficulty, which turned out to be crucial for the findings. Most of the threats to internal validity have been eliminated by the use of random assignment, but some must still be considered, including instrumentation, diffusion of treatment, local history, and treatment replications. There was very good control of variables for conducting the study in a school setting. There is poor external validity, since the results are heavily dependent on the teachers at this one school. Appropriate inferential statistical tests were used. The design could be strengthened by including more schools and more teachers.

5. a. Much more detail about the design is needed, for example, time frame, how instruments were administered, how the intervention condition was administered.

b. It is not possible to use a randomized design in this setting, even if students could be randomly assigned to classes, because the intervention was done by class and groups within classes.

c. There was no disscussion of potential threats to internal validity.

d. No. Several key threats were not addressed, including selection, treatment replications, diffusions of treatment, subject effects, and experimenter (teacher) effects.

e. No explanations were provided.

f. This design is the best that could be used in this school.

g. No, since there was inadequate effort to show that the classes did not differ with respect to student characteristics, and control of the implementation of the intervention was not examined.

h. There was little indication of any emphasis on external validity.

i. No. Other procedures, such as matching, could be used to ensure group equivalency.

CHAPTER 11

1. There are three groups in this study. The researcher would hence use one-way ANOVA or an appropriate nonparametric analog, depending on the nature of the dependent variables. Most likely, means would be reported for the groups, and the parametric procedure would be acceptable, followed by post hoc comparisons if necessary.

2. Since the same group of students is assessed twice, a dependent samples t-test is the statistical procedure. If there were more than one dependent variable (i.e., several facets to sex education), then the teacher should employ a multivariate test.

3. The teacher should now use a 2 × 2 ANOVA (group × gender). The analysis will provide a test for each main effect and a test for the interaction between group and gender.

4. There would be two ways to analyze this data: First, a correlation could be computed between self-esteem and frequency of visits and tested by a t-test to see whether the correlation is significantly different from zero; or second, groups of students could be identified (e.g., high, low, medium self-esteem), and a 1 × 3 ANOVA computed on the mean frequencies of each group.

5. There are two independent variables and eight related dependent variables, resulting in the need for a 2 × 4 MANOVA, with appropriate post hoc tests if necessary.

6. a. 2
   b. 1
   c. 1.6
   d. 1.08

7. a. There was a statistically significant difference between Group A and Group B. Or Group B demonstrated significantly greater scores than Group A. Or there is a 1/50 probability that the researcher is wrong in concluding that Group B was significantly higher than Group A.

   b. There was a statistically significant difference in SAT scores among Groups A, B, and C. Or there is 1 chance out of 1,000 that the researcher is wrong in concluding that there is a significant difference in SAT scores among Groups A, B, and C. Or depending on post hoc analyses, Group C had SAT scores that were significantly higher than those of Groups A and B.

   c. In a comparison of five groups, there was a statistically significant difference between Group A and Group E. Or there is 1 chance in a 100 that the researcher is wrong in concluding that there is a difference between Group A and Group E.

CHAPTER 12

1. a. Purposeful sampling is appropriate because the interest is only with *these* parents and *this* program. There is no interest in generalizability.

   b. Comprehensive sampling is appropriate because there is only a director, one teacher of the class, and twelve households. The twelve households are also maximum variation sampling because there are three types of households. The researcher needs to locate within each household who is actually attending the child and his or her schooling in the parent education program.

   c. Interview, documents of the program, records of parent/teacher contracts, and materials sent to the parent.

2. Elementary school principals are the key informants. The research question focuses on how, which suggests obtaining information on the process of decision making, who is consulted, which records are used, and copies of school and district guidelines for retention. The design would require use of in-depth interviews and documents analysis. A purposeful sample should be used, but the sample size will depend on locating principals who have had experience with making retention decisions.

3. a. Purposeful sampling is appropriate because the focus is on understanding a concept and a process.

   b. Reputational sampling. Knowledgeable central office personnel who planned, selected the six schools, and did the orientation sessions could select the school where a team is operating on a regular basis. Other cases could be added—such as a negative case or typical case—depending on the information obtained from this site.

   c. Field observations of the monthly team meetings, in-depth interviews with the principal and the facilitator, and documents (e.g., records of all meetings, district guidelines, and others).

4. a. Extension of findings can be enhanced by specifying the researcher role, informant selection, multimethods employed, and data analysis strategies in the report. Data collection strategies that could increase extension are obtaining verbatim accounts, using low-inference

descriptors, having the teacher keep records (participant researcher), and participant review.

b. Strategies to minimize threats to validity are use of participant language, visiting the households and the program, and techniques to enhance reflexivity.

c. The researcher needs to specify how typical are these households and the common and contrasting features of this parent education program to other programs.

5. a. Validity can be enhanced by specifying in the study the researcher role, site selection, social context of the team meetings, data collection and analysis strategies, and analytical premises—concept of site-based school management. Data collection strategies that could increase validity are verbatim accounts, low-inference descriptors, mechanically recording data, and member checking with team members and others.

b. To minimize threats to validity, the researcher can collect data on team meetings for a year, use the language of the site, do all data collection in the field, and keep a reflex journal. Obtaining baseline data is important in a process study.

c. The researcher needs to describe the typicality of the school and the contrasting dimensions of site-based management with that of other management approaches. Of interest is this district's definition of site-based management contrasted to that of other districts and to the theory of site-based school management. Because prior research has been done on site-based school management, the results of this study can be contrasted to prior research.

CHAPTER 13

1. The researcher can collect data by observations and casual conversations with the other teachers and school personnel. Rapport can be maintained with the sixth teacher by indicating interest without demanding her to use the curriculum in the researcher's presence. Sufficient data about the curriculum can be obtained from other sources. Further, for confidentiality of the data, the ethnographer should not tell other district officials of the teacher's reluctance.

2. A researcher tries to observe all the happenings, formal and informal, in the setting, although the major foci may be on the processes within the photography class and the evening programs. Thus, social activities, meals, and extracurricular activities are also potential sources of data. Student photographs are sources of data, as well. Field notes of all observations and conversations should be made because the ethnographer will not know what is important at the time it occurs.

3. The researcher can remind the director of the agreement established at entry into the field—that all data are confidential and all names and places will be coded. Second, the ethnographer does not know what the remarks mean or if the remarks will be reported in the findings, which will reflect only patterns established through cross-checking with other sources. Third, the ethnographer could use the occasion to encourage the director to talk more about these adults so the researcher could assess the trustworthiness of the adult testimony. The ethnographer could also use the occasion to have the director talk about her concerns regarding the public image of the adult education program.

4. The question may be as follows:
   a. How do you feel when your principal visits your class? Probe: Could you tell me why?
   b. Principals usually have a conference with teachers after observing their instruction. Can you tell me what these conferences are like?
   c. Do you think that your principal's evaluation of your teaching is fair?
      Probe: Why is it fair or unfair?
   d. How do you think evaluation relates to your idea of being a professional teacher?

5. a. The interview questions are both descriptive and open ended because they are phrased as *what, how,* and *why* questions.
   b. Yes. Probes were used to clarify the questions and to get to the meanings of student perceptions.

CHAPTER 14

1. a. Beliefs about child development: lines 1–3, 15–16.
   b. Beliefs about the possibility of catching up: lines 4–5, 17–18.
   c. Beliefs about the possibility of influencing a child's preparation for school: lines 6–9, 19–21.
   d. Beliefs about what teachers can do: lines 10–14, 22–24.
2. Some patterns that need confirmation are as follow:
   a. Teacher beliefs about child development relate to beliefs about the possibility of catching up.
   b. Teacher beliefs about the possibility of influencing a child's preparation for school relate to beliefs about what teachers can do.
   c. Teacher beliefs about the possibility of catching up relate to beliefs about what teachers can do.

CHAPTER 15

1. a. Secondary data analysis
   b. Mixed-method design
   c. Mixed-method design
   d. Action research
   e. Secondary data analysis
2. (Individual student answer, e.g., exploratory—using teacher interviews to construct a survey given to teachers about math specialists; explanatory—observing students with special needs following a survey of teachers' perceptions; triangulation—assessing counselors' use of time with interviews and self-report surveys).
3. To extend the study to be an exploratory design, a quantitative phase should be instituted and emphasized more than the qualitative phase. One way to accomplish this would be to use the findings of the interviews to create a quantitative survey that could be administered to a large

group of teachers. A triangulation design could be implemented by asking each teacher to complete a survey right before or after his or her interview.

4. a. Action research
   b. Action research
   c. Traditional research
   d. Traditional research
   e. Action research
   f. Action research
   g. Traditional research

5. (individual student answer)

6. a. To ensure credibility, it would be important to have a systematic way of recording student attention. It would also be excellent if the teacher could have another teacher do some observing to verify her findings. Six weeks total of observing is not very long, and a novelty effect may be present. The teacher could extend the study across more weeks. It would be important to ensure that nothing else was introduced or changed at the same time as the technology. Credibility would be strengthened by adding different ways of measuring student attention, such as using interviews or student self-reports.

   b. Teacher bias can be controlled by asking other professionals to verify her findings. Additional teachers, for example, could also observe or ask students questions. The less the other teachers know about the study, the better.

   c. This is not an example of cyclical research because there is no indication that new research questions were posed upon reflection.

   d. This could become a more traditional study if there was implementation in several schools and many classrooms, if there was a control group that did not receive the technology, if the observation of students was done by observers blind to the study, if the observational procedure had reliability and validity, if the technology was based on a theory of increasing student attention, and if the results were analyzed using inferential statistics.

CHAPTER 16

1. a. The research problem could be stated as follows: The research problem is to analyze the concept of the student in the past 50 years with references to moral development.

   b. Specialized bibliographies for history include *The Historian's Handbook: A Descriptive Guide to Reference Works* and *A Bibliography of American Educational History*.

2. a. A historical analyst would question the accuracy of statements made at a testimonial dinner. Considerations of good taste probably influenced statements such as (1) "due solely to," (2) the junior college system meets state needs and provides a better general education, (3) "alone established" minimum competency testing, and (4) the innovation raised standards and so on.

   b. Other documents about the junior college system, teachers' salaries and certification requirements, and the minimum competency testing program from 1959 to 1979 would confirm, reject, or modify statements made in the newspaper account. The private oral testimonies of the dinners speakers and members of the educational agencies and associations might vary from the public statements.

CHAPTER 17

1. The evaluators should have monitored and noted the changes in purpose and procedures as they occurred. The evaluators could have met periodically with the supervisor to review the purposes and data needs and to check on the procedures that were not directly under their control. Near the end of the evaluation, the evaluation staff could have met with the supervisor and department chairpersons to consider the changed purpose and procedures in preparation for forming recommendations.

2. a. Small-group instruction and advanced organizers
   b. Face validity
   c. Both the teachers and the students were highly motivated.
   d. Objectives-oriented approach

3. a. The authors recommend (1) that the same-age contrast group be used, (2) that participants be asked to evaluate the GREAT program, (3) that teachers' and parents' opinions be recorded, and (4) that school administrators should correlate participation in the GREAT program with incidents of classroom misbehavior.

4. a. The limitations are (1) selection bias, because of the voluntary student response rate of 49 percent and the administrator response rate of 40 percent, and (2) the use of descriptive information only.

   b. Two competencies of concern are technology and inclusion. These areas could be reviewed because (1) additional data of responsibility level versus preparation level were provided, (2) both students and administrators agreed on technology, and (3) additional data (e.g., inclusion trends and research cited for the benefits of technology for special education students) suggest their importance, despite the low response rate.

5. a. The three concepts are task perception, self-efficacy, and goal orientation selected from educational psychology.

   b. The design is a multiple-case study. The levels of purposeful sampling are (1) researcher selection of teachers in different schools with whom they had prior connections, (b)teacher selection of several assessment techniques, and (3) teacher selection of students to interview for each assessment, including some more able and some less able individuals.

   c. Classroom assessment environment
   d. Participant-oriented approach

A

Guidelines for Writing Research Proposals

Writing a research proposal can be the most difficult yet exciting step in the research process. In writing the proposal, the entire inquiry is synthesized into a specific form. Researchers demonstrate that they know what they are seeking, how they will seek and recognize it, and why the research is worthwhile. This appendix describes a general proposal format and provides guidelines first for quantitative proposals and then for qualitative proposals. The preparation and criticism of a proposal is also described.

QUANTITATIVE RESEARCH PROPOSALS

Quantitative research proposals generally follow this format:

I. Introduction
    A. General statement of the problem
    B. Review of the literature
    C. Specific research questions and/or hypotheses
    D. Significance of the proposed study
II. Design and Methodology
    A. Subjects
    B. Instrumentation
    C. Procedures
    D. Data analysis and presentation
    E. Limitations of the design
III.   References
IV.   Appendices

Each main section will be discussed in a following section.

I. Introduction   The *general problem statement* is a clear, precise statement of the research problem, which identifies for the reader the importance of the problem and the area of education in which it lies. A concise and direct statement of the problem is made very early in the introduction, ideally in the first paragraph, and is followed by a description of the background of the problem.

    The *literature review* presents what is known about the problem from theoretical discussions and prior research, thus providing the background and the need for the study. The literature review concludes with a discussion of the knowledge to date on the problem and offers the researcher's insights, such as criticisms of designs of prior research and identification of gaps in the literature.

    Specific research questions and/or hypotheses are stated next and, they should clearly indicate the empirical nature of the investigation, such as the specific type of research design. Definitions—preferably operational definitions—of variables follow.

The *potential significance of the proposed study* notes the importance of the study in terms of (1) the development of knowledge and (2) general implications for further research and educational practices. The researcher discusses how the results of the study could add to theory and knowledge in the area of research.

II. Design and Methodology

The design and methodology include the subjects, instrumentation, procedures for obtaining the data, data analysis and presentation, and design limitations. The researcher also identifies the type of design to be used—survey, correlational, experimental, quasi-experimental, and the like. This orients the reader to expect certain design components to be discussed in the proposal.

The *subjects* are identified by describing the population of interest and how the probability sample will be drawn from this population. The sample size is stated, as well. A rationale for the sampling procedure and the sample size is given. Most proposals state how the protection of the rights of human subjects will be accomplished.

The *instrumentation* section of the proposal identifies the instrument(s) to be used and explains why the instrument(s) was selected as the most appropriate operational definition of the variable(s). If the instrument(s) is already established, then reliability and validity evidence are given. If the instrument(s) must be developed, then the steps for obtaining validity and reliability data are outlined.

The *procedures* section describes how the study will be conducted, often providing a list of steps. Procedures for the replacement of subjects are also noted.

The *data analysis and presentation* states the statistical techniques to be used and specifies how the data will be presented. The statistical test is stated for *each* research question and/or hypothesis and, if necessary, the rationale for the choice of the test. Nothing is gained by using a complicated technique when a simple one will suffice.

The section about *limitations of the design* cites those issues that can be identified at this time: the scope of the study, the design, and/or the methodology. Stating the design limitations illustrates the researcher's knowledge of the threats to internal and external validity in the proposed design. Limitations are tempered with reasonableness and should not be so extensive that the study seems pointless or unimportant. Sometimes, the researcher may prefer to state the research assumptions that were made in order to conduct the study, rather than point out the limitations.

III. References

The references section lists the sources that the researcher actually used to develop the proposal and that are cited in the text of the proposal. That is, every source cited in the proposal *must* be included in the references, and every entry listed in the references *must* appear in the proposal. An ethical researcher does not cite abstracts as references.

IV. Appendices

The appendices provide supplementary materials that are needed for clarity and that allow for economical presentation. When these materials are placed in the appendices, the reader can refer to them as needed, rather than be distracted by them while attempting to follow the logical flow of the proposal. Included in the appendices may be such items as the following:

- Instructions to subjects
- Informed subject consent forms
- Letters of permission to conduct the study in an educational agency
- Pilot studies
- Copies of instruments
- Instructions for and training of data collectors
- Credentials of experts to be used in the study
- Diagrammatic models of research design or statistical analysis
- Chapter outline for the final report
- Proposed time schedule for completing the study

QUALITATIVE RESEARCH PROPOSALS

The degree of specificity in a qualitative research proposal depends on the extent of preliminary work (i. e., gaining access to a site or persons to interview and previewing archival collections). Qualitative research proposals may be more tentative and open ended than quantitative research proposals, allowing for an emergent design.

Qualitative research proposals generally follow this format:

I. **Introduction**
    A. General problem statement
    B. Preliminary literature review
    C. Foreshadowed problems
    D. Significance of proposed study

II. **Design and Methodology**
    A. Site or social network selection
    B. Research role
    C. Purposeful sampling strategies
    D. Data collection strategies
    E. Data management and analysis
    F. Limitations of the design

III. **References or Bibliography**

IV. **Appendices**

Again, each of the main sections will be described in a following section.

I. Introduction   The introduction consists of the general problem statement, the literature review, a description of foreshadowed problems, and a discussion of the potential significance of the proposed study.

The *general problem statement* is phrased as "to describe and analyze" an ongoing event, process, or concept in a discovery orientation. The direct statement of the problem is followed by a description of its background.

The *preliminary literature review* presents the *initial* conceptual frameworks used in phrasing foreshadowed problems/questions as well as the need for the proposed study by identifying gaps in knowledge. The literature review is *not* exhaustive but is rather a preliminary review that makes explicit the initial focus at the beginning of observing and interviewing. The literature review clearly justifies the need for an in-depth descriptive study.

The *foreshadowed problems* are stated as broad, anticipated research questions to be reformulated in the field. These problems are based on the researcher's general, preliminary information about what is likely to occur initially at the site or in interviews.

The *potential significance of the proposed study* describes how the study can (1) add to the development of knowledge and theory and (2) suggest general implications for further research and educational practices. Most qualitative proposals suggest further possibilities for research.

II. Design and Methodology   The design and methodology section includes the site or social network selected, the research role, purposeful sampling strategies, data collection strategies, data analysis, and design limitations. The researcher identifies the proposal as a *case study design* to orient the reader to expect certain design components to be discussed.

The *site selected* is described in terms that illustrate its suitability for investigating the phenomena. A description of the site characteristics is essential—for instance, public or private agency, typical activities and processes, kinds of participants, and the like. The *selected social network* is described to justify that the group members are likely to be informed about the foreshadowed problems. There should be a logical relationship between the potential information to be elicited through personal contact and the foreshadowed problems.

The researcher states the *research role* to be assumed for data collection. The researcher, at this time, can describe the role only in general terms—for example, participant observer or interviewer.

The intent to use *purposeful sampling strategies* is stated in the proposal, and examples are given of possible strategies. Most proposals also state how the rights of human subjects will be protected.

Planned *data collection strategies* are stated next. Although specific data collection strategies will emerge in the field, the intent to use multiple methods should be stated explicitly, to enable corroboration of the data. The researcher also states the expected length of field work and the forms that the data will take, such as field notes and interview records. Finally, the researcher states how data will be catalogued, stored, and retrieved either manually or electronically.

The description of *data management and analysis* includes strategies to facilitate discovery in the field with interim analysis, coding and developing categories, and pattern-seeking techniques. Sometimes, the software programs for data management are stated.

The section on *limitations of the design* notes the limitations that can be identified at this time: the scope of the study, the methodology, and the design. Methodological limitations refer to possible difficulties in assuming the research role, in conducting purposeful sampling, and in conducting observations and interviews. Findings from a case study design are not generalizable, but without a case study design, other research purposes could not be achieved. Researchers discuss the strategies they intend to use to minimize threats to validity, researcher bias, and extension of results.

III. References or Bibliography   Researchers may use one of the two documentation styles: (1) that of the American Psychological Association, known as the *APA style* (APA, 2001) or (2) that of the *Chicago Manual of Styles*, known as CMS style (2003).

IV. Appendices   The appendices in a qualitative proposal provide supplementary materials for clarity and economical presentation, as in a quantitative proposal. The items in the appendices may include the following:

- Letters of permission granting access to the site
- Agreements of informed rights of human subjects from key participants
- Protocols for obtaining informed consent in a social network
- Brief hypothetical examples of field notes and interview records
- A few pages of a coded transcript or field notes from a pilot study
- Lists of records and artifacts known to be available at the site or through a social network
- Proposed schedule for completing the study

PREPARATION AND CRITICISM OF A PROPOSAL

Most institutions either have their own format and style manual or designate a style manual to be followed, such as the *Publication Manual of the American Psychological Association* (2001) and the *Chicago Manual of Style* (2003). *Format* refers to the organization of the proposal. *Style* refers to the rules of spelling, capitalization, punctuation, and word processing employed.

Reference style and format, the treatment of headings and sections, and writing style all differ from one manual to the other. Whereas APA style practically eliminates footnotes, CMS style provides for extensive use of explanatory footnotes to cite specific sources, methodological insights, and comments. And while an APA-style reference list contains only those sources that are cited in the text, a CMS-style list can include sources that provided background knowledge for the problem. The appropriate manual should be consulted for specific directions about these matters as well as grammar, use of personal pronouns, writing of numbers, and table presentations.

Format also addresses the preliminary pages of the proposal: The title page and the table of contents, including sections, references, and appendices. All proposals are typed, and the same standards of scholarship are applied to the typing of a proposal as to the writing of a proposal. The final typed draft should be proofread carefully by the author.

After the final draft of a proposal has been completed, it is submitted to colleagues who read it critically in terms of research criteria, many of which were discussed in prior chapters. They may make observations such as these:

1. The problem is trivial.
2. The problem is not delimited.
3. The objectives of the proposal are too general.
4. The methodology is lacking in detail appropriate for the proposed study.
5. The design limitations are addressed insufficiently.

Guidelines for Writing Research Reports

Writing a good research report or article begins with a thorough understanding of the style, format, conventions, and requirements of the relevant journal, association, or audience. This is best accomplished by carefully reading and reviewing previously published reports and articles in whatever outlets the researcher is considering. For example, most journals that publish educational research use APA style and format, which are explained and illustrated in the *Publication Manual of the American Psychological Association* (2001). If the manuscript is targeted to a specific association, the researcher should check the association's website for directions regarding styles and formats and to review journals published by the association. For example, if the researcher is writing a manuscript for mathematics educators, he or she should check the National Council of Teachers of Mathematics (NCTM) website for guidelines and to obtain some examples of empirical studies in journals published by NCTM.

WRITING STYLE

While the style of writing that is best will depend in part on whether the research is quantitative or qualitative, the goal is the same regardless: to provide a clear and accurate report of what was done and what was found. By presenting different aspects of the study in an orderly manner, the researcher can lead readers logically from one aspect of the study to the next, which enhances their comprehension and understanding.

In sum, while the style of writing in a research report should not be boring, but neither should it contain flowery adjectives and phrases. A research report is not a creative essay; it is a straightforward summary of what was planned, what happened, and what the results mean. The researcher should aim to have interesting and compelling writing that will hold readers' attention and flows smoothly. Quantitative reports should be written in passive voice (i.e., not *I* or *we*) and be concise and technical. Standard headings and parts should be used. In qualitative reports, the writing should be more personal and active, more elaborate, and more detailed to reflect the context and the participants' perspectives.

Here are some general guidelines to improve the writing style of research reports:

- Use simple, easily understood language.
- Avoid jargon, wordiness, and redundancy.
- Use correct spelling, grammar, and punctuation.
- Avoid the use of abbreviations and contractions, except for well-known ones such as IQ and SAT.
- Refer to sources using only the author's last name.
- When a number is the first word in a sentence, it should be spelled out.
- A number of 9 or less should spelled out (i.e., *nine*).
- Avoid overusing of one type of punctuation, such as a comma or dash.
- Avoid shifting verb tense in the same paragraph.

- Avoid using colloquial expressions.
- Only use a pronoun when the referent is obvious.
- Avoid the use of metaphors, rhyming, alliteration, and clichés.
- Avoid ambiguity in identifying sex identity or sex role; also avoid sex bias.
- Use appropriate terms for racial and ethnic identities.
- Avoid language that equates a disabling condition with the person (e.g., "This learning-disabled child . . . ").

PARTS OF THE MANUSCRIPT

Title Page   The title page should contain, at a minimum, the title, the author(s), the author's institutional affiliation, and the date. With multiple authors, the order of authors' names may be important in knowing which person is the primary author. When the order of authors is not alphabetical, the first person listed should be the primary author. When submitting an article for publication, the name of the journal is usually included. The title of the article should be a concise statement of the main idea of the research, written with a touch of style.

Abstract   The abstract is typically 100 to 150 words. It should be dense with information yet concise, providing a summary of the purpose, participants, method, findings, and conclusions. Each sentence should provide information that is essential to understanding the research.

Introduction   The introduction should be one to several paragraphs and should summarize the purpose, background, and significance of the study. The author(s) should indicate why the study is important.

Review of Literature   The review is intended to provide a theoretical foundation and to summarize, critique, and relate other primary studies to the current one. The review should be an analysis and synthesis of previous research. Usually, the most closely related studies are reviewed last. The review should be written in the past tense. For qualitative studies, the review should be brief, and additional literature should be integrated into the paper as findings are presented.

Research Questions and/or Hypotheses   For quantitative research, specific research questions and/or hypotheses are listed following the review of literature. The questions and hypotheses should be consistent with the data analyses. It is usually not necessary to include null hypotheses.

Method—Participants   The methodology section should contain subsections with headings. The first subsection concerns the participants in the research or the data source. Using past tense, all participants are described using age, gender, socioeconomic status, grade level, aptitude, and other characteristics relevant to the study. The sampling procedure and assignment procedure are also described, if appropriate.

Method—Instrumentation   This section describes the data collection measures and procedures. For a quantitative study, it should contain a discussion of the validity and reliability of the obtained scores.

Method—Design   The design is the specific method (e.g., case study, quasi-experimental, longitudinal, nonexperimental, etc.).

Method—Procedure   This subsection is often combined with that on design and includes the steps taken to carry out the study. It also contains instructions to participants; how random assignment was done, if appropriate; how the researcher gained entry into the setting; and how interventions were carried out. Sufficient detail should be provided to enable other researchers to replicate the study. Past tense should be used.

Results   The results section contains a description of the techniques used to analyze the data collected and the findings from those analyses. Written in past tense, the results should only present the findings, not analyze or interpret them. Presentation of the results should parallel the research questions, presenting sufficient detail to support the conclusions drawn. Individual scores are not usually included in quantitative studies. Self-explanatory tables and figures are often used; they should be uncluttered and provide detail that would be cumbersome to include in the narrative. Qualitative results are descriptive and often contain quotations from participants. Results from qualitative studies are also presented with tables and graphs, and findings are typically discussed when presented, integrating the relevant literature as appropriate. For quantitative studies, descriptive statistics should be included when presenting inferential analyses, along with confidence intervals and effect size measures.

Discussion   The discussion section includes an evaluation and interpretation of the findings, weaknesses or limitations of the study, conclusions, and implications for further research and professional practice. The findings are not simply repeated in this section. Interpretations are discussed in relation to previous studies, and theoretical implications are presented. Support for hypotheses is summarized, if appropriate. It is important in this subsection to avoid overgeneralizing the findings and to point out limitations and cautions in making inferences about the meaning of the results (e.g., alternative explanations). The importance of the study is often mentioned, as well.

References   An established style for references should be used—such as APA or CMS—and the conventions of that style should be strictly adhered to. The references list should contain only those sources that are actually cited in the paper. A bibliography can be added to indicate related sources, but that is not common in research. Sources are ordered alphabetically according to first author's last name, and when there is no author, sources are alphabetized by the title of the document. See the References section of this book for examples of APA format.

A-B design   A single-subject design that compares frequency of behavior during the baseline (A) with treatment (B) conditions

A-B-A design   A single-subject design that compares the baseline (A) with treatment (B) and then baseline (A)

achievement tests   Tests that measure knowledge, skills, or behavior

action research   Studies undertaken by practitioners in schools that address an actual problem or issue in the school or classroom

agreement   A type of reliability based on the consistency of ratings or observations among two or more persons

alpha level   Predetermined level of probability to reject null hypothesis

alternative assessment   Procedures used to measure performance through constructed-response answers, unlike traditional paper-and-pencil tests

alternative hypothesis   A statistical statement that is opposite the null hypothesis

analysis of covariance (ANCOVA)   An inferential statistical test used to adjust statistically the effect of a variable related to the dependent variable

analysis of variance (ANOVA)   An inferential statistical procedure for determining the level of probability of rejecting the null hypothesis with two or more means

analytical research   An analysis of documents to investigate historical concepts and events

applied research   Research that is conducted in a field of common practice and is concerned with the application and development of research-based knowledge

aptitude test   A test used to predict behavior

artifact collections   Material objects of a current or past event, group, person, or organization that reveal social processes, meanings, and values

attenuation   The lowering of a measure of relationship between two variables because of the unreliability of the instruments used

attrition   A threat to internal validity in which loss of subjects affects the results

audibility   A record of data management techniques and decision rules that documents the "chain of evidence" or "decision trail."

authenticity   The faithful reconstruction of participants' multiple perceptions

bar graph   A graphical presentation of frequency of nominal variables

baseline   The first phase of single-subject research, in which behavior is recorded before any changes are introduced

basic research   Research that tests or refines theory; not designed to be applied immediately to practice

behavioral objectives   Objectives of a practice that are stated in terms of observable terminal performances, which can be measured; also called *performance objectives* or *measured objectives*.

beta weight   A standardized regression coefficient

bivariate   Refers to correlation between or testing of two variables or categories for differences

bivariate regression   A regression analysis in which the dependent variable is predicated by a single independent variable

box-and-whisker plot   A graphic illustration of variability of a set of scores

career and life history interviews   Interviews that elicit the narratives of individuals' lives or the career histories of professional

case   A particular situation selected by the researcher in which some phenomena will be described by participants' meanings of events and processes

case study   Qualitative research that examines a bounded system (i.e., a case) over time in detail, employing multiple sources of data found in the setting

case study design   A research design in which the researcher selects one phenomenon to understand in depth, regardless of the number of settings, social scenes, or participants in a study

categorical variable   A variable used to divide subjects, objects, or entities into two or more groups

category   An abstract term that represents the meaning of a set of related topics

checklist   A type of questionnaire item in which subjects check the appropriate response from the range of responses provided

chi-square   A nonparametric statistical procedure that is used with nominal data to test relationships between the frequency of observations in categories of independent variables; also called *goodness of fit*

closed form   A type of questionnaire item in which the subject chooses between or among predetermined options

cluster sampling   A form of probability sampling in which subjects are first grouped according to naturally occurring traits

code A descriptive name for the subject or topic of a data segment

coefficient of determination A squared correlation coefficient that indicates the percentage of variance accounted for in a relationship

coefficient of multiple correlation An indicator of the combined relationship of several variables to another variable

comparison group One of the groups whose behaviors are compared in an experiment

comparative *See* comparative research

comparative research A type of nonexperimental quantitative research that examines differences between groups

complete observer An observer who remains completely detached from the group or process of interest

comprehensive sampling The type of sampling in qualitative research in which every participant, group, setting, event, or other information is examined

concept analysis A study that clarifies the meaning of a concept by describing its generic meaning, different meanings, and appropriate use; also called *philosophical research*

confidence interval A range that describes probable population values

construct A complex abstraction that is not directly observable, such as anxiety, intelligence, and self-concept; a meaningful combination of concepts

construct irrelevant variance The extent to which an assessment measures facets that are not related to its purpose

construct underrepresentation The extent to which an assessment fails to incorporate important facets that are related to its purpose

construct validity A type of external validity that refers to the extent to which a study represents the underlying construct

context A description of the site and selected settings, social scenes, participants, and time period of data collection

contingency questions Questions that when answered in a certain way, provide directions to subsequent questions

continuous observation An observational data-gathering technique in which the observer records all important behaviors

continuous variable A variable in which the property or attribute of an object, subject, or entity is measured numerically and can assume an infinite number of values within a range; also called a *measured variable*

control group The subjects in an experiment who receive no treatment

control group interrupted time-series design A quasi-experimental time-series study that compares the treatment group to a control group

controlled vocabulary The use of systematic and consistent definitions of subjects and terms for describing entries in a database

convenience sampling A nonprobability method of selecting subjects who are accessible or available

correlation A measure of relationship that uses a correlation coefficient

correlation coefficient A calculation that represents the size and direction of the degree of relationship between two variables

correlational research Research in which information on at least two variables is collected for each subject in order to investigate the relationship between the variables

cost-effectiveness analysis An evaluation that involves comparing the outcomes of similar programs and practices in relation to their costs when the programs have the same objectives and measures

credibility The extent to which the results of a study approximate reality and are thus judged to be trustworthy and reasonable

criterion variable In a prediction study, the variable that is predicted

criterion-referenced Refers to instruments whose scores are interpreted by comparing them to set criteria or standards, rather than to the performance of others

critical studies Qualitative research in which the researcher is committed to exposing social manipulation and changing oppressive social structures and in which he or she may have emancipatory goals

Cronbach alpha A measure of internal consistency reliability for items with scaled responses

cross-sectional Refers to a research strategy in which several different groups of subjects are assessed at the same time

crystallization An analytical style in which the researcher combines segmenting, categorizing, and pattern seeking into an extensive period of intuition-rich immersion within the data

data The results obtained by research from which interpretations and conclusions are drawn

data management Using a system to retrieve data sets and to assemble coded data in one place

decision-oriented evaluation An evaluation that supplies information for prespecified decisions, such as needs assessment, program planning, program implementation, and outcomes

degrees of freedom A mathematical concept that indicates the number of observations that are free to vary

demand characteristics A possible source of bias when any aspect of a study reveals its purpose and may influence subjects to respond differently because they know that purpose

dependent samples *t*-test An inferential statistical procedure for determining the probability level of rejecting the null hypothesis with two samples of subjects that are matched or related; also called *correlated samples t-test*

dependent variable The measured variable that is the consequence of or depends on antecedent variables

descriptive Refers to research that describes an existing or past phenomenon in quantitative terms

descriptive designs Research that describes the current status of something

descriptive statistics Statistical procedures used to describe something

developmental studies Research studies that investigate how subjects change over time

diffusion of treatment   A threat to internal validity in which the subjects are influenced by other conditions of the independent variable

documents   Records of past events, whether written or printed, such as letters, diaries, and journals, newspapers, and regulations; usually preserved in collections

double-barreled questions   Single questions that contain two or more ideas to which the subject must make one response

duration recording   A type of observer recording procedure in which the duration of behavior is recorded

ecological external validity   The extent to which the results of research can be generalized to other conditions and situations

effect size   A statistical index of the practical or meaningful differences between groups

effect magnitude measures   Statistical procedures that are used to indicate the practical significance of research results

electronic resources   Literature that is stored in a computer database

elite interviews   A special application of in-depth interviewing to persons in an organization or community who are considered to be influential, prominent, or well informed

emergent design   A research plan in which each step depends on the results of the field data obtained in the previous step

emic   Refers to insider's views (e.g., terms, actions, and explanations) that are distinctive to the setting or people

empirical   Refers to what is guided by evidence, data, and sources

equivalence   A type of test reliability in which the scores from equivalent or parallel forms of the same instrument, obtained at about the same time, are correlated

ERIC (Educational Resources Information Center)   A comprehensive database and index of education literature

ERIC digest   Short reports that synthesize the available education literature on a topic

ethnography   A description and interpretation of a culture, social group, or system

etic   Refers to outsider's views of the situation (e.g., the researcher's concepts and scientific explanations)

evaluation   A study that uses a formal design to collect and analyze data about a practice or anticipated practice and then determines the worth of that practice; *see also* evaluation research

evaluation approach   A strategy used to focus evaluation activities and produce a useful report

evaluation research   Research that is designed to assess the worth of a specific practice in terms of the values operating at the site

evidence based on contrasted groups   Validity evidence based on scores from groups expected to show differences

evidence based on internal structure   Validity evidence that shows appropriate correlations among items

evidence based on relations to other variables   Validity evidence that shows appropriate correlations with other measures

evidence based on response processes   Validity evidence that shows consistency between intended and actual response processes

evidence based on test content   Validity evidence in which scores represent an underlying meaning, interpretation, trait, or theory

exhaustive search   A literature search about a narrowly focused problem that spans 10 or more years and uses the most relevant reference services

experimental design   Research in which the independent variable is manipulated to investigate a cause-and-effect relationship between it and the dependent variable

experimental group   The subjects who receive the condition that the researcher hypothesizes will change behavior

experimental variable   The variable in an experimental or quasi-experimental design that is manipulated or changed by the researcher to see the effect on (i.e., relationship to) the dependent variable

experimenter effects   A threat to internal validity in which the researcher's differential treatment of the subjects affects results, also called *experimenter contamination*

explanation   A theory or analytical generalization that states cause-and-effect relationships in simple statements

explanatory design   A mixed-method design in which a quantitative phase is followed by a qualitative phase

exploratory design   A mixed-method design in which a qualitative phase is followed by a quantitative phase

evidence-based inquiry   A search for knowledge that uses systematically gathered empirical data and that reports them in such a way that the reasoning can be examined

ex post facto **design**   *See ex post facto* research

ex post facto **research**   Research that investigates events that have already occurred and implies a cause-and-effect relationship from the results

extension of the findings   Using the results of a qualitative study to enable others to understand similar situations and to apply them in conducting subsequent research

external criticism   Analytical procedures that are carried out to determine the authenticity of the source—that is, whether the source is the original document, a forged document, or a variant of the original document

external validity   The extent to which the results of a study can be generalized to other subjects, conditions, and situations

factorial ANOVA (analysis of variance)   An analysis of variance statistical procedure using two or more independent variables that permits testing each independent variable and the interaction among the variables

facts   In analytical research, descriptions of who, what, when, and where an event occurred; obtained from decisive evidence

field notes   Data that the researcher obtains through participant observation in the actual setting

field research   Research that views the setting as a natural situation in which the researcher collects data over a prolonged time

field residence   In ethnography, the researcher's being present in the field or site for an extensive time to collect data

focus group interview   A group interview of selected individuals to assess a problem, concern, new product, program, or idea

foreshadowed problems   Anticipated research problems that will be reformulated during data collection

formative evaluation   Evaluation that is used to improve an ongoing practice or program

frequency-count recording   A type of observer recording procedure in which the frequency of a behavior is recorded

frequency distribution   A display of a set of scores that is organized by the number of times each score was obtained

frequency polygon   A graphic representation of a frequency distribution formed by connecting in a line the highest frequency of each score

generalization   The extent to which the results of one study can be used as knowledge about other populations and situations

grounded theory   Qualitative procedures that are used to develop detailed concepts or conditional propositions for substantive theory

Hawthorne effect   The tendency of people to act differently upon realizing that they are subjects in a study

high inference   A type of observation in which observer records judgements about what has occurred

histogram   A graphic illustration of a frequency distribution in which a bar is used to represent the frequency of each score

historical analysis   The application of analytical methodology to the study of the past, as in biographies and studies of movements, institutions, and concepts

history   A threat to internal validity in which incidents or events that occurred during the research affect results

historiography   A study of the procedures that different historians use in their research; also a study of the changing revisions and interpretations of the past

holistic emphasis   In ethnography, the relating of subcases of data to the total context of the phenomenon being studied

inadequate explication of the constructs   A threat to the construct validity of a study in which insufficient explanation is provided of the nature of the construct being measured or manipulated

independent samples chi-square test   An inferential statistical procedure for independent variables; also called a *contingency table*

independent samples *t*-test   An inferential statistical procedure for determining the probability level of rejecting the null hypothesis using two samples of subjects that have no relation to each other

independent variable   A variable that is antecedent to or that precedes the dependent variable; in experimental design, also called the *experimental* or *manipulated variable*

in-depth interview   A purposeful conversation that uses a general interview guide with a few selected topics and probes (i.e., not a set of standardized questions); should last for at least an hour

inductive analysis   An analysis in which categories and patterns emerge from the data, rather than being imposed on them prior to data collection

inferential statistics   Procedures that are used to indicate the probability associated with saying something about a population based on data from a sample

informal conversational interview   Questions that emerge from the immediate context and are asked in the natural course of events; there is no predetermination of question topics or phrasing

informed consent   Obtaining permission from individuals to participate in research before the research begins

institutional review board (IRB)   An organization that reviews research involving human subjects to ensure that ethical and legal practices are followed

instrument reliability   An indication of the consistency of measurement

instrument validity   An indication of the extent to which inferences made on the basis of scores are appropriate

instrumentation   A threat to internal validity in which changes in instruments and unreliability affect the results

interaction   The unique effect that different levels of independent variables have on the dependent variable

interactive strategies   The use of participant observation, direct observation, in-depth interviewing, artifacts, and supplementary techniques to study participants' perspectives

intercorrelation matrix   A table that presents intercorrelations among many variables

interim analysis   The regular and frequent use of qualitative data analysis to help make data collection decisions and to identify emerging topics

internal consistency   A type of test reliability in which the homogeneity of the items of an instrument is assessed after it has been administered once

internal criticism   The use of analytical procedures to determine the credibility of the statements in a source; the accuracy and trustworthiness of the facts

internal validity   The degree to which extraneous variables are controlled

Internet   A network of interconnected computers through which information can be obtained worldwide

interval   A type of measurement scale in which numbers are rank ordered with equal intervals between ranks

interval recording   A type of observer recording procedure in which behavior that occurs during a given time interval is recorded

interview elaborations   Reflections by interviewers on their role and rapport, interviewees' reactions, additional information, and extensions of interview meanings

interview guide approach   An approach in which the researcher selects interview topics in advance but decides the actual sequence and wording of the questions during the interview

interview probes   Brief questions or phrases that elicit elaborations of detail, further explanations, and clarifications of responses

key-informant interview   In-depth interview of individuals who have special knowledge, status, or communication skills

Kuder-Richardson   A type of internal consistency reliability for items that are scored right or wrong

leading questions   In qualitative interviews, questions in which the wording encourages certain responses

level of significance A value that is selected to indicate the chance that it is wrong for the purpose of rejecting the null hypothesis; also called *level of probability* or *level of confidence*

Likert scale A type of scale in which subject expresses a degree of agreement or disagreement with a statement

literature review A summary and analysis of related literature that is conducted to provide insights about a study

logistic regression A type of regression analysis in which the dependent variable is dichotomous

longitudinal A research strategy in which quantitative data are collected on subjects over a period of time

low inference Refers to a type of observation in which the observer records the occurrences of specific behaviors

mailing lists (listservs) Shared lists of individuals that are contacted through e-mail to communicate about specific topics

manipulated variable The independent variable in an experiment, as determined by the researcher

mapping the field In qualitative research, the process of acquiring data about the social, spatial, and temporal relationships of a given site to gain a sense of the total context

maximum variation sampling (quota sampling) In qualitative research, a strategy that is used to sample the anticipated different meanings of the research phenomenon or concept

maturation A threat to internal validity in quantitative research in which maturational changes in the subjects (e.g., growing older or becoming tired or hungry) affect the results

MAXMINCON An acronym for maximizing systematic variance, minimizing error variance, and control extraneous variance

mean A measure of central tendency; the arithmetical average of the scores

measured variable *See* continuous variable

measurement scales Properties that describe the relationships between numbers

measures of central tendency Summary indices of a set of scores that represent the typical score in a distribution

measures of variability Numerical indices that describe the degree of dispersion of scores from the mean

median A measure of central tendency; the point or score in a distribution that is the midpoint

meta-analysis A research procedure that uses statistical techniques to synthesize the results of prior independently conducted studies

metasearch engines Research tools that allow conducting multiple Internet searches at one time

mixed-method Refers to a study that combines qualitative and quantitative techniques and/or data analysis within different phases of the research process

mode A measure of central tendency; the most frequently occurring score

mono-method bias A threat to construct validity due to the use of a single exemplar or measure

mono-operation bias A threat to construct validity due to the use of a single method in implementing an intervention or measuring the dependent variable

multimethod In qualitative research, refers to the use of multiple strategies to corroborate the data obtained from any single strategy and/or ways to confirm data within a single strategy of data collection

multiple-base line designs A type of single-subject design that uses several subjects, types of behavior, or situations simultaneously

multiple regression A statistical procedure for using several variables to predict an outcome

multisite evaluation A type of qualitative research designed to report the practices at each site and to make generalizations across sites

multistage cluster sampling The use of several stages of clustering in selecting a sample

multivariate Refers to a family of statistics that are used when there is more than one independent variable and/or more than one dependent variable

narrative descriptions Detailed narrations of people, incidents, and processes

negative relationship A relationship in which an increase in one variable corresponds to a decrease in another variable

negatively skewed A distribution of scores that has a disproportionately large number of high scores

network sampling (snowball sampling) A qualitative strategy in which each successive participant or group is named by a preceding group or individual

newsgroups Electronic forums where information, messages, and questions on shared interests are communicated

nominal A type of measurement scale in which objects or people are named, classified, or numbered

noncognitive Refers to areas other than mental processes, such as affect and emotions

nonequivalent group posttest-only control group design A preexperimental design in which one or more groups of subjects (who have not been randomly assigned) receives a treatment and a posttest and another group of subjects receives only a posttest

nonequivalent groups pretest–posttest control and comparison group designs Quasi-experimental designs in which groups that have not been randomly assigned to treatments are compared

nonexperimental Research that requires no direct manipulation of variables, such as descriptive and correlational research

nonparametric Refers to the types of statistical procedures used when the assumptions necessary to use parametric procedures have been violated

nonprobability sampling A sampling procedure in which the probability of selecting elements from the population is not known

nonproportional sampling Stratified sampling in which the number of subjects selected from each stratum is not based on the percentage of the population represented by that stratum

nonreactive *See* unobtrusive measures

norm-referenced Refers to an interpretation of test results in which a score or group of scores is compared with the typical performance of a given (i.e., norm) group

normal distribution   A symmetrical, bell-shaped distribution of scores that have the same mean, median, and mode

null hypothesis   A formal statistical statement of no relationship between two or more variables

objectives-oriented evaluation   An evaluation that determines the degree to which the objectives of a practice have been attained by a target group

objectivity   Refers to data collection and analysis procedures from which only one meaning or interpretation can be made

observational research   Field research in which observational data are collected using noninterfering procedures

odds ratio   The nature of the results from a logistic regression that indicates the probability of some outcome

open form   A type of questionnaire item in which the subject writes in a response to a question

operational definition   A definition of a variable that is produced by specifying the activities or operations necessary to measure, categorize, or manipulate it

oral history   A form of historical research in which individuals' spoken words and testimonies about the past are recorded

oral testimonies   The records or interview transcripts of witnesses or participants to past event that is being studied

ordinal   Refers to a type of measurement scale in which the objects or persons are rank ordered from lowest to highest

outlier   A data point that is extremely high or low and thus very different from the other data collected

parametric   Refers to types of statistical procedures that assume normality in population distributions, homogeneity of variance, and interval or ratio scale data

participant observation   A combination of interactive data collection strategies such as limited participation, field observation, interviewing, and artifact collection

participant-oriented evaluation   A holistic approach to evaluation that uses multiple methods to uncover the divergent values of a practice from the various participants' perspectives

participants   Individuals from whom data are collected; also called *subjects* in quantitative studies

path analysis   A statistical procedure that uses correlations among a set of variables that are logically ordered to reflect causal relationships

pattern   A relationship among categories

percentile rank   The point in a distribution at or below which a given percentage of scores is found

performance-based assessment   A type of assessment in which student proficiency is evaluated by observing performance in original, authentic contexts

phenomenological interview   A specific type of in-depth interview to examines the meaning or essence of a lived experience

phenomenological study   Research that describes the meanings or essence of a lived experience

planned comparisons   Predetermined statistical tests of selected pairs of means

plausible rival hypotheses   Possible explanations (i.e., other than the effect of the independent variable) for cause-and-effect relationships

policy analysis   An evaluation of government policies to provide policy-makers with practical recommendations

population   A group of individuals or events from which a sample is drawn

population external validity   The extent to which the results of a research study can be generalized to other people

portfolio   A form of alternative assessment in which the materials demonstrating student performance are purposefully collected, organized, and evaluated

positionality   A researcher's display of position or standpoint by describing his or her own social, cultural, historical, racial, and sexual location in the study

positive relationship   A relationship in which an increase in one variable corresponds to an increase in another variable

positively skewed   A distribution of scores that has a disproportionately large number of low scores

post hoc comparison   Statistical tests that are used with pairs of means that are usually conducted after statistical test of all means together; also called *multiple comparisons*

prediction studies   Research in which behaviors or skills are predicted by one or several variables

predictor variable   The antecedent variable in a prediction study

pre-experimental designs   Experimental designs that generally have weak internal validity

preliminary search   A search limited by use of one or two reference services, the number of years to be reviewed, or the number of sources desired; usually conducted to select a research problem

pretesting   A threat to internal validity in which taking a pretest can affect the results

primary literature   The original research studies or writings by researchers and theorists

primary source   In analytical research, a document or the testimony of an eyewitness to an event

probability   A statement of the degree of confidence about predicting some outcome

probability sampling   A type of sampling in which subjects are drawn from a population in known probabilities

probing: *See* interview probes

proportional sampling   A type of stratified sampling in which the number of subjects selected from each stratum is based on the percentage of subjects in the population in that stratum

purposeful sampling   A type of sampling that allows choosing small groups or individuals who are likely to be knowledgeable and informative about the phenomenon of interest; selecting cases without needing or desiring to generalize to all such cases

qualitative   Refers to an in-depth study using face-to-face techniques to collect data from people in their natural settings

qualitative field records   Data that are recorded as participant observation field notes, in-depth interview records, or researcher notes of historical documents

quasi-experimental designs   Research designs in which there is no random assignment of subjects; rather, cause-and-effect relationships are examined by manipulating the independent variable

questionnaire   A written set of questions or statements that is used to assess attitudes, opinions, beliefs, and biographical information

quota sampling   A nonprobability method of sampling in which subjects are selected in proportion to the characteristics they represent in the general population

random assignment   A procedure used to assign subjects to different groups so that every subject has an equal chance of being assigned to each group

random sampling   A procedure for selecting subjects from a population in such a way that every member of the population has an equal chance of being selected

randomized experiments   Experiments in which the subjects are randomly assigned to groups, at least one independent variable is manipulated, and extraneous variables are controlled to investigate the cause of one or more independent variables on the dependent variable or variables

randomized posttest-only control and comparison group design   A true experimental design in which one or more randomly assigned groups of subjects receives a treatment and a posttest and one randomly assigned group of subjects receives only a posttest

randomized pretest–posttest control group design   A true experimental design in which one or more randomly assigned groups of subjects receives a pretest, a treatment, and a posttest and one randomly assigned group of subjects receives only a pretest and posttest

range   A measure of variability; the difference between the highest and lowest scores in a distribution

ratio   A type of measurement scale in which the numbers are expressed meaningfully as ratios

real time   Communication that occurs immediately, without delay via technology; also called *synchronous communication*

refereed   Refers to a review procedure for journal articles by experts in the field

reflexivity   Refers to the researcher's rigorous self-scrutiny throughout the entire qualitative research process

reflex records   Records the researcher makes immediately after leaving the field; contain summaries of observations, addresses quality of data, suggest next steps, and provide for self-monitoring

regression coefficient   A factor used in multiple regression to weight the contribution of each variable in the equation

related literature   Literature that is relevant to the research problem or related to the design in some essential way

reliability   The extent to which scores from an insrument are consistent

relics   In historical research, objects that provide information about the past, such as textbooks, equipment, and examinations

replication   A study that duplicates the findings of a prior study using different settings or techniques

report literature   Documents other than journals that are in the ERIC Document Microfiche Collection and indexed by *Resources in Education;* that is, presentations, final reports of projects, or evaluation studies

research   A systematic process of collecting and logically analyzing data for a specific purpose

research design   The plan that describes the conditions and procedures for collecting and analyzing data

research hypothesis   A tentative statement of the expected relationship between two or more variables

research methods   The procedures used to collect and analyze data

research problem   A formal statement of the question or hypothesis that will be investigated through empirical research

research roles   The relationships acquired by and ascribed to the researcher during interactive data collection; should be appropriate for the purpose of the study

research synthesis   A procedure used to systematically evaluate and summarize comparable studies in narrative or statistical form

responsive evaluation   An evaluation designed to supply information about the issues and concerns of the audiences; uses an emerging design to provide an understanding of the program

restriction in range   A set of scores that represents only part of the total distribution

retrieval algorithms   Used to determine the number of pages and organization of materials found during an Internet search

reversal designs   In single-subject research, involves ending a treatment condition and reinstituting the base-line condition; also called *withdrawal designs*

sample   The group of subjects from which data are collected; often representative of a specific population

sampling distribution   The frequency distribution of possible samples from a given population

scale   Questionnaire items for which the responses consist of gradations, levels, or values that describe various degrees of something

scatterplot   A graphic representation of the intersections of subjects' scores on two variables

search engines   Services that allow for cataloging and retrieving Internet information from the Internet

secondary data   Data that were collected previously and are available in a database for further use

secondary data analysis   Statistical analysis that is conducted using secondary data

secondary literature   A synthesis of existing research literature; can be theoretical, empirical, or both

secondary sources   In historical research, documents and testimonies of individuals who did not actually observe or participate in the event being studied

segment   A part of a data set that is comprehensible by itself and contains one idea, episode, or piece of information relevant to the study

selection   A threat to internal validity in which differences between groups of subjects affect the results

semantic differential   A type of scale in which subjects respond by choosing between adjective pairs in relation to a concept or object

semi-structured questions   A type of interview question that allows for individual, open-ended responses to fairly specific questions

significance of the problem The rationale for a research problem or the importance of a study as it relates to developing educational theory, knowledge, and/or practice

simple random sampling *See* random sampling

single-group interrupted time-series design A quasi-experimental design in which multiple observations of the dependent variable are made before and after the treatment

single-group posttest-only design A pre-experimental design in which a single group of subjects receives a treatment and a posttest

single-group pretest–posttest design A pre-experimental design in which a single group of subjects receives a pretest, a treatment, and then a posttest

single-subject designs Research done with individual subjects in order to study the changes in behavior that are associated with the intervention or removal of a treatment

site selection The specification of site criteria implied in the foreshadowed problems; used to obtain a suitable and feasible research site

skewed *See* positively skewed *and* negatively skewed

social desirability The tendency of subjects to respond to items in ways that will seem desirable to others

sources of variability Systematic, error, and extraneous influences related to research design

split-half reliability A type of internal consistency reliability in which equal halves of a test are correlated

spurious correlation A correlation that overrepresents or underrepresents the true relationship

stability A type of test reliability that correlates scores from the same instrument given on two occasions

standard A level of performance commonly agreed on as typical by experts

standard deviation A measure of variability; a numerical index that indicates the average dispersion or spread of scores around the mean

standard error The standard deviation of a sampling distribution

standard scores Numbers that have been converted from raw distributions; have constant means and standard deviations

standardized open-ended interview A form of qualitative interview in which participants are asked the same questions in the same order to obtain data about participant meanings; *see also* in-depth interview

standardized tests Tests that are administered and scored according to highly structured, prescribed directions

statistical conclusion validity The extent to which statistics provide accurate information about the relationship being studied

statistical hypothesis The hypotheses that is stated in terms of statistical results

statistical regression The tendency for extreme scores to move closer to the mean score on a second testing

statistically significant Refers to evaluating the results of inferential statistics and indicating that the differences noted are not likely due to chance

statistics Procedures for organizing and analyzing quantitative data

stem-and-leaf display A method of showing a frequency distribution

strategies Qualitative sampling and data collection techniques that are continually refined throughout the data collection process to increase the validity of data

stratified random sampling A form of random sampling in which a population is first divided into subgroups (i.e., strata) and then subjects are selected from each subgroup

structured question A type of interview question that provides a predetermined set of responses from which the participant is to choose; also called *limited-response questions*

subject directories Lists of cataloged Internet resources

subject effects Changes in subject behavior that results from being in a study

subjects The person or persons from whom data are collected in a study

summative evaluation An evaluation designed to determine the merit, the worth, or both of a developed practice and to make recommendations regarding its adoption and widespread use

survey The use of a questionnaire or interview to assess the current opinions, beliefs, and attitudes of members of a known population

synthesized abstractions Summative generalizations and explanations of the major research findings of a study; format varies with the selected qualitative tradition

systematic sampling A form of sampling in which subjects are selected from a continuous list by choosing every nth subject

t-test An inferential statistical procedure for determining the probability level of rejecting the null hypothesis that two means are the same

target group The group whose behavior is expected to change as a result of a given practice

test research Research in which subjects' test scores are used as data

theory A prediction and explanation of natural phenomena

thesaurus A publication that lists and cross-references the key terms used in an index for a reference service (database), such as ERIC or *Psychological Abstracts*.

time sampling A type of observer recording procedure in which behaviors are observed for specific time periods

time-series designs Quasi-experimental designs in which one group of subjects is measured repeatedly before and after a treatment

treatment fidelity The extent to which an experimental intervention was completed as planned

treatment group *See* experimental group

treatment replications A threat to internal validity that occurs when the number of treatment replications does not equal the number of subjects

triangulation Qualitative cross-validation among multiple data sources, data collection strategies, time periods, and theoretical schemes

triangulation design A type of mixed-method design in which quantitative and qualitative methods are used simultaneously

Type I error The error that results from rejecting the null hypothesis when it is in fact true

Type II error The error that results from failing to reject the null hypothesis when it is in fact false

typicality The degree to which a phenomenon may be compared or contrasted with other phenomena along relevant dimensions

univariate Refers to a statistical analysis in which there is a single dependent variable

unobtrusive measures Methods of collecting information in which the subject is unaware of being a participant in the research; also called *nonreactive measures*

unstructured question A type of interview question that is broad and allows for open-ended responses

validity of qualitative designs The degree to which the interpretations have mutual meanings between the participants and the researcher

variability *See* measures of variability

variable An event, category, behavior, or attribute that expresses a construct and has different values, depending on how it is used in a study

variance Generically, the degree of spread or dispersion of scores; mathematically, the square of the standard deviation

verification Confirming or modifying the results of a research study in subsequent research

visual representation An organized assembly of information (e.g., figures, matrices, integrative diagrams, and flow charts) that assists in qualitative data analysis

withdrawal design *See* reversal design

worth The value of a practice in relationship to the values, standards, and practical constraints of a site that has the potential for adoption

z-score A type of standard score that has a mean of 0 and a standard deviation of 1

Calculations for Selected Descriptive and Inferential Statistics

In this appendix, we will present a step-by-step guide for performing calculations for several simple statistical procedures.* Our intent is not to derive formulas but to show how the statistics are calculated. We believe that being able to apply these formulas assists greatly in understanding the meaning of the statistics.

MEASURES OF CENTRAL TENDENCY

Measures of *central tendency* are descriptive statistics that measure the central location or value of sets of scores. They are used widely to summarize and simplify large quantities of data.

The Mean

The *mean* is the arithmetical average of a set of scores. It is obtained by adding all the scores in a distribution and dividing the sum by the number of scores. The formula for calculating the mean is

$$\bar{X} = \frac{\Sigma X}{n}$$

where

$\bar{X}$ is the mean score
ΣX is the sum of the X_s (i.e., $X_1 + X_2 + X_3 \ldots X_n$)
  n is the total number of scores

Example: Calculation of Mean   If we have obtained the sample of eight scores—17, 14, 14, 13, 10, 8, 7, 7—the mean of this set of scores is calculated as

$$\Sigma X = 17 + 14 + 14 + \ldots + 7 = 90$$
$$n = 8$$

Therefore,

$$\bar{X} = \frac{90}{8} = 11.25$$

*Statistical tables are located at the end of the appendix.

The Median

The *median* is the score in a distribution below which half the scores fall. In other words, half the scores are above the median and half are below the median. The median is at the 50th percentile.

To calculate the median, the scores are rank ordered from highest to lowest; then one simply counts, from one end, one half of the scores. In distributions with an odd number of scores, the median is the middle score, as illustrated here:

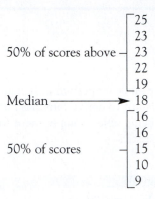

If the distribution has an even number of scores, the median is the average of the two middle scores. In this case, the median is a new score or point in the distribution, as shown here:

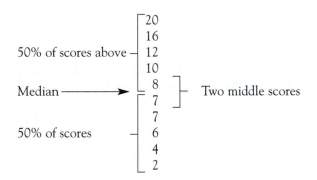

Thus, the median in this example is

$$7 + \frac{8}{2} = \frac{15}{2} + 7.5$$

The median is relatively easy to find in studies with a small number of subjects. As the number of scores increases, the calculation is done either by a formula or by placing the scores into intervals of scores and using the intervals to make the calculations. Computers are able to apply these more complicated calculations easily, quickly, and reliably.

The Mode   The *mode* is simply the most frequently occurring score in a distribution, and it is found by counting the number of times each score was received. The mode in this distribution, for example, is 22:

23   22   22   22   20   18   18   17   16

MEASURES OF VARIABILITY

Measures of variability are used to show the differences among the scores in a distribution. We use the term *variability* or *dispersion* because the statistics provide an indication of how different, or dispersed, the scores are from one another. We will discuss three measures of variability: range, variance, and standard deviation.

The Range

The *range* is the simplest but also least useful measure of variability. It is defined as the distance between the smallest and the largest scores and is calculated by simply subtracting the bottom, or lowest, score from the top, or highest, score:

$$\text{Range} = X_H - X_L$$

where

$$X_H = \text{the highest score}$$
$$X_L = \text{the lowest score}$$

For the following scores, then, the range is $26 - 6 = 20$:

$$6 \quad 8 \quad 10 \quad 11 \quad 15 \quad 20 \quad 26$$

The range is a crude measure of variability and is unstable. Because the range can be biased, it is rarely used as the only measure of variability.

Variance

The *variance* (s^2 or σ^2) is a measure of dispersion that indicates the degree to which scores cluster around the mean. The variance provides the researcher with one number to indicate, in a sense, the average dispersion of scores from the mean. Computationally, the variance is the sum of the squared deviation scores about the mean divided by the total number of scores:

$$s^2 = \frac{\Sigma(X - \bar{X})^2}{N}$$

where

$$s^2 \quad \text{is the variance}$$
$$\Sigma(X - X)^2 \quad \text{is the sum of the squared deviation scores}$$
$$(X - \bar{X}) \quad \text{is the deviation score}$$
$$N \quad \text{is the total number of scores}$$

For any distribution of scores, the variance can be determined by following these five steps:

1. Calculate the mean: $(\Sigma X/N)$.
2. Calculate the deviation scores: $(X - \bar{X})$.

3. Square each deviation score: $(X - \bar{X})^2$.
4. Sum all the deviation scores: $\Sigma(X - \bar{X})^2$
5. Divide the sum by N: $\Sigma(X - \bar{X})^2/N$.

These steps are illustrated with actual numbers as follows:

(1) Raw Scores	(2) $(X - \bar{X})$	(3) $(X - \bar{X})^2$	(4)	(5)
20	7	49		
15	2	4		
15	2	4		
14	1	1		
14	1	1	$\Sigma(X - \bar{X})^2 = 120$	$\dfrac{\Sigma(X - \bar{X})^2}{N} = 12$
14	1	1		
12	−1	1		
10	−3	9		
8	−5	25		
8	−5	25		

$\Sigma X = 130$
$N = 10$
$\bar{X} = 13$

Substituting directly in the formula:

$$s^2 = \frac{120}{10} = 12$$

Here is another formula that can be used to calculate the variance that is computationally more simple:

$$s^2 = \frac{\Sigma \bar{X}^2 - N\bar{X}^2}{N}$$

Because the variance is expressed as the square of the raw scores, not the original units, it is not usually reported in research. To return to units that are consistent with the raw score distribution, we need to take the square root of the variance. Taking the square root of the variance yields the standard deviation.

Standard Deviation

The *standard deviation* (s, σ, or SD) is the square root of the variance. It is a measure of dispersion that uses deviation scores expressed in standard units about the mean; hence the name *standard deviation*. The standard deviation is equal to the square root of the sum of the squared deviation scores about the mean divided by the total number of scores. The formula is

$$s = \sqrt{\frac{\Sigma(X - \bar{X})^2}{N}}$$

where

s	is the standard deviation
$\sqrt{}$	is the square root
$\Sigma(X - \bar{X})^2$	is the sum of the squared deviation scores
$(X - \bar{X})$	is the deviation score
N	is the total number of scores

To calculate the standard deviation, simply add one step to the formula for variance: take the square root. In our example for variance, for instance, the standard deviation would be

$$s = \sqrt{\frac{\Sigma(X - \bar{X})^2}{N}} = \sqrt{\frac{120}{10}} = \sqrt{12} = 3.46$$

The standard deviation is commonly reported in research and, with the mean, is the most important statistic in research. It tells the number of scores (i.e., the percentage of scores) that are within given units of the standard deviation around the mean. This property of standard deviation is explained in the section called "Normal Distribution," which follows.

STANDARD SCORES

Standard scores are numbers that are transformed from raw scores to provide consistent information about the location of a score within a total distribution. They are numbers that are related to the normal distribution.

Normal Distribution

The *normal distribution* is a set of scores that, when plotted in a frequency distribution, result in a symmetrical, bell-shaped curve with precise mathematical properties. The mathematical properties provide the basis for making standardized interpretations. These properties include possessing a mode, mean, and median that are the same; having a mean that divides the curve into two identical halves; and having measures of standard deviation that fall at predictable places on the normal curve, with the same percentage of scores between the mean and points equidistant from the mean.

This third characteristic is very important. We know, for example, that at +1s, we will always be at about the 84th percentile in the distribution. (The percentile score is the percentage of scores at or below the designated score.) This is because the median is at the 50th percentile, and +1s contains an additional 34 percent of the scores (50 + 34 = 84). Similarly, the percentage of scores between +1s and +2s is about 14 percent, which means that +2s is at the 98th percentile. These characteristics are illustrated in Figure D.1, the graph of the standard normal distribution.

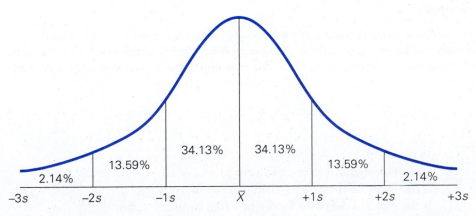

| FIGURE D.1 | Graph of the Standard Normal Distribution or Normal Curve |

The pleasing aspect of this property is that for any raw score distribution with unique units, such as 1 or 2 as s, the interpretation is always the same. If one distribution has a mean of 10, therefore, and a standard deviation of 3, and a second distribution has a mean of 50 and a standard deviation of 7, a score of 4 in the first case is at about the same percentile (the second) as a score of 36 in the second case.

z-Scores

The most basic standard score is called a z-score, and it is expressed as a deviation from the mean in standard deviation units. A z-score of 1 is thus at one standard deviation, –1 is at minus one standard deviation, +2 at two standard deviations, and so forth.

After the mean and standard deviation are calculated for a set of scores, it is easy to convert each raw score to a z-score, which then indicates exactly where each score lies in the normal distribution.

The formula for calculating a z-score is

$$z = \frac{X - \bar{X}}{s}$$

where

z is the z-score value
X is any particular score
$\bar{X}$ is the arithmetic mean of a distribution of scores
s is the standard deviation of that same distribution

Taking the scores used to illustrate variance and standard deviation, the z-scores would be found as follows:

For the raw score of 20: $z = \dfrac{20 - 13}{3.46} = 2.02$

For the raw score of 14: $z = \dfrac{14 - 13}{3.46} = 0.29$

For the raw score of 10: $z = \dfrac{10 - 13}{3.46} = -0.87$

Once the z-score has been calculated, it is easy to refer to conversion tables to find the percentile rank corresponding to each z-score.

T-Scores

One limitation of using z-scores is the necessity for being careful with the negative sign and with the decimal point. To avoid these problems, other standard scores are used by converting the z-scores algebraically to different units. The general formula for converting z-scores is

$$A = \bar{X}_A + s_A(z)$$

where

A is the new standard score equivalent to z
$\bar{X}_A$ is the mean for the new standard-score scale
s_A is the standard deviation for the new standard-score scale
z is the z-score for any observation

For T-scores, $\overline{X}_A = 50$ and $s_A = 10$. The equation for converting z-scores to T-scores is thus

$$T = 50 + 10(z)$$

For example, the T-scores for our earlier illustration would be as follows:

For the raw score of 20: $T = 50 + 10(2.02) = 70.2$
For the raw score of 14: $T = 50 + 10(0.29) = 52.9$
For the raw score of 10: $T = 50 + 10(-0.87) = 41.3$

Other Standard Scores

Other common standard scores include the following:

1. Normal Curve Equivalent (NCE) has a mean of 50 and s of 21.06. Thus, NCE = 50 + 21.06 (z-score).
2. IQ score has a mean of 100 and s of 15 or 16. Thus, IQ = 100 + 15 (z-score).
3. College Entrance Examination Boards (CEEB, such as SAT) use a mean of 500 and an s of 100. Thus, CEEB = 500 + 100 (z-score).
4. ACT (American College Testing Program) uses a mean of 20 and an s of 5. Thus, ACT = 20 + 5 (z-score).
5. Stanine. The stanine is also commonly reported. Stanines are standardized on a mean of 5 and s of 2, but unlike other standard scores, the numbers refer to intervals rather than to specific points on the normal distribution. Stanine 5 is located in the center of the distribution and includes the middle 20 percent of scores; stanines 4 and 6 include 17 percent of the scores; 3 and 7, 12 percent; 2 and 8, 7 percent; and 1 and 9, 4 percent. Stanines are illustrated in Figure 7.11, the normal curve.

MEASURES OF RELATIONSHIP

Measures of relationship are used to indicate the degree to which two sets of scores are related, or covary. We intuitively seek relationships by such statements as "If high scores on variable X tend to be associated with high scores on variable Y, then the variables are related" and "If high scores on variable X tend to be associated with low scores on variable Y, then the variables are related." As indicated in Chapter 7, the relationship can be either positive or negative and either strong or weak.

We use correlation coefficients as a statistical summary of the nature of the relationship between two variables. They provide us with an estimate of the quantitative degree of relationship. The numbers are almost always between -1.00 and $+1.00$. We will show how to calculate two common correlation coefficients: the Pearson product-moment and the Spearman rho correlations.

Pearson Product-Moment (Pearson *r*)

The *Pearson product-moment correlation coefficient* is the most widely used measure of relationship. The Pearson r is calculated to show the linear relationship between two variables. To compute the Pearson r, two measures on each subject are needed. Suppose, for example, we have a group of 10 subjects, and for each subject we have measures of self-concept and achievement. We can then calculate the Pearson r between self-concept and achievement for these 10 subjects using the following formula:

$$\text{Pearson } r = \frac{N\Sigma XY - (\Sigma X)(\Sigma Y)}{\sqrt{N\Sigma X^2 - (\Sigma X)^2} \cdot \sqrt{N\Sigma Y^2 - (\Sigma Y)^2}}$$

where

ΣXY is the sum of the XY cross-products
ΣX is the sum of the X scores
ΣY is the sum of the Y scores
ΣX^2 is the sum of the squared X scores
ΣY^2 is the sum of the squared Y scores
N is the number of pairs of scores

This formula may appear complex but is actually quite easy to calculate. The scores can be listed in a table, as follows. To use it, one simply finds the values for each summation in the formula, substitutes where appropriate, and performs the math indicated.

Subject	Self-Concept Score X	X^2	Achievement Score Y	Y^2	$X \cdot Y$
1	25	625	85	7,225	2,125
2	20	400	90	8,100	1,800
3	21	441	80	6,400	1,680
4	18	324	70	4,900	1,260
5	15	225	75	5,625	1,125
6	17	289	80	6,400	1,360
7	14	196	75	5,625	1,050
8	15	225	70	4,900	1,050
9	12	144	75	5,625	900
10	13	169	60	3,600	780
	$\Sigma X = 170$	$\Sigma X^2 = 3,038$	$\Sigma Y = 760$	$\Sigma Y^2 = 58,400$	$\Sigma X \cdot Y = 13,130$
	$(\Sigma X)^2 = 28,900$		$(\Sigma Y)^2 = 577,600$		

To conduct the Pearson r, follow these steps:

1. Pair each set of scores; one set becomes X, the other Y.
2. Calculate ΣX and ΣY.
3. Calculate X^2 and Y^2.
4. Calculate ΣX^2 and ΣY^2.
5. Calculate $(\Sigma X)^2$ and $(\Sigma Y)^2$.
6. Calculate $X \times Y$.
7. Calculate $\Sigma X \times Y$.
8. Substitute the calculated values into the formula.

$$\text{Pearson } r = \frac{10(131,300) - (170)(760)}{\sqrt{10(30,380) - 28,900} \cdot \sqrt{10(58,400) - 577,600}}$$

$$= \frac{131,300 - 129,200}{\sqrt{30,380 - 28,900} \cdot \sqrt{584,000 - 577,600}}$$

$$= \frac{2,100}{\sqrt{1,480} \cdot \sqrt{6,400}}$$

$$= \frac{2,100}{(38.47) \cdot (80)}$$

$$= \frac{2,100}{3,078}$$

$$= .68$$

The value of 0.68 shows a moderate positive relationship between self-concept and achievement for this set of scores. The level of significance of correlation coefficients are indicated in Table D.2 at the end of this appendix.

Spearman Rank (r ranks or Spearman rho)

The *Spearman rho* is used when ranks are available on each of two variables for all subjects. Ranks are simply listings of scores from highest to lowest. The Spearman rho correlation shows the degree to which subjects maintain the same relative position on two measures. In other words, the Spearman rho indicates how much agreement there is between the ranks of each variable.

The calculation of the Spearman ranks is more simple than calculating the Pearson r. The necessary steps are as follow:

1. Rank the Xs and Ys.
2. Pair the ranked Xs and Ys.
3. Calculate the difference in ranks for each pair.
4. Square each difference.
5. Sum the squared differences.
6. Substitute calculated values into formula.

The formula is:

$$\text{Spearman rho} = 1 - \frac{6\Sigma D^2}{n(n^2 - 1)}$$

For the data used in calculating the Pearson r, the Spearman rho would be found as follows:

Subject	Self-Concept Rank X	Achievement Rank Y	Difference D	D^2
1	1	2	−1	1
2	3	1	2	4
3	2	3.5	−1.5	2.25
4	4	5.5	−1.5	2.25
5	6.5	8	−1.5	2.25
6	5	3.5	1.5	2.25
7	8	8	0	0
8	6.5	5.5	1	1
9	10	8	2	4
10	9	10	−1	1
				$\Sigma D^2 = 20$

Note: When ties in the ranking occur, all scores that are tied receive the average of the ranks involved.

$$r \text{ ranks} = 1 - \frac{6(20)}{10(100 - 1)}$$

$$= 1 - \frac{120}{990}$$

$$= 1 - 0.12$$

$$= .88$$

In most data sets with more than 50 subjects, the Pearson r and Spearman rank will give almost identical correlations. In the example used here, the Spearman is higher because of the low n and the manner in which the ties in rankings resulted in low difference scores.

CHI-SQUARE

Chi-square (χ^2) is a statistical procedure that is used as an infererential statistic with nominal data, such as frequency counts, and ordinal data, such as percentages and proportions. In the simplest case, the data are organized into two categories, such as *yes* and *no, high* and *low, for* and *against*. If, for example, a researcher is interested in the opinions of college professors about tenure and asks the question Should tenure be abolished? then all responses could be categorized as either *yes* or *no*. The total frequency in each category (observed frequencies) is then compared to the expected frequency, which in most cases is chance. This means that with two categories, half the responses should be *yes* and half *no*. Assume the following results:

Should tenure be abolished?

	Yes	No
Observed	40	60
Expected	50	50

These values are then used in the following formula to calculate the chi-square statistic:

$$\chi^2 = \Sigma \frac{(f_o - f_e)^2}{f_e}$$

where

χ^2 is the chi-square statistic
Σ is the sum of
f_o is the observed frequency
f_e is the expected frequency

Inserting the values from the table, the result is

$$\chi^2 = \frac{(40 - 50)^2}{50} + \frac{(60 - 50)^2}{50}$$

$$= \frac{100}{50} + \frac{100}{50}$$

$$= 2 + 2$$

$$= 4.0$$

The obtained value, in this case 4, is then used with the degrees of freedom in the problem ($df = k - 1$, where k equals the number of categories; in our example, $df = 2 - 1$, or 1) to find the value of the chi-square in the critical values of chi-square table (Table D.3 at the end of this appendix) to determine the level of significance of the results. By referring to the table and locating 4.00 within the table with 1 df, the result is significant at just less than a p value of .05. Consequently, it would be appropriate to say that there is a significant difference in the number of professors responding *yes* as compared to the number responding *no*.

Suppose the researcher wanted to go a step further with this problem and learn whether administrators and professors differ in their responses to the question about abolishing tenure. The researcher would then have what is called a contingency table, which is a cross-tabulation of the frequencies for the combinations of categories of the two variables. A hypothetical contingency table is shown below for administrators and professors. Should tenure be abolished?

	Professors	Administrators	Raw Totals
Yes	$40(p = 0.40)$	$40(p = 0.80)$	$80(p_e = 0.53)$
No	$60(p = 0.60)$	$10(p = 0.20)$	$70(p_e = 0.47)$
	$n = 100$	$n = 50$	$n = 150$

Notice in the table that the proportion of responses in each response category (*yes* and *no*) is shown for both professors and administrators, and the total proportions are shown in the last column. These proportions are used in the following equation:

$$\chi^2 = \frac{\Sigma n (P - P_e)^2}{P_e}$$

where

χ^2 is the chi-square statistic

Σ is the sum of all cells in the problem (in our example, there are four cells)

n is the number of total observations in each column

P is the proportion of observed frequencies in each cell

P_e is the expected proportion for each row

For our example, therefore, the result would be

$$\chi^2 = 100 \frac{(.4 - .53)^2}{.53} + 100 \frac{(0.60 - .47)^2}{.47}$$

$$= 50 \frac{(.80 - .53)^2}{.53} + 100 \frac{(.20 - .47)}{.47}$$

$$= 100 \frac{.017}{.53} + 100 \frac{.017}{.47} + 50 \frac{.07}{.53} + 50 \frac{.07}{.47}$$

$$= 3.19 + 3.61 + 6.60 + 7.45$$

$$= 20.85$$

In contingency tables, the degrees of freedom are equal to $(r - 1)(c - 1)$, where r is the number of rows and c is the number of columns. In our example, the $df = (2 - 1)(2 - 1) = 1$. By locating 22.08 with 1 degree of freedom in the critical values of chi-square table (Table D.3), we note that the result is highly significant, $p < .001$. This result indicates that there is a significant association or relationship between the two variables (*professors* and *administrators*, and *yes* and *no*).

t-TEST

The *t*-test is used to indicate the probability that the means of two groups are different. We will present two common forms of the *t*-test: one used with independent samples and the other with dependent samples.

Independent Samples *t*-test

The *independent samples t-test*, or *t*-test for independent groups, is used to determine whether the mean values of a variable on one group of subjects is different from a mean value on the same variable with a different group of subjects. It is important to meet three statistical assumptions: (1) that the frequency distributions of scores for both the populations of each group are normal, (2) that the variances in each population are equal, and (3) that the observation of scores in one group is independent from the other group. If the sample size is greater than 30, violating the assumption of normality is not serious, and as long as the sample sizes are equal, violation of the assumption of homogeneity of variance is not a problem. It is crucial, however, that the observations for each group are independent.

The formula for calculating the *t*-test statistic is

$$t = \frac{\bar{X}_1 - \bar{X}_2}{s_{\bar{X}_1 - \bar{X}_2}}$$

where

t is the *t*-test statistic
$\bar{X}_1$ is the mean of one group
$\bar{X}_2$ is the mean of the second group
$s_{\bar{X}_1 - \bar{X}_2}$ is the standard error of the difference in means

The standard error of the difference in means is estimated from the variances of each distribution. This part of the formula is calculated by pooling the variances of each distribution to result in s. This is done using the following formula:

$$s = \sqrt{\frac{\Sigma x_1^2 + \Sigma x_2^2}{df_1 + df_2}}$$

Then,

$$s_{\bar{X}_1 - \bar{X}_2} = s\sqrt{\frac{1}{n_1} + \frac{1}{n_2}}$$

As an example, consider the data we present below:

Group x_1		Group x_2	
$\bar{X}_1$ =	18	$\bar{X}_2$ =	25
n_1 =	20	n_2 =	20
ΣX_1^2 =	348	ΣX_2^2 =	425

From this point, we can calculate the *t*-test statistic using the following steps:

1. Calculate *s*:

$$s = \sqrt{\frac{348 + 425}{19 + 19}}$$

$$= \sqrt{20.34}$$

$$= 4.51$$

2. Calculate $s_{\bar{X}_1 - \bar{X}_2}$:

$$s_{\bar{X}_1 - \bar{X}_2} = 4.51\sqrt{\frac{1}{20} + \frac{1}{20}}$$

$$= 4.51\sqrt{\frac{1}{10}}$$

$$= 4.51(0.32)$$

$$= 1.44$$

3. Substitute into t-test formula:

$$t = \frac{18 - 25}{1.44}$$

$$= \frac{7}{1.44}$$

$$= 4.86$$

Once the t-test statistic is calculated, it is found in the critical values for t-table (Table 11.1) with corresponding degrees of freedom (which for the independent samples t-test is $n_1 + n_2 - 2$, or in our example, $20 + 20 - 2 = 38$) to determine the significance level of the results. In this example, the t-test statistic of 4.86, with 38 df, is significant at $p < 0.001$.

Here is another example of a computation with the t-test, beginning with raw data:

Group 1		Group 2	
x^1	x_1^2	x_2	x_2^2
7	49	7	49
8	64	7	49
8	64	8	64
6	36	6	36
5	25	6	36
5	25	4	16
6	36	4	16
6	36	3	9
9	81	5	25
8	64	5	25
$\Sigma x_1 = 68$	$\Sigma x_1^2 = 480$	$\Sigma x_2 = 55$	$\Sigma x_2^2 = 325$
$n = 10$	$n = 10$	$\overline{X}_2 = 5.5$	
$\overline{X}_1 = 6.8$			

Following the three steps outlined earlier:

$$s = \sqrt{\frac{480 + 325}{9 + 9}} = \sqrt{44.72} = 6.69$$

$$s_{\overline{X}_1 - \overline{X}_2} = 6.69\sqrt{\frac{1}{10} + \frac{1}{10}} = 6.69\sqrt{\frac{1}{5}} = (6.69)(0.45) = 2.99$$

$$t = \frac{6.8 - 5.5}{2.99} = \frac{1.3}{2.99} = 0.43$$

In this case, the t-test statistic of 0.43, with 18 df, is not statistically significant. Even though the means for the groups are different, therefore, there is a good possibility that they can be different by chance alone.

Dependent Samples t-Test

When two groups that have been matched are being compared, as in a pretest-posttest design, the t-test formula must take into account the interrelationship between the groups: that is, the groups are not independent but rather related. The formula for this type of t-test is easier to calculate than for the independent samples t-test:

$$t = \frac{\bar{D}}{\sqrt{\dfrac{\Sigma D^2 - \dfrac{(\Sigma D)^2}{N}}{N(N-1)}}}$$

where

$\bar{D}$ is the mean difference for all pairs of scores
ΣD^2 is the sum of the squares of the differences
$(\Sigma D)^2$ is the square of the sum of the differences
N is the number of pairs of scores
$N-1$ is the degrees of freedom (one less than the number of pairs of scores).

Consider the following example and steps:

Subjects	Posttest Scores x_1	Pretest Scores x_2	$\bar{D}$	D_2
1	22	15	7	49
2	21	16	5	25
3	20	17	7	49
4	23	16	7	49
5	19	14	5	25
6	21	15	6	36
7	18	12	6	36
8	22	18	4	16
			$\Sigma D = 47$	$\Sigma D^2 = 285$

To perform the first step, calculate $\bar{D}$:

$$\bar{D} = \frac{\Sigma D}{N} = \frac{47}{8} = 5.9$$

To perform step 2:

$$(\Sigma D)^2 = 47^2 = 2{,}209$$

Finally, substitute into the formula:

$$t = \frac{5.9}{\sqrt{\dfrac{285 - \dfrac{2{,}209}{8}}{8(8-1)}}}$$

$$= \frac{5.9}{\sqrt{\dfrac{285 - 276}{56}}}$$

$$= \frac{5.9}{\sqrt{\dfrac{9}{56}}}$$

$$= \frac{5.9}{0.40}$$

$$= 14.75$$

The calculated t-test statistic (14.75) is located in the critical values of the t-table, with the degrees of freedom ($N - 1$, or in this example, $8 - 1 = 7$). The result from the table is that the group means are clearly different from each other and statistically significant at $p < .001$.

TABLE D.1   Random Numbers

03	47	43	73	86	36	96	47	36	61	46	98	64	71	62	33	26	16	80	45	60	11	14	10	95
97	74	24	67	62	42	81	14	57	20	42	53	32	37	32	27	07	36	07	51	24	51	79	89	73
16	76	62	27	66	56	50	26	71	07	32	90	79	78	53	13	55	38	58	59	88	97	54	14	10
12	56	85	99	26	96	96	68	27	31	05	03	72	93	15	57	12	10	14	21	88	26	49	81	76
55	59	56	35	64	38	54	82	46	22	31	62	43	09	90	06	18	44	32	53	23	83	01	30	30
16	22	77	94	39	49	54	43	54	82	17	37	93	23	78	87	35	20	96	43	84	26	34	91	64
84	42	17	53	31	57	24	55	06	88	77	04	74	47	67	21	76	33	50	25	83	92	12	06	76
63	01	63	78	59	16	95	55	67	19	98	10	50	71	75	12	86	73	58	07	44	39	52	38	79
33	21	12	45	29	78	64	56	07	82	52	42	07	44	38	15	51	00	13	42	99	66	02	79	54
57	60	86	32	44	09	47	27	96	54	49	17	46	09	62	90	52	84	77	27	08	02	73	43	28
18	18	07	92	46	44	17	16	58	09	79	83	86	19	62	06	76	50	03	10	55	23	64	05	05
26	62	38	97	75	84	16	07	44	99	83	11	46	32	24	20	14	85	88	45	10	93	72	88	71
23	42	40	64	74	82	97	77	77	81	07	45	32	14	08	32	98	94	07	72	93	85	79	10	75
52	36	28	19	95	50	92	26	11	97	00	56	76	31	38	80	22	02	53	53	86	60	42	04	53
37	85	84	35	12	83	39	50	08	30	42	34	07	96	88	54	42	06	87	98	35	85	29	48	39
70	29	17	12	13	40	33	20	38	26	13	89	51	03	74	17	76	37	13	04	07	74	21	19	30
56	62	18	37	35	96	83	50	87	75	97	12	25	93	47	70	33	24	03	54	97	77	46	44	80
99	59	57	22	77	88	42	95	45	72	16	64	36	16	00	04	43	18	66	79	94	77	24	21	90
16	08	15	04	72	33	27	14	34	09	45	59	34	68	49	12	72	07	34	45	99	27	72	95	14
31	16	93	32	43	50	27	89	87	19	20	15	37	00	49	52	85	66	60	44	38	68	88	11	80
68	34	30	13	70	55	74	30	77	40	44	22	78	84	26	04	33	46	09	52	68	07	97	06	57
74	57	25	65	76	59	29	97	68	60	71	91	38	67	54	13	58	18	24	76	15	54	55	95	52
27	42	37	86	53	48	55	90	65	72	96	57	69	36	10	96	46	92	42	45	97	60	49	04	91
00	39	68	29	61	66	37	32	20	30	77	84	57	03	29	10	45	65	04	26	11	04	96	67	24
29	94	98	94	24	68	49	69	10	82	53	75	91	93	30	34	25	20	57	27	40	48	73	51	92
16	90	82	66	59	83	62	64	11	12	67	19	00	71	74	60	47	21	29	68	02	02	37	03	31
11	27	94	75	06	06	09	19	74	66	02	94	37	34	02	76	70	90	30	86	38	45	94	30	38
35	24	10	16	20	33	32	51	26	38	79	78	45	04	91	16	92	53	56	16	02	75	50	95	98
38	23	16	86	38	42	38	97	01	50	87	75	66	81	41	40	01	74	91	62	48	51	84	08	32
31	96	25	91	47	96	44	33	49	13	34	86	82	53	92	00	52	43	48	85	27	55	26	89	62
66	67	40	67	14	64	05	71	95	86	11	05	65	09	68	76	83	20	37	90	57	16	00	11	66
14	90	84	45	11	75	73	88	05	90	52	27	41	14	86	22	98	12	22	08	07	52	74	95	80
68	05	51	18	00	33	96	02	75	19	07	60	62	93	55	59	33	82	43	90	49	37	38	44	59
20	46	78	73	90	97	51	40	14	02	04	02	33	31	08	39	54	16	49	36	47	95	93	13	30
64	19	58	97	79	15	06	15	93	20	01	90	10	75	06	40	78	78	89	62	02	67	74	17	33
05	26	93	70	60	22	35	85	15	13	92	03	51	59	77	59	56	78	06	83	52	91	05	70	74
07	97	10	88	23	09	98	42	99	64	61	71	62	99	15	06	51	29	16	93	58	05	77	09	51
68	71	86	85	85	54	87	66	47	54	73	32	08	11	12	44	95	92	63	16	29	56	24	29	48
26	99	61	65	53	58	37	78	80	70	43	10	50	67	42	32	17	55	85	74	94	44	67	16	94
14	65	52	68	75	87	59	36	22	41	26	78	63	06	55	13	08	27	01	50	15	29	39	39	43
17	53	77	58	71	71	41	61	50	72	12	41	94	96	26	44	95	27	36	99	02	96	74	30	83
90	26	59	21	19	23	52	23	33	12	96	93	02	18	39	07	02	18	36	07	25	99	32	70	23
41	23	52	55	99	31	04	49	69	96	10	47	48	45	88	13	41	43	89	20	97	17	14	49	17
60	20	50	81	69	31	99	73	68	68	35	81	33	03	76	24	30	12	48	60	18	99	10	72	34
91	25	38	05	90	94	58	28	41	36	45	37	59	03	09	90	35	57	29	12	82	62	54	65	60
34	50	57	74	37	98	80	33	00	91	09	77	93	19	82	74	94	80	04	04	45	07	31	66	49
85	22	04	39	43	73	81	53	94	79	33	62	46	86	28	08	31	54	46	31	53	94	13	38	47
09	79	13	77	48	73	82	97	22	21	05	03	27	24	83	72	89	44	05	60	35	80	39	94	88
88	75	80	18	14	22	95	75	42	49	39	32	82	22	49	02	48	07	70	37	16	04	61	67	87
90	96	23	70	00	39	00	03	06	90	55	85	78	38	36	94	37	30	69	32	90	89	00	76	33

Source: Taken from Table XXXII of Fisher and Yates': *Statistical Tables for Biological, Agricultural and Medical Research* (6th Edition 1974) published by Longman Group UK Ltd. London (previously published by Oliver and Boyd Ltd, Edinburgh) and is reprinted by permission of the authors and publishers.

TABLE D.2 Critical Values for the Pearson Correlation Coefficient

	Level of Significance for a One-Tail Test				
	.05	.025	.01	.005	.0005
	Level of Significance for a Two-Tail Test				
df	.10	.05	.02	.01	.001
1	.9877	.9969	.9995	.9999	1.0000
2	.9000	.9500	.9800	.9900	.9990
3	.8054	.8783	.9343	.9587	.9912
4	.7293	.8114	.8822	.9172	.9741
5	.6694	.7545	.8329	.8745	.9507
6	.6215	.7067	.7887	.8343	.9249
7	.5822	.6664	.7498	.7977	.8982
8	.5494	.6319	.7155	.7646	.8721
9	.5214	.6021	.6851	.7348	.8471
10	.4973	.5760	.6581	.7079	.8233
11	.4762	.5529	.6339	.6835	.8010
12	.4575	.5324	.6120	.6614	.7800
13	.4409	.5139	.5923	.6411	.7603
14	.4259	.4973	.5742	.6226	.7420
15	.4124	.4821	.5577	.6055	.7246
16	.4000	.4683	.5425	.5897	.7084
17	.3887	.4555	.5285	.5751	.6932
18	.3783	.4438	.5155	.5614	.6787
19	.3687	.4329	.5034	.5487	.6652
20	.3598	.4227	.4921	.5368	.6524
25	.3223	.3809	.4451	.4869	.5974
30	.2960	.3494	.4093	.4487	.5541
35	.2746	.3246	.3810	.4182	.5189
40	.2573	.3044	.3578	.3932	.4896
45	.2428	.2875	.3384	.3721	.4648
50	.2306	.2732	.3218	.3541	.4433
60	.2108	.2500	.2948	.3248	.4078
70	.1954	.2319	.2737	.3017	.3799
80	.1829	.2172	.2565	.2830	.3568
90	.1726	.2050	.2422	.2673	.3375
100	.1638	.1946	.2301	.2540	.3211

Source: Taken from Table VII of Fisher and Yates: *Statistical Tables for Biological, Agricultural and Medical Research* (6th Edition, 1974) published by Longman Group UK Ltd. London (previously published by Oliver and Boyd Ltd, Edinburgh) and is reprinted by permission of the authors and publishers.

TABLE D.3 Critical Values of Chi-Square

df	.99	.98	.95	.90	.80	.70	.50	.30	.20	.10	.05	.02	.01	.001
1	.0002	.0006	.0039	.016	.064	.15	.46	1.07	1.64	2.71	3.84	5.41	6.64	10.83
2	.02	.04	.10	.21	.45	.71	1.39	1.41	3.22	4.60	5.99	7.82	9.21	13.82
3	.12	.18	.35	.58	1.00	1.42	2.37	3.66	4.64	6.25	7.82	9.84	11.34	16.27
4	.30	.43	.71	1.06	1.65	2.20	3.36	4.88	5.99	7.78	9.49	11.67	13.28	18.47
5	.55	.75	1.14	1.61	2.34	3.00	4.35	6.06	7.29	9.24	11.07	13.39	15.09	20.52
6	.87	1.13	1.64	2.20	3.07	3.83	5.35	7.23	8.56	10.64	12.59	15.03	16.81	22.46
7	1.24	1.56	2.17	2.83	3.82	4.67	6.35	8.38	9.80	12.02	14.07	16.62	18.48	24.32
8	1.65	2.03	2.73	3.49	4.59	5.53	7.34	9.52	11.03	13.36	15.51	18.17	20.09	26.12
9	2.09	2.53	3.32	4.17	5.38	6.39	8.34	10.66	12.24	14.68	16.92	19.68	21.67	27.88
10	2.56	3.06	3.94	4.86	6.18	7.27	9.34	11.78	13.44	15.99	18.31	21.16	23.21	29.59
11	3.05	3.61	4.58	5.58	6.99	8.15	10.34	12.90	14.63	17.28	19.68	22.62	24.72	31.26
12	3.57	4.18	5.23	6.30	7.81	9.03	11.34	14.01	15.81	18.55	21.03	24.05	26.22	32.91
13	4.11	4.76	5.89	7.04	8.63	9.93	12.34	15.12	16.98	19.81	22.36	25.47	27.69	34.53
14	4.66	5.37	6.57	7.79	9.47	10.82	13.34	16.22	18.15	21.06	34.68	26.87	29.14	36.12
15	5.23	5.98	7.26	8.55	10.31	11.72	14.34	17.32	19.31	22.31	25.00	28.26	30.58	37.70
16	5.81	6.61	7.96	9.31	11.15	12.62	15.34	18.42	20.46	23.54	26.30	29.63	32.00	39.25
17	6.41	7.26	8.67	10.08	12.00	13.53	16.34	19.51	22.62	24.77	27.59	31.00	33.41	40.79
18	7.02	7.91	9.39	10.86	12.86	14.44	17.34	20.60	22.76	25.99	28.87	32.35	34.80	42.31
19	7.63	8.57	10.12	11.65	13.72	15.35	18.34	21.69	23.90	27.20	30.14	33.69	36.19	43.82
20	8.26	9.24	10.85	12.44	14.58	16.27	19.34	22.78	25.04	28.41	31.41	35.02	37.57	45.32
21	8.90	9.92	11.59	13.24	15.44	17.18	20.34	23.86	26.17	29.62	32.67	36.34	38.93	46.80
22	9.54	10.60	12.34	14.04	16.31	18.10	21.34	24.94	27.30	30.81	33.92	37.66	40.29	48.27
23	10.20	11.29	13.09	14.85	17.19	19.02	22.34	26.02	28.43	32.01	35.17	38.97	41.64	49.73
24	10.86	11.99	13.85	15.66	18.06	19.94	23.34	27.10	29.55	33.20	36.42	40.27	42.98	51.18
25	11.52	12.70	14.61	16.47	18.94	20.87	24.34	28.17	30.68	34.48	37.65	41.57	44.31	52.62
26	12.20	13.41	15.38	17.29	19.82	21.79	25.34	29.25	31.80	35.56	38.88	42.86	45.64	54.05
27	12.88	14.12	16.15	18.11	20.70	22.72	26.34	30.32	32.91	36.74	40.11	44.14	46.96	55.48
28	13.56	14.85	16.93	18.94	21.59	23.65	27.34	31.39	34.03	37.92	41.34	45.42	48.28	56.89
29	14.26	15.57	17.71	19.77	22.48	24.58	28.45	32.46	35.14	39.09	42.56	46.69	49.59	58.30
30	14.95	16.31	18.49	20.60	23.36	25.51	29.34	33.53	36.25	40.26	43.77	47.96	50.89	59.70

Source: Taken from Table IV of Fisher and Yates': *Statistical Tables for Biological, Agricultural and Medical Research* (6th Edition 1974) published by Longman Group UK Ltd. London (previously published by Oliver and Boyd Ltd, Edinburgh) and is reprinted by permission of the authors and publishers.

References

Altheide, D. L., & Johnson, J. M. (1998). Criteria for assessing interpretative validity in qualitative research. In N. K. Denzin & Y. S. Lincoln (Eds.) *Collecting and interpreting qualitative materials* (pp. 283–312). Thousand Oaks, CA: Sage.

American Educational Research Association. (1999). *Standards for educational and psychological tests*. Washington, DC: Author.

American Psychological Association. (1999). Statistical methods in psychology journals. *American Psychologist, 54(8)*, 594–604.

American Psychological Association. (2001). *Publication manual of the American Psychological Association* (5th ed.). Washington, DC: Author.

Audience Dialogue (2004, February 24). *Software for qualitative research* (pp. 1–8). Retrieved April 21, 2004 from http://www.audiencedialogue.org/soft-qual.html

Babbie, E. R. (1998). *The practice of social research*. (8th ed.). Belmont, CA: Wadsworth.

Bailey, J. S., & Burch, M. R. (2002). *Research methods in applied behavior analysis*. Thousand Oaks, CA: Sage.

Barlow, D. H., & Hersen, M. (1984). *Single case experimental designs: Strategies for studying behavior change*. New York: Pergamon.

Basit, T. (2003). Manual or electronic? The role of coding in qualitative data analysis. *Educational Research, 45(2)*, 143–155.

Berg, B. L. (2004). *Qualitative research methods for the social sciences* (5th ed.). Thousand Oaks, CA: Sage.

Berliner, D. C. (2002). Educational research: The hardest science of all. *Educational Researcher, 31(8)*, 18–20.

Best, S. J., & Krueger, B. S. (2004). *Internet data collection*. Thousand Oaks, CA: Sage.

Bogdan, R., & Biklen, S. K. (2003). *Qualitative research for education* (4th ed.). Boston: Allyn & Bacon.

Boraks, N., & Schumacher, S. (1981). *Ethnographic research on word recognition strategies of adult beginning readers: Technical Report*. Richmond: Virginia Commonwealth University, School of Education. (ERIC Document Reproduction Services No. ED207007)

Boruch, R. F., & Cecil, J. S. (1979). *Assuring the confidentiality of social research data*. Philadelphia: University of Pennsylvania Press.

Boston College. (2004, February 26). *Qualitative research software* (pp. 1–2). Retrieved April 21, 2004, from http://www.bc.edu/offices/ats/rits/research/software/descriptions/qualitative

Campbell, D. T., & Stanley, J. C. (1963). *Experimental and quasi-experimental designs for research*. Chicago: Rand, McNally.

Charmaz, K. (2000). Grounded theory: Objectivist and constructivist methods. In N. K. Denzin & Y.S. Lincoln (Eds.), *Handbook of qualitative research* (2nd ed., pp. 509–535). Thousand Oaks, CA: Sage.

Chicago manual of style (15th ed.). (2003). Chicago: The University of Chicago Press.

Christians, C. (2000). Ethics and politics in qualitative research. In N. K. Denzin & Y. S. Lincoln (Eds.), *Handbook of qualitative research* (2nd ed., pp. 133–155). Thousand Oaks, CA: Sage.

Clandinin, D. J., & Connelly, R. M. (2000). *Narrative inquiry: Experience and story in qualitative research*. San Francisco: Jossey-Bass.

Code of Federal Regulations for the Protection of Human Research Subjects. (2004). Office For Human Research Protections Code of Federal Regulations, Title 45: Public Welfare, Department of Health and Human Services, National Institutes of Health.

Cohen, J. (1988). *Statistical power analysis for the behavioral sciences*. Hillsdale, NJ: Erlbaum.

Comrey, A. L., Backer, T. E., & Glaser, E. M. (1973). *A sourcebook for mental health measures*. Los Angeles: Human Interaction Research Institute.

Connelly, F. M., & Clandinin, D. J. (1990). Stories of experience and narrative inquiry. *Educational Researcher, 19(5)*, 2–14.

Conoley, J. C., & Kramer, J. J. (Eds.). (1989). *The tenth mental measurements yearbook*. Lincoln: University of Nebraska Press.

Cook, C., Heath, F., & Thompson, R. (2000). A meta-analysis of response rates in web or Internet-based surveys. *Educational and Psychological Measurement, 60*, 821–836.

Cook, T. D., & Campbell, D. T. (1979). *Quasi-experimentations: Design and analysis issues for field settings*. Chicago: Rand McNally.

Cooper, H. (1998). *Synthesizing research*. Beverly Hills: Sage.

Cousins, J. B., & Whitmore, E. (1998). Framing participatory evaluation. *New Directions for Evaluation, 80*, 5–23.

Creswell, J. W. (1998). *Qualitative inquiry and research design: Choosing among five traditions*. Thousand Oaks, CA: Sage.

Creswell, J. W. (2002). *Educational research: Planning, conducting, and evaluating quantitative and qualitative research*. Upper Saddle River, NJ: Merrill/Prentice-Hall.

Daniel, L. G. (1999). *A history of perceptions of the quality of educational research: issues and trends with implications for the teaching of educational research*. Paper presented at the annual meeting of the American Educational Research Association, San Diego, CA.

Denzin, N. K. (1997). *Interpretative ethnography: Ethnographic practices in the 21st century*. Thousand Oaks, CA: Sage.

Denzin, N. K., & Lincoln, Y. S., (Eds.) (2000). *Handbook of qualitative research* (2nd ed.). Thousand Oaks, CA: Sage.

Dexter, L. (1970). *Elite and specialized interviewing*. New York: Basic Books.

Dillman, D. (2000). *Mail and Internet surveys: The tailor-designed method* (2nd ed.). New York: Wiley.

Eisenhart, M., & Towne, L. (2003). Contestations and change in national policy on "Scientifically Based" educational research. *Educational Researcher, 32*(7), 31–38.

Erickson, F. (1973). What makes school ethnography "ethnographic?" *Anthropology and Education Quarterly, 9*, 58–69.

Erickson, F., & Gutierrez, K. (2002). Culture, rigor, and science in educational research. *Educational Researcher, 31*(8), 21–24.

Fabiano, E. (1989). *Index to tests used in educational dissertations*. Phoenix: Oryx Press.

Fetterman, D. M. (2000). *Foundations of empowerment evaluation: Step by step*. Thousand Oaks, CA: Sage.

Fine, M. (1998). Working the hyphens: Reinventing self and other in qualitative research. In N. Denzin & Y. Lincoln (Eds.), *The landscape of qualitative research* (pp. 130–155). Thousand Oaks, CA: Sage.

Finn, J. D., & Achilles, C. M. (1990). Answers and questions about class size: A statewide experiment. *American Educational Research Journal, 27*, 557–577.

Fitzpatrick, J. L., Sanders, J. R., & Worthen, B. R. (2004). *Program evaluation: Alternative approaches and practical guidelines* (3rd ed.). Boston: Allyn & Bacon.

Franklin, R. D., Allison, D. B., & Gorman, B. S. (1997). *Design and analysis of single case research*. Mahwah, NJ: Erlbaum.

Gall, M. D., Gall, J. P., & Borg, W. R. (2003). *Educational research: An introduction*. (7th ed.). Boston: Allyn & Bacon.

Gibbons, J. D. (1993). *Nonparametric statistics: An introduction*. Newbury Park, CA: Sage.

Giesne, C., & Peshkin, A. (1992). *Becoming qualitative researchers: An introduction*. New York: Longman.

Goldman, B., & Mitchell, D. (2002). *Directory of unpublished experimental mental measures*. (Vol. 8). Washington, DC: American Psychological Association.

Goodwin, W. L., & Driscoll, L. A. (1980). *Handbook for measurement and evaluation in early childhood education*. San Francisco: Jossey-Bass.

Gorden, R. (1981). *Interviewing: Strategies, techniques, and tactics*. Homewood, IL: Dorsey.

Green, J. C. (2000). Understanding social programs through evaluation. In N. K. Denzin & Y. S. Lincoln (Eds.), *Handbook of qualitative research* (2nd ed., pp. 981–999). Thousand Oaks, CA: Sage.

Greenberg, D., Meyer, R. H., & Wiseman, M. (1995). Multisite employment and training program evaluations: A tale of three studies. *Industrial and Labor Relations Review, 47*, 679–691.

Grele, R. J. (1996). Directions for oral history in the United States. In D. K. Dunway & W. K. Baum (Eds.), *Oral history: An interdisciplinary anthology* (pp. 60–75). Walnut Creek, CA: AltaMira.

Guba, E. G., & Lincoln, Y. S. (1989). *Fourth generation evaluation*. Beverly Hills, CA: Sage.

Halperin, S. (1978, March). *Teaching the limitations of the correlatin coefficient*. Paper presented at the annual meeting of the American Educational Research Association, Toronto.

Hersen, M., & Bellack, A. (1988). *Dictionary of behavioral assessment techniques*. New York: Pergamon.

Hopkins, K. D., & Gullickson, A. R. (1992). Response rates in survey research: A meta-analysis of the effects of monetary gratuities, *Journal of Experimental Education, 61*, 52–62.

House, E. R., & Howe, K. R. (2000, Spring). Deliberative democratic evaluation. In K. E. Ryan & L. DeStanfano (Eds.), *New directions for evaluation: Promoting inclusion, dialogue, and deliberation 85*(pp. 3–12). San Francisco: Jossey-Bass.

Hunter, J. E. (2004). *Methods of meta-analysis* (2nd ed.). Newbury Park: Sage.

Interviewer's manual. (1999). Ann Arbor: Survey Research Center, Institute for Social Research.

Johnson, O. G. (1976). *Tests and measurements in child development: Handbook II*. San Francisco: Jossey-Bass.

Joint Committee on Standards for Educational Evaluation (1994). *The program evaluation standards* (2nd ed.). Thousand Oaks, CA: Sage.

Kazdin, A. E. (1982). *Single case research designs: Methods for clinical and applied settings*. New York: Oxford University Press.

Kerlinger, F. N. (1979). *Behavioral research: A conceptual approach*. New York: Holt, Rinehart & Winston.

Kerlinger, F. N. (1986). *Foundations of behavioral research* (3rd ed.). New York: Holt, Rinehart & Winston.

Keyser, D. J., & Sweetland, R. C. (Eds.). (1984–94). *Test critiques*, (Vol. 1–10). Kansas City, MO: Test Corporation of America.

Kiecolt, K. J., & Natham, L. E. (1985). *Secondary analysis of survey data*. Beverly Hills, CA: Sage.

Kleinman, S., & Copp, M. A. (1993). *Emotions and fieldwork*. Newbury Park, CA: Sage.

Krueger, R. A., & Casey, M. A. (2000). *Focus group interviews: A practical guide for applied research* (3rd ed.). Thousand Oaks, CA: Sage.

Lather, P. (1991). *Getting smart: Feminist research and pedagogy with/in the postmodern*. New York: Routledge.

Lawrence, S., & Giles, C. L. (1999). Accessibility and distribution of information on the web. *Nature 400*(6740), 107–109.

LeCompte, M. D., & Preissle, J. (1993). *Ethnography and qualitative design in educational research*. (2nd ed.). San Diego: Academic Press.

Lincoln, Y. S. (1990). Toward a categorical imperative for qualitative research. In E. W. Eisner & A. Peshkin (Eds.), *Qualitative inquiry in education* (pp. 277–295). New York: Teachers College Press.

Lincoln, Y. S. (1995). *Emerging criteria for quality in qualitative and interpretive research*. Paper presented at the annual meeting of the American Education Research Association, San Francisco.

Lincoln, Y. S., & Guba, E. G. (1985). *Naturalistic inquiry*. Beverly Hills, CA: Sage.

MacBeth, D. (2001). On reflexivity in qualitative research. *Qualitative Inquiry, 7*(1), 35–68.

Maddox, J. (Ed.). (2003). *Tests: A comprehensive reference for assessments in psychology, education, and business* (10th ed.). Kansas City, MO: Test Corporation of America.

Malone, S. (2003). Ethics at home: Informed consent in your own backyard. *International Journal of Qualitative Studies in Education, 16*(6), 797–816.

Maltby, J., Lewis, C. A., & Hill, A. (Eds.). (2000). *Commissioned reviews of 250 psychological tests*. New York: E. Mellen.

Marascuilo, L. A., & McSweeney, M. (1977). *Nonparametric and distribution-free methods for the social sciences*. Monterey, CA: Brooks/Cole.

Marcus, G. E. (1998). What comes (just) after "post"?: The case of ethnography. In N. K. Denzin & Y. S. Lincoln (Eds.), *The landscape of qualitative research: Theories and issues*. (pp. 383–406). Thousand Oaks, CA: Sage.

Marshall, C., & Rossman, G. R. (1999). *Designing qualitative research* (3rd ed.). Newbury Park, CA: Sage.

Mason, J. (1996). *Qualitative researching*. Thousand Oaks, CA: Sage.

McMillan, J. H. (2000). *Educational research. Fundamentals for the consumer* (3rd ed.). New York: Longman.

McMillan, J. H. (2004, April). *Teachers' classroom assessment and grading practices decision making*. Paper presented at the Annual Meeting of the National Council of Measurement in Education, New Orleans.

Miller, D. C., & Salkind, N. J. (2002). *Handbook of research design and social measurement* (6th ed.). Newbury Park, CA: Sage.

Miller, J., McKenna, M., & McKenna, B. (1998). A comparison of alternatively and traditionally prepared teachers. *Journal of Teacher Education, 49*, 165–176.

Mills, G. E. (2003). *Action research: A guide for the teacher researcher* (2nd ed.). Upper Saddle River, NJ: Merrill/Prentice-Hall.

Moustakas, C. (1994). *Phenomenological research methods*. Thousand Oaks, CA: Sage.

Murphy, L. L., Plake, B. S., Impara, J. C., & Spies, R. A. (2002). *Tests in print VI*. Lincoln, NE: Buros Institute of Mental Measurements.

National Center for Educational Evaluation and Regional Assistance. (2004). *A new generation of rigorous evaluations* (pp. 1–4). Retrieved May 12, 2004, from http://www.ed.gov/print/rschstat/evid/resources/studyplans.html

National Commission on Excellence in Education. (1983). *A nation at risk: The imperative for educational reform*. Washington, DC: United States Department of Education.

National Research Council, Committee on Scientific Principles for Education Research. (2002). *Scientific research in education*. Washington, DC: National Academy Press.

Nord, D. P. (1998, September). Uses of memory: An introduction. *Journal of American History*, 409–410.

Oja, S. N., & Smulyan, L. (1989). *Collaborative action research: A developmental approach*. London, England: Falmer Press.

Osborn, J. W., & Overbay, A. (2004). The power of outliers (and why researchers should always check for them). *Practical Assessment, Research, and Evaluation, 9*(6). Retrieved June 5, 2004, from http://PAREonline.net/getvn.asp?v=9&n=6

Patton, M. Q. (1996). *Utilization-focuses evaluation* (3rd ed.). Thousand Oaks, CA: Sage.

Patton, M. Q. (2002). *Qualitative evaluation and evaluation methods* (3rd ed.). Thousand Oaks, CA: Sage.

Peshkin, A. (1993). The goodness of qualitative research. *Educational Researcher, 22*(2), 23–29.

Pillow, W. (2003). Confession, catharsis, or cure? Rethinking the uses of reflexivity as methlological power in qualitative research. *International Journal of Qualitative Studies in Education, 16*(2), 175–197.

Popham, W. J. (1981). *Modern educational measurement*. Englewood Cliffs, NJ: Prentice-Hall.

Punch, M. (1994). Politics and ethics in qualitative research. In N. K. Denzin & Y. S. Lincoln (Eds.), *Handbook of qualitative research* (pp. 83–97). Thousand Oaks, CA: Sage.

Reynolds, A. J., Temple, J. A., Robertson, D. L., & Mann, E. A. (2000). Age 21 cost-benefit analysis of the Title 1 Chicago child-parent centers. *Educational Evaluation and Policy Analysis, 24*(4), 267–303.

Richardson, L. (1998). Writing: A method of inquiry. In N. K. Denzin & Y. S. Lincoln (Eds.), *Collecting and interpreting qualitative research* (pp. 345–372). Thousand Oaks, CA: Sage.

Rist, R. C. (2000). Influencing a policy process with qualitative research. In N. K. Denzin & Y. S. Lincoln (Eds.), *Handbook of qualitative research* (2nd ed., pp. 1000–1017). Thousand Oaks, CA: Sage.

Rosenthal, R., & Jacobson, L. (1968). *Pygmalion in the classroom: Teacher expectation and pupil's intellectual development*. New York: Holt, Rinehart & Winston.

Rowntree, B. S. (1941). *Poverty and progress: A second social survey of York*. London: Longman, Green.

Rue, G., Dingley, C., & Bush. H. (2002). Inner strength in women. Metasynthesis of qualitative findings and theory development. *Journal of Theory Construction and Testing, 4* (2), 36–39.

Ryan, G. W., & Bernard, H. R. (2000). Data management and analysis methods. In N. K. Denzin & Y. S. Lincoln (Eds.), *Handbook of qualitative research: 2nd ed.*, (pp. 769–802). Thousand Oaks, CA: Sage

Schonlau, M., Fricker, Jr., R. D., & Elliot, M. N. (2002). *Conducting research surveys via e-mail and the web*. Santa Monica, CA: Rand.

Schumacher, S. (1984). *Evaluation of CoTEEP field-testing of workshop-seminar series and principles for summative evaluation*. Richmond: Virginia Commonwealth University, School of Education. (ERIC Document Reproduction Service No. ED252499)

Schumacher, S., & Esham, K. (1986). *Evaluation of a collaborative planning and development of school-based preservice and inservice education, Phase IV*. Richmond: Virginia Commonwealth University, School of Education. (ERIC Document Reproduction Services No. ED278659)

Schumacher, S., Esham, K., & Bauer, D. (1985). *Evaluation of a collaborative teacher education program: Planning, development and implementation, Phase III*. Richmond: Virginia Commonwealth University, School of Education. (ERIC Document Reproduction Service No. ED278659)

Schuman, H., & Presser, S. (1996). *Questions and answers: Experiments in the form, wording and context of survey questions*. Thousand Oaks, CA: Sage.

Schwandt, T. A. (2001). *Dictionary of qualitative inquiry* (2nd rev. ed.). Thousand Oaks, CA: Sage Publications.

Seidman, I. E. (1998). *Interviewing as qualitative research: A guide for researchers in education and the social sciences* (2nd ed.). New York: Teachers College Press.

Shadish, W. R., Cook, T. D., & Campbell, K. R. (2002). *Experimental and quasi-experimental designs for generalized causal inference*. Boston: Houghton Mifflin.

Shepard, L. A. (1993). Evaluating test validity. *Review of Research in Education, 19*, 405–450.

Siegel, S. (1956). *Nonparametric statistics for the behavioral sciences*. New York: McGraw-Hill.

Smith, J. K. (1993). *After the demise of empiricism: The problem of judging social and education inquiry*. Norwood, NJ: Ablex.

Smith, L. M. (1990). Ethics in qualitative field research: An individual perspective. In E. W. Eisner & A. Peshkin (Eds.), *Qualitative inquiry in education: The continuing debate* (pp. 258–276). New York: Teachers College Press.

Smith, M. L., & Shepard, L. A. (1988). Kindergarten readiness and retention: A qualitative study of teachers' beliefs and practices. *American Educational Research Journal, 25*(3), 298–325.

Spradley, J. P. (1979). *The ethnographic interview.* New York: Holt, Rinehart & Winston.

St. Pierre, E. A. (2002). "Science" rejects postmodernism. *Educational Researcher, 31*(8), 25–26.

Stake, R. E. (1975). *Program evaluation, particularly responsive evaluation.* Kalamazoo, MI, Evaluation Center, Western Michigan University. (Occasional Paper Series, No. 5.)

Stake, R. E. (1995). *The art of case study research.* Thousand Oaks, CA: Sage.

Stake, R. E. (2000). Case studies. In N. K. Denzin & Y. S. Lincoln (Eds.), *Handbook of qualitative research* (2nd ed., pp. 435–454). Thousand Oaks, CA: Sage.

Stinger, E. T. (1996). *Action research: A handbook for practitioners.* Thousand Oaks, CA: Sage.

Strauss, A., & Corbin, J. (1998). *Basics of qualitative research: Grounded theory procedures and techniques* (2nd ed.). Thousand Oaks, CA: Sage.

Stringer, E. (2004). *Action research in education.* Columbus, OH: Pearson Education.

Stufflebeam, D. L., Foley, W. J., Gepart, W. J., Guba, E. E., Hammond, R. L., Merriman, H. O., & Provus, M. (1971). *Educational evaluation and decision-making.* Itasca, IL: F. E. Peacock.

Stufflebeam, D. L., Madeus, G. F., & Kellaghan, T. (2000). *Evaluation models: Viewpoints on educational and human services evaluation.* (2nd ed.). Boston: Kluwer.

Tashakkori, A., & Teddlie, C. (1998). *Mixed methodology: Combining qualitative and quantitative approaches.* Thousand Oaks, CA: Sage. (Applied Social Research Methods Series No. 46)

Thompson, A. (1998, September). Fifty years on: An international perspective on oral history. *The Journal of American History,* 581–595.

Tobin, K., & LaMaster, S. U. (1995). Relationships between metaphors, beliefs, and actions in a context of science curriculum change, *Journal of Research in Science Teaching, 32*(3), 225–242.

Touliatos, J., Perlmutter, B. F., Straus, M. A., & Holden, G. W. (Eds.). (2000). *Handbook of family measurement techniques.* Newbury Park, CA: Sage.

Tuckman, G. (1998). Historical social science: Methodologies, methods, and meanings. In N. K. Denzin & Y. S. Lincoln (Eds.), *Strategies of qualitative inquiry* (pp. 225–260). Thousand Oaks, CA: Sage.

Van Manen, M. (1990). *Researching lived experience.* New York: State of New York Press.

Viadero, D. (1999, June 23), New priorities, focus sought for research. *Education Week, 18*(41), 1, 36–37.

Wainer, H., & Robinson, D. H. (2003). Shaping up the practice of null hypothesis significance testing. *Educational Researcher, 32*(7), 22–30.

Walker, D. K. (1973). *Sociomotional measures for preschool and kindergarten children.* San Francisco: Jossey-Bass.

Wax, R. H. (1971). *Doing fieldwork: Warnings and advice.* Chicago: University of Chicago Press.

Webb, E. J., Campbell, D. R., Schwartz, R. D., & Sechrest, L. (2000). *Unobtrusive measures* (rev. ed.). Thousand Oaks, CA: Sage.

Weiss, H. B., Mayer, E., Kreider, H., Vaughan, M., Dearing, E., Hencke, R., & Pinto, K. (2003). Making it work: Low-income working mothers' involvement in their children's education. *American Educational Research Journal, 40*(4), 879–901.

Weston, C., Gandell, T., Beauchamp, J., McAlpine, L., Wiseman, C., & Beauchamp, C. (2001). Analyzing Interview data: The development and evolution of a coding system. *Qualitative Sociology, 24*(3), 381–400.

Wijnberg, M. H., & Weinger, S. (1998). When dreams wither and resources fail: The social support systems of poor single mothers. *Journal of Contemporary Human Services, 79*(2), 212–223.

Wolcott, H. F. (1973). *The man in the principal's office: An ethnography.* New York: Holt, Rinehart & Winston.

Wolcott, H. F. (1995). *The art of fieldwork.* Walnut Creek, CA: AltaMira.

Wolcott, H. F. (1999). *Ethnography: A way of seeing.* Walnut Creek, CA: AltaMira.

World Health Organization (WHO). (2002). *Health behavior in school-aged children: 1997–1998 (United States)* [Computer file]. Calverton, MD: Macro International. (Distributed by Inter-University Consortium for Political and Social Research, University of Michigan, Ann Arbor)

Yin, R. K. (2004). *The case study anthology.* Thousand Oaks, CA: Sage Publications.

Name Index

Subject Index